STUDIES IN PUBLIC COMMUNICATION

A. WILLIAM BLUEM, GENERAL EDITOR

MASS MEDIA AND COMMUNICATION

STUDIES IN PUBLIC COMMUNICATION

MASS MEDIA AND COMMUNICATION

EDITED, WITH AN INTRODUCTION
AND SPECIAL NOTES BY

Charles S. Steinberg, Ph.D.

COMMUNICATION ARTS BOOKS

HASTINGS HOUSE, PUBLISHERS · NEW YORK

CONTENTS

B) *Motion Pictures*

STUDIES IN PUBLIC COMMUNICATION

AN INTRODUCTION

ACADEMIC CONCERN about communication has a long tradition. Throughout history—notably in rhetoric, literature and the arts—communicative acts and artifacts have been subjects of inquiry and speculation. Not until the middle of this century, however, has communication been studied in an independent context which first frames these broad and persuasive systems we have come to call the public or mass media, and which subsequently forces re-examination of all other aspects of human communication insofar as they are related to these systems. From such a core of inquiry and assessment, bounded by its own limits of specialization, is emerging the discipline of *public communication.*

The great public media, together with many attendant services and contributing agencies, have reached their greatest evolution within the past half-century. And while the press, broadcasting and motion pictures, separately, have engaged the serious attention of various schools and departments, only recently has common need decreed the practicality of investigating these mechanical and electronic enterprises within a wholeness of structure and purpose. As the public media continue to take increasing hold of our civilization—giving definition and thrust to the very quality of personal and social existence—we realize that they must be assessed by men of varied scholarly interests.

A critical perspective on the technological extensions of the communicative process cannot be derived from narrow bases. Social and cultural theorists, behavioral scientists, media practitioner-controllers, philosophers and artists—all contribute to our understanding. Their theories, research findings and discussions have already expanded the possibilities of analysis. The problem before us, in *Studies in Public Communication*, is to gather into meaningful relationship some part of this wealth of considered opinion and clear fact.

In his essay, "The Great Debate on Cultural Democracy," Bernard

Berelson advises us that critical examination of the media has begun to cluster in three discernible patterns of commentary. Taken together, these patterns supply a rubric partially useful to the purpose and organization of the *Studies*.

Berelson points out that the behavioral scientist regards the public media as instruments for achieving social and political stability—while the philosopher-humanist sees in them the potential for liberation of mind and spirit, for enlargement of human vision. There is also the media-controller who is beginning to share respect for the magnitude of power invested in him by the course of events. Each has his position and "point of view," each his convictions and private fears, each the mechanisms for defending incapacities. But missing from Berelson's tri-partite division of attitude toward the media is the viewpoint of the artist, who must consider techno-logical systems only as means of expressing his creative personality and who can be concerned neither with an empirically established social function nor a humanistically established moral purpose in his use of the media.

Following the outline suggested by Berelson, the *Studies in Public Communication* series will encompass the empirical knowledge we have of the effects of the media, the philosophic insights required for their purposeful shaping, and the practical problems which govern their internal control and direction. And we will include the discoveries of those creative artists who have sought expression through technology. What we hope to accomplish in this series of anthologies and individually authored volumes is a total view of the media as physical systems, as social and cultural forces, and as outlets for man's creative energies. Upon the fulfillment of this purpose depends the value of the *Studies* for teachers and students of public communication.

Charles S. Steinberg has provided the most valid point of departure for the series in this cogently edited first volume. He begins where we must all begin—by concentrating upon certain operative communications systems as they are an integral part of the social structure. In so doing, Dr. Steinberg establishes, at the outset, an essential delimitation of our subject.

A. WILLIAM BLUEM, PH.D.
General Editor, *Studies in Public Communication*
Newhouse Communication Center
Syracuse University

PREFACE

ALTHOUGH THE twentieth century is more than a decade beyond the mid-century mark, it is still too early for historians to begin any appraisal from perspective of those distinguishing and definitive characteristics which may have emerged. This is an age in which man's increasing conquest of the universe has reached so startling a degree of efficiency as to cause many philosophers and scientists to wonder whether man has not created a scientific revolution in which, like the sorcerer's apprentice, the miracles of science may be beyond human control. It is an age in which the dogma of the theologian and the empiricism of the scientist must find a basis upon which to reconcile man's conquest of the finite with his aspirations toward the infinite. And fundamental to the age are the art and the science of mass communication.

The inordinate curiosity of man is not a phenomenon of any one century. New worlds and new modes of aesthetic experience were discovered in the Renaissance. Man sought a rational explanation of the cosmos in the Age of Reason. He hitched his wagon to a star in the Romantic Revolution and brought it down to earth again in the Age of Realism. These designations are, of course, the historian's way of capsulizing a whole nexus of factors—aesthetic, sociological, psychological, political, scientific and economic—that give an era its descriptive quality or "tone."

From this descriptive point of view, the distinguishing feature of the twentieth century is the phenomenon of mass communication. Indeed, the enormous scientific conquests which developed after World War II have been made possible by the perfecting of the science and technic of mass communication. An electronic screen operated by remote control determines whether a multi-million dollar missile will rise into orbit or be destroyed by a flick of the finger in a blockhouse. Control towers, tuned by radio to approaching aircraft, guide planes to safe landings. Man's increasing knowledge of outer space and weather comes, not merely from launching a satellite into invisible flight, but from delicate transmission devices which communicate knowledge of conditions in a world traditionally presumed to be beyond the finite.

Beyond the technical proficiency of the science of communication, however, is the social impact of the art of communication. The communications revolution has had implications far beyond those that arose from the physical application of steam to transportation and production. The social and economic consequences of the Industrial Revolution in the nineteenth century were so far reaching that their impact is only now being fully recognized, a hundred years after the event. The ultimate results of the communications revolution are still conjectural, largely because the headlong rush of events has made any real perspective an impossible task. One of the fundamental concerns of the television industry, for example, is simply that there has been no time, in the tumultuous growth of the medium, for an historical or critical evaluation. In the short span of one decade, there is obviously no time for productive scholarship or for establishing causal relationships between the medium and society. Yet, it is recognized that television, like other mass media, has an enormous and growing potential, both as an entertainment and an informational catalyst. As a medium it uniquely reflects the society it serves. The print media, too, have their problems, stemming largely from the paradox of decreased competition within their own area, along with increased competition from the astonishing effectiveness of electronic journalism.

The crux of the matter seems to be that the technical achievement of the communications revolution, like the technical achievement of the Industrial Revolution, must be evaluated not only in terms of its purely scientific implications, but in terms of its implications and consequences for society. Its ultimate thrust is as an art form, not a technic; it is sociological rather than scientific. The potential of the mass media for constructive social action is without parallel, because the media of mass communication are implicit and explicit instruments of knowledge. The ubiquitousness of mass communication leaves virtually no corner of the civilized world without access to news and information. The concept of the "power of the press" has a contemporary meaning which reaches far beyond its original connotation. For, in the broadest sense, this concept embraces both printed and electronic journalism. Between them these communications phenomena offer the most powerful and widely disseminated funnels of information the world has ever known. Almost no one need be lacking in the basic facts about the crises, the decisions and the great personalities of our time. Almost no one need be without access to information, even about the minutiae of contemporary events.

Yet, the power of the media of mass communication—their sheer, overwhelming driving energy to inform—can be self-limiting. There is an implicit possibility, and it is a clear and immediate possibility, that this plethora of words may be acting as a soporific, rather than as a stimulus to reflective thought and a prelude to intelligent action. There is, therefore, a fundamental responsibility inherent in the application of the media of mass communication. It is the responsibility not only to inform, but also to contribute to the whole spirit of inquiry which is integral to the functioning of a democracy. There is always the possibility that bombardment with the verbiage of communication content, particularly in advertising and public relations, may result in mass stereotyping. But it is a possibility which, recoginzed, is avoidable. For intelligent application and use of mass media can also move society forward into new and exciting frontiers of knowledge. Mass media have given a new orientation to the social sciences.

The material in this volume is predicated on the conviction that there are affirmative social values implicit in an understanding and proper utilization of the media of mass communication. For the fact is that we are enveloped in a welter of mass media and we cannot, under any circumstances, exclude them from our senses. The individual and the social group must learn, therefore, to evaluate them properly, use them wisely and develop their fullest potential in the service of a democratic society. Such ends come from historical perspective and critical perception. The substance of this volume aims to develop an understanding of how the media of mass communication both serve and reflect society; to describe how they function; to delineate some of their problems and their potential, and finally to chart out a possible course whereby mass media may be utilized, not merely to keep us better informed, but also to serve as a stimulus to reflective thought, to intelligent value judgments and to constructive action.

CHARLES S. STEINBERG

THE STRUCTURE AND DEVELOPMENT OF MASS COMMUNICATION

Eugene L. Hartley and Ruth E. Hartley
THE IMPORTANCE AND NATURE
OF COMMUNICATION

Wendell Johnson
WORDS AND NOT-WORDS

Wilbur Schramm
ITS DEVELOPMENT

Theodore Peterson
WHY THE MASS MEDIA ARE THAT WAY

1

THE STRUCTURE AND DEVELOPMENT

OF MASS COMMUNICATION

DESPITE the increasing literature and research on the structure, function and effects of mass media, there are relatively few studies which concern themselves with the nature of the communication process and with the historical development of the mass media. The studies included in this section delineate, respectively, the nature of interpersonal communication, the significance of semantics in the communication process, the development of mass communication and the nature of the mass media.

"The Importance and Nature of Communication" approaches the process of communication from the standpoint of the psychologist and sociologist since Eugene L. Hartley and Ruth E. Hartley consider the subject in terms of the frame of reference of the social sciences. Wilbur Schramm's chapter on the development of mass communication is introductory to Dr. Schramm's total consideration of the problem of responsibility in mass communication. Dr. Peterson discusses the media in terms of their institutional character.

Basic to a consideration of the structure and function of the mass media is the communication process itself. Dr. Eugene L. Hartley and Dr. Ruth E. Hartley discuss the communication process and its importance in contemporary society. The authors' approach is particularly significant in the light of recent divergent opinions on the effects of mass media. Some studies tend to stress communication between individuals as perhaps of equal or greater importance than group communication. Here, communication—the means by which individuals influence each other and are influenced in turn—is the basic "carrier" of social process. It makes individual interaction possible and comprehensible. It is the basis on which man is considered a social being, able to cooperate with others and to engage in socially useful activity. Communication also makes art, science, literature and politics possible and comprehensible. As the authors show, direct experience, significant as it is, is not as important in a complex society as

3

communication in weaving together the totality of experience. For, individual experience is necessarily delimited in terms of total experience—and this totality, which involves the experiences of others, can only be realized by means of the communication process. Communication makes experience predictable and produces a semblance of order out of implicit chaos.

Through communication, man avoids the frustrating loneliness of isolation and finds a way of satisfying his needs and wants. Communication is a social process. Communications "pattern" the environment for the individual. Mass media reflect that environment. Communication "relates" the individual to other individuals. Mass media, such as the press, reveal certain relationships between individuals and their social environment. Mass media, particularly in education, help to relate group behavior to the environment.

The basic tool of communication which relates the individual to the social environment is language, "the accumulation of symbolized human experiences." Group communication develops out of individual communication. And, as communication makes possible social intercourse between individuals, so mass communication makes possible a kind of cohesion among groups. Unfortunately, semantic barriers to effective communication tend to develop tensions between nations whose stereotypes differ. These barriers to communication, operative also in regional differences within a given country, can become barriers to social progress. They can induce stagnation, rather than progress. It is evident, then, that an understanding of the semantic principles of the communication process is important to the effective use of the media of mass communication. For, mass media can perpetuate stereotypes as effectively as they can help to eliminate them.

Four factors are necessary for the communication process to function. There must be the communicator. There must be the recipient. There must be the communication content. And, there is ultimately the question of the effect of communication. "Who says what to whom and with what effect," is a classic description of the communication process. There is constant interaction between communicators, for communication is a two-way street.

The problem central to effective communication is stated succinctly by Wendell Johnson: to know, and to understand, there must be prior knowledge of the relationship between symbol and fact, between language and reality. Indeed, Dr. Johnson's "modest" aims express what might well be considered a categorical imperative for all students of the communication process. First, communication, on the human level, is concerned with aspects and shades of meaning. Secondly, it is known that words represent facts and that facts are non-verbal. Thirdly, words (or facts) express implicit or explicit evaluations. Finally, communication has effect—a phenomenon which is of increasing interest to social scientists and which has been generating an increased amount of research on the impact of mass media on opinion and behavior.

Semanticists are careful to point out that facts are not always what they purport to be, but are frequently overlaid with opinion. When the propaganda analyst points out, however, that facts should dissipate emotional appeals, he is giving what Dr. Johnson calls "disarmingly simple" advice. The beguiling "fact" is, simply, that communication, however effective, cannot embrace all of the facts in a given situation all of the time. To indicate a need for all the facts, as many public relations and advertising messages do, is frequently to frustrate effective communication, rather than to develop it. Facts are facts only with regard to a specific situation as defined. The vital factor for the recognition of fact as fact is agreement by another party or parties involved in the communications situation.

Effective human communication, of course, involves language—words that stand for, or represent, reality. But here, again, it is important to understand that words are not things, but symbols that stand for things. This is the heart of the matter for effective communication—the notable difference between language and reality or between "words and not-words" as Johnson puts it. Difficulties in the communication process arise from the tendency to confuse words and things, as well as from the tendency to make "two-valued" orientations. As a result, communication may be reduced to either/or and black/white distinctions. There are, however, many valued orientations and many alternatives in a free society. And it is the recognition of the many choices available which makes communication not only effective but also essential to the vital function of a democracy.

Wilbur Schramm's excellent discussion of responsibility in the mass media includes a comprehensive survey of their history, structure and function. As Professor Schramm indicates, mass communication is inevitably related to basic technical change—the changing relationship between the human organism and the machine. The overwhelming factor in this change was the development of methods of intelligible reproduction where "interpersonal communication" could be disseminated more widely to the group and, eventually, to the mass audience.

A significant factor in the development of mass communication was the communications-reproducing machine which moved outward from its identification with sacred interests to an identification with public affairs. It veered from the service of the Church to secular utilization. From the Gutenberg Bible of 1450, technical developments of later centuries saw the gradual emergence of the wireless, the telephone and the audion tube. The point of great change, Dr. Schramm points out, from person-to-person communication to mass communication came with the use of machines which, thrust into the "communication chain," were able to listen and see for the individual. The new machines followed changes in social ethics and orientation from individual to group, from monistic to pluralistic, from a society where the peer group loomed more powerful in importance. From a device of sheer communication, the mass medium became an instrument of entertainment, as well as of information.

Dr. Schramm is concerned in this chapter, with what he terms the "first two waves of communication"—the development of printing, allowing for the mass dissemination of information; and the utilization of the newer techniques which emphasized a basic shift from recipient to sender. In these developments, mass media functioned primarily to inform and subsequently, and collaterally, to entertain.

There is a basic reason for this emphasis on the "first two waves." It is predicated on the development of technology to a degree where mass media became an integral part of our daily lives, where they became "big business" to a point that the entire economy became identified with them.

Dr. Theodore Peterson, in his illuminating discussion on how the mass media got to be the way they are takes a wholly fresh—and refreshing—approach to the development and status of the mass media of communication. In a balanced presentation of the many factors which contributed to the developmental status of mass media, Dr. Peterson evaluates the now commonplace attitudes which many students and critics of mass communication have taken and which, in substance, reach easily arrived at but untenable conclusions. Perhaps those who cavil at the performance of mass media are occasionally right, Dr. Peterson points out, but significantly, he goes on to say that his agreement is often with "the uneasy feeling that they are right for the wrong reasons."

Peterson offers alternatives for a more rational evaluation of mass media and for a better understanding of why they behave as they do. He examines, in turn, the repeated stricturing, including the argument about over-commercialization, the stigma of advertising and the concept of control by a so-called power elite. None of these strictures, however, explains precisely why the mass media *are* that way. Recognizing the fact that mass communication is a formidable business enterprise, Peterson suggests an institutional approach which reveals mass communication as reflecting society. From an "institutional perspective," mass media are not autonomous, but "adjuncts of other orders or institutions in our society. The media are part of the social matrix or fabric of society." This unusual approach gives a new perspective to the structure and function of mass communication, for mass media are shown to be part of human communication in general, and an outgrowth and reflection of the social environment.

*   *   *   *

RELATED READING

Berelson, B., & Janowitz, M. *Reader in Public Opinion and Communication.* Glencoe, Ill.: Free Press, 1950.

Bryson, Lyman (ed.). *The Communication of Ideas*. New York: Harper, 1948.

DeFleur, Melvin L., & Larsen, Otto N. *The Flow of Information*. New York: Harper, 1958.

Hovland, C. I. "Social Communication," *Proc. Amer. Philos. Soc.*, 92 (1948), 371-375.

Hovland, C. I., Lumsdaine, A. A., & Sheffield, F. D. *Experiments on Mass Communication*. Princeton: Princeton University Press, 1949.

Katz, Elihu (1957). "The Two-Step Flow of Communication: An Up-to-Date Report on an Hypothesis," *Public Opinion Quarterly*, XXI, 61-78.

Schramm, Wilbur. *Communications in Modern Society*. Urbana: University of Illinois Press, 1948.

Schramm, Wilbur (ed.). *Mass Communications*. Urbana: University of Illinois Press, 1949.

Seldes, Gilbert. *The Great Audience*. New York: Viking, 1950.

Wiebe, G. D. "Mass Communications," in E. L. Hartley & R. E. Hartley, *Fundamentals of Social Psychology*, pp. 159-195. New York: Knopf, 1952.

Wiener, Norbert. *Cybernetics, or Control and Communication in the Animal and Machine*, Chapter 8: "Information, Language and Society." New York: Wiley, 1948.

THE IMPORTANCE AND NATURE OF COMMUNICATION

By Eugene L. Hartley and Ruth E. Hartley

THE BASIC SOCIAL PROCESS

THE IMPORTANCE of communication in the study of social processes would be difficult to overemphasize. Because communication is the means by which one person influences another, and is in turn influenced by him, it is the actual carrier of social process. It makes interaction possible. Through it men become and maintain themselves as social beings.* Without it they could not band together, undertake co-operative enterprises, or advance their mastery of the physical world. Since inventions and discoveries are almost always dependent upon an accumulation of information and a gradual development of concepts transmitted from one generation to the next, only the simplest inventions and most elementary thought processes could be achieved without communication.

When we compare what we have learned from direct experience with what we have acquired by communication from others (printed words, conversations, and the whole range of communication) the scope of our own experience seems startlingly limited. Communication makes it possible for one individual to draw on what has been called the "experience of the nervous systems of others [9]" and thus to learn what his own nervous system may have missed. Because man has the ability to communicate, human societies may be regarded as intricate, co-operative nervous systems.

Society itself may be defined as "a vast network of mutual agreements." They may be written contracts or they may be unwritten understandings about what one should or should not do—for instance, what is suitable behavior in specified situations; what is, and what is not, regarded as a crime. The effectiveness of these agreements depends upon the ability of men to communicate with one another. By the use of words, communication makes possible a relatively predictable pattern of behavior; we know what to expect from others and they know what to expect from us.

---

* Since "culture" is an abstraction commonly agreed to refer to the products, knowledge, traditions, skills, and beliefs that are shared by a group of people and passed on from generation to generation, its very existence is predicated on the functioning of communication. Without communication there could be no sharing, either with contemporaries or successors.

COMMUNICATION AND THE INDIVIDUAL

Let the reader imagine, if he can, how he would feel if suddenly he were cut off from all communication with his fellows past or present. His would be a completely solitary existence, since it is only through communication that he is able to make and maintain contact with other individuals. No messages of any kind could come to him. He could have no sense of "belonging." He could feel no stir of community living; nor could he in any situation obtain help. Able neither to serve nor be served, it is likely that in a short time he could no longer even continue to exist.

Communication Is Interrupted: The Case of Helen Keller

Only a person who has experienced a position similar to this could describe its powerful impact. Helen Keller, deprived of her sight and hearing in infancy, describes in her autobiography an existence in which the communication channels are blocked. Yet, it must be remembered that although she could not see or hear, she could feel and smell, and in these ways she could achieve some degree of contact with persons about her. When but two of the major channels for expression and reception of impressions were cut off, however, an almost intolerable sense of frustration developed. She describes her reactions during early childhood, before she learned to communicate by use of the manual alphabet:*

> Soon I felt the need of some communication with others and began to make crude signs. A shake of the head meant "No" and a nod, "Yes," a pull meant "Come" and a push, "Go." Was it bread that I wanted? Then I would imitate the acts of cutting the slices and buttering them. If I wanted my mother to make ice-cream for dinner I made the sign for working the freezer and shivered, indicating cold. [*10, p. 9*]
>
> Meanwhile the desire to express myself grew. The few signs I made became less and less adequate, and my failures to make myself understood were invariably followed by outbursts of passion. I felt as if invisible hands were holding me, and I made frantic efforts to free myself. I struggled—not that struggling helped matters, but the spirit of resistance was strong within me; I generally broke down in tears and physical exhaustion. If my mother happened to be near I crept into her arms, too miserable even to remember the cause of the tempest. After a while the need of some means of communication became so urgent that these outbursts occurred daily, sometimes hourly. [*10, p. 17*]

These experiences reveal the strength of the personal needs that drive an individual to communicate with others. When deprived of access to an existing tool for communication, he tries to create his own.

In general, we take for granted both our ability to communicate and the forms of this communication. We acquire communication habits so

* From: *The Story of My Life* by Helen Keller. Copyright 1903, 1931 by Helen Keller, reprinted by permission of Doubleday & Company, Inc.

early, so gradually, and so easily that we have no sense of learning and no recollection of the time when we could not make ourselves understood. It is only through experiences such as Helen Keller's that we glimpse the enormous complexity and effort involved in learning a new system of communication. She presents the groping, the frustration, and the despair inherent in a desire to communicate and an inability to do so. However, the successful grasp of a means by which ready communication can be achieved brings a unique euphoria, a stimulation of the senses, and an eager pursuit of more and more of the same experience.

These indicia of seeking, despair, and joy imply that immediate contact with others is of primary importance to the organism. The poignancy of the quest and the hopelessness and panic when it fails are akin to the reactions frequently coupled with serious deprivations of basic organic needs. This is understandable when we recognize that communication is an important tool in the individual's adaptation to his environment. Through it, he controls the means for satisfying his basic needs. With communication, he need not be isolated. He can get what he needs from others. Without it, he is dependent on his own inadequate powers.

Communication Re-established

In the following passages, Helen Keller conveys the quality of the seeking process, which is essentially a groping for communication, and reports the happiness she felt when the barriers were finally surmounted:*

> The morning after my teacher came she led me into her room and gave me a doll. . . . When I had played with it a little while, Miss Sullivan slowly spelled into my hand the word "d-o-l-l." I was at once interested in this finger play and tried to imitate it. When I finally succeeded in making the letters correctly I was flushed with childish pleasure and pride. Running downstairs to my mother I held up my hand and made the letters for doll. I did not know that I was spelling a word or even that words existed; I was simply making my fingers go in monkey-like imitation.

> · · · · ·

> One day, while I was playing with my new doll, Miss Sullivan put my big rag doll into my lap also, spelled "d-o-l-l" and tried to make me understand that "d-o-l-l" applied to both. Earlier in the day we had had a tussle over the words "m-u-g" and "w-a-t-e-r." Miss Sullivan had tried to impress it upon me that "m-u-g" is *mug* and that "w-a-t-e-r" is *water*, but I persisted in confounding the two. In despair she had dropped the subject for the time, only to renew it at the first opportunity. I became impatient at her repeated attempts and, seizing the new doll, I dashed it upon the floor.

* From: *The Story of My Life* by Helen Keller. Copyright 1903, 1931 by Helen Keller, reprinted by permission of Doubleday & Company, Inc.

. . . . .

We walked down the path to the well-house, attracted by the fragrance of the honeysuckle with which it was covered. Some one was drawing water and my teacher placed my hand under the spout. As the cool stream gushed over one hand she spelled into the other the word *water*, first slowly, then rapidly. I stood still, my whole attention fixed upon the motions of her fingers. Suddenly I felt a misty consciousness as of something forgotten—a thrill of returning thought; and somehow the mystery of language was revealed to me. I knew then that "w-a-t-e-r" meant the wonderful cool something that was flowing over my hand. That living word awakened my soul, gave it light, hope, joy, set it free! There were barriers still, it is true, but barriers that could in time be swept away.

I left the well-house eager to learn. Everything had a name, and each name gave birth to a new thought. As we returned to the house every object which I touched seemed to quiver with life. That was because I saw everything with the strange, new light that had come to me. *[10, pp. 22-4]*

Other examples of the frustration and rage of which Miss Keller speaks can be found in young children who have come to a new culture with an unfamiliar language. For example, children from rural, Spanish-speaking sections of Puerto Rico were confronted with a combination of strange ways and strange speech when they were brought by their parents to American cities. During the day, while their parents went out to work, they were often left in child-care centers where they exhibited inexplicable rages in unpredictable, wild behavior. Usually such behavior subsided as the children learned English and could communicate more freely with their teachers and peers *[7]*.

Anyone who has traveled in a foreign country without knowing the native language has felt the frustration and helplessness that accompany an inability to communicate. To be unable to communicate with persons around one is like living inside a glass container. One can see what other persons are doing but one cannot get through to them. It represents a most basic kind of isolation.

Implications of Communication for the Individual

For the developing individual, communication with his fellows performs three major functions: 1) it patterns the world about him, 2) it defines his own position in relation to other people, and 3) it helps him adapt successfully to his environment. In the last two functions it exerts a critical influence on the formation of his personality and his sense of self. It offers him cues and bench marks by which he can guide his behavior. Through communication the standards and values of his group are transmitted, and an awareness of these makes it possible for him to phrase his needs in ways that will bring him satisfaction. . . .

The tool through which communication is most frequently achieved—language—contains both the definitions and the limitations that direct the individual's approach to the external world. It may be considered an accumulation of symbolized human experiences and as such reflects the life of the group. Each new member is introduced to the experiences of his elders and given directives for his own thinking through the very words that are provided by the group for the transmittal of experiences. The interrelations among these words, the structure of the language, also hold important implications for the individual's approach to the world. In time he comes to think and to feel in terms of these symbols—to think and to feel about himself as well as about external objects and events.

The impact on the individual of communication with his fellows is suggested by observations of those who have been long isolated from human companionship. Several accounts of so-called "feral" children, apparently reared by animals, and of children reared in almost complete isolation, indicate that all these children seemed "unhuman" and retarded in development when they were first found [2, 3, 18]. Many of them never achieved normal human levels of functioning; some may, of course, have been biologically deficient. Nevertheless, it is striking that a few of them made great gains in a short time after they were restored to human contacts and after they had experienced intensive attempts to communicate with them.*

Communication and Intelligence

Recent studies of apparent shifts in the intelligence level of young children, following a change in environment, are equally suggestive. The environmental changes were usually complex, involving in some cases moving from a restrictive, completely unstimulating orphanage to a modern progressive nursery school. The environments differed in factors such as freedom of movement and material resources, but they offered also striking contrasts in the amount of communication to which the children were exposed. In the institutions where the children lived before they first attended nursery school they were isolated in their cribs much of the time, with little opportunity for communication with adults. Contacts with adults were limited to those involving essential services. In the nursery school, on the other hand, communication with both the teacher and other children was encouraged. The teacher often initiated contacts through the medium of verbal communication, and the very nature of the material environment made communication on the part of the children necessary and rewarding. Since there were many attractive kinds of equipment and ma-

---

* It is entirely possible, of course, that the feral children seemed inhuman because they had learned a different system of communication, i.e., one used by the animals among whom they lived. The "gains" they appeared to have made may have been the effect of learning the system of communication prevalent among socialized humans.

terials, the children were motivated to talk about them, to establish bases for sharing them, or for participating co-operatively in their use. In view of other observations of isolated children, it is highly probable that the impetus to increased communication was largely responsible for the striking results shown.

Communication and Behavior

One of the most dramatic demonstrations of the effect of communication can be found in the case of Gua, the ape:

> Gua was reared along with a human child from the age of seven and a half months to sixteen months, by the parents of the child. Both were treated alike. By the time the experiment was terminated, the ape had learned to respond correctly to over 50 verbal phrases. She mastered bladder and bowel control easily, and learned to be obedient. She played co-operatively with the child, and handled the physical environment at least as well as he. More significantly perhaps, her emotional reactions were also similar to those of the child, running a gamut through loyalty, jealousy, docility, anxiety, and negativism. [11]

From the various kinds of evidence here presented, it seems fair to assert that communication is basic to functioning in a manner we conceive of as "human."

Importance of Communication in Specific Situations

The occasions in day-to-day living when successful communication is of crucial importance are legion. For the student, the ability to communicate what he has learned is of primary importance. The following student's plaint could be multiplied many times in many classrooms:

> I was supposed to give a book review in one of my classes for my term report. I slaved over that book. I read it and I outlined it and I could swear I knew it backwards. Yet when I got up in front of the class I couldn't seem to get going. I stuttered and stammered and I could see by the expressions on the faces in front of me that I was incoherent, but I couldn't seem to do anything about it. That sure was one time when I failed to communicate.

Similarly, for the young man and woman seeking a job, the ability to describe their skills and to communicate their objectives convincingly is essential. In social life, in heterosexual contacts, success often depends on accurately transmitting one's meaning and motives. Sometimes ludicrous, often tragic, misunderstandings grow out of a lack of skill in communication.

When students in several college psychology classes were asked for specific instances in which communication had been of critical importance for them both on and off the campus, a wide variety of situations was described. They ranged from attempts to convince instructors that the students deserved higher grades than they had received, to descriptions of emergencies involving immediate danger of destruction. The following illustrative responses may indicate the range of experiences:

> Last semester when I ran for Student Council office, communication played an important part in my election. We spent a great deal of time preparing a single leaflet which was distributed to the students and which I think was a decisive factor in my election. In addition, the campaign statements that I wrote for the college newspapers helped. In both cases I had to introduce myself to the students and at the same time convince them that I was the one they should vote for, always taking care not to antagonize anyone in the smallest way.

> · · · · ·

> While serving as a volunteer firefighter in the mountains of California five of us got separated from the main group. We proceeded down the side of one of the mountains into a huge valley. However, it was not the valley we were acquainted with and we realized we were lost. As we sat there pondering what fate had in store for us one of the men spied a figure in the distance. We called to him but imagine our dismay when after he arrived we discovered he was unable to speak English. However, through the use of signs and all sorts of wild and ludicrous gestures we were able to inform him of our plight, whereupon he, being a native of the area, promptly led us to the safety of the main road. Crucial? Perhaps not, but it certainly seemed so to us at the time.

> · · · · ·

> I was in Quebec and went into a French restaurant and attempted to order, without speaking or understanding French. It was evening and I wanted to ask for a dinner menu. I thought I remembered the French word for dinner. However, when the waitress brought me the breakfast menu at 9 P.M. I realized that I had failed to communicate.

> · · · · ·

> We received orders that the Germans were planning a counterattack that evening. A red flare sent up into the sky by the enemy meant that the attack would take place in two minutes, and a yellow flare meant that the attack would take place in a "code" sector, not mentioned.
> I was sitting at the observation post with a friend. Our position was in no-man's-land, in front of our own troops and near the enemies'.
> My duty was to phone my company when the red or yellow flare went up. My friend had fallen asleep and I alone was awake. In a few minutes I saw dark shadowy forms moving around me. There was no flare warning. This was the attack.
> I grabbed the phone and tried to speak. The lives of many of my friends depended on a warning. I could make no sound. My tongue seemed frozen.

Suddenly a dark form crawled close to my feet—it was a German. In desperation I yelled into the phone, but my words were hardly intelligible, they were so disjointed. Fortunately, my company took the warning.

We could continue with stories of the student who failed to obtain the telephone number he wanted because the girl misunderstood his intentions, the sailors who overstayed their shore leave because they could not get directions for returning to their ship and thus lost shore privileges for thirty days, and the girl who inadvertently insulted her teacher through an ineptitude in phrasing—but it scarcely is necessary. It seems obvious that, no matter what our special interests might be, to this extent we have a common interest: in so far as no individual is completely self-sufficient, as long as we must live with each other, we must depend on each other for succor, for guidance, and for satisfactions, and for these things we must learn to communicate with each other.

COMMUNICATION AND THE GROUP

The importance of communication is not confined to the individual. It is the force that enables groups to cohere. In interpersonal relations it performs functions similar to those of cement, mortar, glue, or the charges of a magnetic field. Not only do small informal associations depend upon it for their continued existence, but every formal organization, every industrial unit, every governmental body functions effectively only when it communicates with ease and facility. The following excerpt from a newspaper account of "practice war games" particularly illustrates this:

> Washington, March 14, 1950. One of the greatest lessons learned in Portrex—the Puerto Rican amphibious air-borne exercises just completed—was that communications—the nerve system of any military force—are still the key to success in battle.
>
> Probably more difficulty was encountered with communications than in any other single item. . . .
>
> Perhaps even more important was the lesson that communications or electronics counter-measures—jamming, the dispatch of false radio orders and the like—can create havoc in any operation. . . .
>
> During the maneuver, the defending enemy broke into the landing "invaders'" wave net, countermanded orders for landing craft, brought down the invaders' artillery fire on the heads of their own troops and at the end of the maneuver, the "enemy" was about to control the naval gunfire support of the "invaders."
>
> The possibilities of communications' and electronics' counter-measures are enormous, and to us it is a fledgling art. . . . [14]

Communication in Industry

The basic importance of communication in the efficient functioning of industrial groups is illustrated by B. B. Gardner's analysis of human relations in industry. He points out that a major function of the "line of authority" or "chain of command" is "that of providing channels of communication extending from top to bottom throughout the structure [5]." These channels play a critical part in two kinds of relationships that are essential to the smooth operation of the organization—relationships between each person and his job, and those between each person and his superior. If communication breaks down in relation to matters which the workers need to know about their jobs, goods are not produced. If communication in the worker-foreman relationship is not satisfactory, co-operation is hampered and efficiency impaired. Speaking of the relationship between foremen and top-management levels, Gardner says:

> They [the foremen] . . . feel that, while top management often talks of them as being part of management and expects them to identify with the interests of the company and top management, it does not make them feel that they really belong. They feel that they are expected to take whatever is handed down to them from above no matter how arbitrary it may seem to them, nor how difficult it may make their jobs. Obviously these feelings of resentment interfere with cordial relations between superiors and subordinates and lead to a less than optimal performance . . . and they arise essentially from *a lack of communication* between status levels. (Italics ours.) [5, p. 46]

The reason assigned by Gardner for this impairment in relations is the fact that foremen rarely participate in the making of decisions or the determination of policy. Moreover, he says, often "they are not well informed" as to the whys and wherefores of decisions. While theoretically the foreman's ideas or feelings are indicated to his superiors, actually he knows that his ideas do not often penetrate to top-policy levels and that they rarely influence decisions. In Gardner's words: "He almost never has the satisfaction of *communicating them directly* or seeing that they are actually considered." (Italics ours.) [5, p. 67]

For the executive, efficient communication with his staff is essential if he is to be well informed. To make proper decisions, to settle conflicts, and to function properly, he needs adequate information. He must rely on verbal communication from subordinates for detailed knowledge of the work and the conditions which might affect it, in order to interpret properly his cost reports and production records. (Note that the latter are in themselves forms of communication.) Since a top executive of a large plant cannot have contact with all the workers, it is *from what other people say* that he must learn about their attitudes. The need for effective communication in any industrial organization is so acute that some sections of it "are primarily concerned with gathering certain types of information and communicating it to top levels [5]." Some of the chief values of personnel counselors and labor-management committees lie in their facilitation of communication among different divisions and different management levels in large organizations.

The Importance of Communication on National and International Levels

The international scene provides striking demonstration of the vital part communication plays in group interaction. During World War II, friction developed between GI's and the English among whom they were stationed. Therefore, a specialist was employed by the United States government to analyze the sources of this friction and to develop ways of overcoming the barriers to communication. She discovered that American soldiers and English civilians did not understand each other because in conveying their intentions they used the same language in different ways. Starting from different premises, each party thought that the other meant to imply something besides the simple content of his words, and it was this "something" which was so frequently unacceptable to the recipient. Margaret Mead, the investigator, analyzed the intentions imputed to each party, and traced the bases for these imputations to characteristic differences in custom and use of speech [13]. Thus her task was to find, without antagonizing either side, a means of making each side aware of the other's intentions. . . . Here the significant facts are that even with the same language, people living in different cultural frameworks often fail to understand each other, and their lack of understanding hinders their ability to work together.

How often since the beginning of the United Nations have we heard: "*If we could only communicate with the Russians.*" This reflects the common belief that if you can talk with a man, you can find a way of working with him. The very purpose of a device to prevent contacts between peoples such as a ban on listening to foreign broadcasts, is to keep groups apart and to stifle the development of sympathetic understanding. In a recent appraisal of the problem, T. M. Newcomb suggests that hostility toward other peoples is encouraged by barriers to communication. He points out that group-shared hostilities toward the members of other groups are kept alive by the segregation which emphasizes the group differentiation. The effect is to block communication between the groups and to make any development of fellow feeling with their members impossible [15]. In arbitration or mediation of disputes it is a truism that the opportunity for peaceful settlement can be maintained only so long as communication channels remain open. Indeed, the basic task of the arbitrator, and particularly of the mediator, is to keep the channels of communication open between the antagonistic factions while seeking to find a possible common ground for agreement.

Communication as a Test of Reality

Ample evidence exists of the way in which barriers to communication maintain social illusions and prevent social change. One study of social attitudes [17] found that each member of a certain church denomination in a small town assumed that all the other members disapproved of card playing. In fact, however, each one played cards himself. Each, therefore, maintained in public a disapproving attitude, unaware that his fellow church-members were personally in agreement with his private views.

With this study in mind, it seems clear that communication is a means of testing notions and prejudices against reality, and for setting each individual straight concerning the nature of the real world and the motives of his fellows. Newcomb's study of the effect of social norms on socio-political attitudes of college students [16] found a fairly consistent shift in a liberal direction between freshman and senior years. These shifts were smaller in some colleges than in others. It is a suggestive observation that where smaller shifts were found, little overt expression was given to such matters, while on the campus showing the largest changes they were the subject of much discussion. Newcomb suggests that in colleges showing little change, those students whose attitudes did move away from their freshman norms were unaware of the extent of community support which they had, and consequently tended to feel rather isolated. When social norms are discussed in detail, it will be seen that awareness of the norms of the group can be a very potent factor in inducing individual conformity and effecting changes in an individual's attitudes. Lack of communication would, of course, militate against such awareness.

One study of public opinion in the United States during the early years of World War II, for instance, [1] showed that Congressional action lagged behind the opinions of the public as reflected in the public opinion polls. Since there was no well-established and regularized channel for free communication between citizens and members of Congress, it is very likely that the latter were not even aware that they were out of step with their constituents. Whatever the success of public opinion polls, they can at least serve as points of contact between citizens and their government.

The foregoing discussion underscored the importance of communication in social living. We turn next to a consideration of the actual process.

DEFINITIONS AND CONCEPTS

Many definitions of communication have been proposed. Of these the relatively simple ones are probably the most useful. C. I. Hovland, for example, suggests that communication be defined "as the process by which an individual—the communicator—transmits stimuli (usually verbal symbols) to modify the behavior of other individuals—communicatees [8]." Henry Pratt Fairchild's Dictionary of Sociology includes the following definition:

> The process of making common or exchanging subjective studies such as ideas, sentiment, beliefs, usually by means of language, though also visual representations, imitations, and suggestions. . . . Communi-

cation in human groups becomes the chief factor in their unity and continuity and the vehicle of culture. . . . Good communication is the very basis of human society. *[4, p. 50]*

"Communication" is used by Warren Weaver to include "all of the procedures by which one mind can affect another *[22, p. 11]*." Still another author calls all meaningful social interaction "communication." Noel Gist writes: "When social interaction involves the transmission of meanings through the use of symbols, it is known as communication." He further defines "social interaction" as "the reciprocal influences that human beings exert on each other through interstimulation and response *[6, p. 363]*."

Common to all these definitions are four factors involved in effective communication: (1) the *communicator*—the person who initiates the process; (2) the *communicant,* that is, the recipient; (3) the *content* of the communication—this might be called the *communiqué;* and (4) the *effect* achieved by the communication. Implicit in all definitions are the concepts of *interaction* and *effect.*

MODES OF COMMUNICATION

Although communication usually takes place by means of verbal symbols, the actual forms of stimuli responsible for the contact are numerous. In the words of one scientist: "A nod or wink, a drumbeat in the jungle, the blinking of a signal light, a bit of music that reminds one of an event in the past, puffs of smoke in the desert air, the movements and posturing in a ballet—all of these are means men use to convey ideas *[22, p. 11]*."

Intonations, facial expression, and bodily gesture are all, in themselves, excellent communication media. Their use, moreover, together with words, is often necessary to convey precisely the intended meaning of the communiqué. Sometimes they are inextricable aspects of language. It is reported, for example, that Zuñi Indians "require much facial contortion and bodily gesticulation to make their sentences perfectly intelligible." It is claimed that the language of the Bushman requires so many signs to make clear its meanings that it is "unintelligible in the dark *[20, p. 706]*."

Non-verbal Forms of Communication

Signs other than language are often employed in a complex way to indicate feelings and attitudes. Among the Orokaive tribes of New Guinea, for example, each individual has a symbol—a "vegetable signature," a sprig of some plant which he wears and uses in communicating under given circumstances. He may leave the sprig in his neighbor's garden, for example to inform him that he has taken some produce. He may also use it to indicate the state of his feelings.*

* By permission from *Primitive Behavior,* by W. I. Thomas. Copyright, 1937, McGraw-Hill Book Company, Inc.

It is used by individuals as a sign of abstinence, a sort of self-inflicted tabu, whenever such abstinence has been the outcome of some quarrel or grievance. The Orokaive is very prone when his feelings are hurt to punish himself rather than the man who has hurt him; or, perhaps better, to take revenge upon the other party by punishing himself.

Thus if a man fall out with his wife, he will thrust a sprig of his *heratu* through his armlet, and while he continues to wear it will receive no food of her cooking. Not that he altogether starves himself into relenting; some friend will cook for him until his mood softens, and then there are inter-changes of gifts between the wife's people and his own, and as I am assured, invariable reconciliation. Similarly a wife who has been accused by her husband of sponging on him, not working for her keep, will advertise her grief and indignation by wearing her heratu, and will for the time being refuse to eat another taro out of his garden.

.   .   .   .   .

A bunch of drooping leaves may be tied to a coconut palm in the village. The owner has fallen out with his neighbor over the boundary of his garden. The row of tree trunks which constitutes the usual garden border has been displaced and shows an encroaching and unwarrantable bulge. Therefore he has set up his heratu to indicate that he has been imposed upon and has broken off friendly relations with his neighbor; he will accept no hospitality from him (and give none) until the matter has been adjusted. Another man nurses some resentment against a near-by village. If he were bidden to a feast there he would go, but with his heratu in his armlet; and when the wooden dish of savory taro was placed before him, he would wave it aside, or lay his heratu upon the food to show that he could not accept the hospitality of those who had wronged him. Then the offender would be put to shame and punished, and be sorry for what he had done. *[21, p. 71-2]*

The potency of such relatively subtle forms of communication as body stance and muscular variations are indicated by the responses of nonseeing and nonhearing individuals to persons with whom they are in contact. The teacher of Helen Keller tells of her pupil's extreme sensitivity to the emotional reactions of other persons in her presence even when these reactions were expressed only through body movement and set. The following instances are striking examples of the communication value of these muscular variations:*

One day, while she was walking out with her mother and Mr. Anagnos, a boy threw a torpedo, which startled Mrs. Keller. Helen felt the change in her mother's movements instantly and asked, "What are we afraid of?" On one occasion, while walking on the Common with her, I saw a police officer taking a man to the station house. The agitation which I felt evidently produced a perceptible physical change; for Helen asked excitedly, "What do you see?"

* From: *The Story of My Life* by Helen Keller. Copyright 1903, 1931 by Helen Keller, reprinted by permission of Doubleday & Company, Inc.

· · · · ·

A striking illustration of this strange power was recently shown while her ears were being examined. . . . Several experiments were tried, to determine positively whether or not she had any perception of sound. All present were astonished when she appeared not only to hear a whistle, but also an ordinary tone of voice. She would turn her head, smile, and act as though she had heard what was said. Thinking that she was receiving impressions from me, I put her hands upon the table, and withdrew to the opposite side. The aurists then tried their experiments with quite different results. Helen remained motionless throughout them all, not once showing the least sign that she realized what was going on. [10, pp. 353-4]

Communication by Empathy

Some psychologists are interested in even more subtle modes of communication. In speaking of the relationship between the infant and the adult and the importance of communication in the development of the self, Harry Stack Sullivan points out that long before there are any signs of understanding emotional expression, an infant will show the effects of emotional contagion or "communion." He states that the adequacy of language to serve as a medium of communication stems from the primitive empathic response of the organism. In this connection he says:

It is biological for the infant when nursing to show certain expressive movements which are called the satisfaction response, and it is probably biological for the parent concerned to see these things. Due to the empathic linkage, this, the reaction of the parent to the satisfaction-response of the infant, communicates good feeling to the infant and thus he learns that this response has power. [19, p. 8]

Similarly, Margaret Mead, in discussing her observations in Bali, has commented:

A child's display of fear in the arms of a young-girl nurse which is not paralleled by similar behavior in the arms of a different nurse may be placed against the knowledge that the nurse has just quarreled with her guardian and been expelled from the temple society of unmarried girls. [12, p. 678]

Objective analyses of this "empathic" communication would probably reveal it to be compounded of facial expression, postural elements, and muscular tensions, and to present a system of nonverbal symbols to the child which is similar in many ways to the manual alphabets of the deaf-mute and the blind-deaf. Regardless of how it is achieved, the existence of this type of interaction emphasizes the contribution of nonverbal elements to the communication process.

SITUATIONAL FACTORS IN COMMUNICATION

Although the number of available communication tools is large, each communication situation may call for a particular mode of expression uniquely effective for it, or again, it may preclude the use of some modes, thus laying a greater burden on the communicator by reducing the number of useful tools. Significant differences, for example, exist between the modes of communication possible in small, intimate groups meeting face-to-face, and those required by mass communication.

Again, the channels through which communication is attempted involve differences in the use of communication tools. Those which necessitate written language—newspapers, books, letters, and the like—eliminate the aids to communication provided by intonation, facial expression, or gestures. Even when oral forms of communication can be used, some situations involving large distances between the communicator and the recipient or recipients of the communication, such as the telephone or radio, preclude the use of bodily gestures and facial expressions. In other situations which may permit a fully integrated impact of bodily gestures, facial expression, and vocal intonations—such as the motion picture or television —another extremely important aspect of communication is absent. This is the observation by the communicator of the effect of the communication, which we may call the "feedback."

The Function of the Feedback

The "feedback" is of critical importance in testing the success of any attempt at communication, for only by some such device is it possible to observe its effect. If the communicator is face-to-face with the communicant, it is possible for him to judge the success of the communication by the latter's reaction.

When the communication gives directions or persuades to a line of conduct, it is easier to gauge its success than when it involves the transmission of an experience or the sharing of an idea. In the first instance, A can estimate whether he has "put over" what he intended, by what B does. In the second instance, however, A has no way of knowing what he has conveyed to B, unless B responds with a communication of his own. It is not sufficient for A to ask "Do you understand me?," for even if B says, "Certainly I do," this does not necessarily mean that the desired effect has been achieved—for the reason that A has no way of knowing what B thinks A has wanted him to understand.

The point of this discussion will become clearer if the reader will substitute for the words "Do you understand me?" and "Certainly I do" some other set of verbal symbols, such as "Quo me hie munipa me?" and "Hu mampaki quo." This absence of immediate "feedback" is precisely what concerns those who invoke mass communication for the purpose of achieving specific effects, such as persuading people to buy more of a product, to espouse a point of view, or to adopt a social attitude.

COMMUNICATION IS INTERACTION

We come now to a point made earlier: communication is interaction. It is usually a two-way process, involving stimulation and response among organisms, and it is both reciprocal and alternating. The response evoked by one communiqué in turn becomes a stimulus and a communiqué in its own right. In this way, in a series of communications, each may be both response and stimulus.

This statement holds true even for mass communication situations, where the audience is not present to answer back. If the communication is at all successful, the audience responds in some way, and its response affects future communications. The length of time between the inception of a communiqué and the response does not alter the fact that the latter takes place and that it has an effect on the communicator. An advertiser, for example, may have to wait before the response of his audience to an advertisement becomes evident, but once it does, it then affects the course of future advertisements. Actually, the main difficulty that the advertiser faces is devising ways of checking an audience response. The propagandist must know the effect of his propaganda in order to plan future successful campaigns. A response of "No" is in itself a message to the initiators of messages.

The importance of interaction can be illustrated further by the manner in which a young child acquires the communication symbols used in its group. Sullivan [19] points out that as soon as an infant picks up a verbal trick—such as saying "Ma"—he receives a strong response from the adult. The latter is important to him and he soon senses the power implicit in his accomplishment. Because of the power of the responses he evokes he is stimulated to develop the rudiments of communication habits. He learns the meaning of his own words and gestures from the responses that others give to them. If one mode of communication does not achieve the response he desires, he experiments with another. Thus he builds up a collection of sounds and bodily expressions that "stand for" objects, acts, and needs. These are symbols of the feelings he experiences, the things he wants or has, and the behavior he wishes to elicit. The child learns how to obtain results by using these symbols, and thereby he learns what others mean by the same sounds or movements when they use them.

The socialization of the individual largely depends on his acquiring meanings for symbols that are commonly used; he can understand what is wanted of him only after he has acquired such meanings. In other words, the individual develops habits of communication and acquires the tools for communication as a result of his interaction with other people. His learning to communicate is based on a two-way process that involves the response of other people to his behavior and his response to theirs.

COMMUNICATION IS RECIPROCAL

A constant reversal of roles takes place in communication. In a conversation, the communicant becomes the communicator and the latter in turn becomes the communicant. As the roles of these two are interchanged, each takes on the functions of the other. The communicator, whose first job is the sending of the message, becomes the person who receives the message. The communicant, who has been on the receiving end, often by his very response becomes the initiator of a subsequent message. Thus, in reversing their roles, both communicator and communicant contribute to the communication process, and both are equally important.

This raises for consideration the criteria of the success or effectiveness of communication. It might very simply be stated that communication takes place successfully when the effect produced by the communiqué is that intended by the communicator. If the communication was designed to instigate action or to persuade, it is successful if the outcome suffices for the purposes of the communicator. If the latter sought to transmit an experience or to share an idea, the communication may be considered successful if there is evidence of at least approximate understanding by the recipient. It is obvious that the criteria for success in communication are fairly gross. This, however, cannot be avoided since it is often impossible to convey with complete exactness the inner experience of the communicator or to invoke in the recipient precisely the state sought by the initiator. If even pragmatic or partial success is to be achieved, the communicator must solve an impressively complicated problem. . . .

COMMUNICATION AND EXPRESSION

We assume, in our discussion, that the originator of a communication has a purpose in initiating the process. That purpose may be varied or multiple, but an intention of creating some sort of effect on another person or persons is always present. One may, however, witness the production of stimuli resembling communication stimuli that lack the intention of communication. Under such conditions the originator of the stimuli may be expressing something, but he will not intentionally be communicating anything. The cry of the newborn infant exemplifies the type of expression from which any intent to communicate is absent. The infant cries because of an internal state of feeling, not because of any desire to produce an effect. Only after this cry has been repeatedly followed by gratifying effects can it be regarded as being used as a communication device.

In like manner many an individual has addressed himself verbally to the stone on which he has just stubbed his toe, or to a baulky automobile motor. Here too there is no intent to communicate. Lecturers in college classes sometimes give the impression that they are talking because of the need to talk rather than to communicate with their hearers. Exclamations of pain, grimaces, postural attitudes, writings, paintings, drawings, sculptures, musical compositions—all these may be merely expressions or reflections of internal states. Only when they are intended to produce effects, or when they succeed in producing effects, may they be considered forms of communication.

Voluntary and Involuntary Communication

At this point the reader may ask: "Is there no involuntary communication?" We would have to agree that there is. Whenever an observer reacts to the expressional activity of another individual in a way that indicates the observer's awareness of the internal state of the originator of the stimulus, a communication has taken place. He may look sympathetic, or do something to help the originator, or he may merely register internally—for instance, "He looks worried"—but as long as his reaction is congruent with the state of the individual he is observing, he may be considered a communicant. When, however, his reaction has no relevance to the state of the latter, although he may have perceived and responded to the emitted stimulus, no communication can be said to have occurred. The crying of an infant may cause a nearby child to strike it, or cause an adult to leave the room. In these situations, while the infant has expressed a state of feeling, and while the observer has reacted to the form of the expression, no communication, voluntary or involuntary, has taken place, since the reaction has no relevance to the internal state of the communicator.

It should now be obvious that the study of the communication process can be very complicated. However, the real obstacles to successful communication have not yet been mentioned. They will emerge as we consider all the implications of the process in terms of the four major components involved—communicator, communicant, communiqué, and effect.

Summary

The communication process is the basis of all that we call social in the functioning of the living organism. In man, it is essential to the development of the individual, to the formation and continued existence of groups, and to the interrelations among groups.

Although there is no complete agreement by social scientists on a single definition of communication, all the major definitions imply both interaction and effect. Analysis shows that at least four factors are involved in effective communication: (1) the communicator, (2) the communicant, (3) the content, and (4) the effect.

Communication is usually thought of as taking place by means of verbal symbols, but the social-psychological analysis requires that attention be paid to the full range of symbols that may be used by man, including gestures, tone, facial expression, drumbeats, telegraph clicks, flag and smoke signals, etc.

The interaction that is involved in communication, the return to the communicator of some clue to the effect of the communiqué on the communicant, is seen in the "feedback." Analysis of this process reveals the complexity of communication, for it requires that the communicator be also communicant and the communicant be also communicator.

* * * *

BIBLIOGRAPHY

1. Cantril, H.: "Public Opinion in Flux," *The Annals of the American Academy of Political and Social Science*, Vol. 220 (1942), pp. 136-52.
2. Davis, K.: "Extreme Social Isolation of a Child," *American Journal of Sociology*, Vol. 45 (1940), pp. 554-65.
3. Dennis, W.: "The Significance of Feral Man," *American Journal of Psychology*, Vol. 54 (1941), pp. 425-32.
4. Fairchild, H. P. (Ed.): *Dictionary of Sociology* (New York: Philosophical Library, Inc., 1944).
5. Gardner, B. B.: *Human Relations in Industry* (Chicago: R. D. Irwin, 1946).
6. Gist, N., in S. Eldridge (Ed.): *Fundamentals of Sociology* (New York: Thomas Y. Crowell Company, 1950).
7. Hartley, R. E.: Personal Observations.
8. Hovland, C. I.: "Social Communication," *Proceedings of the American Philosophical Society*, Vol. 92 (1948), pp. 371-5.
9. Johnson, W.: *People in Quandaries* (New York: Harper and Brothers, 1946).
10. Keller, H.: *The Story of My Life* (New York: Doubleday, Page and Company, 1908).
11. Kellog, W. N. and L. A. Kellog: *The Ape and the Child* (New York: McGraw-Hill Book Company, Inc., 1933).
12. Mead, M.: "Research on Primitive Children," in L. Carmichael (Ed.): *Manual of Child Psychology* (New York: John Wiley and Sons, Inc., 1946), pp. 667-706.
13. Mead, M.: "The Application of Anthropological Techniques to Cross-National Communication," *Transactions of the New York Academy of Sciences*, Vol. 9 (1947), pp. 133-52.
14. *The New York Times*, March 14, 1950.
15. Newcomb, T. M.: "Autistic Hostility and Social Reality," *Human Relations*, Vol. 1 (1947), pp. 3-19.
16. Newcomb, T. M.: *Personality and Social Change* (New York: The Dryden Press, Inc., 1943).
17. Schank, R. L.: "A Study of a Community and its Groups and Institutions conceived of as Behaviors of Individuals," *Psychological Monographs*, Vol. 43 (1932), No. 2.
18. Singh, J. A. L. and R. M. Zingg: *Wolf Children and Feral Man* (New York: Harper and Brothers, 1943).

19. Sullivan, H. S.: *Conceptions of Modern Psychiatry* (Washington, D. C.: William Alanson White Foundation, 1947).
20. Thomas, W. I.: *Source Book for Social Origins* (Boston: Richard G. Badger, 1909).
21. Thomas, W. I.: *Primitive Behavior* (New York: McGraw-Hill Book Company, Inc., 1937).
22. Weaver, W.: "The Mathematics of Communication," *Scientific American,* Vol. 181 (1949).

WORDS AND NOT-WORDS
The World of Not-Words—The World of Words

By Wendell Johnson

THE WORLD OF NOT-WORDS

IT HAS BEEN SAID by many, and in various ways, that the problems of knowing and of understanding center around the relation of language to reality, of symbol to fact. These ink marks over which your eyes are racing, these ink marks that we agree to call words, and these words that we agree to accept as "legal tender" for the exchange of information, by what magic, or by what humdrum rules, do they serve their strange functions? If you stare at a word long enough, it does indeed become, for you, mere ink marks, a peculiar pattern of lines. At first it looks as though it were spelled correctly, then you cannot be sure, and finally you are overcome with the feeling that to consider its spelling at all is to enter into the most entangled mazes of humanity.

Of course if you stare at anything sufficiently long and thoughtfully, as a calf stares at a new gate, it tends to appear at last as though it were utterly unaccountable. A great philosopher once remarked that the strangest invention in all history was that peculiar covering for the human foot that we call a sock. He had been looking at one for several minutes. There are times when it seems impossible, however, that any other human invention could be more astonishing and strange than a word—the word *sock*, for example.

One may wonder how words came to exist in the first place, and how they "get" their "meaning." One may wonder, as C. K. Ogden and I. A. Richards wondered throughout a sizable book, about "the meaning of meaning." And we can be sure that at least one would discover sooner or later that a word "means" something more than other words. People who are accustomed, for example, to look in a dictionary for the meanings of words proceed under a great delusion if they suppose that what they find in a dictionary is a word's full meaning. What they find is that the dictionary definition of a word consists of other words. Moreover, a dictionary is a closed system. In it, not only is a word defined in other words, but these, in their turn, are also defined in other words—and if you follow far enough this trail of definitions of words, you find that it is a trail that goes in a great circle, so that finally you make the enlightening discovery that the words are defined by each other. *Space* is defined in terms of *length* and *length* is defined in terms of *space*, *beauty* is defined in terms of *good* and *good* in terms of *beauty*, etc. When you have energetically explored a dictionary, what you know are words, and what you know about them are words, too. And if all you know are words, you are left with the question with which you started, the question of what words "mean"—besides other words.

The question is incredibly complex, and our stupidity has been expressed persistently in the unduly simple answers we have given to it. We can avoid a repetition of that stupidity, at least in part, by the easy means of announcing that we do not propose here to exhaust the subject. Our aims are modest. We are concerned chiefly with three aspects of "meaning": with the non-verbal *facts* which words represent, with the *evaluations* which they express, and with the *effects* which they have on those who hear or read them, including their effects on the persons who speak or write them. The word *blonde*, for example, may refer to a particular person, or it may be spoken in such a way as to express evaluations ranging all the way from love to disgust, or its utterance may lead to any reaction from cheery smiles to homicide. What *blonde* "means" according to the dictionary is something else again, and it is not our primary concern. It is the primary concern of certain other students of language, and the work they do is important. Moreover, there are many other ways of considering the "meaning" of a word. The problem is as profound and as intricate as the problem of humanity itself. Certainly we shall not attempt to exhaust it. Within the limits of our major interests, however, we shall deal with it in an orderly way.

What Is a Fact?

Let us begin by looking briefly at the main steps involved in the seemingly simple process of Mr. A speaking to Mr. B—the process of communication. First, there is a "fact," which is to say that something happens to stimulate Mr. A. He feels it and interprets it. He speaks, verbalizing his interpretation. In speaking, Mr. A produces sound waves which serve to vibrate certain membranes and fluids in Mr. B's ear. This sets up activity in Mr. B's auditory nerve, and so in his brain cortex, and then he interprets what goes on in his cortex. Finally he says something or does something— to which Mr. A in turn reacts, and then Mr. B reacts again to Mr. A, etc. This sort of thing has been going on among hundreds of millions of people for thousands of years, with the result that human society has been growing more and more complex. Mr. A talking to Mr. B is a very important matter. Around it center practically all our problems of human understanding and disagreement, of cooperation and conflict, of knowledge and stupidity, of peace and war.

Just what goes on when Mr. A speaks to Mr. B? We said that, to begin with, there is a fact. It is this part of the process that we shall consider in the present chapter. The basic question we have to examine is simply this: What is a fact? Propaganda experts, so-called, keep warning us about the dangers of what they call emotional appeals. They urge us to look at the facts, to insist on the facts, to keep our eyes on the facts. This advice is so disarmingly simple. It leaves so much to chance, takes so much for granted. Behind it lies the assumption that a fact is a fact, and that everyone knows a fact when he sees one. In the meantime, there are some very elementary considerations to be taken into account. One is that knowing the facts is impossible if one means knowing *all* the facts about anything. Whenever anyone advises you not to act until you know the facts, he puts you under a spell of inaction forever unless he indicates which facts and how many of them you are to know, because you will never know them completely. Then, too, what we call facts have a way of changing, so that yesterday's statistics become today's fairy tales. Furthermore, a fact appears different depending on the point of view; your facts are not exactly like those of someone else. Actually, one man's fact is not infrequently another man's fiction. This means, finally, that facts are, in important measure, a matter of social agreement. Unless these elementary points are clearly recognized, telling people to stick to the facts is usually a sure-fire way of getting them embroiled in hopeless argument.

If you would recognize a fact when you see one and make the most of it, there are, then, four things about any fact that you must be clear about: It is necessarily incomplete, it changes, it is a personal affair, and its usefulness depends on the degree to which others agree with you concerning it.

A fact is necessarily incomplete. There are definite limitations to our ability to observe the world about us, to say nothing of our ability to observe ourselves. There are certain air waves that we do not register as sound. There are energy radiations that we do not see, or feel, or in any other way recognize. In order to see beyond certain limits of magnitude we must use microscopes, and even microscopes have their limitations. In other words, we get only as much of the facts as we can with the sensory organs—and the magnifying devices—we have to work with. Beyond the directly observable lies the microscopic world, and beyond even that the submicroscopic realm extends to limits, if there are limits, that we can imagine scarcely better than a blind child can imagine the appearance of trees in autumn.

What we observe as a fact is necessarily an abstract, an expurgated version, so to speak, of something concerning which we can only conjecture. "If he is ingenious he may form some picture of a mechanism which could be responsible for all the things he observes. . . ." Thus, indeed, and inescapably, "in our endeavor to understand reality we are somewhat like a man trying to understand the mechanism of a closed watch" which he has no way of opening. So far we may go and no farther in our explorations of reality. Our "facts" are incomplete. The argument against intolerance and dogmatism is not, in the final analysis, a "moral" argument; it rests solidly upon the simple consideration that it is humanly impossible to know *all* the facts, or even all of any one fact. The carrier of dogma is deluded; he may or may not be "immoral."

We can know something, however. Facts change, and yet a semblance of yesterday remains in today's sounds and visions. Facts change, but sufficient unto the day are the facts thereof. Indeed change itself would appear to be the most important fact of all. Facts as we observe them are little more than quick glimpses of a ceaseless transformation—as if we viewed the separate frames of a moving picture without quite realizing that what we were viewing was, in fact, a *moving* picture. Looking closely at a motion picture film we see that each successive frame is slightly different from the last. Just so, looking closely at a "fact" we see that it appears slightly—or markedly—different from time to time. The grasses grow, the fruit ripens, the boy becomes a man. A person, as we know him, is a kind of average, a fusion or blending, an abstract, of many different observations that we have made of him. Like the sting of a bee, each fact occurs but once. Because *facts* change, any one fact is unique. Actually, to say that facts change is to say simply that no two facts are completely alike. Generally speaking, however, all the facts within our range do not change so utterly or so suddenly as to leave us dumb with surprise. True, there are times when change takes us quite unawares; that is the basis of comedy—and of tragedy. But so long as we remain responsive to the fact of change itself, the ever-changing facts are not, as a rule, unnerving.

In a basic sense a fact is an observation. An observation is the act of an individual. So it is that a fact is a personal affair. After all, that is why a fact (considered as a personal observation) is necessarily incomplete: The individual who observes it is limited in observational capacity. And that, in part, is why a fact changes: The individual who observes it is himself changing continuously, and so he observes differently from time to time. To paraphrase Heraclitus, the same man cannot step in a river twice. Having learned this lesson for the first time, we bewail our disillusionment, and having learned it well, we treasure our foresight. We do not merely discover facts; in some degree we fashion them. "The world as known to us is a joint product of the observer and the observed." The basic importance of the personal equation in what we call facts is illustrated in homely and effective terms in the following passage from the introductory chapter in the fifth volume of *Colloid Chemistry*, edited by Jerome Alexander:

> Lest we be too confident of all our sensory knowledge, let it be recalled that Blakeslee and Fox demonstrated that the ability of persons to taste phenylthiocarbamid is heritable as a Mendelian recessive, and that even those who get any taste at all from it (about 70 per cent) describe it

variously as bitter, sweet, salty, or sour. This indicates that there is a relativity of sense impressions. H. C. Moir tested sixty persons as to their ability to recognize by taste four simple flavors—orange, lemon, lime, and vanilla. Only one person had a perfect score. Five had records of over 75 per cent, but forty-eight failed to reach 50 per cent. Vanilla was variously identified as black currant, lime, apricot, greengage, damson, lemon, pineapple, orange, tangerine, almond, red currant, strawberry. Only a limited number of persons can taste sodium benzoate, and wide differences exist in the ability to detect and recognize such odors as verbena and to distinguish between wines. R. J. Williams reports (*Science*, Dec. 11th, 1931) that a man whose sense of smell appeared otherwise normal could not detect the odor of a skunk, while *n*-butyl mercaptan, the "perfume" carried by skunks, had no unpleasant odor for him. Laselle and Williams in attempting to identify a substance as creatinine, found it tasteless, though the literature states that creatinine is bitter. It was not until they had tried the sample on several others that they located someone who found it bitter. Since lean meat contains much creatinine (about 2 grams per pound), and soups made from lean meat contain extracted creatinine, we have another possible basis of differences in taste. Williams believes that the problem is associated with the more general one of individual metabolic idiosyncrasies, which crop up at times in medicine (*e.g.*, reactions to morphine, novocaine, iodoform) or in industry (reactions to cosmetics, "chemicals," etc.).

There is, indeed, no accounting for taste, unless we recognize the fact that it is an individual matter in a fundamental physiological sense. And the individul differences, great as they are to begin with, become tremendously confounded when the factors of training, or so-called psychological conditioning, are brought into play. What is true in this respect of the sense of taste is likewise true in varying degrees of all the other sense modes. Individual differences in sensory capacity in its various aspects have been heavily documented by scientific investigators in many laboratories. This is to say that a fact, as an observation, is a personal affair, to be trusted as such and not as a universal truth.

What this means, in practical terms, is that a fact is useful, or dependable, to the degree that other persons agree with you concerning it. (We are referring here, of course, to first-order facts, not to conclusions that might be drawn from them. One man's conclusions can be better than those of the people who disagree with him.) If the majority say something is green every time you say it is red, you had best take their word for it. If a doctor, two internes, and a nurse all agree that there are no grasshoppers on your suit jacket, you might as well quit trying to brush them off. Generally speaking, the larger the number of people who agree as to a fact, the more dependable the fact is.

This is to be said, however, with two qualifications. The first is that some observers are more reliable than others. If you were a factory personnel manager hiring inspectors whose job was to detect flaws in metal plates, you would not employ applicants indiscriminately. In a sample pile of 100 metal plates there might be 27, for example, that were defective as determined by ten experienced inspectors. An applicant who would find only 17 or as many as 36 defective plates in the pile would not be as reliable an observer as one who would find 27. Modernized factories use various kinds of so-called aptitude tests in determining the reliability of applicants for work requiring observational ability. The general principle underlying such tests is that the reliability of an observer is to be measured in terms of his agreement with other observers. Fundamentally, what we mean by a good observer is one with whom other observers of experience and established competence tend to agree. It is not necessarily true that one man's report of a fact is as good as another's.

Another aspect of this general point is that agreement in making observations depends in part on similarity in the conditions under which they are made. If you have a microscope and I have none, you may disregard my disagreements with you. But if I use the same microscope as you, our disagreements become important. Every newly discovered microbe, every new synthetic substance, every newly discovered fact of any sort is for a time known to only one person. No one else may dispute it simply because others have not observed it, so long as these others have not used the proper method for observing it. Its dependability as a fact increases, however, as more and more other persons do observe it. In fact, until it is observed by at least two individuals, it remains unsubstantiated. What all this amounts to is that some observers are more reliable than others, not only because of differences in ability to use the same equipment and techniques, but also because of differences in available equipment and technique.

The other qualification is that some observations simply cannot be verified *directly* by a second party. If I tell you that I have a toothache, you have to take my word for it so far as any direct confirmation by you is concerned. You cannot feel my toothache. Nor can I tell you the toothache; I can only tell you about it. How, then, is a fact of this sort to be verified? Indirectly. We commonly say, "He says he has a headache, but he doesn't act like it." Or "He says he has a headache, but there certainly doesn't seem to be any reason for it." Physicians distinguish two major types of condition of this kind: malingering and hysteria. When a person says that he is unable to hear, he may be deaf in the ordinary sense, but also he may be pretending (malingering), or he may be suffering from hysterical deafness. The proper examination methods give strong indirect evidence as to whether the condition is one or the other of these types. Essentially, if it can be shown that the accepted physical causes of deafness are absent and, further, that the person can hear, we say he is malingering—not only is he giving a false report, but he knows he is. If, however, the accepted physical causes are absent and the person cannot hear, at least not under conditions sufficient to demonstrate hearing in a malingerer, we say he is either genuinely deaf, or else hysterically deaf. Absence of the accepted or known physical causes of deafness is strong evidence that he is not genuinely deaf, of course, but there remains in such a case the possibility that medical history is on the verge of being made by the discovery of some physical cause of deafness not previously recognized. Generally speaking, hysterical deafness is the diagnosis made when, so far as can be determined, physical causes are absent and the person is honest in reporting that he cannot hear. What we mean essentially by saying that a person is hysterically deaf is that, although he has the physical equipment for hearing, he does not hear because of emotional conflicts which make hearing intolerable for him. The fact that, when the emotional conflicts are cleared, the person hears and freely admits it is taken as good evidence that he is not, or was not, malingering.

The report of any so-called inner experience—as of an ache, pain, itch, etc., that cannot be observed directly by a second party—may, then, be (a) reliable, (b) deliberately false, or (c) hysterical. Whether it is the one or the other has to be determined by indirect evidence. We accept it as reliable when it is consistent with the conditions and the behavior associated with it. Whether or to what degree it is consistent, and so reliable, depends, even in this case, on agreement among the persons who are in a position to observe its consistency.

With these qualifications granted, therefore, we may say that a fact is an observation agreed upon by two or more persons situated, qualified, and equipped to make it—and the more persons agreeing, the better.

THE WORLD OF WORDS

So THOROUGHLY DO WE take speech for granted as an exclusively *human* characteristic, so thoroughly do we take it for granted as a *personal* characteristic, that it scarcely ever occurs to us to "speak about speaking." We learn to speak, for the most part, without conscious effort, and by the time we are old enough to understand in any mature fashion those strangely powerful and direful noises that we call speech and that give us, somehow, control over others from a distance, it has become so much like reflex behavior, like breathing or chewing or coughing, that it hardly occurs to us that there is anything about it to be understood. Consequently most of us, by far, never do come to understand our speech in any deep or comprehensive manner. Mostly we just talk. As a noted professor once expressed it, "I seldom know what I am going to say until I hear myself saying it." Most persons could add to that that sometimes they don't know what they have said a moment or so after they have said it. A day after they have said it, it has, except for a few stray fragments, become lost in the mists of no-more.

One of the advantages of writing over speaking lies, as a matter of fact, in the increased awareness of language that writing involves. At least, language that is written is not so likely to be forgotten, and it is not so likely to be uncritically accepted, as is language "writ in the water" of speech. Certain primitive societies have managed to achieve rudimentary forms of culture and to survive for centuries without written language, but no advanced civilization was possible until the invention of writing and other methods of making more or less permanent records of symbolization, such as painting, geometry and other mathematics, etc. Professor John Dewey once declared that the invention of symbols was the oustanding event in human history.

Our world of words, to which we become so unreflectively accustomed, is indeed not something to be taken for granted. Our common belief that language is an exclusively human characteristic is for all practical purposes true, and precisely because it is true we have to face the fact that our problems, as individuals and as social groups, insofar as they are *human* problems, tend largely to arise out of the nature or structure of our language and the ways in which we make use of it. Whether we speak of our problems as economic, or political, or educational, or personal, we imply that they are to be described and understood and solved largely in terms of various methods of dealing with symbols.

The crucial point to be considered in a study of language behavior is the relationship between language and reality, between words and not-words. Except as we understand this relationship, we run the grave risk of straining the delicate connection between words and facts, of permitting our words to go wild, and so of creating for ourselves fabrications of fantasy and delusion. The importance of these considerations is heavily underscored by the fact that we obtain the overwhelming bulk of our information and convictions by purely verbal means. It is also to be recognized that by far the greater part of what we communicate to others in the form of language is not words about facts in a direct sense; rather, it is predominantly made up of words about words. Firsthand reports of direct experience comprise a relatively small proportion of the speech of most of us. Nevertheless, firsthand reports of direct experience must form the basis of our entire language structure, unless we are to live in a world of words that bears a gravely disordered relationship to the world of non-verbal reality.

This does not mean that our statements must always refer directly to immediate experience, to facts that can be pointed to or tangibly demonstrated. The referents of *electron*, for example, are not tangible things. The referents of *if, to, and, yet*, etc., are seldom very obvious. Just where does one usually find the referent of such a word as *ability?* One cannot, while speaking in Boston about rice culture in China, point to the referent of *China*. We should be as clear as possible about this. The "tyranny of words" does not lie chiefly in the fact that frequently referents for them cannot be found immediately in the form of solid objects or well-defined events. What is important is that *eventually*, by means of some sort of interlocking definitions, some rules for using one word in relation to another, we tie our statements down to first-order facts. These facts will not as a rule be observable at the moment they are referred to, but they should be observable in principle. Language is never so boring, however, or so ineffectual, as when it is kept on the level of sheer enumeration of first-order facts. In order to say anything significant, one simply has to rise above that level, and the higher above it one can rise the more significant one's remarks become—provided the steps taken in rising, so to speak, are taken in an orderly fashion and can be readily traced back to the level of factual data.

The relationship between language and reality is a *structural* relationship. For purposes of personal adjustment or effective social organization, the structure of our language must correspond essentially to the structure of reality. Structure, in this sense, can best be discussed under three headings: (a) degree of differentiation, (b) variability, or extent and rate of change, and (c) relationships among the parts (organization). In these respects, how does the structure of our language compare with the structure of reality? This is the fundamental question to be asked, from the point of view of general semantics, concerning the relation of words to facts.

Language Structure: Degree of Differentiation

As we have said before, a fact occurs but once. This is a way of stating that no two things are exactly alike and no one thing remains exactly the same. It is a way of expressing the process character of reality. Thus, the structure of reality shows a practically infinite degree of differentiation.

The structure of our language, on the other hand, is much less highly differentiated. Even though the English tongue, for example, contains many thousands of words and many of these have more than one recognized dictionary meaning, yet we are far from having one word for each fact. Each word, and even each dictionary meaning of each word, must do heavy duty, representing a great number and variety of facts.

In this respect, then, there is a fundamental lack of correspondence between the structure of our language and the structure of reality. It is a lack of correspondence that makes for considerable difficulty. Much of our more apparent confusion is due to this simple fact: that there are more things to be spoken of than there are words with which to speak of them. A rather large share of our misunderstandings and disagreements arises not so much because we are constitutionally stupid or stubborn, but simply because we have to use the same words to refer to so many different things. Thus, the word *intelligence* has been used—and is currently used—to refer to a most bewildering variety of activities and assumed qualities. Discussion about intelligence therefore drips with controversy, invective, and obfuscation: animals have intelligence; animals cannot have intelligence; intelligence is hereditary; it is environmentally determined; the rate of mental growth is increased in an enriched environment, decreased in an impoverished one; it is not; intelligence is comprised of a general factor together with a number of specific factors; it consists of specific factors only; of a general factor only; it is mainly a verbal affair; its verbal aspects are relatively unimportant, etc. To ask innocently, "Just what is all this talk about?" is to cry into the teeth of a typhoon. Such a question, if recognized at all, is met by a gale of definitions and variegated examples. It is only by painstaking care that one might conduct an "intelligent" discussion of intelligence.

Moreover, what is called intelligence by one person may be called by one of many other names by someone else. The general principle in this connection is that not only may the same word be used to refer to many different things, but also many different words may be used to refer to the same thing. Two witnesses in a court trial, one five feet in height and the other six feet five inches, are likely to disagree, one contending that the suspect was tall and the other insisting that he was short. What is sauce to the goose may be soup to the gander. The deacon glowers when the alderman laughs.

The difficulties in communication—and in understanding—thus created are due, fundamentally, to the structural difference, with respect to degree of differentiation, between language and reality. So far we have considered this structural difference in its more apparent aspects. It has a still more serious form: our language, as used, tends strongly to be two-valued at best, seldom more than three-valued. That is to say, we deal largely in terms of black and white, good and bad, beautiful and ugly. Our language, in other words, tends to assume an either-or form, to provide for differentiation into only two categories. We talk, not always but often, and particularly in decisive matters, as though there were only two alternatives, so that anything must be classified as *either* A *or* B (the so-called law of the excluded middle). We pride ourselves on being willing to consider *both* sides of a question, as though a third, or even a tenth or a fifty-fourth, were inconceivable. Not infrequently, of course, we do recognize a third possibility: high, low, and medium; good, bad, and so-so. In such a case, our language assumes a three-valued structure. This makes possible a middle-of-the-road policy, the so-called golden mean. The view that moderation in all things is a virtue expresses the conviction that an either-or form of language is not conducive to wisdom. Many a man's claim to immortality rests fundamentally on his recognition of the undue limitations imposed upon us by a two-valued language, and his counsel that we avoid extremes by choosing a middle course, a third alternative. Even this slight break with linguistic tradition, however, has so far been achieved by few, and leaves most of us with a feeling of verbal awkwardness, at least in many situations.

In American politics, for example, a third party seldom makes a strong appeal. The great majority of the voters find it difficult enough to decide between two parties; a third complicates matters beyond the practical capacity of our common language. Our racial conflicts, to choose another obvious example, operate within the well-worn grooves of a verbal frame of reference within which people are sorted into opposing groups of black or white, Jew or Gentile, Catholic or Protestant, etc. We mentioned still another illustration of the practical consequences of our two-valued orientation: the personal maladjustments we tend to create for ourselves by restricting our self-evaluations to the two terms of "success" and "failure." In the meantime, reality consists of *degrees* of political belief, of "racial" or religious difference, of personal accomplishment. The actualities to be dealt with in political, or religious, or personal terms present a highly differentiated structure. Our inability to deal effectively with these actualities stems in no small part from our misguided persistence in attempting to order and understand an infinite-valued reality by means of a two-valued or three-valued language structure.

Certain simple devices are used in general semantics to counteract in some degree the ill effects of this particular lack of structural correspondence between our world of words and the world of not-words.

Language Stucture: Variability

All our words are in some measure "abstract" or generalized. In part, as we have seen, this is because there are at any given moment more facts than there are words with which to refer to them. The word *chair*, for example, names no one unique object, but a very large array of objects. Even such a supposedly exact term as $10.51 does not specify *which* $10.51. The "abstractness" of our words is due to another reason, however. This other reason is the difference between language and reality with respect to the variability of structure, or rate of change. Reality is process-like; language, by comparison, is static. The world in which we live and we who live in it change faster than does the language we use to speak about our world and ourselves. So it is that words become generalized because the conveyer belt of time brings under their spell a changing inventory of "meanings."

Even a proper name, such as *National Broadcasting Company*, which we may at first glance take to be unambiguous on the ground that there is only one National Broadcasting Company, is seen on closer examination to refer to something different every day, every hour, every minute. Your own name signifies something at least slightly different every time it is used by you or by anyone else. These considerations become particularly important with reference to the pronoun *I*. "I was a shy and homely child" involves, as it stands, a fantastic misstatement of fact. I_{1946} never was a child. It was I_{1910} who was shy and homely. Certainly I_{1946} and I_{1910} are not the same. When *I* is used without a date, however, it tends to express identity, or lack of difference, between clearly different stages of a growing, changing individual. This is one of those perfectly obvious things that we so commonly overlook. When we do learn to take it into account, it is impressive how often we find beneath a festering point of personal maladjustment an unqualified, undated, generalized personal pronoun.

It is true that with the passage of time our language changes in some degree. That is why dictionaries are revised and brought more or less up to date occasionally. A perennial complaint of the older generation is that the younger generation is vulgarizing the language, is rudely deficient in respect for the mother tongue. Even the imposing and reverently preserved bulwarks of Shakespeare, the King James version of the Bible, Wordsworth, and Matthew Arnold do not completely stay the tide of linguistic innovation. The teachers of English struggle valiantly against an avalanche of jive. Migrations and wars, conquests and colonizations, new experiments in government, increased diversity of industrial and professional pursuits, and the rise of the sciences have all served to introduce new words and to alter the sense of old ones. In each professional field with which I am associated there are one or more special dictionaries, and as this is being written still newer glossaries are being compiled; and each of these will be, on its date of publication, in some measure out of date. If Benjamin Franklin could return tomorrow to Philadelphia, not only would he see all about him the imprint that he long ago left upon the city, but he would also find, even in the pages of his own *Saturday Evening Post,* a vocabulary strange to his tongue.

Yet it would not be the language of Philadelphia that would seem most strange to Benjamin Franklin, were he suddenly to reappear in its streets tomorrow. What he would find most unfamiliar would be the responses of the people to their new language—and to the old terms once known to him. The general countenance of the city, the activities of its inhabitants, their tools, their aspirations, from these he would gather most clearly the impression of being in a foreign land. Even the loaf of bread under his arm would be different from the one he carried in the Philadelphia of the pre-vitamin eighteenth century. Our language in its codified forms changes at a tortoise pace compared to the hare-like transformations of material and social reality. In driving his third automobile, my father still said, "Giddap" and "Whoa." In 1946 jitterbugging is essentially a mystery to people who call it dancing. Under the spigots of cultural evolution the old categories bulge, spill over, and collapse.

Viewing reality through the lenses of language we get at best a blurred and jerky picture. Against a misty background a few bulky shapes appear, and as the winds of living history play upon the mists the shapes seem suddenly to change, or they disappear and new ones come into view. But it always takes us some time to see the changes; it is as though we remain unaware of them until some time after they have occurred. We experience an irregular series of greater and lesser surprises, for astonishment is only the child of miscalculation imposed by words which have come to imply what no longer recurs. The moving finger of actuality writes faster than the tongue can herald. The structure of language is less fluid than the structure of reality. Just as the thunder we hear is no longer sounding, so the reality we speak about exists no more.

Maladjustment, for the individual or for society, lies in mistaking the verbal record of the past for the description of the present. Because the words we speak today are quite the same as the ones we spoke yesterday, we tend to create the illusion that what we speak about is also quite the same. It can be serious enough when change takes us by surprise; what is even more serious is to have change escape our notice entirely. That is the condition of persistent delusion. There is a theory that schizophrenia in the adult consists of a reversion to childhood modes of behavior. What would seem to be a more apt statement of the case is that the disorder lies in a failure to recognize and take into account the changes that constitute the passage from childhood to maturity. There are maladjusted individuals —and societies—who live as though they looked upon the present as a temporary deviation from the past. Their norm being as of yesterday, they treat the here and now as though it were a condition of abnormality. The new wine sours in their old bottles.

The essential forms of our language were devised by ancient men who were remarkably unfamiliar with present-day knowledge. The pictures they imagined of "the mechanism inside the watch" appear today as a fanciful mythology. Because they had not been driven to assume the superdynamics of the submicroscopic realm which we accept, the world in its visible aspects seemed far more static to them than it does to us. In devising our language, they created a world of words that implied a relatively static world of not-words. That language, still with us so far as its basic structure is concerned, still plagues us. It is reflected in our institutions, our customs, our common modes of conduct and evaluation: we prepare ourselves rather better for a history that might repeat itself than for brave new days.

It is one of the purposes of general semantics to stimulate basic revisions in our language structure, revisions that will provide for evaluative reactions of greater adjustive value in a world which we now know to be far from static and unchanging.

Language Structure: Organization

As we have seen, a structure may be described in terms of its degree of differentiation (number of parts) and its fluidity or rate of change. It may be described also in terms of its organization, the relationships among its parts.

There are a few very important features of the organization of our language which all of us have learned from our grammar books. Of course, we learned them as grammar and perhaps we find it easier to recall the distractions of the classroom than the details of the lessons. For our present purposes, however, memory need not be unduly sharp and clear. It will not be difficult to recall that in our grammar books words were classified, in part, as nouns and adjectives, as verbs and adverbs. One of the verbs was *to be*, which took the forms of *is, was, were*, etc. These particular few details of grammar are the ones that most concern us here. In fact, a large part of what we have to say with regard to the organization of our language structure can be illustrated by the simple statement: "John is smart."

We classify *John* as a noun, *is* as a verb, and *smart* as an adjective. To put it simply, a noun refers to a thing, an adjective refers to a quality of a thing, and a verb refers to a relationship between a quality and a thing, or between one thing and another. Now, one might take off from this modest beginning and whirl away into an elaborate dissertation on the intricate complexities of grammar, but this will not be necessary for our purposes. In keeping it simple, however, we should appreciate the fact that a tremendous number of details are being left out of account. They are being left out only because they are not crucial to our discussion.

To say that *John* is a noun is to say, according to the traditional rules of language usage, that John is a thing of some sort. To say that John is smart, and to say that *smart* is an adjective, is to say that smartness is a quality of John. This leaves *is* implying a relationship of inclusion, or possession: the smartness is possessed by John, or is included in him. This sort of language structure implies that reality is made up of things that possess qualities. In other words, the qualities—the colors, shapes, odors, etc.— *belong to the things*. The ancient men who devised our language doubtless regarded this as a "self-evident" truth. They probably constructed the kind of language they did simply because they took for granted that just such a language was needed in order to give a true account of reality. So far as they could see, it was true that reality consisted of things with attributes.

So it was that a great delusion came to be embedded in the very structure of our language so that, simply by using the language, we maintain the delusion, working it continuously into our beliefs and attitudes, our habit systems, our institutions and culture patterns. Probably this was not emphasized, perhaps it was not even mentioned, in your grammar book. It is likely that you were, as I was, permitted to acquire the uncritical view that grammar is a fact of nature rather than a creation of human beings. What impressed us most when we were school children was that the more "correctly" we used grammar, the better marks we got. It escaped our notice, in all likelihood, that using grammar "correctly" might involve certain disadvantages. We should be clear on the point, however, that the errors made by our teachers, innocent of them as they must have been, were errors chiefly of omission. It was not that we were taught too much grammar; rather, we were not taught enough of it. We were not brought up to date.

We were not made sufficiently aware of the fact that, contrary to the incomplete grammar books, reality does not consist simply of things with attributes. The relationships that characterize the structure of our common language are not altogether like those which characterize the structure of reality. The ancient wise men notwithstanding, the sort of language that appears to be needed in order to represent the relationships to be found in the world of not-words is one which expresses a space-time order among facts, and between the observer and the observed, between the speaker and what he speaks about. To put it quite simply, the venerable designers of our language left out of account, in large part, the human beings who were to use the language. And in conceiving of the nature of reality they overlooked the part which they themselves played in abstracting it. They were like a potter who bows down before the idol he has made with his own hands, forgetful that he himself has fashioned it. Even today we continue to revere the semantic apparitions molded in the contours of our verbal forms.

"John is smart" leaves out of account, or seems to deny, two very important considerations. One is that the smartness is not entirely *of John*; it is "a joint product of the observer and the observed." The other is that *John* and *smartness* properly represent, respectively, not a thing and a quality of that thing, but a comprehensive on-going series of events (John) and some part of that series (the smartness). It is not to be proposed that we abolish nouns and adjectives and *is*. At least, I shall leave that to someone far less impressed with the forces of tradition than I am. It is rather to be suggested that in using our language we remain aware of its structural implications, and where they tend to mislead we avoid being misled by seeing steadily those facts which the language would obscure and distort. In saying, "John is smart," let us remember that we are not simply calling attention to a quality of John; in part, we are reporting our personal evaluations. The same consideration holds when we say that John is good or that he is wicked. In judging others we express to an important degree simply our own standards of judgment.

We run a slighter risk of delusion, of course, if we replace *is* with certain other verbs. When, for example, we say, "John appears smart," we more definitely indicate that, in part, we express a private judgment. If, to go further, we say, "John appears smart to me," we indicate still more definitely that the judgment is personal and not necessarily universal.

Our language is made still more adequate if we replace *smart* with other terms more nearly descriptive of John's behavior. Thus, what is to be communicated is more clear if we say, "John scored an I.Q. of 140 on Form L of the 1937 revision of the Stanford-Binet intelligence test yesterday," or "John is only eight years old and he can name and locate all of the forty-eight states." It is simply a matter of being more or less clear. Adjectives like *smart, good,* etc., tend to imply qualities of things and to fall into a two-valued usage, and so what they imply in the way of events or behavior is not always apparent. It is with an appreciation of this fact that they are to be used.

One further point is to be emphasized. "John is smart" tends to imply something about John besides his alleged smartness. As it stands, the statement strongly indicates that John is always the same. Nothing is said about when, where, in what respects, or from what point of view John is smart. One is left with the implication that John is smart all the time, everywhere, in all respects and from any point of view: John is John. Beneath the particular words used we see the basic structure of identity: A is A. In the meantime, John ₜₒdₐy *is not* John yₑₛₜₑᵣdₐy. John playing tennis is not John computing his income tax. What is meant by *John* depends in some measure on who speaks the word and on who hears it; it depends on time, place, and circumstance. *John* refers ultimately to a series of events. To the extent that this is appreciated and reflected in our statements about John, they tend to imply and create more and more effective understanding.

ITS DEVELOPMENT

By Wilbur Schramm

———

ABOUT THE YEAR 1450, in Mainz, Germany, there occurred one of those con-junctions of an idea, skills, and materials that historians later write about. In this case, the materials were the wine press used for centuries in Western Europe; cast metal type, invented 50 years earlier in Korea but rediscovered independently at Mainz; and paper and ink, both of which had been de-veloped many centuries earlier in China and brought to Europe by way of the Near East. The skills were those of calligraphy and block printing, de-veloped to a high level by Asians and by Europeans especially in the medieval monasteries. The new idea was to print from movable metal type, so that a piece of type might be used interchangeably, in many jobs. The result was a machine for the rapid duplication of writing—the writing being standardized into type faces.

That was the beginning of modern communication. The story of those 500 years of development in communication is a story of man's changing relation to machines in the communication process. The differ-ence between communication before and after 1450 was simply that man had finally made an efficient machine to duplicate interpersonal communi-cation. Then, a long time after 1450, man made a machine which he could interpose in the communication process to see and listen for him. That was the second great step in the history of modern communication. A lit-tle later he developed the skills and techniques that make possible efficient communication between man and machines. And in our time he has un-locked the wonders of machine-to-machine communication, and we have automatic factories and devices that remember facts and make decisions. Those four steps are the ones that have made modern communication what it is.

But let us return to the events just after 1450. That first step into modern communication—how did man take it? What was the first thing he printed from movable metal type, there beside the River Main in Ger-many? Was it something like "What hath God wrought?" which Samuel Morse sent over the first telegraph line? Was it a medieval version of "Now is the time for all good men. . . ."? Was it the printer's name, set in a stick of type to be marveled at? We do not know. The earliest dated piece of printing that remains is a papal indulgence, struck by Fust and Schoeffer, in 1454. The first book was apparently the 42-line Bible, which was done not later than 1456, and of which the printer is believed to have been Johann Gutenberg.

Thus at its very birth the new art was pressed into the service of the chief power center of the times: the Church. And if the printing press had been a different kind of machine, it could have been restricted—as certain other communication devices, like heraldry, or the semaphor, have been —to one master, or one class, or a certain kind of job, or a certain topic. But the peculiar characteristic of machine-duplicated communication was that it became involved everywhere with all the public affairs of man. How swiftly that converted wine press spread from the Rhineland around the world! Caxton was printing in England, Aldus in Italy, by 1494; Juan Pablos in Mexico City less than 50 years after Columbus first saw the new continent. Everywhere it went, the printing press involved itself in the matters that exalted or stimulated or troubled man. It served the parties in power, but it also served all the revolutions of the spirit and the body politic. It served the Church and also carried the great debate on the Reformation. It circulated the precious books of Aristotle, which had been chained to the library desks of the Middle Ages. It carried far and wide the extraordinary intellectual output of the Renaissance. It carried commercial news to the merchants of England and North Germany, and also revolutionary pamphlets—in fact so many of them that anonymous pamphlets are even today the symbol of revolution in many European countries. Without the press there might possibly have been an Enlightenment, but it is a matter of grave doubt whether there could ever have been a French or American revolution.

The press served all masters who would have it. In the great ground swell of democracy toward the end of the eighteenth century, the press led the people toward their new-found importance. And just at that time, shortly after 1800, man succeeded in making the first major modification in his remodeled wine press. He added a new source of power to it. This was the gift of the industrial revolution. Steam—later electricity—replaced man's muscles. It was the same old press, but it worked faster; the same product, but more of it. The exciting thing about the power press was that it came at just the time when it was needed to reach the masses of new voters. To those who couldn't read, it offered an easily seen incentive to learn to read, and thus it was closely involved with the growth of public education. Then smart merchandisers found out they could sell papers for a penny and still make a profit if they sold enough, and if they sold enough they could also sell advertising, and so we had "mass" communication— prices at a level the common man can pay, enormous circulations, advertising, large publishing organizations, the attractive concept of the new machine as the voice and servant of democracy, and the misleading and erroneous concept of a "mass audience."

Meanwhile, in the mid-century, the telegraph and the cable had speeded communication, and the camera and photo-engraving had added vividness to the printed word. But all this was still nothing fundamentally new. The Washington hand presses that rode west in the American covered wagons were essentially only a hardier version of the press that Gutenberg had at Mainz in 1450. The presses that printed the Gettysburg Address were essentially the same machines, run by steam. They were still a part of the great wave of communication that began to break at Mainz in 1450. And the accomplishment of that first wave, as we have said, rested entirely on its ability to make very swift duplicates of writing on paper.

The first fundamentally new development came three quarters of the way through the nineteenth century. As the first wave of modern communication can be dated back to Gutenberg in 1450, so the second can be dated, if not to Samuel Morse and the telegraph, at least to Alexander Graham Bell in 1876. He gave us the telephone. A few years later, Edison's phonograph and his movie camera and projector made it possible to store sounds and moving sights. DeForest's triode vacuum tube in 1907 opened the world of radio and television.

The difference between communication before and after 1876 was that man had finally begun to make efficient machines that could be interposed in the communication chain, and trusted to listen and see for him. In a sense, of course, the printing machine had been interposed in a communication chain, but it merely duplicated; it did not communicate directly. It made a product that could be read at leisure, the reader taking the initiative, setting his own pace, selecting from the copy as he wished. The second wave of modern communication made a profound change in that it shifted the initiative, partly at least, from receiver to sender. Once the receiver had made his basic choice, the sender was in charge. The machine, or the force behind it, controlled the pace, the repetitions, the emphasis, the timing.

The new machines were faster than the press. They brought tidings more quickly, answered an argument more swiftly. They had about them a sense of reality, a sense of immediacy, that print never had. They had an emotional quality that was hard to get into print. And yet we must admit that the second wave has not yet involved itself in social change as the first wave did. While print is five centuries old, we have had the telephone only three quarters of a century, and radio and television are newcomers within our time. These newer media came into being when Western countries were being urbanized. They came into being when the work week was being greatly shortened, and people began to have more leisure. They came into being at a time when America was on the verge of a striking change from what David Riesman[1] calls "inner-directedness" to "other-directedness"—from an individualistic work-success ethic and a future-time orientation, to a hedonistic present-centered ethic concerned greatly with group relationships and opinions. These new machines were exactly what people needed to keep them informed of the other people around them. They were sociable little machines. They brought personalities into one's living room, and transported one into countless other living rooms and chambers of state. More than print, this new machine-interposed communication extended man's environment and dominated his leisure. More than print, it offered opportunities to manipulators.

When one tries to add up the social impacts of machine-interposed communication, he concludes that as print had come to play a part in certain great revolutions of the mind and the state, so films and broadcasts came to play parts in a great change within our way of life. It is still too early to assay the exact part they have played in the change to "other-directedness," but it must have been significant. This, I think, we can say: that while print first commended itself to man for its ability to inform, films and broadcasts commended themselves for their ability to entertain. And, whereas print began as the most private and the smallest of media and grew into mass communication, films and broadcasts were born into mass communication and never knew anything else. Even more than print, they demanded large communicating organizations to produce them.

These are the parts of modern communication with which we are going to be concerned in this book. But we should be telling less than the whole truth if we did not fill in the rest of the picture, the other two waves.

The third wave of modern communication was developing at the same time as the second, but came slowly and reached its crest only in the twentieth century. This was communication between men and machines. It developed slowly as man became more ingenious at making dials and gauges that would give him information, and instruments on which he could register his wishes. It now seems ordinary to us, but it would have seemed fantastic only a few decades ago, that a man would be able to fly an airplane when ground and horizon were completely invisible to him, simply by means of messages sent him by a panel of instruments designed to say how high he is, how fast he is going, where he is heading, whether his wings are level, and how fast his engine is turning. If that would have seemed fantastic in 1915, the idea of ships seeing the shoreline or planes seeing the ground quite clearly through clouds and fog would still have seemed fantastic in 1935. Yet in the 1940s we had a machine that operated through an electronic screen and conveyed exactly this kind of information, in the most minute and exacting detail, to humans. We call it radar.

The third wave in modern communication, then, developed slowly for a hundred years and came to a peak in the fourth decade of the twentieth century. The fourth wave has broken really only in the last ten years. It can pretty well be dated to a paper by Claude Shannon in the *Bell System Technical Journal* for 1948.[2] The article began modestly: "The recent development of various methods of modulation . . . has intensified the interest in a general theory of communication." That is exactly what Shannon set about providing. The effect of his paper, and the formulas in it, was to stimulate a great outpouring of developments in the area of communication between machines.

Let us not say arbitrarily that we are uninterested in any communication that seems not to involve humans, because this fourth wave has the most direct and important implications for humans. As machines in the early nineteenth century had come to do the work of man's muscles, so now these new machines were able to do some of his thinking for him. In our own time, therefore, we have had the excitement of watching a major scientific idea develop into use. The great computers, with their brain-like qualities, have all come into being in the last two decades. The concept of feedback of information, which made possible such relatively simple devices as the thermostat, has been so developed that it is now possible to put a machine in charge of other machines and to build a factory to run itself. It is mathematically possible even to build a machine to duplicate itself. Literally we have built machines able to take over many of the qualities thought previously to be man's unique prerogative. Under the name of automation, this fourth wave of modern communication has already had great effects on American industry, and may have profound effects on man's concepts of himself and his place in the world.

Let us be clear that the reason we are limiting ourselves to the first two waves of modern communication is not that the third and fourth are any less exciting. Indeed, the most exciting communication developments ahead of us are undoubtedly in the area of machine-to-machine communication, and 25 years from now this may well be the largest branch of the communication industry. Nor are we limiting ourselves because the two later areas do not furnish ethical problems. On the contrary, we may expect automation and the "thinking" machines to provide ethical problems at least as severe as any of the other kinds. We are limiting ourselves precisely because the two newest kinds of communication are so new. Young as machine-duplicated and machine-interposed communication may be when measured against the whole history of man's communicating, they are still old when compared to man-machine and machine-to-machine communication. They are old enough to have acquired an ethic and to have been incorporated into philosophies.

For another reason too we are particularly concerned with the first two waves of modern communication. The great voice of print was caught up in the ground swell of democracy and the sharply breaking waves of revolution in the 17th and 18th centuries; and the impressive new technology of the media (the power press, photoengraving, stereotyping, sound and sight recording on film and transmission by airwaves) was caught up in the almost unbelievable growth curve of economics in the 19th and 20th centuries. As a result, the tiny hand press, the squeaking earphones, the flickering film, have in our time grown into vast business enterprises: daily newspapers, publishing houses, radio and television stations and networks, and film studios and theater chains. We call these developments mass communication because of their massive product and the enormous audiences they have come to serve.

At the beginning, print was used mostly to meet *specific* needs and *specific* interests. Thus the merchants needed business information, the Church needed certain religious documents in a form that could be more readily circulated, the government needed a way to duplicate certain products of legislation and executive authority. Gradually print began to have more general uses. The newspaper came into being. As Robert E. Park pointed out, the first newspapers were mostly devices for organizing gossip.[3] And yet they were more than that because their growth was intertwined with the growth of schools and cities and people's governments. It is no accident that Shakespeare talked about schools and printing, together, or that early newspapers in this country tended to appear where there were post offices and to grow as school population grew.

The social history of newspapers is the history of a battle for circulation. As communities grew larger, the newspapers began to take over some of the functions that were served in villages by face-to-face contact. Villages operate by the kind of public opinion that grows out of gossip and the understanding that grows out of familiarity. And so the newspaper tried to organize gossip and keep its readers familiar with what they could not themselves see or find out. To do this, it needed an audience that could read, which was gradually provided by public education. It needed a way to circulate speedily and cheaply, which was gradually provided by the clustering of people in large communities and by postal services. It needed a way to print fast and cheaply, which was provided at last by the power press. And it needed a way to become important to large numbers of readers, a way which was provided by the growth of political democracy.

In its first century the newspaper was essentially a newsletter. Political pamphlets circulated separately and often surreptitiously because the political content of the newspapers was controlled by authority. In the 18th century, these functions of print were married, and there was born the party paper. This was a journal of opinion which took over from the broadside and pamphlet the task of representing political discontent. It developed in time to be fired at the Bastille and at the Stamp Tax and to lead the great movement toward popular government and democracy.

Thus all the dams broke at once and loosed the torrent of communication. More people went to school. There they learned to read and become more deeply interested in their governments and in the world beyond the realm of their eyes and ears. The growth of popular governments required people to inform themselves and helped them to do so by providing schools and facilitating the distribution of newspapers. And newspapers, given cities full of people, many of whom now could read, and most of whom felt a need for political information in order to take part in government, helped break their dam by developing the power press. Thus the newspaper grew on the mighty yeasts both of the industrial revolution and the democratic political revolution.

The newspaper in this country and Western Europe has evolved beyond the party press to a more general newspaper. As Park pointed out, when someone in the 19th century referred to "the power of the press" he was referring to the power of the editor and the editorial.[4] On the other hand, when someone today speaks of the power of the press, he is almost certainly talking about the power of the reporter and the news. In the 19th century, our influential papers were journals of opinion. At best, these papers were like Horace Greeley's New York *Tribune*, which Charles Francis Adams said "during those years was the greatest educational factor, economically and morally, this country has ever known." [5] At worst, they were journals in which news was regarded very much as it is regarded in present-day Communist papers: as merely an excuse for editorial comment.

In several ways the party papers were anachronistic. For one thing, there tended to be so many of them. Each such paper tended to gather a party, or a splinter of a party, behind it. The little town of 12,000 persons in which I grew up had at one time five newspapers, all representing different political viewpoints. The tendency of papers was, therefore, to proliferate, to divide their potential audiences in terms of ever more sharply defined differences of opinion. On the other hand, the tendency of the industrial revolution, in which the growing newspaper was involved, was toward consolidation. Greater profits were to be made by selling more units of a single kind. Furthermore, costs were swiftly rising, partly because of increasing mechanism requiring greater skill on the part of a staff, partly because more machines and more complicated machines had to be bought, partly because the public learned to demand more expensive services (for example, wire news, syndicated columnists, feature services, pictures, cartoons, and a good local news coverage). Many newspapers also came to have a revulsion against subservience to a political machine or party, and to note on the part of the people a decreasing appetite for the owners' ready-made, one-sided opinions and an increasing appetite for news.

For all these reasons, the party press was not a suitable mold for the future. More and more papers broke away from it and began to serve larger segments of the people with a product in which news was more important than opinion, and feature news often more important than hard news, and in which advertising grew rapidly with circulation and came to be an important determinant of the paper's success. Many American papers went through a period of "yellow" journalism, in which they subordinated other services to the production of sensation, fantasy, highly emotionalized news. They were trying to reach the people, as Walter Lippmann said, "who find their own lives dull, and wish to live a more thrilling existence." [6] Under the competition of the machine-interposed media and the pressure of needs for other kinds of service, our press has come through its "yellow" age and now exists in a spectrum which extends from the *New York Times*, which tries to carry "All the news that's fit to print," to the most sensational tabloid and *Confidential* magazine. Some of the inheritance of the "yellow" period remains with us, however, in comic strips, in the high proportion of feature and human-interest stories, and in the playing-up of sensational news as a stimulus to circulation.

It is important to notice that the general pattern of the industrial revolution (toward larger and fewer manufacturing units) has been reflected in newspapers. Even while the national population has more than doubled, and while total circulation of daily newspapers has increased twelvefold in 75 years, the number of daily newspapers has significantly decreased. The number is still decreasing, through mergers, sales, and suspensions, and very few new dailies are being started. Thus we have fewer and larger newspapers.[7] Indeed, only 6 per cent of all the daily newspaper cities in this country now have competing dailies. The figures in the table below show what the trend is in relation to the national population. They are assembled from the N. W. Ayer *Guide to Periodical Literature*, the yearbooks of *Editor and Publisher*, and the United States Census reports. Here is the story:

	Number of Dailies	Total Circulation	U. S. Population
1888	1,442	4,543,713	61,000,400 (est.)
1900	2,120	9,330,930	75,994,575
1914	2,442	25,426,911	96,000,000 (est.)
1920	2,042	27,790,656	105,710,620
1930	1,942	39,589,172	122,775,046
1940	1,878	41,131,611	131,669,275
1950	1,772	53,829,072	150,697,361
1956	1,760	56,147,359	162,000,000 (est.)

The trend with respect to competitive ownership of daily newspapers in the United States is indicated in the table on the next page.

This is a dramatic development indeed, and it makes for an obvious difference in the relation of a newspaper to its public. The whole essence of the party press was the ability of each opinion group to be represented by its own paper. This would be very hard to accomplish in

	Total Dailies	Total Daily Cities	Cities with Competing Dailies	Percentage of Cities with Noncompetitive Ownership
1909-10	2,202	1,207	689	42.9
1920	2,042	1,295	552	57.4
1930	1,942	1,402	288	79.4
1940	1,878	1,426	181	87.3
1944-5	1,744	1,396	117	91.6
1953-4	1,785	1,448	87	94.0[a]

[a] This table is from an article by Ray B. Nixon, "Concentration and Absenteeism in Daily Newspaper Ownership," *Journalism Quarterly*, 22 (June 1945) 97-114, updated by the same author, "Trends in Daily Newspaper Ownership since 1945," *Journalism Quarterly*, v. 31 (Winter 1954) pp. 3-14.

the 94 per cent of our cities which do not have competing dailies. The kind of service that a paper in a single-ownership town sells therefore must be different from the kind of service a party paper sold. By its very nature it has to be big. It has to sell many copies, to sell large amounts of advertising to pay its bills, and to serve more people better. The process is obviously circular. In order that it may sell many copies it must serve many kinds of people representing many political viewpoints. Therefore, it cannot afford to represent one political viewpoint only, as could the party press. It finds that representing all significant viewpoints on controversial questions is usually profitable, whether or not otherwise desirable.

Even though its publisher may be anti-Roosevelt or -Truman or -Eisenhower, the paper cannot afford to carry only anti-Roosevelt or -Truman or -Eisenhower news. Even though it is big business by virtue of the costs of producing it (which we shall have occasion to discuss in greater detail in a later chapter), it cannot afford to be an apologist only for big business. This is a new kind of responsibility, one which the party press never had to think of, and to which the yellow press paid little attention. The effort of newspapers to analyze this new obligation has made for much of the preoccupation with ethical problems in the mass media during recent years, and indeed represents much of the reason for this book.

We have been talking about print. The machine-interposed media came along relatively late in the industrial revolution and therefore had relatively short histories of smallness and fewness. They were caught up in the tidal wave of growth almost as soon as they had a marketable product. Motion pictures were already in 1920 attracting weekly audiences equivalent nearly to one third of the people in this country. Radio, which had 30 stations and 60 thousand receivers in 1922, had 3400 stations and over 100 *million* receivers in 1956. Television reached barely 75,000 homes in 1947, but in 1956 went into three quarters of the homes of the country—

about 36 million. The later these media came along, the more fantastically swift was their growth. . . .

Another way to show the swift growth of mass communication in this country is to tabulate the estimated size of the advertising pool, a very large part of which, of course, goes to the support of the mass media. These are the best figures it is possible to assemble on one of the more dramatic growth curves of the industrial revolution:

Year	Estimated Total Advertising (*in millions*)
1880	200
1890	360
1900	542
1910	1,200
1920	2,935
1930	2,607
1940	2,087
1950	5,710
1955	8,500[a]

[a] These are *Printers' Ink* estimates.

This is what we mean by the growth of mass communication. Dramatic as they are, the figures are merely incidental to what has happened. For the truth is that we have, in the lifetime of many of us, been presented with a *new* system of public communication. The social bulk of these new enterprises is as different from that of the tiny printing enterprises of the 16th century as the 16th-century enterprises were different from the *Acta Diurna*, the wall newspaper used to record the decisions of the Roman Senate. But it is not necessary to go back as far as the 16th century to find a contrast with our present mass communications. One hundred years ago there was no radio, no television, no movies; newspapers were mostly party papers, and magazines and books were small industries indeed. Only 50 years ago there were no radio and no television; movies were represented by a few nickelodeons; newspapers were a combination of party papers and yellow press, and still growing in numbers. The dramatic coming of largeness and fewness to newspapers was still in the future, and so was the passing of the party press. Radio and television were still to be born, and the days of mass audiences for films were still to come. All these developments have come about in the last 50 years.

There is another way to symbolize what has happened. What would people have thought a century ago, if someone had predicted that it would be possible not too far in the future to buy for five cents a newspaper connected by leased wires and reporters to all the principal cities of the world, no more than minutes removed from a news event anywhere, and indeed only a few hours from news pictures wherever they are taken, and maps and charts wherever they are available? What would people have thought 50 years ago, if someone had told them that in the future most homes would contain a relatively inexpensive little box into which one could look and see and hear the Metropolitan Opera, the New York Music Hall stage, the Olympic games in Melbourne, the meetings of the United Nations, the fighting in a distant part of the world, and the candidates for national office?

There is yet another way. What would anybody have thought, if someone had predicted that these little boxes we have been talking about ·would be used, on the average, about four hours a day in every American home where they are available; that another box called a radio would be used, on the average, a little over two hours a day; and that the average American adult would spend, on the average, thirty minutes a day with his newspaper? On the basis of various data, it has to be concluded that most Americans now spend between three and six hours a day, on the average, with mass communication. This probably compares with not much more than an hour 50 years ago, and considerably less 100 years ago.[8]

These developments in communication have made a profound difference in the way we receive information, and in the kind and amount of information we receive. For communicators they have made a profound difference in the opportunities they offer and the responsibilities they enjoin.

*   *   *   *

BIBLIOGRAPHY

1. David Riesman, *The Lonely Crowd* (New Haven: Yale Univ. Press, 1950), see especially Chap. I.
2. Claude E. Shannon, "The Mathematical Theory of Communication," *Bell System Technical Journal*, July and October 1948. Reprinted as a book (Shannon and Weaver, *The Mathematical Theory of Communication* [Urbana, Illinois: 1949]).
3. This famous essay is now most readily available in the collected papers of Robert Ezra Park, Vol. 3, *Society* (Glencoe, Illinois: Free Press, 1955), pp. 89-104. It was originally published in Park, Burgess, and McKenzie, *The City* (Chicago: Univ. of Chicago, 1925).
4. Park, *op. cit.*, p. 96.
5. Quoted in Park, *op. cit.*, p. 97.
6. Walter Lippmann, *Public Opinion* (New York: Macmillan, 1927, 1944), pp. 331-32.
7. It is only fair to point out, however, that whereas the number of *general* newspapers (both daily and weekly) has notably decreased in the last 40 years, the number of *special* newspapers and other publications has greatly increased. Many of these are the publications of corporations, trade unions, trade associations, community organizations, and similar

groups and organizations which have a need to communicate frequently among their own members. Much of the news in these publications used to get into the local newspapers, but it has been crowded out as the newspapers have grown larger and a larger proportion of their space has been given over to wire news and advertising. These house organs, organization bulletins, and private newspapers sometimes reach a very high circulation and are often highly valued and influential with their audiences.

8. Estimates for television (4:06) and radio (2:12) are from A. C. Nielsen 1955 figures. The figure of 40 minutes a day for newspaper reading is the average of several estimates made in connection with readership surveys. For example, see Schramm and White, "Age, Education, and Economic Status as Factors in Newspaper Reading," *Journalism Quarterly*, v. 26, (Spring, 1949) pp. 149-59. The most recent national survey (by Sindlinger and Company, in 1957) came up with an average of 34 minutes.

WHY THE MASS MEDIA ARE THAT WAY

By Theodore Peterson

———

IN THE PAST FEW YEARS a good many persons have been lining up, like sailors at a shooting gallery, to draw a bead on the various mass media of communication. A. J. Liebling, for one, has published his essays about our "monovocal, monopolistic, monocular press." Newton Minow has spoken about television fare with such vehemence and frequency that he has given the term "wasteland" a currency that T. S. Eliot never did. And Robert Lekachman, in the greatest heresy of all, has charged that our good magazines, our *Harper's* and *Atlantic* and *Nation*, are not good enough, are not the equal of their British counterparts.

Editors, publishers, and broadcasters have learned to live with this criticism, but they have seldom learned to like it. Their reactions have varied from surprised hurt and mild petulance on the one hand to red-faced indignation and savage counterattack on the other.

I cannot agree with those publishers and broadcasters who seem to think that finding fault with the mass media is somehow un-American, like setting out poisoned Ken-L-Ration for Lassie. My aim is not to argue that the American mass media are the best in the world, although I think they are. It is evading the issue to say that our media are the best or even good. The word "good," after all, has many meanings, as G. K. Chesterton reminds us with his remark that a man who shoots his grandmother at five hundred yards may be a good shot but not necessarily a good man.

The truth is that I sometimes agree with what the critics have to say about press performance. But when I do, I often have the uneasy feeling that they are right for the wrong reasons and that one may as well look to Dr. Seuss for richness of character and complexity of plot as to look to them for sensible prescriptions. So what I propose to do is to touch on a major stream of press criticism that I think is bound to be futile, to examine its assumptions and shortcomings, and then to suggest, a little hesitantly, a direction that I think holds greater promise.

The strain of criticism that strikes me as essentially futile blames publishers and broadcasters for all of the shortcomings of the mass media. In its many variations, this line of criticism sees the men who own and operate the media as merely foolish, as irresponsible, or as downright evil. The

Reprinted by permission from the *Antioch Review*, Volume XXIII, No. 4.

common denominator of the variations is that the media are bad because the men who own and operate them are in some way bad.

That idea is almost as old as printing itself. In the sixteenth century, even before the newspaper came to England, critics were grumbling about the half-penny chroniclers who scampered off to scribble verses for its precursor, the broadside. When newspapers did appear, the men who ran them came in for some abuse. Samuel Johnson, who had opinions on all subjects worth having opinions about and on a good many that were not, delivered his views on newsmen in 1758: "The compilation of News-papers is often committed to narrow minds, not qualified for the task of delighting or instructing; who are content to fill their pages with whatever matter, without industry to gather, or discernment to select." His observations were mild compared with the American variety, especially those in the period of bitter partisan journalism in the late eighteenth and early nineteenth centuries, when the press deserved all of the criticism it got. James Ward Fenno, an old newspaperman himself, said in 1799:

> The American newspapers are the most base, false, servile, and venal publications, that ever polluted the fountains of society—their editors the most ignorant, mercenary and vulgar automatons that ever were moved by the continually rusting wires of sordid mercantile avarice.

In our own century, by far the great bulk of press criticism, I think, has blamed the owners and operators for the shortcomings of the media. A good deal of it arises from what we might call the conspiratorial theory of press malfunction—the notion that publishers and broadcasters have conspired with big business to promote and to protect their mutual interests, that in exchange for suppressing and distorting media content they share in such handsome rewards as advertising contracts, social position, and political prominence.

Will Irwin set the themes for much of such criticism in a series of articles about newspapers that he wrote for *Collier's* back in 1911. Advertisers had come to realize their power over the press, he said, and in some instances they had been taught it by the newspapers themselves. To attract customers for advertising space, some papers had made concessions to advertisers. In time advertisers came to take these concessions as special privileges—insertion of publicity; biased news accounts; suppression of news harmful to the advertiser, his family, his associates and his business interests; and, in rare instances, a complete change in editorial policy. Irwin was perceptive enough to recognize that many shortcomings of the newspaper arise not from the harmful influence of advertising but from the commercial nature of the press, and he observed that simply because publishers are businessmen, the newspapers they control might be expected to reflect the viewpoint of business.

Irwin was followed by a succession of critics who reiterated his charges, although not always with his perception. In 1912, after he had already clubbed the packing industry with his wooden prose, Upton Sinclair brought out *The Brass Check*, which likened the press to a vast brothel in which truth was the virtue for sale. *The Brass Check* has been almost as durable as its author, who has written a book for each of his eighty-four years, for it went through several editions and was revised in 1936. Sinclair's pitch was that the "Empire of Business" controls journalism by four devices—by direct ownership of the press, by ownership of the owners, by advertising subsidy, and by direct bribery.

The "empire of business" idea was a favorite one in the Depression of the 1930's, when businessmen were low in popular esteem, and critic after critic described how knights of that empire worked hand in hand with the press to thwart the common good. Harold L. Ickes contended that publishers made up America's House of Lords, a body enriching and enhancing the power of the economic royalists whose ideology had a well-filled purse as its core. George Seldes saw the lords of the press as polluting the fountain of truth by suppressing news or distorting it and plotting evil behind closed doors at meetings of the American Newspaper Publishers Association. Ferdinand Lundberg wrote scathingly of Imperial Hearst, and other writers did portraits of other publishers in acid.

Today critics seldom speak of "lords of the press," a term that sounds a little dated, but they sometimes do number media owners among "the power elite." And quite a few critics evidently do assume that Sinclair and Seldes and Ickes were right in blaming the owners and operators for a good share of what is wrong with the media.

Their line of thought, let me confess, is rather appealing. For one thing, there is enough truth in it to make it seem valid. The media *are* big business, and their outlook *does* tend to be that of big business generally. For another thing, the way to improvement is then comparatively easy: Somehow, through punishment or persuasion, we must make the media owners pure of heart; then the press will be as great as publishers say it is during National Newspaper Week, and television will become man's greatest achievement since the pyramids. Charles Dickens had a similar explanation for the ills of nineteenth-century England, and his solution was equally simple: Let evil-doers be shown their errors, and they will join their nobler fellows in a merry dance of brotherhood around the Christmas tree.

Criticism that does little more than blame the men who own and operate the mass media is bound to be futile, I think, for it rests on debatable if not downright erroneous assumptions.

One is that most owners and operators lack a sense of social responsibility. Now, some publishers do show a deeper concern over what paper costs than over what they print on it, and some broadcasters do regard the public airwaves as their personal, exploitable property. Even so, I am prepared to argue that most publishers and broadcasters have a greater sense of public responsibility than a good many critics give them credit for having—one as high as that of most leaders in business and government, and perhaps higher. At times their standards of performance may not be the ones that most intellectuals would set if they were running the media, but the eggs that make one man's souffle make the next man's omelet.

A second assumption is that the nature of the communications system is determined primarily by the men who now own and operate the media. They of course do have a good deal to say about what the mass media pump out. But in one sense what they choose to include and omit, as I will try to show, is not entirely of their own doing.

Let me make it abundantly clear that I am not suggesting that publishers and broadcasters are sacrosanct, like Harvard, J. Edgar Hoover, and the Marines. I am not defending the shortcomings of the media for which they can be held accountable. What I am saying is this: Criticism that concentrates on them and their motives at best can explain only a small part of reality and at worst can obscure a genuine understanding of why the mass media are what they are.

Jay Jensen, in an article in the *Journalism Quarterly*, argued that genuine criticism of the press must begin with an understanding of the mass media as an institutional order.* His approach enables us to see the mass media from an entirely different perspective. It changes our focus from the transitory, short-term effects of the media to the relationships of the communication system to society in their most fundamental form. It enables us to see that the communication system performs certain objective functions quite irrespective of the intents and interests of the men who operate it.

For criticism to be valid and fruitful, Jensen said, it must meet three requirements. First, it must be objective. It must be conducted without bias or censure arising from ideological presuppositions. Second, it must take into account the influence of social, political, and cultural forces in the historical development of the media. And finally, it must put the media into the context of their environment; it must take note of the demands, values, aspirations, and life interests of the society in which the media operate.

Criticism meeting those three tests can come about, he said, if we will look at the mass media from an institutional perspective. Man has devised various institutions to help solve different aspects of the problem of human existence. Each institution is a complex pattern of values and behavior designed to meet some persistent and pressing social need. The family exists to sustain life, the church to give it meaning and direction. An institutional order is simply a larger and more complex pattern of values and behavior, for it is made up of several institutions by which man attacks the over-all problem of existence. In that functional sense, then, the mass media are

* Jay W. Jensen, "A Method and a Perspective for Criticism of the Mass Media," *Journalism Quarterly* 37 (Spring 1960), 261-66.

an institutional order. They are a way of dealing with one phase of existence—the necessity for social communication. So wrote Jensen.

In a sense, human societies arose from and are maintained by communication. What makes man unique among all creatures is his capacity for
creating symbols. Throughout history, in all societies, mankind has had
certain fundamental means of communicating—gesture, imitation, what
Sapir calls social suggestion, language. Using them, both primitive man and
civilized man have surrounded themselves with a web of symbols.

Man, in fact, seems to have some inner compulsion to create symbols.
They give him his image of himself and locate him in the vast stream of
time. As Kenneth Boulding reminds us, a dog has no idea that there were
dogs before him and that there will be dogs after him. But man, through
his symbolic creations, has a sense of the past that stretches centuries behind him and a concept of the future. Symbols are man's chief means of
communicating with his fellow man, the carrier of the social process.
Through them, he can express his fears, his hopes, his plans, his ideas of
the world he lives in, and through them he achieves the consensus that is
necessary if he is to get along with his fellow men. They are the means
whereby man copes with his environment and gives meaning to his existence.

Man's propensity for creating symbols has given human beings a
whole new environment. For man, alone of all creatures, reacts not just to
his physical surroundings but to a pseudo-environment, a symbolic environment, and it may be more important than the actual one in governing
what he thinks and does. Only with comparative rarity does man deal with
physical reality at first hand; for the far greater part, he deals with ideas
about reality. In short, he interposes a symbolic system between himself and
his purely physical universe. This is not to say, of course, that he moves in a
world of utter fantasy. The symbols he has developed are his attempts to
organize his sensations and experiences into some meaningful form, to
bring some order and meaning to his existence, and thus to deal with his
environment. And indeed through the use of symbols man can alter and
shape his environment.

What one sees from the institutional perspective is that the mass media are but one aspect of human communication in general. Like the sem-
aphore and tribal drum, they are technical extensions of this primary social
process that I have been talking about. As purveyors of symbols, the mass
media help society to function. They are carriers of the values, the beliefs,
the distinctive tone of the society in which they operate. As Walter Lippmann observed some forty years ago, they interpose a sort of pseudo-environment between man and physical reality. But if they are a force for
stability, they are also a force for change. And because they are technical extensions, they can transmit their message across vast sweeps of space and
time.

What one further sees from his institutional perspective is that the mass media are not really autonomous but are adjuncts of other orders. Looking back through history, one sees how various dominant institutions, unwittingly or by conscious design, have used the media to maintain and strengthen their power. So it was when the church used the printing press to reinforce and extend its influence. So it was when the Crown held the press of England in thrall. So it is today in Soviet Russia, where the mass media are an adjunct of the political order, or in the United States, where they are an adjunct of the industrial.

What one sees still further, however, is that the media are a force for disrupting the status quo as well as for perpetuating it. Under the bejeweled but firm hand of Queen Elizabeth I, the press was a means of consolidating the power of the Crown and of achieving the nationalism that echoes so gloriously through the chronicle plays of Shakespeare. Yet in the hands of dissidents the press became a powerful weapon for wresting the scepter from the monarch and reducing his presence on the throne to the largely ceremonial. Or consider another instance. When printing came along, its immediate effect seems to have been to disseminate and perpetuate the very superstitions that scientists were trying to combat. In the November 1962 issue of *The American Behavioral Scientist*, Livio C. Stecchini summarized the effects in this way:

> In the sixteenth century books of geography consolidated the outmoded conceptions, just when navigators and discoverers were revealing completely new worlds. The press was greatly responsible for the general wave of opposition to the Copernican doctrine. Copernicus' book *De revolutionibus orbium coelestium*, published in 1543 A.D., was not reprinted for twenty-three years, while in the interval there appeared a cataract of popular works on astrology. Not until the beginning of the seventeenth century did the non-academic public, reading in vernacular, become sufficiently enlightened to make it possible for Galileo to impose his views by appealing especially to them. The surprising epidemic of witch trials which began in the sixteenth century can be blamed partly on enterprising publishers who discovered that there was an excellent market for books on magic and witchcraft.

Yet true as all of that may be, few persons would dispute the subsequent influence of the press on the dissemination and advancement of learning.

If we look at the press from an institutional perspective, we should be especially concerned, I think, with the forces that have helped to make our mass communications system what it is. From here on, I would like to talk about two environments in which our communications system grew up. Both of those environments, as I will try to show, have played a tremendous part in determining the nature of our communications system. On the one hand, the mass media have been conditioned by an environment that exists largely in the minds of men. They have been profoundly influenced, that is, by the way we have answered such fundamental questions as the nature of man, the ideal relationship of man to the state, and the nature of truth and knowledge. On the other hand, the media have been shaped by such powerful social and economic forces as the rise of democracy, urbanization, and the industrial and technological revolution.

The classical libertarian theory of the press derived from the ideas of the Enlightenment, and among its several assumptions are these: That man is a creature of reason who wants to know the truth and will be guided by it, that he can find truth by applying his reason, that he is born with certain inalienable natural rights, that he forms governments of his own volition to protect those rights, and that hence the best government is that which governs least.

In brief, the libertarian theory of the press came to be something like this: The press must have only the most minimum of restraints imposed upon it because man can find truth only if there is free trade in information and ideas. No one need worry about the wide arena of freedom, though, for the natural working of things provides certain built-in correctives and safeguards. If some parts of the press lie and distort, if some parts abuse their freedom, other parts will find it expedient or profitable to expose them. And, after all, man puts all information and ideas to the powerful test of reason. He may find some truth amidst falsehood, some falsehood amidst truth, but over the long pull truth will prevail.

The government should keep its hands off the press for several reasons. For one thing, free expression is a natural right, one the state must preserve and protect. For another, the state has traditionally been a foe of liberty and is always likely to use the press for its own selfish purposes. For yet another thing, the state by intervening would surely upset the delicate dialectic by which truth emerges. The press, then, is best left in private hands, to make its own way in the market-place, free from the pressures of any one group or interest. In short, freedom under libertarian theory consists simply of the absence of restraint; to put it another way, a negative freedom is an effective freedom.

As that theory evolved, certain social functions came to be ascribed to the press. The press, for instance, is charged with enlightening the public and providing it with some entertainment. It is charged with servicing the political system by carrying the information and discussions that the electorate needs for its decisions. It is charged with protecting individual rights by sounding the alarm whenever they are threatened or infringed. It is charged with servicing the economic system, largely through advertising, and with earning its own financial support.

In the twentieth century especially, many of the assumptions of traditional theory have been seriously challenged if not indeed actually undermined, and some of us have found signs that a new theory of the press, a social responsibility theory of the press, has begun to emerge. But social responsibility theory is still largely theory, and our traditional ideas still guide a good deal of thinking about the press and still influence its workings in many ways. Let me give just one rather detailed example.

One tenet of Anglo-American theory is that the government should stay out of the communications business. My purpose is not to debate whether or not that idea is a good one. My point is that the idea has profoundly affected the nature of our communications system, although someone from another society may find it as quaint as we find the Yurok salmon fisherman's belief that he must not eat in his boat. From his parochial viewpoint, the Yurok has good reason for that bit of dietary abstinence: eating on the water violates his tribe's belief that various channels of nature must be kept apart. From our parochial viewpoint, so ingrained are the laissez faire doctrines of Adam Smith and the experiences of men who fought for press freedom in the past, we think we have good reason for keeping the government's hands off communications; for control necessarily follows support, we reason, and the government can weigh the scales on which truth is measured. In each case, a sacrosanct belief has affected life's crucial affairs—getting enough to eat in one, communicating with our fellows in the other.

Let me give just one illustration of how our faith in laissez faire has affected our communications system. Broadcasting depends upon the use of a limited number of channels, and other countries have handled the ownership of radio and TV facilities in various ways. The assumption is that the airwaves belong to the people. There is nothing in the nature of the medium demanding that it be left to private entrepreneurs, or, if it is, that its programs be surrounded by and punctuated with pleas to buy this product or that.

But broadcasting costs money, and someone has to pick up the tab. In our society the financing, described crudely, goes something like this: Broadcasters pay for programing and all of the equipment for transmitting it, but they are more than reimbursed by advertisers. Presumably the advertisers are not out of pocket, though, for they are reimbursed by listeners and viewers, who also must invest in receiving equipment. So ultimately the consumer bears the cost of broadcasting, but his money is channeled through private rather than governmental hands. True, the government regulates broadcasting, but the Federal Communications Commission has severe legal and practical limitations on its powers.

So strong is the conviction that communications must be kept in private hands that the federal government was reluctant to assign frequencies for educational and other non-commercial broadcasting. When it did, it acted in accord with the negative tradition of our press theory. It simply granted schools and communities permission to operate stations, but it made no provision for getting them on the air or keeping them there. Many stations got their money from state funds, a form of government support that was only partially taboo, since the cause was "education."

Once a year the Yurok suspends his tribal taboos, and in 1962 Congress waived one by authorizing the expenditure of $32,000,000 to encourage the growth of educational TV. Even though that sum was only about 60 per cent of what Procter & Gamble spent on network TV in 1961, Congress hesitated for months before actually appropriating just a small part of it.

Although critics have found fault with our system of broadcasting, attack is not my aim here. My object is simply to show how an idea, central to public thinking about the press, has contributed to the nature of the system.

It is not just ideas, however, that have given us the sort of communications system we have. Social, economic and political forces shaped the media too, and a combination of ideas and these other things made the media what they are.

In a way, it is not surprising that the mass media should be described as an adjunct of the industrial order. The rise of journalism paralleled the rise of capitalism, and printing itself was one of the earliest forms of mass production. Many early printers in England and America were primarily businessmen. Indeed, the fight for press freedom in England arose not just from political causes and the philosophical principles of free inquiry; it also came about from the trade demands of London printers and stationers who wanted to pursue wealth without state interference.

Today our communication system is characterized by bigness, fewness, and costliness. Small units have grown into huge ones. The *Reader's Digest*, for instance, began publication in a Greenwich Village basement in 1921 with a capital of $5,000 and a list of 1,500 charter subscribers. Today it publishes more than forty editions around the world, and its domestic edition alone reaches slightly more than one in four of U.S. adults. As the media have grown, there has been need for fewer of them. Three networks serve the great majority of TV stations, and two major wire services supply the great bulk of international, national, and regional news to the nation's dailies. As the media have grown, they also have become costly. A century ago one could start a metropolitan daily like the New York *Times* for $50,-000 to $75,000. Today one can spend more than a million getting a daily going in a medium-sized town such as Jackson, Mississippi, and then have it fail.

In all of those things, the media are not much different from other businesses and industries. Bigness, fewness, and costliness are characteristics of much of our economic order. The electronics industry is dominated by a few huge complexes, and the automotive industry has its short list of giants. Most cities have a few large department stores, and it would be about as quixotic to establish a new one as to run a Republican in an Alabama election.

What happened is that the media were moulded by forces that conditioned American industry generally and that tremendously affected other social, economic, and political institutions. These forces wrought a powerful revolution that affected virtually every aspect of American life, especially after the Civil War, although their foundations were laid long before that.

Those forces, closely interrelated, were the rise of democracy, the spread of popular education, the industrial and technological revolution, urbanization, and, in this century, the redistribution of income.

In the nineteenth century, the electorate broadened as restrictions on voting gradually broke down, although it was not until 1920 that women got the right to vote. Meanwhile, qualifications on the right to hold office were giving way; no longer did a candidate need to own property or meet religious tests before he could hold office. One result of all of this was that the common man, for the first time in history, achieved effective political power. Another was that he was called upon, at least in theory, to make innumerable decisions that once had been made for him, decisions that required information, decisions that countless special pleaders were anxious to help him make.

A concomitant of universal suffrage was the spread of free popular education. By 1850, in principle if not in practice, the issue of a common-school education for all children at public expense was settled in the North and in parts of the South. In the half-century after 1860, the number of high schools increased a hundredfold, from 100 to 10,000, and a growing proportion of children entered their classrooms. After the Civil War, assisted by the land-grant movement, colleges began a period of expansion that has made the bachelor's degree a commonplace. All of this gave the media a vast audience equipped at least with the rudimentary tools of literacy and at best with far-ranging intellectual interests.

Between the end of the Civil War and the start of the new century, industrialization and mechanization hit America with all the force of revolution. So pervasive were the changes they brought about that a man of George Washington's time would probably have been more at home in the Holy Land of Jesus Christ than in the America of Teddy Roosevelt. A web of shiny rails held the nation together, and factories sprouted up where once corn had grown. Inventor after inventor came up with machines and gadgets to do the tasks that man once had performed by hand. Steam power replaced water power; electricity and the internal-combustion engine replaced steam. In the sixty years after 1850, the average manufacturing plant increased its capital more than thirty-nine times, its number of wage earners nearly seven times, the value of its output more than nineteen times.

Beneath much of that change, of course, lay a system of mass production and mass distribution. The system depended upon standardization and mass consumption; so long as consumers would accept goods tailored to averages instead of to individual preferences, they were treated to a profusion of products at relatively low cost. Mass production changed the conception of markets from areas to people. The typical manufacturer no longer produced only for his own locality; he sought out buyers wherever they lived. Now, all of the characteristics of mass production—greater use of product, standardization, and so on—had implications for the mass media, as I plan to show.

But one is so important that I wish to mention it now—the development of advertising. For one thing, mass production and mass distribution needed some kind of inexpensive mass salesmanship. For another thing, the media and appeals that worked when markets were regional or local did not suffice when markets became widely-scattered consumers. For still another thing, manufacturers had no great need of advertising when their production was barely above subsistence level. But as assembly lines turned out a seemingly endless flow of products of seemingly endless variety, as consumption became essential to keeping the stream of goods flowing, manufacturers had to make consumers conscious of dimly-sensed needs and desires, had to channel human drives to exploit the psychic values of their wares, had to make the consumer want to consume. For yet another thing, as unlabelled merchandise gave way to the brand-name product, the manufacturer saw the financial advantage inherent in his name and trademark. If he could convince the consumer that his product was more desirable than all others, he could charge a premium for it. Advertising grew, and as it did the media clutched at it for financial support.

Along with the industrial and technological revolution came the crowding of Americans together in cities. Farm workers put down the plow to tend the machines of the factory. Boat after boat brought immigrants seeking new opportunities—some 11½ million of them in the thirty years before 1900—and although many of them huddled together on the coast, many others ventured inland, some no doubt encouraged by the special rail fares that let them journey from New York to Chicago for as little as a dollar. All in all, the nation's population just about doubled between 1870 and 1900, and the city became home for an increasing proportion of it. Gathered in one place, people were natural markets for the media. And the immigrant, in many ways, had an influence on the media. The foreign-language newspaper, for instance, provided a link with the homeland and with others from it, helped adjustment to a strange land but also encouraged reading of regular American dailies. The early movies, low in price and heavy on pantomime, were an ideal medium for the foreign-born struggling with a new tongue and wanting escape from the drudgery of the factory.

In our own century, we have seen a redistribution of income so apparent that it probably is unnecessary to document it. It is true, of course, that despite all of our talk about the affluent society, poverty stubbornly exists and that many Americans still live in actual want. It is also true that disparities of income still exist, although not on the grand scale of 1900 when Andrew Carnegie's personal tax-free income of $20,000,000 was at least 20,000 times that of the average workingman. The middle-class American is considerably better off financially than he was in 1900, and that point is important to the mass media, not only because he has money for TV sets, transistor radios, and newspaper and magazine subscriptions but also because he has money for the advertisers' washing machines, hi-fi sets, and automobiles.

My little excursion into history has turned up little that is unfamiliar, I am sure. I have dwelt on the past at such length because critics have looked back to it surprisingly little when they have tried to explain why the media are what they are. My pitch is that the communications industries, like other industries, were affected by the social and economic forces I have just outlined; they changed, in short, from personal craft industries to impersonal mass-production industries, and today they share many of the characteristics of other mass-production enterprises.

First, the mass media usually carve out little markets of their own, much as manufacturers and retailers do. The publisher of a confessions magazine no more expects every literate American to curl up with his tales of sin and redemption than an overall manufacturer expects every American to wear his blue jeans. Each has a pretty clear idea of who is a good prospect for what he turns out, and he fashions his product accordingly.

Usually the market of a medium coincides with that of its advertisers. A newspaper typically concentrates its circulation in the trade area served by local retailers, for instance, and a magazine like *Farm Journal* aims at people who buy the tractors and chemical fertilizers extolled on its advertising pages. Even TV programers do not necessarily expect the people who guffaw at the Beverly Hillbillies to sit entranced by Meet the Press.

Media that do not carry advertising quite often pick out specialized markets, too. The book clubs neatly illustrate the point. Sired by that middle-aged grandfather, the Book-of-the-Month Club, their tribe has multiplied to include clubs for antique collectors, gardeners, cooks, farmers, educators, salesmen, executives, Civil War buffs and other amateur historians, Irishmen, outdoorsmen, drama and art lovers, science fans, yachtsmen, writers, Catholics, Jews, Lutherans and other Protestants, young children, teenagers, and grapplers of prose in its original French and Spanish.

A second consequence is what we might rather grandiosely call a democratization of content. In simple words, the mass media as a whole turned from a class audience to a mass audience and adjusted their content accordingly. Newspapers began their transition from sober organs for the mercantile class to lively sources of news for quite literally the man on the street in the early nineteenth century. Magazines began their change about a half-century later. Movies, radio, and television, born into a world of cities and technology, went after a mass market from the start.

As I have already said, the media seek out their own little publics. But in speaking to those publics, the media tend to address themselves to some center point, to some common denominator of taste, interest, and capability. In the nature of things a publisher or broadcaster must conduct his business pretty much as any other manufacturer must. A magazine publisher and a refrigerator maker, say, both want maximum saturation of their chosen markets. The media need audiences to exist, and to get and hold them they must please the majority of their chosen market. They can no more tailor their product to the specifications of a single individual or tiny group than can the dressmakers in New York's garment district. Over-all, then, they tend to reflect the concerns, values, beliefs, and tastes of the great majority, and therein lies their essential conservatism.

Third, the mass media have become standardized in content and in technique. Newspapers across the land are pretty much alike in size, format, and over-all appearance; in the ways in which they get their news; in the ways in which they write it, headline it, and present it; even in the relative play they give to national and international events. Magazines depend upon a pattern of content that carries over from issue to issue, and the big ones play a relatively small scale of major themes. Television programs are remarkable more for their basic sameness than their variety; the past season offered more than a dozen series in which Western badmen found death on the dusty streets of frontier towns, for instance, and depending on how one counted them, between twenty-three and thirty situation comedy series. And TV programs themselves, as any viewer knows, are developed in familiar, standardized ways. This standardization seems an almost inevitable result as the media increased their reach, their speed, and their efficiency by adopting such techniques of mass production as division of labor and mechanization, but consumer convenience and expectation also have probably played some part.

Fourth, as content became democratized, as technological advances enabled speedy output, there has been an increased use of the media. Today the typical American spends more time looking at and listening to the mass media than at anything else except his work or sleeping, and the typical youngster leaving high school has spent more time in front of a TV set than in the classroom. Newspapers, magazines, radio, and television all penetrate deep into the population.

Fifth, the media have become more efficient, just as many other mass-production enterprises have. The telegraph, wireless, train, and plane have enabled the media not only to take the entire world for their beat but to cover it with astonishing swiftness. Until the middle of the last century, England was still two or three weeks away, and at home news was slow in traveling from one part of the country to another.

When Andrew Jackson successfully defended New Orleans in the War of 1812-14, New Yorkers did not read about the outcome until a month afterwards. And as they learned from their papers five days later, the battle itself had been fought two weeks after the peace treaty was signed in London. But when the Korean War broke out in June, 1950, Jack James's United Press dispatch reached Washington almost at once—several minutes before the State Department's own cable, in fact.

New means of communication and improvements in the old ones have made possible vast audiences for the media. High-speed presses and mechanical typesetting allowed newspapers and magazines to seek their large circulations, and the electronic media have put a speaker into instantaneous touch with millions of persons. We often forget how very recent some of these changes are. In my own childhood, in 1919, when President Woodrow Wilson wanted to sell the Treaty of Versailles to the nation, he spent twenty-seven days traveling more than 8,000 miles in seventeen states to deliver forty formal speeches and many more informal talks, only one of them with benefit of public address system. In December, 1962, when three TV networks carried "Conversation with the President," John F. Kennedy was in instantaneous touch with an estimated 21,960,000 American homes, according to A. C. Nielsen figures.

Finally, the mass media, like other industries, have used the assembly-line technique of division of labor. Once even the publisher of a metropolitan daily could operate as James Gordon Bennett did in 1835, when he gathered his own news, wrote it up, handled business affairs, and waited on customers at a desk made of two barrels with a plank across them. By the 1870's those days were largely gone, and by the 1890's the large-city dailies had staffs about as specialized as they are today. All of the other media, too, have come to depend upon a variety of specialists to put together the finished product. As they have, the individual employee has lost most of whatever chance for self-expression he ever had. He became one of a team turning out mass-produced images, and too large an investment rides on his efforts for him to produce with anything but the market in mind.

Those, then, are the forces that have joined to give us the sort of communication system we have, and in large measure they are responsible for the many strengths we too often take for granted. They have contributed to the development of a communication system that reaches virtually the entire population and that in the aggregate makes available an astonishing amount of entertainment and an astonishing array of information, viewpoint, and interpretation on a wide array of subjects with incredible swiftness and superb technical skill. They have contributed to the important part that the media have played in bringing about our high material standard of living.

But in large measure those forces also are responsible for the faults that have sent many a critic reaching for his thesaurus of epithets. They have contributed to the superficiality, the sameness, the blandness, and the blindness that characterize a good deal of media content. They have contributed to the bigness, fewness, and costliness that some critics see as jeopardizing the free trade in information and ideas, putting control of a powerful social instrument into the hands of the few and converting the personal right of press freedom into a property right.

All of what I have said, I immodestly think, has some implications for those who are serious in their criticism of the mass media.

First, those who examine the press should try to achieve objectivity in two meanings of the term. On the one hand, as they set out to discover what the mass media are and why they are what they are, they should leave their ideological baggage behind, much as a good cultural anthropologist does. They should look deep into the past for clues to present understanding. They should examine the interrelationships of the media with other parts of society. On the other hand, they should explore the objective social functions that the media perform, quite apart from those ascribed by normative press theory. As Jensen suggested, the media have a reality of their own. Although they are man-made creations, they have developed certain objective functions distinct from the tasks assigned them by their operators and by society. Desirable or not, those functions exist, and it is the duty of the serious critic to understand them.

Second, critics should put up for serious examination our traditional theory of the press, which in many ways seems out of joint with the times. That theory may have been adequate in the eighteenth and nineteenth centuries, when both the world and the communication system were far less complex than today, but one might ask if it is in accord with contemporary thought and reality. Some such examination has already begun; and as publishers and broadcasters themselves have discarded parts of traditional theory as outmoded, there are indications that a new theory of social responsibility is emerging. As a part of this intellectual overhaul, which should begin with the questioning of basic assumptions, I hope we could also re-examine some of the notions that have long surrounded traditional theory. For instance, are we right in the notion that although the media have a responsibility to enlighten the public, the public has no special responsibility to be enlightened? Are the media right in their notion that in enlightening the public, the demands of the market are the best test of how well the job is being done? Are we right in the notion that bigness is necessarily badness? Does a multiplicity of communications units necessarily mean a multiplicity of viewpoints? Are small media operators necessarily more socially responsible than large ones? Does control necessarily follow financial support?

In conclusion, let me say that I am not proposing that we grant the media absolution for all their sins, venal or otherwise. Some, I know, will read my message that way. In looking at the press from an institutional perspective, some will conclude that publishers and broadcasters are swept inexorably along by powerful, impersonal social and cultural forces and that there is nothing that they or we can do about it. That conclusion implies a degree of predestinarianism I am quite unwilling to accept. Man with brain and hand has given the media the milieus in which they operate, and man if he will can change them.

2

PUBLIC OPINION

Paul F. Lazarsfeld
PUBLIC OPINION AND THE CLASSICAL TRADITION

Hans Speier
HISTORICAL DEVELOPMENT OF PUBLIC OPINION

Walter Lippmann
STEREOTYPES

2

PUBLIC OPINION

THERE have been two basic approaches to the problem of public opinion. One is the speculative approach, predominant in the nineteenth century. The other is the empirical method, characteristic of the current era. Although both speculative and functional methods have been applied to public opinion research, the term has almost as many definitions as there are studies on the subject. What precisely is public opinion? Whose opinions constitute public opinion? What is meant by consensus? According to Dr. Samuel Johnson, "the majority of a society is a true definition of the public." This would mean, logically, that public opinion is the true expression of the majority, but it would also eliminate significant minorities.

In his discussion of "Public Opinion and the Classical Tradition," Paul F. Lazarsfeld compares the contemporary experimental approach to public opinion research with the theoretical or speculative approach of the nineteenth century—an approach which continues to have some advocates even today when scientific method is being applied vigorously to communication research. Professor Lazarsfeld shows, in this analysis, how the classical tradition of opinion research was confronted by the empiricists who postulated the concept of "attitudes" and of "attitudes and opinions." The arena for this confrontation of classicism and empiricism was the field of public opinion research. According to Bernard Berelson, public opinion research today is the result of a process which began with the recognition that public opinion is a significant phenomenon and has moved forward to the present empirical or scientific method of approaching the whole area of public opinion research.

Public opinion is not easily amenable to scientific definition. It is an outgrowth of educational processes as well as of the growth of mass media. Its substance and the way it functions in terms of the individual and the group are still described in terms of intangibles. While empirical research has yielded more data than speculative method, there are still questions to be answered. How do the public and its opinions interact? How do mass media reflect public opinion? How—and to what extent—are mass media influenced by public opinion? These questions leave room for considerable research. As additional data come to light, we shall understand more thoroughly the nature of goals and values and learn to distinguish and select those values which are worth seeking and preserving.

According to Hans Speier, public opinion, in terms of this historical review, is a phenomenon of middle class civilization. It is a way whereby the citizens may communicate with their government. It is government by consent of governed.

Speier's concept of public opinion is that it is a political phenomenon, a consequence of habits in economic and social strata, culminating in the emergence of the "common man" or middle class citizen who made his demands and opinions articulate to the government. The factor which distinguishes this rendering of public opinion from purely private opinion is communication. For public opinion in this sense means communication from groups of citizens to those selected to represent these groups, i.e., the government. It is not opinion circulating privately among private citizens. Nor is it diplomacy, or communication between governments. Speier does recognize communication and opinion formation among individual citizens, but this he terms a secondary, rather than a primary, communication process.

It might be determined from his analysis, therefore, that public opinion became operative when citizens were free to communicate opinions to the government without censorship. It is interesting to note, parenthetically, that John Locke, a philosopher of the Era of Enlightenment, did not view public opinion as an operative influence from the governed (the group) to the government, but rather as a form of "private censure" from the individual to the government. In point of fact, the government recognized and responded to public opinion only after economic and social inequalities were reduced, and after large groups began to enjoy greater economic and social freedom. As a result, political influence by citizens on the government became significant. Finally, the development of public opinion was inevitably woven into the development of mass communication. Hence, Hans Speier's view of the development of public opinion is primarily an economic one, a phenomenon growing out of the "struggle for budget control." The major factors involved are growing economic equality, the rise of literacy and the growth of social meeting places such as the coffee houses in England and the salons in France.

Walter Lippmann, in his volume *Public Opinion*, was probably the first student of this area to dwell on the importance of the stereotype, a short-hand method of influencing opinion by reinforcing the pathways of well-traveled responses to verbal and visual stimuli. Stereotyping is possible because of the tendency of the public to abstract symbols from the verbal environment. No expression of opinion stands alone. Its development involves an observable fact, plus imagined projection, along with an acceptance of the statements of others. Facts as such are illusory. They are facts only with reference to habitual perceptive responses at the particular time when data are revealed to our senses.

How, then, do definition and meaning result from the vast, buzzing confusion of the immediate environment? Our perception is, to some degree, a priori—"we pick out what our culture has already defined for us and we tend to perceive that which we have picked out in the form stereotyped for us by our culture." The individual's reaction to an event or an idea, in other words, is not without conditioning. It is based upon that individual's past conditioning to what that event was like—or what he thought it was like.

Stereotyping, of course, is a dangerous phenomenon. Its less savory aspects were clearly revealed in some of the early motion picture presentations of policemen, servants, bankers and other spurious representations of reality. But stereotyping is also comprehensible in our welter of communication content, because it tends to give form to our reactions to the events in the outside world as these events relate to the images in our heads. Carried to extreme, stereotyping is an indolent way of reacting to the world around us. It tends to result in uncritical acceptance of appearance for reality. If it is impossible to see everything freshly and see it whole, it is nevertheless possible to learn to avoid casual convictions about the people and events that shape our environment. Since stereotypes are abstractions, they should be approached with a healthy skepticism. In this way, empirical evidence becomes significant and opinions take on significance. As Walter Lippmann indicates, stereotypes as such are neither good nor bad. It is the knowledge that they are only stereotypes that makes them capable of absorption and modification.

Lippmann's analysis of the stereotype is of great significance to our understanding of the public opinion process today, particularly with respect to the growing influence of public relations techniques. Students of semantics have taken pains to emphasize that stereotyping is a lazy and spurious process at best, for it not only minimizes and short-circuits intelligent effort and action, but tends to leave us prey to the more predatory aspects of propaganda.

Walter Lippmann's *Public Opinion* was written before the advent of television, but he anticipated the power of visual communication in his comment on the moving images conveyed by the motion picture. Today, the combined auditory and visual prowess of television not only carry forward the graphic power of the film, but also enlarge the scope of journalism.

* * * *

RELATED READING

Albig, William. *Public Opinion*. New York: McGraw-Hill, 1939.
Berelson, Bernard. "Communications and Public Opinion," in Waples, *Communication in Modern Society*. Urbana, Ill.: University of Illinois Press, 1948.

Dollard, John. "Under What Conditions Do Opinions Predict Behavior?" *Public Opinion Quarterly*, 12 (Winter 1948-49), pp. 623-32.

Markel, Lester (ed.). *Public Opinion and Foreign Policy.* New York: Harper, 1949.

Powell, John Norman. *Anatomy of Public Opinion,* New York: Prentice-Hall, 1951.

Smith, B. L., Lasswell, H. D., & Casey, R. D. *Propaganda, Communication. and Public Opinion.* Princeton: Princeton University Press, 1946.

PUBLIC OPINION AND THE CLASSICAL TRADITION

By Paul F. Lazarsfeld

QUITE POSSIBLY the emergence of empirical social science will one day be considered an outstanding feature of the twentieth century. But its birth has not been without travail. Hardest have been its struggles with what we shall call the classical tradition. After all, for two thousand years or more people have thought and written about human and social affairs. Has the empirical trend been an enriching innovation? Has it had a pernicious effect? The matter has certainly been much discussed in recent years.

The debate over the study of public opinion probably provides the best case in point. Since about the beginning of the eighteenth century a steadily increasing amount has been written on this subject by political scientists, by historians and, recently, by sociologists. Toward the beginning of the twentieth century, however, this classical tradition was confronted by the empiricists, who rallied around the notion of attitudes.

The empirical tradition in opinion and attitude research began modestly enough in Germany with simple laboratory experiments on problem solving, in which the notion of "mental sets" was carved out. It gained strength from the work of the Chicago school of sociologists, which brought the study of attitudes and values into play. Immediately thereafter, the psychometricians under the leadership of Thurstone introduced the portentous problem of measurement. And finally came the public opinion research people who, on the one hand, narrowed the conceptual range but, on the other, greatly extended the field of practical applications.[1]

About ten years ago the aspiring new science and the classical tradition confronted each other like petulant antagonists. Our professional organizations certainly took cognizance of the matter. Three presidential addresses delivered at AAPOR annual meetings since 1950 have been devoted to the discussion of the relation of public opinion research to history, political theory and social theory, respectively. Nor did exponents of the classical

[1] For an excellent brief history of the empirical position see Gordon Allport's essay on "Attitudes" in the *Handbook of Psychology*, edited by Carl Murchison (Worcester, Mass.: Clark University Press, 1935).

Reprinted by permission from *Public Opinion Quarterly*, Spring 1957. Copyright 1957 Princeton University Press. This may also be identified as publication No. A-230 of the Bureau of Applied Social Research, Columbia University.

tradition let us forget their claims: Lindsay Rogers made violent attacks, Herbert Blumer articulated his complaints, and the historians showed their contempt for public opinion research by their neglect, speaking about it only occasionally and upon request. This contentious situation has been ably summarized by Bernard Berelson in an unusually thoughtful and informative paper.[2] Were we to review where we stand now, hardly anything could be added to Berelson's remarks, and if we want to discuss how to proceed from here his essay is still the most suggestive.

Berelson sees the present state of public opinion research as the seventh phase of an unfolding process which began with a general feeling that something called public opinion was important. As a result, prominent writers developed broad speculations about it during a second phase of development. In a third phase empirical data were drawn on wherever they were available: magazine articles, speeches, or other documents. The shortcomings of these data led, fourthly, to intense interest in the methodology of the field. At this point a fifth phase set in, during which specialized commercial agencies as well as university institutes took the lead in research. Next, contact was made with intellectual neighbors such as anthropology and psychology. This makes possible the seventh phase, into which we are just entering, a phase in which systematic propositions on public opinion are being developed: public opinion research has become an empirical social science.

If we were dealing with a field like chemistry, or any other natural science, we would be rather confident that any new phase incorporated what was of value in past work; only the historian of natural science must actually turn back to earlier stages. In the social sciences the situation is not as simple. Progress in the clarity of formulations and the respect for evidence is often accompanied, at least temporarily, by an insensitivity to the broader visions and the more general concerns characteristic of an older tradition.

The resulting clash between modern empiricists and spokesmen for the classics recurs in many other fields, and is almost always productive. This is true for three distinct reasons. First, empirical development usually furnishes sharper conceptual tools that enable us to see the classics from a new vantage point: what was only dimly perceived before can now often be discerned with clarity and, as a result, new implications of all sorts can be brought to light. Secondly, the very act of inspecting this classical material brings to our attention ideas which might otherwise have been overlooked, either because of preoccupation with the work of the day, or because empirical researchers are likely to be guided too much by what is a manageable topic at the moment, rather than by what is an important issue. Finally, the classical tradition, as exemplified by Berelson's first two phases, is by no

[2] In *The Study of the Social Sciences*, edited by Leonard White (Chicago: University of Chicago Press, 1956).

means over. We hope that scholars will keep on thinking about problems with a broad scope, irrespective of whether data or precise modes of reasoning about these problems are available. Theorizing itself can make progress, and the logic of empirical research can contribute to it. Thus, our conceptual task is to bend Berelson's phases into a loop to see how the early phases mesh with the later ones.

COMPLEXITIES OF THE CLASSICAL NOTION

We may profitably begin by paying heed to the discussions centering around the definition of public opinion. It is no coincidence that both Blumer and Rogers make this big point: when the pollsters use the term public opinion, they do not know and cannot say what they mean. Now, in principle, this is not a picayune objection. Definitions, whether implicit or explicit, do indeed have great influence on scholarly activities. In another respect, however, the objection is a strange one. Neither of the two authors proposes a definition. And if one looks at the collection of quotations which Rogers provides in one of his chapters in *The Pollsters*, one is impressed by the fact that few of the classics offered a definition. As a matter of fact, earlier writers overflow with comments about the mysterious and intangible character of public opinion.

Why is public opinion so difficult to define? It is generally agreed that it was the rise of the middle class, the spread of democratic institutions, the expansion of literacy, and the growth of mass media of communication which gave rise to concern with what was loosely called public opinion. By this term many authors of the classical school referred to people who did not belong to the ruling classes from which the government personnel was recruited and yet claimed a voice in public affairs.[3]

But two matters became puzzling. One is a normative problem: What is the best relation between this "public opinion" and the government? The second is a descriptive problem: How does public opinion actually exercise its influence? The term "public opinion" came into use in just the casual way in which we have introduced it now. While ostensibly a concept, it actually signified only a complicated congeries of observations, practical problems, and normative concerns. It is very much worth while to follow closely this startling piece of intellectual history: how the complexity of a developing historical situation was experienced as a linguistic difficulty be-

[3] In a book by Emden on the people and the constitution, to which we shall come back later, an interesting appendix on this history of the term "The People" can be found. He shows that at various periods in English history the people were always those who hadn't yet the right to vote but were about to get it at the next turn of parliamentary reform. In Germany, prior to the First World War, the liberal intellectuals were, for all practical purposes, excluded from government. It is therefore not surprising that the German sociologist Toennies defined public opinion as the opinion of experts (*Gelehrte*), the men who thought about public issues but did not have direct access to the centers of power. Cecil S. Emden, *The People and the Constitution*, 2nd edition (London: Oxford University Press, 1956).

cause no appropriate logical categories existed to cope with it. In modern parlance one would say that there was a confusion between the subject language dealing with factual observations, and the meta-language dealing with the way the observations should be analyzed.[4]

We shall take our main example of this problem from an essay by the German historian Hermann Oncken on "The Historian, the Statesman, and Public Opinion." According to Oncken, the statesman is concerned mainly with the enduring interests of his country; therefore when he writes history he should be mistrusted. The historian is mainly concerned with truth; he should not become too involved in politics or he runs the risk of a conflict of values. "Public opinion"—watch the personification—stands for the ever-shifting qualities of the human mind not encumbered by either scholastic or national responsibilities.

Oncken goes on to discuss public opinion as follows:

> The vague and fluctuating cannot be understood by being clamped into a formula; certainly not when it is a very characteristic of the concept that it embodies a thousand possibilities of variation. But when all is said and done, everyone knows, if put to it, what public opinion means. If it must be set in words, then it can only appear hedged around by many restricting clauses: public opinion is a complex of similar utterances of larger or smaller segments of society concerning public affairs (1, 2); at times spontaneous, at times artfully manipulated (3); expressed in a multitude of ways, in clubs, assemblies, above all in the press and in journals, or perhaps only in unspoken feelings of each one of us (4); of the common man in the street or of a small circle of the cultured (8); here a true power factor, which statesmen must take into account, or something of no political significance (5); something again to be evaluated differently in every country (5 or 6); sometimes united, rising up like a tidal wave against the government and the experts, sometimes divided, concealing conflicting tendencies (7); at one time bringing out the simple and natural sentiments of the people, at another time being the rowdy thoughtless manifestations of wild instincts (6); always leading and always being led (5, 3); looked down upon by the sophisticated, yet forcing the hands of men (6, 5); contagious like an epidemic (10); capricious, treacherous (9); and power mad (resembling man himself) (6); and then again only a word by which those in power are bewitched (5).[5]

[We have inserted numbers after the sentences in this passage so that we can refer to them easily.] Now, what is interesting about this bewildering formulation is that it can be disentangled easily as soon as one matches

[4] Interestingly enough, at least one historian has dealt in detail with a similar difficulty for an earlier epoch. Lucien Febvre makes the point that in 16th century France it was impossible to develop a system of religious scepticism because the language did not provide the necessary intellectual base for it. See his *Le Probleme de l'Incroyance en XVIe Siecle*, pp. 383-401.

[5] *Essays on Politics and History* (Berlin, 1914), Vol. I, pp. 203-204.

it against what one might call a complete attitude distribution. It is a commonplace for most of us that polling does not consist merely in finding out how many people are for or against something. We need to know the social and demographic characteristics of the respondents, and we take great care to distinguish between people who are informed and concerned with the problem and those who are not. In other words, a good public opinion poll ends up not with one distribution of attitudes but with many of them for different sectors of the population. In this sense, Oncken undoubtedly gives a definition of public opinion. It is a statistical distribution of utterances (No. 1 and No. 7), expressed by various segments of the population (No. 2), and these segments can and should be classified by the degree of their competence (No. 8).

But intermingled with this definition are a number of empirical problems which are encountered in investigations more complicated than cross-sectional surveys. What factors determine a given attitude distribution at any given time (No. 3)? What effect does it have on statesmen and on the legislative process in general (No. 5)? How are opinions communicated and diffused (No. 10)?

Two further elements in this passage foreshadow topics which are now of great technical concern to us. How should one choose among the various sources and devices which can be used to ascertain an attitude distribution (No. 4)? Oncken mentions only expressions at meetings and in the printed mass media. Today we would add questionnaires and other more systematic research procedures. And we would now translate the phrase "capricious, treacherous" (No. 9) into the terminology of panel techniques, distinguishing people who upon repeated interviews show constant attitudes from those whose attitudes fluctuate. Finally (No. 6), Oncken is obviously concerned with the normative problem of how certain opinions should be evaluated.

It is this intertwining of matters of definition and factual problems which is so characteristic of the classical tradition. We are probably faced here by an irreversible development. Now that we have the reality of public opinion polls we will undoubtedly keep on calling public opinion a well analyzed distribution of attitudes. But certainly no one denies that we still know very little about how such complete attitude distributions come into being, and what role they actually play in the governmental process. And under the general heading of the "mass society phenomenon" we certainly keep on worrying about the role it *should* play. Thus the issue of definition resolves itself in an interesting way. The critics of polling are worried that the joy of having found greater conceptual clarity will lead us to forget some of the grave philosophical and empirical problems with which the classics dealt (and well these critics might worry as far as some pollsters are concerned). But what is overlooked is something that has happened often in intellectual history: a new technique has permitted the sorting out of various aspects of a diffused concern and has prepared the way for a more rational approach to its different elements.[6]

THE "PUBLIC OPINION SYSTEM" AS A BRIDGE

There has recently been an interesting effort to find a formulation which will bridge the gap between the classical tradition and the modern turn of events. MacIver has introduced the term "public opinion system." [7] It implies a clear understanding that the multiplicity of facts and problems by which earlier writers were confused can be structured only by distinguishing different dimensions in the concept of public opinion. One is "the opinion alignment," corresponding to the type of information which modern public opinion polls provide. The second dimension is the "structure of communication." This refers to a set of questions with which many sociologists are concerned: the role of associations and leadership; the way in which the mass media and their public influence each other. The third dimension is "the ground of consensus" which takes account of a distinction that has perturbed other writers. Some of the attitudes relevant to the study of specific historical situations are of long enduring character: people are hardly conscious of them, take them for granted, and they come to the fore only in situations where these basic sentiments are somehow threatened. Such "grounds of consensus" should be distinguished from opinions on current controversial issues.

The three components together form the "public opinion system." Two of them are clearly parallel to the two groups of elements we found in Oncken. The third component aims at taking care of another difficulty which has plagued writers during the last century: What aspects of popular sentiment are significant for the analysis of social events? The French social psychologist, Gabriel Tarde,[8] has proposed a three-way distinction: tradition, opinion, and fashion. The German sociologist Toennies has paralleled the well known distinction between *Gemeinschaft* and *Gesellschaft* by coordinating religion with the former and opinion with the latter.

[6] An interesting parallel could be developed with the invention of the Arabic number system. This was also of a highly technical nature, but it permitted the formulation and later the solution of problems which were unmanageable with the numerical symbolism of antiquity.

[7] Robert M. MacIver, *Academic Freedom in the United States* (New York: Columbia University Press, 1954). The "structure of communication" as part of the "public opinion system" is a felicitous way to bring out a feature common to many writers steeped in the classical tradition. Hans Speier, *e.g.* (in the American Journal of Sociology, 1950) takes an "historical approach to public opinion"; he mainly provides valuable material on ways in which opinion was formed, for instance, in coffee houses, salons, etc. Only tangentially is he concerned with "opinion alignment."

[8] His book on *Opinion and the Crowd* has never been translated. It is, however, well summarized in Sorokin's *Survey of European Sociology*. Herbert Blumer's paper on "mass and opinion" is a rendition of the Tarde point of view. (See "The Mass, the Public, and Public Opinion," included in *Reader in Public Opinion and Communication*, edited by Bernard Berelson and Morris Janowitz. Glencoe, Ill.: The Free Press, 1953.)

The problem was always to place "public opinion" somewhere between the rather permanent and subconscious value system of a society and the fleeting reaction of a people to the passing events of the day.

Probably the most productive formulation of this kind has been taken over and developed by historians under the term "climate of opinion." [9] This concept became fashionable in the seventeenth century, and acquired prominence through Carl Becker's analysis of the eighteenth century Enlightenment in France. It is often drawn on by historians when they explain why they are not interested in contemporary polling: they assert that we do not investigate quasi-permanent sentiments out of which grow opinions on specific events. A sociologist giving the presidential address at the annual meeting of AAPOR recently acknowledged the existence of the issue by admonishing us to pay more attention to the study of "mentality."

Researching the "Climate of Opinion"

Now this is indeed a topic on which the classics have much to teach us. Here they were certainly in their element, because historical documents, laws and customs are an important source of insight into climates of opinion. But again, the situation is rather complex. Some of our more sophisticated contemporaries like to answer that we can discover the basic values of any population group by applying methods like projective tests; anthropologists, especially, incline toward this point of view. But such procedures are costly, even on a small scale, and almost unmanageable with a reliable sample. There is, however, a possible compromise; this consists in the development of fairly simple projective *items* which can be handled within the frame of a sampling survey procedure. We have not yet made a great deal of progress along this line, and it is therefore worthwhile to review where we stand.

Some examples can be taken from current studies of "national character." We find considerable differences between nations if we ask such questions as: Can people be trusted? Is it possible to change human nature? Should children consult their parents before they get married? Is it dangerous to contradict one's superiors? Should clergymen or teachers be more respected in the community? Would you rather live in another country? What do you approve or disapprove of most in your neighbors?

Within a single country, class differences have been made the object of special investigation. What should children be punished for? How much do adolescents confide in their parents? What decisions does the husband make without consulting his wife? The answers indicate whether the "mores" vary between social strata. In addition, tensions between classes can be investigated using projective items. Are the courts and the police considered impartial, or do they favor the rich? Does a worker or a busi-

[9] For some historical references on the term "climate of opinion" see R. K. Merton's essay on *Social Structure and Anomie* (Free Press, Glencoe, Illinois), p. 378, footnote 6.

ness man feel he has more in common with people of the same class in other countries, or with people of a different class in his own country? Is it especially interesting to read stories and books about people of one's own class? [10]

Attention should be drawn to findings which deserve to be followed up as the historical scene changes. In a survey conducted in Germany in 1946, a sample of the population was asked whether they considered physical courage an important quality in a man. More than 90 per cent said "no." This probably reflected disillusion with the Nazi ideology, as well as an effort to guess what the American interviewer wanted to hear. It would be highly instructive to repeat this question a few years after the revival of a German army. If physical courage gains rapidly in prestige, we may have to start worrying about the consequences of German rearmament.

DICEY REVISITED: THE FEED-BACK EFFECT

Behind the battle over definitions, then, lie the serious difficulties involved in selecting problems that are important. The choice of problems, in turn, helps determine what type of techniques need development and what data should be gathered. But there is also another relationship between the style of thinking in a social science and its technical development. The propositions which the classics developed were of a broader and altogether different nature from the more microscopic findings with which we concern ourselves today. Only rarely is the discrepancy small enough to allow the problems of interest in the older tradition to be approached with the techniques and orientations of the newer one.

An exception is found in one of the most famous of the older books: Dicey's *The Relations Between Law and Public Opinion in England During the 19th Century*.[11] The title clearly presents the scope of the work. The author's main interest is in the changes which came about in England between 1840 and 1880. The earlier date represents the peak of *laissez faire*, when efforts were made to minimize governmental interference with economic affairs. By 1880 a great deal of social legislation had been enacted, and an era had started which Dicey dislikes, and interchangeably calls the era of collectivism or of socialism. He not only tries to trace the effects of prevailing trends of opinion on legislation; he also seeks to account for changes in opinion, and formulates a number of "characteristics"—generalizations purporting to explain the ways such changes come about. One of these rules covers what we today might call a feed-back effect: "laws foster or create opinion."

[10] The general role of such questionnaire items is discussed and exemplified by Jean Stoetzel in an article on the use of polls in social anthropology (UNESCO *International Social Science Bulletin*, Vol. V, No. 3). Stoetzel, incidentally, was the first, in his dissertation in France, to stress the relation of history and political science to attitude research.
[11] Second edition (London: Macmillan Co., 1920).

Now it happens that we have by now a considerable amount of data showing that Dicey was right. Cantwell and Hyman have demonstrated that immediately after Congress enacts a law there tends to be an increase in the number of people who approve of it. (Their examples range from the debates on enlarging the Supreme Court to the Marshall Plan.) Planck gives us similar data from France, where public opinion polls showed increasing approval of a series of international agreements right after they had been signed. But how did Dicey know this when obviously no such evidence was available to him? Again, a careful reading of his argument permits separation of the "old-fashioned" from the creative and enduring element. On the one hand, he calls his rule an "undeniable truth" and seems to think that he can derive it from basic principles. On the other hand, he supports his contention with examples, developing various interesting ideas in the course of his argument. According to him, most people are sufficiently uncertain enough about their opinion, so that when a law is enacted "its underlying principle derives prestige from its mere recognition by parliament." As a matter of fact, he says, the less clearly this underlying principle is formulated the more likely it is to be accepted. Casual legislation on marginal matters often "surreptitiously introduces ideas which would not be accepted if brought before the attention of the nation" in a more explicit form.

Here is something like the beginning of a theory of how an accomplished fact finds support. Modern notions like "legitimation," "redirection of attention" and "the nature of an unstable equilibrium in a weak opinion structure" can easily be read into Dicey's discussion. But the most interesting fact from our point of view is that in none of the modern publications presenting data on this feed-back phenomenon has there been the slightest effort to explain it. Thus "Dicey revisited" shows a serious gap in our contemporary approach and gives the first hint on ways to fill it.

Empirical Verification of Classical Insights

Sensitized by one such episode, we can now again raise the question of where we can find further material to apply to the observations of classical authors. Obviously this material cannot come from one single public opinion poll, and the time periods covered by empirical research are usually too short to be of much help. But we are now beginning to collect *comparative* public opinion data, and these are likely to lead to broader generalizations. The impetus for this has come largely from other fields. The cross-cultural files gathered at Yale by anthropologists have yielded a number of interesting books comparing the social structure or the child rearing practices of a large number of primitive tribes. Industrial sociologists have compared the productivity of work teams under varying conditions of leadership and personal interaction among members. Political scientists have begun to use the forty-eight states as a kind of political laboratory. A very interesting example is a study which attempts to show that the weaker the two party system is in a state the more influential are the pressure groups.[12]

Slowly, attitude research is being included in this new movement. One of the ways in which Bryce compared England with America was in regard to political participation. He felt that in each country one could distinguish three strata: those who make political decisions; those who seriously discuss them and influence the decision makers through the press, books, meetings, and so on; and finally, the politically inert and uninterested masses. Bryce thought that the middle group was considerably larger in the United States than in Europe; but he had no evidence.[13] Today it might, however, be supplied by the "index of political activity" constructed by Julian Woodward and Elmo Roper.[14] They obtained information on their respondents' activities in parties and pressure groups, the extent to which they discussed politics with friends, their frequency of voting, etc. Finally, they divided the American population into four groups: Those who were very active (10 per cent), those who were active (17 per cent), those who were inactive (35 per cent), and those who were very inactive (38 per cent). Probably the real decision makers were not included in their sample, but reasonable reading of the questions asked by Woodward and Roper would make the active 27 per cent correspond to Bryce's second group and the inactive 73 per cent to his third. As usual, the division has to be somewhat arbitrary, but such an index, once constructed, would be suitable for making comparisons over time and space.

In the international field, our best example comes from an attitude survey which UNESCO carried out in nine countries during 1948.[15] We select one phase of this study because it relates attitudes to an economic index. The respondents in nine countries were asked which country in the world would give them the life they wanted to live. For each of the nine nations the proportion of respondents who named their own country was computed as an "index of satisfaction." This then was related to a set of statistics made available by another agency of the United Nations showing the "per capita calory supply." The measure of economic well-being had a correlation of .75 with the index of satisfaction. Even the deviations suggest interesting speculations. For instance, Mexico had the lowest food standard but was relatively high in the satisfaction of its citizens. Perhaps this may be explained by the high morale possibly engendered by the revolution and also by an improvement over past stand-

[12] "Report of the Committee on American Legislatures," Belle Zeller, editor, American Political Science Association. See also P. T. David, "Comparative State Politics and the Problem of Party Realignment" in Research Frontiers in Politics and Government, The Brookings Institution, 1955.
[13] American Commonwealth, Part IV, Ch. X.
[14] "Political Activity of American Citizens," American Political Science Review, Vol. XIV, December 1950, p. 872.
[15] Buchanan and Cantril, How Nations See Each Other. Urbana: Univ. of Ill. Press, 1953.

ards of living. The Netherlands, on the other hand, were low in satisfaction in spite of a relatively good food supply. This might be due to war devastation, the loss of Indonesia, or the high population density in Holland.

We now must return to one element in the picture which we by-passed before. The classical tradition is very much concerned with the problem of what the proper relation between public opinion and democratic government *should* be. Rogers' most valid objection against contemporary pollsters is exactly on this issue: they either do not think about it or they make naive statements to the effect that the government should actually do what the public opinion polls tell them the people want. This is a normative problem, and therefore it is important to know what the relation between the discussion of values and the factual findings of empirical research can be. The more we know about the probable consequences of various measures, the more certain can we be as to whether they will realize the values we strive for, and the more wisely can we choose among the conflicting values themselves.[16]

In the earlier writings on public opinion, value problems such as this one were discussed in a pseudo-factual language which made communication between generations especially difficult. Consider, for example, the first major American book on the topic: A. Lawrence Lowell, *Public Opinion and Popular Government*.[17] In the initial eighty pages or so of this book, Lowell proposes to find out what "true" opinion is. The first reaction of a modern reader is to think the question absurd (what is true electricity?), and to discard the book. This, however, would be a mistake. For, upon considerable effort, one learns that by "true" Lowell means the kind of public opinion which a democratic government should take into account.

Following this lead, one discovers that Lowell has three very different criteria of "true" public opinion. In modern terminology they are: (a) opinions should count only after proper general discussion, and only those people should be included who have given the matter considerable thought. Applied to current polling practices, this means that while thoughtful persons can readily be identified by good polls, the *timing* of polls, if they are to be used by government officials, raises quite a number of important problems. (b) Neither elections nor referenda really ascertain people's attitudes properly; the former fail because they are not centered around issues, and the latter because we do not know whether the

---

16 While there is agreement on the general logic of the problem, little work has been done to analyze in detail how arguments are actually supported by facts in the discussion of social affairs. Obviously this is not identical with the rule of formal logic. But we also do not mean the misuses of propaganda, which have been described by content analysts. What we have in mind is the systematic description of efforts to come to reasonable conclusions from necessarily insufficient data. The problem is similar to the question of how policy decisions are related to factual information in government and business. This has not been well investigated either.

17 (New York, 1913.)

"right" (informed) people participate. Clearly, Lowell would have welcomed polls if properly analyzed and interpreted. (c) Certain topics should never be the subject of legislation and, therefore, cannot be objects of "true" public opinion; religion is an example specifically mentioned by the American constitution. Here the intricate decision of excluding certain topics confronts us. Should "true" opinion in these areas be ascertained by a public opinion poll, historical analysis of the tradition of a country, or by general philosophical consideration? Lowell does not raise or answer these questions, but he suggests interesting problems about what people consider private and what they consider public issues under various circumstances.

Public Opinion and Government Policy

The relationship of opinion to government policy has been discussed in another type of literature, to which we could profitably pay more attention than we have previously. There are writers who try to approach normative questions by the careful analysis of historical events where the consequences of measures actually taken were first described and then judged. Before considering concrete examples, attention should be drawn to the historical aspect of the problem itself. Emden's history[18] reveals the big changes which came about in the British climate of opinion on such matters. A century-and-a-half ago, for instance, it was illegal to publish any reports on the debates of the British parliament. After a while summaries were permissible, but the votes of individual members could not be published. Only since 1845, and after serious debate, were official reports issued. Conversely, up to about 1880 it was considered inadmissible for politicians, including cabinet ministers, to address the population at large. They could appeal to their own constituencies, but otherwise only parliament itself was thought to be the proper place for debate.[19]

Three detailed monographic studies have analyzed the relation between governmental policy and contemporary expression of opinion in an especially interesting way. One was published in 1886 and is often quoted, but it is rarely read because of its inordinate length.[20] Its setting is the Russian-Turkish conflict in the late 1870's which led up to the Congress of

[18] See footnote 3. This book contains much interesting information, for instance, the history of petitions in the 19th century (pp. 74 ff.). Petitions fell out of usage because it was impossible to know which sector of the population the signers represented. A reading of the controversy, almost a hundred years old, shows that everyone was groping for something like representative sampling carried out by politically neutral agencies.

[19] Even today the English tradition is quite different from the American. If a law is under discussion in Congress radio and television overflow with panel debates and press interviews on the issue. The British Broadcasting Corporation does not permit a discussion of laws within a period of two weeks prior to a parliamentary debate to prevent the influence of the public voice on the deliberations of the legislature.

[20] Geo. C. Thompson, *Public Opinion and Lord Beaconsfield 1875-1880* (London: Macmillan Co., 1886).

Berlin. The issue between the two countries was the protection of the Christian population of the Balkans, then part of the Turkish Empire. According to the author, the British people were for the liberation of the Balkan provinces, a wish which corresponded to the demands of the Russian government. Disraeli (Lord Beaconsfield) feared an extension of Russian influence into Europe, and his policy was essentially to help the Turks. Thus a situation arose in which the British government acted avowedly against the advice of the majority of the British press and of most civic organizations concerned with foreign affairs. Thompson gives a vividly documented description of the dramatic interplay of the two partners to the conflict: how events sometimes strengthened the one and sometimes the other and how they reacted to each other's moves. The normative problem with which the author is concerned is whether even if a government has the majority support of its own party in parliament, it shall be required to resign when there are unmistakable signs that the population at large does not agree with its policy. In the 1880's this was not yet the British tradition; it probably would be today.

The data on which Thompson drew are speeches, resolutions, editorials, and similar documents. His contribution consists in the minute analysis of the different phases of the conflict. But he has to look at the matter, so to say, from the outside; he has no information on how the decisions were made in either the British cabinet or in the various groups which organized what he called the "agitations," the anti-Turkish movement.

A much more recent book by Lynn M. Case is outstanding because it has just this kind of information.[21] Under the Second Empire the French government had a detailed system for obtaining reports on public opinion from its administrative officials in all parts of the country. These were not the usual reports of the Secret Police, denouncing individuals, but rather were detached impressions of how various social groups responded to the policy of Napoleon III.[22] In times of crisis these reports came in as often as once a week. Case not only gives a very good picture of these interesting reports; he also tells of the effect they had on the foreign policy of the Second Empire, citing minutes of cabinet meetings during which these reports were discussed and used as arguments by the participants.

This book includes one dramatic episode in which the normative implication comes out with particular clarity. In 1866, Napoleon wanted to interfere in the Austro-Prussian War, in order to avoid a Prussian victory. Public opinion reports, however, indicated such a strong desire in the

---

[21] *French Opinion on War and Diplomacy During the Second Empire*, University of Pennsylvania Press, 1954.
[22] In the historical part of his book, Toennies has a section on France (pp. 375-401). He quotes there a letter by Mirabeau urging Louis XVI to set up just this kind of an organization. Whether the reporting system of Napoleon III goes back to these early stages cannot be seen from Case's book.

population for peace and so much danger of a revolution in case of war
that the group in the cabinet which was against intervention prevailed. As
a result, Prussia became so powerful that four years later it could provoke war with France which, in turn, led to the defeat of Napoleon III and
to the end of his regime. Case calls into doubt the wisdom of having a
foreign policy guided by public opinion.[23]

Finally, we have W. P. Davison's study of the Berlin Airlift. There he
reports actual polling data from Berlin cross-sections and interviews with
policy makers on various levels among Americans as well as Germans. He
shows how public reaction went from incredulity through hesitancy to a
decision to stick it out on the side of the Western powers. Davison stresses
a complex interplay: American determination was strengthened by favorable German attitudes; in turn, the Airlift increased the German expectation that the Allies would not desert them and that the Russians would
not be able to take over the city. This made many cautious souls willing to
take part openly in anti-communist activities. The main practical applications of this study turn on the relation of leadership and public opinion in
a crisis; because of the need for swift action, Davison feels that those in
command of the administrative machinery have to take chances and trust
that the people at large will support them eventually.[24]

Need for a Classical-Empirical Synthesis

In sum, valuable thinking on the relation between governmental decision
and public opinion is available. It falls short of an ideal type of research
only insofar as the information on public opinion itself is more or less in-
ferential. Undoubtedly, it will take a considerable length of time before we
have a joining of the two trends: a careful analysis in the classical tradition
supported by modern empirical data. Still, it does not seem unjustified to
conclude these remarks in a somewhat Utopian mood. During a debate on
the relation between history and public opinion, a historian remarked that
even in the future his colleagues will not need attitude studies; they will
know what actually has happened and from that they can infer what
"effective public opinion" was at the time. However, the French economic
historian Ferdinand Braudel provides us with the pertinent rejoinder:

> Victorious events come about as a result of many possibilities, often con-
> tradictory, among which life finally has made its choice. For one possi-
> bility which actually is realized innumerable others have drowned. These
> are the ones which have left little trace for the historians. And yet it is
> necessary to give them their place because the losing movements are
> forces which have at every moment affected the final outcome, sometimes

23 He takes a position quite similar to that of Almond and Speier in their writings on
the topic.
24 In its yet unpublished form the study is the first to combine poll data with traditional historical analysis. A preliminary summary of some of the findings is available
from a paper identified as P-851, The RAND Corporation, Santa Monica, California.

by retarding and sometimes by speeding up its development. The historian should also be concerned with the opposing elements, its incipient waves which at the time were not easily arrested. Ideas which couldn't be realized at one time still might have made the subsequent victory of another idea possible.[25]

In other words, if an event is the result of several potential trends, none of which have been fully realized, then it cannot be really understood unless the "tendencies" are known. It is illogical to reverse the analysis and to derive the potential from the actual, because various combinations of trends might have led to the same outcome. Only attitude data can provide the components which produced the final result.

Thus, from all sides the need for broad gauge opinion studies becomes increasingly obvious. But the complexity of this task also becomes more evident. While modern empiricists have reason to be pleased with their progress, there is no doubt that they can gain much from close contact with the classical tradition. We should not be deterred by the classicists' sometimes outmoded style of reasoning. The essence of progress, it has been said, consists in leaving the ashes and taking the flames from the altars of one's forebears.

[25] From a discussion remark on "historical economics" contributed to the French *Revue Economique*, 1952.

HISTORICAL DEVELOPMENT OF PUBLIC OPINION

By Hans Speier

I

PUBLIC OPINION is often regarded as opinion disclosed to others or at least noted by others, so that opinions which are hidden or concealed from other persons may be called either private or clandestine opinions. The criterion for distinguishing between private and public opinion thus appears to lie in the realm of communication. In expressions like "public good," "public ownership," "public law," however, our point of reference is not communication but rather a matter of general concern or, more precisely, *res publica*. This political meaning of the word is older than the meaning we customarily associate with the term "public opinion."

Thomas Hobbes, for example, distinguishing public worship from private worship, observed that public is the worship that a commonwealth performs "as one person." [1] According to this usage, the distinctive mark of private worship need not be secrecy; it might rather be heresy. Hobbes mentions indeed that private worship may be performed in "the sight of the multitude," which is an old-fashioned, if more concrete, way of saying "in public." Private worship performed in public he regarded as constrained either by the laws or by the "opinion of men." Correspondingly, in considering the nature of heresy, Hobbes remarked that it "signifies no more than private opinion." [2] If we follow the lead Hobbes gives us, we may arrive at an understanding of public opinion that makes political sense and is useful for the purposes of this historical review.

Let us understand by public opinion, for the purposes of this historical review, opinions on matters of concern to the nation freely and publicly expressed by men outside the government who claim a right that their opinions should influence or determine the actions, personnel, or structure of their government. In its most attenuated form this right asserts itself as the expectation that the government will publicly reveal and explain its de-

[1] *Leviathan*, II, 31.
[2] *Ibid.*, I, 11.

Reprinted from the *American Journal of Sociology*, Volume LV (January 1950) No. 4, by permission of the University of Chicago Press. Copyright 1950, the University of Chicago.

cisions in order to enable people outside the government to think and talk about these decisions or, to put it in terms of democratic amenities, in order to assure "the success" of the government's policy.

Public opinion, so understood, is primarily a communication from the citizens to their government and only secondarily a communication among the citizens. Further, if a government effectively denies the claim that the opinion of the citizens on public matters be relevant, in one form or another, for policy-making or if it prevents the free and public expression of such opinions, public opinion does not exist. There is no public opinion in autocratic regimes; there can only be suppressed, clandestine opinion, no matter how ingenious or careful the government may be in permitting an organized semblance of its true nature for the sake of democratic appearances.[3] Finally, for public opinion to function, there must be access to information on the issues with which public opinion is concerned. This means, above all, that the actions of the government must not be kept secret. Thus, Jeremy Bentham demanded full publicity for all official acts so that what he called "the tribunal of public opinion" could prevent misrule and suggest legislative reforms. Public communication of governmental acts (*Oeffentlichkeit*) was demanded by the political philosophers of enlightenment. The practice of submitting a budget to popular representatives, if not to the public at large, was established in England by the time of the revolution in 1688 and in France at the time of the French Revolution of 1789. The more democracy progresses and the more intensely public opinion is cherished as a safeguard of morality in politics, the louder become the demands for the abolition of secrecy in foreign policy as well. After the first World War such demands led to the so-called "new diplomacy." Under the system of the League international treaties had to be registered so as to prevent the inclusion of secret clauses.[4]

If public opinion be regarded primarily as a public communication from citizens *to* their government, it may be distinguished from policy counseling by policy advisers or governmental staff members, which is one of the processes of communication bearing on decision-making *within* the government (whether it is democratic or not). Public opinion is also distinguished from diplomacy, which may be regarded as communication *among* governments. Finally, one may speak of government information and propaganda activities as communications *from* a government to

[3] By way of illustration, no German public opinion existed in occupied Germany after the second World War under the rule of military governments, despite the speedy liberalization of press and radio, especially in the American Zone, and despite the expression of many opinions in public, because the Germans were neither free to act politically according to their own decision, having been deprived of sovereignty, nor were they free to criticize the actions of the American Military Government or of the Allied Control Council.

[4] For a discussion of secrecy in international negotiations versus secrecy of international agreements see Harold Nicolson, *Diplomacy* (London: T. Butterworth, 1939) and *Peacemaking 1919* (new ed.; New York, 1939), pp. 123 ff.

its own citizens, other government personnel, or foreign audiences in general.

Public opinion can of course also be studied with a view to what I have called its secondary communications process, i.e., with respect to the communications it involves *among* the citizens. In this context questions of the relations between opinion leaders and followers arise; so do problems of the size and anonymity of the public, the competence and representativeness of its organs, the direction and intensity of the interest taken in matters of public concern, the level and organization of public discussions, etc. On many of these aspects of public opinion our historical knowledge is limited. The absence of a history of public opinion, which combines descriptive detail with analytical clarity, makes it doubly necessary not to lose sight of the most conspicuous landmarks in this history, namely, the dates when governments ceased to censor the public expression of political dissent. In France free communication of thought and opinion was proclaimed as "one of the most valuable of the rights of men" during the Revolution of 1789. In England censorship in the form of licensing was abolished with less fanfare about a century earlier (1695).

II

Older discussions of our subject do not differ much from modern writings in estimating the influence popular opinions exert upon the actions of men; they differ in assessing the influence popular opinions have or should have upon the actions of statesmen and philosophers. It was common knowledge among older writers that opinions hold sway over the success, conduct, and morals of men. Shakespeare called opinion a mistress of success, and Pascal regarded it as the queen of the world. John Locke pointed out that men judge the rectitude of their actions according to three laws, namely, the divine law, the civil law, and the law of opinion or reputation, which he also called the law of passion or private censure. He attributed overwhelming power to the third law, the law of opinion, because man fears the inexorable operation of its sanctions. Dislike, "ill opinion," contempt, and disgrace, which violators of the law of censure must suffer, force men to conform. When Locke was attacked for his allegedly cynical view of morality, he defended himself by saying that he was not laying down any moral rules but was "enumerating the rules men make use of in moral relations, whether these rules are true or false." "I only report as a matter of fact what *others* call virtue and vice." [5]

Locke did not advance the view, however, that popular opinion should govern the actions of governments. Characteristically, he used the phrase "the law of *private* censure" as a synonym for "the law of opinion." Moreover, he described the law of opinion "to be nothing else but

[5] John Locke, "The Epistle to the Reader," in *An Essay concerning Human Understanding*, ed. A. C. Fraser (Oxford, 1894), I, 18 (The italics are Locke's.)

the consent of private men, *who have not authority enough to make a law*." [6]

Locke did not say that he shared popular opinions about morality. He knew that independent minds examine such opinions, although they cannot lightheartedly provoke the censure of others in whose company they live by showing disregard for what others consider to be right and wrong; the philosophers would otherwise "commit the fault of stubbornness," as Montaigne charmingly put it.[7]

Sir William Temple's essay *On the Original and Nature of Government*, written in 1672, has often been cited as an early discussion of public opinion. Temple observed that it cannot be that "when vast numbers of men submit their lives and fortunes absolutely to the will of one, it should be want of heart, but must be force of custom, or opinion, the true ground and foundation of all government, and that which subjects power to authority." "Authority rises from the opinion of wisdom, goodness, and valour in the persons who possess it." [8]

But Temple did not speak of public opinion. He spoke of opinion or "general opinion." As a matter of fact, he used the term "vulgar opinion" when he wished to designate opinions critical of authority. "Nothing is so easily cheated," he said in his essay *Of Popular Discontents*, "nor so commonly mistaken, as vulgar opinion." [9] Temple's concern was with the nature and stability of government. He opposed the contractual theories of government, no matter whether they advanced a sociable or bellicose view of man in the state of nature. If men were like sheep, he once wrote, he did not know why they needed any government; if they were like wolves, how they could suffer it. Contending that political authority developed out of habits and feelings formed in relation to the father of the family, he regarded opinion as a conserving force which helped the few to govern the many. The word "public," however, he reserved for the common good or the common interest of the nation: the "heats of humours of vulgar minds" would do little harm if governments observed the public good and if they avoided "all councils or designs of innovation." [10] It was precisely such innovation with which public opinion was concerned when it came to be called "public opinion" in the eighteenth century.

Even Rousseau, who put public opinion in its modern political place, demanding that law should spring from the general will, still spoke of opinions also in the traditional, predemocratic way. In his *Nouvelle Héloïse* he equated "public opinion" with vain prejudices and contrasted them with the eternal truths of morality; and in his *Considerations*

[6] *Ibid.*, Book II, chap. xxviii, sec. 12. (Our italics.)
[7] *Essays*, Book III, chap. 8.
[8] *The Works of Sir William Temple: A New Edition* (London, 1814), I, 6-7.
[9] *Ibid.*, III, 39.
[10] *Ibid.*, p. 44.

about the Government of Poland he said: "Whoever makes it his business to give laws to a people must know how to sway opinions and through them govern the passions of men." [10a]

The discussions of popular opinions up to the eve of the French Revolution lay much stress upon the power of opinions as means of restricting freedom, upon their prejudicial character, their changeability as to both time and place; they also indicate that men of judgment, whether philosophers or statesmen, deal prudently with popular opinion, and especially during the eighteenth century there are discussions to the effect that governments should take account of popular opinion instead of merely imposing their laws on the people. Finally, in the traditional discussions popular opinion was seen in close relation to imagination and passions rather than to intelligence and knowledge. Jacques Necker, who was the first writer to popularize the notion and the term "public opinion" throughout Europe at the eve of the French Revolution, still spoke of "imagination and hope" as "the precious precursors of the opinions of men." [11]

It did not occur to older writers that the "multitude" should know more about government than a good ruler, an experienced counselor, or a political philosopher. Only when economic and social inequalities were reduced and the rising elements in the population became unwilling to put up with political inequality could the claim be advanced that the government should make concessions to public opinion. Public opinion is a phenomenon of middle-class civilization. At the end of the *ancien régime* in France, Count Vergennes, one of M. Necker's colleagues, wrote in a confidential report to the king: "If M. Necker's public opinion were to gain ascendancy, Your Majesty would have to be prepared to see those command who otherwise obey and to see those obey who otherwise command." [12] With reference to Locke's remark about "the law of opinion" one might say that Count Vergennes warned the king of public opinion, because the people who formed it had gained enough authority to make a law.

[10a] Rousseau regarded public opinion as "the standard of free society," but as questionable from a "transpolitical point of view." Cf. Leo Strauss, "On the Intention of Rousseau," *Social Research*, XIV (December, 1947), 473.

[11] A *Treatise on the Administration of the Finances of France* (3d ed.; London, 1787), I, xvii. The two best expositions of the treatment of "opinion" and "public opinion" by political theorists are Paul A. Palmer, "The Concept of Public Opinion in Political Theory," in *Essays in History and Political Theory in Honor of Charles H. McIlwain* (Cambridge, Mass., 1936), and Hermann Oncken, "Politik, Geschichtsschreibung und öffentliche Meinung," in *Historischpolitische Aufsätze und Reden*, I (Berlin and Munich, 1914), 203-44.

[12] Cited from Soulavie's *Mémoires historique* in F. Tönnies, *Kritik der öffentlichen Meinung* (Berlin, 1922), p. 385.

III

In his fierce criticism of Edmund Burke's ideas on the French Revolution, Thomas Paine remarked that "the mind of the nation had changed beforehand, and the new order of things has naturally followed the new order of thoughts." [13] The observation that the habits of Frenchmen had become republican while their institutions were still monarchical is well sustained by modern research, although it should be borne in mind that it was a numerically small class which had slowly changed its habits.

Lord Acton attributed the growing influence of public opinion in eighteenth-century France to the rise of national debts and the increasing importance of the public creditor.[14] It is curious that this important insight into the origin of public opinion has not led to more detailed research by the historians of public opinion. The history of public opinion has been written primarily with reference to channels of communication, e.g., the market place in ancient Greece; the theater in Imperial Rome; the sermons, letters, ballads, and travels in the Middle Ages; pamphlets, newspapers, books and lectures, telegraph, radio, and film in modern times. We know more about the history of literacy, the press, the law of sedition, and censorship than about the relationship between the struggle for budget control and the history of public opinion or about the emergence of social institutions other than the press which were instrumental in the political rise of public opinion.

In some older sources the close interconnection between public finance and public opinion is fully recognized. In the French *ancien régime* publicists and financiers no less than the middle classes at large condemned public loans. Bankruptcy was demanded by courts of justice and by political philosophers like Montesquieu. "It was a reaction against these proposals of bankruptcy that the French constitutions at the end of the eighteenth century proclaimed that the public debt was sacred." [15]

Jacques Necker had occasion to observe as minister of finance that his contemporaries were much concerned with his fiscal policies. He, in turn, regarded it as the "dear object" of his ambition to acquire the good opinion of the public. He contrasted the "extensive horizon" of the public with the court at Versailles, the place of ambition and intrigue, and made the interesting observation that the minister of finance could not consider the court as a "suitable theatre" for himself; Versailles, he said, was a place appropriate perhaps for ministers of war, the navy, and for-

[13] *Rights of Man* ("Modern Library" ed.), p. 141.
[14] "The Background of the French Revolution," reprinted in *Essays on Freedom and Power*, ed. Gertrude Himmelfarb (Boston, 1948), p. 267.
[15] Gaston Jeze, "Public Debt," in *Encyclopaedia of the Social Sciences*, XII, 602. Cf. also Thomas Paine's remark: "The French nation, in effect, endeavored to render the late government insolvent for the purpose of taking government into its own hands: and it reserved its means for the support of the new government" (*op. cit.*, p. 175).

eign affairs, "because all the ideas of military and political glory are more connected with the pageantry of magnificence and power." [16] By contrast, the minister of finance "stands most in need of the good opinion of the people." Necker recommended that fiscal policies should be pursued in "frankness and publicity" and that the finance minister "associate the nation—as it were, in his plans, in his operations, and even in the obstacles that he must surmount." [17] Necker's great contribution to the history of public opinion was not so much what he wrote about its power but rather his important innovation of publishing fiscal statements (*compte rendu*) so that the merits and faults of government policy in this field could be appraised in public. He did so "to calm the public which began to distrust the administration of finances and feared that the income of the treasury would not offer any security to the capital and interests of its creditors." [18] Mme. de Staël, Necker's daughter, regarded this innovation as an important means for pacifying public opinion. The government, she observed, was forced by its need for public credit not to neglect public opinion; but Necker did not yet hold the view that the general will of the public should take the place of the government. He represents a transitional phase between the predemocratic and the revolutionary-democratic views of public opinion.

The institutional changes which preceded the restriction of absolutist rule and contributed to the rise of public opinion can be stated in this historical sketch only in bare outline. Gains in economic power of the middle class and the gradual spread of literacy are merely two aspects of this process.

The first impetus toward increasing literacy was given by the Reformation, which created a broad reading public seeking edification without the mediation of priests in religious literature written in the vernacular.[19] During the eighteenth century popular religious literature was gradually replaced by secular reading materials. Content and style of fiction changed in the process. The novel of manners and the epistolary novel, both primarily addressed to women, made their appearance, and the moral concern of the readers was shared by their authors. It became possible for them to earn a livelihood by writing. The professionalization of writing was furthered by the breakdown of the patronage system and its replacement by the collective patronage of the anonymous public.[20]

Parallel with the formation of a broader literary public, the middle classes transformed musical life. Public concerts to which an anonymous

16 *Op. cit.*, p. liv.
17 *Ibid.*, p. lxxiii.
18 August Wilhelm Rehberg, *Über die Staatsverwaltung deutscher Länder* (Hanover, 1809), p. 58.
19 Herbert Schöffler, *Protestantismus und Literatur* (Leipzig, 1922).
20 See Charlotte E. Morgan, *The Rise of the English Novel of Manners* (New York, 1911).

audience paid admission fees took the place of concerts given by the personal orchestras at the courts of European rulers and in the luxurious resi-
dences of distinguished aristocrats.

The expansion of the reading public was accompanied by the development of related social institutions such as reading societies, reading clubs,
circulating libraries, and secondhand book stores. The establishment of
the first circulating library in London coincided with the publication of
Richardson's *Pamela*. Secondhand book stores appeared in London during
the last third of the eighteenth century. European reading societies were
influenced by the model of the American subscription libraries, the
earliest of which was founded by Franklin in Philadelphia in 1732. Thirty
years later there were several *cabinets de lecture* in France, and the first
German reading circle seems to have been established in 1772.[21] In addition
to fiction—the favorite literature of the ladies—books on history, belles-
lettres, natural history (i.e., science), and statistics were read in these circles. But the favorite reading matter was political journals and scholarly
magazines. In fact, the reading societies of the eighteenth century must
be considered as the collective patrons of the moral weeklies which contributed so much to the articulation of middle-class opinion on matters of
moral concern.

In German social history one looks in vain for the social institutions
which in England and France contributed powerfully to the formation of
public opinion, the coffee-house and the salon, respectively. Germany's
middle classes lacked the commercial strength that made the coffee-house
so important in England. In Europe, coffee-houses date back to the middle of the seventeenth century; they became popular as centers of news-
gathering and news dissemination, political debate, and literary criticism.
In the early part of the eighteenth century, London is said to have had no
fewer than two thousand coffee-houses. Addison wanted to have it said
of him that he had brought philosophy out of closets and libraries "to
dwell in clubs and assemblies, at tea tables and in coffee houses." [22] The
English middle classes began to accomplish their own education in
the coffee-houses.

Like the history of the coffee-house in England, that of the French
salon goes back to the seventeenth century and even farther to the Italian
courts of the Renaissance. In the history of public opinion the French
eighteenth-century salons were important because they were the gathering
places of intellectually distinguished men and women who cherished con-

[21] Walter Götze, *Die Begründung der Volksbildung in der Aufklärungsbewegung* (Ber-
lin-Leipzig, 1932), p. 64.
[22] On the history of coffee-houses in England see E. F. Robinson, *The Early History of
Coffee Houses in England* (London, 1893); Ralph Nevill, *London Clubs: Their History
and Treasures* (London: Chatto & Windus, 1911); Hermann Westerfrölke, *Englische
Kaffeehäuser als Sammelpunkte der literarischen Welt im Zeitalter von Dryden und
Addison* (Jena, 1924).

versation, applauded critical sense, and did not regard free thought or irreverent ideas as shocking unless they were advanced pedantically. During the second half of the eighteenth century the salons governed opinion in Paris more effectively than the court. Men of letters were received regardless of their social origin and met on terms of equality with the most enlightened members of society. The salon, a place where talent could expect to outshine ancient titles, was an experiment in equality that assumed paradigmatic importance within a hierarchically organized society.[23] As D'Alembert said in his *Essay upon the Alliance betwixt Learned Men and the Great,* "the man of quality, whose ancestors are his only merit, is of no more consequence in the eye of reason, than an old man returned to infancy, who once performed great things." [24]

In Germany the salon never exercised the influence on the dignity and the literary style of authors or on the manners and opinions of their public which it did in France. Germany was a poor, divided, and in part overmilitarized country; it had neither a Versailles nor a Paris. The social institutions which helped to pave the way toward the social recognition of the ideas of enlightenment in Germany were the predominantly aristocratic language orders of the seventeenth century and the stolid moral and patriotic societies of the eighteenth century in which civil servants played an important role. Both of them may be regarded as forerunners of the Masonic lodges in Germany. They practiced egalitarian rituals, opposed the conventional customs of the courtier, extolled merit and virtue as the new principles of prestige, read and discussed John Locke, and cultivated mutual confidence as a bulwark against the dangerous intrigues in politics.

These institutional changes in European society which led to the emergence of public opinion as a prominent factor in politics may be summed up without regard to national differences as follows. A closed and restricted public gradually developed into an open one, enlarging both its size and its social scope as illiteracy receded. This movement ran its full course only during the nineteenth century. It extended to the lower classes much later than the late eighteenth-century attempts to parade the Third Estate as the nation would make us believe. From the end of the eighteenth century we have glowing accounts of the widespread eagerness of people to read and to learn, but illiteracy was still widespread. It has been estimated that about 57 per cent of the men and 27 per cent of the women could read and write in France at the time.[25]

[23] Cf. Helen Clergue, *The Salon: A Story of French Society and Personalities in the Eighteenth Century* (New York and London, 1907); Erich Auerbach, *Das französische Publikum des XVII. Jahrhunderts* (Munich, 1933); Chauncey B. Tinker, *The Salon and English Letters* (New York, 1915); Conférences du Musée Carnavalet, *Les grands salons littéraires* (Paris, 1928).

[24] Jean d'Alembert, *Miscellaneous Pieces in Literature, History and Philosophy* (London, 1764), p. 149.

[25] As Aulard has pointed out, "it was by the political song, sung in the theatre, in the cafes and in the street, that the Royalists and Republicans succeeded, principally at

Geographically, the process of diffusion spread out from urban centers, with the United States, England, and Germany taking the lead over France, where printing presses as well as the socially influential circles were concentrated in Paris.

The economic and technical landmarks of this process of diffusion are reflected in the cost of mass communication to the poorer classes of society. Here again progress was made more rapidly during the nineteenth century than the eighteenth century. Taxes on newspapers and advertisements were fairly high until 1836 and partly until 1845; the poor could not afford to buy them. Even postal service was not readily available to them until 1839, when penny postage was introduced. Harriet Martineau said at the time that the poor now can "at last write to one another as if they were all M.P.'s." [26]

As regards the men of letters and the publicists, the prerequisite of their wider influence was the recognition of merit as a criterion of social status, so that authors could climb the social ladder regardless of origin merely on the strength of performance. It might be added that the rise of public opinion presupposed a redefinition of scholarship and a program of its missionary diffusion to laymen, a process in which "the world" took the place of "the school" and education became a technique for the establishment of a classless society.

One of the earliest and most radical instances illustrating this missionary zeal can be found in Christian Thomasius' *Einleitung zur Vernunftlehre*, published in 1691. Thomasius' believed that it was only due to differences in social status that not everybody arrived at wisdom; science ought to be the common property of all mankind. Everybody was capable of becoming learned, and the scholar should disseminate rather than attain knowledge.[27]

Thomasius' notion of scholarship is close to Condorcet's doctrine of education or Sieyès views of public opinion. Condorcet's aim was to

---

Paris, in influencing the people," during the French Revolution (quoted by Cornwall B. Rogers, *The Spirit of Revolution in 1789* [Princeton, N. J.: Princeton University Press, 1949], p. 26). Cornwall's book is a monographic study of the propagandistic importance of oral communication, especially lyrics, during the French Revolution.
[26] Quoted by Howard Robinson, *The British Post Office* (Princeton, 1948), p. 302.
[27] In chap. xiii Thomasius discussed the origin of error, distinguishing between the "prejudice of human authority" and "the prejudice of precipitation." (Cf. the reprint of this chapter as well as of the equally relevant chap. i of Thomasius' *Ausübung der Sittenlehre* [1696] in F. Brüggemann [ed.], *Aus der Frühzeit der deutschen Aufklärung* ["Deutsche Literatur, Sammlung literarischer Kunst und Kulturdenkmäler, Reihe Aufklärung," Vol. I (Berlin and Leipzig, 1928)]). It has been said that Thomasius repeated "the Lutheran teaching of general priesthood in the secularized form of general scholarship" (Götze, *op. cit.*, p. 20). For the relation between prejudice and the demand for enlightening education, cf. also especially Thomas Hobbes, *Elements of Law*, ed. Ferdinand Tönnies (London, 1889): "The immediate cause . . . of indocibility is prejudice; and of prejudice, false opinion of our own knowledge" (I, 10, §8); and *Leviathan*, chaps. xiii and xv.

render it impossible through education to use the masses as "docile instruments in adroit hands" and to enable them to avoid the "philosophic errors" on which he believed "all errors in government and in society are based." [28] And Sieyès wrote: "Reason does not like secrets; it is effective only through expansion. Only if it hits everywhere, does it hit right, because only then will be formed that power of public opinion, to which one may perhaps ascribe most of the changes which are truly advantageous to mankind." [29]

IV

The elimination of prejudice, ignorance, and arbitrary government which the advocates of enlightenment wrote upon their banner in order to base the commonwealth upon reason and civic virtue is frequently regarded as a rationalistic program in which no cognizance was taken of the so-called "irrational" factors of human nature. For this reason, propaganda has often been presented as the counterpart to the process of public opinion. It is erroneous, however, to believe that the advocates of enlightenment neglected or overlooked the emotional facets of life.

The advocates of enlightenment themselves proposed the equation of government with adult education. They proposed, for example, that the government should engage orators for political instruction as it paid priests for religious service (Weckherlin); that attendance of courses on the nature of society should be made obligatory for the acquisition of citizenship (Mercier de la Rivière); that the government should control and publish newspapers to increase loyalty to the sovereign (Quesnay); and that historical works should be written to increase patriotism and national pride (Voss).

Perhaps even more important than these suggestions of political indoctrination were the proposals for the organization of public spectacles and celebrations in order to evoke enthusiasm for common causes and enlist the sentiments of those who did not think. Dupont de Nemours in *Des Spectacles nationaux* developed a theory of national celebrations based on the idea that the desire for pleasure is the driving force of mankind. The people should be brought to develop their patriotic virtues by way of exaltation over public celebrations in which they were to participate—an idea, one might say, which was realized in both the institutionalized public celebrations of the French Revolution and in the Nuremberg festivals of the Nazis or in May Day celebrations. Other writers who pointed to the educational function of national festivals and public plays were Dide-

---

[28] For a convenient summary of Condorcet's views on education, contained in his "Report on Education," presented to the Legislative Assembly on April 20-21, 1792, see Salwyn Schapiro, *Condorcet* (New York, 1934), chap. xi, pp. 196-214. On the educational views of leading writers in the eighteenth century see F. de la Fontainerie (ed.), *French Liberalism and Education in the Eighteenth Century* (New York, 1932).
[29] *The Third Estate*, chap. vi.

rot, Condorcet, and Rousseau, and, in Germany, among others, Stephani, Voss, and Zachariä.[30]

In view of these facts it cannot be maintained without qualification that the modern advocates and practitioners of totalitarian government propaganda have superseded the theory and practices of the reformers who helped public opinion on its way to political prominence. It would be more correct to say that the participation of large masses of the population in public affairs, characteristic of both government by public opinion and modern tyranny, is spurious in character under totalitarian regimes in that it is demonstrative rather than determinative of government action. It may also be said that in totalitarian regimes mass participation in politics is regarded by the intellectuals as a design to conceal the truth about power processes, whereas in the eighteenth century such participation was considered as a measure toward the ultimate elimination of the irksomeness of power, if not of power itself.

It was believed that man guided by reason and inspired by rectitude would reduce politics to a calculation in happiness and do away with war. Nevertheless, the French Revolution gave rise to war and to war propaganda. It created what William Pitt called "armed opinions" and Jomini "wars of opinion." Liberty, equality, and fraternity were not the aims of Frenchmen; they were held to be rights of man regardless of political and national affiliation. The French revolutionary armies did not wage war against other countries but for the liberation of man from old, oppressive governments.[31] Foreign exiles in sympathy with the new regime were admitted to the French clubs, the National Guard, and the public departments. They could even be found in the Ministry for Foreign Affairs.[32] They were organized in foreign legions fighting the battle for France. The Girondists imagined that foreign nations in their desire to be delivered from the tyranny of their rulers and priests would rally in support of the revolutionary principles. Robespierre's program of April 24, 1793, envisaged a universal republic in which all citizens in all countries unite against the aristocrats and the tyrants.[33] As Burke pointed out, before the time of the French Revolution there had been no instance "of this spirit of general political factions, separated from religion, pervading several countries, and forming a principle of union between the partisans in each." [34]

---

[30] Götze, *op. cit.*, pp. 97 ff.
[31] According to Alexis de Tocqueville, the Revolution "a considéré le citoyen d'une façon abstraite, en dehors de toutes les sociétés particulières, de même que les religions considèrent l'homme en général indépendamment du pays et du temps" (*L'Ancien régime et la Révolution* [8th ed.; Paris, 1877], p. 18).
[32] Albert Mathiez, *The French Revolution* (New York, 1928), p. 217.
[33] Corneliu S. Blaga, *L'Évolution de la technique diplomatique au dix-huitième siècle* (Paris, 1937), p. 421.
[34] Edmund Burke, "Thoughts on French Affairs," in *Reflections on the French Revolution and Other Essays* ("Everyman's Library" ed.), p. 289.

Nor were the enemies of France capable of restricting the war to its former, military dimensions. They responded to the ideological challenge. In October, 1793, His Majesty's Government sent a declaration to the commanders of the British forces in which France was accused of attacks on "the fundamental principles by which mankind is united in the bond of civil society." [35] And William Pitt found the most eloquent expression for the ideological issue raised by the French Revolution. On June 7, 1799, he spoke in the House of Commons, moving that the sum of £825,000 be granted to His Majesty to enable him to fulfil his engagements with Russia. Pitt pointed out that this subsidy would be used for the deliverance of Europe. In reply Mr. Tierney contended that the funds were to be used against the power of France "not merely to repel her within her ancient limits, but to drive her back from her present to her ancient opinion." Mr. Pitt rose once more and said, among other things:

> It is not so. We are not in arms against the opinions of the closet, nor the speculations of the school. We are at war with armed opinion; we are at war with those opinions which the thought of audacious, unprincipled and impious innovations seeks to propagate amidst the ruins of empires, the demolition of the altars of all religion, the destruction of every venerable, and good, and liberal institution, under whatever forms of policy they have been raised; and this, in spite of the dissenting reason of men, in contempt of that lawful authority which, in the settled order, superior talent and superior virtue attain, crying out to them not to enter on holy ground nor to pollute the stream of eternal justice;—admonishing them of their danger, whilst, like the genius of evil, they mimic their voice, and, having succeeded in drawing upon them the ridicule of the vulgar, close their day of wickedness and savage triumph with the massacre and waste of whatever is amiable, learned, and pious, in the districts they have overrun.[36]

V

After the Congress of Vienna the utilization of public opinion in international affairs became, as it were, respectable also among statesmen who did not pursue any revolutionary cause. Once the importance of public opinion was discovered as a new factor in international relations, it became tempting on moral as well as on expediential grounds to utilize it. Neither Canning, who believed that public opinion should be invoked in the pursuit of British foreign policy, nor Palmerston, who held that public opinion founded on truth and justice would prevail against the force of armies, realized that they were continuing to revolutionize European diplomacy

[35] Quoted in W. Allison Hillet and Arthur H. Reede, *Neutrality*, Vol. II: *The Napoleonic Period* (New York, 1936), p. 8.
[36] *British Historical and Political Orations from the 12th to the 20th Century* ("Everyman's Library" ed.), pp. 146-48.

by their actions. A diplomat of the old school like Metternich was appalled by Canning's enthusiasm and could see only preposterous folly in the Englishman's notion of public opinion as "a power more tremendous than was perhaps ever yet brought into action in the history of mankind." [37]

The art of arousing public opinion became nevertheless a valued skill during the nineteenth century even of statesmen like Bismarck, who failed to respect public opinion, remained indifferent to its moral claims, and made no attempt to raise its level of competence. Bismarck condemned policies inspired by sentiments or moods. He regarded public opinion as dependent, to a large extent, on mood and sentiment, incapable of the calm calculations that had to precede political decisions. Nor did he believe in the political insight of public opinion. "As a rule," he said, "public opinion realizes the mistakes that have been committed in foreign policy only when it is able to review in retrospect the history of a generation." [38] Given the political constitution of Prussia and the Reich, Bismarck could afford to make foreign policy against public opinion, if he regarded it as necessary and if he had the confidence of his monarch. Thus, in 1866 he waged war against the will of almost all Prussians, but he also refused to risk war against Russia by interfering in Bulgaria, a course rashly sponsored by the liberal press. Similarly, in the Boer War, Chancellor von Bülow disregarded German public opinion, which strongly favored interference, in the well-considered interest of the country.

The scope of governmental influence upon public opinion was limited throughout the nineteenth century and, if compared with recent activities in this regard, had an almost patrimonial character. In nineteenth-century Europe public opinion was a synonym of opinions expressed by the political representatives of the electorate, by newspapers and by prominent members or organizations of the middle class. In England their faith in the beneficial effects of discussion and the persuasiveness of liberal opinion upon the conduct of domestic affairs grew particularly under the influence of Bentham and his followers.[39] Toward the end of the nineteenth century Lord Bryce pointed out that in England the landowners and "the higher walks of commerce" not only form the class which furnish the majority of members of both houses but also express what is called public opinion. He held that in Germany, Italy, and France as well public opinion was "substantially the opinion of the class which wears black coats and lives in good houses." [40] He contrasted these conditions with those prevailing in the United States, where he believed government by pub-

---

[37] Nicolson, *Diplomacy*, p. 73.

[38] *Memoirs*, III, 157.

[39] The Benthamites did not share the belief in natural rights. Bentham had deplored the Declaration of Rights in France because he regarded them as metaphysical and did not believe that political science was far enough advanced for such declarations (cf. A. V. Dicey, *Law and Opinion in England* [New York, 1930], p. 145, n. 1).

[40] Lord Bryce, *The American Commonwealth*, II, 260.

lic opinion to exist, because "the wishes and views of the people prevail even before they have been conveyed through the regular law-appointed organs." [41]

Like De Tocqueville and other nineteenth-century writers,[42] Lord Bryce recognized the decisive importance of class distinctions in limiting participation in public opinion, although he failed to appreciate the limiting influence upon public opinion exercised by pressure groups in the United States. He also lacked the perspicacity of De Tocqueville, who detected the threats to freedom of thought which public opinion in conditions of social equality presents. Reactionaries, romantics, and Marxists attacked liberal convictions and threw doubt upon the morality, disinterestedness, and representativeness of middle-class opinions in the nineteenth century. They were not concerned, however, with freedom of thought; they contributed, in fact, to its modern decline. De Tocqueville, however, clearly saw that in "ages of equality" the liberation of the people from ignorance and prejudice by enlightenment may be purchased at the price of equalizing thought.

> There is, and I cannot repeat it too often, there is here matter for profound reflection to those who look upon freedom of thought as a holy thing and who hate not only the despot, but despotism. For myself, when I feel the hand of power lie heavy on my brow, I care but little to know who oppresses me; and I am not the more disposed to pass beneath the yoke because it is held out to me by the arms of millions of men.[43]

VI

In its early phase public opinion showed a marked preoccupation with domestic affairs, i.e., with issues of immediate concern to the life of the citizens. Foreign policy issues appeared less relevant, but they were expected to be ultimately relegated from the realm of power to that of discussion and agreement, as governments would become more enlightened. Power politics and professional diplomacy became designations of various evils, and war was expected to vanish, since only power-hungry governments uncontrolled by public opinion would embark upon them. If wars did occur, governments by public opinion would enter them in the conviction that the national interests they defended were the interests of enlightened mankind. While this picture is simplified, it remains basically true that, according to the theory of public opinion, it is the function of

---

[41] *Ibid.*, p. 257.

[42] Thus Bluntschli in the *Staatswörterbuch* (1862) said of public opinion that "it is predominantly the opinion of the large middle class." This notion was predicated upon the conviction that public opinion was a matter of free judgment. "Without training of the reasoning power and the capacity to judge there is, therefore, no public opinion." For the same reason, Bluntschli observed that public opinion is possible in political matters but alien to religious piety (*Ergriffenheit*). Cf. Oncken, *op. cit.*, pp. 229 ff.

[43] Alexis de Tocqueville, *Democracy in America* (New York, 1948), II, 11-12.

government in foreign affairs to make the world safe for the rule of public opinion.

The expectation that public opinion safeguards morality and promotes reasonableness in foreign affairs was nowhere entertained with greater optimism than in the United States. In 1909 President Taft said about the compulsory arbitration of international disputes: "After we have gotten the cases into court and decided, and the judgments embodied in a solid declaration of a court thus established, few nations will care to face the condemnation of international public opinion and disobey the judgment." [44] Above all, Woodrow Wilson stated the gospel of public opinion as a purifying force in world politics. Said he about the first World War:

> National purposes have fallen more and more into the background; and the common purpose of enlightened mankind has taken their place. The councils of plain men have become on all hands more simple and straightforward, and more unified than the councils of the more sophisticated men of affairs, who still retain the impression that they are playing a game of power and are playing for high stakes. That is why I have said that this is a people's war, not a statesman's. Statesmen must follow the clarified common thought or be broken.[45]

Since the end of the first World War, however, the faith in the power of public opinion to render world politics reasonable has been shaken. There are many events which contributed to this demoralization: the failure of the League of Nations; disillusionment concerning the lofty war aims of the Allies and the general distrust of propaganda which spread between the two world wars; the rise of fascism and national socialism in countries of old civilization and with no lack of liberal traditions; the absence of inspiring peace aims during the second World War; the sterility of the resistance movements in the realm of political ideas; the use of weapons of mass destruction in the attainment of victory; and the quick transformation of the wartime coalition into intense hostility between its main partners even before peace was formally established. Despite war crimes trials, attempts to re-educate the conquered peoples and the insistence on world-wide freedom of information, the moral energy of the liberal faith in the moralization of foreign as well as domestic affairs by means of enlightenment appears to have been spent. The hope that public opinion will be able to solve the problems of international policy has waned. Do we still maintain the belief in the perfectibility of man, faced, as we are, with the overwhelming experiences of the twentieth century, in

---

[44] Quoted from W. H. Taft's *The United States and Peace* in C. H. Carr, *The Twenty Years' Crisis, 1919-39* (New York, 1942), p. 32.
[45] Quoted from *Intimate Papers of Colonel House*, ed. C. Seymour, IV, 291, in Carr. *op. cit.*, p. 44.

man's manageability, and with the advances in both the technology of destruction and moral apathy?

In democratic countries, foreign policy-makers continue to address public opinion in order to obtain ultimate approval of their actions and, on a deeper level, absolution from the qualms and moral uncertainty which public opinion demands of them until they do so. Public opinion does not permit the enjoyment of power, because it suspects that its enjoyment indicates its abuse. Public opinion, which appropriated to itself the moral standards to be applied to power, wants power to be a burden which it alone can lighten; but the complex structure of world politics in which the individual citizen finds himself involved, often beyond his understanding, does not permit an easy transfer of moral rules from the domain of his private concern to actions of larger consequence. Moreover, the reduction in moral energy which I have mentioned further emaciates the effective functioning of public opinion in foreign policy.

When governments attempt to unburden themselves on foreign policy matters to the people and its representatives, they find it trying and difficult to foster the formation of a responsible public opinion on issues demanding action or on actions that have been taken. There is first the need for secrecy which is felt to be a prerequisite of national security. I do not wish to question the urgency of this need, but, when information vital for intelligent and critical judgment on policy matters is kept from the public, it is not possible to have government by public opinion. Recently, Senator Brian MacMahon pointed out that informed policy decisions affecting our defense budget depend on information concerning our atomic stockpile, which is withheld from both Congress and the American people. He said, "When we debate the necessity of a 65,000 ton aircraft carrier or a 70 group air force or universal military training, I fear that we quite literally do not know what we are talking about." [46]

Less far-reaching in consequence than the safeguarding of vital secrets, but no less in conflict with the prerequisites of an intelligent public opinion, is the manner in which measures requiring sacrifices on the part of the people are presented and justified. It is easy and rewarding to engage public opinion in consideration of ultimal success or gains or of progress. It is difficult to have the public face the dangers to cherished forms of life in true perspective. It is even more difficult to present such dangers when they are not temporary but require continuous alertness because they are a permanent price to be paid for active participation in world politics. During war, patriotism and national self-interest can be more readily counted upon to support policies involving sacrifice. In times of peace, however, privations imposed by the government are easily unpopular or believed to be so. It is, therefore, tempting to policy-makers to justify minor sacrifices,

[46] *Bulletin of Atomic Scientists*, Vol. V, No. 3 (March, 1949).

which they deem necessary, in terms of major risks to national safety, in order to arouse and gain the support of public opinion.[47]

By the same token policy-makers are likely to present their actions in the field of foreign affairs to public opinion in short-range perspective, because the public responds to immediate issues most readily. Thus, the true time range of political action may be lost sight of by the public if not by policy-makers as well. The point in time to which the planning of foreign policy must extend differs, of course, from issue to issue. But it does not seem paradoxical to say that it lies characteristically between the two extremes with which public opinion seems most preoccupied, namely, the immediate and the remote. If it is true that moral apathy, secrecy, preoccupation with safety, and lack of an appropriate time perspective interfere with effective government by public opinion in the field of foreign affairs, public opinion cannot perform the function which its eighteenth-century advocates envisaged; but this situation should not be viewed as a verdict but as a challenge to seek and attain improvement as far as it can be attained.

[47] When Secretary of State Dean Acheson appeared before the Senate Foreign Relations and Armed Services committees to discuss the program of foreign military aid on August 8, 1949, the following discussion took place:

Senator H. Alexander Smith said that the administration's handling of the program had led "many people to think that there must be some crisis imminent that we don't know about."

"The state of the world," Mr. Acheson responded, "is not one to allow anyone to relax. There has never been a more hazardous world in peacetime."

"But you want no war scare?" asked Senator Smith.

"Nobody," replied the Secretary, "is attempting to give anybody a war scare. I repeat that the situation in the world is hazardous and unstable" (*New York Times,* August 9, 1949).

STEREOTYPES

By Walter Lippmann

1

EACH OF US lives and works on a small part of the earth's surface, moves in a small circle, and of these acquaintances knows only a few intimately. Of any public event that has wide effects we see at best only a phase and an aspect. This is as true of the eminent insiders who draft treaties, make laws, and issue orders, as it is of those who have treaties framed for them, laws promulgated to them, orders given at them. Inevitably our opinions cover a bigger space, a longer reach of time, a greater number of things, than we can directly observe. They have, therefore, to be pieced together out of what others have reported and what we can imagine.

Yet even the eyewitness does not bring back a naïve picture of the scene.[1] For experience seems to show that he himself brings something to the scene which later he takes away from it, that oftener than not what he imagines to be the account of an event is really a transfiguration of it. Few facts in consciousness seem to be merely given. Most facts in consciousness seem to be partly made. A report is the joint product of the knower and known, in which the rôle of the observer is always selective and usually creative. The facts we see depend on where we are placed, and the habits of our eyes.

---

[1] E. g. cf. Edmond Locard, *L'Enquête Criminelle et les Méthodes Scientifiques*. A great deal of interesting material has been gathered in late years on the credibility of the witness, which shows, as an able reviewer of Dr. Locard's book says in *The Times* (London) Literary Supplement (August 18, 1921), that credibility varies as to classes of witnesses and classes of events, and also as to type of perception. Thus, perceptions of touch, odor, and taste have low evidential value. Our hearing is defective and arbitrary when it judges the source and direction of sound, and in listening to the talk of other people "words which are not heard will be supplied by the witness in all good faith. He will have a theory of the purport of the conversation, and will arrange the sounds he heard to fit it." Even visual perceptions are liable to great error, as in identification, recognition, judgment of distance, estimates of numbers, for example, the size of a crowd. In the untrained observer, the sense of time is highly variable. All these original weaknesses are complicated by tricks of memory, and the incessant creative quality of the imagination. *Cf.* also Sherrington, *The Integrative Action of the Nervous System*, pp. 318-327.

The late Professor Hugo Münsterberg wrote a popular book on this subject called *On the Witness Stand*.

An unfamiliar scene is like the baby's world, "one great, blooming, buzzing confusion." [2] This is the way, says Mr. John Dewey,[3] that any new thing strikes an adult, so far as the thing is really new and strange. "Foreign languages that we do not understand always seem jibberings, babblings, in which it is impossible to fix a definite, clear-cut, individualized group of sounds. The countryman in the crowded street, the landlubber at sea, the ignoramus in sport at a contest between experts in a complicated game, are further instances. Put an inexperienced man in a factory, and at first the work seems to him a meaningless medley. All strangers of another race proverbially look alike to the visiting stranger. Only gross differences of size or color are perceived by an outsider in a flock of sheep, each of which is perfectly individualized to the shepherd. A diffusive blur and an indiscriminately shifting suction characterize what we do not understand. The problem of the acquisition of meaning by things, or (stated in another way) of forming habits of simple apprehension, is thus the problem of introducing (1) *definiteness* and *distinction* and (2) *consistency* or *stability* of meaning into what is otherwise vague and wavering."

But the kind of definiteness and consistency introduced depends upon who introduces them. In a later passage[4] Dewey gives an example of how differently an experienced layman and a chemist might define the word metal. "Smoothness, hardness, glossiness, and brilliancy, heavy weight for its size . . . the serviceable properties of capacity for being hammered and pulled without breaking, of being softened by heat and hardened by cold, of retaining the shape and form given, of resistance to pressure and decay, would probably be included" in the layman's definition. But the chemist would likely as not ignore these esthetic and utilitarian qualities, and define a metal as "any chemical element that enters into combination with oxygen so as to form a base."

For the most part we do not first see, and then define, we define first and then see. In the great blooming, buzzing confusion of the outer world we pick out what our culture has already defined for us, and we tend to perceive that which we have picked out in the form stereotyped for us by our culture. Of the great men who assembled at Paris to settle the affairs of mankind, how many were there who were able to see much of the Europe about them, rather than their commitments about Europe? Could anyone have penetrated the mind of M. Clemenceau, would he have found there images of the Europe of 1919, or a great sediment of stereotyped ideas accumulated and hardened in a long and pugnacious existence? Did he see the Germans of 1919, or the German type as he had learned to see it since 1871? He saw the type, and among the reports that came to him from Germany, he took to heart those reports, and, it seems, those only, which fitted the type that was in his mind. If a junker blustered, that

---

[2] Wm. James, *Principles of Psychology*, Vol. 1, p. 488.
[3] John Dewey, *How We Think*, p. 121.
[4] *Op. cit.*, p. 133.

was an authentic German; if a labor leader confessed the guilt of the empire, he was not an authentic German.

At a Congress of Psychology in Göttingen an interesting experiment was made with a crowd of presumably trained observers.[5]

> "Not far from the hall in which the Congress was sitting there was a public fête with a masked ball. Suddenly the door of the hall was thrown open and a clown rushed in madly pursued by a negro, revolver in hand. They stopped in the middle of the room fighting; the clown fell, the negro leapt upon him, fired, and then both rushed out of the hall. The whole incident hardly lasted twenty seconds.

> "The President asked those present to write immediately a report since there was sure to be a judicial inquiry. Forty reports were sent in. Only one had less than 20% of mistakes in regard to the principal facts; fourteen had 20% to 40% of mistakes; twelve from 40% to 50%; thirteen more than 50%. Moreover in twenty-four accounts 10% of the details were pure inventions and this proportion was exceeded in ten accounts and diminished in six. Briefly a quarter of the accounts were false.

> "It goes without saying that the whole scene had been arranged and even photographed in advance. The ten false reports may then be relegated to the category of tales and legends; twenty-four accounts are half legendary, and six have a value approximating to exact evidence."

Thus out of forty trained observers writing a responsible account of a scene that had just happened before their eyes, more than a majority saw a scene that had not taken place. What then did they see? One would suppose it was easier to tell what had occurred, than to invent something which had not occurred. They saw their stereotype of such a brawl. All of them had in the course of their lives acquired a series of images of brawls, and these images flickered before their eyes. In one man these images displaced less than 20% of the actual scene, in thirteen men more than half. In thirty-four out of the forty observers the stereotypes preempted at least one-tenth of the scene.

A distinguished art critic has said [6] that "what with the almost numberless shapes assumed by an object. . . . What with our insensitiveness and inattention, things scarcely would have for us features and outlines so determined and clear that we could recall them at will, but for the stereotyped shapes art has lent them." The truth is even broader than that, for the stereotyped shapes lent to the world come not merely from art, in the sense of painting and sculpture and literature, but from our moral codes and our social philosophies and our political agitations as well. Substitute in the following passage of Mr. Berenson's the words 'politics,' 'business,' and 'society,' for the word 'art' and the sentences will be no less true:

[5] A. von Gennep, *La formation des légendes*, pp. 158-159. Cited F. van Langenhove, *The Growth of a Legend*, pp. 120-122.
[6] Bernard Berenson, *The Central Italian Painters of the Renaissance*, pp. 60, et seq.

". . . unless years devoted to the study of all schools of art have taught us also to see with our own eyes, we soon fall into the habit of moulding whatever we look at into the forms borrowed from the one art with which we are acquainted. There is our standard of artistic reality. Let anyone give us shapes and colors which we cannot instantly match in our paltry stock of hackneyed forms and tints, and we shake our heads at his failure to reproduce things as we know they certainly are, or we accuse him of insincerity."

Mr. Berenson speaks of our displeasure when a painter "does not visualize objects exactly as we do," and of the difficulty of appreciating the art of the Middle Ages because since then "our manner of visualizing forms has changed in a thousand ways." [7] He goes on to show how in regard to the human figure we have been taught to see what we do see. "Created by Donatello and Masaccio, and sanctioned by the Humanists, the new canon of the human figure, the new cast of features . . . presented to the ruling classes of that time the type of human being most likely to win the day in the combat of human forces. . . . Who had the power to break through this new standard of vision and, out of the chaos of things, to select shapes more definitely expressive of reality than those fixed by men of genius? No one had such power. People had perforce to see things in that way and in no other, and to see only the shapes depicted, to love only the ideals presented. . . ." [8]

2

If we cannot fully understand the acts of other people, until we know what they think they know, then in order to do justice we have to appraise not only the information which has been at their disposal, but the minds through which they have filtered it. For the accepted types, the current patterns, the standard versions, intercept information on its way to consciousness. Americanization, for example, is superficially at least the substitution of American for European stereotypes. Thus the peasant who might see his landlord as if he were the lord of the manor, his employer as he saw the local magnate, is taught by Americanization to see the landlord and employer according to American standards. This constitutes a change of mind, which is, in effect, when the inoculation succeeds, a change of vision. His eye sees differently. One kindly gentlewoman has confessed that the stereotypes are of such overweening importance, that when hers are not indulged, she

---

[7] *Cf.* also his comment on *Dante's Visual Images, and his Early Illustrators* in *The Study and Criticism of Italian Art* (First Series), p. 13. "We cannot help dressing Virgil as a Roman, and giving him a 'classical profile' and 'statuesque carriage,' but Dante's visual image of Virgil was probably no less mediaeval, no more based on a critical reconstruction of antiquity, than his entire conception of the Roman poet. Fourteenth Century illustrators make Virgil look like a mediaeval scholar, dressed in cap and gown, and there is no reason why Dante's visual image of him should have been other than this."
[8] *The Central Italian Painters*, pp. 66-67.

at least is unable to accept the brotherhood of man and the fatherhood of God: "we are strangely affected by the clothes we wear. Garments create a mental and social atmosphere. What can be hoped for the Americanism of a man who insists on employing a London tailor? One's very food affects his Americanism. What kind of American consciousness can grow in the atmosphere of sauerkraut and Limburger cheese? Or what can you expect of the Americanism of the man whose breath always reeks of garlic?" [9]

This lady might well have been the patron of a pageant which a friend of mine once attended. It was called the Melting Pot, and it was given on the Fourth of July in an automobile town where many foreign-born workers are employed. In the center of the baseball park at second base stood a huge wooden and canvas pot. There were flights of steps up to the rim on two sides. After the audience had settled itself, and the band had played, a procession came through an opening at one side of the field. It was made up of men of all the foreign nationalities employed in the factories. They wore their native costumes, they were singing their national songs; they danced their folk dances, and carried the banners of all Europe. The master of ceremonies was the principal of the grade school dressed as Uncle Sam. He led them to the pot. He directed them up the steps to the rim, and inside. He called them out again on the other side. They came, dressed in derby hats, coats, pants, vest, stiff collar and polka-dot tie, undoubtedly, said my friend, each with an Eversharp pencil in his pocket, and all singing the Star-Spangled Banner.

To the promoters of this pageant, and probably to most of the actors, it seemed as if they had managed to express the most intimate difficulty to friendly association between the older peoples of America and the newer. The contradiction of their stereotypes interfered with the full recognition of their common humanity. The people who change their names know this. They mean to change themselves, and the attitude of strangers toward them.

There is, of course, some connection between the scene outside and the mind through which we watch it, just as there are some long-haired men and short-haired women in radical gatherings. But to the hurried observer a slight connection is enough. If there are two bobbed heads and four beards in the audience, it will be a bobbed and bearded audience to the reporter who knows beforehand that such gatherings are composed of people with these tastes in the management of their hair. There is a connection between our vision and the facts, but it is often a strange connection. A man has rarely looked at a landscape, let us say, except to examine its possibilities for division into building lots, but he has seen a number of landscapes hanging in the parlor. And from them he has learned to think of a landscape as a rosy sunset, or as a country road with a church steeple and a silver moon. One day he goes to the country, and for hours he does not see

[9] Cited by Mr. Edward Hale Bierstadt, *New Republic*, June 1, 1921, p. 21.

a single landscape. Then the sun goes down looking rosy. At once he recognizes a landscape and exclaims that it is beautiful. But two days later, when he tries to recall what he saw, the odds are that he will remember chiefly some landscape in a parlor.

Unless he has been drunk or dreaming or insane he did see a sunset, but he saw in it, and above all remembers from it, more of what the oil painting taught him to observe, than what an impressionist painter, for example, or a cultivated Japanese would have seen and taken away with him. And the Japanese and the painter in turn will have seen and remembered more of the form they had learned, unless they happen to be the very rare people who find fresh sight for mankind. In untrained observation we pick recognizable signs out of the environment. The signs stand for ideas, and these ideas we fill out with our stock of images. We do not so much see this man and that sunset; rather we notice that the thing is man or sunset, and then see chiefly what our mind is already full of on those subjects.

3

There is economy in this. For the attempt to see all things freshly and in detail, rather than as types and generalities, is exhausting, and among busy affairs practically out of the question. In a circle of friends, and in relation to close associates or competitors, there is no shortcut through, and no substitute for, an individualized understanding. Those whom we love and admire most are the men and women whose consciousness is peopled thickly with persons rather than with types, who know us rather than the classification into which we might fit. For even without phrasing it to ourselves, we feel intuitively that all classification is in relation to some purpose not necessarily our own; that between two human beings no association has final dignity in which each does not take the other as an end in himself. There is a taint on any contact between two people which does not affirm as an axiom the personal inviolability of both.

But modern life is hurried and multifarious, above all physical distance separates men who are often in vital contact with each other, such as employer and employee, official and voter. There is neither time nor opportunity for intimate acquaintance. Instead we notice a trait which marks a well known type, and fill in the rest of the picture by means of the stereotypes we carry about in our heads. He is an agitator. That much we notice, or are told. Well, an agitator is this sort of person, and *so he* is this sort of person. He is an intellectual. He is a plutocrat. He is a foreigner. He is a "South European." He is from Back Bay. He is a Harvard Man. How different from the statement: he is a Yale Man. He is a regular fellow. He is a West Pointer. He is an old army sergeant. He is a Greenwich Villager: what don't we know about him then, and about her? He is an international banker. He is from Main Street.

The subtlest and most pervasive of all influences are those which create and maintain the repertory of stereotypes. We are told about the world before we see it. We imagine most things before we experience them. And those preconceptions, unless education has made us acutely aware, govern deeply the whole process of perception. They mark out certain objects as familiar or strange, emphasizing the difference, so that the slightly familiar is seen as very familiar, and the somewhat strange as sharply alien. They are aroused by small signs, which may vary from a true index to a vague analogy. Aroused, they flood fresh vision with older images, and project into the world what has been resurrected in memory. Were there no practical uniformities in the environment, there would be no economy and only error in the human habit of accepting foresight for sight. But there are uniformities sufficiently accurate, and the need of economizing attention is so inevitable, that the abandonment of all stereotypes for a wholly innocent approach to experience would impoverish human life.

What matters is the character of the stereotypes, and the gullibility with which we employ them. And these in the end depend upon those inclusive patterns which constitute our philosophy of life. If in that philosophy we assume that the world is codified according to a code which we possess, we are likely to make our reports of what is going on describe a world run by our code. But if our philosophy tells us that each man is only a small part of the world, that his intelligence catches at best only phases and aspects in a coarse net of ideas, then, when we use our stereotypes, we tend to know that they are only stereotypes, to hold them lightly, to modify them gladly. We tend, also, to realize more and more clearly when our ideas started, where they started, how they came to us, why we accepted them. All useful history is antiseptic in this fashion. It enables us to know what fairy tale, what school book, what tradition, what novel, play, picture, phrase, planted one preconception in this mind, another in that mind.

4

Those who wish to censor art do not at least underestimate this influence. They generally misunderstand it, and almost always they are absurdly bent on preventing other people from discovering anything not sanctioned by them. But at any rate, like Plato in his argument about the poets, they feel vaguely that the types acquired through fiction tend to be imposed on reality. Thus there can be little doubt that the moving picture is steadily building up imagery which is then evoked by the words people read in their newspapers. In the whole experience of the race there has been no aid to visualization comparable to the cinema. If a Florentine wished to visualize the saints, he could go to the frescoes in his church, where he might see a vision of saints standardized for his time by Giotto. If an

Athenian wished to visualize the gods he went to the temples. But the number of objects which were pictured was not great. And in the East, where the spirit of the second commandment was widely accepted, the portraiture of concrete things was even more meager, and for that reason perhaps the faculty of practical decision was by so much reduced. In the western world, however, during the last few centuries there has been an enormous increase in the volume and scope of secular description, the word picture, the narrative, the illustrated narrative, and finally the moving picture and, perhaps, the talking picture.

Photographs have the kind of authority over imagination to-day, which the printed word had yesterday, and the spoken word before that. They seem utterly real. They come, we imagine, directly to us without human meddling, and they are the most effortless food for the mind conceivable. Any description in words, or even any inert picture, requires an effort of memory before a picture exists in the mind. But on the screen the whole process of observing, describing, reporting, and then imagining, has been accomplished for you. Without more trouble than is needed to stay awake the result which your imagination is always aiming at is reeled off on the screen. The shadowy idea becomes vivid; your hazy notion, let us say, of the Ku Klux Klan, thanks to Mr. Griffith, take vivid shape when you see the Birth of a Nation. Historically it may be the wrong shape, morally it may be a pernicious shape, but it is a shape, and I doubt whether anyone who has seen the film and does not know more about the Ku Klux Klan than Mr. Griffith, will ever hear the name again without seeing those white horsemen.

5

And so when we speak of the mind of a group of people, of the French mind, the militarist mind, the bolshevik mind, we are liable to serious confusion unless we agree to separate the instinctive equipment from the stereotypes, the patterns, and the formulae which play so decisive a part in building up the mental world to which the native character is adapted and responds. Failure to make this distinction accounts for oceans of loose talk about collective minds, national souls, and race psychology. To be sure a stereotype may be so consistently and authoritatively transmitted in each generation from parent to child that it seems almost like a biological fact. In some respects, we may indeed have become, as Mr. Wallas says,[10] biologically parasitic upon our social heritage. But certainly there is not the least scientific evidence which would enable anyone to argue that men are born with the political habits of the country in which they are born. In so far as political habits are alike in a nation, the first places to look for an explanation are the nursery, the school, the church, not in that limbo inhabited by Group Minds and National Souls. Until you have thoroughly

[10] Graham Wallas, *Our Social Heritage*, p. 17.

failed to see tradition being handed on from parents, teachers, priests, and uncles, it is a solecism of the worst order to ascribe political differences to the germ plasm.

It is possible to generalize tentatively and with a decent humility about comparative differences within the same category of education and experience. Yet even this is a tricky enterprise. For almost no two experiences are exactly alike, not even of two children in the same household. The older son never does have the experience of being the younger. And therefore, until we are able to discount the difference in nurture, we must withhold judgment about differences of nature. As well judge the productivity of two soils by comparing their yield before you know which is in Labrador and which in Iowa, whether they have been cultivated and enriched, exhausted, or allowed to run wild.

3

THE NEWSPAPER

Robert E. Park
NEWS AS A FORM OF KNOWLEDGE

Walter Lippmann
THE NATURE OF NEWS

Summary of Principle:
A STATEMENT BY THE COMMISSION ON FREEDOM
  OF THE PRESS

3

THE NEWSPAPER

THE newspaper is the oldest medium of mass communication, except for the book. In the contemporary world of mass communication, it is probably more accurate to use the term "newspaper," rather than the term "press." "Press" has been given wider latitude to embrace newspapers, electronic journalism and national magazines. The term "newspaper" distinguishes this particular medium from other mass media.

It was not until the latter part of the eighteenth century that the newspaper became a medium of information, opinion and advertising. Printed journalism in the form of newsletters, however, circulated in England in the seventeenth century. Mass circulation, on a limited basis, began in the nineteenth century and laid the basis for contemporary American journalism.

Three analyses of newspaper journalism are included in this volume. Walter Lippmann explores the nature of news and relates it to the public relations function. Robert E. Park explores news as a form of knowledge—its function being "to orient man and society in an actual world." Concluding is the statement of the Commission on Freedom of the Press which emphasizes the principle of freedom of the press as "close to the central meaning of all liberty."

Mr. Lippmann's concern is with the essence or nature of news. Beyond the pragmatic aspect of the news—the evanescent copy that appears in the daily newspaper—what makes news? Before a series of events become newsworthy, they usually make themselves noticeable by means of a more or less overt act. This act is what distinguishes news from opinion, the assumption of form or shape by means of a tangible event. Otherwise, one is dealing not with fact but simply with "possible" truth. Experienced journalists know where the news lies. They know where to find it and, frequently, when to generate it.

Does the news reflect social conditions? Not if it is viewed as an "aspect" of those conditions which, in the course of human events, become overt and obtrusive. In this sense, news bear a similarity to public opinion,

which does not become meaningful until it centers about an area of implicit controversy. News does not become news until an "issue" of some
kind is joined. An opinion becomes news when that issue becomes overt
through a public statement, a startling fact, an accusation or an interchange
of contested points of view.

Here, Mr. Lippmann, unlike many students of this area, recognizes the
existence and the contribution of what he terms the "press agent," now
known more deferentially as the public relations man. Lippmann was
perhaps the first to recognize and to point out the validity of publicity as a
catalyst between mass media and the public. When this catalyst is well
trained in the ethos of journalism, he serves as a valuable adjunct to the
news-gathering process. It is precisely because reporting is not simple separation of fact from opinion that the public relations function has become
increasingly important.

More often than not, the very nature of news makes "at the source"
reporting all but impossible. For example, the fact that a large number of
buildings in a given city may be fire hazards becomes news primarily through
an "exposé." Or, it may become explicit news through the exciting cause of
a fire, a flagrant violation or through the opinion-generating stimulation
of public relations. The use of an automated shuttle train in New York
City is not news beyond the initial announcement until the engineers'
union threatens to strike. An overt event, articulated by a statement or a
press release, generates the news.

What restricts most newspapers in covering the news? The answer,
broadly, is human interest—the second half, or audience part, of the inevitable interaction between the organism (the newspaper) and its environment (the reader). Like other media, the newspaper gives its reader partly
what the reader wants, partly what the editors believe he ought to have.
The nature of news, unfortunately, is made interesting for the reader because of—and in spite of—the fact that it must rely to a great extent on
stereotyping and standardization.

Dr. Park, in his discussion of "news as a form of knowledge," predi-
cates his discussion of the news as reported in the daily newspaper on
psychologist William James' distinction between "acquaintance with" and
"knowledge about." The former is intuitive, informal knowledge. The latter is empirical, scientific and documented. The former, too, is pragmatic,
yet unsystematic. There is an immediate response to communication, and
it is personalized. But, according to Park, this informal knowledge is
neither articulate—nor is it communication.

James' "knowledge about" is formal and systematic. It is, therefore,
scientific, because it is based on observation which has been checked and
rechecked, and it is communicable and articulate. Because it uses symbols
(words to represent things) it is communication. It makes possible not
merely the ability to communicate in the present, but also to predict the

future on the basis of its findings. Its validity is tested, not merely by formal logic but by "practical" identification with tangible objects in the world of things or reality. This quality makes it communicable knowledge. Although there is a distinction between formal and informal knowledge, as James noted, there is also a continuum or relationship. News, in the form of data communicated by an organ such as the press, is part of this continuum. What makes news is its interest for people, for without human identification it is not news, but inert data. News as knowledge reaches the reader as communication, rather than as perception, and this distinction underscores the difference between informal knowledge and formal knowledge—knowledge of and knowledge about. Nor is it individualized. News as a form of knowledge reaches the group or public and, as a result of discussion, public opinion occurs. If news does not always result in action, it results in discussion from which opinions emerge.

Finally, for news to be news it must be published. It must appear in print. And news serves as literature, as folklore and as history because it is a way of preserving the "permanence of society in a volatile world." News today is characterized particularly by its speed, a result of highly perfected means of communication such as television's reporting of events, not after the fact, but as they occur.

The Statement of Principle of the Commission on Freedom of the Press applies not only to the newspaper, but to all of the mass media. Freedom of expression, freedom to communicate, is shown to be inextricably connected to all liberty. Conversely, the thwarting of free discussion is implicit in the growth of authoritarianism. As the media of communication grow, the meaning and significance of free speech and of a free and responsible press emerge more strongly as fundamental to a democratic society.

The Commission statement is particularly significant in that it attaches to "freedom" a negative as well as a positive meaning. In other words, the meaning of freedom includes the right not to participate, not to read, not to listen—and, if one chooses to become a participant, the right not to accept uncritically what one reads, sees and hears. The audience may, in a free society, reject as well as accept communication content. It can be active as well as passive. Freedom recognizes a healthy interaction between the communicator and the audience. In this context, the Commission statement is one of the first documents which goes beyond the historical acceptance of the issuer as the one to be protected to the receiver as one whose freedom is equally in need of protection.

As the Commission points out, "freedom is destined not to repress social conflict but to liberate it . . . from the plane of discussion." Furthermore, freedom to communicate in any medium requires courage on the part of the issuer and the receiver. Basic to the protection of freedom is a responsible government, for the pressure against free expression is frequently oppressive. The Commission statement indicates that the government must protect and, in order to liberate expression, must set limits on its own capacity to regulate. For self-limitation by government is coherent with public interest. It is also the responsibility of editors to respond to what the public believes should get a hearing, not to any particular bias of their own.

And, finally, the most significant point is made that, where issuers of communication ignore their moral obligations, then moral rights to freedom no longer inhere. The venal voice, therefore, has no right to freedom of expression for it does not adhere to the moral standards of freedom of expression in a free society. But, even here, paradoxically, "the abuse of a right does not ipso facto forfeit the protection of the legal right," although there are limits to the protection or the tolerance of such abuses of freedom of expression.

*   *   *   *

RELATED READING

Larson, Otto N. and Hill, Richard J. "Mass Media and Interpersonal Communication in the Diffusion of a News Event," *American Sociological Review*, XIX (1954), 426-33.

Lee, Alfred McClung. *The Daily Newspaper in America: The Evolution of Social Instrument*. New York: Macmillan, 1937.

Lundberg, George A. "The Newspaper and Public Opinion," *Social Forces*, IV (1926), 709-15.

Mott, Frank Luther. "Newspapers in Presidential Campaigns," *Public Opinion Quarterly*, VIII (1944), 348-67.

Mott, Frank Luther. *American Journalism: A History of Newspapers*. New York: Macmillan, 1941.

Park, Robert E. "The Natural History of the Newspaper," *American Journal of Sociology*, 22, Nov. 1923, pp. 273-89.

NEWS AS A FORM OF KNOWLEDGE:

A Chapter in the Sociology of Knowledge

By Robert E. Park

I

THERE ARE, as William James and certain others have observed, two fundamental types of knowledge, namely, (1) "acquaintance with" and (2)
"knowledge about." The distinction suggested seems fairly obvious.
Nevertheless, in seeking to make it a little more explicit, I am doubtless doing injustice to the sense of the original. In that case, in interpreting the
distinction, I am merely making it my own. James's statement is, in part, as
follows:

> There are two kinds of knowledge broadly and practically distin-
> guishable: we may call them respectively knowledge of acquaintance and
> knowledge-about. . . . In minds able to speak at all there is, it is true,
> some knowledge about everything. Things can at least be classed, and the
> times of their appearance told. But in general, the less we analyze a
> thing, and the fewer of its relations we perceive, the less we know about it
> and the more our familiarity with it is of the acquaintance-type. The two
> kinds of knowledge are, therefore, as the human mind practically exerts
> them, relative terms. That is, the same thought of a thing may be called
> knowledge-about it in comparison with a simpler thought, or acquaint-
> ance with it in comparison with a thought of it that is more articulate
> and explicit still.[1]

At any rate, "acquaintance with," as I should like to use the expression,
is the sort of knowledge one inevitably acquires in the course of one's personal and firsthand encounters with the world about him. It is the knowledge which comes with use and wont rather than through any sort of
formal or systematic investigation. Under such circumstances we come
finally to know things not merely through the medium of our special
senses but through the responses of our whole organism. We know them in
the latter case as we know things to which we are accustomed, in a world to

[1] William James, The Principles of Psychology (New York: Henry Holt & Co., 1896),
I, 221-22.

which we are adjusted. Such knowledge may, in fact, be conceived as a form of organic adjustment or adaptation, representing an accumulation and, so to speak, a funding of a long series of experiences. It is this sort of personal and individual knowledge which makes each of us at home in the world in which he elects or is condemned to live.

It is notorious that human beings, who are otherwise the most mobile of living creatures, tend nevertheless to become rooted, like plants, in the places and in the associations to which they are accustomed. If this accommodation of the individual to his habitat is to be regarded as knowledge at all, it is probably included in what we call tact or common sense. These are characters which individuals acquire in informal and unconscious ways; but, once acquired, they tend to become private and personal possessions. One might go so far as to describe them as personality traits—something, at any rate, which cannot well be formulated or communicated from one individual to another by formal statements.

Other forms of "acquaintance with" are: (1) clinical knowledge, in so far at least as it is the product of personal experience; (2) skills and technical knowledge; and (3) anything that is learned by the undirected and unconscious experimentation such as the contact with, and handling of, objects involves.

Our knowledge of other persons and of human nature in general seems to be of this sort. We know other minds in much the same way that we know our own, that is, intuitively. Often we know other minds better than we do our own. For the mind is not the mere stream of consciousness into which each of us looks when, introspectively, he turns his attention to the movements of his own thoughts. Mind is rather the divergent tendencies to act of which each of us is more or less completely unconscious, including the ability to control and direct those tendencies in accordance with some more or less conscious goal. Human beings have an extraordinary ability, by whatever mechanism it operates, to sense these tendencies in others as in themselves. It takes a long time, however, to become thoroughly acquainted with any human being, including ourselves, and the kind of knowledge of which this acquaintance consists is obviously not the sort of knowledge we get of human behavior by experiments in a psychological laboratory. It is rather more like the knowledge that a salesman has of his customers, a politician of his clients, or the knowledge which a psychiatrist gains of his patients in his efforts to understand and cure them. It is even more the sort of knowledge which gets embodied in habit, in custom, and, eventually—by some process of natural selection that we do not fully understand—in instinct; a kind of racial memory or habit. Knowledge of this sort, if one may call it knowledge, becomes, finally, a personal secret of the individual man or the special endowment of the race or stock that possesses it.[2]

[2] "The biologist ordinarily thinks of development as something very different from such

One may, perhaps, venture this statement since the type of intuitive or instinctive knowledge here described seems to arise out of processes substantially like the accommodations and adaptations which, by some kind of natural selection, have produced the different racial varieties of mankind as well as the plant and animal species. One may object that what one means by knowledge is just what is not inherited and not heritable. On the other hand, it is certain that some things are learned much more easily than others. What one inherits therefore is, perhaps, not anything that could properly be called knowledge. It is rather the inherited ability to acquire those specific forms of knowledge we call habits. There seems to be a very great difference in individuals, families, and genetic groups as to their ability to learn specific things. Native intelligence is probably not the standardized thing that the intelligence tests might lead one to believe. In so far as this is true studies of intelligence in the future are, I suspect, more likely to be concerned with the idiosyncrasies of intelligence and the curious individual ways in which individual minds achieve essentially the same results than in measuring and standardizing these achievements.

It is obvious that this "synthetic" (i.e., the knowledge that gets itself embodied in habit and custom, as opposed to analytic and formal knowledge) is not likely to be articulate and communicable. If it gets itself communicated at all, it will be in the form of practical maxims and wise saws rather than in the form of scientific hypotheses. Nevertheless, a wide and intimate acquaintance with men and things is likely to be the bulwark of most sound judgment in practical matters as well as the source of those hunches upon which experts depend in perplexing situations and of those sudden insights which, in the evolution of science, are so frequently the prelude to important discoveries.

In contrast with this is the kind of knowledge that James describes as "knowledge about." Such knowledge is formal, rational, and systematic. It is based on observation and fact but on fact that has been checked, tagged, regimented, and finally ranged in this and that perspective, according to the purpose and point of view of the investigator.

"Knowledge about" is formal knowledge; that is to say, knowledge which has achieved some degree of exactness and precision by the substitution of ideas for concrete reality and of words for things. Not only do ideas constitute the logical framework of all systematic knowledge but they enter into the very nature of the things themselves with which science—

---

modification of behavior by experience, but from time to time the idea that the basis of heredity and development is fundamentally similar to memory has been advanced. . . . Viewed in this way the whole course of development is a process of physiological learning, beginning with the simple experience of differential exposure to an external factor, and undergoing one modification after another, as new experiences in the life of the organism or of its parts in relation to each other occur" (C. M. Child, *Physiological Foundations of Behavior*, pp. 248-49; quoted by W. I. Thomas in *Primitive Behavior* [New York: McGraw-Hill Book Co., 1937], p. 25).

natural as distinguished from the historical science—is concerned. As a matter of fact, there seem to be three fundamental types of scientific knowledge: (1) philosophy and logic, which are concerned primarily with ideas; (2) history, which is concerned primarily with events; and (3) the natural or classifying sciences, which are concerned primarily with things.

Concepts and logical artifacts, like the number system, are not involved in the general flux of events and things. For precisely that reason they serve admirably the purpose of tags and counters with which to identify, to describe, and, eventually, to measure things. The ultimate purpose of natural science seems to be to substitute for the flux of events and the changing character of things a logical formula in which the general character of things and the direction of change may be described with logical and mathematical precision.

The advantage of substituting words, concepts, and a logical order for the actual course of events is that the conceptual order makes the actual order intelligible, and, so far as the hypothetic formulations we call laws conform to the actual course of events, it becomes possible to predict from a present a future condition of things. It permits us to speculate with some assurance how, and to what extent, any specific intervention or interference in a present situation may determine the situation that is predestined to succeed it.

On the other hand, there is always a temptation to make a complete divorce between the logical and verbal description of an object or a situation and the empirical reality to which it refers. This seems to have been the cardinal mistake of scholasticism. Scholasticism has invariably tended to substitute logical consistency, which is a relation between ideas, for the relation of cause and effect, which is a relation between things.

An empirical and experimental science avoids a purely logical solution of its problems by checking up its calculation at some point with the actual world. A purely intellectual science is always in danger of becoming so completely out of touch with things that the symbols with which it operates cease to be anything more than mental toys. In that case science becomes a kind of dialectical game. This is a peril which the social sciences, to the extent that they have been disposed to formulate and investigate social problems in the forms in which they have been conventionally defined by some administrative agencies or governmental institution, have not always escaped. Thus investigation has invariably tended to take the form of fact-finding rather than of research. Having found the facts, the agencies were able to supply the interpretations; but they were usually interpretations which were implicit in the policies to which the agencies or institutions were already committed.

These are some of the general characteristics of systematic and scientific knowledge, "knowledge about," as contrasted with the concrete knowledge, common sense and "acquaintance with." What is, however, the unique character of scientific knowledge, as contrasted with other forms of knowledge, is that it is communicable to the extent that common sense or knowledge based on practical and clinical experience is not. It is communicable because its problems and its solutions are stated not merely in logical and in intelligible terms but in such forms that they can be checked by experiment or by reference to the empirical reality to which these terms refer.

In order to make this possible, it is necessary to describe in detail and in every instance the source and manner in which facts and findings were originally obtained. Knowledge about, so far at least as it is scientific, becomes in this way a part of the social heritage, a body of tested and accredited fact and theory in which new increments, added to the original fund, tend to check up, affirm, or qualify, first of all, in each special science and, finally, in all the related sciences, all that has been contributed by earlier investigators.

On the other hand, acquaintance with, as I have sought to characterize it, so far as it is based on the slow accumulation of experience and the gradual accommodation of the individual to his individual and personal world, becomes, as I have said, more and more completely identical with instinct and intuition.

Knowledge about is not merely accumulated experience but the result of systematic investigation of nature. It is based on the answers given to the definite questions which we address to the world about us. It is knowledge pursued methodically with all the formal and logical apparatus which scientific research has created. I might add, parenthetically, that there is, generally speaking, no scientific method which is wholly independent of the intuition and insight which acquaintance with things and events gives us. Rather is it true that, under ordinary circumstances, the most that formal methods can do for research is to assist the investigator in obtaining facts which will make it possible to check up such insights and hunches as the investigator already had at the outset or has gained later in the course of his researches.

One of the functions of this methodical procedure is to protect the investigator from the perils of an interpretation to which a too ardent pursuit of knowledge is likely to lead him. There is, on the other hand, no methodical procedure that is a substitute for insight.

II

What is here described as "acquaintance with" and "knowledge about" are assumed to be distinct forms of knowledge—forms having different functions in the lives of individuals and of society—rather than knowledge of the same kind but of different degrees of accuracy and validity. They are, nevertheless, not so different in character or function—since they are, after all, relative terms—that they may not be conceived as constituting together a continuum—a continuum within which all kinds and sorts of knowledge find a place. In such a continuum news has a location of its own. It is obvious that news is not systematic knowledge like that of the physical sciences. It is rather, in so far as it is concerned with events, like history. Events, because they are invariably fixed in time and located in space, are unique and cannot, therefore, be classified as is the case with things. Not only do things move about in space and change with time but, in respect to their internal organization, they are always in a condition of more or less stable equilibrium.

News is not history, however, and its facts are not historical facts. News is not history because, for one thing among others, it deals, on the whole, with isolated events and does not seek to relate them to one another either in the form of causal or in the form of teleological sequences. History not only describes events but seeks to put them in their proper place in the historical succession, and, by doing so, to discover the underlying tendencies and forces which find expression in them. In fact, one would not be far wrong in assuming that history is quite as much concerned with the connections of events—the relation between the incidents that precede and those that follow—as it is with the events themselves. On the other hand, a reporter, as distinguished from a historian, seeks merely to record each single event as it occurs and is concerned with the past and future only in so far as these throw light on what is actual and present.

The relation of an event to the past remains the task of the historian, while its significance as a factor determining the future may perhaps be left to the science of politics—what Freeman calls "comparative politics" [3]— that is to say, to sociology or to some other division of the social sciences, which, by comparative studies, seeks to arrive at statements sufficiently general to support a hypothesis or a prediction.[4]

News, as a form of knowledge, is not primarily concerned either with the past or with the future but rather with the present—what has been described by psychologists as "the specious present." News may be said to exist only in such a present. What is meant here by the "specious present" is suggested by the fact that news, as the publishers of the commercial press know, is a very perishable commodity. News remains news only until it has reached the persons for whom it has "news interest." Once published and its significance recognized, what was news becomes history.

This transient and ephemeral quality is of the very essence of news

[3] Edward A. Freeman, *Comparative Politics* (London, 1873).
[4] The sociological point of view makes its appearance in historical investigation as soon as the historian turns from the study of "periods" to the study of institutions. The history of institutions—that is to say, the family, the church, economic institutions, political institutions, etc.—leads inevitably to comparison, classification, the formation of class names or concepts, and eventually to the formulation of law. In the process history becomes natural history, and natural history passes over into natural science. In short, history becomes sociology (R. E. Park and E. W. Burgess, *Introduction to the Science of Sociology* [Chicago: University of Chicago Press, 1921], p. 16).

and is intimately connected with every other character that it exhibits. Different types of news have a different time span. In its most elementary form a news report is a mere "flash," announcing that an event has happened. If the event proves of real importance, interest in it will lead to further inquiry and to a more complete acquaintance with the attendant circumstances. An event ceases to be news, however, as soon as the tension it aroused has ceased and public attention has been directed to some other aspect of the habitat or to some other incident sufficiently novel, exciting, or important to hold its attention.

The reason that news comes to us, under ordinary circumstances, not in the form of a continued story but as a series of independent incidents becomes clear when one takes account of the fact that we are here concerned with the public mind—or with what is called the public mind. In its most elementary form knowledge reaches the public not, as it does the individual, in the form of a perception but in the form of a communication, that is to say, news. Public attention, however, under normal conditions is wavering, unsteady, and easily distracted. When the public mind wanders, the rapport, grapevine telegraph, or whatever else it is that insures the transmission of news within the limits of the public ceases to function, tension is relaxed, communication broken off, and what was live news becomes cold fact.

A news item, as every newspaperman knows, is read in inverse ratio to its length. The ordinary reader will read a column and a half of two- or three-line items about men and things in the home town before he will read a column article, no matter how advertised in the headlines, unless it turns out to be not merely news but a story, i.e., something that has what is called technically "human interest."

News comes in the form of small, independent communications that can be easily and rapidly comprehended. In fact, news performs somewhat the same functions for the public that perception does for the individual man; that is to say, it does not so much inform as orient the public, giving each and all notice as to what is going on. It does this without any effort of the reporter to interpret the events he reports, except in so far as to make them comprehensible and interesting.

The first typical reaction of an individual to the news is likely to be a desire to repeat it to someone. This makes conversation, arouses further comment, and perhaps starts a discussion. But the singular thing about it is that, once discussion has been started, the event under discussion soon ceases to be news, and, as interpretations of an event differ, discussions turn from the news to the issues it raises. The clash of opinions and sentiments which discussion invariably evokes usually terminates in some sort of consensus or collective opinion—what we call public opinion. It is upon the interpretation of present events, i.e., news, that public opinion rests.

The extent to which news circulates, within a political unit or a political

society, determines the extent to which the members of such a society may
be said to participate, not in its collective life—which is the more inclusive
term—but in its political acts. Political action and political power, as one
ordinarily understands these terms, are obviously based not merely on such
concert and consensus as may exist in a herd or in a crowd. It rests ultimately, it seems, on the ability of a political society, aside from whatever of
military or material resources it possesses, to act not only concertedly but
consistently in accordance with some considered purpose and in further-
ance of some rational end. The world of politics, it seems, is based, as
Schopenhauer has said of the world in general, on the organic relation of
will and idea. Other and more material sources of political power are obviously merely instrumental.

Freeman, the historian, has said that history is past politics and politics
is present history. This puts a great deal of truth into a few words, even if
the statement in practice needs some enlargement and some qualification.
News, though intimately related to both, is neither history nor politics.
It is, nevertheless, the stuff which makes political action, as distinguished
from other forms of collective behavior, possible.

Among other kinds of collective behavior are the recognized and
conventional forms of ceremonial and religious expression—etiquette and
religious ritual—which, in so far as they create unanimity and maintain
morale, play directly and indirectly an important role in politics and in political action. But religion has no such intimate connection as politics with
the news. News is a purely secular phenomenon.

III

There is a proverbial saying to the effect that it is the unexpected that
happens. Since what happens makes news, it follows, or seems to, that
news is always or mainly concerned with the unusual and the unexpected.
Even the most trivial happening, it seems, provided it represents a departure from the customary ritual and routine of daily life, is likely to be
reported in the press. This conception of news has been confirmed by
those editors who, in the competition for circulation and for advertising,
have sought to make their papers smart and interesting, where they could
not be invariably either informing or thrilling. In their efforts to instil into
the minds of reporters and correspondents the importance of looking
everywhere and always for something that would excite, amuse, or shock
its readers, news editors have put into circulation some interesting examples
of what the Germans, borrowing an expression from Homer, have called
geflügelte Wörter, "winged words." The epigram describing news which
has winged its way over more territory and is repeated more often than
any other is this: "Dog bites man"—that is not news. But "Man bites dog"
—that is. *Nota bene!* It is not the intrinsic importance of an event that
makes it newsworthy. It is rather the fact that the event is so unusual that

if published it will either startle, amuse, or otherwise excite the reader so that it will be remembered and repeated. For news is always finally, what Charles A. Dana described it to be, "something that will make people talk," even when it does not make them act.

The fact that news ordinarily circulates spontaneously and without any adventitious aids—as well as freely without inhibitions or censorship—seems to be responsible for another character which attaches to it, distinguishing it from related but less authentic types of knowledge—namely, rumor and gossip. In order that a report of events current may have the quality of news, it should not merely circulate—possibly in circuitous underground channels—but should be published, if need be by the town crier or the public press. Such publication tends to give news something of the character of a public document. News is more or less authenticated by the fact that it has been exposed to the critical examination of the public to which it is addressed and with whose interests it is concerned.

The public which thus, by common consent or failure to protest, puts the stamp of its approval on a published report does not give to its interpretation the authority of statement that has been subjected to expert historical criticism. Every public has its local prejudices and its own limitations. A more searching examination of the facts would quite possibly reveal to a more critical and enlightened mind the naïve credulity and bias of an unsophisticated public opinion. In fact, the naïveté and credulity thus revealed may become an important historical or sociological datum. This, however, is merely another and further illustration of the fact that every public has its own universe of discourse and that, humanly speaking, a fact is only a fact in some universe of discourse.[5]

An interesting light is thrown on the nature of news by a consideration of the changes which take place in information that gets into circulation without the sanction which publicity gives to it. In such case a report, emanating from some source not disclosed and traveling to a destination that is unknown, invariably accumulates details from the innocent but mainly illicit contributions of those who assist it on its travel. Under these circumstances what was at first mere rumor tends to assume, in time, the character of a legend, that is, something which everyone repeats but no one believes.

When, on the other hand, reports of current events are published with the names, dates, and places which make it possible for anyone concerned to check them, the atmosphere of legend which gathers about and clothes

[5] A universe of discourse is, as the term is ordinarily used, no more than a special vocabulary which is well understood and appropriate to specific situations. It may, however, in the case of some special science include a body of more precisely defined terms or concepts, which in that case will tend to have a more or less systematic character. History, for example, employs no, or almost no, special concepts. On the other hand, sociology, and every science that attempts to be systematic, does. As concepts assume this systematic character, they tend to constitute a "frame of reference."

with fantastic detail the news as originally reported is presently dispelled, and what is fact, or what will pass for fact, until corrected by further and later news reports, is reduced to something more prosaic than legend and more authentic than news, i.e., historical fact.

If it is the unexpected that happens, it is the not wholly unexpected that gets into the news. The events that have made news in the past, as in the present, are actually the expected things. They are characteristically simple and commonplace matters, like births and deaths, weddings and funerals, the conditions of the crops and of business, war, politics, and the weather. These are the expected things, but they are at the same time the unpredictable things. They are the incidents and the chances that turn up in the game of life.

The fact is that the thing that makes news is news interest, and that, as every city editor knows, is a variable quantity—one that has to be reckoned with from the time the city editor sits down at his desk in the morning until the night editor locks up the last form at night. The reason for this is that the news value is relative, and an event that comes later may, and often does, diminish the value of an event that turned up earlier. In that case the less important item has to give way to the later and more important.

The anecdotes and "believe it or nots" which turn up in the news are valuable to the editor because they can always be lifted out of the printer's form to make way for something hotter and more urgent. In any case it is, on the whole, the accidents and incidents that the public is prepared for; the victories and defeats on the ball field or on the battlefield; the things that one fears and things that one hopes for—that make the news. It is difficult to understand, nevertheless, considering the number of people who are killed and maimed annually by automobile accidents (the number killed in 1938 was 32,600) that these great losses of life rarely make the front page. The difference seems to be that the automobile has come to be accepted as one of the permanent features of civilized life and war has not.

News, therefore, at least in the strict sense of the term, is not a story or an anecdote. It is something that has for the person who hears or reads it an interest that is pragmatic rather than appreciative. News is characteristically, if not always, limited to events that bring about sudden and decisive changes. It may be an incident like that of the colored family in Philadelphia, Frances and Ben Mason, who won a fortune in the Irish sweepstakes recently.[6] It may be a tragic incident like the battle off the coast of Uruguay which resulted in the destruction of the German battleship, the "Graf Spee," and the suicide of its captain. These events were not only news—that is, something that brought a sudden decisive change in the previously existing situation—but, as they were related in the newspapers

[6] See *Time*, December 25, 1939, p. 12.

and as we reflected upon them, they tended to assume a new and ideal significance: the one a story of genuine human interest, the other that of tragedy, something, to use Aristotle's phrase, to inspire "pity and terror." Events such as these tend to be remembered. Eventually they may become legends or be recorded in popular ballads. Legends and ballads need no date line or the names of persons or places to authenticate them. They live and survive in our memories and in that of the public because of their human interest. As events they have ceased to exist. They survive as a sort of ghostly symbol of something of universal and perennial interest, an ideal representation of what is true of life and of human nature everywhere.

Thus it seems that news, as a form of knowledge, contributes from its record of events not only to history and to sociology but to folklore and literature; it contributes something not merely to the social sciences but to the humanities.

IV

The sociological horizon has recently taken on new dimensions. Social anthropology, no longer interested in primitive society merely, has begun to study not only the history but the natural history and function of institutions. In doing so it has appropriated more and more the field of sociological interest and research. Psychiatry, likewise, has discovered that neuroses and psychoses are diseases of a personality which is itself a product of a social milieu created by the interaction of personalities. Meanwhile there has grown up in the United States and in Europe a sociology of law which conceives as natural products the norms which the courts are seeking to rationalize, systematize, and apply in specific cases. Finally, there have been some interesting recent attempts to bring the subject of knowledge itself within the limits of a sociological discipline.

Theories of knowledge have existed since the days of Parmenides. They have, however, been less interested in knowledge which is a datum than in truth or valid knowledge which is an idea and an ideal. The question with which the sociology of knowledge is concerned is not what constitutes the validity of knowledge—of a statement of principle or of fact —but what are the conditions under which different kinds of knowledge arise and what are the functions of each.

Most of the forms of knowledge that have achieved the dignity of a science are, in the long history of mankind, of very recent origin. One of the earliest and most elementary forms of knowledge is news. There was a period, and not so long ago, either, when there was neither philosophy, history, nor rational knowledge of any sort. There was only myth, legend, and magic. What we now describe as the exact sciences did not exist until the Renaissance. The social sciences have, roughly speaking, only come into existence in the last fifty years. At least they have only begun within the last half-century to achieve, with the wider use of statistics, anything like scientific precision.

News, so far as it is to be regarded as knowledge at all, is probably as old as mankind, perhaps older. The lower animals were not without a kind of communication which was not unlike news. The "cluck" of the mother hen is understood by the chicks as signifying either danger or food, and the chicks respond accordingly.

This is not to suggest that every kind of communication in a herd or flock will have the character of news. What is ordinarily communicated is merely a kind of contagious excitement—sometimes merely a sense of well-being and security in the gregarious association of the herd, at others a sense of unrest or malaise, manifested and often intensified in the milling of the herd. It seems likely that this pervasive social excitement, which is essential to the existence of the herd as a social unit, serves, also, to facilitate the communication of news, or what corresponds to it in the herd.

There is in naval parlance an expression, "the fleet in being," which means, apparently, that the ships which constitute a fleet are in communication and sufficiently mobilized, perhaps, to be capable of some sort of concerted action. The same expression might be applied to a community, a society, or a herd. A society is "in being" when the individuals that compose it are to such an extent *en rapport* that, whether capable of united and collective action or not, they may be described as participating in a common or collective existence. In such a society a diffuse social excitement tends to envelop, like an atmosphere, all participants in the common life and to give a direction and tendency to their interests and attitudes. It is as if the individuals of such a society were dominated by a common mood or state of mind which determined for them the range and character of their interests and their attitudes or tendencies to act. The most obvious illustration of this obscure social tension or state of mind in a community is the persistent and pervasive influence of fashion.

At certain times and under certain conditions this collective excitement, so essential to communication if not to understanding, rises to a higher level of intensity and, as it does so, tends to limit the range of response but to increase the intensity of impulses not so inhibited. The effect of this is the same as in the case of attention in the individual. Exclusive attention to some things inhibits responses to others. This means in the case of a society a limitation of the range and character of the news to which it will either collectively or individually respond.

The rise of social tension may be observed in the most elementary form in the herd when, for some reason, the herd is restless and begins to mill. Tension mounts as restlessness increases. The effect is as if the milling produced in the herd a state of expectancy which, as it increased in intensity, increased also the certainty that presently some incident, a clap of thunder or the crackling of a twig, would plunge the herd into a stampede.

Something similar takes place in a public. As tension arises, the limit of public interest narrows, and the range of events to which the public will respond is limited. The circulation of news is limited; discussion ceases, and the certainty of action of some sort increases. This narrowing of the focus of public attention tends to increase the influence of the dominant person or persons in the community. But the existence of this dominance depends upon the ability of the community, or its leaders, to maintain tension. It is in this way that dictators arise and maintain themselves in power. It is this that explains likewise the necessity to a dictatorship of some sort of censorship.

News circulates, it seems, only in a society where there is a certain degree of rapport and a certain degree of tension. But the effect of news from outside the circle of public interest is to disperse attention and, by so doing, to encourage individuals to act on their own initiative rather than on that of a dominant party or personality.

Under ordinary circumstances—in a time of peace rather than of war or revolution—news tends to circulate over an ever widening area, as means of communication multiply. Changes in society and its institutions under these circumstances continue to take place, but they take place piecemeal and more or less imperceptibly. Under other conditions—in war or revolution—changes take place violently and visibly but catastrophically.

The permanence of institutions under ordinary conditions is dependent upon their ability, or the ability of the community of which they are a part, to adapt themselves to technological and other less obvious changes. But these changes and their consequences manifest themselves not only directly but rather indirectly in the news. Institutions like the Catholic church or the Japanese state have been able to survive the drastic changes of time because they have been able to respond to changes in the conditions of existence, not merely those physically and obviously imposed upon them but those foreshadowed and reflected in the news.

I have indicated the role which news plays in the world of politics in so far as it provides the basis for the discussions in which public opinion is formed. The news plays quite as important a role in the world of economic relations, since the price of commodities, including money and securities, as registered in the world-market and in every local market dependent upon it, is based on the news.

So sensitive are the exchanges to events in every part of the world that every fluctuation in fashion or the weather is likely to be reflected in the prices on the exchanges. I have said that news is a secular phenomenon. But there come times when changes are so great and so catastrophic that individuals and peoples are no longer interested in worldly affairs. In such cases men, frustrated in their ambitions and their hopes, turn away from the world of secular affairs and seek refuge and consolation in a flight from the great world into the security of the little world of the family or of the church. The function of news is to orient man and society in an actual world. In so far as it succeeds it tends to preserve the sanity of the individual and the permanence of society.

Although news is an earlier and more elementary product of communication than science, news has by no means been superseded by it. On the contrary, the importance of news has grown consistently with the expansion of the means of communication and with the growth of science.

Improved means of communication have co-operated with the vast accumulations of knowledge, in libraries, in museums, and in learned societies, to make possible a more rapid, accurate, and thoroughgoing interpretation of events as they occur. The result is that persons and places, once remote and legendary, are now familiar to every reader of the daily press.

In fact, the multiplication of the means of communication has brought it about that anyone, even in the most distant part of the world, may now actually participate in events—at least as listener if not as spectator—as they actually take place in some other part of the world. We have recently listened to Mussolini address his fascist followers from a balcony of Rome; we have heard Hitler speaking over the heads of a devout congregation in the Reichstag, in Berlin, not merely to the President, but to the people, of the United States. We have even had an opportunity to hear the terms of the momentous Munich agreement ten seconds after it had been signed by the representatives of four of the leading powers in Europe and the world. The fact that acts so momentous as these can be so quickly and so publicly consummated has suddenly and completely changed the character of international politics, so that one can no longer even guess what the future has in store for Europe and for the world.

In the modern world the role of news has assumed increased rather than diminished importance as compared with some other forms of knowledge, history, for example. The changes in recent years have been so rapid and drastic that the modern world seems to have lost its historical perspective, and we appear to be living from day to day in what I have described earlier as a "specious present." Under the circumstances history seems to be read or written mainly to enable us, by comparison of the present with the past, to understand what is going on about us rather than, as the historians have told us, to know "what actually happened."

Thus Elmer Davis in a recent article in the *Saturday Review* announces as "required reading" for 1939 two volumes: Hitler's *Mein Kampf* and Thucydides' *History of the Peloponnesian War* (431 B.C.). He recommends the history of the Peloponnesian War because, as he says, "Thucydides was not only a brilliant analyst of human behavior both individual and collective" but was at the same time "a great reporter." [7]

One notes, also, as characteristic of our times, that since news, as re-

[7] "Required Reading," *Saturday Review of Literature*, October 14, 1939.

ported in American newspapers, has tended to assume the character of literature, so fiction—after the newspaper the most popular form of literature—has assumed more and more the character of news.[8]

Emile Zola's novels were essentially reports upon contemporary manners in France just as Steinbeck's *The Grapes of Wrath* has been described as an epoch-making report on the share-cropper in the United States.

Ours, it seems, is an age of news, and one of the most important events in American civilization has been the rise of the reporter.

[8] See Helen MacGill Hughes, *News and the Human Interest Story* (Chicago: University of Chicago Press, 1940).

THE NATURE OF NEWS

By Walter Lippmann

1

ALL THE REPORTERS in the world working all the hours of the day could not witness all the happenings in the world. There are not a great many reporters. And none of them has the power to be in more than one place at a time. Reporters are not clairvoyant, they do not gaze into a crystal ball and see the world at will, they are not assisted by thought-transference. Yet the range of subjects these comparatively few men manage to cover would be a miracle indeed, if it were not a standardized routine.

Newspapers do not try to keep an eye on all mankind.[1] They have watchers stationed at certain places, like Police Headquarters, the Coroner's Office, the County Clerk's Office, City Hall, the White House, the Senate, House of Representatives, and so forth. They watch, or rather in the majority of cases they belong to associations which employ men who watch "a comparatively small number of places where it is made known when the life of anyone . . . departs from ordinary paths, or when events worth telling about occur. For example, John Smith, let it be supposed, becomes a broker. For ten years he pursues the even tenor of his way and except for his customers and his friends no one gives him a thought. To the newspapers he is as if he were not. But in the eleventh year he suffers heavy losses and, at last, his resources all gone, summons his lawyer and arranges for the making of an assignment. The lawyer posts off to the County Clerk's office, and a clerk there makes the necessary entries in the official docket. Here in step the newspapers. While the clerk is writing Smith's business obituary a reporter glances over his shoulder and a few minutes later the reporters know Smith's troubles and are as well informed concerning his business status as they would be had they kept a reporter at his door every day for over ten years." [2]

When Mr. Given says that the newspapers know "Smith's troubles"

[1] See the illuminating chapter in Mr. John L. Given's book, on "Uncovering the News," Ch. V.
[2] Op. cit., p. 57.

and "his business status," he does not mean that they know them as Smith knows them, or as Mr. Arnold Bennett would know them if he had made Smith the hero of a three volume novel. The newspapers know only "in a few minutes" the bald facts which are recorded in the County Clerk's Office. That overt act "uncovers" the news about Smith. Whether the news will be followed up or not is another matter. The point is that before a series of events become news they have usually to make themselves noticeable in some more or less overt act. Generally too, in a crudely overt act. Smith's friends may have known for years that he was taking risks, rumors may even have reached the financial editor if Smith's friends were talkative. But apart from the fact that none of this could be published because it would be libel, there is in these rumors nothing definite on which to peg a story. Something definite must occur that has unmistakable form. It may be the act of going into bankruptcy, it may be a fire, a collision, an assault, a riot, an arrest, a denunciation, the introduction of a bill, a speech, a vote, a meeting, the expressed opinion of a well known citizen, an editorial in a newspaper, a sale, a wage-schedule, a price change, the proposal to build a bridge. . . . There must be a manifestation. The course of events must assume a certain definable shape, and until it is in a phase where some aspect is an accomplished fact, news does not separate itself from the ocean of possible truth.

2

Naturally there is room for wide difference of opinion as to when events have a shape that can be reported. A good journalist will find news oftener than a hack. If he sees a building with a dangerous list, he does not have to wait until it falls into the street in order to recognize news. It was a great reporter who guessed the name of the next Indian Viceroy when he heard that Lord So-and-So was inquiring about climates. There are lucky shots but the number of men who can make them is small. Usually it is the stereotyped shape assumed by an event at an obvious place that uncovers the run of the news. The most obvious place is where people's affairs touch public authority. De minimis non curat lex. It is at these places that marriages, births, deaths, contracts, failures, arrivals, departures, lawsuits, disorders, epidemics and calamities are made known.

In the first instance, therefore, the news is not a mirror of social conditions, but the report of an aspect that has obtruded itself. The news does not tell you how the seed is germinating in the ground, but it may tell you when the first sprout breaks through the surface. It may even tell you what somebody says is happening to the seed under ground. It may tell you that the sprout did not come up at the time it was expected. The more points, then, at which any happening can be fixed, objectified, measured, named, the more points there are at which news can occur.

So, if some day a legislature, having exhausted all other ways of im-

proving mankind, should forbid the scoring of baseball games, it might
still be possible to play some sort of game in which the umpire decided
according to his own sense of fair play how long the game should last,
when each team should go to bat, and who should be regarded as the winner. If that game were reported in the newspapers it would consist of a
record of the umpire's decisions, plus the reporter's impression of the
hoots and cheers of the crowd, plus at best a vague account of how certain
men, who had no specified position on the field moved around for a few
hours on an unmarked piece of sod. The more you try to imagine the logic
of so absurd a predicament, the more clear it becomes that for the purposes of newsgathering (let alone the purposes of playing the game), it is
impossible to do much without an apparatus and rules for naming, scoring, recording. Because that machinery is far from perfect, the umpire's
life is often a distracted one. Many crucial plays he has to judge by eye.
The last vestige of dispute could be taken out of the game, as it has been
taken out of chess when people obey the rules, if somebody thought it
worth his while to photograph every play. It was the moving pictures which
finally settled a real doubt in many reporters' minds, owing to the slow-
ness of the human eye, as to just what blow of Dempsey's knocked out
Carpentier.

Wherever there is a good machinery of record, the modern news service works with great precision. There is one on the stock exchange, and the
news of price movements is flashed over tickers with dependable accuracy.
There is a machinery for election returns, and when the counting and
tabulating are well done, the result of a national election is usually known
on the night of the election. In civilized communities deaths, births, marriages and divorces are recorded, and are known accurately except where
there is concealment or neglect. The machinery exists for some, and only
some, aspects of industry and government, in varying degrees of precision
for securities, money and staples, bank clearances, realty transactions, wage
scales. It exists for imports and exports because they pass through a custom
house and can be directly recorded. It exists in nothing like the same degree for internal trade, and especially for trade over the counter.

It will be found, I think, that there is a very direct relation between
the certainty of news and the system of record. If you call to mind the
topics which form the principal indictment by reformers against the press,
you find they are subjects in which the newspaper occupies the position
of the umpire in the unscored baseball game. All news about states of
mind is of this character: so are all descriptions of personalities, of sincerity, aspiration, motive, intention, of mass feeling, of national feeling,
of public opinion, the policies of foreign governments. So is much news
about what is going to happen. So are questions turning on private profit,
private income, wages, working conditions, the efficiency of labor, educational opportunity, unemployment,[3] monotony, health, discrimination,

[3] Think of what guess work went into the Reports of Unemployment in 1921.

unfairness, restraint of trade, waste, "backward peoples," conservatism, imperialism, radicalism, liberty, honor, righteousness. All involve data that are at best spasmodically recorded. The data may be hidden because of a censorship or a tradition of privacy, they may not exist because nobody thinks record important, because he thinks it red tape, or because nobody has yet invented an objective system of measurement. Then the news on these subjects is bound to be debatable, when it is not wholly neglected. The events which are not scored are reported either as personal and conventional opinions, or they are not news. They do not take shape until somebody protests, or somebody investigates, or somebody publicly, in the etymological meaning of the word, makes an *issue* of them.

This is the underlying reason for the existence of the press agent. The enormous discretion as to what facts and what impressions shall be reported is steadily convincing every organized group of people that whether it wishes to secure publicity or to avoid it, the exercise of discretion cannot be left to the reporter. It is safer to hire a press agent who stands between the group and the newspapers. Having hired him, the temptation to exploit his strategic position is very great. "Shortly before the war," says Mr. Frank Cobb, "the newspapers of New York took a census of the press agents who were regularly employed and regularly accredited and found that there were about twelve hundred of them. How many there are now (1919) I do not pretend to know, but what I do know is that many of the direct channels to news have been closed and the information for the public is first filtered through publicity agents. The great corporations have them, the banks have them, the railroads have them, all the organizations of business and of social and political activity have them, and they are the media through which news comes. Even statesmen have them." [4]

Were reporting the simple recovery of obvious facts, the press agent would be little more than a clerk. But since, in respect to most of the big topics of news, the facts are not simple, and not at all obvious, but subject to choice and opinion, it is natural that everyone should wish to make his own choice of facts for the newspapers to print. The publicity man does that. And in doing it, he certainly saves the reporter much trouble, by presenting him a clear picture of a situation out of which he might otherwise make neither head nor tail. But it follows that the picture which the publicity man makes for the reporter is the one he wishes the public to see. He is censor and propagandist, responsible only to his employers, and to the whole truth responsible only as it accords with the employer's conception of his own interests.

The development of the publicity man is a clear sign that the facts of modern life do not spontaneously take a shape in which they can be known. They must be given a shape by somebody, and since in the daily routine reporters cannot give a shape to facts, and since there is little disinterested

[4] Address before the Women's City Club of New York, Dec. 11, 1919. Reprinted, *New Republic*, Dec. 31, 1919, p. 44.

organization of intelligence, the need for some formulation is being met by the interested parties.

3

The good press agent understands that the virtues of his cause are not news, unless they are such strange virtues that they jut right out of the routine of life. This is not because the newspapers do not like virtue, but because it is not worth while to say that nothing has happened when nobody expected anything to happen. So if the publicity man wishes free publicity he has, speaking quite accurately, to start something. He arranges a stunt: obstructs the traffic, teases the police, somehow manages to entangle his client or his cause with an event that is already news. The suffragists knew this, did not particularly enjoy the knowledge but acted on it, and kept suffrage in the news long after the arguments pro and con were straw in their mouths, and people were about to settle down to thinking of the suffrage movement as one of the established institutions of American life.[5]

Fortunately the suffragists, as distinct from the feminists, had a perfectly concrete objective, and a very simple one. What the vote symbolizes is not simple, as the ablest advocates and the ablest opponents knew. But the right to vote is a simple and familiar right. Now in labor disputes, which are probably the chief item in the charges against newspapers, the right to strike, like the right to vote, is simple enough. But the causes and objects of a particular strike are like the causes and objects of the woman's movement, extremely subtle.

Let us suppose the conditions leading up to a strike are bad. What is the measure of evil? A certain conception of a proper standard of living, hygiene, economic security, and human dignity. The industry may be far below the theoretical standard of the community, and the workers may be too wretched to protest. Conditions may be above the standard, and the workers may protest violently. The standard is at best a vague measure. However, we shall assume that the conditions are below par, as par is understood by the editor. Occasionally without waiting for the workers to threaten, but prompted say by a social worker, he will send reporters to investigate, and will call attention to bad conditions. Necessarily he cannot do that often. For these investigations cost time, money, special talent, and a lot of space. To make plausible a report that conditions are bad, you need a good many columns of print. In order to tell the truth about the steel worker in the Pittsburgh district, there was needed a staff of investigators, a great deal of time, and several fat volumes of print. It is impossible

[5] Cf. Inez Haynes Irwin, *The Story of the Woman's Party*. It is not only a good account of a vital part of a great agitation, but a reservoir of material on successful, non-revolutionary, non-conspiring agitation under modern conditions of public attention, public interest, and political habit.

to suppose that any daily newspaper could normally regard the making of Pittsburgh Surveys, or even Interchurch Steel Reports, as one of its tasks. News which requires so much trouble as that to obtain is beyond the resources of a daily press.[6]

The bad conditions as such are not news, because in all but exceptional cases, journalism is not a first hand report of the raw material. It is a report of that material after it has been stylized. Thus bad conditions might become news if the Board of Health reported an unusually high death rate in an industrial area. Failing an intervention of this sort, the facts do not become news, until the workers organize and make a demand upon their employers. Even then, if an easy settlement is certain the news value is low, whether or not the conditions themselves are remedied in the settlement. But if industrial relations collapse into a strike or lockout the news value increases. If the stoppage involves a service on which the readers of the newspapers immediately depend, or if it involves a breach of order, the news value is still greater.

The underlying trouble appears in the news through certain easily recognizable symptoms, a demand, a strike, disorder. From the point of view of the worker, or of the disinterested seeker of justice, the demand, the strike, and the disorder, are merely incidents in a process that for them is richly complicated. But since all the immediate realities lie outside the direct experience both of the reporter, and of the special public by which most newspapers are supported, they have normally to wait for a signal in the shape of an overt act. When that signal comes, say through a walk-out of the men or a summons for the police, it calls into play the stereotypes people have about strikes and disorders. The unseen struggle has none of its own flavor. It is noted abstractly, and that abstraction is then animated by the immediate experience of the reader and reporter. Obviously this is a very different experience from that which the strikers have. They feel, let us say, the temper of the foreman, the nerve-racking monotony of the machine, the depressingly bad air, the drudgery of their wives, the stunting of their children, the dinginess of their tenements. The slogans of the strike are invested with these feelings. But the reporter and reader see at first only a strike and some catchwords. They invest these with their feelings. Their feelings may be that their jobs are insecure because the strikers are stopping goods they need in their work, that there will be shortage and higher prices, that it is all devilishly inconvenient. These, too, are realities. And when they give color to the abstract news that a strike has been called, it is in the nature of things that the workers are at a

---

[6] Not long ago Babe Ruth was jailed for speeding. Released from jail just before the afternoon game started, he rushed into his waiting automobile, and made up for time lost in jail by breaking the speed laws on his way to the ball grounds. No policeman stopped him, but a reporter timed him, and published his speed the next morning. Babe Ruth is an exceptional man. Newspapers cannot time all motorists. They have to take their news about speeding from the police.

disadvantage. It is in the nature, that is to say, of the existing system of industrial relations that news arising from grievances or hopes by workers should almost invariably be uncovered by an overt attack on production.

You have, therefore, the circumstances in all their sprawling complexity, the overt act which signalizes them, the stereotyped bulletin which publishes the signal, and the meaning that the reader himself injects, after he has derived that meaning from the experience which directly affects him. Now the reader's experience of a strike may be very important indeed, but from the point of view of the central trouble which caused the strike, it is eccentric. Yet this eccentric meaning is automatically the most interesting.[7] To enter imaginatively into the central issues is for the reader to step out of himself, and into very different lives.

It follows that in the reporting of strikes, the easiest way is to let the news be uncovered by the overt act, and to describe the event as the story of interference with the reader's life. That is where his attention is first aroused, and his interest most easily enlisted. A great deal, I think myself the crucial part, of what looks to the worker and the reformer as deliberate misrepresentation on the part of newspapers, is the direct outcome of a practical difficulty in uncovering the news, and the emotional difficulty of making distant facts interesting unless, as Emerson says, we can "perceive (them) to be only a new version of our familiar experience" and can "set about translating (them) at once into our parallel facts." [8]

If you study the way many a strike is reported in the press, you will find, very often, that the issues are rarely in the headlines, barely in the leading paragraphs, and sometimes not even mentioned anywhere. A labor dispute in another city has to be very important before the news account contains any definite information as to what is in dispute. The routine of the news works that way, with modifications it works that way in regard to political issues and international news as well. The news is an account of the overt phases that are interesting, and the pressure on the newspaper to adhere to this routine comes from many sides. It comes from the economy of noting only the stereotyped phase of a situation. It comes from the difficulty of finding journalists who can see what they have not learned to see. It comes from the almost unavoidable difficulty of finding sufficient space in which even the best journalist can make plausible an unconventional view. It comes from the economic necessity of interesting the reader quickly, and the economic risk involved in not interesting him at all, or of offending him by unexpected news insufficiently or clumsily described. All these difficulties combined make for uncertainty in the editor when there are dangerous issues at stake, and cause him naturally to prefer the indisputable fact and a treatment more readily adapted to the reader's in-

[7] Cf. Ch. XI, "The Enlisting of Interest" in Lippmann's *Public Opinion*.
[8] From his essay entitled *Art and Criticism*. The quotation occurs in a passage cited on page 87 of Professor R. W. Brown's, *The Writer's Art*.

terest. The indisputable fact and the easy interest, are the strike itself and the reader's inconvenience.

All the subtler and deeper truths are in the present organization of industry very unreliable truths. They involve judgments about standards of living, productivity, human rights that are endlessly debatable in the absence of exact record and quantitative analysis. And as long as these do not exist in industry, the run of news about it will tend, as Emerson said, quoting from Isocrates, "to make of moles mountains, and of mountains moles." [9] Where there is no constitutional procedure in industry, and no expert sifting of evidence and the claims, the fact that is sensational to the reader is the fact that almost every journalist will seek. Given the industrial relations that so largely prevail, even where there is conference or arbitration, but no independent filtering of the facts for decision, the issue for the newspaper public will tend not to be the issue for the industry. And so to try disputes by an appeal through the newspapers puts a burden upon newspapers and readers which they cannot and ought not to carry. As long as real law and order do not exist, the bulk of the news will, unless consciously and courageously corrected, work against those who have no lawful and orderly method of asserting themselves. The bulletins from the scene of action will note the trouble that arose from the assertion, rather than the reasons which led to it. The reasons are intangible.

4

The editor deals with these bulletins. He sits in his office, reads them, rarely does he see any large portion of the events themselves. He must, as we have seen, woo at least a section of his readers every day, because they will leave him without mercy if a rival paper happens to hit their fancy. He works under enormous pressure, for the competition of newspapers is often a matter of minutes. Every bulletin requires a swift but complicated judgment. It must be understood, put in relation to other bulletins also understood, and played up or played down according to its probable interest for the public, as the editor conceives it. Without standardization, without stereotypes, without routine judgments, without a fairly ruthless disregard of subtlety, the editor would soon die of excitement. The final page is of a definite size, must be ready at a precise moment; there can be only a certain number of captions on the items, and in each caption there must be a definite number of letters. Always there is the precarious urgency of the buying public, the law of libel, and the possibility of endless trouble. The thing could not be managed at all without systematization, for in a standardized product there is economy of time and effort, as well as a partial guarantee against failure.

It is here that newspapers influence each other most deeply. Thus when the war broke out, the American newspapers were confronted with a

[9] *Id., supra.*

subject about which they had no previous experience. Certain dailies, rich enough to pay cable tolls, took the lead in securing news, and the way that news was presented became a model for the whole press. But where did that model come from? It came from the English press, not because Northcliffe owned American newspapers, but because at first it was easier to buy English correspondence, and because, later, it was easier for American journalists to read English newspapers than it was for them to read any others. London was the cable and news center, and it was there that a certain technic for reporting the war was evolved. Something similar occurred in the reporting of the Russian Revolution. In that instance, access to Russia was closed by military censorship, both Russian and Allied, and closed still more effectively by the difficulties of the Russian language. But above all it was closed to effective news reporting by the fact that the hardest thing to report is chaos, even though it is an evolving chaos. This put the formulating of Russian news at its source in Helsingfors, Stockholm, Geneva, Paris and London, into the hands of censors and propagandists. They were for a long time subject to no check of any kind. Until they had made themselves ricidulous they created, let us admit, out of some genuine aspects of the huge Russian maelstrom, a set of stereotypes so evocative of hate and fear, that the very best instinct of journalism, its desire to go and see and tell, was for a long time crushed.[10]

5

Every newspaper when it reaches the reader is the result of a whole series of selections as to what items shall be printed, in what position they shall be printed, how much space each shall occupy, what emphasis each shall have. There are no objective standards here. There are conventions. Take two newspapers published in the same city on the same morning. The headline of one reads: "Britain pledges aid to Berlin against French aggression; France openly backs Poles." The headline of the second is "Mrs. Stillman's Other Love." Which you prefer is a matter of taste, but not entirely a matter of the editor's taste. It is a matter of his judgment as to what will absorb the half hour's attention a certain set of readers will give to his newspaper. Now the problem of securing attention is by no means equivalent to displaying the news in the perspective laid down by religious teaching or by some form of ethical culture. It is a problem of provoking feeling in the reader, of inducing him to feel a sense of personal identification with the stories he is reading. News which does not offer this opportunity to introduce oneself into the struggle which it depicts cannot appeal to a wide audience. The audience must participate in the news, much as it participates in the drama, by personal identification. Just as everyone holds his breath when the heroine is in danger, as he helps Babe Ruth swing

[10] Cf. A Test of the News, by Walter Lippmann and Charles Merz, assisted by Faye Lippmann, New Republic, August 4, 1920.

his bat, so in subtler form the reader enters into the news. In order that he shall enter he must find a familiar foothold in the story, and this is supplied to him by the use of stereotypes. They tell him that if an association of plumbers is called a "combine" it is appropriate to develop his hostility; if it is called a "group of leading business men" the cue is for a favorable reaction.

It is in a combination of these elements that the power to create opinion resides. Editorials reinforce. Sometimes in a situation that on the news pages is too confusing to permit of identification, they give the reader a clue by means of which he engages himself. A clue he must have if, as most of us must, he is to seize the news in a hurry. A suggestion of some sort he demands, which tells him, so to speak, where he, a man conceiving himself to be such and such a person, shall integrate his feelings with the news he reads.

"It has been said" writes Walter Bagehot,[11] "that if you can only get a middleclass Englishman to think whether there are 'snails in Sirius,' he will soon have an opinion on it. It will be difficult to make him think, but if he does think, he cannot rest in a negative, he will come to some decision. And on any ordinary topic, of course, it is so. A grocer has a full creed as to foreign policy, a young lady a complete theory of the sacraments, as to which neither has any doubt whatever."

Yet that same grocer will have many doubts about his groceries, and that young lady, marvelously certain about the sacraments, may have all kinds of doubts as to whether to marry the grocer, and if not whether it is proper to accept his attentions. The ability to rest in the negative implies either a lack of interest in the result, or a vivid sense of competing alternatives. In the case of foreign policy or the sacraments, the interest in the results is intense, while means for checking the opinion are poor. This is the plight of the reader of the general news. If he is to read it at all he must be interested, that is to say, he must enter into the situation and care about the outcome. But if he does that he cannot rest in a negative, and unless independent means of checking the lead given him by his newspaper exists, the very fact that he is interested may make it difficult to arrive at that balance of opinions which may most nearly approximate the truth. The more passionately involved he becomes, the more he will tend to resent not only a different view, but a disturbing bit of news. That is why many a newspaper finds that, having honestly evoked the partisanship of its readers, it can not easily, supposing the editor believes the facts warrant it, change position. If a change is necessary, the transition has to be managed with the utmost skill and delicacy. Usually a newspaper will not attempt so hazardous a performance. It is easier and safer to have the news of that subject taper off and disappear, thus putting out the fire by starving it.

11 On the Emotion of Conviction, *Literary Studies*, Vol. III, p. 172.

SUMMARY OF PRINCIPLE

A Statement of the Commission on Freedom of the Press

———

FREEDOM of speech and press is close to the central meaning of all liberty. Where men cannot freely convey their thoughts to one another, no other liberty is secure. Where freedom of expression exists, the germ of a free society is already present and a means is at hand for every extension of liberty. Free expression is therefore unique among liberties as protector and promoter of the others; in evidence of this, when a regime moves toward autocracy, speech and press are among the first objects of restraint or control.

There are obvious reasons for bracketing freedom of the press with freedom of speech, as in the First Amendment. The press was at first hardly more than a means for extending the speaker's audience: the printed word could go far beyond the reach of his voice and to greater numbers and, through its durability, could continue to speak at all later time. This space-time extension alters nothing in the relation of the speaker to his audience or the nature of his message. And while today the voice, by the aid of radio, is freed from its natural limitations—it can reach as far as print, at least as many, and in far shorter time—it is the more evident that the two social functions merge.

Equally obvious are important differences between speech and press. Speech is natural and inseparable from the human person, the breath of his social existence, and so intimate a tool of all mental life that without free speech thought itself could not be fully free. The press, by contrast, is an institution of developed society, a machine-using institution, and one whose role tends to enlarge as new instruments are devised. Extending many fold the working environment of personal life, it creates an appetite for its own increasing services. It has done much to make possible the unity of large states; without its aid the incipient order of mankind would be inconceivable. The problems it faces today are in large part the problems of its own achievements. It is incumbent upon us to inquire whether the traditional groundwork of principle which has inspired our existing law and our social attitudes is adequate to the period we now enter.

We shall begin by analyzing the situation of the press within society into its elements, in order to find the bare essentials of the actual fact we call "the press."

It will be understood that we are using the term "press" to include all means of communicating to the public news and opinions, emotions and beliefs, whether by newspapers, magazines, or books, by radio broadcasts, by television, or by films.

I. The Parties Directly at Interest

When we use the phrase "freedom of the press," we mention but one party at interest; the term "press" indicates an *issuer* of news, opinions, etc., through the media which reach mass audiences. But since no one cares to utter news or opinions into the void, there must be at least one other party at interest, the reader or listener as *consumer* of news, opinions, etc.; we shall refer to him collectively as the *audience*.

The interest of the issuer is, typically, to express his mind without external constraint or restraint—his ideas and reports of events, also his feelings, judgments, protests, business proposals, appeals, visions, prophecies. . . . To the press, the implied audience is seldom visibly present or personally known; it is an imagined audience, and it is hopefully considered a representative audience. For, while it is commonly called "the public," it is at most a fair sample of the actual public. From this fragment, given freedom of speech, the message will spread to others and, with good luck, find the listeners to whom it belongs.

The interest of the consumer is, in detail, highly variable and personal. Yet, in any mentally alert society, there is a fairly universal desire for access to a world of experience, thought, and feeling beyond the range of private observation. And also beyond the range of private concern, for it is the genius of the human animal to "take an interest" in what does not immediately concern him. It may be a random and marginal curiosity; it may amount to an insistent hunger. In any case, since the nature of the appetite is such that it exceeds any actual satisfaction, the issuer can usually count on a latent demand; he may develop a demand where none pre-exists.

Wherever there are two parties, within a community, there is always a third party, the community itself. As a social totality including all pairs of (domestic) issuers and consumers, the community has a stake in the impact of all conversation, but especially in that of speech addressed to a mass audience. For all communication, apart from its direct meaning, has an effect on the communicators, on the social fabric, and on the common standards which measure the free cohesion of the group.

II. Freedom of the Parties at Interest

Though the issuer's interest cannot be realized without an audience, his interest carries with it no claim whatever to compel the existence of an audience but only to invite an audience from men free not to listen. Freedom of the press must imply freedom of the consumer *not to consume* any particular press product; otherwise, the issuer's freedom could be at the expense of the consumer's freedom.

As the issuer cannot compel an audience, so the consumer cannot compel the existence of a speaker. Nor does it usually occur to him that he has a claim upon anyone for more light and leading than is spontaneously offered. The expresser is offering a gift. Nevertheless, the consumer is not a passive receptacle. Since the issuer cannot survive without his free attention, the consumer has power to encourage or discourage his advances. Through the consumer's willingness to pay for the successful divination of his appetites, he lures out the yield of thought-products; it is his free suffrage that builds up the great press and sustains a mass production in which thought and pseudo-thought devised for the market mix in varying proportions. He may go to the extent of setting up, with a like-minded group, a press organ to meet special group needs, interests, or prejudices; here the consumer controls, or perhaps becomes, the issuer. But the birth of opinion the consumer cannot control; the genesis of thought is incurably free and individual. For its abundance and pertinence he must take his chances as with the fertility of his native soil. He is necessarily interested in the freedom of the sources of opinion, because if they are unchecked and unwarped, even by himself, he will have, other things being equal, the widest and most honest offering to select from or to piece together or to mix with his own thought. His interest here coincides with that of the issuer, actual or potential.

Hence it is that, although there are these two direct interests, *only one of them, in simple conditions, needs protection*. To protect the freedom of the issuer is to protect the interest of the consumer and in general that of the community also. Hitherto in our history, it has been sufficient to protect the "freedom of the press" as the freedom of issuers.

But, as this analysis is intended to indicate, under changed conditions the consumer's freedom might also require protection. If his need became more imperative, and if at the same time the variety of sources available to him were limited, as by concentration of the press industry, his freedom not to consume particular products of the existing press might vanish. It would then be no longer sufficient to protect the issuer alone. This theme is resumed in Section XI below. Meantime we trace the theory in terms of the issuer's freedom.

III. Freedom of the Issuer Requires Protection

The utterance of opinion is not merely the announcement of an "I think . . ." It is a social force and is intended to be such.

Since civilized society is a working system of ideas, it lives and changes by the consumption of ideas. It is vulnerable to every shock to the fortunes of the ideas it embodies. And since there is usually less motive for uttering ideas with which everybody and every institution is in accord than for uttering those destined to change men's minds, a significant new idea in the social field is likely to arouse resistance. The issuer will have need of protection. But of what protection?

Freedom of expression can never be made a costless immunity by shackling hostile response, for response is also expression. Free expression is destined not to repress social conflict but to liberate it. But its intention is that the *level of social conflict shall be lifted from the plane of violence to the plane of discussion.* It should mean to the issuer that he is protected, not from anger, contempt, suffering, the loss of his clientele, for in this case his critic would be unfree, but from types of harm not an integral part of the argument or relevant to the argument (wrecking the issuer's shop, threatening his employees, intimidating his patrons . . .).

There are those who would define freedom of expression as meaning no pain and no opprobrium to the issuer, no matter what he proposes. This ideal, if it is such, could be realized only in a society to which all ideas had become either impotent or indifferent. In any actual society free speech will require courage. And the first danger to free expression will always be the danger at the source, the timidity of the issuer, or his purchasability.

IV. THE EFFECTIVE AGENCIES FOR PROTECTING FREE EXPRESSION ARE THE COMMUNITY AND THE GOVERNMENT

The community acts, by routing social conflict through the ballot box, encouraging the method of discussion by making it a preliminary to action, and, then, by such traditions of self-restraint and toleration as may exist.

But, in the steadiest of communities, the struggle among ideas tends to become physical as it becomes prolonged; there is an incessant downtrend of debate toward the irrelevant exchange of punishments—malicious pressures, threats and bribes, broken windows and broken heads. Government is the only agency which, through its monopoly of physical force, can measurably insure that argument in speech and press will continue to be argument and not competitive injury. The elementary function of government in simply maintaining public order and the rights of person and property must be noted as the cornerstone of free expression, inasmuch as the cruder menaces to freedom are always from within the community.

Wherever in society there is an institution, a body of belief or interest, an organized power—good, bad, or mixed—there is a potential (we do not say actual) foe of the free critic—good, bad, or mixed. This potential hostility to the challenger is due not simply to the fact that it is easier and more natural for the obstinate vein in human nature to discourage or repress the critic than to meet his arguments. It is due also to irrational elements commonly present in the critic and the critic's audience. Freedom of the press to appeal to reason is liable to be taken as freedom to appeal to public passion, ignorance, prejudice, and mental inertia. We must not burke the fact that freedom of the press is dangerous. But there is no cure for bad argument either in refusing to argue or in substituting irrelevant pressures upon, or repression of, the free critic for the patient attempt to reach the elements of reasonableness in the mass mind, as long as the belief persists that such elements are there. The only hope for democracy lies in the validity of this belief and in the resolute maintenance, in that faith, of the critic's freedom.

The first line of defense for press freedom is government, as maintaining order and personal security and as exercising in behalf of press freedom the available sanctions against sabotage, blackmail, and corruption.

V. Government as Protecting Freedom Against Government

Any power capable of protecting freedom is also capable of infringing freedom. This is true both of the community and of government. In modern society the policy of government vis-à-vis the free expression of its citizens is in peculiar need of definition.

For every modern government, liberal or otherwise, has a specific position in the field of ideas; its stability is vulnerable to critics in proportion to their ability and persuasiveness. To this rule, a government resting on popular suffrage is no exception. On the contrary, just to the extent that public opinion is a factor in the tenure and livelihood of officials and parties, such a government has its own peculiar form of temptation to manage the ideas and images entering public debate.

If, then, freedom of the press is to achieve reality, government must set limits upon its capacity to interfere with, regulate, control, or suppress the voices of the press or to manipulate the data on which public judgment is formed.

What we mean by a free society is chiefly one in which government does thus expressly limit its scope of action in respect to certain human liberties, namely, those liberties which belong to the normal development of mature men. Here belong free thought, free conscience, free worship, free speech, freedom of the person, free assembly. Freedom of the press takes its place with these. And all of them, together with some stipulations regarding property, constitute the burden of our bills of rights.

VI. Free Expression as a Right

If government accepts a limitation of its range of action in view of such interests, the reason is that they are not only important interests but also moral rights. And they are moral rights because their exercise, besides being valuable to both the citizen and the community, has an aspect of duty about it.

The motives of expression are certainly not all dutiful; they are and should be as multiform as human emotion itself, grave and gay, casual and purposeful, artful and idle. In a modern state all social activity, including the conduct of business, requires use of the press as well as of speech and assumes its natural freedom. But there is a vein of expression which has the added impulsion of duty, namely, the expression of thought and belief. If a man is burdened with an idea, he not only desires to express it, he ought to express it. The socially indispensable functions of criticism and appeal may be as abhorrent to the diffident as they are attractive to the pugnacious, but for neither is the issue one of wish. It is one of obligation—to the community and also to something beyond the community, let us say, to truth.* It is the duty of the scientist to his result and of Socrates to his oracle; but it is equally the duty of every man to his own belief. Because of this duty to what is beyond the state, freedom of speech and press are moral rights which the state must not infringe.

While dutiful utterance bears the burden of the claim of right as against the state, that right extends its coverage over all legitimate expression.

This self-limitation of the state cannot in the long run be contrary to the public interest. For, whatever its judgment of the opinions expressed, no nation can have a net interest in repressing the conscience of its citizens. On the contrary, the modern state recognizes that the citizen's conscience is a source of its own continued vitality. And, wherever the citizen has a duty of conscience, there the soverign state has also a duty, namely, to that conscience of its citizen. Thus both its interest and its duty require the state to give the moral right a legal status.

This consideration is logically prior to the traditional ground of a free press, namely, that the unhampered publication of opinion promotes the "victory of truth over falsehood" in the public arena. Public discussion is indeed a necessary condition of a free society, and freedom of expression is a necessary condition of an amply furnished public discussion. It is not a sufficient condition, for the co-presence of a variety of opinions is not equivalent to debate; it may well be questioned whether the actual process we now call public discussion is functioning as the health of a democracy requires. In any case, it is a process which elicits mental power and breadth in those consumers whom it does not baffle or confuse; it is essential to building a mentally robust public; and, without something of the kind, no self-governing society could operate. But the original source of supply for this very process is the duty of the individual thinker to his thought; here is the primary ground of his right.

* For brevity, we shall use the concern for "truth" as token of a group of interests having a similar claim on expression, such as belief regarding "right," or justice of feeling, or public policy, or the advocacy of a legitimate personal interest. To make "truth" the symbol of all this will bring our discussion into close relation with the classical argument for freedom of expression, which has been chiefly concerned with the contest of opinions in respect to truth and falsehood. "Truth" is beyond the state and may symbolize whatever is, in similar fashion, obligatory on individual and state alike.

While it is not, like the right of speech, a universal right that every citizen should own a press or be an editor or have access to the clientele of any existing press, it is the whole point of a free press that ideas deserving a public hearing shall get a public hearing and that the decision of what ideas deserve that hearing shall rest in part with the public, not solely with the particular biases of editors and owners. In any populous community a vigorous trimming-out process among ideas presenting themselves for wide public hearing is obviously essential; but freedom of the press becomes a mockery unless this selective process is free also. This means that free speech, with its informal emphasis, is the natural vestibule to a free press and that the circumstance of ownership of press instruments confers no privilege of deafness toward ideas which the normal selective processes of the community promote to general attention.*

VII. THE MORAL RIGHT OF FREEDOM OF EXPRESSION IS NOT UNCONDITIONAL

If reasons can be given for a claim of right—and there are reasons for all of them—those reasons constitute the condition on which the right can be claimed. The absence of that condition, therefore, automatically removes the basis for the claim.

By this logic, since the claim of the right of free expression is based on the duty of a man to his thought, then when this duty is ignored or rejected—as when the issuer is a liar, an editorial prostitute whose political judgments can be bought, a malicious inflamer of unjust hatred—the ground for his claim of right is nonexistent. In the absence of accepted moral duties there are no moral rights.

It may reasonably be doubted whether any man is capable of a thoroughgoing repudiation of duty. His experiments in the rejection of good faith are likely to be sporadic; a single lie does not make a man a liar nor a single acceptance of bribe a prostitute. Further, if a man is stung into reckless or inflammatory speech by a genuine grievance which ought to be made known, his bedeviled utterance may contain an important piece of truth. Still, if we define a liar as a man who habitually tells the truth except when it suits his policy to deviate, the press liar is not a mythical person. His ultimate humanity and freedom he cannot alienate; but he has used his freedom to undermine his freedom. His claim of right as an issuer of opinion has by his own choice become groundless.

Since all rights, moral or legal, make assumptions regarding the will of the claimants, there are no unconditional rights. The notion of rights, costless, unconditional, conferred by the Creator at birth, was a marvel-

---

* It is worth noting that the Soviet Constitution, while limiting publishable ideas within a fixed orthodoxy, undertakes within these limits to implement press expression for a wide segment of the people who own no presses. It provides (Art. 125) that "printing presses, stocks of paper . . . communications facilities, and other material requisites" shall be put at the disposal of working people and their organizations.

ous fighting principle against arbitrary governments and had its historical work to do. But in the context of an achieved political freedom the need of limitation becomes evident. The unworkable and invalid conception of birthrights, wholly divorced from the condition of duty, has tended to beget an arrogant type of individualism which makes a mockery of every free institution, including the press. This conception has concealed the sound basis of our liberal polity, the one natural right, the right to do one's human task. From this one right, the others can be derived so far as they are valid; and into this right the ingredient of duty is inseparably built.

VIII. A Right of Liberty Includes a Right to Be in Error

Liberty is experimental, and experiment implies trial and error. Debate itself could not exist unless wrong opinions could be rightfully offered by those who suppose them to be right. For social purposes, the cutting edge of the right of free expression is its demand for what is called "toleration" on the part of those who see, or think they see, error in others. What is required is something more positive than toleration—respect for the process of self-correction as against any authoritatively imposed correctness.

The assumption of this respect is that the man in error is actually trying for the truth; and this effort on his part is of the essence of his claim to freedom. What the moral right does not cover is a right to be deliberately or irresponsibly in error.

IX. The Abuse of a Right Does Not Ipso Facto Forfeit the Protection of the Legal Right

Legal protection cannot vary with the inner fluctuations of moral direction in individual wills; it does not cease whenever the moral ground of right has been personally abandoned. It is not even desirable that the whole area of the responsible use of freedom should be made legally compulsory, even if such a thing were possible, for in that case free self-control, necessary ingredient of any free state, would be superseded by mechanism.

The attempt to correct abuses of freedom, including press freedom, by resort to legal penalties and controls is the first spontaneous impulse of reform. But the dangers of the cure must be weighed against the dangers of the disease; every definition of an abuse invites abuse of the definition. The law might well be justified in acting against malicious public criticism; but if courts were called on to determine the inner corruptions of intention, honest and necessary criticism would proceed under an added peril and the "courage of disclosure" incur a new cost.

Hence many a lying, venal, and scoundrelly public expression must continue to find shelter under a "freedom of the press" built for widely different ends. There is a practical presumption against the use of legal action to curb press abuse.

X. There Are, However, Limits to the Legal Toleration of Abuse of the Liberty of Expression

The already recognized areas of legal correction of misused liberty in this field—libel, misbranding, obscenity, incitement to riot, sedition in case of clear and present danger—have a common principle, namely, that an utterance or publication invades in a serious, overt, and demonstrable manner recognized private rights or vital social interests. If new categories of abuse come within this definition, the extension of legal remedies is justified. In view of the general presumption against legal action above stated, the burden of proof will rest upon those who would extend these categories; but the presumption is not intended to render society supine in the face of all new types of misuse, actual or possible, of the immense powers of the contemporary press.

Today a further question of public responsibility in the use of freedom is raised in view of the extent to which the function of the press is affected by a public interest. Not only positive misdeeds but omissions and inadequacies of press performance have now a bearing on general welfare. Freedom to express has hitherto included freedom to refrain from expressing; for the press this liberty is no longer perfect.

XI. The Work of the Press as Clothed with a Public Interest

As observed at the beginning (Sec. I), the work of the press always involves the interest of the consumer; but, as long as the consumer is free, his interest is protected in the protection of the freedom of the issuer. Today, however, the conditions affecting the consumer's freedom have radically altered. Through concentration of ownership the flow of news and opinion is shaped at the sources; its variety is limited; and at the same time the insistence of the consumer's need has increased. He is dependent on the quality, proportion, and extent of his news supply not alone for his personal access to the world of thought and feeling but also for the materials of his business as a citizen in judging public affairs. With this situation any community in which public opinion is a factor in policy, domestic and international, must be deeply concerned.

Clearly a qualitatively new era of public responsibility for the press has arrived; and it becomes an imperative question whether press performance can any longer be left to the unregulated initiative of the issuers. The moral and legal right of thinkers to utter their opinions must in any case remain intact; this right stands for the kernel of individualism at the heart of all free social life. But the element of duty involved in the right requires a new scrutiny. And the service of news, as distinct from the utterance of opinion, acquires an added importance. The need of the consumer to have adequate and uncontaminated mental food is such that he is under a duty to get it; and, because of this duty, his interest acquires the stature of a *right*. It becomes legitimate to speak of the moral right of men to the news they can use.

Since the consumer is no longer free not to consume, and can get what he requires only through existing press organs, protection of the freedom of the issuer is no longer sufficient to protect automatically either the consumer or the community. The general policy of laissez faire in this field must be reconsidered.

XII. The Accountable Press and the Responsible Community

The press today, as the Supreme Court has recently recognized in the case of news services, has responsibilities to the general spread of information which present analogies to those of a common carrier or of a trustee, though the likeness in either of these cases is limited. The analogy is closer to an educational enterprise in which private schools, enjoying the advantages and risks of experimental initiative, are yet performing a necessary public function for which a measure of social accountability would be appropriate. Do these analogies suggest that for the press also some degree of public oversight and co-operation and possibly of regulation must be the way of the future?

An over-all social responsibility for the quality of press service to the citizen cannot be escaped; the community cannot wholly delegate to any other agency the ultimate responsibility for a function in which its own existence as a free society may be at stake.

At the same time, the main positive energy for the improvement of press achievement must come from the issuers. Although the standards of press performance arise as much from the public situation and need as from the conscious goals of the press, these standards must be administered by the press itself. This means that the *press must now take on the community's press objectives as its own objectives*. And for the correction of abuses the maxim holds good that self-correction is better than outside correction, so long as self-correction holds out a reasonable and realistic hope, as distinct from lip service to piously framed paper codes.

How shall this realism be implemented? And how shall the objectives of the press be held to identity with the necessary objectives of the community? By a recognition on the part of the press that, while its enterprise is and should remain a private business, its efforts to define and realize its standards are also a community concern and should be systematically associated with corresponding efforts of community, consumers, and government.

—With those of consumers and community, acting through specialized organs, as responsible critic, gadfly, and source of incentive.

—With those of government in various ways whose principles we may indicate as follows:

1. Without intruding on press activities, government may act to im-

prove the conditions under which they take place so that the public interest is better served—as by making distribution more universal and equable, removing hindrances to the free flow of ideas, reducing confusion and promoting the reality of public debate.

2. New legal remedies and preventions are not to be excluded as aids to checking the more patent abuses of the press, under the precautions we have emphasized. Such legal measures are not in their nature subtractions from freedom but, like laws which help to clear the highways of drunken drivers, are means of increasing freedom, through removing impediments to the practice and repute of the honest press.

3. Government may and should enter the field of press comment and news supply, not as displacing private enterprise, but as a supplementary source. In so doing, it may present standards for private emulation. While in our experience a democratic government is one in which government itself is one of the main objects of public discussion and can therefore never be allowed to control or to regulate the debate, it is not inconceivable that a government by the people should also be a powerful instrument for the people, in respect to educational and other noncommercial possibilities of the developing press.

XIII. Resulting Conception of Freedom of the Press

The emerging conception of freedom of the press may be summarized as follows:

As with all freedom, press freedom means freedom from and also freedom for.

A free press is free from compulsions from whatever source, governmental or social, external or internal. From compulsions, not from pressures; for no press can be free from pressures except in a moribund society empty of contending forces and beliefs. These pressures, however, if they are persistent and distorting—as financial, clerical, popular, institutional pressures may become—approach compulsions; and something is then lost from effective freedom which the press and its public must unite to restore.

A free press is free for the expression of opinion in all its phases. It is free for the achievement of those goals of press service on which its own ideals and the requirements of the community combine and which existing techniques make possible. For these ends it must have full command of technical resources, financial strength, reasonable access to sources of information at home and abroad, and the necessary facilities for bringing information to the national market. The press must grow to the measure of this market.

For the press there is a third aspect of freedom. The free press must be free to all who have something worth saying to the public, since the essential object for which a free press is valued is that ideas deserving a public hearing shall have a public hearing.

XIV. Contemporary Problems of Principle

1. These several factors of an ideal press freedom are to some extent incompatible with one another.

A press which has grown to the measure of the national market and to the full use of technical resources can hardly be free from internal compulsions. The major part of the nation's press is large-scale enterprise, closely interlocked with the system of finance and industry; it will not without effort escape the natural bias of what it is. Yet, if freedom is to remain secure, this bias must be known and overcome.

Again, the growth of the press acts together with the growth of the nation to make more remote the ideal that every voice shall have the hearing it deserves. Concentration of power substitutes one controlling policy for many independent policies, lessens the number of major competitors, and renders less operative the claims of potential issuers who have no press. For this clash there is no perfect remedy. There is relief, to the extent that the wider press, somewhat as a common carrier, assumes responsibility for representing variant facets of opinion. But no listening devices of the human mind have yet secured us from a certain wastage of human genius as the scale of a nation's thinking enlarges; and the contemporary arts of what is called publicity can hardly be acquitted of aiming rather at further lens distortion than at just and proportionate recognition of worth. As commercial arts it is hard to see how they can make justice their supreme object.

2. There is an antithesis between the current conception of the freedom of the press and the accountability of the press.

Accountability, like subjection to law, is not necessarily a net subtraction from liberty; the affirmative factor of freedom, freedom for, may be enhanced. But the liberty to be carefree is gone. Charles Beard could say with accuracy that "in its origin, freedom of the press had little or nothing to do with truth telling. . . . most of the early newspapers were partisan sheets devoted to savage attacks on party opponents. . . . Freedom of the press means the right to be just or unjust, partisan or nonpartisan, true or false, in news column or editorial column." * Today, this former legal privilege wears the aspect of social irresponsibility. The press must know that its faults and errors have ceased to be private vagaries and have become public dangers. Its inadequacies menace the balance of public opinion. It has lost the common and ancient human liberty to be deficient in its function or to offer half-truth for the whole.

* *St. Louis Post-Dispatch Symposium on Freedom of the Press, 1938*, p. 13.

The situation approaches a dilemma. The press must remain private and free, *ergo* human and fallible; but the press dare no longer indulge in fallibility—it must supply the public need. Here, again, there is no perfect solution. But the important thing is that the press accept the public standard and try for it. The legal right will stand if the moral right is realized or tolerably approximated. There is a point beyond which failure to realize the moral right will entail encroachment by the state upon the existing legal right.

XV. THE ENDURING GOAL AND THE VARIABLE REALIZATION

A free press is not a passing goal of human society; it is a necessary goal. For the press, taken in sum, is the swift self-expression of the experience of each moment of history; and this expression ought to be true. Much of the content of the press is intended solely for its own day; and the journalist sometimes reflects that his art is one of improvisation, and that its products, being destined to pass with the interest of the moment, require no great care in their workmanship. Yet, just because it is the day's report of itself, it is the permanent word of that day to all other days. The press must be free because its freedom is a condition of its veracity, and its veracity is its good faith with the total record of the human spirit.

At the same time, freedom of the press is certainly not an isolated value, nor can it mean the same in every society and at all times. It is a function within a society and must vary with the social context. It will be different in times of general security and in times of crisis; it will be different under varying states of public emotion and belief.

The freedom we have been examining has assumed a type of public mentality which may seem to us standard and universal, but which is, in many respects, a product of our special history—a mentality accustomed to the noise and confusion of clashing opinions and reasonably stable in temper when the fortunes of ideas are swiftly altered. But what a mind does with a fact or an opinion is widely different when that mind is serene and when it is anxious; when it has confidence in its environment and when it is infected with suspicion or resentment; when it is gullible and when it is well furnished with the means of criticism; when it has hope and when it is in despair.

Further, the consumer is a different man when he has to judge his press alone and when his judgment is steadied by other social agencies. Free and diverse utterance may result in bewilderment unless he has access —through home, church, school, custom—to interpreting patterns of thought and feeling. There is no such thing as press "objectivity" unless the mind of the reader can identify the objects dealt with.

Whether at any time and place the psychological conditions exist under which a free press has social significance is always a question of fact, not of theory. These mental conditions may be lost. They may also be created. The press itself is always one of the chief agents in destroying or in building the bases of its own significance.

ROBERT M. HUTCHINS

ZECHARIAH CHAFEE, JR.

JOHN M. CLARK

JOHN DICKINSON

WILLIAM E. HOCKING

HAROLD D. LASSWELL

ARCHIBALD MACLEISH

CHARLES E. MERRIAM

REINHOLD NIEBUHR

ROBERT REDFIELD

BEARDSLEY RUML

ARTHUR M. SCHLESINGER

GEORGE N. SHUSTER

4

THE AMERICAN MAGAZINE

James Playsted Wood
MAGAZINE PUBLISHING TODAY

Roland E. Wolseley
SOCIAL EFFECTS OF MAGAZINES

4

THE AMERICAN MAGAZINE

THE MOST STRIKING characteristic of the contemporary magazine does not lie in its editorial content. It is in the area of advertising. The degree of success or failure in securing advertising is a matter of life or death for almost every mass circulation periodical. Other mass media have made serious inroads into the economics of magazine publishing, simply by cutting into the advertising revenue of almost all national magazines. The result has been the demise of some major American magazines over the past decade, while others—once giants—are in a precarious situation.

Some observers claim that this change was inevitable and that the inroads of other media have been largely fortuitous and incidental. The fact remains that, whatever the basic reasons, magazines showed a significant loss in revenue for several years and have had to undertake their own agonizing re-appraisal as television became the world's largest advertising medium. Like the movies, however, this has resulted in an improvement in magazine publishing from an editorial viewpoint. Challenged, many magazines have developed more definitive personalities of their own. But most significant has been the increase in interest on the part of the public in the more seriously edited publications. Despite problems of circulation due to competition and increased costs, the American magazine is still big business and the editorial influence of the major publications on public opinion is enormous.

In his consideration of the magazine, James P. Wood examines these publications by type. Certain general changes, responding to the needs of contemporary readers, have been recognized—shorter and more pithy articles, emphasis on popular culture, articles of a quasi-educational nature, greater emphasis on pictorial values, attractive make-up and increased stepping-up of promotional activities. Such publications as *Harpers* and *The Atlantic* continue to attract discriminating readers, while relatively newer publications like *The Reporter* and rejuvenated ones such as *The Saturday Review* are finding a selective audience. *The Saturday Review*, in keeping with the interest in mass media, has added a communication section to its articles and book reviews. Special publications, such as business and professional magazines, also continue to attract specialized publics.

In the main, however, the popular magazine has not had easy sledding. It would be extremely difficult to start a new magazine today—almost as difficult as it would be to publish a newspaper. Competition and costs make both such ventures too risky to undertake. Indeed, the major mass circulation magazines, like the movies, have had to do considerable reorientation in order to maintain respectable circulation and advertising.

The problems of the popular magazine have given added significance to the stature of the more serious publications. The well-edited and thought-provoking publications have attracted a growing public and have become increasingly important in the area of public opinion. As organs of enlightenment, as grist for a thoughtful public, these magazines have made their mark in the world of ideas.

The social effects of magazines tend to parallel, to some extent, similar effects of other mass media. These effects depend, of course, on the orientation of the audience, but there is a qualitative difference between the magazine reader and the audience for other mass media. As Roland Wolseley indicates, the magazine reader tends to respond more overtly, there is more "intellectualizing over the content of the magazine" than, for example, the daily newspaper. This is because there is always a strong possibility of opinion change as a result of reading the magazine, particularly with respect to the more seriously oriented magazines.

Professor Wolseley points out that the editor of the better magazine writes and edits with a specific end in view. His purpose is to influence his reader, to create a "social effect" upon his audience. The question, still widely debated, is whether magazines ought to be edited with such specific social effect as an end in view. These publications have a more selective public. Next to the book, they command a relatively small audience in terms of mass media. Furthermore, the magazine can be re-read and pondered over. It can stimulate social discussion and controversy out of which consensus may emerge.

The social purpose of magazines depends in turn on their economic and editorial objectives. The more popular the objective, the less of an endowed educational institution the magazine will tend to be. Its purpose is human interest. But even the more serious magazines, if they are to command audience, cannot ignore the eternal trilogy of advertising-promotion-editorial, each of which impinges upon and influences the other. Some students of the American magazine have concluded that magazine publications, of all the mass media, have the greatest social effect—although, as television continues to mature and refine its informational techniques, it must undoubtedly be considered in terms of its significant contribution to an informed public opinion.

There is need for more intensive research on the effects of magazines to parallel earlier studies on the newspaper and on radio listening. Like other media, the magazine gives the reader partly what the reader wants and partly what the editor would like the reader to have. Only through this kind of interaction can either the magazine or the newspaper stay in business. But what a magazine is and what it ought to be in terms of its social impact is the basic responsibility of its editors and publishers. The ultimate responsibility rests with its management. Whether the proposal of Dr. Lazarsfeld ("the best solution would be to have mass media aimed just slightly above what would be the simplest level at any time") is pragmatically possible still remains to be determined. Most magazines, in recent years, have certainly tried to put that proposal to the test.

*   *   *   *

RELATED READING

Hoult, T. F. "Comic Books and Juvenile Delinquency," *Sociology and Social Research*, XXXIII (1949), 279-84.

Lazarsfeld, P. F., & Wyant, Rowena. "Magazines in 90 Cities—'Who reads What?'" *Public Opinion Quarterly*, 1 (1937), 29-41.

Spiegelman, Marvin; Terwilliger, Carl; and Fearing, Franklin. "The Content of Comic Strips: A Study of a Mass Medium of Communication," *Journal of Social Psychology*, XXXV (1952), 37-57.

Wolf, Katherine N., & Fiske, Marjorie. "The children talk about comics," in Lazarsfeld, P. F. & Stanton, F. N. (eds.), *Communications Research 1948-1949*, pp. 3-50. New York: Harper, 1949.

MAGAZINE PUBLISHING TODAY

By James Playsted Wood

THOUGH IT WILL not compare to basic industry, the national magazine to-day is big business. No current figure on the total gross or net income of the periodical publishing industry as a whole is available, but as long ago as 1945, the estimated total gross receipts from magazine publishing before deduction of any items of cost was $739,000,000.[1] The president of the National Association of Magazine Publishers estimated in 1947 that total magazine income would approximate or exceed one billion dollars yearly within a few years' time. It has probably done so. About a quarter of a million people, according to the NAMP president, are directly supported by the magazine industry, while two million depend on it in whole or in part for their livelihood.

There are 23 national magazines with circulations of 2 million or more, 53 with circulations exceeding 1 million.[2] More than 3¾ billion copies of magazines are sold every year. In 1955 the total per issue circulation of all the 267 members of the Audit Bureau of Circulations was 166 million. This contrasts with a figure of less than 18 million copies per issue in 1914, when the A. B. C. was founded with 54 general and farm magazines reporting. During and since World War II magazine circulation has increased 62 per cent, and magazine advertising has mounted year by year. Over $653,400,000 was spent for national advertising in magazines in 1955.[3] The number of large advertisers has also risen; in 1954, 2,163 advertisers spent more than $25,000 each for advertising in magazines.[4]

Despite these increases in circulation and in advertising revenue, magazine profits have fallen as a result of mounting production and distribution costs. Second-class postal rates, accorded newspapers and magazines by the Postal Act of 1879, have been increased by Congressional leg-

[1] The Magazine Publishing Industry in the United States, 1945," Bureau of the Census, Department of Commerce, October 6, 1947.
[2] Farm magazines included; comics excluded. A. B. C. figures.
[3] Leading National Advertisers, Inc.
[4] *Sales Management*, October 15, 1955.

islation; rates now are almost one-third higher than in 1951; and there is pressure, fought by the magazine publishers, for further increases. Subscription and single-copy prices of magazines and the rates charged for magazine advertising space have not increased in proportion to magazine publishing expenses or in ratio with the price advance of most other commodities. Magazine net profit, profit after taxes as a percentage of sales, stood at about 6.7 per cent in the middle 1930's. This figure climbed during the war years, profitable years for magazines, to 8.3 per cent in 1946. It has gradually declined since that time. Although a few publishers are earning more, magazine net profits averaged 2.8 per cent in 1954.[5]

The number of magazines stays constant at over 7,000, though the mass periodicals are concentrated in the hands of a relatively few large publishers. The Curtis Publishing Company covers the general weekly, the women's, the recreational, and the children's field with *The Saturday Evening Post, Ladies' Home Journal, Holiday,* and *Jack and Jill.* Its subsidiary, the Curtis Circulation Company, distributes an additional fourteen magazines, including *Harper's,* the *Atlantic, Look, Esquire, Coronet, American Home,* and *Field and Stream.* Time, Inc., has *Time, Life, Fortune, Architectural Forum, House and Home,* and *Sports Illustrated.* The Crowell-Collier Publishing Company has a general biweekly and a general monthly as well as a woman's monthly: *The American Magazine,* and *Woman's Home Companion.*[6] Hearst Magazines, Inc., has *Good Housekeeping, Harper's Bazaar, House Beautiful, Cosmopolitan,* and *Town and Country;* while the McCall Corporation publishes *Redbook* in addition to *McCall's Magazine;* and Meredith Publishing Company puts out *Successful Farming* and *Better Homes and Gardens. Reader's Digest,* biggest of them all, *Farm Journal* and *Town Journal,* the farm periodicals of Capper Publications, the publication of Esquire, Inc., and the large Macfadden group (detective story magazines, magazines retailing true life stories, and their ilk) must be added to the list of magazines and publishers reaching very large circulations.

It is a far cry from the days when a magazine editor and publisher could almost count, as could Noah Webster, on the early financial failure of his venture. It is a far cry, too, from the days when magazine contributors were unpaid, or the days, a little later, when Edgar Allan Poe was paid ten dollars for "The Raven" by the *American Review.* Longfellow sometimes received twenty dollars a poem from *Graham's,* and Lowell got ten dollars at first, more somewhat later. When Lowell himself became an editor, he paid such contributors as Emerson, Longfellow, and Bryant about five dollars a page for their work in the *Atlantic.* "Couldn't you," he wrote in 1864, as editor of *The North American Review,* to John Lothrop Motley, who was then minister to Austria, "Write on the natural

---

[5] Magazine Publishers Association.
[6] These two magazines have since gone out of publication.

history of the diplomatic cuttlefish of Schleswig-Holstein without forfeiting your ministerial equanimity?" Again he offered five dollars a page.

Today the mass magazines compete with each other in purchasing manuscripts, usually the memoirs of public men, at announced prices running into the hundreds of thousands of dollars. A magazine paid $60,000 for "Admiral Halsey Tells His Story," $175,000 for the war diary of General Eisenhower, and $102,000 to another general and his collaborator for their series of six articles on World War II. Though no price was announced, *Life, The New York Times,* and a book publisher are reported to have paid $1,000,000 for Winston Churchill's war memoirs. *The Saturday Evening Post* paid $100,000 for Lindbergh's "33 Hours to Paris," and $75,000 for Bing Crosby's "Call Me Lucky." Press reports stated that ex-President Truman was paid about $600,000 for his memoirs which were published in *Life.*

The larger magazines pay from a few hundred dollars up to $1,500 for a single story or article, and up to $2,500 for a cover painting. *The New Yorker,* though it has a comparatively small circulation, pays regular contributors fifteen to thirty cents a word, half as much again for pieces of less than 2,000 words, and an additional bonus of 25 per cent to writers placing six or more pieces with the magazine in the same year. The *Post* pays $750 for the first article accepted from a writer; $850 for the first short story. *Reader's Digest* pays writers of articles condensed from other magazines a minimum of $200 a *Digest* page. After a free-lance writer has sold the *Digest* five articles, he gets an additional $500 bonus on every article he sells the magazine. *Ladies' Home Journal* pays a minimum of $850 for short stories.

Rufus Wilmot Griswold's salary as editor of *Graham's* was $1,000 a year. James Russell Lowell received what was at the time the very large salary of $2,500 as editor of *The Atlantic Monthly.* The salary proved more than the magazine could support. A chief reason for supplanting Lowell with James T. Fields, a member of the firm which then published the *Atlantic,* was to save this salary. The successful editors of the modern national magazines receive salaries reputed to be somewhat larger. According to a fact sheet released by *The Saturday Evening Post* in 1954, "Editorial pay ranges downward from the editor's salary of more than $100,000 a year." Top editors of *The Reader's Digest* get both large salaries and large bonuses. Roving editors get $10,000 to $20,000 a year, travel expenses, and a minimum of $1,200 for each piece accepted.

The product put forth by an industry of this size cannot be manufactured by hit-or-miss methods. Every device is used to insure a product which will be approved by the mass public which it serves and which supports it. Modern means of assistance to editorial judgment are in use throughout magazine activity. National sample surveys are used to measure public reaction to magazine contents. The purpose of these interviews, conducted through personal interrogation and by mail, is to discover what stories, articles, and features are read, how closely they are read, and by what kinds of people. Editors use the findings to help them decide what new departments to inaugurate or what old ones to drop, and what types of fiction and articles will be most widely and appreciatively read. Through reader research, now in use by almost all the larger magazines, the editors can discover what magazine covers their audience likes best, what stories men prefer, which women like best, and a hundred other things; and the knowledge thus gained serves as a guide in the selection of new material for publication. Each month *Reader's Digest* queries 4,000 of its subscribers on their likes and dislikes in a current issue. Personal interviews are conducted among a sample of the magazine's readers every month on *The Saturday Evening Post*. Several of the women's magazines have used this poll and sampling technique to discover what women think about subjects often avoided in magazine discussion—divorce, moral standards, birth control—and to find out what material, outside the purely domestic sphere, women wish to read. Months of such research into the probable audience and market go into the planning before any new large magazine is inaugurated. Painstaking work of this type was done before *Holiday* began publication in 1946. Research is done monthly on every *Holiday* issue. "Reader research," the executive editor of a weekly magazine remarked somewhat ruefully, "has become a great leveler among editors."

With such a research device at their disposal, it might be thought that editors now can put out their magazines by slide rule and tabulating machine, avoiding by simple arithmetic the possibility of serious errors in editorial judgment. It is conceivable that they could. It is fortunate that they do not, for the tendency would undoubtedly be to level downward to the lowest common denominator and to publish only writing of some kind approved in the past, as there is yet no reliable way of estimating the potential readership of new material.

Editors accept or reject the findings of reader research in the light of their experience and editorial judgment. They will deliberately publish a story or an article whose value they recognize, despite foreknowledge that it will have a low readership. In doing so they are motivated not so much by an altruistic desire to raise the public taste as by an intent to maintain and improve the editorial quality of their individual magazines. Competition among magazines for vital material in itself obviates the possibility of dependence upon mechanical editing. The modern magazine editor practices what is still very much an art and not an exact science. Reader research is an aid to editorial judgment, not a substitute; but it is an aid which the editor is finding helpful as a quick and useful check on features and qualities of his periodical.

When he visited the United States in 1908, Lord Northcliffe, originator of the tabloid, astute publisher of the *London Daily Mail* and *The Times* [London], was outspoken in his opinion that even then American magazines were "infinitely better than those of England." The next great advance in American magazine production, he prophesied, would take place when some method of printing photographs accurately in color could be devised. His prophecy was correct. The increased use of full color, the increased emphasis on graphics generally, is one of the most noticeable changes in the modern magazine. Not only the picture magazines like *Life* and *Look* but the general weeklies and monthlies, the women's magazines, the shelter magazines, and the fashion magazines are using more and more photographs both in black and white and in color. In all of these magazines, color photography has become not an added decoration but an essential editorial element. The increased use of photographs and more profuse use of illustration have been accompanied by a general streamlining and refurbishing of the mass magazines. Type faces have been modernized, new logotypes devised to replace older ones. Margins have disappeared with the increased use of bleed for color and picture pages.[7] Physically the national magazine has been made as attractive as expert photography and reproduction, expert makeup and printing, expert styling, and capable art work, done for both editorial and advertising use by the country's finest illustrators, can make it.

The change is more than superficial. All the sensuous appeal of color and art work is being used by the magazine, used skillfully and with psychological knowledge carefully applied. The whole appeal of the mass magazines has become one of speed. Articles have been shortened to balance the quickness of impression provided by pictures. Magazine fiction, too, has been shortened. The ratio of articles to fiction has been increased. Clarity, brevity, and sharpness have been substituted for prolixity, in some cases for thoroughness. A greater variety of short features, cartoons, quips, puzzles, has been introduced, and the accent on timeliness has been stressed.

The American public has proved that it will read, at least tolerate and support, a great variety of magazines. It has shown its favor to long-established periodicals, to certain relatively new magazines, and to some so changed in content and format as to seem new. It accepts the pretentious, the cultural, and at the other extreme, the crudest of periodical publications. There is the simple fact that the United States population is far larger than it was, and is growing rapidly. It is affluent and can afford to indulge its fancies. The spread and dilution of education has at least made

[7] Too often page numbers seem also to have disappeared. Full bleed pages are not numbered, nor are full pages in four-color. On other type pages, numbers are shifted from the upper outside corner to the bottom middle of the page, or to some other position where they are almost impossible to detect. There are mechanical reasons for this annoyance, but it often seems as though a magazine has been made up by someone careless of arithmetic or by a layout editor who just does not like people.

more people susceptible to print and pictures in pleasing format. Acceptance of certain of these magazines by at least a substantial segment of the population that reads at all reflects something of our changing social interests. The response to others reflects the perennial appeal of other subject matter to basic humankind.

One of the most outstanding of the post-World War II magazines is *Holiday*, founded in 1946. Calling itself a "class-mass" magazine, it steadily maintains a substantial circulation of about 850,000. *Holiday*, the elaborate, lushly dressed, fifty-cent Curtis-owned magazine, is difficult to classify. It is not a fashion magazine, a travel magazine, a shelter book, or a literary monthly, though it shows some of the aspects of all of these. It has some of the glamour of *Vogue*, some of the substance of *National Geographic*, some, though it is worn unsurely, of *The New Yorker's* urbanity. It falls into none of the established magazine categories. In part, this may be because *Holiday* is devoted not to a particular subject or directed to a specific audience, but is based on a practically indefinable concept, the concept of leisure and recreation. It is published on the factual premise that the mid-twentieth century American has an increased and increasing amount of leisure time, and edited with the conviction that there are certain ways in which he can be taught to use it gracefully.

Holiday describes itself as "the magazine of creative leisure." Its purpose is to instruct people how best to use the new leisure with which they are blessed or confounded. In the words of Ted Patrick, its editor, "Creative use of leisure time includes travel, but also other activities . . . all sports, the theater, movies, television and radio, music, painting or writing indulged in as a pastime, the reading of good books, the preparation and pursuit of food, party-giving and attending, the fixing of one's home to make it more rewarding and relaxing to live in, and the making or acquisition of the clothing best designed for any of these activities."

This description about fits the *Holiday* menu. Served for the aspiring epicure and *bon vivant*, the correctly attired lawn or field sportsman, the self-conscious cosmopolitan, and the suburbanite who would be socially sophisticated, the menu offers caviar, the approved wines, and some more substantial fare, usually in a night-club setting.

Place articles are the *Holiday pièces de résistance*. They are full, informative, sometimes charming, sometimes pretentious, often seductive —objective and subjective descriptions of Atlanta or Rome, café and resort society in Philadelphia or on Capri, the romance of Africa, Asia, Indianapolis, or Kansas City. Most of these pieces are pleasantly and skillfully written. Some are superficial and brilliant; others, like the E. B. White piece on New York (April, 1949), J. P. Marquand on Boston (November, 1953), and Frank O'Connor on Ireland (December, 1949), have greater depth, strength, and virtue.

Holiday standards of writing are high, and the magazine uses some of

the best and best-known writers of the day: Faulkner, Dunsany, Hemingway, Steinbeck, O'Faolain, Joyce Cary. More characteristic of the magazine's tone and attempt are Bemelmans, Perelman, Fadiman, Lucius
Beebe, Strong, Michener, Guthrie, Schulberg, Wechsberg, and Jerome
Weidman. *Holiday* has published notable issues on Paris (April, 1953),
on Italy (April, 1955), on London (April, 1956). From the standpoint
of layout, illustration, and reproduction, every issue of *Holiday* is attractive. Photographically, *Holiday* compares favorably with the best of
its competitors.

The McGraw-Hill Publishing Company, founded in 1917 by the merger of two older organizations, is a unique and greatly influential periodical
publishing enterprise, the country's largest publisher of technical, scientific, and business magazines. Through a subsidiary company, the McGraw-
Hill Book Company, which has over 3,500 active titles and publishes perhaps 300 new books a year, it is also one of the country's largest book
publishers. Currently McGraw-Hill issues twenty-nine industrial, trade,
and technical magazines, most of them the best-known publications in the
fields they cover. *American Machinist, Chemical Engineering, Electrical
Merchandising, Electrical World, Engineering News-Record, Engineering and Mining Journal, Textile World,* and a few of the others are old
and highly respected magazines with reputations transcending their immediate fields of interest. McGraw-Hill can well claim to have kept pace
with, and perhaps even assisted, the advance of technology, engineering,
and business in the United States.

In 1929 McGraw-Hill established *Business Week.* The company's
other magazines deal with specific management, engineering, production,
maintenance, and selling functions in business. They are intended as
vehicles to communicate applicable information to men at work within
given industries or professions. *Business Week,* described by its publishers
as "essentially a news service," has by the nature of its coverage a wider
appeal. Because business in some form is the primary American occupation and preoccupation, the magazine's emphasis on business and its handling of most subjects from an economic viewpoint makes it function in
some degrees as an important news weekly.[8] Timely, accurate, authorita-
tive, *Business Week* covers production, finance, labor, and marketing. It
gives, in what has become the standard telegraphic inset form, used early
by *U. S. News,* "Washington News," "International Outlook," and "Business Outlook." The American businessman seems to thirst always for fore-
casts, tips, and the interpretations of portents; he wants the news of the
day after tomorrow, of the month after next if he can get it and anything
that gives him the impression he is "in the know." *Business Week's* "Personal Outlook" is chatty in content despite the flash form which it also

[8] Standard Rate and Data service lists *Business Week* as a consumer magazine, as well
as listing it among business publications.

wears: "Your morning grapefruit will have 10% more juice this year.
. . . Note for football fans: At your bookstore now is one of the more
vivid histories of the game's development. . . . Try daffodils for an effective display on sloping lawns. . . . Tip for your wife. Here are a few
hints to help avoid unscrupulous salesmen. . . ."

Featured articles in *Business Week,* whether on automation, television, or the crowded Ohio River (illustrated in full color), are full and informative. In terms of advertising revenue, which was estimated at over
$14.5 million for 1954, *Business Week* has become by far the largest busi-
ness magazine in the United States.[9]

Business Week does well at one pole of American interest, the office,
the plant, the job. Another magazine, its success renowned in the trade,
does as well at the other pole of American interest, the home.

There are a number of handsome "shelter" magazines. Some are older
and more pretentious, affect a more patrician pose and appeal. None has
achieved greater popular success in recent years than *Better Homes & Gardens,* founded 1922 and published in Des Moines by the Meredith Publishing Company. Heavy, thick with advertising, diversified in skillfully
chosen editorial content, *Better Homes & Gardens* has a monthly circulation of well over 4,000,000.

Since World War II the United States has been building houses at an
unprecedented rate. Through G.I. loans purchase was made easy for ex-
servicemen. Small down payments and small monthly charges have brought
new houses within the range of most people. Home ownership has become the rule even among people of an age and income scale which previously would have caused delay in the acquisition of a new house. Social
conditions are such that an attractive and practical magazine about the
home appeals to a wide audience. Founded by E. T. Meredith, who had
been Wilson's Secretary of Agriculture, with idealistic pronouncements
about the home and its place in American life, *Better Homes & Gardens* is
a very practical success.

When the magazine was twenty-five years old it printed a folksy editorial statement in which it could claim that for years it had printed more
about food than any other magazine in the world, that one out of four subscribers clipped and saved its recipes—560,000,000 clipped recipes in ten
years. A study had found it the magazine gardeners most often turned to
for help. It was the magazine most read by families building new homes.
More than a million families had used the complete home-planning centers
set up by the magazine with department stores in various cities. Five to six
thousand people wrote the magazine monthly "for help on anything from
smoky fireplaces to keeping frogs through the winter." [10] Every month

---

9 "McGraw-Hill," *Barron's,* February 7, 1955. *Barron's* called *Business Week* "the work-
horse of the [McGraw-Hill] company."
10 *Better Homes & Gardens,* September, 1947.

Better Homes describes in detail a "Five Star" home. Complete plans and specifications after designs by leading architects are offered for $7.50. Hundreds of thousands of these plans have been sold. Most popular of all was Number 2001, published in January, 1950. By March, 1955, 28,982 sets of plans for this house had been sold. This one house plan has accounted for the building of almost 6,000 homes for a total building cost of nearly $120,000,000. Some 3,600 families still planned to build Number 2001 at a future estimated building cost of another $73,000,000.

Hundreds of homes have been remodeled, miles of landscaping have been done, scores of community beautification projects have been undertaken and completed, thousands of shrubs and trees have been planted as a result of *Better Homes* contests, advice, and suggestions. The magazine, which does a thorough job of reader and marketing research as a continuing program, gives its readers plenty of luscious illustrations, plenty of how-to-do-it hints, plenty of practical home remodeling ideas, plenty of articles on family problems, plenty of green-thumb tips on bulbs, perennials, parasites, and sprays, and takes in plenty of profitable advertising. *Better Homes* holds first place in advertising revenue among all monthly magazines.

Two other magazines, one new, the other revamped, are comparable neither in size, focal interest, nor influence on things material to those just discussed. They do not tell anybody how to do anything, not even how to succeed. They do not read the future. One carries no advertising; the other, little. The point is that the American public will respond to other appeals besides those of play, work, and home. It will patronize, if not extravagantly, publications of a very different kind from *Holiday*, *Newsweek*, and *Better Homes & Gardens*.

From 1920 to 1924 Yale professor of English Henry Seidel Canby edited the Saturday night *Literary Review*, a supplement of the *New York Evening Post*. On the staff of the *Post*, writing a column called "The Bowling Green," was Christopher Morley. In 1924 the *Literary Review* broke away from the *Post* and became *The Saturday Review of Literature* with Henry Seidel Canby as editor and Christopher Morley and William Rose Benét as associates. Under Canby, who retired as editor in 1936 but is still chairman of the magazine's editorial board,* *The Saturday Review of Literature*, which had a difficult time financially for some years, was a thin, scholarly paper, on newsprint, primarily a collection of book reviews. Bernard De Voto succeeded Canby as editor. In 1942 the editorship went to Norman Cousins, who for two years had been the magazine's executive editor and before that managing editor of *Current History*. Since that time *The Saturday Review* has dropped "of Literature" from its title and bravely has taken all culture within reach for its province.

The Saturday Review covers travel, music, recordings, television, and

* Henry Canby died.

movies as well as the new books. It has liberal opinions. It fights for causes. It seems to consider its mission the dispensation of knowledge and the generation of ideas. It is still very literary but seems more vital. Page size cut down, slick paper front and back, illustrated with line cuts and halftones, it looks more like a magazine than the supplement from which it stemmed. Popular opinion used to link *The Saturday Review* with the Sunday *Herald Tribune* "Books" and *The New York Times Book Review*. *The Saturday Review* has left this group to become a periodical entity. It carries signed articles as well as reviews, the humor of Bennett Cerf, anagrams, cryptograms, the mellow conversation of bibliophiles, and pieces which its table of contents lists proudly as "SR Ideas." Even its book reviews are not merely reviews. *The Saturday Review* takes literary criticism seriously as an art in itself. The "personals" in its classified advertising columns, long the warmest and most amusing page of the publication, seem less colorful. The magazine calls itself now a "magazine of ideas, entertainment, and the arts." *Time* has called it a bookworm that turned and described it as "a sort of last haven for the sprightly American essay." [11] Like the *Atlantic* and *Harper's* (and it is not far behind the older monthlies in its weekly circulation), *The Saturday Review* carries a kind of hallmark of prestige for readers who take their culture seriously in conversation. A point at issue when Henry Seidel Canby and his fellows started what used to be referred to affectionately as the *SRL* was to see whether the United States would support a purely literary weekly. The answer, apparent in the revamped magazine, is that it can and does; in moderation, of course. It is in great moderation that nationally circulated magazines of literature, ideas, and the arts are tolerated in mid-twentieth century United States. The *Atlantic*, *Harper's*, and *The Saturday Review* are about all there is, where a generation ago there were also *Scribner's*, *The North American Review*, *The Dial*, the *Forum*, and the *Century*.

In December, 1954, appeared the first handsome issue of *American Heritage*, a bimonthly magazine between hard covers, with full color illustrations, no advertising, and a subscription price of $12 a year; single copies, $2.95. *American Heritage* had been founded in 1949 by the American Association for State and Local History. About to founder, it was combined with a projected magazine called *History*, planned as organ of the Society of American Historians. Backed by both organizations, the new *American Heritage* is dedicated to history. Its editor, Bruce Catton, Civil War historian, said in a preface to the first issue that it was published in ". . . the belief that our heritage is best understood by a study of things that the ordinary folk of America have done and thought and dreamed since they first began to live here. Our beat is . . . anything that ever happened in America."

Contributors to *American Heritage* are popular historians, commenta-

11 "A Bookworm Turned," August 1, 1949. The bookworm has really not turned much.

tors on American manners and mores, novelists, and politicians: Allan Nevins, Carl Carmer, Paul Horgan, Adlai Stevenson, Mark Van Doren, Bernard De Voto. History here is dramatized as colorful narrative and incident. During its first year the magazines described the boyhood and youth of Alexander Hamilton, gave a previously unknown account of the death of John Brown, a medical report on George Washington, a Civil War correspondent's story of an off-duty Grant during the siege of Vicksburg, and published Albert Lasker's account of his life in advertising. Unlikely as it seems, public response to an expensive magazine of limited appeal made the venture a quick success. The print order for *American Heritage*, sold in bookstores as well as through subscription, went from 55,000 for the first issue to 115,500 a year later.

Another large group of magazines does better than that. If the circulation they have attained and the hold they have on their addicts is reasonable evidence, they reflect even more of what the United States approves and prefers to read than *Holiday*, *Newsweek*, *Better Homes & Gardens*, *The Saturday Review*, and *American Heritage* combined. Harried and bedeviled, attacked as depraved, violent, sadistic, obscene, accused of fomenting juvenile delinquency, preying on the immaturity of adults, and pandering to the lowest instincts and impulses of the human animal, the so-called "comic books" sell at the rate of 60 to 90 million copies a month.[12]

The comic magazines are an offshoot of the newspaper comic strips and pages which began late in the last century in the New York *World* with R. F. Outcault's "Yellow Kid." He took the Kid to the *New York Journal*, later developed the famous Buster Brown for the *New York Herald*. Today's Superman, L'il Abner, Blondie, Orphan Annie, *et al.* are direct descendants of Buster Brown, Foxy Grandpa, Happy Hooligan, and the rest. The comics have been powerful circulation builders for the newspapers for a long time. The comic monthly magazine originated in the 1930's when the Eastern Color Printing Company in New York, printers of Sunday newspaper comic supplements, conceived the idea of printing comics in book form in small page size. They successfully published *Funnies on Parade*, and followed that with *Famous Funnies*, issued for distribution through variety stories. The book proved so popular that the publishers began to put it out monthly. Then came the deluge. By 1950 a Fawcett Comics Group advertisement could be headlined in true comic book style: "The comic magazines bought each month laid end to end would reach 1/25th the space from the earth to the moon." [13]

The agitation against the worst of the comic books started in magazines.[14] Horror and crime comics have been condemned in the newspaper

[12] *Barron's*, January 17, 1955. *Time*, September 27, 1954, said 80 million; the New York *Herald Tribune*, December 29, 1954, said 60 million. Accurate circulation figures are available only for those comic magazine publishers reporting to the Audit Bureau of Circulations.

[13] Advertisement in *Advertising Age*, May 8, 1950.

[14] "What Parents Don't Know About Comic Books," by Frederic Wertham, M. D.,

press. Parents' groups rose in protest against them. The comics have been legislated against in a dozen states, banned from the newsstands of some large cities, policed in others. Leading comic book publishers were quizzed by a Senate subcommittee on juvenile delinquency. Under fire and complaining bitterly that their attackers did not discriminate between good and bad comic magazines, they formed the Comics Magazine Association of America and appointed a New York magistrate, who had specialized in juvenile delinquency, to act as czar and censor for the industry.

As a result of all this agitation by outraged public opinion, some of the worst of the horror comics ceased publication. Others edited out some of their more offensive material. In England, where millions of copies of American comic magazines had been reprinted each month, the activity came to an end.[15] There has been a considerable reduction in the number of comic book titles reaching the newsstands. There had been overproduction, anyway, both in number of titles—as many as 350 in one month—and in number of copies of a title printed. The newsstands could not handle them all.

The comics have been seriously defended as a new kind of American folklore, as a survival of primitive adventure narrative. They have been looked upon as inheritors of the tradition of the dime novel, now sanctified in wreaths of nostalgia. The comic technique has been praised for its educational uses. The comic magazine idea has been used as a teaching device by both the army and the navy and for purposes of government propaganda. Literary classics and Bible stories are presented in comic magazines. Used in these ways, the comics have been defended as exerting a benevolent social force.[16] As it usually is when censorship is applied or threatened, "the freedom of the press" has been invoked, this time by the indignant publishers of "good" comic books. The one thing which, in all the dispute, no one has called the comic magazines is comical. Humor is seldom their intent.

The comic books provide breathtaking, fantastic adventure, prolonging suspense until the hero finally triumphs over a long, long series of obstacles. The comics, a psychologist explains, are picture-story fantasies

---

Ladies' Home Journal, November, 1953. The article came out in book form as *Seduction of the Innocent* and was condensed by *Reader's Digest*, May, 1954. The *Digest* also published another exposé, "The Face of Violence" by T. E. Murphy, in November, 1954. In the horror comics, magazines have an example of magazine influence which they would gladly disavow. Reputable and responsible magazines have done their best to correct an abuse of the power of the periodical press.

[15] One of the two big English publishers of comic magazines said the outcry against his wares had made it so difficult to get comics printed and distributed that his costs had become prohibitive. He pointed out that the comic magazines were not intended for children anyway. Among his customers, he said, were two army colonels, some majors, and a number of people in public life. "An analysis of my sales would almost certainly reveal that the main readers are young married women with too much time on their hands." "Britons Drop Publication of Horror Comics," *Advertising Age*, December 6, 1954.

[16] Sidonic Matsner Gruenberg, "The Comics as a Social Force," *The Journal of Educational Sociology*, December, 1944.

appealing directly to human desires and aspirations, to wish fulfillment. "Superman and his innumerable followers satisfy the universal human longing to be stronger than all opposing obstacles . . . to experience vicariously the supreme gratification of the *deus ex machina* who accomplishes these monthly miracles of right triumphing over not-so-mighty might.[17] It all depends, the moralist might add, on what kinds of wishes are to be fulfilled and what kinds of obstacles overcome.

Whatever the ethical, moral, or civic solution to the problem, the comic magazines prevail. Dell, the largest publisher, has a circulation of over 9,000,000 for its group, which includes: *Gene Autry, Tom and Jerry, Little Lulu, Mickey Mouse, Donald Duck, Lone Ranger, Roy Rogers,* and *Tarzan*—all very respectable characters. National Comics, which issues 49 titles, has a circulation of over 6,000,000. *Bob Hope, Nutsy Squirrel, Martin and Lewis,* and *Mr. District Attorney* are all in the National Comics stable. Marvel Comics, with 59 titles, among them *Annie Oakley, Black Rider, My Friend Irma,* and *Cowboy Action,* has a circulation of nearly 5,000,000. Harvey Comics, with *Joe Palooka, Little Audrey, Dick Tracy, Blondie, Dagwood, Ripley's Believe It Or Not,* and 20 other titles, go to over 4,000,000 buyers for each issue.

Whether the comic magazines are the textbooks in crime and depravity many think them or educational periodicals with traditions going back to paleolithic times, as their admirers claim, they are read. Seemingly, at this stage in the cultural development of the United States these crudely written, crudely illustrated and reproduced magazines gratify the literary and artistic tastes of a large part of the population. In 1946 Professor Harvey Zorbaugh of the School of Education, New York University, stated that at post exchanges during World War II comic books outsold *The Saturday Evening Post, Life,* and *Reader's Digest* combined by ten to one. A study done by *Puck* in 1948 showed that four out of five American adults read comics. No more than in England are comic magazines read only by children and adolescents, though one study by Marvel Comics showed over 90 per cent readership for boys and girls aged eight to sixteen. According to survey results released by the Bureau of Public Administration of the University of California in 1955, about $100 million is spent yearly for about one billion copies of comic magazines. They are read by one quarter of American high school graduates, 16 per cent of the country's college graduates, and 12 per cent of its teachers.[18]

Magazine publishing today is larger than ever it was. Profits have fallen, but the industry's product is diversified, pervasive, and influential; and like any other commodity, it is accepted in proportion to its ability to please the many or the few.

[17] William Moulton Marston, "Why 100,000,000 Americans Read Comics," *The American Scholar,* Winter 1943-44.
[18] Survey findings reported in *Time,* March 1, 1955, and *The Reader's Digest,* June 1955.

SOCIAL EFFECTS OF MAGAZINES

By Roland E. Wolseley

FREDERICK LEWIS ALLEN, editor of *Harper's*,* once described a frequent editorial experience: "We at *Harper's* are called from time to time, communists, fascists, New Dealers, reactionaries; brutally savage toward the nation's enemies, pacifistically tender toward the nation's enemies; anti-Russian, anti-British; victims of conspiratorial propaganda of the Russians, of the British; anti-business, anti-farmer, or the tools of each." [1]

Every once in a while the editors of *Time* print letters that fall into two distinct groups of reactions to some article. One set of writers interprets a particular article as having a given bias. Another bevy of correspondents succeeds in finding the opposite bias in the same article. An example was a long feature on the Puerto Ricans in New York City. One letter called the article "a sensible report," even expressed gratitude for it. Another, the same week, said "Shame on your article," accused the magazine of being as sensational as the tabloid New York *Daily News*, and complained that the Puerto Ricans of Gotham were being attacked by *Time*, which now had "at last put in its two cents of cowardice." [2]

Editors who get such reactions may well think they have succeeded in being impartial. In any case they are having a social effect; they are reaching people's minds.

At times, no doubt, any editor would prefer such outright praise as Francis Parkman gave Edwin Lawrence Godkin of *The Nation:*

"I have always regarded *The Nation* as the most valuable of all American journals, and I ought to know, for I have read every number since it first appeared. I feel—and others feel also—that every educated and right-minded American is doubly in your debt." [3]

---

* The current editor of *Harper's* is John Fischer.
[1] Frederick Lewis Allen, "The Function of a Magazine in America," address prepared for delivery at the Thirty-sixth annual Journalism Week, University of Missouri. *University of Missouri Bulletin*, Vol. 46, No. 23, Journalism Series No. 101. Aug. 10, 1945.
[2] Letters. *Time*, July 3, 1950, p. 2.
[3] Rollo Ogden, *Life and Letters of Edwin Lawrence Godkin*. New York: Macmillan, 1907, pp. 251-2.

But if the magazinist believes that a man is known by his enemies, and if he has not made many an enemy among wrongdoers, he may tire of complimentary letters and be eager for some that find fault. The magazine publisher, writer, or editor does not work in a vacuum, nor can he for long content himself with making (or losing) money. His presence in journalism, in fact, is likely to mean that he has other motives: to express himself, to influence others, to provide guidance or entertainment or information. He wants to have some influence upon and relationship to his day, i.e., to have a social effect.

THE MEANING OF SOCIAL EFFECT

All publications, as do all other institutions and all persons, have some social effect. Nothing, in our interdependent world, functions without bearing directly or indirectly upon society or some segment of it. A magazine publishing company may or may not be a social institution, that is, one with a social purpose. Whether a magazine firm should have a social purpose at all or whether such a purpose should be the main reason for being is a constantly debated matter.

A social institution may be defined as one devoted to the whole good of the whole people. Theoretically, that is the purpose of all properly run organizations. It is the guiding principle of the school, the church, the professions.

The magazine world is part of the world of business. At its best, business benefits all the people. But if a magazine publishing company is a part of an economic scheme which makes it dependent upon public support through purchase of subscriptions, single copies, and advertising space, the magazine can be socially beneficial only to the extent that this dependence permits.

William L. Chenery, for many years editor of *Collier's*, observed while speaking at the University of Virginia in 1936 that "The national magazine of mass circulation can treat only those national problems about which millions of people are willing to read. . . . [The magazine] is not an endowed educational institution. It is a business operated primarily for profit. If it does not interest its readers, it cannot endure." [4]

Therefore if the public will not read certain types of content, it will not be exposed to ideas and facts of that withheld content. Here is one of several points of contact between magazine and public that relates to the publication's social effect.

CONTENT AND SOCIAL EFFECT

The magazine, long a vigorous tool in special propaganda jobs, has been accused of a save-the-world complex. John Reed, while an assistant editor

---

[4] William Ludlow Chenery, "The Magazine and Public Opinion," address delivered at the University of Virginia, July 13, 1936. *Vital Speeches of the Day*. Aug. 15, 1936, p. 718. See also "Causes and Effects," *Collier's*, Dec. 15, 1950, p. 70.

of the *American* (before he became a famous political writer), wrote a hymn for "Everymagazine: An Immorality Play," a satirical work he produced before the Dutch Treat Club in New York in 1913:

> When God the earth created
> And saw that it was good
> He was naturally elated;
> He did the best He could.
> But not to knock Jehovah
> (He wisely used His means)
> It had to be done over
> By all us magazines.
> We do not mean to be unkind—
> How could He know the public Mind?
> We do not mean to give offense,
> He hadn't our experience.
>
>   *   *   *
>
> God made the earth and heaven
> And things that creep and crawl.
> It took but mornings seven;
> It wasn't bad at all.
> But not to criticize Him
> The world was raising hob
> Till the magazines came forward
> And finished up the job.[5]

That magazines have not saved the world needs no proving; that many have made a brave effort is easily demonstrated. General and specialized magazines alike have championed countless good causes, conducting crusades the year around. Some have given analysis and advice, others have raised money, supported political parties, undertaken exploration or under dangerous conditions sponsored investigations of crime or political corruption. A segment has explored unpopular social ideas, often surviving to see them widely accepted.

The effects, good or bad, have been accomplished largely, however, through magazine content rather than organized action. Three departments have been influential: advertising, editorial, promotion.

The advertising department has offered word, camera, and brush pictures of new products and services, has conveyed general information and ideas. Through its literature, the promotion department has supported the advertising. Both have stimulated desires for products and services, affecting the progress of modern business and industry. Living standards of readers have been affected in consequence.

The editorial department has influenced the language of readers, has been a creator or molder of cultural standards and interests, and has purveyed facts and ideas that readers might not otherwise have been exposed

[5] Jack Goodman, *While You Were Gone*. New York: Simon & Schuster, 1946, p. 409.

to. Editorial content has affected prople's dress, eating habits, and entertainment plans.

What might be called the official concept of the influence of the general magazine comes from the Magazine Advertising Bureau. Placed first among general effects is the shaping of public opinion. "The national magazine does not have the spot news function of either the newspaper or the radio. But being edited with deliberation, it is read with equal deliberation, and therefore has the unique ability to form a *mature* public opinion, nationally." It also is a reflector of American life. Said the Bureau: "Life is not the daily headlines of the newspaper, nor is it the artificial dramatics thrown out daily, hourly by radio. The solid values of the lives of millions of American families are reported by the national magazine, unsensationally but vividly and accurately, in articles and fiction, in pictures and illustrations." [6]

James Playsted Wood in his study of American magazines declares that the magazine is one of "three major forces affecting and controlling national public opinion." With newspaper and radio it "first created the public opinion they affect." He reminds his readers that it is read more persistently than other media, is less perishable, and is read attentively. It provokes results, gets reactions. Much magazine material later goes into books and motion pictures; reprints also are made.

"The character of a given magazine limits its audience," he says, "thus, to some extent, the spread of its influence, its educational force, its persuasion to belief, and possibly to individual or social action." [7]

EFFECTS BY TYPES

Wood properly qualifies his generalization by using the word *given*. The effects of the pulps are unlike those of literary magazines, and within the specialized magazine world the effects of one technical journal only in a superficial way resemble those of another.

Led by the *Reader's Digest*, condensed and pocket-size magazines have stimulated popularized reading by the middle-class public, have spread certain social ideals and standards, and have increased the demand for short, quickly-read units. The digests have had both an internal and an external influence. They have made the portable magazine popular and demonstrated that gigantic circulations and sensationally successful publishing businesses can be achieved without carrying advertising.

With magazines of four or five million circulation setting the pace, the women's group, with which may be associated the service and shelter books, has been principally responsible for influence wielded by advertising departments on homes and families of the middle class. They have to some

[6] Undated bulletin of the Magazine Advertising Bureau. No. 2, p. 2.
[7] James Playsted Wood, *Magazines in the United States*. New York: Ronald, 1949, p. 252.

extent standardized housekeeping tools, widened the variety of cookery, introduced or popularized certain habits (such as frequent bathing and shaving), and called attention to books, motion pictures, and art works, considerably broadening their effect. Not a minor result has been the introduction of fictional stereotypes: heroes and heroines of fiction in women's magazines are seldom like realities. An internal effect has been to put more authors on a sounder financial basis.

The confession magazine, imitator of much of the slick magazine content, has had a changing influence. In its early days it played a psychological role: it offered spiritual release for uneducated or immature readers (whether adults or adolescents), enabling them to experience adventures of the more daring and unorthodox without personal risk. Now, except for a surviving group offering stories of crime detection, it is achieving on its own economic level a standardization in reader habits and practices similar to the women's slicks.

The majority of pulps continue the function attributed to the confessions in their early years: to provide escape into adventure for persons whose lives are dull. Their effect is to regularize moral concepts—virtue is victorious, evil is punished in the end—and to reduce life to black and white, ignoring the usual gray. Comic magazines, closely associated with pulps, have the similar effect of ignoring subtleties and reducing life to elemental conflicts or providing escape from reality. Pulps and comics help perpetuate slang and the cliché.

The success magazines, with such titles as *Success Today*, *Your Personality*, and *Your Life*, and a segment of the religious magazine world (notably *Guideposts*) provide psychological guidance of a sort to persons with such problems as failure in marriage, sexual maladjustment, and tendencies to minor criminality. By a more nearly direct approach than pulps or confessions, they serve somewhat the same purpose of allowing a reader to relive his personal experiences or his drifting fancies through the experiences of others. They simplify attempts of the individual to adjust himself to society.

Literary magazines have started literary movements, erected critical standards and founded schools of criticism, introduced new writers, maintained the following of older ones, and provided an outlet for work not marketable to the public through general or consumer magazines. Henry Mills Alden lists the following writers as owing their first publication to magazines: Samuel Johnson, Walter Scott, Coleridge, De Quincey, Lamb, Hazlitt, Shelley, Keats, Wordsworth, Leigh Hunt, Eliot, Landor, Trollope, Thackeray, Poe, Twain, and Longfellow.[8]

Literary magazines long have been accepted as arbiters of fashion in language; many a dispute about words has been ended by the *Atlantic*

[8] Henry Mills Alden, *Magazine Writing and the New Literature*. New York: Harper, 1908, p. 42-52.

Monthly's usage. Editors of literary magazines often are asked to settle literary disputes.

Magazines for juveniles have had definite effects, since their readers are in formative years. A youngster's heroes once were provided almost solely by books and magazines; today the radio, motion picture, and television have equal if not stronger influence. The religious juveniles have built concepts of right and wrong in human conduct and of individual responsibility at home and in church. They have aroused loyalties. The secular juveniles in more recent times have been simplified versions of magazines for grown-ups—witness the departments in *Seventeen,* for example. Their effect has been at once to create little adults and to encourage youthful independence if also standardization of mores among adolescents.

Newsmagazines have freed some newspaper readers from wading through the mass of newsprint issued daily and have intended to provide understanding of current events. They have provided continuity in news developments and background for those events. Like the digest, they have given readers concise material to read, with elimination of fine distinctions that interfere with simplified summaries.

The newspapers' entry in the race for magazine advertising is the Sunday supplement or newspaper magazine (*American Weekly, Parade, This Week*). This type of publication has not only obtained some of the advertising it sought but also has provided leisure time reading similar to that in some magazines. Originated in 1896, these supplements at first provided sensational articles and conventional fiction, but in our time they have settled into imitations of picture magazines (*Parade*) or of general weeklies (*This Week*) or of women's magazines (*Pictorial Review* or *Home*). Their effects, somewhat less intensive because they are taken less seriously, are not unlike those of the magazines they resemble.

The effects of specialized magazines are vertical, rather than horizontal. A clothing publication or a food magazine (*Infants' and Children's Wear*) affects the profession, industry, business, or other group it serves by conveying news created by the group, evaluating trends within, and providing an outlet for ideas.

EVALUATING THE EFFECTS

This analysis of social effects of magazines has not to this point attempted evaluation. Little attention has been given by scholars or critics of the magazine to these effects or to their merits. Journalism in general, or specifically the newspaper, radio, or television, has been subject to evaluation, but not much space has been accorded the magazine. For many years there has been an open season for judging the effects of journalism as a whole. Almost all the judges have been adversely critical of newspapers, and may have lumped the magazines with them, without so stating.

During its early days the magazine in the United States was criticized, both at home and in England, for the low quality of its content. Dean Mott, for example, quotes Charles Astor Bristed, who contributed to *The Galaxy* under the name of Carl Benson. In an article in the *Edinburgh Review* in 1848, Bristed wrote: "In examining the causes of the inferiority of American periodical literature the most readily assignable and generally applicable is that its contributors are mostly unpaid." [9] Bristed assumed that readers agreed about the inferiority. But except for complaint about an occasional article, the periodical as an institution has either been praised or ignored, for the most part.

Individual magazines or groups sometimes have drawn attack, as shown by the histories of *Woodhull and Claflin's Weekly* or of *The Masses,* to cite two widely different periodicals of distinctly separated periods. The pulps, comics, slicks in general, newsmagazines, digests, and women's magazines occasionally have been attacked. Whereas newspapers as a group are evaluated for their ethics or their alleged failure to live up to the guarantees of the freedom of the press, magazines are dealt with through appraisals of individual editors and publishers. Harold Ross, Henry Luce, William Randolph Hearst, H. L. Mencken, and George Horace Lorimer have not always been kindly treated in the literature about them.

The few appraisals bear such titles as "What Happened to the Slicks," by Wilma Shore in *The New Masses;* "The Time the Lady Writer Imagined Me," by Dorothy McKenzie in *Politics;* "The Women's Magazines," by Elizabeth Bancroft Schlesinger in the *New Republic;* "The Magazines Women Read," by Ann Griffith, in the *American Mercury,* and "Up the Ladder from *Charm* to *Vogue*" by Mary McCarthy in *The Reporter.* Two books may be considered evaluations of magazines: *Little Wonder* by John Bainbridge, which is about the *Reader's Digest,* and Wood's *Magazines in the United States.* An older volume, Algernon Tassin's *The Magazine in America,* has an overtone of evaluation, but is more heavily historical and descriptive.

Insubstantial as criticism of the effect of the magazine has been, what is its point? A few views commonly held are these.

[9] Frank Luther Mott, A *History of American Magazines.* New York: Appleton, 1930. Vol. I, pp. 511-12.

Credo for a Magazine

By Norman Cousins

Fundamentally, to publish a magazine that people will read and respect;

To believe, not as rote or strained slogan, but as rigid fact, that a magazine is by natural right the property of its readers;

That, because of this, editors are but temporary custodians, their tenure related to and dependent upon their confidence in the judgment and intelligence of the reader;

That such confidence is best established by avoiding both the condescension of talking down and the presumption of talking up;

That a magazine, like a person, requires, in order to be effective, certain qualities—readily identifiable and beyond obliteration;

That high among these qualities is a response to values, the capacity to create values, and the passion to defend values;

That other essential qualities include clarity, curiosity, insight, incisiveness, integrity, good taste, good will, conviction, responsibility;

That what is written is believed by the writer and written to be believed by the reader;

That the magazine should reflect a sense of adventure and excitement about life in general and about books and ideas in particular;

That honest sentiments, honest passions, and honest indignations are among the highest expressions of conscience, that there is no need to feel shy or awkward or embarrassed in their presence, and that they are not to be waved aside by mock austerics;

That cynicism at best is a waste of time; at worst, a dangerous and potentially fatal disease for individuals and civilizations both;

That ideals are the main business of writers, and that people will respond to ideals far beyond the anticipations of their nominal leaders;

That believing all this need neither limit nor inhibit a sense of fun and the enjoyment of laughter;

That editing, finally, is not paring but creating.

Mr. Cousins is editor of the Saturday Review of Literature. This editorial is reprinted by permission from that magazine, where it appeared under the head "Credo for SRL."

Critics who detect adverse effects declare that the magazine is too much inclined to give the public what it wants, that it deprives the public of the fullest knowledge of facts and ideas, that through its advertising content it stimulates desires for possessions that cannot be gratified by the average reader's income, that it presents only conventional or ultra-conservative viewpoints, that it evades its duty to provide leadership in the solution of social problems, that it is time-wasting, distracting the reader from more valuable uses of his leisure.

The critics who see positive effects point to the comparatively high standard of living in this country and declare that magazines, through their advertising copy, have helped produce it by stimulating mass consumption of goods and, thereby, mass production; that prices have thus been lowered; that the public, through the popular education materials in magazines, is better informed than ever before; that new ideas are "merchandised," as one proponent put it, through magazines, and that they play an important role in every national crisis, be it war, depression, or flood.

As with so many arguments this is not a clear case for either pro or con. After analysis, some parts of each may be accepted as true. The charge that the magazine is but a mirror of the public mind cannot be disputed; as Godkin of *The Nation* put it in a letter to Charles Eliot Norton of Harvard: ". . . the press would not be what it is without a public demand for it as it is." Because the magazine depends upon public support, it must gratify public demand to assure support. It follows that unpopular ideas will get short shrift in the mass magazine, such ideas as the consumer cooperative movement, non-violent means of dealing with aggression, and mental telepathy, to mention three more or less ignored in the mid-years of the twentieth century. The subject of racial and religious intolerance likewise was ignored, except by certain specialized magazines, until progress was made in the United States toward decreasing such intolerance, and so the press ran less risk in discussing it. With progress came open discussion in countless magazine articles and even fictional treatment in the women's magazines.

Magazine advertising sometimes *does* make readers dissatisfied with their present washing machines, food mixers, vacuum cleaners, and refrigerators; the less responsible consumers *do* implicate themselves in endless installment buying. To balance these detriments, however, are the greater sanitation and efficiency made possible in part by the lower prices and greater availability of tools resulting from better merchandising. Magazines are time-wasting to time-wasters; other readers should not be deprived of occasional trivial reading.

The assertion that the public is better informed because of magazine reading can be accepted as correct if *better informed* is taken relatively. "Better informed about what?" and "Better informed than who else?" are legitimate questions. The American people as a whole may be better informed about current affairs than the inhabitants of Patagonia or Pakistan or Paraguay, but are they well informed enough to make democracy work to the limit and to the full interests of the people? The discovery, for example, that many millions in the late 1940's had no knowledge of the United Nations is not too encouraging. Yet the magazine does not exist in isolation; it is only one medium of mass communication. It should not carry full blame for failures shared by all other media. It is blameworthy to the extent that it makes no attempt to provide information, to the degree in which editors and publishers lack interest or courage in dealing with controversial subjects, unorthodox ideas, and topics of limited appeal.

A single, all-inclusive statement about the social effect of the magazine in the United States is difficult to frame. No comprehensive studies have been undertaken. The magazine of our time has lost the dynamics that made it powerful in the days when it was a personal organ or a tool for social pioneers. As the general or consumer magazine has become a business it has had to follow business methods lest it not survive. As the specialized periodical has become a spokesman for business or a textbook for industry it, too, has had to give increasing attention to its own business survival. The magazine is likely, under such conditions, to invoke blessings upon the existing social order and make readers wary of experiments threatening to change the fundamental economy upon which they are dependent.

The Magazine's Social Role

If the magazine, as has been said, does not exist in a vacuum but shares its social role with other media, those who produce and use it must have some idea what that social role might be.

A business society prevents the magazine from fulfilling the role of the institution that is wholly devoted to the welfare of society as are, for example, the church and the school. It is left to play a part short of full devotion to the public good. If magazines indiscriminately use the fear motive in advertising they are not bettering society; if they ignore significant social ideas for fear of adverse reader reaction, they are doing less than their best to help mankind. But where shall they position themselves? How far ahead of the public may they safely be?

Paul F. Lazarsfeld and Robert K. Merton tackle this problem in a general manner and point out a procedure for the magazine, among other media of mass communication. They examine the argument that the level of esthetic taste has deteriorated in "the measure that the size of these audiences has increased." They say there is fear "that the mass media deliberately cater to these vulgarized tastes, thus contributing to further deterioration." [10] They declare that they have been able to find little knowledge

---

[10] Lyman Bryson, Editor, *The Communication of Ideas*. New York: Harper & Brothers and the Institute for Religious and Social Studies, 1948, pp. 113-114.

about the social role of mass media and their effect upon the community.

Many critics of mass media make them "targets for hostile criticism because they feel themselves duped by the turn of events." Reformers have helped make available more leisure but people use it in radio listening, movie going, and, the authors might have added, television gazing. Such media seem somehow to have "cheated reformers of the fruits of their victories." Instead of spending its time to read Shakespeare or listen to Beethoven's music the public turns to Faith Baldwin or Johnny Mercer or Edgar Guest.

Messrs. Lazarsfeld and Merton ask how best to use mass media "for moving toward designated types of social objectives." They answer by suggesting that propaganda, whether for good or bad social motives, must satisfy one or more of three conditions if it is to be effective: 1. Monopolization; 2. Canalization rather than change of basic values; and 3. Supplementary face to face contact.

Monopolization they illustrate by war-time censorship in a democracy, the taking over or use of channels of communication for war propaganda. Creation of popular idols by mass media is another example, this one in the commercial area. Kate Smith, the authors say, is thought to be a "woman with unparalleled understanding of other American women, deeply sympathetic with ordinary men and women, a spiritual guide and mentor, a patriot whose views on public affairs should be taken seriously."

There is no counter propaganda to this; ". . . there are none who set themselves systematically to question what she has said. In consequence an unmarried radio entertainer with an annual income in six figures may be visualized by millions of American women as a hard working mother who knows the recipe for managing life on $1,500 a year."

Canalization perpetuates existing behavior patterns or attitudes. Magazine fiction offers an example. In most short stories the heroine is beautiful and desirable; the hero, handsome and virile.

Supplementation is a follow-up on the presentation of a point of view through mass media, achieved through local centers of organized face to face contact, such as reading rooms and clubs. It "serves to reinforce the prevailing culture patterns."

Dr. Lazarsfeld went a step further, in an address before the Institute of Communications Research at the University of Illinois, when he said:

> Do we "give the people what they want" or do we believe that there are experts who know the best balance for the total supply which the mass media provide? It is not too difficult to suggest an answer. Obviously, we do not want magazines and radio programs in this country to drive audiences away. But almost no one would propose that the media be based on the lowest common denominator; publishers and broadcasters have a cultural responsibility. Their business is affected by public interest. Thus the best solution would be to have mass media aim just slightly

above what would be the simplest level at any time. In this way, we shall have a general acceptance of media content, as well as a slow, systematic intellectual progress to which the media, themselves, will contribute.[11]

He admits that the recommendation is more easily made than carried out. Consciously or unconsciously, however, Dr. Lazarsfeld's philosophy seems to be followed by certain editors. The increasing quantity of material dealing with such social problems as divorce, lack of interest in religion, juvenile delinquency, low pay for school teachers, child labor, and many phases of bad health has increased the popularity of women's magazines, notably *Woman's Home Companion* and *McCall's*. And other magazines, particularly *Mademoiselle* and *Harper's Bazaar*, have dared to print such unconventional fiction as psychological short stories. *The New Yorker* has torn up all the rules about pleasing the public and thrives on the results, devising its own pattern for personality sketches and setting a fashion for fiction that once was thought to have no popular appeal whatsoever.

The progress made in introducing new ideas through magazines can be judged by the difference in the climate of public opinion during two periods in magazine history. The first was in the days when Edward Bok was editor of the *Ladies' Home Journal*. The social effect of some of his policies was tempestuous. He relates in his autobiography the medical opposition to a department of questions and answers for prospective mothers. He published the material in the 1880's. He describes, also, the results of a policy of refusing patent medicine advertising advocated by John Adams Thayer, advertising manager, and supported by Cyrus H. K. Curtis, the publisher. Mr. Curtis returned a check for the equivalent of five pages of advertising because it came from a patent medicine manufacturer, although the money would have met the magazine's payroll for three weeks. When Bok launched a campaign to improve small-house architecture he found architects unalterably opposed to his plan. Finally obtaining the assistance of one, he offered readers full building specifications and plans to scale.

"A storm of criticism now arose from architects and builders all over the country, the architects claiming that Bok was taking 'the bread out of their mouths' by the sale of plans, and local builders vigorously questioned the accuracy of the estimates. But Bok knew he was right and persevered. Slowly but surely he won the approval of the leading architects." [12]

Bok's campaigns would be considered mild today; their results are commonly accepted. Far more controversial problems are now dealt with, yet public opinion has so changed that the effect on the magazine is not harmful. In 1949 *Woman's Home Companion* published an article titled,

[11] Wilbur Schramm, Editor, *Communications in Modern Society*. Urbana, Illinois: University of Illinois Press, 1948, p. 195.
[12] Edward W. Bok, *The Americanization of Edward Bok*. New York: Scribner's, 1922, p. 241.

"Is Prejudice Poisoning Your Children?" William A. H. Birnie, editor-in-chief, described to Quincy Howe, of the Columbia Broadcasting System staff, the origin of this article, on which the magazine had received many letters.

"We investigated the subject very carefully," he told Mr. Howe in a broadcast,[13] "and found out that even in many well-meaning homes the children were subjected to overtones and echoes of racial and religious prejudices that were harming them and harming their future as citizens. We felt that this was an important thing to call to the attention of people who didn't realize what they were allowing to go on in their own homes."

"You had that idea as a result of an editorial conference or an editorial inspiration," Mr. Howe observed and then asked: "Then what did you do? Did you write to somebody? Did you attach that idea to a person, or had somebody already said something that suggested the idea?"

"That particular article," Mr. Birnie replied, "I happen to recall very definitely. All of us on the *Companion* feel that the subject of racial discrimination is something we should come back to from time to time; that no matter how hard you hit it in any given article, some vestiges of the problem still remain, and it's worth coming back to."

Howard Whitman, author of the article, had noted traces of prejudice in his own children and, realizing the magazine's policy, had proposed the piece. Later in the conversation Mr. Birnie told Mr. Howe that the subjects that were attracting attention more and more were politics, atomic energy, "social problems, civic improvement, family relationships, psychiatric and psychological handling of children, all of those have very greatly interested women in the last few years."

[13] "You and Magazines," third in a series of interviews on WCBS, New York, Feb. 1, 1950. Script released by *Woman's Home Companion*, New York.

5

THE MOTION PICTURE

Ruth Inglis
THE SOCIAL ROLE OF THE SCREEN

Hortense Powdermaker
HOLLYWOOD AND THE U. S. A.

5

THE MOTION PICTURE

THE history and economics of the motion picture are closely related to the social role of the screen, more so perhaps than prevails in the case of other mass media. The consent decrees, for example, by which the government determined the divorcement between production-distribution and exhibition had a cataclysmic effect on the economic and social role of the motion picture. Indeed, these decrees, coming almost simultaneously with the rise of television, changed the character of the motion picture radically from what it had been in the thirties or early forties. That the medium has survived is partly a result of an influx of younger and more imaginative producers and partly a result of public interest in foreign and art films. It is a result of an enforced maturity in which motion pictures, for the first time, began to eliminate major stereotypes and face the multifarious problems of the real world.

The early rise of the motion picture was bewilderingly rapid. New techniques, such as CinemaScope, were known to the studios many years before their actual use, but producers saw no need to prod a successful economy while audiences stood in line to see the Hollywood product. But competition from television and the government decision forced the industry to take a new look in the direction of the public interest, particularly the minority audience.

Many of the patterns and stereotypes prevalent in the motion pictures of an earlier period, described by Ruth Inglis, have all but disappeared. But the inertia of a few older producers who still remain in Hollywood, along with the influence of special interest groups, have continued to keep many pictures close to proven molds and traditional formulae.

In the last decade, however, the screen has shown signs of a new maturity. There is a fresh recognition of responsibility and of the potential of the screen as an art form. Particularly in some of the foreign pictures, there has been a greater awareness of values and a wider area of experiment. As Miss Inglis' study adumbrates, the consent decrees, along with competition from other media, resulted in an improved Hollywood product. In addition, social changes wrought by the last war along with the enormously rapid growth of television have given the motion picture industry a new sense of direction. Also responsible, however, is a more critical and sophisticated audience, freshly oriented by the realism and artistry of the better foreign films.

Hortense Powdermaker's analysis of the motion picture industry is from the perspective of the anthropologist. It is concerned with the mores and the behavior patterns of those people who have been responsible for movie-making—the executives, the producers, the directors, stars and agents. The author is careful to indicate, however, that Hollywood, although insular, is still a segment of the larger framework of the American society. While Hollywood may have been a world unto itself, there has always been a degree of interaction between the movie society and other elements of the public. Hollywood is not viewed in sheer isolation, as writers have tended to look upon it, but as part of a larger world which it reflects and which, to some extent, is reflected in it.

There are three parts to this "circular interaction"—Hollywood, the U.S.A. and the movies themselves. The author makes the shrewd observation that Hollywood reflects and contributes to the age of anxiety which is exaggerated, in the movie colony, beyond what it would be in any other field of endeavor. This is shown in the tendency to "run scared"; in the fear of discipline; the emphasis on the haphazard; and the lack of faith in the public or in the movie colony's own product.

Paradoxically, the lack of discipline is offset by the simultaneous presence of the Puritan tradition, exemplified in the would-be censors, ethnic and educational pressure groups and special interest groups. The Production Code, recently defied by some producers, is still a restraining factor.

How does Hollywood reflect the major areas of society? First, by its emphasis on its quest for pleasure, a kind of new hedonism. Secondly, by its emphasis on cost rather than on qualitative values. Furthermore, Hollywood's behavior is almost invariably opposite to Hollywood's product. Frequently, the affluent tend to be the villains in motion pictures. Love tends to triumph over all. The emphasis on affluence in Hollywood is counterbalanced by a de-emphasis in its product.

Perhaps Hollywood's greatest problem has always been that the artist has no real function in movie-making, the economic and executive climate being what they are. Until recently, techniques have been stressed over creativity. Hollywood met its time of difficulty, not by better pictures, but by new techniques such as 3-D and large screen.

Hollywood is here depicted as a kind of authoritarian society. However, as the older executives leave, there has been a gradual replacement by a new group—more realistic, more cognizant of artistic and ethical values. Hollywood has slowly been moving away from its ancient stereotypes of rich and poor, love and hate, toward a new responsibility. The change has been slow, but it has been sure.

*   *   *   *

RELATED READING

Cooper, Eunice & Dinerman, Helen. "Analysis of the Film 'Don't Be a Sucker':
  A Study in Communication." *Publ. Opin. Quart.*, 14 (1951), 234-264.
Handel, Leo. *Hollywood Looks at Its Audience.* Urbana: University of Illinois
  Press, 1950.
Jacobs, Lewis. *The Rise of the American Film: A Critical History.* New York:
  Harcourt, Brace, 1939.
Ramsaye, Terry. *A Million and One Nights.* New York: Simon & Schuster,
  1926.

THE SOCIAL ROLE OF THE SCREEN

By Ruth Inglis

---

1. THE MOTION PICTURE: HISTORY AND ECONOMICS

COMPARED with the long history of the printed word, the emergence of the screen as a full-fledged agency of mass communication has been very rapid. Fifty years ago motion pictures were virtually unknown. Many film pioneers are still living who can give firsthand accounts of the early days of the movies. With radio, new techniques of rapid printing, and television, they are part of a revolution in communications.

Early History

In 1889 Edison invented the kinetoscope, the immediate forerunner of the modern motion picture. Similar machines were developed in France and England. The American invention was a type of peep-show machine with an aperture through which one person at a time could see pictures move. A few years later the projector and screen were perfected, and the first public commercial showing took place in New York City in 1894.

At first the "flickers" were closely associated with vaudeville, but by 1902 penny-arcade owners were presenting all-movie programs. During this period three companies—Edison, Biograph, and Vitagraph—made short pictures in the streets using crude equipment. For the most part they were simple plots with staged episodes which were improvised on the spot.

Almost all the future uses of the films can be seen in embryo during these early years. Fact as well as fiction was employed. The depiction of current events was common. Among the earliest newsworthy pictures were flashes of the inauguration of President McKinley. Nor were the early movie-makers afraid to express themselves on the social issues of the day. For example, there were several films ridiculing the movement for women's rights, one being entitled *Why Mr. Nation Wants a Divorce*. Films were used for religious purposes, too.

Reprinted from *Freedom of the Movies* by Ruth Inglis, by permission of the University of Chicago Press. Copyright 1947, the University of Chicago.

The problems of today also plagued pioneer producers. A famous and lengthy kiss aroused fervent moralistic protest the like of which was to be seen again. As the screen became recognized as a social force, pressure for its control arose. At first, of course, it was as sporadic and unorganized as was the business itself.

By 1903, however, the screen had achieved popularity with a steady audience, heavily weighted toward the lower end of the economic scale. It was a new and different kind of entertainment commodity.

Lewis Jacobs in his *Rise of the American Film* has designated the period from 1903 to 1908 as that in which the foundations of the motion picture industry were established. The movies became a large permanent business with production, distribution, and exhibition as its three different parts. A system of exchanges was created through which films were rented to exhibitors. The year 1905 brought the first "nickelodeon" in Pittsburgh. Designed especially for the showing of movies, these exhibition houses were more adequate than the old makeshift storerooms which had heretofore been used. Soon there were eight to ten thousand exhibitors in the United States. Pictures lasted half an hour or an hour and ran continuously all day. From one of the old notices, "Please do not stamp, the floor may cave in," it would seem that the audience participated actively. They were enthusiastic fans and demanded frequent changes in the program.

The production end of the business boomed. Speed and quantity were of prime importance. Sometimes a picture was made in a day, and the average cost of the best pictures was not more than $500. The product could not be other than of poor quality. At times films were made indoors and with great secrecy. From an artistic point of view they were crude. The techniques of film-making evolved through trial and error. Experimentation with subject matter extended to morality dramas, westerns, episodes from American history, and some literary adaptations. Many of the techniques were invented by Edwin S. Porter, whose picture, *The Great Train Robbery*, Jacobs has described as the first American film story of importance.

The next period in the development of the film ended with the beginning of the first World War. From 1908 to 1914 the movie business was marked by bitter competition for economic control of the medium. The period might be labeled the battle over patents, or the rise and fall of the Motion Picture Patents Company. The Patents Company was the means by which the leading manufacturers of cameras and projectors and the producers of movies pooled their resources. The ten companies in the trust made the rental of their films and the use of their projectors mutually contingent and charged exhibitors two dollars a week for that privilege in addition to rental charges. Opposition, however, was very bitter, and by 1914 the power of the combine was greatly reduced. In 1917, after a long antitrust suit, the Patents Company was legally outlawed.

Competition improved the quality of films, which also became longer. During these early years preceding the first World War great strides were taken in the development of production techniques. David Wark Griffith explored the art of the cinema, introducing new but enduring techniques in lighting and editing. He was the first to make functional narrative use of the close-up and the full panorama.

As newspapers began to notice the new art, movie-making became a more respectable occupation. At first, Griffith, for example, had concealed his connection with movies. Specialization also increased. This period marked the beginning of screen credits. Acting was improved, and the practice of emphasizing stars as individuals began. Fan magazines came into existence. Hollywood was established as a production center.

Although most films were fictional, producers were not afraid to point up moral lessons and to inject their own opinions into films. Compared with later years, the motion pictures of this era before World War I were extremely opinionated. They preached strict late Victorian moral attitudes. With great fervor and earnestness they made hundreds of pictures on the theme that it pays to be good. The values of love and marriage and womanly virtue were extolled, the compensations of poverty were endlessly dramatized, and the good life was presented as somewhat like that which the audience experienced.

At first there was no reluctance to produce films which expressed opinions about the issues of the time. Several, for example, presented union organizers as low characters and in general smeared the labor movement. Soon, however, films friendly toward labor appeared. Sympathetic treatment of minorities also became more common.

Taking sides on current issues was most clear cut in the movie *Escape from the Asylum*, which argued sympathetically for Harry Thaw, principal in the famous Stanford White murder case. Jacobs stated that "observers generally believed that this movie converted many people to the belief that Thaw had been sufficiently punished and that he deserved sympathy."

Setting the Pattern

The period of the first World War was extremely important in the history of the movies. It was one of transition, completely changing the economics, content, and influence of films. In the very brief span of four years the movies became a big business and a national institution. Expansion in all its branches was rapid though confused. It was a time of fantastic successes and failures for individual companies. Most of the corporate names of earlier days disappeared or lost their identity in new ventures. Production, distribution, and exhibition were set in firm new patterns.

In production the business was changed overnight in all its aspects by the substitution of features for short pictures. Exhibitors found that patrons were willing to pay more for longer pictures. This led to much greater production costs and to increased specialization with accompanying larger salaries all along the line.

Faced with the dilemma of creating a product which would have some uniformity and at the same time would be fresh and new, the producers developed several means of standardizing film content. The problem is one which is peculiarly acute in the motion picture business because of the high cost of production and the investment in theaters. A large number of pictures must be produced each year in order to keep theaters supplied, and, if a profitably large audience is to be maintained, the pictures must be of such a nature that patrons do not completely gamble on going to see them. Large audiences definitely limit the range of variability. At the same time, every picture must be different. It must somehow be new and unlike all the ones that have gone before.

The star system, an important solution to the problem of standardization, had been initiated earlier not by the producing companies but by movie fans. Movie-goers began to notice players as individuals and demanded to know their names. Mary Pickford was identified as "the girl with the blonde curls." At first, the movie companies tried to preserve the anonymity of players in order to prevent salary increases. But soon the fact was established that pictures featuring known actors attracted larger audiences. People became fond of John Bunny, Charlie Chaplin, Mary Pickford, and others and were eager to see their latest exploits. Then actors and actresses were identified by name and their personalities highly publicized in order to increase and stabilize their following.

The formula picture was also a partial solution. Certain different types of movies were made and advertised, and patrons began to know what to expect from problem dramas, action pictures, westerns, shockers, or comedies. They became the staples of the business, and companies tried to diversify their product within these types.

Advertising on a wide scale was a necessary part of both solutions. Publicity about stars and pictures was widespread and extravagant. The industry had little trouble keeping itself in the public eye. It also carried on an advertising campaign to make movie-going a national habit so that people would take the whole family no matter what picture was showing.

The changes in distribution were even more revolutionary and far-reaching. Distributors now were more than mere middlemen between producers and exhibitors. They became the key to the whole industry—of greater importance to the big companies than production. Recognized as a means of controlling the market, competition was most intense on this level.

Paramount, one of the largest companies, led the others in consolidating production and distribution. It started the practice of "block-booking," by means of which films were rented to exhibitors in groups, sometimes before the individual pictures were produced. At first the exhibitors liked the system because they were assured of a steady flow of films with a minimum of bother. But the practice became subject to abuse. Poor pictures were lumped with good ones, with little individual choice possible to the exhibitor. Distributors did not always keep their promises, and they began exacting higher and higher rentals. The exhibitors complained but were unable to improve their situation until they themselves organized.

Finally, a group of leading circuits of exhibitors formed First National Pictures (later to be absorbed by Warner Brothers) to compete with Paramount. They obtained pictures from independent producers on an individual basis and subleased them to other exhibitors. Finally, they entered production themselves. This led to a bitter fight between the two giants lasting for several years. Paramount went into exhibition also but was forced to give up block-booking in August, 1917, and temporarily the practice was abandoned.

Block-booking, however, permanently influenced the basis upon which films were rented. Exhibitors selected pictures sight unseen on the basis of written descriptions. In them, well-known stars and directors, stories with a reputation outside the industry, and production costs became the new symbols of merit. They still are, although, at the present writing, block-booking has been eliminated from the industry.

Meanwhile exhibition itself had also assumed new patterns. Longer pictures meant a slower turnover of customers. This in turn led to higher admission prices and larger theaters. It was a period of great expansion with the building of many large and pretentious movie "palaces," which, with rising admission prices and new comforts, began to compete with legitimate plays for a more sophisticated audience. In fact, as time went on, the movies gradually supplanted the provincial theater with its road shows and surpassed the remaining "live" theater in metropolitan areas in terms of attendance.

Formerly the motion picture audience, to a large extent, had been composed of working-class people, many of whom could not read English. Now middle-class audiences were attracted. They, however, were less tolerant of flickering projection, stoppages to mend broken films, and uncomfortable seats. In order to hold the new audiences, the movie-houses became more "refined." This refinement extended to the pictures themselves. Slides with local store advertising were eliminated, and obvious preaching or crude dramas of simple morality were no longer tolerated. A new sophistication was noticeable, and the audiences seemed to accept the standards by which exhibitors measured the worth of pictures.

All these changes in production, distribution, and exhibition reinforced each other and were necessary elements for expansion. They became the inevitable characteristics of a big-scale motion picture industry. No longer was it open to an enterprising young man with slender resources but required a large capital investment and a vast organization.

Meanwhile, the motion picture activities of other countries were practically at a standstill because of World War I. Foreign competition was virtually eliminated during these crucial years, and Hollywood became the film capital of the world. Only recently has there been any foreign competition to challenge seriously the American industry in the field of motion picture entertainment.

The later history of the industry followed the same pattern of expansion and consolidation. The competition was intense, but it was between giants and resulted in ever new mergers of smaller units into larger companies spreading over the three branches of the business. The occasional crises of the between-war years seemed only to establish the pattern more firmly.

Banking interests in these years entered the picture with large-scale financing. At the same time, control in the studios shifted from directors to executive producers who attempted to "rationalize" the business. Although only partially successful, the desire to reduce the financial risks in picture-making resulted in attempts to standardize production. By and large, money was made available only to producers of proved success who could secure the services of stars of established popularity. The development of new talent was costly, and the exploration of untried themes risky. The tendency to imitate former successes too frequently resulted in cycles of cut-and-dried pictures. Unfortunately, the tried and true is seldom fresh or new.

Warner Brothers' introduction of sound was a major change. The first feature picture with sound, *Don Juan*, was released in the summer of 1926. The other companies, although resisting the change from silent pictures for a time, were forced to it by public enthusiasm. By 1928 talking pictures were admittedly here to stay. The change weakened some companies and strengthened others, notably Warner Brothers, but did not alter the fundamental economic pattern of the industry except to concentrate capitalization further.

The same can be said for the depression. Sound delayed the slump for the movie industry until 1933. There was a slight recovery in 1937, but both 1938 and 1939 were lean years. Real prosperity came only with the second World War in spite of the loss of many foreign markets.

The recent history of the motion picture industry has been greatly colored by the war. In the first place, war conditions resulted in increased attendance at movies and in longer runs of films, so that the industry's profits soared to new heights. At the same time, costs were greatly increased—those for labor on a permanent basis. With a shortage of raw film stock and with longer runs, the number of pictures produced declined sharply during the war years. More money per picture was spent than ever before, and the proportion of B (second-quality) pictures decreased. As we shall see, there was a great deal of independent production by experienced producers, actors and actresses, directors, and writers who made releasing contracts with the major companies.

The motion picture industry participated officially in the war through its War Activities Committee, which was an industry-wide organization. Entertainment films were donated for exhibition to the troops abroad, actors and actresses made personal appearance tours, and the industry voluntarily submitted to government censorship. Short pictures, some of them made by the industry and some by governmental agencies, were widely shown in theaters throughout the country and brought to the movie-goers of the nation war information and appeals from the government, the Red Cross, and other similar organizations.

One of the most permanent effects of the war was upon the industry personnel who served in the armed forces. They began to see new opportunities and responsibilities for the films, and their experience should have a profound effect upon the content of movies during the coming years.

2. THE MOTION PICTURE: THE SOCIAL ROLE OF THE SCREEN

The movies are entering a new phase in their development as a mature organ of mass communication. The demands of the second World War tested the medium as never before and demonstrated its great potentialities. As a result, both inside and outside the motion picture industry there is increasing recognition that the movies have an essential role to play in social life and that the freedom of the screen is important because of what the film can do. Freedom finds its meaning not only in liberty but in responsibility, as the leaders in the motion picture industry have publicly acknowledged many times.

In the past the industry has faced a difficult problem in defining its responsibilities. Belief in the power of the movies is so widespread that inevitably they have been drawn into the conflict between those who want to conserve traditional morality, on the one hand, and, on the other, those who are hospitable to the idea of change and would like motion pictures to depict the realities of life, moral or social. In addition, the industry is beset by pressure groups which are sensitive about the screen portrayal of characters like themselves or of their interests. The economic necessity of mass audiences has made the industry eager to please everyone.

Moral Responsibilities

No pressure coming from outside the industry has been more powerful or persistent than that concerned with the moral effects of motion pictures. Since the earliest beginnings of the movies, women's, civic, welfare, and religious groups have worried about the effect of movies upon children, upon the mentally, emotionally, or morally retarded, and upon the whole society. In 1896, two years after the first public commercial exhibition of movies, the film of the then-current stage success, *The Widow Jones*, was condemned as "no more than a lyric of the Stock Yards."

Moralistic pressure groups may be differentiated according to whether they co-operate with the industry or attack it. The former work closely with the National Board of Review of Motion Pictures or the Motion Picture Association of America (formerly the Hays Office, now the Johnston Office). The latter try to gain their objectives by means of censorship statutes and boards or through consumer boycotts.

The usual response of the motion picture industry, if we may anticipate the pages to come and generalize from the history of a quarter of a century of experience, has been to evade the morality issue whenever possible but to yield when necessary. Self-regulation has been evolved as the industry's method of fulfilling its obligations with reference to the moral content of films, as we shall see.

Eric Johnston in his first annual report as president of the Motion Picture Association, indorsed the industry's self-regulation and said: "True freedom is always liberty under law. Its proper exercise is never incompatible with moral principles. Those who want a lawless freedom, a freedom to do whatever they please regardless of the precepts of virtue and the welfare of the community, confuse the privileges of liberty with the indulgences of license."

Responsible Imagery

A second area of responsibility for the movies has been defined by a wide variety of groups which are critical of the portrayal of themselves or their interests on the screen. Protests have come from innumerable individuals and groups who claim that they or their interests have been misrepresented in movies. Pictures casting members of racial, national, professional, occupational, or avocational groups as villains draw hundreds of letters of complaint to the industry from the clubs, fraternities, and associations of these particular groups.

One of the earliest films to arouse such protest was Griffith's famous *The Birth of a Nation*, which was vigorously denounced by the National Association for the Advancement of Colored People. And unfavorable or servile portrayals of Negroes on the screen still spell trouble for the industry.

National groups are equally alert. In peacetime the officials of foreign countries are able to protect what they conceive to be their national interest because of the industry's dependence upon foreign markets. For example, in the case of *Blockade* and *Devil's Island*, General Franco and the French government, respectively, threatened to ban *all* the distributing companies' products in their countries if the pictures in question were shown *anywhere* in the world, including the United States. To this same end foreign states sometimes make film agreements with each other. In 1935, for example, Spain and San Salvador agreed "to prohibit the . . . exhibition in both countries of . . . films . . . which attack, slander, defame, ridicule, insult, or misrepresent directly, or indirectly, the uses, customs, institutions, habits, characteristics, or peculiarities of or incidents occurring in Spain or

San Salvador. . . . Should a foreign film-producing firm repeat the offense
. . . a penalty may be imposed . . . consisting in prohibiting the exhibition of all films produced by the offending firm." [1]

Such agreements are not uncommon. For a time the Italian government protested successfully the use of Italians not only as villains but as
comic characters. Upon occasion, the United States Department of State
has been known to take an interest in films thought by foreign governments to give a disparaging interpretation of their country. *The Forty
Days of Musa Dagh* is a good example.

A slightly different but related problem concerns the portrayal of life
in America to peoples abroad. The recent war revealed what seemed to
many to be an appalling misconception of this country to which—all unwittingly—the American motion picture had contributed. Americans have
been presented as frivolous, wasteful, extraordinarily preoccupied with sex
and irresponsible about marriage, generally given to casual drinking, and
frequently involved in murder and other forms of violence. Although this
picture is partially true, other American qualities belong in any adequate
characterization. As Robert Boothby, a member of Parliament, said recently
on the B.B.C., "anyone who suggests that the American films portray the
American way of living is an enemy of the United States."

Film-makers themselves are coming to realize their international responsibilities. In reference to a proposed United Nations conference on
the free flow of communications, Eric Johnston wrote to Mrs. Roosevelt on
May 7, 1946, that the war had proved that "the motion picture is one of the
most potent instruments ever devised for the dissemination of ideas, information and mutual understanding between peoples. The motion picture
no longer is looked upon solely as a device for mass entertainment." In
discussing the exportation of films abroad, in his first annual report he ad-
vised that pictures be selected "in terms of entertainment value, artistic excellence and social significance." This marks a long step forward in the
definition of foreign policy for the industry.

The presentation of members of occupational groups also creates problems. The sources of complaints range wide to include lawyers, ministers,
plumbers, doctors, grocers, icemen, and newspapermen. A contributor to
School and Society for August 11, 1945, voiced the feeling that school-
teachers should join the chorus of protest. Whenever a script calls for a
schoolteacher, he complained, "the casting office will come up with a
character which is neither animal, vegetable, nor mineral. . . . Everything
points to a clear-cut case of vitamin deficiency. Mentally he is always in a
blue funk. . . .

"Do men teachers really look and act like refugees from an isolation

[1] Quoted from the League of Nations, *Treaty Series*, Vol. CLXV (1935), No. 3818,
by John E. Harley, in *World-wide Influences of the Cinema* (Los Angeles: University
of Southern California Press, 1940), p. 302.

ward? Do women teachers possess the same charm of a gargoyle perched atop the Cathedral of Notre Dame? Is the education of American youths in the hands of persons whom even Havelock Ellis never got around to classifying?"

Interest groups, too, are quick to resent scenes which run counter to their ideas. The Society for the Prevention of Cruelty to Animals is among the most effective of such groups. The British censors ban any picture showing cruelty to animals, apparent or real, and in order to avoid trouble the studios bring in a representative of the S.P.C.A. to witness the filming of all scenes in which animals are used and to issue a certificate that there was no cruelty. Drinking in pictures is another sensitive point. For years it has been the focus of attention by pressure groups otherwise as diverse as the Women's Christian Temperance Union and the American Brewers Foundation.

Business firms and trade associations are likely to feel outraged when their products or industries are displayed in unfavorable ways on the screen. For example, a silver-fox grower protested that the showing of a Negress wearing a silver-fox scarf in a film would hurt the fur business. Walter Wanger in *Foreign Affairs* for October, 1939, cited the example of a Will Rogers picture in which a comedy character used the simile "as thick as flies in a Greek restaurant," and, as a result, "sixteen top-hatted gentlemen, representing the American Society of Greek Restaurateurs, called on the Hays Office to protest." Years ago the industry found itself "behind the eight ball" when the National Billiard Association of America became incensed because of a scene in which the game was played in disreputable surroundings. Trade associations are especially alert to the presentation of the interests of their members on the screen.

And so it goes. The pressures are amazingly varied. As Joseph I. Breen, the director of the industry's program of self-regulation, sensibly remarked: "If we paid serious attention to one tenth of one per cent of what looks like legitimate protest, it would be utterly impossible for us to make any pictures at all, or have any kind of villain unless he were a native born, white, American citizen, without a job and without any political, social, religious or fraternal affiliations of any kind." [2]

The industry's working solution has been to ignore the demands of unorganized or ineffectual groups and to placate the others with a greater number of attractive roles than villainous ones. There are, after all, usually more pleasant than unpleasant characters in fiction—at least in the Hollywood variety. Take newspapermen, for example. At the William Allen White Foundation Dinner held in New York on April 24, 1946, Mr. Francis S. Harmon, vice-president of the Motion Picture Association, reported that, of the 81 journalists in the 398 feature films approved by the Association during 1945, "67 were sympathetic characters, 5 were un-

[2] Quoted by J. P. McEvoy in the *Saturday Evening Post*, December 24, 1938, p. 48.

sympathetic and 9 played indifferent, minor roles. Only one unsympathetic newspaperman had a prominent role, while 37 newspaper people appeared in prominent sympathetic characterizations."

As a further safeguard against unpleasantness for the industry, unnecessary identifying details are avoided. Can anyone remember a movie villain with any fraternal affiliation? Further protection against lawsuits by individuals is sought in the common disclaimer that any resemblance to real persons or situations is purely coincidental.

As part of the policy of self-regulation, certain groups are especially protected. The Motion Picture Production Code specifically mentions judges, officers of the law, ministers of religion, and the prominent people and citizenry of all nations. The Annotations to the Code, prepared by a member of the Association's staff, asserts that "all of the professions should be presented fairly in motion pictures" and that "there shall be no dialogue or scenes indicating that all, or a majority of the members of any professional group, are unethical, immoral, given to criminal activities, and the like." As we have said, one way of handling such situations is to include people with the same identifying characteristics in sympathetic roles. Other devices are to arrange that sympathetic characters condemn their evil counterparts and to show the wrongdoers punished for their evil ways. The industry's expediency sometimes takes precedence over public welfare in evaluating the adequacy of these solutions. Those groups which can harm the industry receive most consideration.

Insignificance and Stereotyping

The third major type of criticism of the movies has gained momentum during the past decade and now constitutes an important problem for producers. As a consequence of meeting the first two types of criticism and attempting to cater to mass audiences, the industry, it is claimed, has retreated to a dream world of unreality, offering a stereotyped and insignificant product.

Among writers, artists, and critics, both within and outside the industry, the movies are accused of being empty and meaningless. In *The Movies on Trial*, a symposium of 1936, William Allen White compared the movies to chewing gum and claimed that the industry offers "little that is much better than the glittering toy for an imbecile giant." Howard Barnes in the *New York Herald-Tribune* a year or two later called the movies the "ostrich of the arts."

Wolcott Gibbs gave up movie reviewing for the *New Yorker* magazine some months ago firm in the belief that "ninety per cent of the moving pictures exhibited in America are so vulgar, witless and dull that it is preposterous to write about them in any publication not intended to be read while chewing gum." Movies are, he charged in the *Saturday Review of Literature* for November 17, 1945, "an astounding parody of life devoted to a society in which anything is physically and materially possible, including perfect happiness, to a race of people who operate intellectually on the level of the *New York Daily News*, morally on that of Dayton, Tennessee, and politically and economically in a total vacuum."

Research likewise discloses that the world of the movies is one of unreality. For example, an analysis of the content of American films in the *Public Opinion Quarterly* for Fall, 1942, by Dorothy Jones revealed that the most common major character was an "independent adult," that is, one economically established, free of parental influence, usually unmarried, and with definitely limited social and economic responsibilities. People so unencumbered with cares and problems are seldom found in real life. Likewise Mrs. Jones found the great American middle class inadequately represented in Hollywood films.

A later analysis revealed that during 1942 about one-fourth of the output from Hollywood had some relation to the war. Half of these films depicted the enemy, but, Mrs. Jones found, they were inconsequential or worse in nature. She reports: "Of the 64 films about the enemy released in 1942, all but two dealt with sabotage and espionage activities, following the time-worn spy formula. . . . There were few which contributed to an understanding of our foes. As a whole, they tended to stereotype them as the usual gangster 'heavy,' identifiable by the fact that he either 'heils Hitler' and speaks with a guttural German accent, or has slant eyes and hisses his 's's.'" As the article in the *Hollywood Quarterly* for October, 1945, points out, however, in 1943 better characterizations of the enemy began to appear in *occasional* first-rate films, and the job of portraying the people of the United Nations was performed somewhat more adequately. *Mrs. Miniver* made Americans more sympathetic toward British people, although Britons themselves did not consider the film typical of middle-class life in England. Pictures like it and earlier films such as *The House of Rothschild, Disraeli, Emile Zola,* and *Imitation of Life* prove that the fictional film can provide well-rounded portrayals of the problems of minorities and other groups in society.

When it comes to the presentation of the major values and goals in society, the record is mixed. Curiously enough, one is forced to agree both with those who praise the movies and with their most severe critics. Like the elephant examined by blind men, the product of the industry is large enough and varied enough in its extremes to present pictures of widely differing degrees of relevance to social morality. The Hollywood movie, as John Grierson has said in *Grierson on Documentary*, "has very successfully debunked some of the lesser evils of society. It has given many salutary lessons in critical citizenship, for it has taught people to question authority, realize the trickery that may parade in the name of justice and recognize that graft may sit in the highest places. . . . It may not have added to the wisdom of the world but it has at least de-yokelised it." This was particularly true during the depression of the early 1930's but seems to be less so now.

On the other hand, the Institute for Propaganda Analysis in 1938 listed the following samples of dubious value-judgments common in the movies:

"1. That the successful culmination of a romance will solve most of the dilemmas of the hero and heroine.

"2. Catch the criminal and you solve the crime problem.

"3. War and the preparation for war are thrilling, heroic, and glamorous.

"4. The good life is the acquisitive life, with its emphasis upon luxury, fine homes and automobiles, evening dress, swank, and suavity."

Pictures contradicting these stereotypes would be easy to name, but they would be in the minority among all the films released during the last ten years. For one picture like *Our Vines Have Tender Grapes* or *The House on 92nd Street* there are a dozen caricatures of society as "café society." Of the war films from Hollywood, Mrs. Jones found only a few "which aided significantly, both at home and abroad, in increasing understanding of the conflict."

Memorable films like *The Good Earth, Pasteur,* and the relatively inexpensive little gem, *A Man to Remember,* prove what Hollywood can do upon occasion and underline the greatness to which the medium can aspire.

HOLLYWOOD AND THE U. S. A.

By Hortense Powdermaker

THE ANTHROPOLOGIST sees any segment of society as part of a whole; he views Hollywood as a section of the United States of America, and both in the larger frame of Western civilization. The problems of the movie industry are not unique to it. But some characteristics of the modern world have been greatly exaggerated in Hollywood while others are underplayed. Hollywood is therefore not a reflection, but a caricature of selected contemporary tendencies, which, in turn, leave their imprint on the movies. It is a three-way circular interaction between Hollywood, U.S.A. and movies.

Many people would agree with the characterization of our society by the poet W. H. Auden as "The Age of Anxiety." The present generation has known two world wars and is worried about the possibility of a third, even more devastating. We won the last war and are probably the strongest nation, and yet we are insecure in our relations with former enemies and allies. Our country is prosperous and we have demonstrated an enormous capacity for production, but we are worried about a possible recession and unemployment. We live in a fast changing world but have lost faith in our belief that change is always for the better, and that progress is inevitable. We are not so sure of the happy ending.

Man has become increasingly lonely. Although people live in close physical contact, their relationships have become more and more depersonalized. We have a sense of being with people, and yet do not feel in any way related to them. In cities we are accustomed to having strange people beside us in street car, bus, or uncomfortably close in the subway. The technique of business and many other organizations, in trying to personalize their selling relationships, such as by announcing the name of employees to customers, really fools no one. The fact that the name of the post office clerk, the bank teller or the person who handles complaints in the department store, is posted, does not really influence their relationship with customers. The market place is still basically impersonal. Over the radio, we listen to the voices of strangers relating intimate domestic stories or giving us their opinions about the latest national or world event. All these factors give an illusion of companionship which, however, only increases the feeling of being alone. This loneliness is particularly striking when we compare modern to primitive man with his web of personal relationships within his clan. From birth to death he was tied through reciprocal duties and responsibilities to his clan kindred. Clan membership could not be lost and was as fixed for the individual as was his sex. He belonged to his group through basic biological ties and isolation was rare.

Many other factors contribute to modern man's anxiety. The traditional American belief that anyone, by working hard and industriously, may rise in the social hierarchy and become rich and successful is being questioned. There is considerable evidence that the American worker realizes that social mobility is decreasing. Workers increasingly believe that hard work no longer counts for as much as it did and that opportunities for advancement are restricted.[1] Many employees do not even understand the immediate aspects of their work situation. A study made at an electric company, which had an unusually good relationship with its employees, showed that there was much that the worker did not understand about his job, even including the method of payment. The author thought that this lack of understanding caused a feeling of exasperation and sense of personal futility on the part of the workers.[2] Modern man lives in a world which is difficult to comprehend. He is prosperous or unemployed in recurring economic cycles about which economists talk in learned words of cause and effect. But the average man sees only the effect, and is confused as to the causes.

In Hollywood there is far more confusion and anxiety than in the society which surrounds it. Even in its most prosperous periods when net profits were enormous, far surpassing those of other businesses, everyone was scared. Now, when diminishing foreign markets, increasing costs of production, competition with European pictures, and changing box-office tastes threaten the swollen profits of past prosperity, fear rises to panic. Anxiety grips everyone from executive to third assistant director. The happy endings of at least 100 per cent net profit for the studio and a relatively long period of employment at high salaries for employees, are becoming less common. Yet, although this is well known, many individuals still cherish the fantasy for themselves. In the movies the happy ending is still almost universal. Perhaps the people who make the movies cannot afford to admit that there can be another kind of ending, and many of those who sit in the audience prefer this fantasy, too. But an increasing number are becoming dissatisfied with the so obviously contrived nature of these endings. The neat and unrealistic movie solution to all problems is neither satisfying nor entertaining.

[1] William Lloyd Warner and J. O. Low, *The Social System of the Modern Factory*, p. 182. New Haven: Yale Univ. Press.
[2] Elton Mayo, *The Human Problems of an Industrial Civilization*, 2nd ed., pp. 119-120. New York: The Macmillan Co.

Attitudes stem from the past and change slowly. In a rapidly changing society such as ours, some attitudes born out of a past situation continue under new conditions, even when inappropriate. Today there are people who will still believe in the *laissez-faire* economy of the frontier days and are hostile to planning designed for a country which no longer has a frontier. But many who stubbornly cling to the old *laissez-faire* thinking are uneasy lest they fight a losing battle, while many of those who plan are afraid that the planning may go too far. Neither side is really very sure of itself. In Hollywood the lack of planning and extemporizing has been carried to extremes probably not known even on the frontier, and greater certainly than in any contemporary industry. Even more important, extemporizing without a plan has long been regarded by many as a necessary and inherent part of movie making. However, the proper accompaniment, the frontier self-confidence and courage in taking chances, is very rare in Hollywood. The distinguished director-producer William Wyler appeals for . . .

> " '. . . men of courage' in Hollywood to reach out for a wealth of picture material which the industry has shunned so far." He continues, "We need men of courage in high places who will not be intimidated or coerced into making only 'safe' pictures—pictures devoid of any ideas whatsoever." Too often he has bunked up against a situation where the top men were forced to decide between two stories and asked the question, "Which is the safest?" Mediocrity in films is the direct result of playing it safe.[3]

The men who make these decisions do not trust the public to like a picture which has ideas in it, Mr. Wyler says, in the same interview. It might be added that the men who do not trust the public usually do not trust themselves.

From the frontier past comes also the tradition of individual aggressive behavior. This persists although industry has become increasingly regimented and co-operation more essential. In the movie industry which depends on the collaborative effort of many people, the aggression is more ruthless than any described on the frontier, although, due to the insecurities of most people, it is masked under "Darlings" and "Sweethearts" and costly presents and parties. In the movies, however, the hatred and aggression comes through with a bang. Here is undiluted violence. This may meet the needs of the makers of our daydreams, as well as of those who consume them. Many people in our society experience a high level of frustration but are unable, either because of social pressures or inner fear, to express their resentment. In the movies they may find comfort and encouragement for their fantasies.

We have also inherited a Puritan tradition, stressing the sinfulness of human nature and giving us taboos to curb it. Today the doctrine of the innate evilness of man has lost much of its force and is far less a part of the

[3] *Variety,* October 12, 1949.

conscious beliefs of many people. There is a growing awareness that babies are born neither sinful nor virtuous, but with potentialities for many different kinds of behavior, and even the definitions of sin and virtue continue to change. Hollywood, however, even more than the rest of society, feels the weight of Puritan traditions. The industry has imposed on itself a set of taboos derived in part from seventeenth-century New England Protestantism, in order to appease the Catholic Legion of Decency and other would-be censors. No one in Hollywood, and very few outside of it, believe in the Code, nor are the censors appeased or pleased. For while the taboos are applied in the production of each movie, they fail completely to achieve the Puritan concepts on which they are based. They serve merely to make movies more dishonest, which is the natural result of any hypocrisy.

The activities of the various censoring groups spring not only from our past Puritanism, but also out of our social system in which pressure groups are accustomed to playing an important role. Labor, big business, farmers, and others try to influence legislation and get what they want through their organizations. Pressure groups are not restricted to modern society. In primitive ones, the whole tribe may bring pressure on recalcitrant individuals to follow the mores. But the pressure groups which try to influence Hollywood represent only a small part of the population and of movie audiences and are always negative in their intentions. They try to enforce a list of "Thou shalt nots." Most people interested in good entertainment usually know enough to realize that good movies cannot be created by such actions and so do not belong to these groups. This raises the whole question of the function of pressure groups in different areas of society. It is possible that legislators can pass adequate laws through balancing the claims of different pressure groups, and the pluralistic theory of government has long been an accepted democratic practice. But legislation is one thing, and making a movie is another.

An important focus for much of the anxiety in our modern world is in our changing values and goals. The anthropologist knows that the important differences between groups of men are not biological, but lie in their goals. Among the same people the goals may change from one historical period to another, such as from Elizabethan to Victorian England, and they obviously vary from one society to another. In the early Middle Ages religion provided the sanctions for most behavior. Since then the church, while still a functioning institution, has continued to lose much of its vitality. As Kluckhohn writes:

> The anthropologist must characterize our culture as profoundly irreligious. More than half of our people still occasionally go through the forms, and there are rural and ethnic islands in our population where religion is still a vital force. But very few of our leaders are still religious in the sense that they are convinced that prayer or the observance of church codes will affect the course of human events. . . . Belief in God's

judgments and punishments as a motive for behavior is limited to a decreasing minority.[4]

Even more important relatively few people today, as compared to a couple hundred years ago, have the kind of relationship with God to bring them security or comfort. Our society stresses the search for a good time rather than the quest for salvation.

Traditions, however, have a habit of living on in the deeper levels of our consciousness, even when they are overtly denied. Comparatively few people give the impression of really enjoying their wealth or their good times. Many of them appear to be consumed with an obsession to merely fill up time with more and more activity, and space with more and more costly objects. The frenzied and compulsive activity in the studios and outside of them is one of Hollywood's most striking characteristics. Another is the evaluation of not only objects, but people too, in terms of how much they cost. In making movies, this is reflected in the idea that the more a picture costs the better it must be. The tendency towards lavish sets, costumes, and other extravagances is now being curtailed because of the need for economy and the trend to shooting on location. But, with a few exceptions, the correlation of the value of pictures with their budgets is still the prevalent type of thinking in Hollywood. The greater the cost the more sure the studio feels of success, and hence high costs become one way of reducing anxiety. Actually, money can no more guarantee dramatic values than it can insure accuracy or significance in research.

The U.S.A. has been labeled by many students as a business civilization as contrasted to a religious one. This is obviously true, but not the whole truth. Roger Butterfield has described the dominant themes of American life as "the desire to see all men free and equal, and the desire to be richer and stronger than anyone else." [5] This conflict between human and property rights has, as this author points out, generated much of the drama of American life. The political idealism and humanitarianism of the eighteenth and nineteenth centuries, as well as the earlier Puritanism, still influence our business civilization. In our Declaration of Independence is the quintessence of idealism, expressing for the first time the idea that all men have a right to happiness. If the anthropologist interested in our contemporary society digs under the top layers of people's beliefs, he will find still surviving the archaic concepts that money is not the road to happiness, or, at least, not the main one. If he is historically minded, he will note that when private capitalism was developing, the man who accumulated wealth through his own hard work was respected and admired; but that later when private capitalism changed to a corporate form, the corporation

[4] Clyde Kluckhohn, *Mirror for Man*, pp. 247-248. New York: McGraw-Hill.
[5] *The American Past: A History of the United States from Concord to Hiroshima*, p. 5. New York: Simon & Schuster.

was regarded as an enemy of the people. Theodore Roosevelt became famous as a "trust-buster." No man in the U.S.A. becomes a national hero just through making a lot of money. He must have made some contribution to the welfare of his fellow men; most of the nation's heroes have been humanitarians.

In Hollywood the concept of a business civilization has been carried to an extreme. Property is far more important than man and human values have to struggle hard to exist at all. But, while the heroes in Hollywood are those with the most money, in the movies we find the opposite extreme. The wealthy tycoon is almost always the villain and the hero is the man of good will. The hero or heroine may be rich, but wealth does not give them their status. Often we are asked to admire the poor little rich girl who breaks away from her luxurious environment to marry the poor hero whom she loves. Hollywood leans over backward to sentimentalize love, which in the movies is always more important than wealth. Earning a living is never shown with any sense of reality and making a fortune is rarely portrayed sympathetically. True, most of the characters in the movies are better dressed and live more luxuriously than do their counterparts in real life. The secretary dresses like a wealthy debutante and the female psychoanalyst like the popular concept of a Hollywood star. But neither they nor any other heroine or hero are shown as fundamentally interested in or concerned about the problem of making a living or becoming rich. It is only possible to speculate on the reasons for this almost complete negation of economic motives which are so prevalent in our society. The very extremes to which most movies go in the negation may mean that the executives who control the contents of the movies have themselves some hidden ambivalence about their goals. After all, the executives, as well as the actors, do belong to the human species and are not completely unaffected by the conflicting values of our society. Or, they may think that this underplaying of economic motives in the movies is desired by the audience. Neither reason precludes the other, and both could be true, as well as other unknown ones. Whatever the reasons, Hollywood represents a caricature and overelaboration of the business motives and goals of our society, while the movies consistently underplay the same characteristics.

Art and aesthetic goals have always been less important in our society than either business or humanitarian ones. The artist in all societies has traditionally been a kind of barometer, more sensitive to nuances and changes than others, because he is more deeply immersed in his culture and more interested in its meanings. Since he rarely completely accepts all the conventions, he has a certain degree of objectivity and freedom, which of course also makes him seem different from other men. While the artist's status declined in all Western societies after the Industrial Revolution, many of the European countries with their older traditions of painting, music and literature, accorded him a higher position than he enjoys in the United States. Here, he is still considered peculiar, abnormal, sometimes feminine, and unimportant unless he achieves a commercial success comparable to that of a businessman. A Hollywood caricature of this concept is portrayed in the movie, *A Kiss in the Dark*. The hero, a successful concert pianist, played by David Niven, is scared, nervous, withdrawn, and obviously infantile. He is saved by noticing, with appreciation, a model's legs (those of Jane Wyman). She has no interest in his music and leads him to her world of jazz and trombones. He finally frees himself from being an artist and wins his girl by using his musician's hands to knock down the heroine's fiancé, a former athlete. The hero is now a he-man, throws his practice keyboard away, and embraces the heroine as the train carries them away on a honeymoon.

So in the actual production of movies in Hollywood, the American concept of the unimportance of the artist is magnified. Those who know most about storytelling, who are gifted with imagination, and who have a knowledge of human beings, all raw materials which the camera transforms into a movie, do not have sufficient status to use their abilities. As one director expressed it, "the environment is hostile to them." The environment favors the latest developments in sound and color, but discourages new ideas from its artists. These men, who traditionally have known considerable freedom in expressing themselves, work under the direction of businessmen.

The movies have to earn their living. Unlike some of the fine arts, they are not privately endowed nor are they an esoteric medium for the enjoyment of the few. The goals of business and art are each justifiable and not necessarily irreconcilable. When art meets the needs of a large number of people in our society, it inevitably makes a profit. Some of our most creative popular artists, such as Chaplin, Gershwin, Walt Disney and Irving Berlin, have made fortunes. The problem is not the simple one of art versus business. The artist can contribute to business. But his stock-in-trade is not only his technical know-how: it includes the ability to interpret man to himself. This is true in folk art, popular art and fine art. But it makes little difference to the businessman whether he assuages man's anxieties by interpretation, or whether he exploits them; but the latter is easier. Or, if phoniness brings in money easily, why bother about the details of honesty? The front-office executives are not completely blind to humanitarian issues, but they seem far more interested in profits than in man. Most of them are not conditioned to be otherwise. Artists have a different kind of conditioning. While they are concerned about money, they must also, in order to be reasonably contented, use their gifts to give their interpretations. It has already been indicated that while only relatively few of the Hollywood writers, directors and actors are artists in this sense, they are far more important than the host of mediocre people.

The social organization of Hollywood has, however, permitted the businessman to take over the functions of the artists and to substitute his values for theirs. The movies are the first art form of any kind, popular, folk or fine, to become a trust. Quite early the major companies combined in their efforts to restrain competition and to blacklist those who would not do their bidding. The struggle between the Independents and the organization of the major studios still continues. At the same time movies increasingly make use of a developing technology and of the heritage from theater and literature. Under any circumstances such a combination would create complex problems. In this particular situation, the men with power have known how to exploit the advantages of a trust better than they could utilize the assets of literature and drama. They have not seemed to realize that the efficiency of the factory is possible because it turns out identical products, whether automobiles or coffeepots, and that this principle cannot be applied to the making of movies. Since these businessmen have neither understanding nor respect for the artists' ability, they attempt to negate or destroy it, partly out of ignorance and partly from a desire to satisfy their urge to dominate men. It is only an exceptional executive who does not give the impression that he would have been equally satisfied as a tycoon in any other industry.

Outside of Hollywood there is a certain freedom in choice of goals. A man can decide to be an artist, a scientist or a college professor, which means that most likely he will never be rich. Or he can plan to be a big business executive and have the possibility of acquiring great wealth. In Hollywood the same freedom of choice does not exist, because whatever role the individual plays, the goals of business are paramount. In the country as a whole there is the combination of humanism and materialism. But in Hollywood, money is always more important than man. It is this difference in goals which accounts for much of the deep hostility between the front-office and the artists' group. People with the same goals may argue and differ on how to achieve them, but they speak the same language. People with conflicting goals speak a different language. The real artist in Hollywood cannot be completely satisfied, even though he earns a fortune, if he is not functioning as an artist, and this the head of a trust cannot understand.

Another trait of our civilization is its high level of ingenuity and inventiveness in the mechanical skills. Our heroes include men like Thomas Edison, Alexander Graham Bell, Eli Whitney and Henry Ford as well as the humanitarian, political figures. We are justly famous for the enormous number of additions to material culture which make life more comfortable. Movies are themselves a remarkable invention in their integration of electricity, photography, color, sound and acting. The history of inventions from the first stone ax is a fascinating story and one peculiar to our species.

For only man is a tool-making and tool-using animal. Each succeeding example of his ingenuity and cleverness has brought, however, its own problems. This has always been true, but only recently has atomic energy forced a public recognition of the serious social consequences of technological developments.

The control of machines and of all our inventions for the benefit of man is one of the most pressing problems of our time. Machines can enslave people or free them. The Industrial Revolution brought young children into sweatshops and kept them and their parents for long hours at machines. Gradually changes in the social and economic organization reduced the hours of work, set age limits for workers, and enabled them, as well as other people, to enjoy the higher standard of living which machines made possible. But even the most casual observer of our society today recognizes its machinelike character. Not only do machines increasingly replace human labor, but what is left of it grows more mechanical. The role of the individual worker on the assembly line tends to be more and more automatic and he has less and less understanding of its relationship or his own to the whole. The ironic climax is his attempt to escape into fantasies and daydreams, themselves manufactured on an assembly line, far more concerned with technology than with meaning.

The way in which Hollywood has mechanized creativity and taken away most of its human characteristics again exaggerates the prevailing culture pattern, which gives little prestige to creativity not technological. This, of course, does not apply to the genius: an Einstein, Picasso, or a Rachmaninoff is given due honor. But we do little to bring out the creativity which lies in all human beings. Most people—just the everyday garden variety, not the geniuses—have far more potentialities for being creative than they use. But very few of them have the courage or desire to carry through their own ideas, big or little, because they have been conditioned to think routinely and follow the crowd. Our society tends, particularly today, to prize uniformity in thinking more than originality. The concern with the "know-how" rather than the "why," with technology rather than meaning, permeates much of the thinking even in the social sciences when method becomes more important than problems. The use of the most exact scientific methods on a sterile and meaningless problem is not too different from the employment of the most technically advanced camera work to produce a banal movie. It is the same when our educational system stresses the accumulation of facts rather than the meaningful relationship between them, and the taking of so many courses that there is little time for thoughtful reflection. It is not that factual knowledge or scientific methods are unimportant, but rather that they are of use only in the larger context of problems and meanings. Hollywood expands these two features of our society to such an extent that it discourages and sometimes even forbids creativity in the very people whom it presumably pays to be creative.

The problem of power has been important since the beginning of mankind's existence. Its history follows no straight line, but lunges forward and backward, always correlated with the concept of what is human nature and with the meaning of freedom. In the very beginning of his history, man was more at one with the natural world than he is today. He might think he was descended from a totemic animal and there was a close tie with other animals and to the world of nature. Primitive man was also more closely linked with his kindred than is modern man. Much of life in Stone Age societies consisted of a series of reciprocal duties and responsibilities between members of an extended family, clan or other social group, which continued even after death. In this system of close relationships there was little room for emphasis on individuality. Differences between people might be noted, but were not considered particularly important. Rebels from traditional customs were few. If head-hunting was a way of proving manhood and becoming eligible for marriage, it would be unusual to find one of the young men of the tribe staying behind, murmuring "I'm not the type," as the others went off on a head-hunting expedition. Some primitive societies do have institutionalized modes of behavior for people who do not fit into the norm, such as homosexuals; but on the whole little attention is paid to the less striking individual differences. Traditions are followed, and power to implement them lies with the elders.

The process of the emergence of the individual from these primary ties Erich Fromm calls "individuation." He points out that the same process occurs in the life history of an individual.[6] Birth involves a biological separation from the mother and the beginning of an individual existence, even though the child is functionally dependent on his mother for a considerable time. Mankind as well as the individual struggles through the ages to free himself from primary ties. Familiar landmarks in this history are Christianity, with its emphasis on the importance and value of each individual's soul to God, the end of Feudalism, the Reformation, the Industrial Revolution, political revolutions with their overthrow of monarchies, and the development of political and economic democracy. During this process power has gone through many re-allocations, from the tribal elders to feudal lords, popes, kings and emperors. Gradually it was diffused from the hands of a few to the many, who include elected political representatives, owners of industry, leaders of labor and others. This century has seen revolutions which reversed the process and concentrated power again in the hands of a few dictators. Man, as Fromm says, both wants and fears freedom; he struggles to gain it and he gives it up.

The meaning of the word "freedom," of course, is not the same to all men, or at all times. There are many freedoms and none is absolute. Most

[6] Erich Fromm, *Escape from Freedom*. New York: Rinehart. Fromm discusses this whole problem and its relation to freedom in detail.

of them connote freedom from some form of constraint, either in society or within man's personality. But, underlying all freedoms, as Ralph Barton Perry writes, is the freedom of thought. This implies choice and an awareness of alternatives, based on both imagination and knowledge.[7] The *exercise* of the freedom of choice may be restricted, by institutions and customs, or by psychological forces within man, due to ignorance and fear. The degree to which freedom of choice is permitted is always linked with society's particular concept of the nature of man. Today, at one end of the power scale is the idea of man as a passive creature without ability to choose for himself, manipulated by a powerful few who claim omniscience. Men are puppets pulled by strings, seen and hidden. They are told what to think politically, scientifically, morally, and aesthetically. Spontaneity in thinking is discouraged and conformity is the goal. Choice of an alternative which involves different values is not presented in the concept. When all the manipulation is done by the state and when the strings are pulled by a dictator, it is called totalitarianism.

The form of thinking underlying totalitarianism and some of its accompanying behavior is not confined to the countries labeled as such. It is present everywhere and not absent from our own society. However, here, it is in conflict with a different concept, the democratic one, which emphasizes the uniqueness of man in his greater capacity for thinking as compared to other species. Both the desire and ability to choose between alternatives is regarded as an innate part of being human, which increases as men grow up and break their dependency on primary ties. This theory of human nature is imbedded in our formal charters, the Constitution and the Declaration of Independence, and is part of our traditional behavior as represented by a multiple-party system; freedom of choice at a secret ballot box; freedom of religion; diversity of ideas in sciences and arts, and choice of different goals.

The democratic concept of the nature of man is in continuous conflict with the totalitarian one, but the struggle is not confined to the political level, or to international relationships. It is part of the texture of our daily lives, in the family, in school and college, in courts, in Congressional and State legislative committees, and in every other area which has responsibility in human relations. There appears to be an increasing tendency in some of these areas to stifle, overtly and subtly, the expression of opinions which are not those of the majority, to overstress conformity, and to so prevent freedom of thought and of choice.

The conflict comes out particularly clearly in education. On one side there is the emphasis on discovering individual aptitudes and developing the unique capacities of each student. The goal of small classes so that more attention can be paid to individual students is everywhere recognized, even if not always attained. But even in graduate work, there is also the

[7] Ralph Barton Perry, *Characteristically American*, pp. 148-149. New York: Knopf.

tendency in the opposite direction: one graduate seminar at a well-known university had eighty members. Still, the idea of the educational process as one which trains the student's capacity for critical and independent judgment is sincerely believed in by some, and given lip service by most educators. The ninetieth birthday of John Dewey, more responsible than any other one person for shaping our concept of democratic education, was celebrated nationally. At the same time there are opposing tendencies, political and pedagogical, which negate the whole concept of developing the students' capacity to think for themselves and to choose between alternatives. The censorship of ideas in books and magazines of which school boards or influential pressure groups do not approve generates an atmosphere of fear for teachers and students, which is hardly conducive to independent thinking. Nor is training in critical judgment necessarily provided by the emphasis on accumulation of facts for ritual examinations.

In family living and bringing up of children, there are also opposing trends, with the democratic one gaining. Implicit obedience to parents and the idea that "children should be seen and not heard" belong to the past mores. In this country, there is the trend, sometimes carried to extremes, of self-expression for children and for parents to be friends or pals with their children, rather than authoritarian figures. The emphasis is on the development of the child's capacity to make decisions for himself, as his knowledge and experiences broaden. This type of thinking, accenting spontaneity rather than conformity, appears to be gradually becoming part of our mores. The family, one of the most significant conditioning forces in the life history of the individual, is decidedly nontotalitarian in our society.

Family life, education, and political organizations have always been conditioning forces molding the lives of people; but mass communications are new. Certainly they have enriched our culture. Without the invention of printing, literacy for masses of people would be impossible. Radio gives a speed and ease of communication undreamed of by our ancestors. Movies can bring drama to millions of people who otherwise would never enter a theater. But the mass communications, like every other advance, bring problems as well as advantages. Among the most serious is the capacity of these communications to manipulate the ideas, opinions and emotions of vast audiences. More and more do people depend on what they read in their daily newspaper or what their radio commentator says, for their opinions. This means that man functions passively, taking over opinions, ideas, and prejudices ready-made from others, rather than actively examining a number of choices and making up his own mind. In a totalitarian society all the mass communications are controlled by a ruling clique, and no choice is permitted the citizen. In the United States there is a choice, but relatively few people avail themselves of it. They do not all seem to realize that almost every newspaper has its own line, whether it be the [New York] *Daily News* or the *Daily Worker,* as has each radio commentator; and many do not bother to examine different lines. Albert Schweitzer thinks that our whole society is geared to what he calls "the renunciation of thinking," and he labels our age one of spiritual bankruptcy. He writes:

> The organized political, social and religious associations of our time are at work to induce individual man not to arrive at his convictions by his own thinking but to take as his own, such convictions as they keep ready-made for him. Any man who thinks for himself and at the same time is spiritually free is to the associations something inconvenient and even uncanny. He does not offer sufficient guarantee that he will merge himself in their organizations in the way they wish. All corporate bodies look today for their strength not so much to the spiritual worth of the ideas they represent and to that of the people who belong to them, as to the attainment of the highest possible degree of unity and exclusiveness. It is here that they expect to find their strongest power for offense and defense.[8]

The tendency of our age is not only to take over our thoughts ready-made and to lazily conform, but to continue the same pattern with our emotions. This is to be expected, since the dichotomy between thought and feeling is, of course, artificial. In manipulating and defining our emotions and ideas about human relations, mass communications are among the most powerful agents. For instance, the pulp literature, advertising and movies all hammer home a similar concept of love. Advertising both uses and abuses man's basic need for love to sell its ware. The young woman who rides the subway or bus to work, daily reads that holding a husband is dependent on using certain soap flakes which will keep the color of her underwear fresh; and in the past, there was the negative campaign of "Always a bridesmaid and never a bride" unless a certain mouthwash was used. Not only does advertising sell its products, but it also sells a concept of love and human relations. The pulps and movies sell their concept of love, too, with the movies being probably far the more powerful, since in them, love objects are dramatically portrayed by glamorous or highly attractive men and women. Love, in most movies, is limited to instant biological attraction without any other elements. The hero sees a girl waiting for a bus; one look at her well-shaped legs, strutting bosom, and golden hair is sufficient to tell him that this is his mate for life, and the pursuit begins. In actual life in Hollywood, and elsewhere, the end of such a pursuit would usually be only the bed, quickly reached. Censorship, of course, forbids this portrayal, and so the ending is transformed into the romantic one of happiness ever after. This confusion between love and infatuation or an adolescent "crush" is repeated over and over again. Another recurring theme in movies is the loss, or threatened loss, of a love object;

[8] Albert Schweitzer, *Out of My Life and Thought,* p. 255. New York: Henry Holt.

the solution is usually suicide, murder, or insanity. Finding another love object rarely occurs, although our divorce and remarriage rate indicate this is a fairly frequent modern solution. Love is also supposed to be the mainspring for all creative work, whether in science or the arts. In the lives of great artists and scientists which have been filmed, the hero is usually dependent for his accomplishment not on his own genius, intelligence, or hard work, but on the loving devotion of his mate, or more colloquially, "the little woman."

The other emotional behavior most frequently emphasized in the movies, besides love, is violence. Radio, comics and headlines are vibrant with it. Like love, violence has long been a part of all drama. But, as John Houseman writes:

> What is significant about our contemporary "tough" films (critics and ladies' organizations to the contrary) is *not* their surface violence but the neurotic reaction that accompanies it. It is not the act of brutality that is repellent, but the indifference with which it is regarded by those who commit it and those whom it affects.[9]

As Houseman points out in his discussion of the characters in *The Big Sleep*, "It is these people—spiritless zombies, utterly lacking in moral or tragic sense—that are really frightening, not their forays with blackjack and pistol."

There are a number of points of view about violence in movies. It may serve as a catharsis for the conscious and unconscious desires of the audience, as all drama does to some degree. But whether or not the function of catharsis is served depends on whether the violence is treated in its tragic and human aspects. As noted earlier, it is possible that a succession of movies in which violence is portrayed by glamorous stars and in which there is no sense of inner morality, even though the "sinners" are punished at the end, may not be cathartic at all but, instead, give this behavior a kind of permissiveness. At least, these movies do not act as a deterrent and movie solutions, other than violent and easy ones for difficult situations, are often ignored.

The problem of aggression in our society is not an easy one. The ordinary frictions of life generate an aggressive attitude and it is a necessary ingredient underlying much success. Yet aggressive behavior in general is not approved. Rarely is an outlet permitted in the family. If an adolescent or person in his late teens is angry with his father or mother, instead of letting his anger out on them, he is more apt to rush out of the house and go to a movie. Here, he can find an outlet for his feelings. But his relationship with parents and the situation which caused his aggression remains unchanged. Many other older people are afraid of showing their aggressive feelings, because they fear loss of love or affection. Movies provide

[9] John Houseman, "What Makes American Movies Tough?" in *Vogue*, January 15, 1947.

a vicarious outlet, but the basic insecurities of the individual are left untouched.

The heightening of suspense is part of most pictures in which violence is a part. These movies aim to increase tensions and their advertisements feature the breathless suspense, excitement and horror. An element of suspense is part of all drama. But never has it been so intense and so exaggerated as in most current thrilling movies. A possible hypothesis is that people cannot permit themselves to be fully aware of all the suspense and fear involved in the atomic bomb, a possible third war, and the future in general for themselves and the world. Although they try to evade the problem, the anxiety remains. The suspense of finding out "who done it" in the movie or detective story may be one way of relieving the greater suspense of what is going to happen to them and their children in the future. The suspense gags of a man dangling on a clothesline between two high buildings and wild hysterical automobile chases, in all of which no one gets hurt, may offer some relief. In a typical Abbott and Costello comedy, *The Buck Private Comes Home,* Costello drives a midget car in a race and through all kinds of fantastic obstacles. He does not know how to drive, is unable to control the car, and throughout the whole race is scared stiff. Through a series of miraculous escapes he comes out safely and wins the race. An audience who feels helpless to control an equally fantastic social situation, would like nothing better than a Costello victory through a miracle.

The manipulation of behavior as well as emotions is common to our society. Salesmen are important in our business civilization and success in selling is attained primarily through the manipulation of people. *How to Win Friends and Influence People,* and all the books similar to this best seller, attempt to give the techniques. Knowing the right people is regarded as more important to success in many jobs than knowledge, experience, or integrity. Many young men go to prestige universities in the East in order to make "contacts," which will help them in Wall Street or business careers after commencement. There is hardly a profession, even those in which skill and knowledge count, that does not number among its successes a goodly number who have come to the top primarily through the slap-on-the-back and similar techniques. Of course, knowing influential people and getting their help is part of human relations in every society. But our society exaggerates the pattern.

While these are some of the totalitarian elements which exist in democratic societies, there are basic differences between them and totalitarian ones. In the latter, the manipulation of people is carried to the greatest extremes and, even more important, is always done by a few powerful men at the head of the state. In democracies, the manipulation is done by many different forces with diverse goals and often in conflict. The differences between the totalitarian philosophy of man as an obedient robot and the traditional democratic concept of man's freedom and independence are very significant. These differences in social organization and in philosophy should not be underestimated. Totalitarian elements in our society, whether in school, home, politics, are only one of a number of alternatives. For, while democratic ideas and behavior are not always implemented or used, there are opportunities for freedom of thought and behavior. It is true that sometimes the citizen merely repeats opinions he hears over the radio or reads in the newspaper. But there are other times when he bursts through all these synthetic ideas and thinks for himself, as he has demonstrated in several presidential elections. The election of President Roosevelt in 1944 and of President Truman in 1948 ran counter to the majority of editorial opinions and radio propaganda. As far as is known, the citizen of the totalitarian state is not given this opportunity to choose or the family and educational conditioning to utilize it. In American society, as in many of the Western European ones, there are present conflicting trends of totalitarianism and democracy.

Hollywood represents totalitarianism. Its basis is economic rather than political but its philosophy is similar to that of the totalitarian state. In Hollywood, the concept of man as a passive creature to be manipulated extends to those who work for the studios, to personal and social relationships, to the audiences in the theaters and to the characters in the movies. The basic freedom of being able to choose between alternatives is absent. The gifted people who have the capacity for choice cannot exercise it; the executives who technically have the freedom of choice do not actually have it, because they usually lack the knowledge and imagination necessary for making such a choice. Much behavior is compulsive, springing from fears, hidden and open. The careful planning and good judgment of the exceptional people have been already described and are in dramatic contrast to the hysterical behavior of the others.

The Hollywood atmosphere of crises and continuous anxiety is a kind of hysteria which prevents people from thinking, and is not too different from the way dictators use wars and continuous threats of war as an emotional basis for maintaining their power. As the late Dr. Harry Stack Sullivan pointed out, there is considerable difference between fear and anxiety. Fear, he said, is often provoked by a new or novel situation and wears off as one becomes accustomed to it. Anxiety, however, arises out of relationships with other people which are disturbed, and "from its mildest to its most extreme manifestations interferes with effective alertness to the factors in the current situation that are immediately relevant to its occurrence, and thus with the refinement and precision of action related to its relief or reduction." [10] Put more colloquially and applied to Hollywood, this

[10] Harry Stack Sullivan, "Multidisciplined Co-ordination of Interpersonal Data," in *Culture and Personality*, p. 179. Proceeding of an Interdisciplinary Conference held under the auspices of the Viking Fund. Published by the Viking Fund, New York.

means that a stage director who directs a movie for the first time might have some fear which would disappear as he became more accustomed to the new situation. In the meantime, the fear would not inhibit his learning as much as possible about the new situation and applying his knowledge and talent to it. But the anxiety of the average producer who has been in movies all his adult life springs out of his character and interpersonal relations, and the Hollywood situation calls forth and increases what is already there. Nor is it possible to become accustomed to anxiety-provoking situations. The very anxiety prevents an awareness of the factors which call it forth and of realistically doing something about them. These anxiety-ridden producers and executives of Hollywood try to reduce anxiety by spending more money, buying a best seller whether or not it is appropriate for a movie, using ten writers instead of one, having three "big name" stars in a movie, and so on. But none of these formulas rids him of his anxiety. Even where a picture is a big success, he knows the same anxiety on the next one.

In *Mein Kampf*, Hitler wrote about Fate as sometimes cruel and other times loving. Whether it is called Fate, destiny, or breaks, the underlying concept is the same: man gives up the attempt to exercise some control over his life through his own intelligence, because he thinks forces beyond his domain completely direct it.

The totalitarian concept of man is not limited to human relationships in Hollywood, but is reflected in many movies. Life, success or misfortune is usually portrayed as caused by luck or an accident. Only rarely does a movie show the process of becoming successful or the process of disintegration. Either one is treated as a *fait accompli* in the beginning of the picture or as caused by accidents during the course of the movie. Most movie characters, whether hero or villain, heroine or jade, are passive beings to whom things happen accidentally. Rarely do they even try to think through the situation in which they find themselves. They are buffeted about and defeated; or Fate smiles on them and almost magically they are successful. A few pictures have freed themselves from this formula. In *Home of the Brave* the Negro hero is shown as suffering realistically from prejudice. His escape is not on a magic carpet into a never-never world but through a painful psychological process, which the movie plainly says is kaleidoscoped. The Negro problem is seen as part of a larger human one. Nor is the problem over at the end of the picture. The hero merely understands it better and has a way of handling it.

The totalitarian concept likewise extends toward the audiences, often regarded as suckers whose emotional needs and anxieties can be exploited for profit. Hollywood producers are, of course, not the only people with undue anxieties and many of the movies cater to the same kind of anxieties in their audiences, strengthening rather than reducing them, and contributing nothing to understanding. Only men who are not completely ridden with anxieties and who have some understanding of their own, as well as mankind's problems, can make other kinds of pictures. "The people," however, are always used as a rationalization—by dictators who say they rule for the good of the people, and by Hollywood producers who say they give the people what they want.

Until recently Hollywood offered very little more choice to audiences than it did to its artist employees. Today, because of competition from both exceptional Hollywood movies and foreign films, there is more choice.

The ultimate in totalitarian power is power for its own sake, although dictators offer various rationalizations for propaganda purposes. Some of the men with power in Hollywood present the same picture. These men have made millions, and more money means very little to them; but they cannot get enough of power: power over human beings in the studio and power over the daydreams of men and women who sit in the darkened theater.

For men of this type there is often enjoyment also in the power to humiliate, which they exercise in their relationships with their employees. There is a story about a well-known director, Mr. John Mighty, who was sleeping with the star of the picture he was directing. One morning she came on the set about a half hour late, and he bawled her out in loud, scolding language before the other actors, a crowd of extras, and the work-men. She tried to tell him that the hairdresser and make-up had taken longer than usual, but he refused to listen. Instead, he made her repeat after him an abject apology to the crowd on the set: "I apologize because I am late, and because I have caused loss of money to the studio and loss of time to all of you, and more particularly, because I know I am an actress without ability." At this point, she broke down and, crying, said, "But please, John!" She got no further. The director bellowed, " 'John' in bed, you bitch; 'Mr. Mighty' on the set!" Humiliation as a technique for main-taining authority and for enjoyment is not confined to big people: assistant directors often show the same pattern in their treatment of extras. Those who take pleasure in degrading other people, whether in Hollywood or in a totalitarian state, are themselves degraded and may be even subcon-sciously aware of it.

Of course Hollywood is no more completely totalitarian than it is completely primitive. The genesis of Hollywood is different from that of any totalitarian state. In the latter the dictators either seize power through revolution, or attain it by making promises to relieve the misery and anx-ieties from which people suffer, or they do both. In Hollywood most of the men who enjoy power have it simply because they got there first and were able to form the social structure of movie making as they desired, rather than in the interests of movie making. The Hollywood dictators have not been able to make converts, in the way of any successful political dictator. He gets his subjects when young, and conversion begins in the kindergarten. The subjects in Hollywood arrive there as adults with fairly well-formulated ideas about how they can best work and live. They accept the dictatorship only nominally, because of the high salaries. They rarely accept it emotionally and, instead, are filled with resentment and bitterness toward it.

The rebels, in this case the artists, do not struggle in underground movements to outmaneuver the studio executives. They fight openly to gain power, that is, to get into positions in which they can make important decisions and influence the movies. A sufficient number of gifted writers, directors and actors are succeeding to indicate at least a trend which offers a variation and may, eventually, modify or change the system.

These exceptional individuals receive little help in their struggles. The Federal Government tries to reduce the monopolistic power of the industry and to regulate its buying and selling practices. Censorship groups attempt to regulate the morality of the pictures and succeed only in making them dishonest. Guilds fight for more money for their members, but do nothing about a contract, which allows the employer almost literally to own his employees for its duration. The exceptional individuals, with great strength of character and drive, with high talent, and with a true morality, work on their own as they try to dent the power situation in Hollywood, alter the human relationships, and give meaning to their movies.

Totalitarianism, whether in a foreign nation or in Hollywood, represents one of the backward swings in history. But primitive societies seldom knew the degradation that modern man can suffer under a dictator. Although primitive cultures have a similar lack of emphasis on the individual, there are wide differences between them and modern totalitarian states. The two situations differ widely in origin and effect. In primitive societies man has not yet emerged sufficiently from his primary ties to his family and clan kindred to emphasize his own individuality. But totalitarianism attempts to negate the individuality of men who *have* broken these primary ties, who *have* known, and valued, freedom. The force of tradition offers very little choice to primitive man. The force of the modern police state also offers very little choice. Primitive cultures lack the knowledge and awareness of man's potentialities. Modern totalitarian societies fear and distrust them. Evolutionary thinking is not in style in the social sciences, but it is possible to view the history of man as a gradual freeing of himself from primary ties and becoming freer to utilize and develop his uniquely human characteristics.

In every society there are a multitude of patterns, some overelaborated and others underplayed. The anthropologist is well aware that either process may be carried to such unnecessary extremes as to threaten the well-being and, occasionally, even the survival of the society. Among the aborigines of Australia the marriage regulations are worked out to such a fine point that it is almost impossible for a native to find a socially approved mate. His way out of this impossible situation is to elope. Some Eskimo tribes are not permitted to hunt seals in summer, and they will not touch seals in this season even if the land game fails and they are starving.

Hollywood has the elaborated totalitarian elements we have described: the concept of people as property and as objects to be manipulated, highly concentrated and personalized power for power's sake, an amorality, and an atmosphere of breaks, continuous anxiety and crises. The result of this overelaboration is business inefficiency, deep frustration in human relations, and a high number of unentertaining second- and third-rate movies.

There are, of course, other patterns in the U.S.A. which Hollywood could elaborate. They are the democratic ones of the dignity of man, the concept of freedom, a belief in man's capacity to think, create, and to exercise some control over his life—a belief that man is more important than property—all part of our cultural heritage. How far will Hollywood utilize them? It is not a matter of more brains and talent or of money, but of generating new modes of behavior and a system in which collaboration is more important than domination. Any changes that will occur will not come out of magical thinking or waiting for breaks. Nor is it possible to be sure of a "happy ending." No anthropologist ever expects a complete break from the past. But he does know that societies assume different forms through contact with others, through technological inventions, and through changes in values and goals. He can predict that Hollywood will not go back to its isolated position and that there will be new technological developments. The really difficult question to answer is, Can Hollywood change its ways of thinking and its values, so that the democratic concept of man becomes more important than a totalitarian one?

6

BROADCASTING MEDIA

George O. Gillingham
THE ABC'S OF RADIO AND TELEVISION

Neil Postman
THE LITERATURE OF TELEVISION

Sydney W. Head
SOME INTER-MEDIA RELATIONSHIPS

6

BROADCASTING MEDIA

No other medium of mass communication has equaled television in the intensity of its appeal to the American people. Television has generated more attention, interest, discussion and controversy than all the other mass media combined. The audience for a television program is almost invariably many times the audience for any of the other media and, frequently, larger than all of the other media of mass communication.

As the world's largest advertising medium, television makes a tremendous contribution to the economy of the nation. As an entertainment form of unusual variety and potential, television embraces drama, comedy, western, action-adventure programs and many other types. As a news and public affairs medium, television has become a unique informational force in our society, presenting the news with an impact and immediacy not equaled by any other medium. As a teaching aid, television has stirred the imagination of educators and—even at this relatively early stage—has contributed to new audio-visual techniques and vastly expanded facilities for learning.

Broadcasting stations operate under licenses to serve "the public interest, convenience and necessity" in spectrum space allocated by the Federal Communications Commission. In this context, television has engendered a vast amount of pro and con discussion relating to problems of freedom and control, censorship, program content and corollary matters. The full potential of television is yet to be realized, but the implications of the medium have stirred the imagination as have few other phenomena since the invention of printing.

Chroniclers of the growth of mass communication begin with the basic premise that the broadcasting industry operates necessarily from a socio-economic base, that it makes a vastly important contribution to a competitive mercantile economy and that it provides an entertainment and information service which is truly national in scope. As Dr. Frank Stanton, President of the Columbia Broadcasting System, Inc., has stated: "One of its most essential functions is to provide instantaneous national interconnection day in, day out, between great cities and small towns throughout the length and breadth of America . . . No such facilities ever existed before the creation of the networks, nothing except networks can serve these functions, and nothing now imagined can take their essential place . . .

"The first, the absolutely primary aspect of a network is its relationship to the public. A network renders its service to nothing else and to nothing smaller, than the national American public. This service is its touchstone. . . ."

Since television's service is so often discussed, a summary of the structure and function of broadcasting is of some relevance. Such a summary is provided in "The ABC's of Radio and Television," provided by Broadcasting Yearbook and prepared by George O. Gillingham, information officer of the Federal Communications Commission. The relevant background of radio, the development of television broadcasting, the problems inherent in the activation of UHF channels, the growth of educational television, or ETV, and the function of the Federal Communications Commission are discussed.

In his discussion of "The Literature of Television," Neil Postman attempts the difficult task of determining what literary forms are to be found in the television medium, particularly in the area of drama. There are some critics, fortunately a small minority, who seem unable to find any literature indigenous to television. Postman's analysis proves otherwise, both in terms of authors and of the original dramas which have appeared on television.

Television drama reflects both the potential and the limitations of the medium, as well as the needs, wants and aspirations of its vast, heterogeneous television audience. The key word is "reflects." While meeting the needs of majority audiences, television is also cognizant of the interests of minority groups and reflects these as well. Particularly in the last few years, television drama has reflected the attitudes and interests of its audiences— just as other art forms, such as the motion picture, the novel and the stage play tend to reflect audience needs. Postman wisely points out that it is extremely difficult to satisfy a wide audience base, particularly in a medium in which there have been certain dramatic and technical limitations on the creative process. These limitations are largely being overcome as television has learned to range from film to live programming to tape, depending upon creative and production needs.

As one author put it, the basis for drama is "intimacy." The creative limitations, rapidly decreasing with new techniques, are the lack of wide scope, the tendency to emphasize the close-up, and the frequent limitations of time and space. Nevertheless, Postman's analysis provides a valuable frame of reference and indicates that there has developed a literature of television. Some viewers may be surprised to discover that contemporary television drama is an outgrowth, however tenuous, of such forms as the early morality play, the early American western and similar dramatic types.

Certainly, one of television's most significant contributions is its unique ability to capture the world of reality, a form revealed occasionally in drama, but more often in the non-fictional forms of news and public affairs programming. In this area, television communicates in the immediate present and with a scope, power and breadth which are unequaled by any other medium of mass communication.

In "Some Inter-Media Relationships," Sydney W. Head essays the somewhat complex job of juxtaposing television and other mass media. Professor Head's evaluation is valuable not only for the analysis of television and other media, but also for what it reveals of other inter-media relationships. It provides, in addition, a summary of the place of each of the mass media in the total framework of the communications field. Head properly places television in a "pivotal position" at which the currents of other mass media intersect. For television both competes with and complements other media such as the newspaper, magazine and, particularly in the area of popular entertainment, the motion picture. Furthermore, broadcasting utilizes and, in many ways, goes beyond in its services, the content of these other related media.

There is provided an interesting and accurate parallel between broadcasting (i.e., both radio and television) and the development of the motion picture—both from a technical and creative point of view. The early tendency of the motion picture to disregard the potentialities of television is particularly relevant in view of the crisis through which Hollywood has been passing in the decade or so since television began. In many ways it was, as Head indicates, "the end of an era" for motion pictures. What must be considered, however, is that, apart from the impact of television, the decline of the motion picture was also a result of Hollywood's own incompetence and its degeneration "into telling myths for children."

Classified as "hybrid" systems, particularly at this juncture, are such experimental efforts as theater television and subscription television. But more significant a development has been the increased tendency of the press to recognize that readers want to read about radio and television, so that newspapers have been printing complete TV logs as a necessary service to the reader. At the same time, many newspaper enterprises also operate radio and television stations, although it has been said that this ownership appears in no way to have influenced editorial judgment. Paradoxically, many newspapers which are owned by the same interests as operate the television station have not been kind to the broadcast media. It is certainly a fact of journalistic life that television's coverage of "spot" news events is unparalleled by any other media, as the on-the-spot coverage of the astronaut shoot clearly revealed.

Professor Head's conclusions are basically sound: ". . . generally speaking, competition among the media seems to have resulted in mutual gains for all" by stimulating each medium. Non-theatrical film production is a case in point. The record industry is another. Adaptation of plays and motion pictures to—and from—television is still another example of inter-media relationships.

*   *   *   *

RELATED READING

Coffin, T. E. "Television's effects on leisure-time activities." *J. Appl. Psycho.*, 32 (1948), 550-558.

Gross, Ben. *I Looked and I Listened*. New York: Random House, 1954.

Head, Sydney W. "Content Analysis of Television Drama Programs," *Quarterly of Film, Radio and Television*, IX (1954), 175-94.

Lazarsfeld, Paul F. and Stanton, Frank, eds. *Radio Research, 1941; Radio Research, 1942-43*. New York: Duell, Sloan, and Pearce, 1941, 1944.

Maccoby, Eleanor E. "Television: Its impact on school children." *Publ. Opin. Quart.*, 15 (1951), 421-444.

Marx, Herbert L., Jr., ed. *Television and Radio in American Life*. New York: H. W. Wilson Company, 1953.

McDonagh, E. C., et al. "Television and the family." *Sociol. & Soc. Res.*, 1950, 35, 113-133.

Riley, J. W., Cantwell, F. V., & Ruttinger, Katherine F. "Some observations on the social effects of television." *Publ. Opin. Quart.*, 13 (1949), 223-234.

Shayon, Robert Lewis. "The Pied Piper of Video," *Saturday Review of Literature*, XXXIII, November 25, 1950, 9-11 and continued.

Siepmann, Charles A. *Radio, Television and Society*. New York: Oxford University Press, 1950.

THE ABC'S OF RADIO AND TELEVISION

By George O. Gillingham

How Radio Began

RADIO COMMUNICATION was born of many minds and developments. In the 1860's, Maxwell predicted the existence of radio waves. Hertz later demonstrated that rapid variations of electric current can be projected into space in the form of waves similar to those of light and heat. In 1895, Marconi transmitted radio signals for a short distance and, at the turn of the century, conducted successful trans-Atlantic tests.

The first practical application of radio was for ship-to-ship and ship-to-shore telegraphic communication. Marine disasters early demonstrated the speed and effectiveness of radiotelegraphy for safeguarding life and property at sea.

This new communication medium was first known as "wireless." American use of the term "radio" is traced to about 1912 when the Navy, feeling that "wireless" was too inclusive, adopted the word "radiotelegraph." Though the British still cling to the older term, "radio" continues to be the American designation. The word "broadcast" stems from early United States naval reference to "broadcast" of orders to the fleet.

There was some military radiotelephony in World War I—between ground and planes and ship and shore—but most early radio communication was confined to ships at sea and to amateurs. The latter were highly instrumental in arousing popular interest in radio and otherwise contributing to its progress.

The first voice broadcast is a subject for debate. Claims to that distinction range from "Hello, Rainey," said to have been sent by Stubblefield to a partner in a demonstration near Murray, Ky., in 1892, to an impromptu program from Brant Rock, Mass., by Fessenden in 1906, which was picked up by nearby ships.

There were other early experimental audio transmissions—such as De Forest putting Enrico Caruso on the air in 1910 and trans-Atlantic voice tests by the Navy station at Arlington, Va., in 1915—but it was not until after World War I that regular broadcasting began. But here, too, there is

Reprinted from an article prepared for *Broadcasting Yearbook* 1961-62 by George O. Gillingham by permission of Broadcasting Magazine.

controversy. Some radio broadcasting stations developed from experimental operations going back to 1912. KDKA Pittsburgh, although not issued a regular broadcasting license until Nov. 7, 1921, carried experimental programs prior to that date under a license issued in 1920. The first station issued a regular broadcast license was WBZ Springfield, Mass., on Sept. 15, 1921.

There was experimental network operation over telephone lines as early as 1922. In that year WJZ Newark, N. J., and WGY Schenectady broadcast the World Series. Early in 1923 WEAF New York and WNAC Boston picked up a football game from Chicago. Later that same year WEAF and WGY were connected with KDKA Pittsburgh and KYW Chicago to carry talks made at a dinner in New York. President Coolidge's message to Congress was broadcast by six stations in late 1923. In 1926 the National Broadcasting Co. started the first regular network with 24 stations. Its first coast-to-coast hookup, in 1927, broadcast a football game. In the latter year the Columbia Broadcasting System was organized. The first round-the-world broadcast was made from Schenectady in 1930. Today, thanks to telephone lines, coaxial cable, microwave and other relay facilities, it is possible to send the same program over many stations at the same time.

FM (frequency modulation) and TV (television) broadcast emerged from their experimental stage just before World War II. Wartime restrictions retarded normal expansion of radio facilities but that emergency produced new techniques and apparatus which have invaluable peacetime application.

Communications Act of 1934

At the request of President Roosevelt, the Secretary of Commerce in 1933 appointed an interdepartmental committee to study the overall interstate and international electrical communications situation. The committee reported that "the communications service, as far as Congressional action is involved, should be regulated by a single body." Accordingly, it recommended the establishment of a new agency which would regulate all interstate and foreign communication by wire and radio, including telegraph, telephone and broadcast. The resultant Communications Act of 1934 created the present Federal Communications Commission for this unified regulation.

Federal Communications Commission

The Federal Communications Commission, an independent federal agency composed of seven commissioners appointed by the President, by and with the advice and consent of the Senate, began operating on July 1, 1934.

What the FCC Does

One of the FCC's major activities is the general regulation of broadcasting—now visual as well as aural. This regulation, largely technical in nature, may be divided into two phases.

The first phase deals with the allocation of spectrum space to the different types of broadcast services in accordance with Commission policies and rules to carry out the intent of international agreements, the Communications Act and other domestic laws affecting broadcasting.

The second phase is concerned more directly with individual stations, and embraces consideration of applications to build and operate; the assignment of specific frequencies, power, time of operation and call letters; the periodic inspection of equipment and the engineering aspects of operation; passing upon transfers and assignments of facilities; also the many varied changes in existing authorizations; modifying and renewing construction permits and licenses; reviewing the general service of each particular station to determine whether it has been operating in the public interest; licensing radio operators, and otherwise discharging domestic regulatory responsibilities.

Broadcast stations are licensed to serve the public interest, convenience and necessity. Because radio channels are limited and are a part of the public domain, it is important that they be entrusted to licensees who have a high sense of public responsibility. The normal license period is three years but, in 1960, Congress authorized the Commission to make shorter term grants at its discretion.

The Communications Act sets up certain basic requirements which must be met by broadcast applicants. In general, applicants must be legally, technically and financially qualified, and show that their proposed operation will be in the public interest. A 1960 amendment to the Communications Act empowers the Commission to fine broadcast licensees up to $10,000 for willful and repeated violations.

The license privilege is limited by law to citizens of the United States. It is denied to corporations wherein any officer or director is an alien or of which more than one-fifth of the capital stock is controlled by foreign interests.

The Commission's broadcast application and hearing procedure is outlined in a separate FCC information bulletin.

Programs: Under the Communications Act it is the responsibility of each broadcast station licensee to arrange his program structure so that his operations will be in the public interest. The Commission does not prescribe any percentages of time which should be devoted to particular subjects, such as news, education, religion, music, public issues, etc. That is something which can vary with the locality. However, the Commission does periodically review the overall performance of a station—engineering and otherwise—when it applies for renewal of its license, to determine whether it has lived up to its obligations and the promises it made in obtaining permission to use the public airwaves.

In 1960 the Commission issued a report and statement of policy on programming. It stated in part:

"In the fulfillment of his obligation the broadcaster should consider the tastes, needs and desires of the public he is licensed to serve in developing his programming and should exercise conscientious efforts not only to ascertain them but also to carry them out as well as he reasonably can. He should reasonably attempt to meet all such needs and interests on an equitable basis. Particular areas of interest and types of appropriate service may, of course, differ from community to community, and from time to time. However, the Commission does expect its broadcast licensees to take the necessary steps to inform themselves of the real needs and interests of the areas they serve and to provide programming which in fact constitutes a diligent effort, in good faith, to provide for those needs and interests.

"The major elements usually necessary to meet the public interest, needs and desires of the community in which the station is located as developed by the industry, and recognized by the Commission, have included: (1) Opportunity for Local Self-Expression, (2) The Development and Use of Local Talent, (3) Programs for Children, (4) Religious Programs, (5) Educational Programs, (6) Public Affairs Programs, (7) Editorialization by Licensees, (8) Political Broadcasts, (9) Agricultural Programs, (10) News Programs, (11) Weather and Market Reports, (12) Sports Programs, (13) Service to Minority Groups, (14) Entertainment Programming.

"The elements set out above are neither all-embracing nor constant. We re-emphasize that they do not serve and have not been intended as a rigid mold or fixed formula for station operation. The ascertainment of the needed elements of the broadcast matter to be provided by a particular licensee for the audience he is obligated to serve remains primarily the function of the licensee. His honest and prudent judgments will be accorded great weight by the Commission. Indeed, any other course would tend to substitute the judgment of the Commission for that of the licensee."

Censorship and free speech: This review of broadcast station performance does not, however, give the Commission authority to direct a station to put a particular program on or off the air. The Communications Act states: "Nothing in this Act shall be understood or construed to give the Commission the power of censorship over the radio communications or signals transmitted by any radio station, and no regulation or condition shall be promulgated or fixed by the Commission which shall interfere with the right of free speech by means of radio communication." The Commission has held that freedom of speech on the air must be broad enough to provide full and equal opportunity for the presentation of both sides of public issues. Under such conditions, licensees of broadcast stations have the right to editorialize.

Advertising: While it does not pass upon the nature or length of commercials on the air, the Commission's review of a station's performance does consider deviation from promised service which tends toward overcommercialization. Also, under a cooperative arrangement with the Federal Trade Commission, which has jurisdiction over false and misleading advertising on the air, the Commission notifies stations concerned of broadcast advertising cited by the FTC so that these stations may take any necessary action consistent with their obligation to operate in the public interest.

Political broadcasts: The Communications Act (sec. 315) expressly provides: "If any licensee shall permit any person who is a legally qualified candidate for any public office to use a broadcasting station, he shall afford equal opportunities to all other such candidates for that office in the use of such broadcasting station: Provided, that such licensee shall have no power of censorship over the material broadcast under the provisions of this section. No obligation is hereby imposed upon any licensee to allow the use of its station by any such candidate. The charges made for the use of any broadcasting station for any of the purposes set forth in this section shall not exceed the charges made for comparable use of such station for other purposes." In 1959, news broadcasts were exempted from the "equal time" provisions of sec. 315. Congress suspended the equal-time provision for nominees for President and Vice President in the 1960 campaign to determine its effect in considering possible permanent waiver.

"Payola" and "Fixed Quiz" show revelations resulted in the Communications Act being amended in 1960 to make it illegal to "plug" records and other commercial services over the air without announcing if payment has been received, and to penalize those who broadcast deceptive programs purporting to be based upon knowledge, skill or chance.

Lotteries, obscenity and fraud: The United States Criminal Code prohibits broadcast of information concerning "any lottery, gift enterprise, or similar scheme," also utterance of obscene, indecent, or profane language, and fraud by wire, radio, or television. A Supreme Court decision on a particular "giveaway" program did not hold it to be a lottery.

Time charges and station management: The Communications Act declares that broadcasting is not a common carrier operation. Consequently, a broadcast station is not required to sell or to give time to all who seek to go on the air. Because programming is primarily the responsibility of broadcast station licenses, the Commission does not ordinarily monitor or pass upon individual programs, or require the filing of radio scripts. However, broadcast stations are required to keep a program log and a technical log, and a record of all requests for political broadcast time. The Commission does not maintain surveillance of the day-to-day internal management of broadcast stations or regulate their time charges, profits, artists' salaries or employe relations.

Networks: The Commission does not license networks as such, but only individual stations. However, its licensees are subject to the chain broadcasting regulations adopted by the Commission in 1941 to further competition in broadcasting and implemented by regulations stemming from its 1957 special study of TV network broadcasting. The major radio networks are: American Broadcasting Co., Columbia Broadcasting System, Mutual Broadcasting System and the National Broadcasting Co. The Commission has indorsed proposed legislation which would enable it to license networks directly.

Monopoly: There is Commission prohibition against the same interest or group from operating more than one network, or more than one AM, FM or TV station in the same area, or more than seven AM, seven FM or, seven TV commercial stations throughout the country as a whole. Not more than five of these TV stations may be in the VHF band.

Receivers: The Commission does not license sets that are for reception only. However, it does impose limitations on their radiations which may interfere with radio or TV service. The advent of "wireless" prompted the use of receiving sets by amateurs and others interested in listening-in on Morse code radiotelegraph transmission. Inexpensive crystal detectors boomed the production of home-made and manufactured receivers. The advent of broadcasting aroused public interest in sets (at first battery-operated) to receive regular programs. Receiving sets operated by house current came on the market about 1928. A 1948 development called the "transistor" has replaced tubes in many sets.

Call letters: International agreement provides for the national identification of a radio station by the first letter or first two letters of its assigned call signal, and for this purpose apportions the alphabet among different nations. United States stations use the initial letters K, N, and W, exclusively, and part of the A series. Broadcast stations are assigned call letters beginning with K or W. Generally speaking, those beginning with K are assigned to stations west of the Mississippi River and in the territories and possessions, while W is assigned to broadcast stations east of the Mississippi.

During radio's infancy, most of the broadcast stations were in the East. As inland stations developed, the Mississippi River was made the dividing line of K and W calls. KDKA Pittsburgh was assigned the K letter before the present system was put into effect. Most of the early broadcast assignments were three letters. This combination became exhausted, making it necessary to add a fourth letter.

Since many AM broadcast licensees also operate FM and TV stations, a common practice is to authorize the use of the call letters of the AM station followed by a dash and "FM" or "TV," as the case may be.

BROADCAST OPERATION

Since radio frequencies differ, the particular qualities of each radio band must be considered in determining the type of service which can best operate on it. Consequently, that portion of the radio spectrum between 535 and 1605 kilocycles is occupied by AM broadcast, FM broadcast is allocated 88 to 108 megacycles, and TV is provided for in 54-216 megacycles (VHF) and 470-890 megacycles (UHF). (A "kilocycle" denotes a thousand wave transmissions a second, while a "megacycle" is a short way of indicating a thousand kilocycles.)

Fm broadcast requires a channel 20 times wider than that used for AM, but TV transmission or combined picture and sound needs about 6 times the spectrum space occupied by the entire AM broadcast band.

The same aural or video broadcast channel can be used in different places if the using stations are far enough apart so as to not cause excessive interference with one another or to stations on adjacent channels. A TV station may be required to operate "offset" 10 kilocycles above or below its normal carrier frequency. The channel assigned to such a station is, in consequence, designated "plus" or "minus," as the case may be. This makes more TV assignments possible and reduces the probability of interference.

HOW TV WORKS

Television broadcasting involves transmission of visual and aural programs so synchronized that at the receiving set they are seen and heard in a manner resembling talking motion pictures.

The picture phase is accomplished by sending a rapid succession of electrical impulses which the receiver transforms into scenes and images. The method is complex, but the following is a brief explanation of monochrome (black-and-white) video operation.

The scene to be televised is focused on a special tube in the television camera which has a small "screen" covered with approximately 367,000 microscopic dots of a special substance. This screen can be likened to a tiny motion picture screen and is called a "mosaic." The varying light from each part of the scene being televised falls upon these dots and charges them with an electrical charge the strength of which depends upon the amount of light falling upon the individual dots. Thus each dot becomes a tiny storage battery and the scene is formed in a pattern of electrical charges on the mosaic.

The mosaic is "scanned" by a tiny beam of electrons, no larger than the head of a pin, moving from left to right and progressing downward (just as the printed page is read by the human eye). This complete process is repeated 60 times per second, and the horizontal lines of alternate complete scanning are interlaced so that 30 complete pictures or "frames" composed of 525 horizontal lines are produced each second. As the electron beam strikes each dot on the mosaic, the dot is discharged through the electron beam and the electrical impulses produced are used to modulate the signals of the TV transmitter. Each time the dots are discharged by the electron beam they are recharged by the light produced by the succeeding scene falling upon them. The succession of individual "still" scenes creates the illusion of motion just as in the case of motion pictures made on film.

The reproduction by the TV receiver of the pictures transmitted is just the reverse of the transmission. The incoming succession of electrical impulses are separated from the "carrier" and, after amplification, impressed on the picture tube grid. The picture tube also has an electron "gun" which shoots out a tiny beam of electrons which moves from left to right and progresses downward on the face of the picture tube.

The face of the tube is coated with a material which fluoresces or gives off light at the point where it is struck by the electron beam. In the absence of a television signal the whole face of the picture tube is illuminated equally by a series of closely spaced horizontal lines. When a television signal is placed on the grid of the picture tube it controls the strength of the electron beam and hence the amount of light on the face of the tube. If the scanning of the electron beam in the picture tube is kept in perfect step with the scanning of the electron beam in the television camera, the picture tube will reproduce the lights and shadows of the subject scene and the succession of such scenes produces the illusion of motion.

In brief, the picture seen by the viewer is actually produced by a flickering spot of light moving rapidly across and down the face of the picture tube. The viewer sees the "whole picture" because the screen continues to glow for a tiny fraction of a second after the electron beam has passed, which coupled with the retentive ability of the eye creates the illusion that the picture is there all the time. The high rate of repetition minimizes flicker and lends smoothness to motion.

The TV transmitter is, in effect, two separate units. One sends out the picture and the other the sound. Visual transmission is by amplitude modulation (AM). The sound portion employs frequency modulation (FM).

In addition to live studio presentations, television uses films. The latter include "kinescope" recordings, a rapid filming process which makes it possible to show scenes of events soon after they tape, which would carry both picture and sound, are now being used as a means of TV programming.

How TV Began

Many persons in many lands contributed to the development of television. Like radio, TV was made possible by electronic discoveries in the late 19th century and early 20th century. In 1884 Nipkow, a German, patented a scanning disk for transmitting pictures by wireless. In our own country, Jenkins began his study of the subject about 1890. Rignoux and Fournier conducted "television" experiments in France in the 1900's. In 1915 Marconi predicted "visible telephone." In 1923 Zworykin applied for a patent on the iconoscope (TV camera tube). Two years later Jenkins demonstrated mechanical TV apparatus. There were experiments by Alexanderson, Farnsworth and Baird in 1926-1927. An experimental TV program was sent by wire between New York and Washington by the Bell Telephone Labs in 1927, in which Herbert Hoover, then Secretary of Commerce, participated. The next year the same laboratories experimentally televised outdoor programs.

The Federal Radio Commission (predecessor of the FCC) reported that "a few" broadcast stations were experimenting with video in 1928. In that year, WGY Schenectady experimentally broadcast the first drama by TV. Large-screen TV was demonstrated by RCA at a New York theater in 1930, and RCA tested outdoor TV pickup at Camden, N.J., in 1936.

Seventeen experimental TV stations were operating in 1937. An experimental mobile TV station was placed in operation that year. The first President seen on TV was Franklin D. Roosevelt, when he opened the New York World's Fair in 1939. That year also saw the first telecast major league baseball game, college football game and professional boxing match. In 1940 the Republican and Democratic conventions were televised, that of the former making pioneer use of coaxial cable for long distance TV relay purposes. Previously, in the same year, WNBT New York and WRGB Schenectady were joined by radio relay for a rebroadcast test.

Meanwhile, in 1939, the *Milwaukee Journal* filed the first application to broadcast TV programs on a commercial basis. At a hearing in 1940, the FCC found the industry divided on the question of whether TV was ready for commercial use and at odds on engineering standards. At that time various TV systems required different receivers. A National Television System Committee considered standardization and reported in 1941. Subsequent Commission hearings showed the industry to be in substantial agreement on commercialization and standards. The latter fixed the present line and frame frequencies at 525 and 30 respectively. On April 30, 1941, the Commission authorized commercial TV operation to start July 1 of that year.

Previously, a number of TV stations which had been operating experimentally applied for commercial authorization. The first grant looking to regular TV operation was issued to WNBT (TV) New York on June 17, 1941, effective July 1 of that year. On June 24, 1941, WCBW (now WCBS-TV) New York was authorized to commence program tests July 1 thereafter. By May of 1942, 10 commercial TV stations were on the air. Six of these continued to provide service during the war.

In 1945 the Commission allocated 13 VHF (very high frequency) channels between 44 and 216 megacycles for commercial television. In doing so, it pointed out that there was insufficient spectrum space below 300 megacycles for an adequate nationwide and competitive TV broadcasting system. Twelve of these channels were to be shared with certain nonbroadcast (fixed and mobile) services. At the same time, that portion of the UHF (ultra high frequency) spectrum between 480 and 920 megacycles was made available for experimental TV operation looking to future television expansion, and between 1245 and 1325 megacycles for TV relay.

In 1948, because of interference to commercial TV operation, the Commission stopped the sharing of television VHF channels with other services, and deleted TV channel No. 1 (44-50 mc) by assigning it to the nonbroadcast services affected.

The TV Freeze

As predicted by the Commission in 1945, it became increasingly evident that the few available VHF channels were inadequate to provide a truly national competitive TV service. Also, operating stations developed interference which had not been anticipated when TV broadcasting began. As a result, the Commission on Sept. 30, 1948, stopped granting new TV stations pending a study of the situation. This was the so-called television "freeze" order.

The resultant study showed that, before additional stations could be authorized, it was necessary to determine various engineering and other questions which would govern future TV operation. Consequently, on July 11, 1949, the Commission proposed comprehensive changes looking to the improvement and extension of TV service. These included new engineering standards; opening UHF channels for TV broadcasting; consideration of color systems; reservation of channels for noncommercial educational use, and a national assignment plan incorporating VHF and UHF channels.

UHF Problems

Economic and technical problems have impeded further utilization of the UHF channels. In addition to the normal TV cost factor, they are caused, chiefly, by the large number of VHF-only receivers in use and which continue to be manufactured; certain performance deficiencies of UHF, and the consequent preference of program and revenue sources for VHF outlets.

In 1950 the Commission outlined a long-range and interim plan to promote comparable TV facilities as a means of extending TV service throughout the nation. It invited comments on the possibility of ultimately shifting all or a major portion of TV operation to the UHF band and, at the same time, enlisted the cooperation of industry in a research and development study to increase the range and coverage of UHF stations. Meanwhile, it increased the maximum power of UHF stations, has made certain areas all-UHF and increased TV competition in others, and has taken other steps to put UHF and VHF operation on a more competitive basis.

On two occasions the Commission sought the release of Government VHF space to augment the present TV broadcast channels but each time a determination was made that national defense considerations do not make this possible. At the Commission's request, Congress appropriated funds to conduct a UHF test in New York City to determine the ability of UHF to provide service to a large metropolitan area. In 1960 the Commission recommended to Congress that TV sets transported in interstate commerce for sale to the public be required to receive UHF as well as VHF channels.

Subscription TV

Subscription TV involves furnishing special video programs to viewers who pay a charge for this service. Such transmission over the air is subject to FCC jurisdiction; closed-circuit (cable) toll-TV operation does not require Commission licensing.

The Commission authorized pay-TV experimentation as early as 1950. Five years later it proposed trial of such service and, in 1957, invited comments on various proposed systems. They differ mainly in how the transmissions are sent in scrambled form and then decoded by special apparatus attached to a subscriber's set, and whether coin boxes, punch cards or tape record is used for billing purposes. Later in 1957 the Commission looked toward considering applications by TV stations to test this service under certain conditions. But in view of resolutions by two Congressional committees, it deferred further action until 1959 when it invited applications by commercial TV stations to test pay-TV under revised requirements.

The latter specify three-year trial authorizations limited to markets in which there are at least four existing commercial TV services, to the trial of any one system in only one market, to one system per market, and to subscription programs being broadcast over only one local station at a time. Also, until the Commission has decided whether toll-TV service should be authorized on a regular basis, it decided that the public should not be called upon to buy any special equipment.

On Feb. 24, 1961, the Commission, after a hearing, granted the only conforming toll-TV application then pending (WHCT [TV] Hartford, Conn.)

EDUCATIONAL BROADCASTING

Educational institutions were among the pioneers in experimental broadcasting, and held a considerable proportion of the early AM licenses.

By 1925, educational groups had 171 such licenses. For various reasons, notably the increased competition from commercial broadcasting, most of these stations were off the air when the Federal Communications Commission was created. However, about 35 educational stations still operate in the AM broadcast band, a score of them on a voluntary noncommercial basis.

As directed by sec. 307(c) of the Communications Act, the Commission made a study of the proposal that Congress should allocate fixed percentages of radio facilities for particular types of nonprofit radio programs and activities, including education. On Jan. 22, 1935, the Commission recommended that no such statutory allocation be made at that time. It held that there was "no need for a change in the existing law to accomplish the helpful purposes of the proposal," but recognized the need for extending broadcasting to education and expressed its intention "actively to assist the determination of the rightful place of broadcasting in education and to see that it is used in that place."

To further the development of noncommercial educational broadcasting, the Commission in 1938 set aside certain AM channels between 41 and 42 megacycles for the exclusive use of educational institutions. Due, however, to the inability of the normal radio set to receive broadcasts on these frequencies, only a few educational institutions secured licenses for such operation. Those which did later changed to frequency modulation operation when provision was made for FM educational broadcasting.

When regular FM broadcasting was authorized to start in 1941, five channels between 42 and 43 megacycles were allocated for noncommercial educational use, in lieu of the educational AM facilities previously provided.

In 1945, as part of an extensive revision of frequency allocations, the Commission reserved 20 FM channels between 88 and 92 megacycles for noncommercial educational FM stations. This educational portion of the FM band is contiguous to that containing the commercial FM stations and present FM receivers are capable of tuning in both noncommercial and commercial stations within range. The number of these noncommercial educational FM stations has grown slowly but steadily.

In 1948 the Commission authorized low power (10 watt) operation on these educational FM channels. With such low power equipment easily installed and operated, schools may begin broadcasting to a limited area of from two to five miles in radius for an outlay of a few thousand dollars. Higher power equipment may be added when desired. In 1951, as a further aid, the Commission authorized remote control operation of low-power educational FM stations.

Stations in the educational FM broadcast service are licensed principally to school systems, colleges and universities for furnishing educational programs to teachers and students, as well as for public educational and informational purposes.

The Commission, for the first time, allocated TV facilities for exclusive noncommercial educational use as a result of its lengthy study of this question in the general television proceedings. The Commission determined therein that "the need for noncommercial educational stations has been amply demonstrated"; that "the record shows the desire and ability of education to make a substantial contribution to the use of television"; that "the actual process of formulating plans and of enacting necessary legislation or of making adequate financing available is one which will generally require more time for educational organizations than for commercial interests . . . and that to insure an extensive rather than a sparse and haphazard development of educational television, channels must be reserved by the Commission at this time." Consequently, in its Sixth Report and Order of April 14, 1952, the Commission made channel assignments to 242 communities exclusively for noncommercial educational purposes. Forty-six of these were made to "primarily educational centers." Of the total of 242 channels then assigned, 80 were VHF and 162 were UHF. There have since been additional assignments.

The Commission expects educational TV licensees to make their station facilities available to other local educational institutions, since such assignments are made to serve the educational and cultural needs of the community. Except in particular cases, TV educational eligibility is not extended to municipal authorities in places where an independent educational authority—such as a board of education—is established. Although there is no requirement that noncommercial educational stations broadcast a specified minimum number of hours, commercial and educational television stations are both subject to the same TV service requirements, such as station separation, antenna height and power, etc.

The first non-commercial educational TV grant was made July 23, 1952, to the Kansas State College of Agriculture and Applied Science (KSAC-TV) at Manhattan, Kan. The first such station to go on the air was KUHT Houston, Texas, May 25, 1953; and the first one licensed was WCET Cincinnati, Ohio, March 11, 1955.

Several colleges and universities hold commercial TV authorizations and operate on a profit or non-profit basis. Many schools have closed-circuit TV systems linking classrooms for instructional purposes.

INTERNATIONAL

Under international agreement, certain high frequency bands are allocated for broadcasts directed between nations.

Authorizations for non-Government international broadcast stations located in the United States are issued by the Federal Communications Commission. A single grant usually authorizes use of a number of frequencies between 5,950 and 26,100 kilocycles as well as several transmitters. This is because of seasonal and other considerations in broadcasting different programs to different parts of the world at the same time. The minimum power for international broadcast stations under Commission jurisdictions is 50 kilowatts.

During World War II, international broadcast stations in the United

States were taken over by the Office of War Information and the Office of Inter-American Affairs of the Dept. of State which operated and programmed them in the interest of the war effort.

"The Voice of America" is the title given to the programs now sent out daily, in many languages, to various parts of the world by shortwave transmitters under the auspices of the United States Information Agency. Transmission is by amplitude modulation.

EXPERIMENTAL BROADCAST SERVICES

Experimental broadcast stations test new techniques and develop broadcast equipment. Information obtained from this experimentation and research helps the industry to evolve and improve equipment and methods and also provides the Commission with useful information about new developments. Because of their temporary nature, the number of these authorizations fluctuates.

THE LITERATURE OF TELEVISION

By Neil Postman

FOR A VARIETY OF REASONS, the phrase, "the literature of television," does not fall gently on the English teacher's ear. For the teacher who confines literature to written or printed forms (as the word's etymology suggests), television, by definition, cannot be properly classified as literature. For the teacher who defines literature as *belles lettres*—the higher arts of literary expression—television is excluded not only by reason of its form but by reason of its unexalted reputation. Even for the teacher whose definition of literature includes written, oral, and visual forms (so as to subsume the living theater), television's claim to the status of literature seems premature, if not presumptuous, because it cannot provide the kind of permanence we normally associate with literature. And yet, clearly, we find on television types of dramatic and narrative programs that serve many of the purposes of literature. Moreover, these programs possess at least some of the distinguishing traits of literature. For if we recognize, as Wellek and Warren do, that fiction, invention, and imagination are characteristics of literary form, then we must concede that these characteristics may be found as abundantly in certain television programs as in certain books. For our purposes then, the word *literature* is used metaphorically and as a description, not as an evaluation. We do not mean to suggest by its use that television is the equivalent of *belles lettres* but rather that certain kinds of television programs employ language and action in ways that duplicate the functions of traditional literary forms. Using words and images, television can, for example, tell stories—long, short, serious, or comic ones—in narration or dramatization. In using the phrase, "the literature of television," therefore, we are referring to those types of programs analogous in many of their purposes, if not in their form, to novels, short stories, plays, even essays. Before examining these types of programs in detail (we have called them "genres"), let us consider, in general, some of the similarities and differences between the literature of television and the more traditional forms with which we are all familiar.

Like all literary types, the literature of television reflects the assump-

From *Television and the Teaching of English* by Neil Postman and The Committee on the Study of Television of the National Council of Teachers of English. Copyright © 1961 Appleton-Century-Crofts, Inc.

tions and values of the men who create it and, to some extent, their assumptions about the audiences for whom they create. Thus, if there were few television plays of "social protest" in the 1950's, neither in literature nor in society were there many powerful and sustained expressions of social protest during the same period. Although we may criticize some of the literature of television for encouraging the acquisition of material comforts as an end in itself, we must concede that this tendency, too, is a genuine reflection of our times rather than an emphasis manufactured by latter-day Medicis. No doubt some of our collective virtues have also been reflected in the literature of television, as for example, our growing awareness of the dangers of class prejudice and ethnic stereotypes. In other words, to the extent that we may trust literature to reveal the prevailing attitudes of an era, television is perhaps as useful an index of the last decade as any other form of literature.

A second similarity is that, like the novel, short story, or play, the literature of television is uneven in quality. At its best, it is truthful and artistic. At its worst, it is trivial and formless. This is not to suggest that the best of television, say, Paddy Chayefsky's *Marty*, is the artistic equivalent of the best of twenty-four hundred years of the theater or even four hundred years of the novel. Such comparisons are unjust as well as unproductive. Rather, we are suggesting that in television, as in other literary forms, there are levels of value. *The Death of a Salesman* is a far cry from *Abie's Irish Rose* but perhaps no farther than is television's *Requiem for a Heavyweight* from *This Is Your Life*.

The literature of television is created within certain limitations, limitations imposed by the form of the medium. Limitations of form are, of course, well known to creators of novels, short stories, poems, journalism, stage plays, and films. The nature and extent of these limitations as they apply specifically to any medium define that medium's difference from other forms. For example, the form of the novel may be flexible enough to integrate, even exploit, lengthy philosophic discourse. The form of the film is not. The film, however, through the process of editing, lends itself to striking manipulations of time and space, while on "live" television such manipulations are less effective. The narrator may serve as a useful, perhaps essential, dramatic device on radio. In the theater, the Greek Chorus of *Electra* and the Stage Manager of *Our Town* notwithstanding, the narrator is less believable or, at least, less conventional.

The main part of this chapter will deal directly with the technical and artistic limitations and resources that make television unique. But some important differences between television and other forms of literature need mentioning before we begin.

In the first place, since the literature of television is transmitted simultaneously to millions of people, its creators are subject to limitations of theme, language, and style more severe than those in other media. In general, the wider the base of the audience, the greater the degree of restriction imposed on the creator, and no contemporary literary form has a more heterogeneous or massive audience than television.

In the second place, the line that separates commercial interests from literary interests in television is less distinct than in most other literary forms. To be sure, the publisher of novels and the producer of stage plays are concerned with making money. But in television the advertiser, the man who pays the bills, is primarily concerned with the sale of a commercial product rather than an artistic one. At the same time, selling products and presenting high quality programs are not necessarily incompatible motives. There are, in fact, numerous examples of sponsors who have done both simultaneously.

The literature of television, unlike most types of literature, is highly ephemeral in character. At the moment, the libraries of television are its "reruns," but even so, a particular show must be seen at a specific time or it cannot be seen at all. As a result, studying or teaching about television presents certain problems not found in the study of other types of literature, except the legitimate stage.

Finally, unlike most types of literature, the literature of television defies easy classification. This poses a problem not only for those who would study or teach it but even for those who would praise it. For example, in 1948, when the National Academy of Television Arts and Sciences presented its first "Emmys," five awards were given, one of which was for "Best Film for Television" and another for "Most Popular Television Program." The following year, neither of these categories was represented even though nine awards were given.

As the number of different types of programs increased through the years, the problem of establishing recognizable "genres" became more difficult. A humorous example of the unwieldy proportions of the problem was provided in 1957 when an award was given for the "Best Continuing Performance (Male) in a Series by a Comedian, Singer, Host, Dancer, M.C., Announcer, Narrator, Panelist, or Any Person Who Essentially Plays Himself." Although this extraordinary award was never repeated, its appearance—even once—suggests the difficulties involved in classifying television programs. Clearly, any coherent treatment of the literature of television must necessarily be selective. Since the purpose of this chapter is to provide the reader with a sense of the significance of what we are calling *the literature of television*, the following discussions are concerned only with those types of television programs which have distinguished themselves by virtue of artistic quality, by reason of their unfailing popularity, or by the clarity with which they express social values.

ORIGINAL TELEVISION DRAMA

In his book, *The Public Arts*, Gilbert Seldes uses the term the *fifty-two-minute hour* to refer to a popular dramatic form which began and matured between the years 1948 and 1958. Approximately 1500 fifty-two-minute plays were performed "live" during those ten years. The term *live* refers, of course, to the fact that these plays were performed at the precise moment that they were seen by the television audience, a condition which since the advent of videotape has become increasingly rare; "fifty-two minutes" describes the actual running time of the play, eight minutes of the hour being subtracted for commercial messages, the listing of credits, and publicity for next week's play.

Undoubtedly, some of television's finest moments were provided by these fifty-two minute hours, particularly by such weekly series as *The Kraft Television Theater* (1947-1958), *The Philco-Goodyear Playhouse* (1948-1955), and *Studio One* (1948-1957). These programs began by presenting adaptations of the classics and established contemporary novels but by 1950 shifted their emphasis from adaptations to "originals." By that time, such producers and directors as Worthington Miner, Fred Coe, Delbert Mann, Arthur Penn, and John Frankenheimer had assembled about them several gifted, young writers who were prepared to devote their collective talents to a serious exploration of television's artistic resources. Included in that group, among others, were Reginald Rose, Tad Mosel, Robert Alan Aurthur, Horton Foote, Rod Serling, J. P. Miller, and Gore Vidal. None, however, wrote more fittingly for television than Paddy Chayefsky.

Chayefsky was to the "original" television drama what Ibsen was to the "social drama," which is to say that he was one of its first creators and certainly its most distinguished one. And, like Ibsen, he achieved an almost perfect union of form and content. Critics have observed, for example, that the effects that Ibsen achieved in *A Doll's House* and *Ghosts* were a function not of his themes alone, with which audiences were certainly familiar in 1879 and 1881, but a result of the stark, simple, and economical form in which he stated his themes. Social dramas had been written before Ibsen, but it remained for him to discover the proper form for dramatizing social problems.

Chayefsky, however, did not write for the proscenium arch which is viewed from a distance in a darkened theater. He wrote for a seventeen-inch screen which was situated in the family living room and on which the only colors were varying shades of gray. He also had to present his story, from start to finish, in fifty-two minutes and could make two assumptions with almost absolute assurance. The first was that his play would be interrupted at least twice for commercial messages. The second was that he would have to attract his audience instantly or lose much of it to other channels. He knew, too, as did his director, Delbert Mann, that the picture on the television screen is considerably cruder in its visual definition than that of the motion picture screen. Thus, Chayefsky wrote his plays in anticipation of the audience's observing the players in almost unrelenting "close-up."

Chayefsky realized that some of these unique technical-aesthetic conditions could create, as perhaps no other medium, a sense of utter and absolute reality, could create the illusion that what the audience was watching was not a mere play but life as seen through a seventeen-inch, nearly square hole. Beginning with *Holiday Song,* which dealt with a rabbi's re-examination of his faith in God, Chayefsky created a series of distinguished dramas that have often been characterized as "small" masterpieces. They were plays about unexceptional people who existed for fifty-two minutes in wholly unexceptional situations. The plots were uncluttered, undaring, and highly compressed. They had few unexpected turns, little action, no treachery, no perversion, and no heroic gestures (in a traditional sense). Chayefsky's stories were "small" in very much the same way that Sherwood Anderson's stories were small. The setting was the Bronx, not small-town Ohio, and Chayefsky was less concerned than was Anderson with "social outcasts." But, like Anderson, Chayefsky explored in economical but meticulous detail the agonizing problems of small people, thus elevating the status of both the problems and the people who suffered them. In fact, Chayefsky has said that "your mother, sister, brothers, cousins, friends—all of these are better subjects for drama than Iago." He was talking, of course, about television drama.

Chayefsky's most widely known play, *Marty,* tells the story of an unmarried and inarticulate Bronx butcher who is attracted to a sensitive but homely girl. Marty's friends attempt to dissuade him from seeing the girl because she is, in their words, "a dog." His mother, who fears being abandoned, resents the girl. Against a backdrop of such universal themes as man's need of loving and being loved, his fear of living alone, and his need of communicating articulately, Chayefsky pursues a "small" story with a persistent literalness, concluding with an equally "small" crisis in which Marty decides, against the protest of his friends and family, to phone the girl and ask her for a date. On the stage or in novel form, the plot alone would probably be too flimsy to carry much dramatic weight. When the play was adapted for the movies, it required more "movement" or action and the addition of at least one subplot. On the television screen, however, the play was an artistic masterpiece, producing an illusion of intimacy that was at once disturbing and edifying. Perhaps no other medium is better suited to the "slice of life" drama than television, and Chayefsky exploited this fact repeatedly.

Chayefsky was not alone in exploring the unique qualities of the television screen, but some of the other writers did not place the same emphasis as he on the explication, in naturalistic terms, of the problems of ordinary people. Reginald Rose, for example, favored the "message" play, such as *Twelve Angry Men* and *Tragedy in a Temporary Town,* in which he exhorted his audience to discard its prejudices. Gore Vidal wrote television's most literate satire, *Visit to a Small Planet,* which in simulated Shavian style condemned man's most persistent talent, the making of war. Rod

Serling examined the motivations and pressures of "big business" in his highly successful *Patterns*. And Alvin Sapinsley experimented with poetic dramas, one of which, *Lee at Gettysburg*, was suggestive, in its rhythm and compression, of the poetic dramas of radio.

Whatever differences existed among these various writers, the success of each may be attributed to his ability to recognize certain inescapable facts about the medium, its audience, and the environment in which the audience characteristically viewed his play. For example, television drama seems to be singularly effective when focused on people rather than plots, places, or even ideas. As mentioned before, the "normal" view of the players on the television screen is the "closeup." As a consequence, the human face is given such continued and forceful presence that it tends to become the overriding emphasis of the play, whether the author intends it or not. Bridges falling down and planes zooming high may be thrillingly pictured in films and novels. On live television, the space limitations of a studio make such actions technically impractical, if not impossible. Even in film sequences, such actions are not as dramatically persuasive because of the smallness of the screen and the relatively crude definition of the image. Television, as one director put it, is the "psychoanalytic medium." What television drama does best is to show faces and to suggest what is behind them. Of this quality, Rod Serling wrote, "The key to TV drama was intimacy, and the facial study on a small screen carried with it a meaning and power far beyond its usage in the motion pictures."

Also, television drama must be highly compressed. There is little time for subplots or for much elaboration of even the main plot. The television dramatist, like the short story writer, has time only to relate a bare narrative and evoke a mood. Of course, unlike the short story writer, he has the camera to help him do both. Occasionally, as in the adaptation of "The Killers," the television writer is faced with the problem of expanding a brief story, but, typically, his problem is the reverse. "Television," Paddy Chayefsky wrote, "cannot take a thick, fully woven fabric of drama. It can only handle simple lines of movement and consequently smaller moments of crisis."

We must remember also that television is family entertainment viewed within the home. This tends to impose limitations on both the language and the themes of television plays. Nymphomania, homosexuality, or incest may be maturely explored in the theater and in other literary forms, but on television such subjects tend to be shocking, not only because of television's unselected audience but especially because of the almost painful explicitness of the medium. "It is far worse," writes Jan Bussell in *The Art of Television*, "to see someone spewing in your sitting room than hear it only." Or, one might add, than to see it in a darkened theater. Similarly, words which would scarcely be remembered when read in novels or heard on the stage can almost never be forgotten when they invade the living room. A now famous example of this fact occurred on February 19, 1956, at which time *The Alcoa Hour* presented Reginald Rose's *Tragedy in a Temporary Town*. One of the actors, Lloyd Bridges, was overcome by the excitement of a particular scene and uttered an expletive that was not in the script but which might have been had the play been performed on the stage. The words themselves would have gone practically unnoticed in a Norman Mailer or Nelson Algren novel. On television, the event was a *cause célèbre*.

Television writers worked for years within these limitations and produced a substantial body of serious drama. But for various reasons, the fifty-two minute live drama has become increasingly rare. In the first place, some writers abandoned television altogether because they felt it did not provide sufficient artistic freedom or financial reward. They objected, for example, to the intrusion of commercial messages and to the imposition of thematic limitations by sponsors. And, of course, they have found that writing for the movies is far more lucrative.

In the second place, many producers abandoned the fifty-two minute hour because a weekly series demanded a constant source of talent that was simply not available. Television is a ravenous consumer of talent and material. It must be fed eighteen hours a day, seven days a week. The most gifted find it difficult to survive such a relentless challenge of their creative resources. Even if Paddy Chayefsky, Tad Mosel, J. P. Miller, and all the others were still writing for television, they probably could not produce distinguished hour-long dramas week after week. Finally, many sponsors abandoned the form because it was more expensive than filmed half-hour shows and not quite as magnetic as the ninety-minute or two-hour "special."

Nevertheless, high quality, "original" drama still exists on television. Reginald Rose and Robert Alan Aurthur write less frequently for television now but are still concerned with it. Rod Serling has turned his attention to the thirty-minute filmed drama in a series called *The Twilight Zone*. *The Hallmark Hall of Fame* and the *Armstrong Circle Theater* have been distinguished for the high quality of their dramas, although the first has emphasized adaptations and the last, semidocumentaries. In addition, gifted new writers have continued to explore the medium in the serious tradition of their predecessors. James Costigan's *Little Moon of Alban*, Alfred Brenner's *Survival* (on the *United States Steel Hour*), and Alvin Boretz's work on the *Armstrong Circle Theater*, among others, suggest that "original" television drama will continue to make an important contribution to American literature.

Moreover, the advent of videotape has given great impetus to the development of an "elite" theater, that is, television drama aimed at special audiences. Such programs as *The Play of the Week*, *The Robert Herridge Theater*, and *Camera Three* may be seen, on tape, in many cities throughout the country. *The Play of the Week* has been particularly distinguished for its adaptations of classics, such as *Medea, Don Juan in Hell, Tiger at the Gates, The Cherry Orchard,* and *The Iceman Cometh.*

In addition to its efforts to present original and serious dramatic programs, television has provided its audiences with an abundance of fiction which, although largely stereotyped in form and in spirit, may fairly be regarded as an important part of television's literature, certainly in terms of popularity. We are referring to westerns, "cops and robbers," and family programs. We call these three types of fiction "genres" because each is a special kind of television literature, possessing a style, form, and purpose that distinguishes it from other types of television fiction.

THE WESTERN

There is an understandable impression among the young of the land that the western is synonymous with television itself. In actual fact, the western did not fully emerge on television until 1955, or approximately seven years after commercial television started nationwide operations. The earliest television westerns—*Hopalong Cassidy, Roy Rogers,* and *The Lone Ranger*—were imported creations from the movies and radio, and were, for the most part, popular only with children. On September 6, 1955, the ABC Television Network introduced Wyatt Earp in an "adult" western, and several evenings later, the CBS Television Network featured another one, *Gunsmoke* (in point of fact, an import from radio). From that month on the western has probably been the most popular literary "genre" on television.

As indicated above, the western did not, as Minerva from Jove's head, spring full grown from the television screen or, for that matter, from the movie screen. On the contrary, the western has been a fully developed mythology for probably close to one hundred years. Its earliest outlines may be identified, for one example, in James Fenimore Cooper's five Leatherstocking Tales, the second of which, *The Last of the Mohicans,* has sold more than two million copies in America alone. Since the frontier did not extend much beyond the Mississippi River when Cooper wrote, the setting of his "easterns" is upper New York State in the latter half of the eighteenth century and not the Southwest in the second half of the nineteenth. But differences in time and place do not obscure similarities of spirit and invention. For example, Cooper insisted that he was writing history, not fiction. In the preface of his first edition of *The Last of the Mohicans,* published in 1826, he wrote, "The reader, who takes up these volumes, in expectation of finding an imaginary and romantic picture of things which never happened, will probably lay them aside, disappointed."

In spite of this disclaimer, Cooper's stories have little enough to do with the realities of life in the wilderness. Cooper wrote pure romances in the guise of history, and in this he set a pattern which was emulated by later writers of frontier tales. Owen Wister, for example, claimed that his *The Virginian,* published in 1902, was a historical novel of the cattle country.

But, as Frank Luther Mott has observed, there is not one cow in the entire book. Similarly, modern-day westerns (whether in novel, film, or television form) claim, at least by implication, to possess a certain degree of verisimilitude. However, historians find little resemblance between their fictions and the literal facts. Cattle, for example, play only an incidental part in the modern western. The main and even minor characters rarely engage in the kind of strenuous labor that dominated the growth of the frontier. And heroes who are supposed to be modeled after men who actually lived bear little relation to their real life counterparts. For example, historical evidence indicates that the actual Wild Bill Hickok, Wyatt Earp, Bat Masterson and Billy the Kid possessed qualities and performed deeds that were considerably less than admirable. Nevertheless, out of this unpromising material, magazines, newspapers, novels, and films fashioned extraordinary "culture heroes," heroes not unlike Cooper's Natty Bumppo. Bumppo preferred the company of men, idealized women, and performed feats that are patently impossible, as Mark Twain clearly demonstrated in his essay on Cooper's literary offenses. He was also virtuous, pious, and almost always correct. These qualities are certainly to be found in our modern cowboys. None, to be sure, can shoot quite so well as Bumppo, who could hit a nail-head at a distance of 100 yards; but generally in skill, motivation, and attitude, the cowboy is clearly a distant relative of Leatherstocking.

A weekly publication, *The National Police Gazette*, is frequently cited as having been one of the original manufacturers of the legendary cowboy, at least as he exists in his present form. Perhaps the prototype is more directly found in Bret Harte's stories of western mining towns, complete with brawls, romances, and hold-ups. Whatever their original source, the legends of the West apparently fascinate Americans and, quite naturally, have been given form on television.

The television western has, for the most part, maintained the spirit of the tradition. In other words, television continues to present the western as the most unsubtle of all modern morality plays. The characters in a typical television western are clearly the embodiments of various virtues and vices. There is, for example, the Good Guy, the Bad Guy, and even the Gray Guy. (According to John Steinbeck, the Gray Guy is one who may start out good and end up bad or start out bad and end up good.) As in the less sophisticated morality play, the symbols of virtue and vice must not only be unambiguous but immediately recognizable. The Good Guy, in general, wears a light hat and clean light clothes (particularly if he is a law man). He knows no fear, is facile with some deadly weapon, and is as courteous to women as he is indifferent to their sexuality. He is tall and handsome and, usually, is not much of a conversationalist. He is rarely troubled by moral ambiguities and is, of course, never called upon to make decisions that involve complex rational processes. In each play, Good is clearly distinguished from Evil, although people of sensibility will easily discern flaws in the dichotomy. For example, frequently the Good Guy defends the Good in questionable ways and thus tarnishes the virtue of his cause. Also, occasionally, the Good Guy equates mere petulance with Evil, dealing with those who are only sources of irritation as if they were serious advocates of the Devil.

Each hero usually has some personal symbol which distinguishes him from all similar types. Paladin (*Have Gun, Will Travel*) distributes at appropriate moments a simple business card which states his name, address, and occupation. Josh Randall (*Wanted: Dead or Alive*) carries in an oversized holster what surely must be the biggest pistol ever manufactured. Tate (*Tate*) has the use of only one arm. Bat Masterson has the use of three, if one counts his all-purpose cane.

The Bad Guy, like the Good Guy, is also enveloped in stock symbols. The Bad Guy may be defined as a man who smokes cigarettes or cigars, is unshaved and unclean, wears black hats, and is the second "fastest gun in town."

Television, as have the novel and the film, has provided some notable departures from these stock characters and simple allegories. In *The Ox-Bow Incident*, for example, Walter Van Tilburg Clark used a western setting in which to probe deeply into the nature of guilt and man's inhumanity to man. Clark's characters—true to the western tradition—are clearly allegorical, but in providing them with complex and entirely believable motivations, he elevated his story to the status of tragedy. Similarly, the film, *High Noon*, although using the standard materials of the formula western, achieved something approaching artistic distinction by its development of characters who react fearfully but humanly to the confrontation of Evil. On television, departures from the formula western have largely taken the form of parody rather than tragedy. In *Have Gun, Will Travel*, the Good Guy is almost a direct refutation of his entire breed. He is materialistic (as a professional gunfighter, he invariably demands payment in advance), sensual (at the beginning of a typical play, he is on the verge of making love to a beautiful woman), and literate (in one show, he out-talked, of all people, Oscar Wilde). But the best example of the parody-western may be found in *Maverick*. Maverick is the family name of two brothers who at first appearance seem to be typical Good Guys. They are handsome, tall, and wear the standard symbols of justice, guns. But beyond this superficial resemblance they are the exact opposite of Matt Dillon of *Gunsmoke* or Wyatt Earp. The brothers Maverick are, in fact, frequently cowardly, conventionally interested in women, and by occupation and temperament, professional gamblers. The tone of the program is invariably breezy, and its intention is clearly to poke fun at the entire "genre." *Maverick*, in short, approaches literary criticism, as parody always does.

Perhaps the best explanation of the wide appeal of the formula western may be found in the psychological needs of the audience. The western's clear moral imperatives, its emphasis on raw physical danger rather than the insecurities of a modern society, its overt rather than suppressed violence, and its evocation of a mythical, but romantic, past no doubt touch something that runs deep in American culture. The western appears to fill a need that in other times for other people may have been satisfied by tales of gallant knights and fair damsels in distress.

Many people have objected to the degree to which violence is depicted on westerns and other "action" programs. Of course, almost by definition, there must be *some* physical contact on an "action" program. The question is whether or not all the shootings or fights are artistically essential to plot or character development. Both industry and citizen pressures have been exerted in behalf of less violence in general and of no "unnecessary" violence in particular. But since the question of what is or is not necessary to a story involves a subjective judgment, the problem is not easily resolved. Certainly, this is a matter to which teachers ought to give careful thought. Apparently, there is no end in sight to the western, even though its lack of variety suggests that the saturation point may have been reached. Perhaps in the immediate years ahead the romantic legends of the West will be replaced by adventures of space travel. Outer space is, after all, the new frontier.

COPS AND ROBBERS

Like the western the "cops and robbers" story that is so ubiquitous on television has a history many years older than television itself. The theme has been explored with creative variety in novels, short stories, and films. In fact, early formulations of this motif date as far back as the fifteenth century when tales of Robin Hood and his relentless pursuer, the Sheriff of Nottingham, took form in poems and ritual dramas. The Robin Hood legends, however, are more properly described as "robbers and cops" stories, since it is the outlaw, not the law officer, who is the object of admiration and emulation. Despite Hollywood's protestations to the contrary, the "gangster" movies of the 1930's were very much in this tradition. Like Robin's discontented band of Saxons, James Cagney's "mob" of public enemies lived romantic, violent, and episodic lives, lives which were largely free from the customary restraints and proscriptions imposed by society. Possibly fifteenth-century Britons, as well as twentieth-century Americans, found these tales appealing precisely because they admired the courage and ingenuity that is required to survive in such a wildly antisocial manner. We may, however, infer important differences between the values of the fifteenth-century Britons and twentieth-century Americans by attending to the manner in which their robber-hero concluded his career. Robin Hood was ultimately pardoned by King Richard I, and thus the outlaw's unconventional style of life was justified. James Cagney (or Paul Muni-Edward G. Robinson) was ultimately mutilated by machine-gun fire, and the audience's conventional style of life was justified.

The television "cops and robbers" story comes in two varieties, both of which are from more recent literary stock than fifteenth-century legends. In fact, both are probably direct descendants of the Sherlock Holmes stories, which is to say, among other things, that the audience's sympathies are enlisted on the side of the detective, not the criminal. Occasionally, in, say, *The Untouchables*, a gangster's breezy disregard of our legal apparatus will perversely engage our admiration, just as, occasionally, Professor Moriarty's resourcefulness commands our affection. But for the most part, the television "cops and robbers" story is focused on the detective and his problems and has a high moral tone.

One of the varieties of television detective literature may be described as being in the "romantic" mode and the other, in the "realistic." Let us consider the romantic first.

Sometimes the romantic detective-hero is a semi-official officer of the law, such as the lawyer Perry Mason. But typically, he is a "private-eye," that is, a self-employed detective whose relation to official legal apparatus is largely informal and frequently antagonistic. Like Holmes, he is a bachelor, possesses an inexhaustible fund of potentially valuable information, and has his own unconventional methods of detection. He also has a friendly but patronizing attitude toward all police officers (for example, Lt. Tragg plays Inspector Lestrade to Perry Mason's Holmes). Like Holmes, some television "private-eyes" are attended by a faithful and ever-admiring friend who appears to have no interests in life other than to pay homage to his companion.

In *77 Sunset Strip*, a frivolous parking-lot attendant—appropriately named Kookie—plays Dr. Watson to Stuart Bailey's Holmes. While Kookie is not nearly so ingenuous as Watson, Watson would undoubtedly be startled by Kookie's lack of taste and education. Moreover, Kookie is rarely as useful as Watson. We may infer important differences between nineteenth-century England and twentieth-century America by attending to the differences in character between Watson and Kookie. The character of Kookie is undoubtedly a concession to the audience's demonstrated taste for well-proportioned and inarticulate heroes, a type that would scarcely be of interest to a Victorian audience. Watson, as well as the chronicler of Monsieur Dupin's adventures, is a mature, literate, and fairly well-informed companion. This difference notwithstanding, both Kookie and Watson serve the same dramatic role—"straight men" who occasionally can be the source of comic relief.

In spite of certain resemblances to Holmes, the modern private-eye has unique characteristics. Holmes was, after all, a Victorian. The private-eye is a reflection of more recently established social values and patterns of behavior. He actively eyes unattached women, rarely expresses surprise or indignation over grotesque crimes, and probably would find violin playing an absurd avocation. Also, unlike Holmes', his powers of observation are hardly impressive, and he employs only the most rudimentary logic in solving crimes, sometimes blundering his way to their solutions. Whereas Holmes is successful because he is cleverer than the criminal he pursues, Stuart Bailey of 77 *Sunset Strip* succeeds because the criminal is stupider than he. Also, Holmes is seldom violent, which of course distinguishes him sharply from those television detectives who have been patterned after types originally found in Raymond Chandler and Dashiell Hammett novels.

And yet, in spite of his blunted sensibilities, the private-eye frequently emerges as a romantic figure. In his own way, he is sophisticated, winsome, unpredictable, well paid, and haphazardly effective. He is also pure myth. Real life private detectives do not normally engage in the kind of work their television counterparts are weekly called upon to do, and might be terrified at the prospect. In short, the private-eye is almost the direct opposite of the realistic Sgt. Joe Friday of *Dragnet*, who along with his imitators represents television's most original variation of the "cops and robbers" theme.

Sgt. Joe Friday was created by Jack Webb, who, in 1952, after several successful years on radio, brought his program, *Dragnet*, to television. Using conventional cinematic and radio techniques, but with important modifications for the purposes of television, Webb achieved an impressive illusion of reality that opened new possibilities to "cops and robbers" literature. With the exception of its standard opening—a long shot view of the City of Los Angeles—almost the entire program was shot in "close-up." Webb was only minimally concerned with the supposedly dramatic ways in which criminals are apprehended. Instead, he focused the audience's attention on the process of interrogation, emphasizing the inherent drama in simple questions and answers by frequently and sequentially cutting from one face to another. Approximately half of the program's dialogue (or so it seemed) consisted of terse questions and guarded answers. Most of the performers on the show were "fresh faces," many of whom pretended to be as uncertain about their own performances as they were about their answers to Friday's questions.

Sgt. Friday, played by Webb himself, functioned also as the narrator of *Dragnet*, addressing the audience in tired, clipped, official, and sometimes technical language. Whether in the role of narrator or detective-hero, Friday was invariably grim and coldly efficient, the embodiment of all the impersonal mechanisms of law enforcement. He did not seek the audience's sympathy or friendship, only its attention. True to the Holmes tradition, Friday was provided with a kindly companion who softened his almost unbelievable dedication to work. But Friday was Holmesian only in the sense that he unfailingly solved his case. Unlike Holmes, Friday did not achieve success through imagination, logic, and daring. Friday appeared to be a cop, a "real cop," his success being a result of hard work and the backing of an efficient scientific machinery, the Los Angeles Police Force.

There are, of course, no cops exactly like Joe Friday, and it is a tribute to Webb's artistry that he was able to convince millions that there are. Nevertheless, with its concern for verisimilitude and its representation (even if stylized) of things "as they really are," *Dragnet* was in the tradition of the realistic movement in literature. Its final season on network television was in 1958, but *Dragnet* set a pattern which has been emulated, with varying degrees of success, by *The Line-up, Naked City, M-Squad,* and *The Untouchables.* In fact, *The Untouchables* has gone even further than *Dragnet* in its efforts at realism. Each *Dragnet* program began with the ominous information that the "story you are about to see is true. Only the names have been changed, to protect the innocent." In *The Untouchables,* real names are used (for example, Al Capone) and the narrator, Walter Winchell, reports the events of the story much as if he were reporting events on one of his news programs. The enormous popularity of this program is a measure of the convincing manner in which it tells an old story.

THE FAMILY SHOW

On television, family life is largely a laughing matter. At least there is no example in the history of television of a weekly program which dealt with the experiences of a family in anything but comic fashion. Occasionally, in the more successful programs, such as *The Goldbergs* and *Mama* (which were originally created in other media), the family would confront situations that were more serious than funny. But for the most part, family programs are classified as "situation comedies."

The *Goldbergs* and *Mama* are notable for two other reasons. They were the first family programs on television, both coming in 1949 (*The Goldbergs* in January, *Mama* in July). And they were clearly "ethnic" family stories, a genre within a genre. *The Goldbergs,* for example, derived much of its humor from the fact that the Goldbergs were a Jewish family living in The Bronx. Just as Leo Rosten's Hyman Kaplan would be pointless and certainly not funny if he were not an immigrant Jew, Uncle David and Molly herself were comprehensible only in terms of a specific cultural and religious context. In their last days on television, the Goldbergs were transplanted to a small suburban town, where, fortunately, they did not last long. Molly and Uncle David were as irrelevant in suburbia as Wyatt Earp would be on Broadway and 42nd Street.

The family programs that followed *The Goldbergs* and *Mama* did not emulate them. The Andersons (*Father Knows Best*), Rileys (*Life of Riley*), Nelsons (*The Adventures of Ozzie and Harriet*), Stevens (*I Married Joan*), and the Henshaws (*December Bride*) have no specific religious or subcultural identification unless it is of a vague, white, middle-class nature.

The reasons for the absence of ethnic stories in current family programs are not hard to find. In the first place, with the exception of the Puerto Rican migration, there have been no new cultural strains assimilated into American life for many years. (Indeed, the only recent family show in which there was an element of a "foreign" culture was *I Love Lucy*, Ricky Ricardo being a Cuban.) Presumably, the adult sons and daughters of immigrant Jews, Swedes, Italians, Poles, Russians, Greeks, Germans, and Irish think of themselves as "Americans" more than as members of a particular subgroup. Thus, they might find ethnic stories more strange than wonderful. In the second place, the wide base of television's audience tends to induce writers to create characters who have something in common with each viewer. This seems to require that characters not possess any quality that might suggest an identification with a particular group. Thus, although we might assume that Chester Riley is of Irish background and Jim Anderson of Swedish, no evidence other than their names confirms this. Ironically, one show which did maintain an ethnic quality, *Amos 'n' Andy*, was frequently accused of perpetuating a grotesque stereotype.

Real families, of course, are identified by more than their religious or cultural backgrounds. They have political biases. Television families have no political preferences, unless by excluding politics from their lives, they do, in fact, make a political gesture. In any case, the families depicted on television remain largely indifferent to any of the larger social and political issues with which most of the audience is familiar. Here again, the explanation is probably to be found in the wide base of the audience, segments of which would undoubtedly feel betrayed if Jim Anderson turned out to be an active member of either the Democratic or Republican party.

Real families, also, find themselves as members of a particular economic class. Some are rich, some are poor, and some, neither. Television families appear to be, almost uniformly, in the last group. With the possible exception of the McCoys in *The Real McCoys*, television families are characteristically surrounded by the symbols of middle-class life in America. The television family is "well fixed," but not so "well fixed" as to offend any members of the audience who might still be struggling to make a living. The Chinese houseboy in *Bachelor Father* is perhaps the only clear-cut symbol of high income in a television family.

In short, the American family as it is portrayed on television is as Norman Rockwell, or perhaps DeWitt Wallace of *Reader's Digest*, claims to see it. It consists of a father and mother and some handsome and "nervy" children. It functions in a house, a school, and an automobile in the "low-priced field." It faces problems, to be sure, but none that are essentially serious and none that cannot be solved through the application of simple good will. And, of course, everything is entirely above board. Jim Anderson would no sooner "fix" a traffic ticket or give himself an advantage on his income tax returns than Matt Dillon would refuse to draw against an evil killer. In other words, the family show, like the western and "cops-and-robbers" programs, is a romance.

Romances, of course, are not expected to be true in the sense of their depicting what actually exists. In our frontier history, we find no such char-

acter as Paladin, the gunfighter. In our police history, we find no such policeman as television's Eliot Ness. In our society, we find no such family as
the Andersons. What "truth" there is in a romance must be an artistic truth,
not a literal one. Cooper's Bumppo, Poe's Dupin, Doyle's Holmes, Tarking-
ton's William Baxter, even Mark Twain's Huck Finn are true only in the
sense of their having a convincing artistic reality. Paladin, Eliot Ness, and
Jim Anderson convey to millions a similar truth. In addition, their actions
express values which the audience finds at least theoretically congenial. Jim
Anderson of *Father Knows Best,* for example, is honest, sympathetic, and
genteel in an unaffected way. He gets along well with others. He is a man
whose convictions will never place him in danger of losing friends, money,
or status in the community. He seems to be educated, but he is not an "egg-
head." He is the head of his household, but he rules it gently. He wears a
smoking jacket in the living room and pajamas in bed, and when roused
from sleep he is invariably well groomed and instantly articulate. If he does
not exist, at least we can say of him that millions wish he did.

THE ACTUALITY NARRATIVE

Although westerns, "cops and robbers," and family stories form an important part of television's literary stock in trade, these types of programs are
not, in the purest sense, native to television. First, these are themes that
were developed in other media long before they were brought to the television screen. But even more important, such programs, almost without variation, are on film, many of them having been produced in Hollywood.
They are essentially twenty-six- or fifty-two-minute movies that are seen on
a television set rather than a movie screen. Of course, in the production of
these films important modifications are made to accommodate some of the
unique conditions imposed by the television screen. For example, there are
many more close-ups than are normally used in films shown in theaters.
Long shots are rarely used. More dialogue is needed. The casts tend to be
smaller, and much less attention is paid to lighting since subtle contrasts of
black and white will go unnoticed on a small, gray television screen.

Yet film and television are by no means identical communication
forms. A movie involves the taking of pictures, pictures which, in the first
place, must be developed in a laboratory, and, in the second place, may be
arranged and then projected in almost any order a director or editor wishes.
Thus, the film director may give to an audience an artfully manufactured
sense of time and space. He may, for example, compress time, expand it,
or even create the illusion of simultaneity. A typical movie technique for
achieving suspense involves alternately projecting different shots onto the
screen so as to create the impression that, for instance, a woman is tied to
the railroad tracks while, at the same time, a train is rushing toward her,
and, also at the same time (and in another part of the country), the hero is
trying to alert a sleepy station master to the impending disaster. In actuality,

each of these events occurs and is photographed separately, their dramatic relationship being established in the director's study and in the film editor's workroom. In this sense, the film as an art form is quite similar to music; time, in the former, and tempo, in the latter, are artificially created, an illusion of eye or ear produced through technical means, just as the painter produces the illusion of depth on a two-dimensional canvas. In another sense, however, the film is like the novel, since the director and the novelist are both limited largely to the past tense. The movie viewer (or reader) is always aware that what he is seeing (or reading) has already happened, that it is a record and reproduction of events rather than the events themselves. Even in "present tense" novels, such as William Faulkner's *As I Lay Dying*, the reader is continually aware of the "pastness" of the events unfolded before him.

Television is different. It introduces an element into literature that cannot be as convincingly expressed in novels or films, namely, real time. On live television the presentation of the action and its perception by the audience are virtually simultaneous. There is no film to be developed, and there are no words to be printed. If we add to this the fact that the aesthetic distance between performer and audience closely approximates the "real" distance that separates people when they are conversing, we may understand why on television the sense of the actual is greater than in any other medium. To put it another way, the grammar of television communicates largely in the "present tense," and, as a consequence, television achieves its most compelling effects when it reveals the illusion of the "thing itself" happening in the here and now.

We have implied earlier that this sense of the actual has been exploited with success by such television dramatists as Paddy Chayefsky. But television plays, even when they are "live," still have the element of "pastness," since the audience can confidently assume that the author, director, and actors have carefully planned each word and action in advance. There are, however, other kinds of television "dramas"—we have called them "actuality narratives"—in which the sense of the actual is not only veritable but essential. Without it the presentations would be pointless. For example, *This Is Your Life*, for all of its artificialities, probably owes as much of its longevity to the inherent drama in an unpredictable situation as it does to its public exposure of what are essentially private matters. Certainly, the campaign debates of the presidential candidates drew much of their excitement from their sense of the actual and unpredictable.

This aesthetic dimension of television was recognized by the drama critic, Walter Kerr, who coined the term *visual essay* to describe programs which draw their main source of appeal from the sense of actuality and immediacy conveyed by television. The term subsumes such diverse programs as Leonard Bernstein's "demonstration-lectures," Mike Wallace's interviews, and the President's press conferences.

It is important to note that these programs have in common not only their sense of immediacy and actuality but (to continue the grammatical analogy) a sense of the "first person"; that is, there is direct, informal, and intimate communication with the audience. This mixture of intimacy and actuality probably accounts for the magnetism of the *Jack Paar Show*, which, despite its frequent commercial interruptions, communicates with a directness and candor that is possible only on television. No doubt the mixture plays a part in the appeal of Dave Garroway's *Today* show, as well as in the effectiveness of the sprightly Huntley and Brinkley commentaries.

This mixture has also been used with notable success for journalistic purposes. For example, probably one of the most dramatic visual essays ever presented on television was the "Army-McCarthy" hearings, in which the television camera, as incisively as any characterization written by Herodotus or Carlyle, penetrated to the essential qualities of public figures. The presentation of the national political conventions has also been a visual essay in which, on one network, Huntley and Brinkley, in the roles of a modern-day Addison and Steele, went beyond the observable events to make deep although humorous comments on American culture.

Whatever they are called—visual essays, actuality narratives, or something else—it would appear that television's most natural and compelling resource is its ability to communicate ideas and reveal events and people with a sense of intimacy and truthfulness. Perhaps the single most important characteristic shared by such television "personalities" as Arthur Godfrey, Jack Paar, Dave Garroway, Chet Huntley, David Brinkley, Edward R. Murrow, Eric Sevareid, Garry Moore, Arlene Frances and Mike Wallace is that they are not typical "show business" people. Neither do they appear to be actors, in a theatrical sense. They "play" themselves, and when their performances approach the histrionic, as occasionally in the case of Leonard Bernstein, there is a corresponding loss in effectiveness for many viewers. Another way of saying this is that on television, the untheatrical frequently tends to be more believable and more dramatic than the theatrical. This is an aesthetic principle which candidates for office ignore at their peril.

COMEDY

No body of literature is quite complete unless humor is amply and artfully represented. Television clearly satisfies this requirement, although its humor may more precisely be referred to as comedy since *comedy* connotes performances whereas *humor* suggests the written word. Aristophanes, for example, wrote comedies; Mark Twain's stories are humorous.

Television comedy has come, and continues to come, in various forms. Indeed, its range of comic forms is so wide that attempts at classification tend to be at an exceedingly high level of abstraction. One might, for example, distinguish between those comedians who essentially play themselves (Bob Hope) and those comedians who portray characters (Red Skelton or Jackie Gleason). Or, one might distinguish between comedians who perform routines, that is, tell jokes, do imitations, and fall on their faces (whether as "characters" or not), and those who act in what are known as "situation comedies."

Because such classifications tend to be vague, the discussion that follows is focused not on comic forms but on selected comedians whose performances have lent distinction to television or, perhaps what is quite as important in any analysis of the medium, whose popularity reflects something of our national character.

One must, therefore, begin with Milton Berle. For eight years—from 1948 to 1956—Berle egotistically but quite properly referred to himself as "Mr. Television." In five of those years his *Texaco Star Theater* was the most popular show on the air, and it was he, more than any other, who made television itself a source of constant conversation in its early years. In part, his success may be traced to the fact that during much of his reign as "King of Television" there were few serious pretenders to the throne. But the sources of his popularity go deeper than the mere absence of competition, as suggested by Gilbert Seldes' characterization of Berle as "the triumph of the hotfoot." Indeed, Berle's comedy often was at about the level of fun that people of unsophisticated sensibilities enjoy when witnessing a well-executed "hotfoot." His milieu was "low" comedy, which he brought to television directly from New York night clubs but which had been a staple in vaudeville. The image he projected was that of a loud, physical, and incipiently vulgar egotist who seemed more amused at his own jokes than anyone else was. For years a substantial segment of the television audience cultivated a curious fondness for this professional "life of the party," admiring, perhaps envying, the abandon with which he "upstaged" his betters and overwhelmed his equals. Possibly it was precisely because the audience believed that Berle was in reality the image he projected on the television screen that they remained fascinated by him for so long. There are few things more destructive to good comedy than manufactured brashness. Berle was genuinely brash, a fact that was unmistakably communicated by the television camera.

The reasons for Berle's decline on the *Texaco Star Theater* are directly related to the reasons for his ascent. The very brashness for which he was noted became too familiar, and because his comedy was uninstructive, it bred at least mild contempt. Also, weekly exposure is a phenomenon to which the television comedian is especially vulnerable. Berle learned, as did Jerry Lewis later, that television performers whose comedy is not about anything except themselves can sustain their popularity only so long as they retain the audience's affection. When affection leaves, obscurity is not far behind.

Whereas Berle was the first to bring the routines and palaver of the night-club floor to television, Sid Caesar was the first to bring to the me-

nore substantial arts of satire and parody. He also brought with
:e Berle, a company of comedians admirably suited to assist him.
9 to 1954, Imogene Coca, Carl Reiner, and Howard Morris, among
,ined the multitalented Caesar in lampooning almost everything
,dern art and Japanese films to quiz shows and westerns. Television, .n particular, provided *Your Show of Shows* with its richest source
of ridicule and, at one time or another, Caesar and his group satirized almost every one of television's literary "genres." The essential quality in
Caesar's comedy was that, like Chaplin, most of his skits made a social comment. As a consequence, for all of its physicalness, often approaching slapstick, Caesar's comedy was invariably edifying. The audience was continually aware that it was observing not merely a funny man but a performer
making fun of man and doing it at the expense of subjects that are not always looked upon as sources of humor. Although Caesar has not made regular appearances on television since 1958, the satiric tradition he began
was carried on most successfully by the recently dissolved Steve Allen
troupe. Not nearly so consistently "serious" as Caesar's *Your Show of
Shows*, the *Steve Allen Show* treated with comic irreverence such subjects
as military organizations, Princess Margaret's marriage, and—in the sturdi-
est tradition of satire—the hand that fed it, the commercial message.

In American culture, marriage is generally regarded as a natural
source of comedy, and it was to this subject that Jackie Gleason turned with
success after an inauspicious beginning on television. Although his character, Ralph Kramden, was the main focus of *The Honeymooners*, Gleason,
like Caesar, enlisted the help of other comedians, each of whom was as
capable as he. Gleason, Audrey Meadows, Art Carney, and Joyce Randolph
played the roles of the Kramdens and Nortons, two improbable but like-
able couples who carried on the battle of the sexes in a more full-bodied
manner than Thurber's line-drawn characters. Unlike Thurber's men,
Kramden, the bus driver, and Norton, the sewer digger, were always and
clearly the inferiors of their respective mates. Whereas the wives appeared
to be eminently sensible, if not always refined, the husbands were consistently boorish and repeatedly fumbled their way to absurd resolutions of
simple and sometimes unnecessary problems. This pattern of the sensible
wife and ineffective husband recurs frequently on television "situation
comedy." One finds this pattern, for example, in *The Life of Riley*, *The
Adventures of Ozzie and Harriet*, and *The Danny Thomas Show*.

Perhaps the most notable exception to this rule of situation comedy
was the *I Love Lucy* show, where the wife, not the husband, appeared consistently clownish. Beginning in 1951 and competently supported by Desi
Arnaz, William Frawley, and Vivian Vance, Lucille Ball romped through
eight years of television's zaniest comedy. Probably the most gifted come-
dienne television has produced, Lucy was most successful at slapstick. Ir-
repressible, unsubtle, loud, and yet eccentrically intelligent, her appeal was

largely to the audience's sense of the absurd. Like the Marx brothers, she represented the nihilistic impulse that dwells beneath the surface in many of us. But whereas Groucho's denial of all conventional standards sprang from a seeming amorality, Lucy's denial of logical standards invariably grew out of good intentions.

Because of this emphasis, we may be assured that exciting comedians will be continually exposed to the public. For example, our newest group of social satirists—sometimes called "sit-down comics"—has found in television an eager outlet for its seriocomic assaults on American values. Mort Sahl, Shelley Berman, Bob Newhart, and Mike Nichols and Elaine May were all catapulted to fame as a result of frequent, although not regular, appearances on television. Their quiet monologues (or, in the case of Nichols and May, dialogues) present an interesting contrast to the more frenetic performances of the Berle-Silvers-Skelton-Gleason type of comedian. However, the new comics are confronted by two obstacles not faced by many of their predecessors. First, the wide base of television's audience —at once a challenge and frustration to all television artists—might require some of these comedians to dilute the pungency of their routines, or even worse, compromise their points of view. Social criticism, in general, and satire, in particular, are not received with equal enthusiasm by all the segments of television's vast audience. Second, the format used by these comedians seems less suited to regular television appearances than the "situation comedy." The monologist requires a new set of jokes for each of his appearances on television, a requirement that would seem exceedingly difficult to fulfill in a thirty-nine week series.

SOME INTER-MEDIA RELATIONSHIPS

By Sydney W. Head

IN MANY WAYS broadcasting has assumed a pivotal position at which the currents of inter-media competition tend to intersect. As an advertising-supported medium with both local and national coverage, broadcasting competes directly with the newspaper and the popular magazine (see graph below). On the other hand, as a primarily entertainment medium, it also competes directly with the motion-picture industry. Yet broadcasting makes considerable use of the basic content material of all three of these competing media. Taking still another point of view, technologically radio contributed to the development of sound pictures, while pictures in turn contributed to the technological development of television.

Historically, the relationship between broadcasting and the competing media has been conditioned by the fact that it was the last to develop. To start with, the older media regarded radio (and later television) with condescension as upstarts and interlopers. An example is the cavalier treatment of radio by the press over the issue of news broadcasting. Another is the smugness which led the motion-picture industry completely to misjudge the potentialities of television.

Having failed to dispose of broadcasting by ignoring it or making jokes about it, the older media have moved into the second stage, adopting the "if you can't lick 'em, join 'em" tactic. Carried to its extreme, this could result in the domination of broadcasting by the press and motion-picture interests through control of strategic necessities such as talent supply, networks and other agencies of syndication, programs, and key stations. Of the two, the motion-picture industry, a naturally monopoly-prone business, perhaps offers the more serious threat to the independence of broadcasting.

RADIO TECHNOLOGY AND SOUND FILM

An interesting parallelism exists between both the technical and the economic histories of the entertainment-film and broadcasting industries. Like broadcasting, the cinema was founded on technological improvements so numerous that no single company could control a complete system. In 1908 patents controlled by the Edison, Biograph, Essanay, and Vitagraph companies were pooled by means of a cross-licensing agreement analogous to the agreements by which the communication companies broke a similar stalemate a dozen years later. The Motion Picture Patents Company, which emerged with a monopoly on film technology as a result of cross-licensing, dominated the industry until 1915. Patents again became a crucial battleground with the introduction of sound in 1927. At this point the former radio rivals, AT&T and RCA, found themselves once more deeply involved in a battle for a new market.

Sound had been combined with pictures as early as the Edison experi-

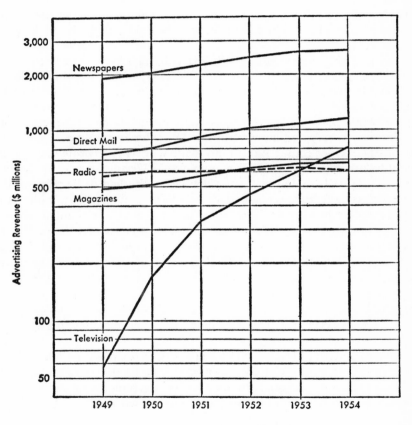

Comparative Growth Rate of TV Advertising Since 1949

Television exceeded both magazines and radio by 1954. Note, however, that the competing media do not show a sharp decline, despite the rapid rise of television.

Source: *Television Factbook No. 21* (Fall-Winter, 1955), p. 22.

ments of the 1890's. But, as in the case of radiotelephony, commercial development of sound had to await the advent of the vacuum-tube amplifier. Significantly, Lee De Forest himself turned from radio to the new field of sound-on-film, and by 1924 was able to demonstrate publicly his "Phonofilm" method.[1] This preceded by four years the marketing of Western Electric's sound system, and was, moreover, a bona-fide sound-on-film system, whereas Western Electric at first depended on disc recordings. De Forest, however, was unable to persuade the motion-picture interests to risk money for commercial development of his invention. The habit of silence was hard to break: "What stone walls of indifference, stupidity, and solid negativity did we unearth among the dead bones and concrete skulls of motion picture 'magnates'!"[2] Despite many successful demonstrations of his system, De Forest failed to acquire the necessary capital in time to forestall AT&T and RCA.

In 1926 the former set up a subsidiary through Western Electric, Electrical Research Products, Incorporated (ERPI), with a working capital of forty million dollars. ERPI's primary purpose was to exploit Western Electric's sound system in the motion-picture field. By 1928, after a year's moratorium while the rival sound systems were investigated, all the major film producers had accepted licenses from ERPI. The license terms were calculated to freeze out competition: films made with WE recording equipment could be projected only on WE equipment; WE equipment could be serviced only by WE representatives; a double royalty had to be paid by WE licensees to project films made with non-WE equipment. In addition to leasing and maintaining the recording and projection equipment and collecting royalties on the use of sound film, ERPI cultivated the market for these services by lending financial assistance, through several subsidiaries, to film producers. In this way AT&T found itself once more in show business, a reminder of the WEAF days. In 1937 a court held that the restrictive provisions of the ERPI licenses, though not at first illegal, later became unlawful when competitive sound equipment was available.[3] In the meantime, however, ERPI had modified its practices under the threat of suit from RCA.[4]

AT&T's attempt to gain exclusive control of sound in the film industry was particularly galling to RCA, for part of AT&T's patent resources in the field derived from the existing cross-licensing agreements between the two companies. In order to assure an outlet for its own products, RCA began

---

[1] Lee De Forest, *Father of Radio* (Chicago: Wilcox & Follett Co., 1950), p. 392. De Forest registered 79 patents connected with sound-on-film.
[2] *Ibid.*, p. 370.
[3] *General Talking Pictures Corp.* v. *AT&T*, 18 F. Supp. 650 (1937).
[4] The rather involved history of ERPI's maneuvers in the early days of sound films is traced in: FCC, *Investigation of the Telephone Industry in the United States* (Washington: Government Printing Office, 1939), pp. 401-415. The contemporary successor to ERPI is Westrex Corporation.

purchasing motion-picture company stock in 1927, and by 1932 it held a controlling interest in Radio-Keith-Orpheum (RKO). RKO had an interest in about 150 concerns involved in motion-picture production, distribution, and exhibition. A few years later, after acquiring an assured place in the film-sound business, RCA sold its interest in RKO.[5]

Meanwhile, in 1928, RCA Photophone, Inc., had been set up by RCA to compete with ERPI. The latter captured an early lead, with installations in 90 per cent of the sound-equipped theatres by the end of 1928. The next year, as the number of theatres capable of exhibiting the new "talkies" rapidly increased, the extent of ERPI's lead fell off sharply. By 1936 resistance to ERPI's highly restrictive contracts had grown to a point where suits amounting to $175,000,000 had accumulated against the company. But ERPI had already begun to relax its contracts under pressure from RCA, and very little in damages was actually collected. Thereafter RCA and AT&T learned to live side by side competitively in this new field.

The Organization of the Film Industry

Although the introduction of sound in 1927 caused a major upheaval and readjustment in the motion picture industry, the basic pattern of the industry had already been set by 1920, the time broadcasting began. Even in the nickelodeon days of the early 1900's it became obvious that the way to make money in motion pictures was (1) to syndicate the product, and (2) to combine theatres into chains. Syndication in this medium is even more essential than in other mass media. Local production analogous to local live broadcast programming or local news coverage is impossible in the motion-picture field because of the irreducibly high cost of picture production. Entertainment-film production facilities are highly centralized both physically and economically, the aggregate output is relatively small (see table), and the risks are considerable. Intervening between the producer and the exhibitor is the distributor. As the middleman he can exert great pressure on both producer and exhibitor. In order to gain economic efficiency and the strength to bargain effectively with the producer and distributor, the exhibitor tends to build up chains of theatres.

Since entertainment films are not a standardized product, the value of the producer's output is not highly predictable. For every hit film which brings in a tremendous profit there may be many mediocre successes and outright failures. In order to iron out the violent fluctuations in the value of the product, film producers and distributors early resorted to the practice of "block booking." This obliged the exhibitor to rent unproduced films in groups, sight unseen. The exhibitor thus found himself involuntarily saddled with a number of second-rate and third-rate releases. Another means of ironing out the erratic economy of motion-picture production is to

[5] FCC, *Report on Chain Broadcasting* (Washington: Government Printing Office, 1941), pp. 13-14.

Feature Output of the Motion Picture Industry, Selected Years

Year	Number of Features	Estimated Production Costs	
		Total ($ thousands)	Per Picture ($ thousands)
1952	324	291,600	900
1948	366	376,336	1,028
1945	350	194,035	554
1942	588	197,921	337
1939	483	149,000	342

Source: Standard & Poor's *Industry Surveys*, March 3, 1955, "Motion Pictures," based on *Film Daily Yearbook* estimates.

combine the production, distribution, and exhibition functions under one economic unit. The producer then has an assured outlet for his product, and the risks of production can be offset by the relative stability of theatre income.

The practice of combining the production-distribution function with the exhibition function, together with block-booking and related restrictive distribution practices, have long been sources of contention within the industry. Antitrust suits dragged out for a decade before a Supreme Court decision in 1948 modified all these practices.[6] One result has been the "divorcement" of the leading companies, known as "The Big Five," by means of consent decrees. In 1950 Paramount Pictures, Inc., was dissolved to form Paramount Pictures Corporation (production and distribution) and United Paramount Theatres (exhibition). In 1950 Radio-Keith-Orpheum (RKO) became RKO Pictures and RKO Theatres, and the next year 20th-Century Fox's 385 theatres were transferred to a new company, National Theatres. In 1953 Warner Brothers became Warner Brothers Pictures and Stanley Warner Corporation (340 theatres). The last of the Big Five to undergo divorcement was Loew's, Inc. (MGM).

THE IMPACT OF TV ON THE FILM INDUSTRY

During World War II and the immediate postwar years the motion picture industry climbed almost to its peak of the pre-depression period (see table). By 1948 the impact of television began to make itself felt. The Supreme Court decision of the same year against block booking was another blow, especially to poor motion pictures, which television also hurt most. In the next four years several thousand marginal theatres closed, box-office receipts fell off alarmingly, production budgets were cut, studios closed down, and the whole motion-picture industry boiled in a ferment of uncertainty and doubt.[7] A symbol of television's effect on motion pictures was the

[6] *U.S.* v. *Paramount Pictures, Inc.*, 334 U.S. 131 (1948).
[7] Cf. "Movies: End of an Era," *Fortune* (April, 1949), pp. 99 ff.; Robert Coughlan,

Average Weekly Attendance at Motion-Picture Theatres Since 1935

Selected Years	Average Weekly Attendance (millions)
1953	50
1952	45
1951*	54
1950*	60
1945	98
1940	80
1935	75

* Total number of seats in open and closed theatres—not comparable with other years.

Source: Standard & Poor's, *Industry Surveys*, March 3, 1955, "Motion Pictures," based on data from *Film Daily Yearbook* and *Motion Picture and Television Almanac*.

demise of the Embassy Newsreel Theatre in New York. Established in 1929, the first of its kind, the Embassy had capitalized on public interest in pictorial news, particularly sports news. Television's first programming success came from on-the-spot coverage of sports events, and the newsreel theatres felt the competition immediately. The Embassy abandoned its news and sports policy on its twentieth anniversary as a newsreel theatre, in November, 1949. It was the end of an era.

One Hollywood reaction to the devastating inroads of television was to dust off some very old film tricks, on the theory that the sheer mechanical superiority of film could beat television at its own game. This theory is in line with the traditional Hollywood notion that mere size and mechanical ingenuity outweigh every other consideration in appealing to the mass public. It ignores the fact that for years the movie industry had been jeopardizing its own future by concentrating on an audience of teen-agers. As audiences matured, they matured away from the movies as a source of entertainment. Instead of telling stories for people, movies had "degenerated into telling myths for children." [8]

Certainly the first efforts at weaning audiences back to the theatres typified this point of view. "Three-D," the first of the "gimmicks," had a brief vogue starting in 1952. Three-D pictures were almost universally con-

"Now It Is Trouble That Is Supercolossal in Hollywood," *Life* (13 August 1951), pp. 102-115. Contrast, however: Freeman Lincoln, "The Comeback of the Movies," *Fortune* (February, 1955), pp. 127-131, 155-158.

[8] Gilbert Seldes, *The Great Audience* (New York: The Viking Press, 1950), p. 88. "The relationship between age and movie attendance is probably one of the most spectacular findings in the whole field of communication behavior . . . confirmed in every study of movie going." Paul F. Lazarsfeld and Patricia Kendall, *Radio Listening in America* (Copyright, 1948, by Prentice-Hall, Inc., New York), p. 11. Reprinted by permission of the publisher.

demned for their content as pictures, but the novelty factor caused a sensation. Based on "a simple optical illusion whose principle was known to Euclid and whose practice put grandfather to sleep on Sunday afternoons," [9] Three-D achieved the illusion of three dimensions by the use of polaroid glasses. The camera takes a double picture through two lenses separated like the two eyes of normal human vision. The two slightly overlapping pictures are separated for the viewer by polaroid glasses. Although the illusion is rather novel, the system is fundamentally impracticable.

However, the unexpected temporary success of Three-D despite the low quality of the pictures set the major studios searching frantically for more practical "gimmicks." The sense of depth in human vision does not depend exclusively on the factor of binocular vision. A one-eyed person does not lose all depth perception. In life a number of different types of "cues" contribute to the perception of the depth dimension.[10] Theoretically, several different cueing devices could be employed, singly or in combination, to secure the depth-illusion.

The most successful system is Cinerama, invented in 1938 by Fred Waller and developed during World War II as a gunnery training device. Cinerama provides a convincing—in fact startling—sense of depth without the use of glasses. It uses the cues provided by peripheral vision—that sense of surrounding objects which the eye normally has even when focussed on a particular object directly in the foreground. The ordinary 3 to 4 aspect ratio of television and motion pictures narrows the width of field down to only about a sixth of the eye's normal arc of vision. Cinerama restores a large part of the scene which is normally seen "out of the corner of the eye." These peripheral cues are provided by a very wide, deeply curved screen. Three synchronized projectors with three separate film strips are required to fill the screen, and the major mechanical defect of the system is the difficulty of blending the three pictures without betraying the fact that they are, indeed, three different pictures. Economically, Cinerama is limited by the fact that it takes a large theatre to seat a small audience; few existing theatres have both the physical dimensions and the necessary audience-turnover potential.

CinemaScope, developed by 20th-Century Fox, is a compromise system adaptable to most theatres. It provides a wide, slightly curved screen filled with a single picture. Anamorphic lenses are used, first to squeeze an image with about a 3 to 8 aspect ratio down to the 3 to 4 ratio of normal film stock, then to spread the image out again for projection on a wide screen. There is little, if any, depth illusion in CinemaScope, but the wide field of view is impressive. Other wide-screen systems introduced to com-

[9] *Time* (8 June 1953), p. 66.
[10] Cf. Thaddeus R. Murroughs, "Depth Perception with Special Reference to Motion Pictures," *Journal of the Society of Motion Picture and Television Engineers*, LX (June, 1953), pp. 656-670.

pete with CinemaScope include VistaVision (Paramount) and Todd-AO (MGM). The latter is the first of the new systems to change the basic 35-mm. film size; it uses double-width film and an aspect ratio of 2 to 1.[11] All the wide-screen systems employ multiple sound tracks to obtain sound perspective, i.e., the illusion that sound is coming from the appropriate sector of the field of view.

Technical improvements mean little, of course, if the basic content is not entertaining or artistically sound. Experience has shown that a simple "flat" black-and-white film can be just as entertaining as one incorporating all the newer gadgets. Even the pre-wide-screen 35-mm. films provide a picture scale and a degree of definition which television cannot duplicate; therefore the competitive value of the various wide-screen processes has been more in terms of ballyhoo than in terms of basic improvement of the film product.

Hybrid Systems

Another approach to the problem of recapturing the theatre audience from television is to bring television into the theatre. Several companies have developed equipment for the projection of television images on theatre-size screens, so that televised events can be incorporated into motion-picture programs or substituted for film programs on special occasions. The Louis-Savold championship fight was televised in nine theatres in seven cities in 1951, and the next year the Marciano-Walcott bout was seen on screens in fifty theatres in thirty-one cities. In 1953, however, the FCC somewhat dimmed the prospects of a really major development of theatre television by refusing to allocate special wide-frequency channels to this service for use in relaying programs. Instead, the FCC ruled, theatres must lease relay facilities from AT&T, just as the broadcast networks do. When confined to the six-megacycle channel standard of broadcasting, theatre television cannot, of course, secure the detail which is desirable for theatrical exhibition. Theatre television seems to have possibilities for permanent but limited use.[12] As an essentially hybrid form of entertainment—combining the disadvantages of both film and television without capitalizing fully on the advantages of either—theatre television gives no promise of affecting either medium profoundly.

A second hybrid medium has been proposed in the form of subscrip-

[11] It is an ironic commentary on the attitude of exhibitors that many of them, after installing wide screens, made it a common practice to project ordinary 3 to 4 ratio films to fit the new screens. This can only be accomplished by blowing up the size of the projected picture to fit the screen width and masking off the overlapping top and bottom of the frame. Thus the highly-skilled, highly-paid Hollywood cameramen spend a great deal of ingenuity and money in carefully composing pictures for the 3 to 4 ratio only to have their artistry nullified by the callousness of exhibitors.

[12] By 1953, 107 theatres were equipped for theatre television and eight producers and syndicates were in operation. *Television Factbook No. 18* (14 January 1954), pp. 276-277.

tion home television. This proposal envisions keeping television's advantages as a home medium while at the same time retaining the economic advantage of motion pictures as a box-office medium. Several systems of subscription television have been proposed. All involve the transmission of a scrambled television picture by an otherwise normal television broadcast transmitter. The picture is unscrambled for the paying customer by any of several unscrambling devices at the home receiver. The subscriber pays a moderate fee per program.[13] The theory of subscription television is that a relatively small fee collected from a relatively small audience (as network television audiences go) would amount to a relatively huge sum of money —much more money than sponsors can normally afford to pay for programs. Subscription television could thus theoretically afford to provide outstanding entertainment, such as first-run feature films, Broadway plays, and major sports events. Proponents originally envisioned an advertising-free service, but later began to waver on this promise.

Subscription television offers more of a threat, as a rival medium, than theatre television. It has been described as "probably the most complex— and the most important—new issue confronting the authorities, because it must inevitably evolve into a new determination of our entire philosophy of broadcasting." [14] Yet subscription television is by no means as simple an answer as might appear at first glance. It leans heavily on the delusion that broadcasting is "free." The fact is, of course, that audiences invest huge amounts in sets, service, power, and replacement parts. Subscription television would add further to the set-owner's economic burdens, since he would have the expense of buying, maintaining, and operating a regular broadcast receiver in the first place even to become eligible to subscribe to the pay-see programs. It seems probable, too, that the proponents of subscription television (insofar as they propose to dispense with commercial announcements) overestimate the opposition of audiences to the advertising content of television programs. In radio at least, it was found that advertising was actually liked by a large proportion of the audience, that only about 10 per cent was in fact aggressively opposed to advertising.[15] Further, subscription proponents are unduly optimistic about the quantity of talent available of a caliber acceptable to mass audiences. Regular broadcasters foresee that subscription-system operators would be in a position to outbid them, and that hence much of the top talent once available "free" to televiewers would become available only at a price.

CROSS-CHANNEL AFFILIATION

A third defensive maneuver by film interests against the competitive inroads of broadcasting is to enter broadcasting themselves. A standard gambit in

---

[13] Subscription television systems are to be distinguished from the coin-operated television sets used in hotels. In the latter case the viewer pays for the use of the *set* as such rather than for the reception of the program.

[14] "Pay-As-You-See Crossroads," *Broadcasting-Telecasting* (20 September 1954), p. 122.

[15] Lazarsfeld and Kendall, *op. cit.*, p. 61.

any business venture, of course, is to buy into related fields as a hedge against possible technological obsolescence. Newspapers bought into radio from the very beginning of broadcasting; later AM radio bought FM on the same principle; still later AM radio bought television. "Cross-channel affiliation," as it has been called,[16] has resulted in complex interrelationships among the media. Early liaisons between the radio and film industries have already been reviewed in connection with the introduction of sound. Since the advent of television a new series of cross-channel affiliations has been made. The merger of the American Broadcasting Company and United Paramount Theatres in 1953, involving combined assets of 144 million dollars, was the biggest transaction of its kind. Paramount Pictures bought a substantial interest in the Dumont Television Network as early as 1939. Other Paramount television interests include Station KTLA in Los Angeles and half ownership of Chromatic Television Laboratories and of International Telemeter (subscription television system). The first major film company to come under the control of broadcasting interests was RKO Pictures, which was purchased for twenty-five million dollars by General Tire and Rubber Company, owner of General Teleradio, which in turn controls MBS. RKO thus came into the broadcasting orbit for the second time in its history. Newspaper interests are connected with about a fifth of all the radio stations in the country, and with an even higher proportion of television stations.

RADIO AND THE PRESS

During the 1930's, when radio was rapidly expanding, newspapers experienced a period of serious decline. The growth of commercial radio also coincided with the depression which followed the stock-market crash of 1929. Hence the difficulties of newspapers during the '30's may have been due as much to prevailing economic conditions as to the competition of radio. Certainly radio did not gain its increasing revenue merely at the expense of the other media. It rode in on a changing economy which favored increased advertising budgets. Moreover, radio created new advertisers, new advertising techniques, new advertising markets. An intensive study of competition among the media led to the conclusion that

> There is no evidence . . . that all or even most of radio's spectacular growth came at the expense of newspapers. Radio probably brought much new money into advertising and also took revenues from magazines, farm papers, car cards and the movies.[17]

The fact is that the economy of newspaper publishing has been undergoing a long-term readjustment ever since the turn of the century. Rising

[16] Harvey J. Levin, "Economies in Cross Channel Affiliation of Media," *Journalism Quarterly* XXXI-2 (Spring, 1954), pp. 167-174.
[17] Harvey J. Levin, "Competition Among the Mass Media and the Public Interest," *Public Opinion Quarterly* XVIII-1 (Spring, 1954), p. 73.

production costs and changing markets have led to a steady decrease in the number of daily papers published. In 1910, competitive daily newspapers were published in 689 cities, but by 1954 only 87 cities were served by competitive daily papers; in the meantime, however, aggregate circulation had gone up from 22 million to 54 million.[18] In short, the trend has been consistently toward fewer but larger newspapers.

Nevertheless, the direct rivalry between newspapers and radio for advertising budgets naturally tends to sharpen the sense of competition between the two media. For example, the broadcasters consider that radio and television station program logs are in the nature of news and should be published as such by the newspapers. Many newspapers, on the other hand, regard program logs as advertising for a rival medium and either charge substantial space rates or refuse to publish them altogether. This narrow view, however, seems to be on the wane, and the more enlightened publishers no longer fear the competition of radio to that extent.[19] Even so, newspapers occasionally resort to unfair tactics in their efforts to freeze out competitive broadcasting stations.[20]

Whatever commercial rivalries exist, the right and duty of broadcasting stations to broadcast the news is no longer questioned by the news services and newspapers. The broadcasters' main difficulty in this respect now comes from some of the sources of the news. Radio and television have long been fighting to establish the principle of "equal access," i.e., the right of radio and television to cover all news events to which reporters of any kind are admitted. The reporters for the radio and television services have secured an equal footing as reporters with those of the news services and print media; but direct radio and television reports by means of remote pickup or recordings have not yet been universally accepted. During the national political conventions and campaigns of 1952, television as an eyewitness reporter made important gains. When television was excluded initially from an important press conference held by General Eisenhower in Abilene, Kansas, in the summer of 1952, CBS forced the issue and won the argument.

Nevertheless, many thoughtful and impartial observers still fear that the presence of television cameras (whether live or newsfilm), microphones, lights, and the rest of the paraphernalia in such places as law courts, Congressional hearings, and important news conferences may do more harm than good. Difficult questions involving rights of privacy, due process of law, and orderly conduct of government arise. With such innovations as televised (though staged) Cabinet meetings and filmed (though edited)

---

[18] Raymond B. Nixon, "Trends in Newspaper Ownership since 1945," *Journalism Quarterly* XXXI-1 (Winter, 1954), p. 7.

[19] An NARTB survey found that in over half of the communities reporting, newspapers published program logs without charge and that most of the newspapers which do charge are in small communities. NARTB, "Newspaper Program Listing Practices" (mimeo., 1954).

[20] Cf. *Mansfield Journal Co.* v. *FCC*, 180 F. (2d) 28 (1950).

Presidential press conferences, broadcasting has recently taken a long step in the direction of equal access. It remains to be seen whether greater familiarity with television as a direct reporting medium will eventually make it more acceptable in more spontaneous situations.[21]

Two other printed products are of particular interest as mass media: comic books and paper-bound books. Comic books came into prominence in 1938, when *Superman* zoomed into print. It is impossible to secure an accurate estimate of the circulation of comic books, but it is believed to be at least as high as a billion per year. Some notion of the value of this output can be gained from the fact that in 1954, when the comic-book industry was under heavy attack because of the presumed bad effects of comics on children, the Comics Magazine Association set up a "czar" after the fashion of Hollywood with an annual budget of $100,000.[22]

Paper-back books represent an even more interesting mass-communication phenomenon, and to some extent offset the negative implications of the comic book. Here the methods of mass merchandising have been applied to a standard product to revolutionize its market.

> Paper-bound publishers say their market is made up mostly of people who used to read only magazines, who are intimidated by the forbidding air of a bookstore, and who can afford perhaps a small fraction of the price of most new hard-cover books. They buy and read on the move, picking books off a rack or newsstand to read while commuting or traveling or during a frenzied day of changing diapers and making meals. They are impulse buyers who pick books at point of sale, and after reading them throw them away or pass them on to someone else. Few paper-bound buyers, say the publishers, want to keep the books as personal possessions or "furniture." [23]

In the "disposable" nature of the books, their adaptation to the tempo of everyday life, their low unit cost, and their method of distribution, we perceive the characteristic features of a mass medium. Their economic success depends on fast turnover; "packaging" aids sales by stressing typical mass appeals. Ludwig Lewisohn's *The Case of Mr. Crump* blossoms forth as *The Tyranny of Sex*, and Voltaire's *Candide* tells how "He chased a virtuous maiden through Europe's most bawdy age." If the merchandising methods are not always in keeping with the dignity of the product, it is significant that such titles as Plato's *Dialogues*, St. Augustine's *Confessions*, the *Iliad*, and the *Odyssey* have sold over half a million copies each.[24]

[21] The issue of equal access was the subject of the first editorial ever broadcast by a network. Cf.: Frank Stanton, *CBS Editorial* (New York: CBS, 1954).
[22] It is significant that the annual cost of comic books is estimated to be about four times the annual book budgets of all U.S. public libraries. "Comic Strips Down . . . ," *Time* (14 March 1955), p. 86.
[23] "The Boom in Paper-Bound Books," *Fortune* (September, 1953), pp. 123-124. © Time Inc.
[24] *Ibid.*, p. 124.

INTER-MEDIA STIMULATION

In the long run, and generally speaking, competition among the media seems to have resulted in mutual gains for all. Nevertheless, in order to meet competition the older media have had to make adjustments in their methods, their price, and the quality of their product. Newspapers have reacted to television competition by increasing production efficiency to reduce operating costs and space rates; the motion-picture industry has curbed some of its more conspicuously wasteful practices, cut back on the production of "Grade B" movies, aimed at fewer but better productions, developed technological improvements, and built 4,000 drive-in theatres since 1948; radio has begun to serve smaller audiences more generously with such limited-appeal programs as classical music.[25]

At the same time, media competition has been found to produce a good deal of cross-channel stimulation. For example, in 1922 there were five popular publications devoted to radio; the next year there were 25. More recently, television has produced a whole swarm of fan magazines, program guides, and the like, just as the motion pictures had done before. The *TV Guide* has become the top-selling publication on the newsstands nationally.[26] News about the doings of television stars, technical developments, and other items about broadcasting constitute a considerable fraction of the news material handled by the press associations and filling out the columns of the daily papers.

Television has tremendously stimulated the non-theatrical side of the motion-picture industry, since it uses far more film footage than the total output of Hollywood feature films. Two trends grow out of this circumstance. One is the conversion of Hollywood theatrical film facilities to the making of films for television. This type of production was pioneered by minor producers, but by 1955 the major film producers had become deeply involved in this new field, which by then represented several hundred millions of dollars annually. The second trend is the expansion of the non-theatrical film industry. During the late 1940's the number of non-theatrical film producers more than doubled.[27] Television created an entirely new demand for filmed commercials, besides creating a new outlet for industrial, public-relations, technical and scientific, travel, conservation and wild life, sports, educational and training, sales, and military films. Business and industrial film producers alone grossed fifty million dollars in 1953 and produced well over a thousand subjects.[28]

One of the most interesting examples of inter-media stimulation is the

[25] Cf.: Harvey J. Levin, "Competition" etc., *op. cit.*, pp. 76-79.
[26] Cf. Earl A. Abrams, "Fan Magazines," *Broadcasting-Telecasting* (22 November 1954), p. 43.
[27] This industry is not as concentrated geographically as the entertainment film industry. Cf. the annual directory of non-theatrical film producers in *Business Screen Magazine*.
[28] "Movies for Business," *Fortune* (August, 1954), pp. 94-98.

story of the near-demise and subsequent flowering of the phonograph-record industry. It will be recalled that the networks bought out the old-line phonograph companies at a time when radio seemed to have doomed home players to technological obsolescence. From a high of $100 million gross, Victor fell to $10 million in 1932. In the long run, however, radio popularized music and stimulated the urge to buy recordings; at the same time, radio provided the technological improvements which reduced the costs of home players and records while tremendously improving their quality. During the 1940's the traditional big three—Victor, Columbia, and Decca—were supplemented by Capitol, Mercury, MGM, and London (English Decca). With the introduction of long-playing records in 1948, still other, smaller companies sprang up rapidly. The classics achieved a hitherto unheard-of popularity.[29] By 1953 record sales had reached $250 million, a quarter of which was in the classical field—a remarkable tribute to both the technological and the aural influence of radio.

Similar inter-media stimulation occurs in the field of talent and programs. The radio program *Dragnet* led to a successful television series and from that to a successful motion picture. A television play, *Marty*, became a hit movie and won an international award. A steady flow of talent and material circulates from one medium to another. At the same time, one medium uses another for advertising purposes, both directly and indirectly. Television manufacturers became for a time one of the biggest radio advertisers; motion pictures use television advertising more and more (much of it donated for the sake of film program material). Walt Disney used inter-media stimulation with startling effect to snowball the "Davy Crockett" craze in 1955. All this emphasizes the fact that there is an essential unity underlying the diversity and competitive singularity of the media. Research has indicated that audiences are more selective with regard to the type of entertainment or information they desire than with regard to the channel by which it reaches them. A person who is a heavy consumer of the product of one mass medium is likely also to be a heavy consumer of the other mass media. Instead of one medium displacing another, one stimulates interest in the other.[30]

[29] Cf.: Dero A. Saunders, "Record Industry: The Classics are Hot," *Fortune* (December, 1952), pp. 128-131, 175-182.

[30] Lazarsfeld and Kendall, *op. cit.*, p. 5. During the winter of 1953, an eleven-day strike stopped publication of all major daily newspapers in New York. The radio and television stations redoubled their news coverage, but the strike "resulted in what amounted to almost a physical hunger for the sight of type. The public denuded the newsstands of magazines and paper-back books, so intense was its yearning for print." Ben Gross, *I Looked and I Listened* (New York: Random House, 1954), p. 299. A very careful survey of readership of major national magazines such as *Life, Look,* and the *Saturday Evening Post* revealed higher readership in television homes than in nontelevision homes. Alfred Politz Research, Inc., *The Audience of Nine Magazines* (New York: Cowles Magazines, Inc., 1955), p. 50.

COMPETITION FOR SPECTRUM SPACE

One species of competition in broadcasting is often overlooked, although it is of vital importance—competition for frequencies in the electromagnetic spectrum. While the development of the broadcasting services was taking place, equally spectacular gains were being made in non-broadcast radio services. As the FCC has pointed out,

> Because it enters the home, broadcasting commands so much popular interest that the average person does not realize that there are now 45 times more non-broadcast than there are broadcast stations, and the former are equally important to the public interest and convenience.[31]

The allocation of services has not followed a rational over-all plan, simply because the practical need for allocation of services has kept ahead of our knowledge of the spectrum and of propagation theory. As a result we have such anomalies as the fragmented television allocation plan, with channels grouped in such widely separated portions of the spectrum that serious practical problems have arisen concerning efficient utilization of the space allotted. It has been estimated that a thorough program of analysis and control for allocations in the United States would cost $50 million a year,[32] which is several times as much as the FCC is allotted annually for its whole regulatory operation.

RADIO V. TELEVISION

Hitherto we have been speaking primarily of broadcasting in relation to other media. Although radio and television are in effect one medium from some points of view, they nevertheless compete sharply with each other for advertising revenue. While television was getting on its feet radio paid the bill, and hence network radio was placed in the unfortunate position of apparently presiding at its own immolation. Even the advertising power of radio became self-destructive as the means for promoting the sale of television sets. By the end of the freeze, in 1952, the position of network radio had begun to deteriorate seriously. It was freely predicted by many observers that network radio was doomed. The networks tried various stratagems to stem the tide. A general overhauling of rates took place, with emphasis on reduction for the nighttime hours, when television has its greatest impact. New sources of business were sought through programming and scheduling devices intended to attract the smaller national and regional advertisers to network radio.

In August, 1953, David Sarnoff addressed a showdown meeting of

[31] FCC, *Eighteenth Annual Report* (Washington: Government Printing Office, 1953), p. 1.
[32] President's Communications Policy Board, *Telecommunications: A Program for Progress* (Washington: Government Printing Office, 1951), p. 27.

NBC radio affiliates in Chicago.[33] NBC had run through several presidents who had been successively outmaneuvered by CBS. In the previous June Sarnoff himself had stepped down from his remote position as Chairman of the Board of both RCA and NBC to take over management of the network in person. His study of the radio network situation had convinced him that a reversal of policy was necessary. The trend had been toward integration of radio and television functions into a single network organization; he now realized that radio tended to be submerged and neglected in a joint operation.

A basic reorientation in the economics of the industry also seemed necessary to Sarnoff. The networks could no longer depend primarily on a limited group of major national advertisers able to spend a million or more dollars a year in the medium. Between 1948 and 1953 radio-network time sales decreased 22 per cent, whereas local sales had gone up 35 per cent. Obviously, as the major network sponsors deserted radio for television, radio networks would have to dip into the local market. This meant, for example, adapting network radio to an advertising technique which had become universal in local radio—participating sponsorship, which distributes program cost over a number of sponsors. Mutual, perforce, had already moved to tap local sources of revenue. The prospective competition in this field by NBC and CBS threatened the very existence of Mutual as a full-scale national radio network.

The new orientation in the economics of network operation calls for a corresponding change in programming. Sarnoff rejected the theory that the future role of radio will be reduced to the "music-and-news" format which has been successfully employed by some local stations. He pointed out that this format works only because such stations depend on a very limited audience. Most big stations have to make a wider appeal, and they depend on network programming for most of that appeal. On the other hand, the network cannot aim any longer for the great mass audience; it must seek relatively large, yet specialized audiences which, though perhaps small in a given market, add up to a respectable size when viewed as a national audience. This point of view opens the door to classes of "highbrow" programming previously regarded by the networks as too specialized in appeal.

The tyranny of program ratings, the natural concomitant of the mass-audience point of view, may become less absolute with this new approach to network programming. "Our industry," said Sarnoff, "from the outset has been plagued by rating systems which do not say what they mean and do not mean what they say." Aside from the question of the validity of the ratings themselves as measurements of audience size, the significance of size itself is questionable, since, as is well known, audience size is not invariably directly related to effectiveness of advertising; it also may be questioned whether it is still appropriate to deal in the family as the unit of measure-

[33] Text published in *Broadcasting-Telecasting*, 21 September 1953, pp. 108-112.

ment, when in point of fact the television set has become the family entertainment, while radio has tended to become more personalized through portables, automobile sets, and small sets in the kitchen, bedroom, children's room, and bathroom. Since as far back as 1947 nearly 50 per cent of all radios sold had been in the small, portable categories. Sarnoff pointed out that the ubiquity of radio—one of its most most telling advantages over television—may well increase with the marketing of transistorized miniature pocket radio receivers.

Perhaps the most disturbing evidence of the impact of television on network radio as Sarnoff looked at it in the summer of 1953 was the prevalence of "rebates," which is a polite term for rate-cutting. This debilitating practice, in one form or another, has always been endemic in broadcasting, but the industry as a whole has fought against it, and hitherto the networks had been relatively successful in maintaining the integrity of the rate structure. The pretense of integrity was still maintained, but under the stress of increased competition the networks as well as individual stations had become prone to "deals" whereby the customer ended up by paying less for time than the published rate. In 1953 Sarnoff could go so far as to say that "deals and concessions are a blight on the radio network business."

On balance, the prospect for network radio is not as hopeless as it seemed in the panicky days of 1952-1953, when the first sweeping cutbacks in network rates occurred. Network radio will find its own level, a level which may not support as many as four full-scale national networks. But television does not replace radio; it revises its scope and function. As a far less expensive medium (and hence one less rigidly committed to mass appeal) the national radio service may well become—in the hopeful slogan of the movies—"better than ever." By 1955 the downward spiral of radio, especially at the local level, seemed to have been halted and this prediction was already coming true.

The Emergent Role of Television

When television first expanded into a national medium, the industry naturally assumed that it would follow rather closely the pattern of radio, with four national networks providing a generalized service and many small, local stations providing localized service. It now appears, however, that television may fall into a somewhat different pattern, a pattern which favors the continued health of radio. The expense of television is so great that the over-all trend seems to be toward a relatively limited number of major stations located in the larger population centers. Most smaller areas may be served either by small non-competitive television stations or, more probably, by various devices for the extension of service from large stations in the population centers. These devices include satellite and booster stations and community antennas, which at relatively modest cost can deliver a station's signal into areas beyond the range of the station's own antenna. This means that highly localized service (in terms of advertising outlets, programs, and community self-expression) may continue to be the peculiar province of radio, with television providing a primarily national and regional service.

Another interesting question is the extent to which film will come to dominate the television service. Hollywood takes an attitude somewhat comparable to that of the Telephone Company back in the early days of radio, i.e., that its prior monopoly of a related art makes it the logical master of the new art. This reasoning, like that of AT&T, is based on a misconception of the nature of the new art. To reduce television to a film medium would be a regrettable national loss. As Sylvester Weaver, President of NBC, has remarked, "We are not like the movies—merchants of dreams, salesmen of escape. We deal primarily with reality." This distinction is vital.

7

BOOK PUBLISHING

Kurt Enoch
THE PAPER-BOUND BOOK: TWENTIETH-CENTURY
   PUBLISHING PHENOMENON

American Scholar Forum:
THE FUTURE OF BOOKS IN AMERICA

7

BOOK PUBLISHING

THE book as a medium of communication has been the subject of fewer critical analyses than have the newspaper or television. While it was the printed book which first brought literacy to the masses, book publishing in America reached relatively small groups until the advent of the paperback book. One reason for this, of course, was the fact that the price of the hard cover volume was too expensive for most readers. Another factor was the paucity of bookstores which, even today, are sorely missing in many urban centers and totally absent from small communities. Still a third was the relatively few public libraries in terms of the total population, and the difficulty in obtaining many books from the average library shelf.

For these reasons, the discussions of books as a mass medium included here deal primarily with the paperback publication, the first genuine instance of the book as a mass medium. Both studies, by implication, consider the paperback book as against the hard cover, or cloth, edition.

Kurt Enoch's summary of the growth of the paperback book in America makes a good case for the publication, both on economic and literary grounds, of cheap, reprint editions. The paperback book is, like television, a basic phenomenon of the twentieth century, although there were sporadic instances of paper-bound books in earlier periods.* Both media emphasize the fact that we are in the eye of a communications revolution which is changing the cultural habits of the nation. The vast diffusion of quick culture via the book club and the pocket edition is not without its paradox. Many critics deplore a lack of genuine culture in the midst of a plethora of popular entertainment. Many readers have yet to learn to reject shoddy literature and select books of genuine literary value. The late Bernard De Voto indicated, in one of his columns for *Harper's*, the shoddy tends to drive out the good, while the good is rarely available on the paperback display stand! This is far less true than it was when De Voto wrote his criticism. Paperback books have become a staple commodity in major

---

* The Haldeman-Julius "little blue" books are an early example of mass distribution of books by direct mail.

bookstores throughout the country, as well as in other outlets, but shoddy paper-bound literature can still be found by those who want to read it.

In any event, the discussion of the paperback book by Mr. Enoch is cogent and thought-provoking. Is the cheap edition a threat to culture? Will it eventually drive fine hard-cover editions out of business? Much depends on the responsibility of the publishers, the process of education and the tastes of the reader. Certainly, the economic and social climate are favorable for cheap editions, which obviously are here to stay. Hard-cover publishing has had to combat increasing costs of production. Good reading facilities are sorely lacking in most cities. The paper-bound book came to pass because the economic and social climate was ripe for it.

Although the paper-bound edition has had a long history in Europe and some small growth in the United States, it is basically a concomitant of the rapid growth of all of the mass media in the twentieth century. While it is true, however, that works of great authors are now being published in cheap editions, it does not follow that they are available. While it is true that cheap editions are to be found on newsstands and drug counters, it does not follow that these volumes are of high quality.

This is the case which Bernard De Voto made against the grandiose claims for the pocket edition. Try to find Hemingway or Faulkner or Cather, he argued, on the drug counters of America. Mass distribution methods are such that only the books that sell steadily remain on display. Other books of high quality may last two or three weeks, but must be returned to make room for inferior volumes in the relentless drive to sell.

On the other hand, successful efforts have been made to keep superior books available. College bookstores have provided a sustained outlet for good paperback literature. Perhaps more significant is the growing recognition, on the part of paperback publishers, of the need to preserve that special integrity which is associated with book publishing and, at the same time, provide a stimulus to book distribution as a medium of mass communication.

"The Future of Books in America" is a verbatim record of a discussion held at the home of Irita Van Doren, Editor of the *New York Herald Tribune* Book Review Section. The following authors, editors and publishers participated: Lester Asheim, Knox Burger, Harold Guinzburg, John Hersey, Walter Pitkin, Jr., and Irita Van Doren.

As early as 1953, Walter Pitkin stated a viewpoint which Bernard De Voto amply corroborated in *Harper's*—that returns exceeded the total annual output of about 260 million paperback books. What point, then, is there in distributing better books when they inevitably will be returned in a few weeks because of lack of sales, while volumes emphasizing sex and violence sell quickly on the drug counters and newsstands? Furthermore, the competition was so keen that more copies were returned than could possibly be sold. This, of course, cannot be compared with hard-cover publishing where there is greater selectivity on the part of the reader and where the differences in subject matter among books produced by various publishers tend to lessen competition.

The earlier proliferation of cheap edition companies has now narrowed down to a somewhat smaller group of still highly competitive concerns. In addition, the hard-cover publishers and university presses are publishing their own paperback lists, thereby improving quality of product. Students are now able to buy cheap editions of classics in college bookstores. Yet, there is validity in the concern expressed by Harold Guinzburg that paperbacks may tend to drive out the better book by responding only to the fancies of a "mass market." Nevertheless, paperbacks have improved both in editorial content and format, while hard-cover books still command a large public from the growing audience of book readers in America. An encouraging sign is that the classic is no longer returned within a few weeks, but has begun to remain on the shelves as a steady seller to meet the needs of significant and growing minorities. And, as Mr. Ascheim stated, "There are books and books, and all books need not be evaluated as an article of culture."

The question, raised obliquely by Mr. Pitkin, is whether paperback books will ultimately become stereotyped as westerns and mysteries, or whether they will become known as purveyors of a broad spectrum of literature of which westerns and mysteries are a part. There is still a large number of books, as Mr. Guinzburg points out, which will never be published in soft covers, whether in original or reprint form, because the specific audience will probably never exist.

The fact remains that paperbacks tend to increase, rather than limit, interest in reading. There are too few bookstores in the United States and too few libraries. The problem, therefore, is not whether there ought to be paperbacks, but what to do about improving their quality. A critical aspect of this problem concerns censorship. As books become a mass medium, they tend to attract more vigorously the interests of special interest groups. The case of a novel, *The Catcher in the Rye,* is cited as one which attracted no censorship in hard-cover or book-club editions, but which ran into trouble in soft-cover reprint because it reached a larger audience. As Mr. Pitkin concludes, this is a serious problem and it concerns the whole future of publishing in America.

* * * *

RELATED READING

Asheim, Lester. "Report on the Conference on Reading Development," *Public Opinion Quarterly,* XV (1951), 305-21.
Brombaugh, Florence H. "Books and TV," *Publisher's Weekly,* CLVII (1950), 2638-44.

Cowley, Malcolm (ed.). *Books That Changed Our Minds.* New York: Doubleday, Doran, 1939.

McMurtrie, Douglas. *The Book: The Story of Printing and Bookmaking,* rev. ed. New York: Oxford University Press, 1942.

Waples, D., Berelson, B., & Bradshaw, F. R. *What Reading Does to People.* Chicago: Univ. of Chicago Press, 1940.

THE PAPER-BOUND BOOK:
Twentieth-Century Publishing Phenomenon

By Kurt Enoch

TODAY the inexpensive paper-bound book is the most widely discussed phenomenon of publishing. It is attacked as a threat to hard-cover publishing and a menace to morals or praised as a revolutionary cultural technique that brings books to a new audience of millions who could not buy them before. Everyone agrees that paper-bound books exert a dynamic influence on contemporary American publishing. Yet, despite the discussion that these ubiquitous volumes have inspired, there has been relatively little thoughtful evaluation of the economic organization, the editorial problems, and the social role of paper-bound publishing.

The inexpensive book in paper binding has a long and honorable history both in Europe and in the United States. In pre-World War II Europe, paper-bound books fell into three broad categories of reprints: in English, in domestic languages, and in local-language editions of public domain titles. The best-known of the English-language reprints were the Tauchnitz Editions, the Albatross Modern Continental Library, both with sales restricted to the non-English-speaking countries, and the British Penguin Books. The famous Tauchnitz Editions, founded in 1837 in Leipzig, contained over 5,000 English-language titles of American and British authors, licensed for reprint on a royalty basis, priced at the equivalent of about 50 cents. This was probably the most complete selection of the classics and of important contemporary American and English literature available in uniform editions published under one imprint.

The Albatross Modern Continental Library, founded in 1932 in Hamburg, followed the same pattern but stressed contemporary writing and created a more attractive format for its series, which eventually included about 400 titles. In 1935, Albatross took over the management of Tauchnitz. These two firms, linking a century of continental reprint experience, established the basic pattern for the modern form of paper-bound book publishing. The Albatross format was adopted by Penguin Books, organized in England in 1935. Penguin quickly became the largest and most

Reprinted from *Library Quarterly*, Volume XXIV, No. 3, July 1954, by permission of the University of Chicago Press and the author.

prominent paper-bound publisher in a domestic language and began not only to change the publishing picture in the British Commonwealth, its home market, but quickly to penetrate the foreign book markets, previously the almost exclusive domain of Tauchnitz and Albatross.

The largest prewar series of inexpensive paper-bound editions of titles mainly in the public domain was Reclam's Universal Bibliothek. Started in Germany in 1867, it published ten titles per month in a slightly smaller size than the standard book of today. The basic price of these books was 20 *pfennig*, equivalent in value to today's dime. Within fifty years the list grew to 6,000 titles. Statistics for this period show a sale of 18 million copies of the German classics, 8½ million of Greek and Roman classics, and 5 million copies of philosophical literature, including 790,000 copies of Kant. Dictionaries and law texts were also very popular. The best-selling single title was Schiller's *Wilhelm Tell*.

Part of this success stems from the close co-operation between Reclam and the Gesellschaft fuer Volksbildung ("Society for Popular Education"), which established during approximately the same period about 137,000 libraries with 4,000,000 volumes and 22,500 traveling libraries with over 900,000 volumes.

The pattern of European paper-bound book publishing changed after the war. Attempts to revive Tauchnitz and Albatross, which had ceased operation during the war, and to continue a number of new English-language series started in neutral Sweden and Switzerland as substitutes for these series, failed or had only limited success. The English-language Continental editions had to yield to the less-expensive and more up-to-date American and English reprints exported to Europe. But the American inexpensive paper-bound book, with its format derived from Tauchnitz and Albatross and a publishing pattern strongly influenced by Penguin Books, began now to be widely adopted by European publishers for domestic-language reprints. Soon after the war, paper-bound reprints hardly distinguishable from their American counterparts, except for language, appeared in almost every European country.

Paper-bound books have substantially as long a history in the United States as they have in Europe. Their beginnings can be traced to the Boston Society for the Diffusion of Knowledge which was founded in 1829 "to issue in a cheap form a series of works, partly original and partly selected in all the most important branches of learning." This society sponsored the American Library of Useful Knowledge, which in 1831 issued the first books in inexpensive paper editions and opened up the so-called "great revolution in publishing," made possible by the invention and improvement of machine-made paper, mechanical typesetting, and fast cylindrical presses. A characteristic of this phase was the publication of books in the form of unbound "supplements" to periodicals. This flowering ended in 1843 when the post office decided to charge book postage instead of the lower newspaper rates for the transportation of these supplements, and overproduction led to a serious price war.

The most flourishing, dynamic, and controversial era of paper-bound book publishing in this country began with a large-scale revival of the industry in the 1870's. A new impulse had come from the development of groundwood paper for book use, which made it possible to exploit inexpensively the wide popular interest in English and French novels, unprotected, incidentally, by copyright.

Following a revival of "extras" published as by-products of the New York *Tribune* in 1873, at prices ranging from 5 cents to 15 cents, and the *Tribune* novels, also in sheet form in quarto and octavo size, at 10 cents or 20 cents, the Chicago firm of Donnelly, Gassett & Lloyd pioneered with its independent and famous Lakeside Library of uncopyrighted quarto paper novels at prices from 10 cents up. Soon fifteen firms were publishing such "libraries." In 1878 Harper and Brothers introduced the Franklin Square Library. Several other trade publishers prominent today, including D. Appleton and Company, Henry Holt and Company, Dodd, Mead and Company, and Funk and Wagnalls, followed suit. These series contained principally standard fiction and current popular novels by foreign, particularly British, authors, on which no royalty had to be paid. Simultaneous publishing of hard-cover and paper-bound editions was customary, and the same titles were often published by several competing publishers in progressively more popular form. The pressure of steadily increasing competition forced editorial expansion to more serious types of reading matter, including biography, poetry, history, travel, and literary history, and also led to the use of more expensive but more appealing duodecimo and sexagesimo formats. Distribution was handled generally by the American News Company, the only national distributor at that time, by newsdealers, and gradually also by bookstores. Use was also made of yearly subscriptions at a price below the cost of the separately purchased volumes.

The enormous significance of inexpensive paper-bound publishing in that era is clearly illustrated by the fact that in 1885, out of a total of 4,500 titles published, almost 1,500 were paper-bound, compared with about 1,000 paper-bound titles out of a total annual production of 12,000 titles today. Yet once again paper-bound books failed. Cutthroat competition, exhaustion of the supply of foreign royalty-free material, and increased production costs prepared the ground for the *coup de grâce* dealt the industry by the Copyright Act of 1891, which for the first time enabled foreign authors to obtain American copyright and hence ended the era of free piracy of foreign writers. From then until the mid-thirties, when the phase of paper-book publishing with which we are here concerned began, no important activity took place in this field.

The contemporary American era of paper-book production, after a few limited or specialized ventures, such as Modern Age Books, Hillman novels, and Mercury Mysteries, began with the establishment of Pocket Books, in 1939. Avon Books followed soon thereafter, and Penguin Books, previously imported from England, organized an American branch from which later on the independent American firm, the New American Library of World Literature, Inc., derived. During the war paper shortages limited the growth of the commercial production of paper-bound reprints.

With the ending of these shortages after the war, a tremendous development took place: In 1939, Pocket Books reported a production of 1,508,000 copies of 34 titles. The census figure for the year 1945 already shows four firms printing 83 million copies of 112 titles. The estimates for 1953 indicate a production of 292 million copies of 1,061 titles by sixteen firms. In 1949, the distribution of paper-bound books approximated that of hard-cover trade books, including book clubs, and in 1953 ran some 100 million copies ahead. Also, compared with library circulation estimated at slightly over 400 million in 1953, the present level of paper-bound book distribution has become impressive. Furthermore, sales of individual titles reached tremendous proportions. An average paper-bound mystery, western, or novel rarely falls below 150,000 to 200,000 copies, and many best sellers, fiction and nonfiction, soar to several million copies. Even scholarly nonfiction and classics frequently reach or surpass half a million in sales. The total amount of royalties paid for reprint rights in 1953 can be estimated at between $5,000,000 and $6,000,000.

The majority of American inexpensive paper-bound books are complete and unabridged editions of copyrighted books originally published in hard covers at $2.50 or higher. They are bound in a flexible laminated or lacquered paper cover, priced at 25 cents, 35 cents, 50 cents, and recently also at 75 cents. They offer a wide and ever-increasing range of reading matter. According to the most recent tabulation, the total 1953 production included 51.3 per cent general fiction, 18 per cent mysteries, slightly over 18 per cent westerns, 6 per cent nonfiction, and about 7 per cent miscellaneous, such as poetry, humor, and short-story collections.

Today, works of virtually every prominent writer and many of the more popular classics are available. Winners of Nobel prizes, Pulitzer prizes, National Book awards, and other literary accolades, and talented novelists from many countries in the world, appear side by side on drugstore display racks. Nonfiction has mushroomed from a few isolated editions of reference, how-to-do, and self-help books to an abundance of books on science, philosophy, religion, history, the arts, the classics, economics, and anthropology. And, recently, experimental and avant-garde writing has found its place in the mass market, first in New American Library's biannual anthology, *New World Writing*, followed by a variety of similar collections by other publishing houses.

Available in nearly 100,000 outlets in the United States and Canada, paper-bound books may be found in drugstores, variety stores, stationery stores, cigar stores, confectionery stores, supermarkets, railway stations, airports, bus terminals, hotel stands, and army and navy installations, as well as in bookstores, department stores, and public libraries. They have actually altered the literary landscape of the United States by making books available in every hamlet, village, and whistle stop, as well as in that disturbingly large number of cities which have no bookstores and only inadequate library facilities. More and more paper-bound books are used by schools, colleges, and adult-education activities, by the armed forces for recreational and informational purposes, and by the United States Information Service for foreign libraries. Substantial quantities are exported commercially to practically all foreign countries outside the Iron Curtain with the exception of the British Commonwealth, where only a limited selection of American titles is available because of agreements between British and American publishers.

This amazing growth of the paper-bound book industry in less than fifteen years raises many questions. What caused this development? What are the editorial impulses or effects? What is the impact on hard-cover book publishing? What do paper-bound books mean to the author and the reader? What are the problems of this adolescent industry? What distinguishes it from former periods of flourishing inexpensive paper-bound book publishing? What is its future?

Although a study of the paper-bound book business is handicapped by the same lack of objective statistics that besets the researcher who investigates any area of book publishing, the answers to most of these questions seem clear—even though experience may vary with the policy of each publisher. Yet I think everyone will agree that the phenomenal growth of the industry may be ascribed to two major conditions—the rapid technical advances in mass production of books and the marriage of book publishing and magazine distribution.

Paper-back books are printed on high-speed magazine presses and, more recently, on huge new special book presses printing from rubber plates at the rate of 18,000 impressions of 128 pages, or 12,000 copies of a 192-page book, per hour. So-called "Perfect" binding machines, which eliminate the expensive process of sewing, have been adapted for the binding of paper books and can turn out approximately 12,000 copies per hour. New types of glue have made this type of binding almost as strong, although not so permanent, as the conventional form. New developments in materials have improved the glossy, dust-repellent, and even washable protection for the paper covers.

These technical advances in inexpensive mass production, however, would have been useless without the vehicle of magazine distribution which makes possible the immediate marketing of the huge quantities of every new title. Magazines, many newspapers, and paper-bound books in this country are distributed either through a network of approximately 800 independent wholesalers or by the American News Company with its 350 branches. Both supply more than 100,000 retail dealers in the United States and Canada, most of whom carry books as only one of many other commodities or services. The books are displayed in racks provided by the publisher and wholesaler. It is estimated that the average dealer has racks containing approximately one hundred pockets holding 3-5 copies per pocket, resulting in slightly less than 10 million pockets with a total capacity for the display of from 30 to 50 million books, or an average capacity of 300-500 books per dealer at any one time. The books are delivered to the dealer by truck or, in certain sparsely populated areas, by mail. The racks are filled and refilled by the wholesaler's personnel, frequently supported by special field representatives of the publishers themselves. Almost every week, sometimes even more often, new releases reach the dealer, and older or less salable titles are returned to the wholesaler.

Since the books are supplied on a fully returnable or exchangeable basis, it is possible to use practically any retail outlet for books, because no special knowledge of books and only a very small, if any, financial investment is required.

This system removes important obstacles which the hard-cover publisher has to overcome to reach his audience. Not only can almost anyone who wants to buy a book find a good variety of reading matter within walking distance of his home or place of work, but he can purchase a book when and where he shops for groceries, cigarettes, drugs, or stationery. Because paper-bound book outlets are self-service operations, the often reported awe of the unfamiliar atmosphere of a bookstore does not discourage the uninitiated from browsing. As a result of this direct exposure to books, many have made their first voluntary book purchase, and this wide distribution has become an important factor in expanding the book audience and developing book-reading habits.

Nevertheless, this system is not perfect. Newspapers and magazines are perishable. They are released on a certain day, on sale for a limited period, and returned to the publisher or destroyed if not sold when the new issues appear. Books are different. Their natural lifetime is limited only by their reader interest and not by the release date of a new title. Consequently, books require longer display than magazines do. Each book has its own appeal and, with the exception of the few works of generally known authors, a new title cannot count on the same kind of automatic acceptance that each new issue of an established magazine can. It has to be introduced to the potential reader from scratch. These requirements are difficult to reconcile with existing conditions of newsstand distribution. It is natural that wholesalers are tempted to treat books and magazines alike. Although their business volume on paper-bound books is substantial, it amounts to only approximately 20 per cent of their total volume, and the economics of their operation makes them prefer bigness to specialization. Every month wholesalers receive from their publishers an allotment of approximately 100 new titles for distribution to their dealers. This multitude of titles makes it difficult to devote attention to specific books.

The average retail dealer's major book activity is to provide the space for the display racks. Because he generally is unfamiliar with the titles that are displayed in those racks, he cannot be expected to do an active selling job. Display space is limited, and older or slower-selling titles, regardless of their permanent value, have to yield prematurely to faster-selling new releases. This makes it extremely difficult to provide permanent display for the so-called "long-pull" titles of fiction and particularly of nonfiction. The result is that frequently the customer looking for specific titles cannot find them and that the publisher has to rely heavily on impulse rather than on selective buying. These problems are under continuous scrutiny, and solutions are being tried and developed in many directions.

Currently, strong efforts are being directed toward increasing the number of dealers, substituting better dealers for unsatisfactory ones, and steadily improving and enlarging the display. Obsolete equipment is replaced by new types of racks that require less floor space for more display pockets. The cost of this equipment, originally totally or partially charged to the dealers, is now underwritten by the publishers or wholesalers. Several million dollars have been invested in such equipment since the end of the war. The display itself is being segregated according to publishers' imprints, permitting easier recognition by the public, as well as more efficient check-ups, title identification, and reorder service by those in charge of servicing these display racks. Separate display units are installed for special categories of books, like New American Library's nonfiction Mentor Books or Pocket Books' Library of Great Art, to attract the substantial audience of readers with special reading interests but previously not aware of the availability of such books. Important titles are highlighted by point-of-sale promotion, such as rack cards and posters attached to the display or by smaller display units which can be placed in other locations of the dealer's store. More and more wholesalers are organizing book departments separate from their magazine operation, with trained personnel familiar with titles and authors. They operate special book trucks carrying a well-assorted stock of books and manned by so-called "bookmen" who regularly check the dealers' racks, rearrange the display, and replace lagging titles with faster-selling books or new issues.

More and more detailed records are being kept by the wholesalers, disclosing the sales and return activity of each dealer and providing other valuable information which helps wholesaler and publisher to establish better controls over distribution and supply.

Side by side with these operational refinements goes the constant penetration into new types of outlets. Along with magazines, paper-bound books are moving into new and untapped retail facilities. But their distribution also expands independently from magazines. Increasingly, bookstores and department stores, originally disinclined to handle paper-bound books because of their low price, have been convinced that these books not only are profitable but also are very potent traffic builders. College bookstores find them a good supplement to textbooks. And lately experiments with special stores handling nothing but paper-bound books and carrying every new or old title of interest seem to be successful in such cities as New York, Detroit, and San Francisco. These developments are encouraging but thus far mainly benefit the most widely popular books. Their effectiveness is more uncertain for the adaptation of mass-distribution methods to the slow but permanent "long-pull" titles or titles with a selective or thinly spread audience. Without the possibility of large printings, many desirable and important books in those categories would have to remain excluded from the lists of paper-bound book publishers. A solution has to be found without resort to the expensive promotion methods of the traditional hard-cover edition, which would defeat the basic low-cost, low-price objective of paper-bound books. It is also necessary to find means of salvaging the substantial numbers of still perfectly salable and useful books which had to yield their display space prematurely to new or faster-moving titles—victims of the fast turnover requirements of mass distribution.

To achieve this, supplementary distribution and promotional activities have steadily gained in importance. By increased publicity the publishers try to widen their audience and to increase its density. They seek the co-operation of organizations and groups that will promote and purchase books of special interest. They recognize the value of better bibliographical material and more information for potential users as to the existence and the sources of supply of such books. The serious publishers have become fully aware of the large potentialities of library, college, school, and adult-education use of paper-bound books and are making great efforts to serve their needs. Increasingly the library profession has experimented with the use of paper-bound books, in spite of their physical shortcomings. Many college and university libraries have used paper-bound books to help solve their reserve problems and to develop an interest in nonassigned reading and student book collecting. Some public libraries are utilizing these books for circulation or adult-education programs, or as fill-in stock, and almost all buy paper-bound books for reference departments when no cloth-bound editions are available.

Paper-bound book publishers are eagerly exploring these areas and seek guidance in making their service more useful. They are fully aware of the necessity of developing reading interest in the young in order to nourish the adult market of the future.

They recognize the great opportunities of export markets. Even where the standard of living is low, the price of American paper-bound books is still within reach of large numbers of people. The higher education which usually accompanies the knowledge of the English language makes the foreign reader an ideal customer for the better book and the foreign market more receptive for back-list titles.

These are some of the opportunities to fill the gaps which still exist and which cannot be filled except by adaptation of magazine-distribution techniques to books. Paper-bound book publishers and their distributors are constantly challenged to seek further perfection in order to tap fully the enormous potential audience for good books and to fulfil the cultural and social obligations which endow publishing with so much of its special traditional and professional character.

In considering the editorial problems of paper-bound publishing, I shall exclude the relatively small number of manufacturers of reading matter who have little or no interest in the literary or cultural value of their product. The nine or ten major paper-bound book firms are responsible publishers with editorial policies as individual as their trade publishing colleagues. Just as magazines are designed to appeal to different types of audiences, so do the lists of the various paper-bound book publishers reflect the varying tastes and standards of each house. Some specialize in books for entertainment—mainly mysteries, westerns, and light fiction. Most, however, try to satisfy the widest possible range of the reading market with variations of emphasis on different categories of interest.

Also, similar to the periodical publication of magazines, the books are issued in monthly groups of eight to twelve assorted titles—the whole group representing the kind of varied literary diet which one finds in an issue of a magazine. Within this monthly package, however, each book has to make its own way, and it is the individual title and not the pattern which decides the success of the publishing enterprise. If the editorial policy of paper-bound publishers in the early stages of the industry may have seemed to reflect the idea that a publisher for the mass market must aim downward, the impressive list of available authors and books indicates that some publishers have always boldly assumed that the taste and interest of the audience for mass-distributed books does not differ radically from that of the audience for hard-cover editions.

In view of the large investment every title requires and the small leeway between profit and loss, many attempts have been made to predetermine the acceptance of books by scientific market analysis. Efforts have been made to determine who buys paper-bound books and what types of books and for what reasons. Do such impulses come from recognition of authors' names, word-of-mouth promotion, the success of a hard-cover edition, a book-club selection, or familiarity with a movie based on the book? Are certain categories preferred to others? Research of this nature can, however, be of only limited value in the practical publishing situation, particularly since the information is necessarily after the fact.

In our own experience, we have found that there is no clear parallel between the sales picture of hard-cover best sellers or book-club selections and that of paper-bound reprint editions of the same books. That is really not so surprising as it might appear at first glance. The status of a best seller is not necessarily determined by merit. It can be pumped up by advertising, it may reflect a special appeal to a particular section of the audience, or, in the case of book clubs, its wide distribution may be secured through pressure on a more or less assured audience. The paper-bound book competes in a market place strikingly free of these influences, is rarely advertised, and seldom reviewed. Of course there are many books which have become best sellers because of their genuine appeal, and in these cases the reprint edition has greatly benefited from the already established reputation of the original hard-cover edition.

Movies have been of help only in cases where an exceptionally good film coincided with the availability of an exceptionally good or widely accepted book on which it was based. Typical examples are *Moulin Rouge*, *From Here to Eternity*, *A Streetcar Named Desire*, *The Cruel Sea*, *Duel in the Sun*, etc.

All this indicates that the paper-bound book publisher in his selection of titles depends on the yardsticks used by the regular trade publisher— his own taste, judgment, flair, courage, and experience, plus assiduous reading. Selecting the best books for a wide audience is as demanding a chore for the reprint editor as the trade editor's hunt for the right original manuscript. In our own firm, for example, our editors read about 4,000 books a year—galleys, advance copies, out-of-print copies, and foreign editions—in order to select the 100-odd titles we will ultimately reprint. However, a paper-bound book publisher is not completely free in developing his program according to his liking. The great majority of paper books are reprints of hard-cover editions for which the original publisher, alone or jointly with the author or agent, controls the decision as to whether and when a paper-bound edition will be authorized. Furthermore, there is stiff competition between the various reprint houses and, more often than not, the reprint rights are awarded to the bidder of the highest royalty guarantee.

In addition, the supply of suitable new titles—at least in the fiction category—is limited, and the number of useful back-list titles is more or less exhausted. This situation has had several important effects. On the positive side, it has become an incentive to widen editorial scope. It has stimulated expansion into new fields, such as anthologies, reference books, and other nonfiction. Also on the positive side, it has been an incentive to bring back to the market through reissues good books which at one time or another had their day in mass circulation but for which a new audience has developed. This periodic reappearance of good titles has done much to alleviate the limitations in time and space imposed by the mechanism of mass distribution.

On the negative side, the limited supply has increased the temptation to publish titles which were not deemed desirable when there was an abundance of material, or which were rejected by the older or better-supplied houses, most of which have no part in such process of downgrading. Nevertheless, even that is not entirely without virtue. As Freeman Lewis, in his Bowker Lecture in 1952[1] pointed out:

> The capacity for enjoying books has almost as many levels as there are readers, and any publisher professing to distribute books to the bulk of our population would be thoroughly remiss in his duty if he did not try to provide titles which would give pleasure to as many levels of reading taste as possible. Furthermore, any improvement in reading taste must have a place of beginning and that place can never be the top. Because of the existence of low-priced books, many people are now reading some books who never read books before. Many other people are reading more books than they ever read before. The result, at all levels, is beneficial and germinant.

Another consequence of the limitation of titles available or obtainable for reprint is an increase in the number of originals published in paper-bound editions. In 1953 it is estimated that 18 per cent of the titles on the lists of ten reprint publishers were originals, and two firms, organized to publish only paper-bound originals, turned out 117 titles between them.

Do paper-bound originals threaten the traditional form of hard-cover publishing? So far the majority of titles are light fiction, and it is quite possible that here the original paper-bounds will indeed cut in on the sales of hard-cover editions. But it is unlikely that a similar trend will develop in the area of more serious fiction. The editorial investment is substantial, and it is doubtful whether the same reviewing space would be available for original paper-bound editions without the advertising support that hard-cover publishers give their publications. It would be impossible to fit these additional costs into the budgetary structure of the paper-bound book without increasing its price. Nor would the rather perishable format of paper-bound originals wholly satisfy the requirements of libraries, schools, and private collections.

One might, of course, think that these problems could be solved if paper-bound book publishers would themselves issue hard-cover editions, or hard-cover publishers paper editions. Examples of both cases exist, but they are far too few to permit any reliable conclusion. The success of a few titles published in that fashion is no yardstick. It would rather seem that such practices might lead to a far-reaching diffusion of paper-bound production that would risk the loss of the advantages of the present method of distribution. Moreover, the natural reluctance of an original publisher to release reprint rights to one who is his competitor in original publishing would restrict the dual edition activity of hard-cover or paper-bound houses more or

---

[1] Freeman Lewis, *Paper-Bound Books in America* (Sixteenth Bowker Memorial Lecture [New York: Public Library, 1952]), pp. 19-20.

less to their own properties and impede a well-planned publishing program with free access to a wide literary market place.

The situation is somewhat different in the field of nonfiction. Most serious nonfiction titles have greater permanence than does average fiction. They represent the bulk of the back lists which are one of the most important assets of hard-cover publishing houses. Therefore the hard-cover publisher of nonfiction is particularly sensitive to the risk that an inexpensive paper-bound edition might harm the sale of the original. Furthermore, many nonfiction titles, although their topics are of wide interest, are written in a style unsuitable for a very wide audience or are too costly to reproduce at a low price. On the other hand, it is less expensive to assign specific nonfiction projects to selected authors or editors than to maintain the substantial editorial department required for a competent original-fiction publishing activity.

These factors create both a greater need and a greater opportunity for original production by the paper-bound book publisher. Here, however, a new pattern of co-operation between the hard-cover and paper-bound book publisher seems to develop. The majority of nonfiction titles, originated on the initiative of paper-bound book publishers for the specific requirements of the mass market, are published jointly with a hard-cover publisher, sometimes before—sometimes simultaneously with—the release in paper. The hard-cover publisher's sales of such titles do not conflict with the paper-bound edition, since less than 10 per cent of their customers overlap, and, of this number, many outlets, such as libraries or schools, prefer more durable binding. This practice results in production savings when the trade publisher uses the composition or printing plates of the paper-bound edition. Such joint editions maintain the reprint pattern, although the procedure itself is reversed. Because of all this, there are strong indications that editorially paper-bound book publishing cannot and will not become a substitute for hard-cover publishing—although it might become predominant in certain limited areas.

But will the paper backs cut in on the sales of hard-cover books? This has long been a controversial issue. Only an industry-wide study would give a fairly conclusive answer. A sampling of cases of about a dozen fiction and nonfiction titles which we had an opportunity to check with original publishers disclosed no adverse effects on the continued sales of their hard-cover editions after the release of our reprints; and in some cases their sales increased. It is also indicative that very often those titles which produced record sales in reprint form had only moderate or average sales as originals. Furthermore, evaluating a statistical survey of hard-cover and paper-bound sales during recent years, Robert W. Frase concluded in his Windsor Lecture in 1953:[2]

2 H. K. Guinzburg, R. W. Frase, and T. Waller, *Books and the Mass Market* (Urbana: University of Illinois Press, 1953), p. 34.

These general statistics would seem to indicate that this vast paper-bound output has had relatively little over-all effect on hard-bound original publishing which has continued to inch ahead in total number of copies during the post-war period. These two types of books may be serving two fairly distinct and separate markets and may not be in direct competition except perhaps in the field of mysteries, and westerns, and light fiction. In other words, the paper-bound books may be attracting new book readers, perhaps from the much larger category of magazine readers.

If one considers also the fact that hard-cover books are distributed through approximately only 1,400 outlets, compared with 100,000 paper-bound outlets, these observations suggest that the continued development of paper-bound book publishing will largely supplement hard-cover publishing and that mutually beneficial co-operation of the two branches will increase.

Another factor influencing the over-all picture is the author's royalty. The standard royalty rate paid by the paper-bound book publisher on 25-cent books is 1 cent per copy on the first 150,000 copies and 1½ cents thereafter. On higher priced editions these rates are increased proportionately. With very few exceptions, however, a minimum guarantee is paid against these royalties, regardless of whether earned by sales or not. These royalties —in case of reprints shared usually 50-50 by the original publisher and the author—have become a very important source of income for the hard-cover publishers and offer many authors the key to the freedom of writing unharassed by the pressure of finding other ways of livelihood.

Competition for titles, however, has often driven the royalty guaranty to levels substantially exceeding the amounts earned by sales. Royalties earned by the average sale of 200,000 copies of a mystery, western, or average novel amount to $2,250.00. Yet guaranties of $4,000.00-$5,000.00 for such titles have been more the rule than the exception. For more important properties the figures are much higher. That does not mean that in certain cases royalty guaranties exceeding the average earnings are not justified and do not remain in the realm of economic reason. The big books obviously have larger than average sales potential, and there are cases where a paper-bound publisher is willing to pay such guaranties in order to obtain a title which would fill a vital gap in his editorial program. But, generally, a guaranty of royalties in excess of those earned is economically unsound. The margin for royalties in the cost breakdown of low-price books cannot be widened any more than can the margins for the cost of paper, printing, binding, and other cost factors without affecting the low retail price—the cornerstone of inexpensive paper-bound book publishing.

Moreover, this margin is not a fixed one. It is narrowed in various degrees by returns of unsold books, which often play havoc with the cost structure—a fact easily overlooked by those who try to make a case for a larger share. It should also be noted that the higher royalty rates offered in a recently widely discussed scheme of simultaneous hard-bound and paper-bound book publishing are not made possible by a new magic formula but by an increase of retail prices above the levels which yield the customary royalty rates (35 cents instead of 25 cents or 50 cents instead of 35 cents). In my opinion this device of overpricing reduces the sales potential of the books and therefore tends to limit rather than increase the total royalty income based on sales.

I have spoken thus far, as it were, from inside the industry, endeavoring to show the operations and the problems of the paper-bound field as they appear to a publisher. I should like now to venture a few remarks, from as detached a point of view as I can achieve, about the social functions of inexpensive books.

We would all, I believe, recognize that books fulfil certain cultural and educational purposes of society not readily served by any other medium. This has been in part because of so simple a quality as length. It is possible in a book to deal extensively, thoughtfully, and in detail with complex ideas and bodies of fact. In part it has been because books afford an unusually effective voice for diversity, with the thousands of titles annually appearing providing a vehicle for every point of view and every form of cultural expression. In part it has been because books have been freer than any other medium from legal and economic pressures toward conformity of manner or of viewpoint. In a word, the peculiar services of the book to society have seemed to derive from the fact that it has not been a "mass" medium.

We now seek to make it one. It seems to me altogether necessary that we do so. As the problems of society become more complex, and a wider segment of the population becomes more really involved in their solution, it is no longer safe, or indeed possible, for the sort of diverse communication "in depth" afforded by books to be confined to an elite. A democracy today cannot be well governed by a people whose insight into contemporary problems and their background is derived solely from newspapers and broadcasts. Nor can it be spiritually whole if it does not have bonds of union growing from such a common experience of the fundamental meaning of Western civilization as can be conveyed only in books.

Yet we have seen other media, as they have been extended by modern technology, suffer distortion and depreciation of meaning. That happens to drama as it reaches the film or the television screen, the short story as it reaches the mass-circulation magazines, the lecture as it reaches the loudspeaker. All are likely to suffer from vulgarization, uniformity, and timidity. By vulgarization I mean the sort of depreciation of quality that arises from the conviction sometimes held that the "mass" audience is of low intelligence and cheap taste; by uniformity, the stale sameness that comes from the illusion that there is but one mass audience, to which there is but one successful formula of appeal.

Timidity is a special problem. Our society allows a wide range of unrepressed expression in all those forms of communication addressed to an elite. In a Broadway play or a university lecture or a five-dollar book one may with little constraint express unorthodox political or social views or speak with candor in those areas of human experience, such as sex, race, and religion, in which taboos are likely to be most pervasive and most violently upheld. But as any form of expression reaches out to a popular audience, pressure rises against it to assure that it does not disturb or offend in these respects. This is universally true: One may not say into a microphone what one may utter from a soapbox. Movies encounter censorship not met by the legitimate stage.

In general, the mass media, confronted with the necessity of holding very large audiences in order to meet heavy costs of production or to satisfy advertisers, have acquiesced in these pressures, often through voluntary codes. They have sought not merely to avoid obscenity but to evade the honest confrontation of many of the more sensitive and taboo-ridden areas of life. There has been a sort of law: the wider the audience, the less provocative or disturbing to established ideas and taboos the medium has to be. If such a conformity is to be the price of the extension of the book audience, obviously there is little gain to the cause of cultural and political freedom which I believe books peculiarly serve.

The fundamental problem of statesmanship, from the social viewpoint, in the paper-bound book industry, is thus to achieve a mass audience while preserving the special virtues of books. It will not be altogether easy. I have pointed out that the assumption has not been absent from the industry that the mass audience is an inferior audience; and many inexpensive books, and more particularly their covers and blurbs, conform to this idea. Unquestionably there is a sterile repetition of formulas in many westerns, detective stories, and historical novels.

But I believe it can be done. One reason for this belief is that even the inexpensive book audience is not really a mass audience as compared with the size of radio or film audiences. Though it may take sales of 200,000 or more to make a paper-bound book profitable, it does not necessarily require any broader public interest to achieve such a sale through 100,000 outlets at 25 cents or 35 cents a copy than it does to achieve 5,000 to 10,000 sales through 1,400 bookstores at $5.00 a copy. As I have pointed out, even quite specialized books can be sold successfully in paper-bound form. Nor is it necessary for a paper-bound publisher, any more than an original publisher, to create a uniform product which will retain the same audience for issue after issue. Each book finds its own audience, and any one publisher may successfully serve quite different and even, so to speak, contradictory audiences with different books.

Finally, the substantial reprint publishers are, like their colleagues, and like librarians, devoted to the book. They do not publish a different product, bowdlerized or with a happy ending tacked on. They publish the books themselves, confident in the belief that the millions who buy inexpensive books want and deserve the same books as those produced in hard covers for a more expensive market. We do not believe that one must be timid in speaking to the mass of Americans and withhold from a larger audience that which is available to a smaller one. In this, of course, we follow and share the faith of librarians, who have found the millions they freely serve to be as eager and mature an audience as exists anywhere.

We have had these principles before us as we have confronted the widespread efforts to apply a special standard of censorship to inexpensive books through police intimidation and through group pressures. There can be no question that a part of the provocation to this alarmingly general pressure has come from or has been helped by a needless and distasteful sensationalism and salacity on covers. But the conception that covers produce censorship is not generally true. Actually the most serious censorship efforts have disregarded covers almost entirely and aimed directly at those works most disturbing to the censoring group. This has, in fact, frequently tended to mean a concentration of censorship efforts on better books which have more effectively penetrated areas of sensitivity.

Though responsible reprint publishers have taken very seriously the sometimes well-founded criticism of means of promotion used in the early days of an industry highly competitive not only within itself but within the whole field of periodicals, they have not been prepared to compromise on content. I am glad to say that in this policy they have had the vigorous collaboration of original publishers who share the conviction that books must retail their essential indivisible character at whatever price and through whatever channels they are distributed.

With all its fantastic gains in sales, distribution, and production techniques, its heavy responsibilities to trade publishers and authors, its sobering moral commitments to the vast public it serves, what is then the future of this adolescent industry—the role of *enfant terrible* or *wunderkind?* Will history repeat itself? Are we again heading toward disaster? Do we not again have overproduction and price wars and too many inferior books which will make us lose our friends? Yes, we have some of all that, to a greater or lesser degree. But we have many other assets which did not exist in earlier periods. We offer predominantly contemporary American literature, without neglecting to make available a good cross-section of the best or most important foreign writing. Informative or scholarly nonfiction is steadily increasing. So is the usefulness of our books for education and enlightenment. We are not the natural enemies but the natural friends of the hard-cover publishers who are our main source of supply. Our publications are books and not only in name in spite of certain limitations in typography and durability of binding imposed by the requirements of mass production. Constant progress in manufacturing equipment and methods makes it possible to improve the format of our books without increasing their low price level. Our distribution benefits from all the advantages of the twentieth century's technological progress—the automobile, airplane, modern communications system, office and warehouse mechanization, etc. Our wholesalers operate efficient, sometimes huge, organizations penetrating into the smallest and farthest corners of the country. We can make use of the refinements of advertising and promotion methods and of the many new modern media at their disposal. We are not dependent upon or limited by special conditions such as influenced the course of events in the past, but operate under the same rules and laws as the rest of the publishing fraternity.

Therefore, to the degree that inexpensive paper-bound book publishers are able to contribute to the objective of bringing books to millions at low cost without in the process sacrificing the tough independence and diversity of thought or the rich variety that books have always meant, they will be participating in an encouraging and significant cultural revolution —another demonstration that in a maturing America we are learning to achieve in matters of the mind and the arts, as we have already achieved in the economic area, the broad and general distribution of goods that are a vital factor in the dynamic expansion of a free society.

THE FUTURE OF BOOKS IN AMERICA

American Scholar Forum

Lester Asheim
Knox Burger
Harold Guinzburg

John Hersey
Walter Pitkin, Jr.
Irita Van Doren

Mrs. Van Doren: I think we are all aware that one of the big trends in publishing these days is the enormous growth of paperbacks. We are here this evening to discuss this trend and its effect. What paperbacks are doing to publishing today, how dependent trade publishing is on them, whether they're helpful or harmful—I'm going to ask each of you to express some opinion on this from your point of view.

Mr. Pitkin, let's start with you. I gather that you are very much interested in this paperback business and not entirely against hard-cover books. What have you got to say about it?

Mr. Pitkin: That is right on both points. I am very sympathetic to the problem of the hard-cover book area, and am hopeful that the hard-cover field may be expanded more than it is at this time.

Would you like me perhaps to give some indication of the present status of paper-backed books?

Mrs. Van Doren: I think that would be good.

Mr. Pitkin: I think that the best place to start perhaps is a simple arithmetical comparison between, let's say, 1946, which was the first postwar year, and 1953. I believe in 1946 there were roughly 60 million paperbacks run off and distributed. That doesn't mean that they were all sold. Sixty million were sent out to the wholesalers and others who put these books on sale. Some percentage was returned in that year, perhaps 10 or 15 per cent.

Mrs. Van Doren: What about 1953?

Mr. Pitkin: In 1953, so far as we can tell, there were about 260 million taken off the presses, an increase of 200 million. Lord knows what percentage of the 260 million were returned. Certainly the sales in 1953, relative to the output, were lower—which is to say that the publishers are taking not just a higher return, but quite a good deal higher return of unsold copies from wholesalers. Partly because of competitive factors in the field, more titles are published than can ever be adequately displayed by the retailer.

MRS. VAN DOREN: And you say part of the reason for that gap is competition: there are more and more soft-cover publishers.

Mr. Burger, you have to do with soft-cover publishing. What is your feeling about that?

MR. BURGER: I would agree with Mr. Pitkin that the turn-back of paperbacks has risen to proportions that are disturbing to a great many soft-cover publishers. I think there are probably too many titles put out. I heard a figure of 1,200 titles published in soft covers in 1953. I don't know if that is correct; that is an estimate. I think there are probably too many companies in the business. I think it was the wartime beginning and the postwar flush of success that made them grow too quickly and get out of bounds.

In the long run, any publishing enterprise or any production technique that makes available very large quantities of an item—particularly an item that has the cultural significance of a book—is good and ought to be fostered and somehow ought to win through the growing pains and difficulties that one encounters on the way up.

It is possible to compare books with the production of automobiles. One of the basic principles of America's beginnings is making available large numbers of needed and wanted articles, and a book is a man-made thing, useful, to a very great degree, to all sorts of people. Some time in the future there will be a shaking-down process: some people will get hurt, and I hope the writer will be hurt less than the publisher, frankly, but I think everybody is going to touch fire and draw back his hand to a degree.

The paperback business is here to stay and here to grow. That is for the same simple reason that more Chevrolets are sold than Chryslers.

MRS. VAN DOREN: Mr. Guinzburg, from the publishers' point of view, the trade-book publishers', what do you think of the influx of paperbacks?

MR. GUINZBURG: I'm not at all sure that I have the right to answer that question from the point of view of trade-book publishers. I think I can answer it only in fairly personal terms, because I know I differ from some of my colleagues in the publishing field.

Offhand, no one can dispute what Mr. Burger has said about the desirability of more books being made available, and in fact what is happening today in the book field is in the pattern of what has happened to other articles in industry as a whole.

It does seem to me, however, that when we get into the realm of ideas we raise a whole set of problems that are not necessarily present when we are talking about automobiles or groceries or almost any of the other things that lend themselves to mass production and mass distribution.

My principal worry about what is happening in the book field is that the success of the paperback may push the whole book business in the direction of a mass industry. The characteristic of a mass industry is that it caters to the largest possible number of customers, and in that process may very well squeeze out those things that do not appeal to large numbers of people. My worry is that you may repeat in the book field what has happened in other fields—in entertainment and communication—you may make it increasingly difficult to do anything that is not geared to appeal to large low common denominators.

It remains to be seen, to be sure, whether it is the low, rather than the large, denominator that is going to govern. Already in this discussion, both Mr. Pitkin and Mr. Burger have referred to the fact that probably too many titles are now being published in the paperback field. It seems to me perfectly clear that if the numbers are going to be reduced, it is not necessarily going to be the poor-quality books that get eliminated; it may rather be those that are less salable.

At the same time, this is a danger: if the whole structure of book distribution shifts to be more and more dependent on the low-priced paperback, it may result in hard-back publishers finding themselves unable to publish much of what they now produce because—well, for a number of reasons. Among them is the possibility that the old-fashioned large bookstore that could carry a large range of assorted titles may find survival much more difficult. Therefore, there may be fewer means of distributing anything, let us say, that doesn't lend itself either to book club, paperback or other large-scale distribution, which would mean that we would find—

Mrs. Van Doren: Mr. Guinzburg, there are all sorts of angles to that, and I think it is a very important point you brought up. Let's go back to it in a minute, but right now let's ask Mr. Hersey how he feels paper-backed books affect the author.

Mr. Hersey: I would like to speak as Mr. Guinzburg did—for myself. I share some but not all of his worries. It seems to me that writing is a kind of reaching out and that the writer, the reacher, wants to touch somebody or something. And so it might be said that the more people he touches, the better; the more readers a book gets, the better; and I think that many writers welcome, are very glad to have, the enormous audience that paper-backed books have made possible.

A difficulty arises. I believe it stems from the relatively commercial nature of the paperback enterprise. Paper-backed books are distributed, as I understand it, through some 100,000, or perhaps even more, outlets. Mr. Burger already tonight has referred to the paper-backed book as an "item." At the meeting that the Authors' Guild had last spring on this problem, he said in passing that it is probably true that these books are less literature than they are (I think his words were) "a brazenly packaged commodity item." And I think that some of the difficulties, from the point of view of the writer who seeks this mass audience, come from the fact that because of the competition not only from magazines and other paper-backed books but from chewing gum, mints and toothbrushes, the paper-back publishers have had to resort to more and more sensational devices.

No, I think you have to say now, "less and less sensational," but in the early years it was "increasingly sensational"—the use of lurid covers and blurbs, which did not reflect in all cases exactly what was in the book, but which were intended to attract the eyes of purchasers.

There are, as I understand it, about 2,000 good bookstores in the country. I don't share Mr. Guinzburg's worry that they will disappear, because I think when a person goes into a bookstore, he goes in to buy a book. When a person buys a paper-backed book, it may be only an auxiliary purchase.

I think there will always be readers and they will look for books wherever they are. The hope is that with an increasing readership which paper-backed books have helped to build, there will be more and more people going directly for books, and that it will be less and less necessary in the long run to use these—well, packaging techniques to attract them, and that there may be a more stable situation than we have at the moment.

MRS. VAN DOREN: Mr. Asheim, you have heard all these different expressions from people who are in one way or another deeply concerned with book publishing. You have a somewhat more detached position, I believe. I wish you would comment a little, after having heard this, on what you think paper-backed books are going to do, how they're going to affect taste, American culture, if you will.

MR. ASHEIM: I'm afraid I'm not competent to deal with as large a subject as that. I would like to react, if I may, to just some of the things that have been said.

One thought that occurred to me immediately as Mr. Burger was speaking is that there seemed to be an underlying assumption that all books are an article of culture. This seems not to be the case. There are books and books. That being so, to create a large audience for the undifferentiated book may or may not be a contribution to the welfare of the community.

This leads us then immediately to make some kind of judgment about the value of the particular content, and it would seem to me that Mr. Guinzburg's distinction between the articles of commerce, "items," and the book as a medium through which ideas are conveyed makes clear what I think are two different levels on which books may be considered.

It seems to me that when we start dealing with the book as a medium for communicating ideas that are perhaps worth preserving—here I suppose my librarianship background comes in—we find that one of the functions of the book has been that it is a very excellent medium for preserving ideas. Tonight, however, we have been talking almost exclusively about the current market: what books will people buy and read right now? But it may take a long, long time for the ideas worth preserving in book form to be accepted or to reach the audience for whom they are intended. To emphasize the immediate market is not the best way to get to the ideas worth preserving.

The question that I would raise is whether the paper-backed book—and what we are really talking about here is not format, of course, but the means of production, the mass production, mass distribution—whether under such a system, the unpopular idea can be held long enough so that the audience that is interested in it will have a chance to know that it is there, to weigh it, to accept it or reject it over a time. As it is now, it seems to me that the mass audience must accept it immediately or this is the end of the idea and it doesn't find expression.

Mrs. Van Doren: You speak of one of the values of a book as a medium in which ideas can be preserved, the ideas that are worthwhile. There is also the need to get acquainted with ideas, and that can sometimes be done in a form that isn't lasting; and perhaps then the reader, if he really becomes interested, can find the book in more permanent form later.

Mr. Asheim: I don't know if I follow what other forms you suggest.

Mrs. Van Doren: The hard-cover book, which can be kept on the shelf or found in the library, after one has first been awakened to an interesting idea perhaps in the soft-cover book.

Mr. Asheim: This is possible, except again—and I think those who know about this ought to correct me if I'm wrong—the chance of coming across it in a soft-cover book is much less, just because the book remains available for so short a period. It is very difficult to get at everything that is in soft covers because those on display are constantly changing under the system of distribution which now obtains.

Mrs. Van Doren: Perhaps one point you have suggested is something Mr. Pitkin might tell us a little more about—the different kinds of soft-cover books. We are assuming that they are all exciting and popular in some way, but there are different kinds.

Mr. Pitkin: Indeed there are many different kinds of soft-cover books. We all, I think, very generally recognize that there are mysteries and westerns, of course, which are statistically a large part of the field, but there are also novels and books of non-fiction. And when we take an area such as the novel and examine it closely, we find that the variation there is as great as the variation within the whole field, because you find everything from the lowest grade of formula-writing—poor magazine writing—to the very best writing that is being done in this country today.

I think there are at least three publishers in the field, at least three important publishers, who are, to a degree, competing for what I consider to be the best sort of fiction—

Mrs. Van Doren: In the soft-cover field, you mean?

Mr. Pitkin: Exactly. I think it is necessarily so; it is necessarily true that the total amount of the best writing that you will find in paper covers is small because there is not enough good writing being done. We are constantly on the lookout for better books of varying kinds. We don't want one book to be like another; but just as a hard-cover publisher, I am sure, always feels that there may be one or two books on his list for the spring or the fall that stand out above the others, we find that when we go through all their lists and attempt to make the best list that we can, only a certain percentage of the books are truly outstanding as creative works.

We believe it is important to find such writing because—I believe this, in any case—the person who is looking for a book, whether it be in hard covers or in soft covers, wants something that is different from magazine fare.

In the area of non-fiction, we find an increasing amount of material available in soft covers. Many publishers today are increasing their non-fiction list, not only in the popular "how to do it" categories, but also in the areas of philosophy and other subjects of interest in adult education. I think the number of titles has gone up and the total sale of important and significant non-fiction has increased.

Mr. Guinzburg: Without going into the broad aspects, I would simply like to register a very strong dissent to what Mr. Pitkin just said, because, although I quite agree with him that a great many excellent books— a great many novels and a great many non-fiction books of the highest quality—have been done by the paperbacks, I think he's quite wrong when he says that they cover the whole range that is covered by hard-back publishing.

There are a lot of books—considered good by those who are supposed to know something about it—that often have sold very well in their original editions and simply won't be considered by any of the reprint publishers, for one reason or another. They'll say, "This isn't the sort of book that goes in our format." They will not say, "It is a bad book." They simply say, "This isn't the sort of thing that we can sell well."

Whether biography, essays or fiction—any hard-back publisher can, by going down his list, put his finger on author after author who is highly regarded, and, as I said, in many cases reasonably popular, who has had no reprints at all and who won't be considered by any of them.

Mr. Pitkin: I didn't intend that my last remarks should be taken to mean that the paperback publishers cover the whole range of hard-cover books. That is not true, and it would be absurd to hold it true.

In the first instance, I was simply discussing fiction. I do agree with you that any publisher who has soft-cover books may say to you and will say to you and to other publishers of hard-back books that a particular book —some book that you like, and a good book, let us say—is not the sort of thing that he can sell in paperbacks. But the fact that he cannot sell it —or he, in his opinion, cannot sell it—does not mean that it can't be done. He is an individual publisher, just as you are an individual publisher, and I am sure that there are many books that you would like to publish but find yourself unable to publish. Let's be frank about this and say right away that different publishers have different talents. Some of the competitors of Bantam Books have people on their staffs who are able to see things and to analyze various areas of fiction and non-fiction which we are unable to handle; but we think there are things we can do that they can't do, and I think they'll admit that, too.

So you have these individual differences, and I think it's good to keep them in mind when we are discussing what can be done in the different areas of hard-cover and paper-backed publishing.

MR. ASHEIM: May I ask a question? I think Mr. Burger might tell us whether he means that he believes that in the future the paper-backed book will replace absolutely the hard-bound book along the whole range of publication. Or did you mean, Mr. Burger, that paper-bound publishing would be a growing phenomenon but that hard-bound books would always cover certain areas of publishing?

MR. BURGER: I would like to evade an immediate, direct answer to your question and maybe work around the bush. Certain of you have mentioned my own use of the phrase "an item" or "a commodity," and I was being deliberately and perhaps defensively hard-boiled about the distribution and the marketing methods for these books.

I feel that the increased number of readers is a forward move made by the paper-backed book business. Mr. Hersey said that he understood that there were 2,000 good bookstores. I don't believe that the American Booksellers Association would agree with those figures. I don't think that there are that many by a good deal. I think they have been diminishing. I think this is very sad, but it happens to be a fact. There are well over 100,000 outlets for soft-cover books. The inventories are very badly kept. There are far too many titles. There is too much competition for the limited space available.

I do not think of books as "items" comparable to chewing gum. I hope I know the difference between a good book and so-called category fiction. I have read a great many of the former and, like most editors, have bought a good deal of the latter.

I think that in the scramble to see these books sell—I am not directly connected with the selling of the books and I am not a publisher, nor a distributor, nor really qualified to speak authoritatively about what sells and what does not sell—in this scramble, which is obviously taking place, I think publishers are being pushed (I mean soft-cover book publishers are being pushed) to exploit the opportunity and try to reach more and more kinds of people. I think that there is an increasing number of books available for 25 to 50 or 80 cents which are not aimed at the man who has come to a drugstore to buy a pack of chewing gum.

Anchor Books are a case in point. Many of the Mentor Books are another case in point. I think that the mass distribution techniques have inspired the cheap reproduction of the world's great treasures, artistic and literary.

To give you a fact about this thing currently, there are several strong indications that the poorer quality books, the books that exploit the lowest possible common denominators, hitting the same nerves over and over again, are hurting the publishers more than the more varied—the more esoteric, if you will—and I think Mr. Pitkin will probably agree.

I have in mind a particular publisher, whom I shall not name, who has material piling up in warehouses, returned copies, a good deal more than the rest of us: his whole slant and approach have been to hit the lowest common denominator. It doesn't displease me that he is hurt to the degree that he is said to be.

Mrs. Van Doren: Do you get reports from authors, through the Authors' Guild, Mr. Hersey, that their books in original hard covers are helped or picked up again by a later soft-cover publication job?

Mr. Hersey: It has been a fairly generally accepted idea for a number of years that in those cases where a book is held for soft-cover publication for two or three years after its original hard-cover publication, there may be a renewed sale that comes probably mostly from the sales of soft-cover books in areas where there are no bookstores at all.

Mrs. Van Doren: But they are not waiting two years now to put a book into soft covers as a rule.

Mr. Hersey: Some publishers still are.

Mr. Burger: Does it not depend upon the book?

Mr. Hersey: Yes, of course. Taking up what Mr. Burger said, I think it is certainly true that some remarkable books, some remarkably good books, are getting on the soft-cover publishers' list now.

I wonder whether part of the difficulty that soft-cover publishers are now facing, from what you said earlier, Mr. Burger, may not come from the kind of illusion that the mass-distribution, mass-production method of paperback sales brought about in the early days when the field was not quite so crowded and there were 150,000 or 200,000 places to sell a book. It was possible in the early days to send out 200,000 copies of a book and be fairly sure that most of them would be sold.

It turned out in the early days that that was even true of books which were not mysteries, westerns and so on. It turned out that books could be distributed and sold even if they were novels and in many cases fairly good novels.

But many new firms have come into the field, and now perhaps it has turned out that the audience for good books is not so solidly developed as we hoped it was; the illusion that *anything* could be sold has had to give way. Perhaps the new reading audience needs time to catch up with the new quality it is being offered.

Mr. Burger: It may well be.

MR. PITKIN: I can pick up right there, if I may. I'm sorry to say that I think there was a time when the audience was miles ahead of the publishers. I have been in the soft-cover book field since 1939 and full-time since 1941, and I don't think anything goes back of 1939 in this country.

I think there was a dividing line in 1947 in the world of soft-covers. Down to that time the soft-cover book was looked upon purely as a book, whether it was a mystery or a novel like Mark Twain's *Life on the Mississippi*, which was published among our first releases.

But in 1947, a number of things started to happen. For the first time we tried adaptation of magazine art on the covers of small books; Bantam Books was the innovator in this particular instance. Thereafter, because results were so good, all the firms went over exclusively to magazine art from the earlier form of more or less abstract representation or typographical covers or simply cartoons or line drawings of one kind or another.

Sales had been growing until then and continued to grow in the aggregate; and it was only two and a half years later that one publisher came into the field with books that weren't books at all, but were simply what I call magazine formula material expanded sufficiently to fill out 160 pages.

Now I believe that down to 1947—and I draw the line very conveniently there, though it may not be too accurate to insist upon that—I believe that down to 1947, everybody who had read a paperback thought of them simply as books at a lower price.

I am very sorry, but I don't believe they think this today. I think that a very important part of our market or our potential market now thinks of paperbacks as low-grade magazine material.

MRS. VAN DOREN: That is an unfortunate trend, if it is true.

MR. PITKIN: I hope it is a trend that is now being reversed. I happen to agree with Mr. Hersey that, for example, the illustrations being used generally on paperback covers are not sensational to the degree that they were, and as a matter of fact, I think that many publishers are now thinking about the abandonment of the adapted magazine illustration for the cover.

At the same time, the publisher who has gone most deeply into the magazine formula book is the publisher who is feeling most severely the effects of the present poor market in paperbacks.

MRS. VAN DOREN: Larger returns?

MR. PITKIN: Larger returns and smaller sales. It has become quite fashionable to talk about the problems of the hard-cover publisher; I think it's going to be a little more fashionable in 1954 to talk about the problems of the soft-cover publisher.

MRS. VAN DOREN: Mr. Guinzburg looks rather happy over there.

MR. GUINZBURG: I think that maybe we are spending a little too much time and emphasis on the year 1954 and its problems with this current over-supply that some publishers are feeling more than others. It is a very short-range problem.

These things happen in all sorts of businesses. Whether the paperback publishers are raising their standards and changing their covers is also a little too new. They may be doing this because there has been a lot of censorship around the country, or it may be a permanent policy, but it seems to me that we cannot talk too intelligently about something that is true of only the current months.

It seems to me that the long-range problems, which may be very difficult to analyze, are nevertheless much more interesting and important.

Mrs. VAN DOREN: I agree with you, and I wish we would talk a little about them.

MR. HERSEY: Well, before we go to that, I would like to pick up one thing that Mr. Guinzburg said in passing, about the attempts to censor certain kinds of paper-backed books.

I think there are indications in this area of censorship that tend to show that the paperback audience is not yet the same audience as that for the hard-cover books. Indeed, there are some curious differences in this area of censorship. Salinger's novel *The Catcher in the Rye* sold, I think, about 45,000 hard-cover copies, and when distributed by the Book-of-the-Month Club sold about 150,000. It was bought by libraries all over the country and was favorably reviewed; and so far as its hard-cover life is concerned, there were, to my knowledge, no questions asked about immorality and so on. But when it got into paperbacks it ran into trouble in many cities over the country, even though its jacket, by the way, was not gaudy. I gather that the censoring body known as the Georgia Literature Commission held hearings on the book, and that it was banned by police chiefs and citizen-censors in several cities.

Why the difference in this treatment between hard-cover and paper-backed book?

MR. ASHEIM: I think that is a typical phenomenon in censorship. The larger the potential audience, the more restricted the subject matter—just as you can say in a book things that you cannot say on the stage when a stage version is made of it. And you can say on the stage some things that cannot be said on the screen.

MR. GUINZBURG: And on the screen, things that cannot be done on television.

MR. ASHEIM: It is not a matter of books or the format, but rather that the potential audience is much greater, that the price is low, and that therefore youngsters may be reached as well as adults. At least this is the rationale that is put forward when a book which has been going around for years in hard covers with no trouble at all suddenly becomes banned when it is put into a paper cover.

MR. HERSEY: I think this is probably a big factor, but I think it is probably more complex than that, because many of the books which have run into censorship trouble in paperback form have been the relatively good

books—that is to say, books which are more or less in the classic area rather
than the really sensational books. And there have been cases of straight por-
nography published (not by these gentlemen, I am sure) in paperback
form which have not run into censorship, while books by Faulkner, Cald-
well and many others have been stopped.

Now, there's a qualitative factor, some kind of cultural factor that operates in censorship—goodness knows. Mickey Spillane is better known to
some of our youngsters than Salinger.

MR. ASHEIM: The question I raised is whether this is a reflection of
the reading audience, which I think is the underlying assumption, or
whether a particular group sets itself up to censor.

MRS. VAN DOREN: You mean that the group that sets itself up to censor is assuming that the large audience is going to be offended or hurt or
something like that?

MR. ASHEIM: That's right.

MR. PITKIN: I think it is a non-reading group.

MR. BURGER: Yes, and they erupt like boils in towns all over the country, and all it takes is half a dozen clubwomen and one chief of police and
you have a big censorship problem.

The best book I have had, in my opinion, is a book that was read in advance of publication by one of Mr. Guinzburg's authors, John Steinbeck,
and he was kind enough to say a good word for it. We put his endorsement
on the cover. It has gotten very good reviews universally, and yet it has
been banned in Detroit—I assume because of the inclusion of a four-letter
word known by every schoolchild.

The book is by no means an attempt to titillate. It is by no means
salacious. It is by no means offensive to morals. It is a story of tremendous
courage.

The censors who set themselves up must find handles, and they must
set up various rules, special lines beyond which the publishers shall not go;
and if a writer or a publisher knows those rules, he can dodge in and out
and put out very meretricious material and still not get banned. I've seen it
happen time and again.

MR. PITKIN: As to your question as to why it is that Mickey Spillane
runs into little or no trouble and books of real literary stature and genuine merit seem to run into somewhat more trouble, I think it can be said
that the people who are most interested in censorship and the activators
are those who are concerned with thought control. They wish to enforce a
kind of conformity on our society, and it is not surprising, if that is so, that
they see little to complain about or be uneasy about in Mickey Spillane.

MR. HERSEY: I still think that the gentlemen who publish paper-
backed books have to take some responsibility in this area, because they
have helped to build up a large new audience. One of the reasons why the
censors are interested—it has been built up primarily, or at least most no-
ticeably, on books that are sensational literature. That has been the main

reason why censorship has been turned to the paper-backed books, along with comic books and some of the more sensational moving pictures, as main targets of its attack.

It does seem to me a different audience from the hard-cover one. The paper-cover audience has defined itself by buying so many books—as David Dempsey of the *New York Times* said at that same meeting last spring—on sex, sensation and statutory rape.

Mr. Pitkin: I am sure there are publishers of hard-cover books that Mr. Guinzburg would hesitate to shake hands with. He can correct me if I'm wrong. There are also publishers of paper-backed books with whom I would hesitate to pass the time of day or be seen with on the street.

I don't like to be roped into a group with my neighbor unless I think my neighbor is a man like me, and I assume that Mr. Burger would feel also that it is not actually fair to look at this field and condemn it on the basis of some sensational books.

I happen to agree with you, however, that some of the most notorious books that have been published have made it much easier for the censors to pick on all paper-backed books, because there has been a tendency to lump paperbacks together—and I think they in fact do lump them together. I think they should be stopped from doing so; I think it is an error for us who are in this room to do so.

Mrs. Van Doren: Don't you think the reason for the tendency to lump them together is that they've sprung up so fast?

Mr. Pitkin: And because they are all for sale in the corner drugstore and candy store.

Mrs. Van Doren: And at a small range of price.

Mr. Pitkin: Exactly.

Mr. Guinzburg: I don't think it is surprising that this has happened. As long as the books were selling at a reasonably high price, they were going almost entirely to sophisticated, educated people who went into bookstores or belonged to a book club. Suddenly these same books, often with lurid covers, are available for sale at candy stores. And when a great many people who've no knowledge of books go in for a Coke and suddenly come upon this rack full of lurid looking things available for a quarter to their kids, then they get upset. They don't know enough to distinguish. They don't know enough to say, "Well, some of these may be very good and some may be very bad." They are outraged by the total thing that they have seen.

I'm not defending censorship, but I think it is perfectly understandable with this new display on every corner. People should worry about it, but should not be dismayed about it.

Mr. Pitkin: It is quite understandable.

Mr. Burger: I think it should be pointed out for the record that about 90 per cent of the books that are on the NODL [National Organization for Decent Literature] banned list, and most other books that have run into trouble in the various communities where there is censorship, are reprints of trade editions which were not considered to be questionable.

Let us not put the rap on soft-covers, for most of them are reprints. Even Mickey Spillane is not an original soft-cover writer.

MR. HERSEY: That is true, but the point I made before still holds, that they are not censored as hard-covered books, for reasons we have discussed.

MR. BURGER: Sure.

MRS. VAN DOREN: Mr. Guinzburg, let's get back to some of the questions you raised just now of the future possibilities and future tendencies, dangers and benefits in all this. That may be more fruitful than some of the present discussion.

MR. GUINZBURG: Well, to go back to some of the more general things. At the beginning of our discussion, the paperback publishers here pointed out the limitation on the number of copies that can be absorbed as far as we know at present by the stationery store, the newsstand, the limited space outlets, in which these books are sold. To be sure, this may change in the future, but that is the present system, a system in which a certain number of square feet are given to this merchandise that might be given to candy bars or something else.

These books are sold at a very low margin of profit to the dealer. That means in turn that it is inevitable that there is no expert advice available; nobody who sells these books can afford clerks who know what is inside of them. These books must sell themselves from their title, their cover, the author's name occasionally. That is the nature of this form of distribution. Now, if it is true that the number of titles that can be handled adequately is limited, and if we don't see any mechanism for keeping them, as Mr. Asheim pointed out before, in permanent or more or less permanent supply, as a great many hard-cover books are, you may very well find that there is only room in this type of outlet for the quick-selling, short-lived book. It may be a very good book; it may be a very bad book.

One of the great problems, as I see it, is what happens to everything else. The bookstore has been declining as an outlet. This year, in New York City, what used to be the two biggest outlets have contracted. Brentano's has given up part of its main store and Macy's has moved its book department from the ground floor to an upstairs floor. This is indicative of what is happening throughout the country.

There are very few new bookstores being started. Those that are being started are much more likely to be smaller stores in a busy neighborhood, which inevitably will handle only the reasonably popular things because they're not like the old-fashioned bookstore that had a large, slow-moving stock; and I think every hard-cover publisher will tell you that it is more and more difficult to get any distribution for any book on his list that isn't in one way or another conspicuous—isn't by a famous author or in some way sensational.

Now remember also that, just as in everything else, costs in publishing have gone up enormously, without a commensurate increase in sale which might have offset the higher costs. It is constantly becoming more difficult for a hard-cover publisher to publish the books which he thinks he would like to publish, which he thinks in some way are worth publishing.

If this goes on, if these trends continue—and I don't blame them entirely on paper-backed books, I merely think they are an important factor in the picture—if these trends continue, you are simply going to have fewer and fewer books being published.

Now people may very well say, "Aren't there too many books being published anyway?" Publishers answer, "Yes, there are," but no two will agree on which ones need to be dropped, and one of the glories of book publishing has been that it's been the one medium in which something that somebody wanted to write could be made available to a relatively small number of people.

I gloomily predict that this will decrease, and it will be harder and harder to do that sort of publishing. In fact, it may become impossible to do it except on a subsidized basis, and although I don't object to the sort of subsidy that is very nobly used by the university presses in many cases and by various other learned groups, I think there is an enormous loss to culture if fewer voices can be heard expressing themselves through books.

Mrs. Van Doren: Isn't it also true, though, Mr. Guinzburg, that many publishers feel that they couldn't publish some books, perhaps even what they consider very good books, if they did not have the chance of the extra income from a cheap paper edition?

Mr. Guinzburg: Of course, it is true. But may I cite one example of a discussion something like this that I was in a while ago, when one of the reprint publishers not present tonight ran to the defense of the paperback and the work which reprint publishers can do? He used the example of Mr. William Faulkner. He pointed out what a small sale he had had and how at last, through inexpensive books, Faulkner was reaching a wide market. This is undoubtedly true. I don't blame him for using that to support his position. It's a very fine case.

The thing I worry about, however, could be explained in terms of that example. I remember that Mr. Faulkner had a very difficult time being published—or I should say, his publishers had a very difficult time publishing him—over the period of a number of books. And I think we have to ask ourselves whether there may not be the next Faulkner, now in his twenties, unable to find a publisher at all because hard-cover publishing by itself is so much more difficult. One can think of the editorial meeting in which somebody says: "Well, yes, this youngster has got an awful lot of talent. But gosh, no book club sale, no reprint sale—we'll probably sell 1,122 copies of this. We can't do it."

Mr. Asheim: This is a question I wanted to raise earlier about the situation if paperback mass distribution took over.

It is quite true that paper-bound books now contain titles of consider-

able stature, but the question is whether they would have ever got into paperbacks without their original publication in hard covers. In other words,
what are the chances in 1980 for that year's Kafka or Joyce or Virginia
Woolf to get published when fiction is published only on a mass-distribution level?

MR. BURGER: This is certainly a very relevant question. I would like to
give two examples from my own list of inventory.

One is a book by a young man in his early thirties—a rather quiet and
serious novel. His first book was published by Scribner's and was well received critically; it didn't sell many copies. Well, I have undertaken to publish this second book; and I confess he has put a title on it which, while very
apt for the book and a fine, symbolic and right title, is also a selling title. If
I seem cynical, I am sorry, but I feel that this title will carry the book. I think
the book is not a natural for mass distribution, but, taking a deep breath,
I'm going to do it.

I suspect it might be a book about which many trade publishers today
would go through the routine that Mr. Guinzburg has just gone through:
"We can't get Book-of-the-Month Club. We may not be able to sell subsidiary rights. Well, can we afford to do it?"

I have a degree of faith that it is not going to fall back on my publisher
and handicap him with return copies, nevertheless it's a chance I'm taking;
and actually we're putting much more money into the first printing of this
book than a trade publisher would be putting into a similar book, for he
might be printing 3,000, and our economics is such that we must do a printing of 200,000 or 300,000.

Another book that I have—I might say in the confines of this room
that I got only by accident—is a book that should have gone to Mr. Guinzburg or another trade publisher, given the present situation of distribution
of paper-backed books and their relatively low degree of literary acceptance.
It happened to come to me. It's a book, I feel, that almost any trade publisher would be very happy to publish. It's a first novel, and it would sell
many copies for the trade publishers and would get good reviews and perhaps bring a very high price from such reprint publishers as Mr. Pitkin and
others. Now, given the present set of circumstances, I will try to arrange
some kind of trade publication for this book almost entirely because of the
author. I feel that he deserves a hearing in the present complex of soft- and
hard-covers. I think he needs to get into hard-covers for the benefit of the
reviews he might get and the chance of making the best-seller lists.

I fully expect that there will be a day when, as in France, there will be
original publication of first-rate, major new novels in soft covers.

This brings me back to the distribution techniques, a basic question.
They may well be in need of revision. I think the possibility of mail order
is only just beginning to be exploited. I think the possibilities of the specialized book in a specialized market, while not to be done in lots of 200,-

ooo and 300,000, are perhaps good for 20,000 to 50,000 to 80,000—I think we'll be driven to that and I think it's a fine thing that we'll be driven to it.

MRS. VAN DOREN: Well, what about Ballantine, in his new plan of publishing hard-covers and soft-covers at the same time, or soft-covers in conjunction with some trade publisher who will simultaneously get out a hard-cover edition?

MR. BURGER: I don't know about the feasibility of publishing the same —forgive me—"item" at $2.50 and again at $.25, $.35, or $.50. The fact that the same book is obtainable at one-tenth of the price is going to hurt terribly when you try to charge $2.00, $3.00 or $5.00 for it simultaneously. I don't think this situation will obtain for long, but if a book deserves to be reviewed, and if sales are increased because of good reviews, under the present circumstances I think a publisher should take it upon himself to try to arrange for hard-cover publication.

MR. PITKIN: It seems to me that Mr. Burger has stated a personal attitude in relation to the problem that Mr. Guinzburg posed. I don't think that that reaction, laudable as it is, is in point of fact an answer to the kind of situation which Mr. Guinzburg foresees as a possibility at least.

MR. GUINZBURG: His cases may be good, but I think he puts them as exceptions rather than as an indication that the basic point I made is not valid.

MR. PITKIN: I would regard them at least as exceptions, and I have some reasons for looking upon them in this light. One of them is that, as Mr. Burger says himself, there are too many publishers in the paperback field; and yet at the moment there are really only about fifteen to twenty firms operating at a good margin, and eight of them don't count because they're simply taking any kind of low-grade material they can lay their hands on and getting it on the stands.

MR. BURGER: They count to the customer.

MR. PITKIN: Quantitatively and statistically only, and what we're left with is a situation in which you have ten or twelve publishers at the outside who are the least bit concerned with any of the problems we have discussed here this evening.

On the other hand, Mr. Guinzburg is in a field where there are—I don't know the figures exactly—well, how many trade publishers would you say there are, Mr. Guinzburg? Upward of fifty?

MR. GUINZBURG: Yes. Actually I think it's eighty that belong to the Book Publishers Council.

MR. ASHEIM: There are thirty of them that actually publish five titles during the year.

MR. GUINZBURG: Many more than that.

MR. PITKIN: It would seem so.

I happen to think that the question we have been discussing here tonight, the future of hard-back books as against the future of paper-backed books, is really the question of the future of reading in America. I wonder how many people in this room saw a survey that Dr. Gallup put out in November. I think it was most likely in the *New York World-Telegram* and syndicated. It showed that in the United States, 17 people out of 100, 17 per cent, when interviewed said they were reading a book. In England, 55 per cent said they were reading a book. That may strike you as a shocking comparison, but I think a more dangerous fact is inherent in another figure, which I think was that a year or two ago in this country 22 per cent said they were reading a book, whereas today only 17 per cent were. I don't know whether those figures are actually indicative of how many people are in point of fact reading books, but I am afraid they are indicative of opinion; and I'm afraid that reading books is a little less respectable than it was two or three years ago, and it is a lot less respectable here than it is in England.

I think it is this kind of problem that we are all dealing with as we look at our own business problems or our problems as writers.

I would like to know—I don't know if there's anybody in this room who can shed any light on this—but I would like to know how Americans can be interested in more and better books and how book-reading can be made a more respectable pastime than it apparently is today.

MRS. VAN DOREN: I am surprised that you use the word "respectable."

MR. PITKIN: Well, I wanted to use the word "respectable" because I thought about it, and I'm sticking to it. I think that the whole climate of anti-intellectualism in this country, which I am afraid has been reinforced considerably in the last four or five years, is closely involved with concepts such as respectability. I just happen to think that if reading books were a more respectable occupation, or pastime, or whatever you choose to call it, more people would identify the thing they were reading as a book, and you'd get a higher figure than 17 per cent.

MRS. VAN DOREN: You don't think it is just a question of other forms of entertainment that are cutting into reading?

MR. PITKIN: I think that that question exists importantly, but I don't think it is just that question. I know too many people who would rather just not be seen with a book and would rather say, as in the case of a printer that I know, a well-educated man, "We print them; we don't have to read them too, do we?"

MRS. VAN DOREN: Surely that question does not mean that the printer was thinking of respectability.

MR. PITKIN: I'm afraid it enters into it.

MR. ASHEIM: There's no implication in what you said, though, that in fact paper-bound books have had any effect in the drop in respectability?

MR. PITKIN: No, I didn't mean to imply that.

MR. ASHEIM: In other words, this is a separate problem, that is not related to one or the other method of publication.

MR. PITKIN: I think anti-intellectualism, as a matter of fact, predated paperbacks. The forces already existed in this country which are pointed toward less emphasis on education beyond a grade-school level, or at least on educational content beyond that level.

MRS. VAN DOREN: On the other hand, the amount of reading of nonfiction books—biography, history, public affairs—has increased steadily while other reading has gone down.

MR. GUINZBURG: You say "increased"—I think we ought to consider the term "increase" in relative rather than in absolute terms. Think of what has happened in this country in the twentieth century in terms of the growth of the well-to-do, literate, leisured population; of a population that has doubled; of the educational level, which has increased so fantastically that there are at present five times as many people in colleges as there were in high schools at the beginning of the century; of the leisure time that has increased tremendously, and all the ease of life—then ask yourself if the reading of non-fiction books has increased or kept anything like the pace of the increased potential that we might have expected in the light of those circumstances. No, I believe you get a very discouraging picture, instead of an optimistic one.

MRS. VAN DOREN: I think that is true, Mr. Guinzburg, but it is a fact that the reading of fiction has gone down in the same period; and though reading of serious non-fiction books may not have increased as it should, the reading of fiction is relatively in a much worse state.

MR. BURGER: How about the writing of fiction?

MR. PITKIN: I would like to ask Mr. Guinzburg a question. I really have only an impression here, and no exact information, but I'd like to know whether any expansion that has taken place in the reading of hard-covered non-fiction hasn't been in the purely inspirational and non-informational books.

MR. GUINZBURG: I think you're quite right. I think that there are a great many kinds of non-fiction that actually sell less well than they used to. I think the total of non-fiction has increased, but that is only true of certain kinds.

MR. PITKIN: Would you say generally of the less profound variety?

MR. GUINZBURG: I think it's frightfully hard to make that sort of qualitative judgment.

MR. BURGER: I do know that in going back over the best-seller lists, back to the turn of the century, you will find certain inspirational material and self-help books of a so-called spiritual nature prominently featured.

MR. PITKIN: That's a recurrent phenomenon.

MR. BURGER: And that has been constantly so with the growth in population.

MR. HERSEY: Don't TV and other cultural factors tend somewhat to decrease reading in the country generally, outside the province of our discussion? It seemed to me that Mr. Burger made some interesting points earlier that may be germane—when he talked about the need for renewed scrutiny of the distribution methods in the paperback field. Evidently, from what Mr. Guinzburg said, that may also be necessary in the hard-cover field; and maybe there is some new kind of publishing that we had better think about for the future, to reach those readers we still have.

MRS. VAN DOREN: Have you any ideas at all as to what sort of publishing that would be?

MR. HERSEY: I would like to ask Mr. Burger whether thinking is being done in the paperback field about the subject of distribution. Are there any discussions among publishers or in the industry?

MR. BURGER: I operate peripherally at that level, and I cannot give you any definitive answers. I do know that at my level, as an editor, this problem is becoming more acute. And as far as all the techniques of publishing are concerned, I am sure that over half of the thirty to eighty trade publishers that Mr. Guinzburg and Mr. Asheim spoke of exist only because of selling subsidiary rights. They would be out of business were it not for this. I think that such a system is somehow bound to get revised and get controlled differently.

The soft-cover publishers have grown up in two different ways, as I see it—little as I know of it. One—Mr. Pitkin's Bantam Books is an example—has been an expansion of interest among various trade publishers, an attempt to capture a new market, to exploit new techniques. Then there is the line of books put out by the publishers for whom I work, for example. This line is an outgrowth of a mass distribution of periodicals, of a massive operation which is very costly. They want to keep the machinery going. They must find the best ways to keep up with what is being done in techniques; and they think more in terms of the point of sale and of the presses and the sales channels—not like the Bantam operation, which started from a publisher's office, where they're thinking directly of the reader.

As far as new techniques for distributing these books go, there are certain signs either for better or worse. There is Anchor Books; there is the new line called Key Books. The first two titles had to do with the life of Gandhi by Louis Fischer and a "success-in-marriage" book. Well, I will put up with every success-in-marriage book if you get an intelligent life of Gandhi to go along with it.

Ballantine has quietly put its books into two different mail-order systems. Obviously, they are for category fiction, the western and science fiction, but a feeler is being put out in this direction.

MR. GUINZBURG: Mr. Burger has mentioned Anchor Books, which was mentioned once before. It seems to be somewhat out of the category we were talking about, because Anchor Books, as I see it, is not really a mass-medium operation. It is an attempt to do relatively inexpensive books for specialized markets, and consequently has to charge three or four times as much as the mass-medium operation does. It is much more on a book basis than on a magazine basis. It is not really in the same class with soft-cover publishing, because the whole distribution method—

Mr. BURGER: It is a distribution method with which I am not entirely familiar, but in the neighborhood where I live there are two *newsstand* outlets for Anchor Books which also feature Dell Books, Bantam Books, Signet Books, etc. Assuming that trade publishing is over here on the right at $4.00, and Anchor Books here in the middle at $.80 or $.90, and over here the reprints and the soft-cover originals at $.25, $.35 and $.50—I would still say that Anchor Books are closer to the soft-covers than to the trade books.

Mr. ASHEIM: Again the thing that concerns me is that Anchor Books are reprints. These have been established by hard-cover publishing and identified with an audience. They are now being brought back into print in an inexpensive format because they are already established. They are not experimenting with new writers.

Mr. BURGER: Do you think that will never come about, that there is a good argument against it?

Mr. HERSEY: It seems to be almost impossible to imagine a Kafka or a Joyce or a Virginia Woolf, to use the examples that Mr. Asheim used, being first sprung at a mass audience. By the very nature of experimental writing, to approach that—

Mr. BURGER: In the case of Anchor Books, they are reprints, they are classics, and they are books that every educated person would be drawn to, has read or would want to read, and would want to own. I don't know what their print orders are—do you know?

Mr. GUINZBURG: They say they have a 20,000 break-even point.

Mr. PITKIN: I think their print orders are in the range of 20,000 to 30,000.

Mr. BURGER: That may be; and they may go under, Ballantine Books may go under, all kinds of books may go under. But I still think that paperback publishers are going to have to continue searching for more and better ways to bring a greater variety of books to people who read, whether they put out 30,000 or 300,000 copies. *Discovery* and *New World Writing* are cases in point.

Mr. HERSEY: While we are on the economics of books, I've waited a very long time to say something that is not news to either of you gentlemen who are in the paperback field—namely, that authors feel very strongly that their share of profits from paper-backed books is not so great as it ought to be.

I don't know whether you know of the standard royalty arrangement, Mr. Asheim. It is 4 per cent to the author and the original publisher on the first 150,000 copies and 6 per cent thereafter. Those royalties are generally shared equally between original publisher and author, and therefore the author's royalty from the paper-backed books is 2 per cent on the first 150,000 and 3 per cent thereafter.

The royalties on hard-cover books start at 10 per cent and generally go to 15 per cent on a sliding scale. Ballantine Books is paying authors 8 per cent on its paper-backed editions. Authors are quite aware of the differences between the economics of publishing paper-backed books and that of hard-cover publishing. Nevertheless, writers generally feel that the paper-back companies can pay a more substantial royalty than they are now paying.

MRS. VAN DOREN: There is one phase of this that hasn't been mentioned at all. We have talked on publishing problems; we have talked about the author's problems; but no one has mentioned the reader and what advantage he may get out of being able to buy a cheaper book.

It is true that he can get a very bad cheap book, but he can also get a very good one; and it seems to me that, on the whole, the advantage to the reader is very significant.

MR. HERSEY: Could I start that off? Although I have been attacking paperback publishing fairly consistently, as a reader I think it is a wonderfully valuable thing.

I started reading paper-backed books in European and English editions before they were very widely published here, and have ever since, whenever I could, bought a paperback in preference to a hard-cover book.

One of the difficulties again lies in distribution, because it is not only hard but sometimes impossible to get the book you want in the paper-backed edition. If you go to a drugstore or to your local outlet for paper-backed books, the chance that the title you want will be there is slight. Mr. Asheim spoke earlier of the perishability of the paper-backed books, because they move through so fast.

Even when you have read an announcement of a recent publication in paper-backed books, it is often very hard to find the book you want. So, from the reader's point of view, there's a kind of chancy nature about the purchase of paper-backed books.

MR. PITKIN: I think that is certainly true. One thing that hasn't been mentioned tonight that is taking place in this country is an increase in the number of outlets—I don't mean to say tens of thousands, but I think probably a few thousand—which are specializing in paper-backed books where you can find not a hundred titles, as you can perhaps in your corner drugstore, but where there are five hundred and even a thousand titles.

I saw such an outlet in Topeka, Kansas, very recently; that one store sold roughly 25 per cent of all the paperbacks sold in the city of Topeka. Well, that made it, I think, one of the big bookstores in the United States in terms of unit sales, though not in terms of dollar sales. There is in many cities today an outlet comparable to that one, and I think there's a trend in that direction.

MR. ASHEIM: I just want to underline what Mr. Hersey said about the difficulty of finding a particular title in a paper-backed edition. I think there are two reasons: one is this problem of distribution. If you look for it immediately after publication, it may not be there; and if you go back three weeks later, it's already gone and won't be replaced.

In addition, the fact that these outlets are manned by people who are not interested in books means that they have no knowledge of the books that they have, no interest in getting the title for you, no way of knowing how to go about it even if they were interested. So, unless you happen by a lucky accident to run upon it yourself, it is a problem. Most readers would not write to the publisher for a book.

MR. PITKIN: That underscores a problem which is being faced by many a paperback publisher, if not by all of them, and that is that the period of sale has been so reduced by the multiplicity of titles that the question today is not whether the production costs can be shaved a tenth of a cent or a hundredth of a cent, but rather whether this or that feature of paperback operations can be modified—whether the paperback industry can exist for the next several years as we know it today in point of volume and range of titles.

MR. GUINZBURG: And, of course, if you reduce your multiplicity of titles, then you have aggravated the very situation that we are worrying about.

MR. PITKIN: Exactly.

MR. GUINZBURG: But I would like to comment on the other point you raised. I am glad it came up, because I think that there has been an enormous amount of exaggeration of the benefit to the reader, as indeed there has been of the benefit to the author. For offhand, it looks as though the existence of the paperback was sheer gain both to author and to reader.

I think that is not at all the case. In the first place, a great deal of paperback publishing is in fact a substitute for the pulp magazine, which has gone down sharply as the paperback has risen. A great deal of the material available in the paperbacks is the same sort of stuff in a different format. The rental library has almost disappeared since the paperback came into existence, which is a loss of distribution to the author and a loss also to readers. Material from the rental library used to be available on a far greater scale than now. But there is also something called the free public library, a place where people could go to get books if they wanted them, offering a far greater choice with none of the disadvantages, or with not as great disadvantage, let us say, of unavailability of title.

People, as we know, habitually borrow books from each other, which is also an inexpensive way of getting books. Finally, from the point of view of the reader, if there is some gain—as I am perfectly willing to concede— it may be offset by the fact that the hard-cover publisher has to charge the reader a good deal more for all the books that don't go into reprint, all that he doesn't think will go into reprint. If he has to break even somehow just on his own original sale through traditional channels, he may have to charge the customer a couple of dollars extra for a book in order to hope to come out ahead, which is certainly at least an offset to the benefit that the reader may get from inexpensive books.

MR. ASHEIM: Here's another aspect of this problem. It seems to me you hinted at it in a sense. One of the things that many of us believe is that the paperback has created a whole new group of readers—that we have reached many people who did not read before. But it would seem at least possible to me that what we have created is perhaps a whole new group of people who are buying books that don't cost very much; that these are people who were reading anyway; that they got them from the library and in other ways, and if they didn't read them as books, they read them as pulp magazines.

And now these same readers happen to be buying these things which we call books and would seem to represent a whole new audience of book buyers, but they do not necessarily represent a great increase in readers as such.

MRS. VAN DOREN: Do you think it possible that during the war, when we had overseas editions in paper which were distributed to the troops all over the world by the millions, a great many men who had possibly never read anything except maybe a comic book or pulp magazine began to read books? Then after they had come home, when they wanted to read a book —having read nothing but paperbacks before and having no money to spend on hard-bound books—they may have gone out and found paperbacks again.

MR. HERSEY: From the figures we have been given tonight, it seems as if they are losing the hang of it.

MR. GUINZBURG: One of the discouraging things, I think, is that we have practically no evidence that these big distributions do make readers for hard-bound editions of books in general or particular authors.

I think you can check that far more accurately in a case of book club distribution. Take the experience that I think all hard-bound publishers have had: an author who has had an average sale of about 10,000 copies per book; and a major book club is suddenly interested in one of his books and distributes a couple of hundred thousand copies. Then the next book isn't a book club selection, and the author is probably right back where he was before. In other words, those couple of hundred thousand people who may have enjoyed the book that they received from the book club do not take note of the author's next book, do not build up substantial additional sales. I say this unhappily, of course, because one of the hopes that everybody in this business had was that the new methods of distribution would spread reading and form reading habits; and all books would benefit from this. But I have seen in just about thirty years no evidence that this happened.

MR. PITKIN: Isn't it partly a question of who goes to bookstores? After all, when a book club puts out 200,000 copies of the work of any particular author, those books are not distributed with regard to the incidence of bookstores; they would simply go out all over the place, into little cities and rural areas where you have to go fifty miles, sometimes a hundred, to find a bookstore.

Mr. Asheim: Isn't it true that bookstore sales increase when a book is distributed through the clubs?

Mr. Pitkin: That is a different question and has to do in part with the heavy promotion given to the book by the book club and the additional attention that the book receives when it is selected by a club. That is a pretty well-known phenomenon.

Mr. Asheim: The point I was making is that there are people who go into bookstores and buy a book club selection, while there is no apparent carry-over to the author's next book.

Mr. Guinzburg: What happens, I think, when the book is taken by the club is that there is then a lot of talk about that book, and some people actually find their way into a bookstore and buy it.

Mrs. Van Doren: Gentlemen, I think we must stop this discussion, and I should like in winding it up to ask you each one thing.

It seems to have developed in one way or another from what you have said here this evening that the American people are losing their interest in reading books. Do you think that is so, and if you think it is so, do you think it has any connection with the advent of paperbacks? Let me ask you first, Mr. Pitkin.

Mr. Pitkin: I think it is possibly so—that we have to assume that it is so—and that it has nothing to do with the advent of paperbacks, but is associated with phenomena such as the tremendous growth of television and other factors in our culture which affect reading, and particularly the reading of books. And these have to do with the area that I mentioned earlier of anti-intellectualism—let us say with the loneliness of the man who is caught reading a good book.

Mrs. Van Doren: What do you think, Mr. Asheim?

Mr. Asheim: I would certainly think that there is no reason to believe that the paper-backed book would cause a decrease in reading books. While I, as you know, have not gone along with the more extravagant claims about the wider audience that is created by the paper-bound book, there is no doubt that it has not reduced the audience, and it certainly has attracted some people who might not otherwise have been reached.

That today there is less interest in reading and that paperbacks abound at the same time is a correlation, but there is no causal factor there at all that can be shown.

Mrs. Van Doren: But you do think there is less interest in reading?

Mr. Asheim: I would fear that is so.

Mrs. Van Doren: Mr. Guinzburg, how about you?

MR. GUINZBURG: I would agree with Mr. Asheim that the paperback isn't in any sense a cause of any decline. I think the paperback is an expression in the book field of what is happening generally in turning the arts of communication into a mass medium rather than a rather relatively selected medium. Serious reading has relatively declined in terms of what we should have expected from the increasingly educated American public. It seems to me that this is all part of a very broad pattern in which there are common factors to be found in the newspaper world, in the magazine world, movies, radio and television—that we are just part of that large pattern.

MRS. VAN DOREN: And you, Mr. Burger?

MR. BURGER: I think that the reading of books has increased tremendously. I think it is largely attributable to the widespread distribution of soft-cover editions of books.

MRS. VAN DOREN: You are optimistic on both scores?

MR. BURGER: Yes, I am, and I regret that the Gallup figures have declined from 1947 to 1953 from 22 to 17 per cent. I think 17 per cent for America in 1954 is a very good figure and quite respectable. And I think that with books printed in the millions—be they partly pulp, partly magazine writing reoriented into a new format, be they serious works of fiction or not—a great many more people are reading books now than they were on any long-term scale going back fifteen, twenty, thirty, forty years ago—a higher proportion of people.

MRS. VAN DOREN: Mr. Hersey, what do you feel about this?

MR. HERSEY: Television.

MRS. VAN DOREN: Not so many are reading?

MR. HERSEY: I think not.

MRS. VAN DOREN: And it's not paperbacks, but television?

MR. HERSEY: I think it's harder to teach reading now. Children see images, not words, and I think there is less reading, less buying of books for that reason. I don't think paperbacks have anything to do with the decline.

MR. PITKIN: I would just like to break in at this point if I might. You asked earlier, Mrs. Van Doren, what was thought about the man who was in service and was introduced to books in paper format, and whether he didn't come out of the Army or the Navy, whatever service, a book reader, having gone in with no background in this field at all. I think that that happened to a great many people who were in service. However, the age of that group of people must be considered: by this time they have taken on families and business, and have such financial responsibilities that they have become, let us say, less important in the book market, and are buying fewer books than they did five years ago.

This is something which apparently happens to people whether they are educated or not. As they take on more and more responsibilities, they read less and less. They may read more selectively and they may read better books, but in the aggregate, so far as I can make out, their total reading tends to decline as they take on family responsibilities.

So, if you take this along with the advent of television and the other factors that have been discussed, I think you might have something that would go far to explain some of the tendencies that have been pointed to here.

MRS. VAN DOREN: Who wants the last word?

MR. ASHEIM: If all these factors militate against reading, it seems to me that Mr. Burger might properly have asked how much less reading there might have been if the paperbacks weren't around.

MR. PITKIN: A fair question.

MRS. VAN DOREN: Any other comments?

Well, thank you all very much; we will look forward to seeing this in type.

8

INTERNATIONAL COMMUNICATION

Llewelyn White and Robert D. Leigh
MERCHANTS OF WORDS AND IMAGES

INTERNATIONAL COMMUNICATION

MOST students of international affairs agree that the technical devices for communication among the countries of the world are now more refined and more readily available than at any other time in the history of mankind. But the "cold war" continues. The disparateness of ideas between nations grows wider, although the communications satellites offer unlimited vistas for international communication.

The problem is not one of technique, but of understanding. It involves semantic differences, as well as ideological differences, in questions of international diplomacy and information. Although the White and Leigh study was written shortly after the end of World War II, it highlights problems very much extant today and offers a comprehensive summary of the development and use of mass media in the area of international communication.

Today, the merchants of words and images are a varied breed—reporters for international news services, free lance observers who became popular with their "inside" stories, special correspondents and international public relations experts. As the authors show, the presence of instruments for the improvement of international understanding has created a genuine need for information and analysis of news and public affairs.

Some of this need is fulfilled by the international press associations and by the television correspondents representing networks in various countries around the world. In addition, books have become valuable items of exchange between countries, and foreign films of superior quality not only challenge American-made movies, but have probably instigated better quality in the home-made product.

The international information area changes constantly. There are improvements in the "raw material" of foreign correspondents, in the "semifinished" press association material and in the quality of newspaper and magazine articles and books which attempt to analyze the foreign social and political scene, as well as in the news and public affairs programs on television and radio.

There is at least one major drawback which frustrates fruitful communication and exchange between nations, apart from language differences. This is the ever-present problem of propaganda and censorship. International understanding has little chance to develop when information is "filtered" or restricted by the propagandist or the government censor. Propaganda plays a major part in world informational exchange, and concepts of the function of the reporter vary widely. A series of interviews in the United States by a Soviet editor turned out in print to be a polemic on differences in ideology, rather than a reportorial account—a procedure which shocked American public opinion, and in particular, the opinion of the American publicist, accustomed to a free and responsible press.

There has been an improvement, however, in the gathering of facts for international information. Owing to the speed of communication and the influence of world opinion, more news has been more readily available in recent years. American correspondents are getting the news through more readily to their home offices. Difficulties will continue to arise, however, partly because of differences in language and ideology, particularly in the area of news interpretation and analysis. Reporters of international affairs have frequently been called to account in many countries, not because of their wire service copy, but because of a book they may have written or a magazine article which has been critical of a particular country or of a particular political regime.

There are also technical problems imposed by the Iron Curtain countries. These problems involve access to news at the source, freedom to travel the country at will, freedom to transmit and receive news without censorship. It may well be that the advent of international television as a practical reality will eliminate many barriers to international communication and open the door to a new phase of "peoples speaking to peoples" throughout the civilized world. Even under the most advanced of conditions, however, the subtle forms of semantic barriers and of implicit censorship in translation will not be eliminated. These barriers to effective international communication will be difficult to eradicate in the foreseeable future.

*   *   *   *

RELATED READING

Desmond, Robert W. *The Press and World Affairs.* New York: Appleton Century, 1937.
Meyerhoff, Arthur E. *The Strategy of Persuasion.* New York: Coward-McCann, 1965.

MERCHANTS OF WORDS AND IMAGES

By Llewelyn White and Robert D. Leigh

THANKS TO THE WAR, the world never had so many instruments which can be used for improving understanding among peoples as it has today. The unprecedented demand for news, background, and interpretation has brought new information agencies into the field and spurred old ones into expanding not only their services but also their concepts of the work to be done. Press associations, which before the war were interested primarily in bringing news of the world to their countries, are now concentrating on selling news throughout the world. Book publishers, who formerly wrote off foreign sales as a "2 per cent nuisance," now regard themselves as vital instruments of international understanding. In a dozen countries, flourishing motion-picture industries are preparing to challenge Hollywood's long-time supremacy—and, in consequence, Hollywood shows signs of being aware that it must do a better job in the export market. The international circulation of finished newspapers and magazines, once regarded as an impractical dream, has become an accomplished fact. Although the future pattern of international broadcasting at the moment is less clear, the next decade is certain to witness the linking of the remotest areas of the world through this modern medium.

In mass communication, information is circulated internationally in three forms: as raw material, as semifinished goods, and as finished product. Raw material may be described as the dispatches of foreign correspondents to their home newspapers and magazines, the pictures of still photographers and newsreel cameramen, the reports of radio newsmen broadcast to their compatriots by their home broadcasting stations or networks, and the materials out of which authors write books and free-lance magazine articles. Semifinished goods may be described as regular press association and picture-feature syndicate services, which the recipient may use in full, cut, combine with material from other sources, or discard. Finished products include books, magazines, newspapers, motion pictures, and direct country-to-country radio broadcasts reaching the consumer in final, unchangeable form.

Obviously, in the three cases the barriers encountered are quite different, both as to form and as to significance. We may agree with alacrity that everyone is entitled to the raw materials of information. We may go a step further and say that, for the sake of obvious economies of effort and expense to the editor and radio-station manager, everyone who wants them should have unhampered access to semifinished goods. But we may hesitate to insist that any people has a right to flood other peoples with finished products, for it is a fact that where no editor can intervene between his compatriots and information-suppliers in other lands to make comprehensible what would otherwise be incomprehensible and to clothe the isolated incident in its historic context, the effect may be to produce misunderstanding rather than understanding; and that where no editor can detect and reject sheer propaganda, governments may be tempted to substitute it for information.

THE NEWS-GATHERERS

It often has been remarked that the interchange of information through mass media will attain its perfect state only when every people is adequately represented throughout the world by competent observers—i.e., when all information starts with imported raw material. Such a system certainly would go far toward checking propaganda, and, assuming an abundance of domestic mass media to air the findings of these observers, most nations probably would subsist very well on nothing but raw material from abroad.

It is interesting to recall that, except for a smattering of books, this is precisely how the world operated until the turn of the century. It is interesting, too, to note the historic sequence in the development of mass media: the coming of new mechanical devices created popular demand for their products rather than the other way around; and government interference with mass media began to assert itself only as the concentration of the means of communication made systematized interference practicable. The first World War began, and the recent war greatly accelerated, a trend away from raw-material imports to the export of finished goods. Doktor Goebbels became the East India Company of our time.

Prior to the invention of printing type, news traveled by word of mouth and by letter, with the choicest bits of court scandal and international intrigue reserved for the safety and embellishment of conversation. The advantages of the confidential courier were preserved long after the coming of the newspaper. In part, this was because editors appreciated that their news-gatherers were protected in the disguise of a bank clerk or a ship's captain. In part, it was because the original purchaser of the news was not an editor at all but an enterprising businessman who let the editor have it only when he could extract no further profit from its exclusiveness. In any event, although governments created the most important news they could not control it in a society in which every other traveler might be a part-time reporter.

I. REUTER, THE PRESS ASSOCIATIONS, AND THE CARTEL

Among the most enterprising businessmen of the pretelegraph period in Europe were the Fuggers and later the Rothschilds, who had discovered early that palace-scullery gossip could sometimes be turned to account in the money mart. In the 1840's a no less enterprising German, named Paul Julius Reuter, found that homing pigeons could beat the Rothschilds' couriers. In 1851, on the advice of the Rothschilds, Reuter took his pigeons to London, where he used them to link the newfangled telegraph lines that could span everything in Europe but the Skagerrak and the English Channel.

Three things immediately became apparent to Reuter: (1) copper wire was going to revolutionize and standardize the whole news-gathering operation; (2) because this would give governments the opportunity to interfere with what was said, the wise news merchant would seek to make himself a partner and confidant of government; and (3) newspapers were becoming so numerous and so bulky that they were better wordage-volume customers than brokerage houses. Armed with such wisdom, Reuter approached the *Times* with a proposition to furnish English newspapers with Continental coverage by his staff of foreign observers. The *Times* was skeptical, but the editor of the *Advertizer* closed a shrewd bargain with him.

Within twelve months Reuter was serving a dozen newspapers in the British Isles and making money at it. But his sights were aimed higher: If the government would permit him to use the new submarine cables that were beginning to link the empire's outposts, the global news service he proposed to develop would cement British ties and help to fill the holds of British merchantmen. He may have added, as an afterthought, that such a plan already had occurred to a Frenchman named Havas.

In any event the British government was quick to see the point. Reuter became a British citizen, a trusted servant without portfolio. Needless to add, Reuter's news service was careful to say at crucial points what the British government wished it to say.

Meantime, Havas, who had been rounding up Continental news for French newspapers since 1835, was also dreaming of world empire. Havas fought Reuter for a year, but the favorite of Westminster held the high trumps—the cables. Then as now, limited facilities argued limited competition. So Havas persuaded Wolff, a German agency founded in 1849, that prudence dictated dividing the world into three parts. Reuter got the British empire, North America, a number of "suzerain" states along the Mediterranean-Suez lifeline, and most of Asia; Havas got the French empire, southwestern Europe, South America, and parts of Africa; Wolff got what was left in Europe, including Austria-Hungary, Scandinavia, and the Slav states.

Reuter soon discovered that he was in for trouble in the United States, where a number of newspaper publishers in 1848 had decided to husband their limited facilities by organizing a co-operative news-gathering agency which they styled the "Associated Press." The British government did not want trouble with America over anything touching United States sovereignty so closely and for such relatively small stakes; so Reuter convinced Havas that the original partners would benefit by letting A.P. into the cartel, since its inclusion would enable them to cover the news of the distant republic without spending a farthing. Even so, A.P. was not formally admitted until 1887.

During the succeeding years there were changes and modifications of the original four-trust agreement. Smaller news agencies, like Italy's Stefani and Belgium's Belga, sprang up, only to be forced to become satellites of Reuter or Havas. Here and there, as in the Caribbean and in Central America, Reuter and Havas agreed to share a market. A.P. was confined to continental United States until after the turn of the century, when it was permitted to venture into Canada and Mexico, and, toward the close of the first World War, into Central and South America. Thus it was that, from 1858 to the first World War, reporting, save in the United States, was never quite free of the taint of government propaganda.

A good many editors, particularly in America, writhed in their strait jackets. They themselves traveled abroad enough to know that they were not getting the facts. Some of the more enterprising, like James Gordon Bennett the elder, sought to gain a measure of independence from the cartel by sending special correspondents to roam the world, as the pre-Reuter couriers had done and as the individual British newspaper correspondents did. A.P. itself was able to place some of its correspondents in foreign capitals with the right of filing their reports directly to the United States. But it was not until a new enlargement of the telecommunications bottleneck coincided with the development of cheap newsprint and high-speed presses to focus a widespread demand for better news coverage that the cartel got its first serious warning of doom.

The break came during the first decade of the present century. The Commercial Cable Company was challenging the Western Union-British stranglehold on the Atlantic cables and preparing to buy into the new Pacific links. Radiotelegraphy was blossoming as a cheap alternative carrier, capable of carrying many thousands of words a day. The improved Hoe high-speed rotary press was shifting the balance of interest to afternoon newspapers, with their multiple split-second editions for street sales. Among the most vigorous of these afternoon papers were those of the midwestern and far western chains owned by the Scripps family, which, because of A.P.'s exclusive-franchise agreements, could not buy that agency's service. In 1907 the Scripps organized the United Press Associations.

U.P. soon was joined in the anticartel fight by Hearst's International News Service.* By 1914, noncartel correspondents dotted the globe, for U.P. and I.N.S. were not alone. Although for political reasons they would not formally break with the monopoly, venturesome British, Dutch, French, Scandinavian, and Japanese editors could and did send their own reporters forth to "supplement" the cartel's coverage. In Canada, Australia, and Japan co-operative news associations were formed, with the partial object of eliminating governmental dominance.

By dint of considerable energy and some good luck, U.P. by 1920 had broken the cartel front at what had been regarded as its strongest point: the non-United States news-buying market. A fortuitous friendship between a U.P. executive and the owners of *La Prensa* of Buenos Aires led, despite Havas' protests, to U.P. contracts with a number of Latin-American newspapers. At about the same time, A.P. extended its membership to include a number of leading South and Central American newspapers. And the forthright demand of several English provincial newspapers for something better than Reuter resulted in the formation of British United Press, an entirely British-owned association having close ties with U.P. with which it exchanged news items.

II. DIVERSIFICATION IN FOREIGN NEWSGATHERING

Although Germany's defeat in 1918 gave Wolff's share of the cartel to Havas and Reuter, the old arrangement was finished. Struggling new agencies like Exchange Telegraph in England and Agency Radio in France had followed the U.P.-I.N.S. example. One-paper special correspondents were becoming commonplace in the world's principal cities. Soon their newspapers, singly or in groups, organized syndicates to sell their global coverage to less venturesome editors. Thus, such newspapers as the *London Daily Mail*, the *London Daily Express*, the *Manchester Guardian*, the *Stockholm Tidningens*, the *Berliner Tageblatt*, the *Züricher Zeitung*, *La Prensa* and *Nación* of Buenos Aires, the *Frankfurter Zeitung*, the *Petit Parisien*, the *Tokyo Nippon Dempo*, the *Philadelphia Public Ledger*, the *New York Evening Post*, the *New York World*, the *New York Herald Tribune*, the *New York Times*, and the *Chicago Daily News* branched out as small press associations in the news-selling, as well as the news-gathering, market.

During the late twenties and early thirties, foreign coverage made rapid strides both in the number of observers roaming the world and in the quality of the best of them. Magazine correspondents joined the ranks of newspapermen. As the importance of pictures increased, news photographers and newsreel cameramen began to apply for admission to the correspondents' corps. In the late thirties, radio newsmen and commentators added their eyes and voices.

The very rapid development of wireless and aviation had made possi-

* These have merged to become United Press International. (Ed.)

ble a flow of words and pictures such as Paul Julius Reuter had never envisioned. The expansion in size and scope of existing periodicals and the creation of many new ones offered a ready outlet for the increased flow. The best of the correspondents departed from time-honored press association methods and began to dig deeply into the social patterns of the countries to which they were assigned. The invention of the "candid" camera and the perfection of fine-screen photographic printing on improved calendar magazine stock called forth a host of first-class photographers, whose art was brought to the home news desk by wire and wireless photo in a matter of minutes. Better book publishing and merchandising methods invited those who roamed the world in search of knowledge to put between covers the best of what they found.

Again, as in Reuter's time, newer and better facilities inspired newer and better uses of the means of international communication; newer and better uses spurred a popular demand for their continuance and improvement. The independent observer and the wireless telegraph had outmoded Reuter's methods, just as Reuter's news network and the cable had outmoded the methods of his predecessors. In the early thirties, A.P. broke away completely from the cartel. In 1940 Havas vanished with the French armies. A year later, British newspaper proprietors took over Reuter. In 1942 Mussolini's puppet, Stefani, disappeared, to be succeeded by the Agenzia Nazionale Stampa Associata, modeled along the lines of A.P. and the new Reuter; and the co-operative association, Agence France Presse, rose from the ruins of the venal Havas. The fall of Deutsche Nachrichten Buro and the Japanese Domei in 1945 left only Spain's E.F.E. and the Russian agency Tass in the field of openly government-controlled news services.

There is every reason to suppose that the development of wireless multiple-address press and voice broadcasting, together capable of carrying tens of thousands of words and scores of pictures daily to literally every corner of the globe at a fraction of a cent a word, will encourage a quantitative flow of information such as the world has never known. It is now possible, mechanically at least, for any publication to receive the equivalent of a hundred thousand words of foreign news daily. The ideal of trained observers roaming the universe, writing freely and fully of what they see and feel, presses impatiently against political barriers which, ironically, bid fair to stifle the flow of information in some areas at the precise moment that science has elected to make the widest flow physically practicable. Will the "irresistible" ideal shatter against the "immovable" barriers? There will be times in the near future when it will seem to in certain areas. But there will be more times and more areas where the barriers will give way. As with any other, this particular ideal will prevail to the extent that men persist through disappointment and compromise.

III. Barriers in Transmission

What are the artificial barriers that impede the flow across national borders of informational raw materials? The shortcomings of the present telecommunications systems have been stressed. Obviously, the most reliable news service in the world cannot reach those who are not reached by cable or wireless; the finest magazines and books and pictures cannot reach those who are not reached by fast plane.

Virtually every nation now forbids foreign radiotelegraph companies the right to maintain their own receiving facilities within its borders. The result is that local companies, usually government owned or controlled, supply reception and internal distribution facilities at whatever rates they can command, with further delays in transmission. Although this situation does not involve multiple-address newscasts or shortwave voice broadcasts (except for automatic relay points) and although radiotelephone has worked out relatively satisfactory reciprocal arrangements for international traffic, it is a serious handicap not only to "trunk-line" news transmissions between two points but also to commercial-message traffic. *What is indicated here is a multilateral agreement, binding all nations to permit authorized wireless telegraph and cable companies (and airlines as well) to maintain suitable terminal facilities wherever they are required, subject only to the regulations binding domestic companies, or to maintain nondiscriminatory two-way connections between its own and foreign companies, as has been developed for wireless telephony.* The Bermuda agreements marked a step in this direction.

The need for automatic wireless relay points has been mentioned. These could be obtained through year-to-year leasing of foreign-owned facilities. But wartime experience with this device has shown that long-time control of the relay transmitters by the sender is the only completely satisfactory solution short of the setting-up of international relay points to be operated under the control of an international telecommunications union. Pending the more ideal solution, which does not appear to be immediately realizable, *a sound proposal would seem to involve bilateral treaties giving those nations which require relay points extra-territorial privileges under long-term lease.*

IV. Access at the Source

Meantime, there are other and more serious barriers to the free flow of informational raw materials across national frontiers. Discrimination and censorship are the two broad headings that cover those evils of which foreign correspondents (and natives, too, for that matter) most often complain. What do newspapermen mean by these terms?

In Nazi Germany reporters could not wander about at will, writing of what they saw and felt. Doktor Goebbels and his press section gave them stereotyped handouts, took them on stereotyped trips. The parts of Germany and German-occupied lands that they did not see were the special province not merely of German newsmen but of "reliable" German newsmen. The defeat of Germany brought an end to Goebbels; but correspondents may face precisely the same type of discrimination, in varying degree, for a long time to come in Russia and the Russian "spheres" in Europe and Asia and in Spain, China, various Latin-American countries, Saudi Arabia, and certain parts of the British, French, Belgian, and Netherlands empires.

It is characteristic of the one-party type of government to fear criticism and to make provisions to exclude it, on the pious ground that not all reporters have the mental capacity to criticize fairly. This is the antithesis of the democratic view. Experience in the United States, Canada, the United Kingdom, Australia and New Zealand, France, Belgium, the Netherlands, Denmark, Norway, Sweden, and Switzerland has built up a reassuring body of evidence that unfair critics sooner or later defeat their own purposes. It may be useless to try to convince Russia and the others that this is so. The Russians already have made it clear that they think Americans and Britons are foolish to permit newsmen so much freedom, and they can quote more than one recent instance of our newsmen's harmful irresponsibility. Reminders from friendly British and American newspapermen that secrecy in itself is likely to breed unwarranted suspicion and give rise to imaginative "news stories" about Russia of the familiar type which, in the twenties and thirties, usually bore Riga datelines apparently do not move the Narkomindell.

This is a problem that will have to be faced and solved. For no news coverage that includes only the "official" versions of events in Russia, Poland, Rumania, Bulgaria, Yugoslavia, Spain, China, Argentina, Iran, Syria and the Lebanon, Palestine, Arabia, Algeria, Tunisia, Morocco, French Equatorial Africa, the Congo, British India, the Malay States, the Netherlands Indies, and Indo-China can pretend to the labels "global" or "complete." The problem is not made easier by the fact that everyone knows that the so-called "free-press" countries sometimes preach more zealously than they practice. Britain, for instance, is a conspicuous example of the paradox that distinguishes between the mother-country and its more "backward" dependencies. However much freedom a newspaperman, foreign or native, may enjoy in the British Isles, the moment he sets foot in India he is in another world. The same contrast is noticeable as between metropolitan France and, say, Syria. Even the benevolent and highly democratic Dutch become "security"-minded when a roving newsman debarks at Batavia or Willemstad.

This is not to say that discrimination was never the practice in the mother-countries. In pre-1939 Britain, France, and many another land by tradition devoted to the principle of a free press, it was not uncommon for government officials to show marked preference to a few hand-picked native reporters and even fewer foreigners. The London papers, for instance, felt the pressure of the Chamberlain government during the appeasement period and responded to it to some extent. The Germans made an effort to systematize this practice. Prior to World War I, a Foreign Office press chief named Hammann was permitted to organize a loose affiliation of a few chosen German newspapermen to "interpret" German foreign policy to the German people. The plan does not appear to have been an unqualified success, in part because newspapers which were left out tended to become even more critical and also because the favored few, which happened to include liberal Opposition papers, frequently declined to follow the official line.

The Hammann technique per se will not be tolerated by most newspapermen. But favoritism for individuals (and sometimes even for groups) is widely practiced not only by all governments (including our own) but by private corporations and individuals as well. Actually, newspapermen connive at forming such useful contacts. Indeed, one suspects that the clamor against discrimination of this sort is loudest from those who have been outwitted by it. It becomes impressive only when, as in Russia, it affects all foreigners equally and thus becomes an instrument of anti-internationalism. It is less impressive when newspapermen roll the phrase "equal and unhampered access to all" off their tongues; for every newspaperman must know that equal access would reduce every story to a mass press conference or a mimeographed handout.

What newspapermen really want is what Kent Cooper, executive director of A.P., calls "the right to roam the world at will, writing freely of what they see and feel." This is quite a different thing. It means that what they want is an equal opportunity to use their wits to create *unequal* access. Within that rather broad framework, they want assurances that certain areas will not be open habitually to the few and closed to the many; that news-givers will carefully distinguish between timely news breaks and background material and will confine their special favors to the latter field; and that in the case of "hold-for-release" stories the release date will be scrupulously respected. Newsmen are not always sure even of these things, for in essence these things represent a compromise between the ever warring considerations of security and opportunity that beset anyone engaged in highly competitive private industry. Sorely tempted, a *New York Times*'s Raymond Daniell will join a pool to receive Army favors; a *New York Herald Tribune*'s Theodore Wallen will beseech a Calvin Coolidge to make an "I do not choose to run" news break exclusive; an A.P.'s Edward Kennedy will double-cross his colleagues by breaking a release date. In sum, carte blanche is the maximum that newsmen dream about, equality of opportunity the minimum for which they will settle.

Either is, of course, more difficult of achievement than mere equal access. Both suggest the need for a degree of organized responsibility on the part of newsmen from which they shrink, using the excuse that freedom of the press does not permit of much self-discipline. The apparent paradox has been shrewdly remarked by the Russians; and there is reason to believe that, as long as it persists, it will be a convenient barrier for Moscow to raise against the democracies in the field of international communication. To press for mass interviews and stereotyped handouts, simply because Russia would be more likely to grant such a demand than any other, would be a disservice alike to the correspondents and to their readers. One is tempted to conclude that any deviation from the expressed ultimate goal of "the right to roam the world at will" would lend credence to Moscow's charge that what the newsmen of the democracies are after is simply a chance to make a little more money. A more honorable strategy would appear to be to hold out for the maximum while admonishing the correspondents to grow up to it and, at the same time, frankly recognize that unsettled conditions during the next few years will not be conducive to achievement of the maximum. *This would seem to involve urging a multilateral accord guaranteeing equality of access as between nationals and foreigners*—knowing that the more enterprising in both categories would use that type of equality to get ahead of their fellows.

How, in the meantime, could those who wish to roam the world and write (or photograph) meet the objection of irresponsibility? *One way might be to tighten the foreign correspondents' corps; adopt a code of professional behavior; and require all newsmen, magazine writers, radio people, authors, and photographers to join the corps and observe the code. Appeals from decisions of a government could be taken by the whole corps rather than by an individual, either to the foreign diplomatic corps or to an appropriate unit of the United Nations Economic and Social Council.* A resolute move in this direction might dispose of the contradiction of newsmen asking for group protection while at the same time declining to organize group responsibility.

V. Censorship

The right to roam the world at all, writing freely, would seem to imply also the right to get what is written to the market. Here we run into another barrier—censorship. Actually, censorship begins at the level of discrimination at the source. But in general usage it is taken to mean the emasculation or total suppression of written and printed matter, pictures and films, and words spoken over a microphone or telephone.

Here, again, the authoritarian powers have been the worst offenders. Before the war, Russia, China, Spain, Portugal, Italy, Germany, Japan, and a number of Latin-American countries openly practiced deletion and suppression. But they did not practice it in the same way. Whereas in Russia correspondents were summoned to discuss cuts and suppressions with the censor who had made them and on occasion were even able to argue him into restoring some of them, in Italy they never knew until they had a chance to check with their home offices from outside what had got through.

More than frank and open censorship itself, newsmen detest the subtler forms. In a sense they have become hardened to a degree of the forthright variety (when a government or corporation official says "Now that's strictly off the record, boys," he automatically becomes a censor); but the honest, conscientious ones will never become resigned to a mixture of censorship, evasion, intimidation, and deceit. They do not like being visited by police who want to "check their papers." They do not like being beaten up in dark alleys. They do not like having their dispatches lie around in telegraph offices until, like ripe fruit, they have lost all market value. They do not like having their houses searched, their families annoyed or terrorized. They do not like clumsy offers of bribes or subtle hints that they might last longer if they were "more correct." But what they like least of all is being forever in the dark, never knowing what the "rules" are, always wondering when they go to work in the morning what they will be able to "get away with" on that particular day.

What can be done to abolish, or at any rate curb, censorship? A *logical first step might be to press for a multilateral agreement pledging the signatories to keep newsmen informed of the rules by which they expect to operate and to abide by them.* If such an agreement could be reached, the climate might encourage *a second and simultaneous step: agreement to limit censorship wherever and as long as it exists to the open deletion or suppression of dispatches in the presence of the writer.* There is little reason to suppose that Russia, which appears to be the key to any multilateral agreement of this sort, would refuse to adhere to either of these provisions. At a favorable moment Moscow might even subscribe to *a third condition: right of appeal by the writer to the correspondents' corps and through it to the United Nations Economic and Social Council.* Meantime, with the ultimate goal of complete abolition of censorship always before us, we could whittle away at the Russian variety, *either through limited multilateral agreement or through a series of bilateral treaties*—although it must be obvious that the former would almost certainly be interpreted by Russia as a revived manifestation of the *cordon sanitaire.*

VI. Barriers in Distribution

The right to roam and write would seem to imply not only the right to get to the market what is written but also the right to sell it there without unjust discrimination. This brings us to another barrier: insistence on interposing a middleman (usually government-controlled) between the wholesaler (press association, news-picture agency, or feature syndicate) and the retailer (newspaper, magazine, or radio station). A.P., U.P., I.N.S., Reuter, A.N.S.A., and A.F.P. have recently announced that henceforth they will deal only with reputable individual newspapers, magazines, and radio stations or with bona fide associations of reputable newspapers, magazines, and radio stations. Anesta of the Netherlands, the Swedish Tidningarnas Telegrambyrå, and several other European agencies are expected to fall into line with this stern decision, aimed at preventing the reappearance of anything like Havas or the old Reuter. *Except for bilateral pacts, which would have the effect of blessing such arrangements*, it is difficult to see what might be accomplished by formal convention at this time, since, obviously, those who wish to do business in Russia and China will be obliged to deal with government agencies, as A.P. and Reuter are doing. One factor which ought to do much to discourage middleman monopolies is multiple-address newscasting, which will bring uncensored news to the very borders of monopoly-ridden countries—and even enable the more daring publishers there, by listening in, to check what their governments give them against what the rest of the world is getting.

What of finished products in international communication, as distinguished from the raw material and semifinished goods? How are newspapers, magazines, books, short-wave radio programs, and motion pictures to be circulated across national frontiers in greater numbers? What are the barriers that presently limit this useful flow?

THE PRINTED WORD

The circulation of printed newspapers across national frontiers dates back to the very beginning of newspaperdom, when every ship brought weeks-old copies from foreign ports which were eagerly scanned by government bureaus and liberally borrowed from by editors who had no better way of getting foreign news. Except for limited areas divided by political but not language barriers or as between mother-countries and their colonies, newspapers were not designed for or shipped in sufficient numbers to reach mass audiences directly. With the development of press agencies, editors began to watch for them less eagerly. In the latter part of the nineteenth century a handful of ambitious publishers founded foreign editions, notably James Gordon Bennett's *New York Herald* and Lord Northcliffe's *London Daily Mail*, both in Paris. But these were edited for, and distributed among, nationals of the countries of origin living abroad; and those natives who deciphered them in the hope of improving their knowledge of other peoples were not usually repaid for their pains. After 1900 a number of independent papers like the *Japan Advertiser*, the *Shanghai Post and Mercury*, and the *Manila Times* were launched by and for aliens of the countries in which they were published. Not until the mid-1930's did it occur to governments to try to reach foreign mass audiences directly through the press—and even then the Germans, Italians, Russians, and Japanese preferred the time-honored technique of hiding behind the mastheads of local organs.

The interchange of printed magazines followed much the same pattern. In the 1920's, however, a number of British, American, and German magazine publishers went into the foreign market with the idea of reaching foreigners rather than expatriates. Their publications fell into two classes: women's magazines like the British Amalgamated group's *Woman's World*, which tried a Paris edition; Condé Nast's British and French *Vogue* and French *Jardin des Modes* (German and Spanish *Vogues* were launched in the thirties, quickly scuttled when they did not pan out); Hearst's British editions of *Good Housekeeping, Harper's Bazaar*, and *Connoisseur*; the German *Die Dame*, which circulated widely in Switzerland and eastern Europe—and "pulps" like Macfadden's British, French, German, and Swedish editions of *True Story*.

The war and a number of technical developments have wrought many changes in the techniques of circulating printed newspapers and magazines. Governments were brought into the international publishing business on a scale hitherto undreamed of—thanks in no small part, to the amazing recent improvements in aviation and offset printing. The German *Signal* at one time boasted a circulation of 7,000,000 outside Germany. Up to 1945 the O.W.I.'s *Victory*, by then jointly sponsored by *Collier's*, had sold 26,-000,000 copies in fifteen languages in forty-six countries. The O.I.A.A.'s *En Guardia* had sold 8,000,000 in two languages in sixteen countries. A score of British and Russian publications had reached comparable totals. Moreover, the war (as well as technological improvements) has supplied the spur to a number of private publishers. Thus, at the beginning of 1946, *Reader's Digest* was printing British, Spanish (for Spain), Spanish (for Latin America), Portuguese (for Portugal), Portuguese (for Brazil), Swedish and Finnish-language editions. *Time, Life*, and *Newsweek* had fourteen, one, and five foreign editions, respectively. *Magazine Digest*, a rapidly growing Canadian monthly, seven-eighths of whose 1,250,000 readers live in the United States, was going forward with plans for several foreign-language editions. The *New York Herald Tribune* and the *London Daily Mail* had revived their Paris editions. The *London Times* was flying a pony edition (greatly reduced in size and printed on thin stock) around the world.

But there were evidences of contraction as well as expansion. The *New York Post*, which entered the Paris afternoon field in August, 1945, was withdrawing for want of American readers. And the *New York Times* apparently had abandoned plans for world-wide facsimile circulation, possibly because its experiments with a facsimile edition at the San Francisco United Nations Conference, while mechanically successful and of great value to the conference, raised a cry of "invasion" from Coast newspapers that caused the A.P. to withdraw the use of its leased wire, over which the edition had been transmitted.

The immediate future for international circulation of newspapers and magazines is far from clear. Government publications (in the United States, at any rate—although the State Department was temporarily continuing *Amerika*, published especially for Russia) did not survive the war. On the other hand, there is an embarrassment of mechanical alternatives which clouds the picture. The sheer bulk and weight of standard-size publications makes their shipment in large quantities by air impracticable. Thus publishers must choose between flying pony editions and printing abroad. Those who elect to print abroad will have a variety of means for getting their copy and pictures to the plant. Whole pages in as many as four colors and in any desired language can be dispatched by wireless in a few minutes. Time, Incorporated, has developed a secret mat of the color and consistency of cellophane, which compresses an entire issue of *Time* or *Life* into a packet which a plane pilot could store in his cap. Printing plates for rotary or flat-bed presses can be pulled with equal facility from facsimile prints or the *Time* mats.

Thus the ease with which periodicals now can be whisked across national borders opens up a prospect of lively competition in this field. What barriers are the enterprising publishers likely to encounter? And how seriously should we take them?

One may eliminate the normal problems that beset foreign-owned business in any country: taxes, licensing, labor troubles, the complicated mechanics of nonpostal distribution which sometimes even in this country involve the payment of premiums to handlers and dealers, local laws requiring the hiring of a certain percentage of natives, and the like. Publishers have somehow got around such obstacles in the past. It is possible that here and there they will be treated worse than native publishers. When that happens, the wise publisher will set up a native subsidiary, with a few prominent native leaders on its board, as Condé Nast did in Paris and London before the war; or publish in a smaller but conveniently located country where the attitude toward business is benevolent, as *Reader's Digest* is doing in Cuba.

Political action is indicated only where discrimination becomes intolerable, where governments go beyond the standards of decency and good taste in exercising arbitrary censorship, where governments attempt to obtain corporate control through what amount to confiscation proceedings, or where governments flatly forbid foreign publishers to print or circulate their products. All but the last are susceptible of immediate regulation by treaty—a multilateral covenant setting the general framework and bilateral treaties dealing with details and special circumstances. It would appear that the opening-up of closed areas must be solved by the patient negotiation of bilateral agreements involving reciprocal inducements not necessarily falling within the mass-communication-field. (A whole list of provisos involving freedom of the press might be tied to Russia's request for rehabilitation loans, for example; it is even possible that such a suggestion would spread less consternation at the Kremlin than in some of the democratic chancelleries.) Diplomatic representatives will be expected, as in the past, to defend the legitimate interests of their countrymen with vigor; but it must be understood by the merchants who take their chances in foreign commerce that any consul or minister would be embarrassed by a request to protest a type of trade-protectionism that has become well-nigh universal.

The flow of books across national frontiers has followed a discernible pattern for the last century, with Britain, Germany, France, and Spain vying for leadership and the United States trailing far behind even such smaller countries as Sweden, Switzerland, and the Netherlands. (In 1941, the last year for which even round-number figures are available, the comparative gross export and re-export figures were: Germany, $35,000,000; Britain, $16,000,000; Spain, $10,000,000; France, $9,000,000; Switzerland, $4,500,000; Sweden, $3,500,000; the Netherlands, $3,000,000; United States, $800,000.) In general this has reflected a combination of language advantages (the Swiss, Swedes, and Dutch have worked extensively in German) and a spirit of enterprise. The Germans believed that if they bombarded school children with scientific and technical books, the children would grow up thinking of Germany as the logical supplier of the types of goods advertised therein. The British, for two centuries blessed with a virtual monopoly of the market for books originally written in English, were a little slow to see the literal truth of the Leipzig *Börsenverein*'s slogan, "Trade follows the book," but are rapidly making amends for their omission. Both British and American publishers were slow to match Spain's traditional cultural ties with Latin America and France's cultural ties with the whole literate world by launching their campaign to make English the lingua franca of the twentieth century. Indeed, it might fairly be said that American publishers were slow to see the value of book exports from any standpoint. No other satisfactory reason can be found for the fact that they allowed themselves to be maneuvered into a position with respect to reprint and translation rights which returns them less than an equitable share of the republisher's profit or for their failure to obtain United States adherence to some equitable international copyright agreement.

The explanation for the adverse reprint situation may have been at one time historically sound. In the early days of our country, we were almost wholly dependent on Europe for books. Until toward the close of the last century the number of books by American authors wanted in Europe was so small compared to the number of books by European authors wanted in America that publishers in this country readily agreed to terms that injured both them and their writers. When the tide began to change, American authors took matters into their own hands and extracted royalty arrangements from the British which made them quite independent of any action by American publishers. The publishers, in consequence, took no action, since they regarded the export business as a "2 per cent nuisance" anyway. By this same spirit of indifference, American publishers for fifty-seven years have permitted the objections, first of the Typesetters Union and latterly of the radio-broadcasting industry, to keep the United States almost alone among leading nations from adhering to the Berne Convention—with the result that American publishers have lost tangible tens of thousands of dollars through the wholesale pirating, notably by the Dutch and Chinese, of books entirely without legal protection outside the United States and its possessions, and with the further result that the United States has permitted the pirating of foreign authors—a circumstance which seriously dilutes American claims to morality and a respect for culture. The Berne Convention is a model of the kind of international agreement which eliminates barriers in a whole area of mass communication. It provides simply that books copyrighted in any signatory country are protected by the copyright in all other signatory countries.

The coming of the cheap paper-bound reprint edition in this country, which has already lowered the forbidding price barrier to mass circulation of books in many countries, may make it possible for more books to flow across national borders than ever before. Aside from the restrictions imposed by different countries operating on different economies, which mean different levels of costs, there are copyright as well as sales-rights restrictions which now bar the free importation of books from one country to another. Already, Sweden and Switzerland are contending for the former German markets. France is waiting only for paper to double her exports. Backed by the British Council, a quasi-governmental body with a "book exploitation" fund of £400,000 sterling, British publishers are off to a good start, and it is rumored that they have plans for world markets. The question mark is the United States, for American publishers can hold the key to the most vexing problems: pirating (nonpayment of royalties where copyright protection is lost through technicalities or carelessness), varying royalty rates based on the selling price of the book, and difference in quality of manufacturing and in costs; and there is a question as to whether the rivalry between British and American publishers may become a dog-eat-dog struggle or a co-operative venture based on allocation of world markets. The chief bones of contention are Australia, New Zealand, and Latin America and possibly the Union of South Africa (the British are practically reconciled to seeing Canada in the American orbit). All these, in addition to the United Kingdom and Eire, to which American publishers lay no claim, together with the United States, form the best markets for English-language books and a consequent exchange of ideas and cultural products.

What appears to be indicated here is an early and amicable settlement of the Anglo-American rivalry, followed by an international copyright and reprint conference at which Britain and the United States would stand together for some formula designed to increase the flow of the books of all nations. The simplest, most forthright formula that suggests itself would involve a rule-of-thumb determination that any piece of literature would remain for a period of years (author's life plus fifty years) the joint property of the author and the original publishers, in all languages and in all countries, effective means to curb pirating; the abolition of block sales, tie-in sales, introductory discounts, and all other unfair competitive devices; establishment of the principle that any publisher has the right to place any original product in any language on any bookstall in any country, subject only to the circumstances governing native publishers—i.e., his ability to persuade the dealer to handle the book at the agreed-on price and discount; a strict limitation on the categories of books that may be sold abroad at below cost or through any other form of dealer subsidy, plus an equally strict limitation on the number of copies of any one title that may be so offered; and an agreement to confine government-inspired gifts of books to schools, libraries, and learned societies. Admittedly, this is an imposing assignment. But when one balances the importance of books as instruments of understanding against the realization that the total book export trade is measured in terms of tens of millions of dollars, it is difficult to see how the governments and publishers involved could justify a less resolute course.

INTERNATIONAL BROADCASTS

The projection across national boundaries of voice broadcasts is, as has been noted, largely a phenomenon of the thirties, although amateurs have been experimenting with short wave for two decades or more. International broadcasting does not necessarily connote direct broadcasting, as nations can exchange programs by mail, cable, radiotelegraph, or radiotelephone for rebroadcast over local facilities. Before the war, American stations concentrated on this method for reaching Latin America, leaving Germany, Britain, Russia, France, and Japan to bring direct short- or medium-wave broadcasting to a peak never approached in the Western Hemisphere.

As has been remarked, the future of international broadcasting is somewhat clouded, although it seems certain that the British, spurred by the wartime expansion of the government-operated B.B.C., will want to saturate as much as possible of the world with direct programming built around straight news, as well as commentary with the British point of view; and that Russia, France, and perhaps also the Netherlands, Belgium, Spain, and Portugal (because of their colonial or cultural ties abroad) will be extremely active in this field. Except for lack of adequate automatic relay points—the unique concern of American broadcasters—barriers to international broadcasting include the possibility that certain nations which are not particularly interested in it may seek to prevent the allocation of sufficient frequencies in the short-wave bands; the unregulated use of outlaw stations in small countries like Luxembourg or Tangier; jamming by clandestine transmitters; limitation of the manufacture or use of receiving sets capable of picking up direct short wave; and, in the field of reciprocal broadcasting, a disinclination on the part of certain countries, notably our own, to allocate adequate time-periods to this type of service. *It would appear that most if not all these barriers could be leveled in time by the In-*

ternational Radio and other conferences presently charged with adjusting such matters—particularly if the conference machinery is brought within the framework of the United Nations Organization and thus given the authority of that body.*

MOTION-PICTURE EXPORTS

The history of the international flow of motion pictures is unique. From the end of the first World War, when earlier bids for mastery by the Swedes and later the British had subsided, until recently, the flow was almost entirely one way: from Hollywood to every habitable part of the globe. From the early 1920's until the mid-thirties, a score of countries seeking to establish their own infant industries fought Hollywood's domination without success. The most obvious government subsidy and protection could not obscure the fact that Hollywood had the most successful writers, the most skilful directors, the ablest cameramen, the best-known stars, and, because it paid the highest salaries, the best chance of picking off foreign stars as soon as they began to show promise. In vain did governments raise import duties and taxes on the operations of those distributing agencies they could reach, institute quotas which required that a certain number of homemade pictures be shown for every American import, devise elaborate fees for the dubbing-in of sound-track in the language of the country by native artists, and extend loans to their own producers. The foreign public wanted Hollywood films and was prepared to make trouble for any government that sought to shut them off altogether. Foreign exhibitors wanted full houses so they could pay their rent, and their landlords wanted the rent. As an example of how a uniquely popular product can override the stiffest protectionism, Hollywood's success was to be compared with that of the French dressmakers and perfume manufacturers.

The coming of talking pictures proved to be a turning-point. Pantomimists like Charlie Chaplin and Buster Keaton, who had been the idols of all the world, dropped from their pinnacles. The emphasis in Hollywood shifted from gesturing to fast-paced dialogue, much of it in an idiom that defied translation. Musical pictures became practicable for the first time. And for the first time Hollywood's rivals found themselves able to compete on something approaching equal terms. Who could sing German *lieder* better than a German? Who could tickle Gallic risibilities better than a Frenchman? It remained only to learn how to produce better pictures mechanically; and in the thirties British and French cameramen and directors who had been concentrating on national audiences began to switch to Hollywood's tried and true formulas to win international favor. Rising young stars like Michael Redgrave, Ralph Richardson, Googie Withers, Esmond Knight, Jean Gabin, and Michele Morgan and veterans like Raimu and Louis Jouvet turned their backs on Hollywood gold (it was the

* Through Telstar, international television is now a reality. (Ed.)

fall of France, not the lure of riches, that brought Gabin and Mlle. Morgan to this country).

The result was better pictures. But the trend was established so shortly before the outbreak of war that few persons even in Hollywood realize the extent to which it is now likely to accelerate after the war. Russian and Swedish, as well as British and French, pictures are improving. Mexico has built up a thriving industry which already is giving American distributors some trouble in Latin America. There is little question that Hollywood is in for a type of competition that will make discriminatory government edicts all the more burdensome. The Department of Commerce listed fifty-eight separate legal restrictions adversely affecting Hollywood's export business at the outset of the war. Few have since been rescinded. Indeed, in the United Kingdom, France, and the Netherlands they have been added to and stiffened. The United Artists' general manager for South Africa, returning in August, 1945, from a fifty-thousand-mile tour of Africa, the Middle East, India, and China, reported that, although American films still were received enthusiastically, new and complex barriers were being raised against them. He discovered that the Russians were financing construction of theaters in several countries through "extremely lenient long-term loans" made with the condition that the theater-owners devote at least 15 per cent of their programs to Soviet pictures.

From the standpoint of promoting the circulation of motion pictures as instruments of understanding, it is difficult to see what can be done—or should be done—to arrest this righting of the balance. The effect of the present trend may very well be to give Americans and others a chance to see more British, Canadian, Swedish, French, Russian, and Latin-American films; and it could scarcely be argued that this would be a bad thing for international understanding. Moreover, the American film industry cannot boast, as can the American press associations, for example, that it leads the world in informational quality. Whatever Hollywood may say about our being admired throughout the world because we have not consciously tried to put our best foot forward in films, the consensus of Americans who lived and traveled abroad during the period between the wars seems to be that American movies have hindered more than furthered an understanding of us.[1] Finally, the United States is hardly in a position to lead a crusade for free trade.

[1] The war product of Hollywood seems not to have overcome these past shortcomings. Interesting in this connection is a recent comprehensive, detailed review of all of the Hollywood war films released during 1942, 1943, and 1944, by Dorothy Jones in the *Hollywood Quarterly*, written from the standpoint of their contribution at home and abroad to an understanding of the conflict. The survey comes to the conclusion that only 4 per cent of the entire output and 10 per cent of the "war" pictures themselves made any such contribution. Although Mrs. Jones found some of the best "war" pictures to be constructive in building understanding among the United Nations and in dramatizing honestly the fine job being done by American fighting men, she concluded that the bulk gave a distorted and inadequate portrayal of the enemy; failed deplorably

The agreements reached during the summer of 1945 between J. Arthur Rank, the outstanding British film distributor and theater-owner, with various Hollywood interests may indicate a significant trend. These include the organization, with Pathe Industries, Incorporated, of Eagle Lion Films to distribute ten American and ten British films a year throughout the world; and the organization, with the Universal Pictures Corporation, of which Rank owns 20 per cent, and International Pictures, of the United World Pictures Company, which will distribute eight pictures from each country annually, for the most part the products of independent producers. Both agreements contemplate an extensive exchange of writing, producing, directing, and acting talent between the two countries; and it is possible that French producers may be drawn into what would seem to be taking the form of an international motion-picture cartel.

PRESS TREATIES

The problem of barriers to mass communication across national borders must be attacked from the national and international viewpoints, not alone that of industry. It must be attacked in a framework of reality. *The first step would appear to be to stake out an area of international agreement sufficiently specific to be meaningful, yet not so all-inclusive that some nations would decline to sign the whole because of objection to a part.*

As has been indicated, *such an area might cover guaranties of the right of all authorized telecommunications companies to operate everywhere with the same lack of discrimination as is accorded movement of the mails; guaranties of equal access at equal rates to all telecommunications and air-mail facilities; guaranties of access of accredited foreign observers to news and other information sources on an equal basis with nationals; satisfactory revision of existing copyright and reprint law and practice; and abolition of all forms of indirect censorship. It might also cover guaranties against arbitrary expulsion; a pledge that all governments will plainly label media owned and operated by them and that they will refrain from the more flagrant forms of propaganda.*[2]

---

in portraying and interpreting the roles of management and labor in winning the war; tended to ridicule, exaggerate, or sensationalize home-front problems; gave unfortunate portrayals of our fighting forces through slapstick treatment or overuse of the swash-buckling American hero conquering single-handed. Interesting, too, is a report from Teheran that 80 per cent of the Hollywood films stockpiled for postwar reissue in Iran were westerns and gangsters; the Russians gave Iran their best.

2 The existing international law of propaganda forms a starting-point from which both multilateral and bilateral treaties can proceed. It is accepted as law, although a "law" flagrantly violated in pre-war international radio broadcasting, that the government of a sovereign state is bound to refrain from spreading propaganda hostile to a foreign country in that country during times of peace. International law is not so settled as to the responsibility of a government with respect to private propaganda activity proceeding from its territory. Lawyers of nineteenth-century European Continental states and more recently in Latin America have attempted to establish governmental responsibility for

The balance—abolition of direct censorship; abolition of discriminatory taxes, tariffs, quotas, and fees; and guaranties of the right of any authorized dealer in mass media to buy and sell without interference from his government—might for the present better be left to bilateral treaties.

---

private propaganda similar to that established for the acts of government. Anglo-American legal opinion and practice, however, have sharply restricted responsibility over private persons and groups to the prevention of organized acts of force in the form of military expeditions and plots for assassination of political figures in a foreign country. Beyond that, these governments recognize no international law creating governmental responsibility with respect to private propaganda activities proceeding from their territory. Such responsibility, however, is at times voluntarily assumed by reciprocal provisions in bilateral treaties. The line between governmental and private propaganda activity is broadly defined so as to include under "government" organizations and agencies receiving governmental subsidy or assistance.

9

THE MOTIVATION OF ASSENT

John Kenneth Galbraith
THE DEPENDENCE EFFECT

Leonard W. Doob
THE NATURE OF PROPAGANDA

Charles S. Steinberg
PUBLIC RELATIONS AND MASS COMMUNICATION

9

THE MOTIVATION OF ASSENT

NEITHER advertising nor public relations is, as such, a medium of mass communication. Yet, both are integral facets of the whole process of mass communication and neither advertising nor public relations techniques could be practiced without the availability and utilization of the mass media. Similarly, while propaganda may be one of the oldest professions, it has acquired a new look owing to the fact that the process and strategy of persuasion can now reach more people more quickly than ever before in history.

The influence of advertising in the American economy has been the subject of a vast body of research and analysis, one of the most notable studies being Professor Neil Borden's definitive work on the economic effects of advertising. Certainly, the contribution of advertising to a competitive mercantile economy is recognized even by those who deplore so-called "Madison Avenue" techniques. But it is the economic base of advertising which has permitted such mass media as television and the press, among other, to provide a unique and unfettered service to the American people —particularly in the contribution of news and public affairs programming in the broadcasting industry.

The point of view toward advertising of John Kenneth Galbraith coheres with the general point of view presented in his widely-discussed volume *The Affluent Society*. At first blush, Galbraith's convictions would not seem to have any direct bearing on the media of mass communication. Yet, one of the basic theses of his book—the creation of wants we do not need to fill needs which are fabricated—has a significant relevance to some contemporary advertising, promotional and publicity techniques. In his presentation of the "dependence effect" Galbraith indicates that, contrary to what it ought to be, the economy as it is now structured creates wants where wants need not exist. Meanwhile, other urgent areas and needs go largely unfulfilled. This is Galbraith's argument against the "conventional wisdom" which is an anachronism in terms of society today.

Our wants, therefore, are self-contrived. This is a phenomenon which can be juxtaposed with the process of mass persuasion, and particularly through the use of techniques of motivation research in order to increase the effectiveness of advertising. The problem posed is that, in the very satisfaction of wants, unnecessary wants are being created. Advertising, according to Galbraith, contributes to this process. As an adjunct of the production-distribution process, advertising urges the public to satisfy its wants by continuously creating a need for more.

Still, the contribution of advertising to the economic growth of the nation cannot be denied. It is advertising and promotion carried to excess, rather than fulfilling their legitimate functions, which creates a problem in values and ethics. For Galbraith, then, the affluent society involves a vicious cycle. Production satisfies wants and, paradoxically, in the very act of satisfying these wants, it creates additional wants artificially. Advertising's part in this process is that it helps to create desires—not only implicit ones, but those which did not exist, thereby adding to the complexity of the vicious cycle. Galbraith's point of view can perhaps be summed up in this paradox: Can wants be very urgent if they can be artificially stimulated by advertising? Would motivation be needed if wants were inherent?

In another, but related, context Professor Leonard Doob discusses the essence of propaganda. There is an immediate difficulty in any attempt to reach a hard and fast definition of the "propagandist," for the term yields easily to stereotyping. If the propagandist is defined as one who influences others, certainly the educator influences others. Obviously, however, there are basic and qualitative differences. There is no doubt that the term "propaganda" in this country takes on negative overtones and often yields to such euphemisms as "information specialist," "psychological warfare," and so forth.

Doob points out that the process by which "true" education is distinguished from propaganda is really a value judgment, involving basic philosophical distinctions between good and bad, right and wrong. Certainly, even formal education, administered in terms of an accepted curriculum, is not without its normative overtones or value judgments. Moreover, there is a basic difference between natural science and social science, the former being verifiable while the latter may not be subject to empirical verification. Since mass media belong more properly in the area of the social sciences, it is easy to see what problems can arise in the determination of what is meant by "All The News That's Fit To Print" and similar value judgments. It should be pointed out, however, that most social scientists would not accept Doob's conclusion that the social sciences do not belong in the broad area of education, since the author's definition of education as being purely "scientific" is limited.

The fact is that, while there are basic differences between education and propaganda, as the author indicates, the social sciences are an admixture of both education and propaganda because, frequently, they present fact heavily overlaid with opinion. Doob properly points out that only a dictatorship is free from propaganda in a literal sense, because there is only one "truth" and only one system of values. Paradoxically, propaganda may be an evil, but it is a necessary one in a free society. There must be a distinction, too, between intentional and unintentional propaganda. The intentional propagandist makes a conscious effort to control behavior. The unintentional propagandist is unwitting, and Doob makes the interesting point that the latter has greater access to media of mass communication because his motives tend to go unsuspected and unknown.

* * * *

RELATED READING

Allport, Gordon, and Postman, Leo J. "The Basic Psychology of Rumor," *Transactions of the New York Academy of Sciences*, VIII (1945), Series II, 61-81.

Brembeck, W. L., & Howell, W. S. *Persuasion*. New York: Prentice-Hall, 1952.

Childs, H. L., & Whitton, J. B. (eds.). *Propaganda by Short Wave*. Princeton: Princeton Univ. Press, 1942.

Doob, Leonard W. *Propaganda: Its Psychology and Technique*. New York: Holt, 1935.

Hovland, C. I., Janis, I. L., & Kelley, H. H. *Communication and Persuasion*. New Haven: Yale Univ. Press, 1953.

Lucas, D. B., & Benson, C. E. "Some sales results for positive and negative advertisements." *J. Appl. Psychol.*, 1930, 14, 363-370.

Lucas, D. B., & Britt, S. H. *Advertising Psychology and Research*. New York: McGraw-Hill, 1950.

THE DEPENDENCE EFFECT

By John Kenneth Galbraith

―――――

I

THE NOTION that wants do not become less urgent the more amply the individual is supplied is broadly repugnant to common sense. It is something to be believed only by those who wish to believe. Yet the conventional wisdom must be tackled on its own terrain. Intertemporal comparisons of an individual's state of mind do rest on doubtful grounds. Who can say for sure that the deprivation which afflicts him with hunger is more painful than the deprivation which afflicts him with envy of his neighbor's new car? In the time that has passed since he was poor his soul may have become subject to a new and deeper searing. And where a society is concerned, comparisons between marginal satisfactions when it is poor and those when it is affluent will involve not only the same individual at different times but different individuals at different times. The scholar who wishes to believe that with increasing affluence there is no reduction in the urgency of desires and goods is not without points for debate. However plausible the case against him, it cannot be proven. In the defense of the conventional wisdom this amounts almost to invulnerability.

However, there is a flaw in the case. If the individual's wants are to be urgent they must be original with himself. They cannot be urgent if they must be contrived for him. And above all they must not be contrived by the process of production by which they are satisfied. For this means that the whole case for the urgency of production, based on the urgency of wants, falls to the ground. One cannot defend production as satisfying wants if that production creates the wants.

Were it so that a man on arising each morning was assailed by demons which instilled in him a passion sometimes for silk shirts, sometimes for kitchenware, sometimes for chamber pots, and sometimes for orange squash, there would be every reason to applaud the effort to find the goods, however odd, that quenched this flame. But should it be that his passion was the result of his first having cultivated the demons, and should it also be that his effort to allay it stirred the demons to ever greater and greater effort, there would be question as to how rational was his solution. Unless restrained by conventional attitudes, he might wonder if the solution lay with more goods or fewer demons.

So it is that if production creates the wants it seeks to satisfy, or if the wants emerge *pari passu* with the production, then the urgency of the wants can no longer be used to defend the urgency of the production. Production only fills a void that it has itself created.

II

The point is so central that it must be pressed. Consumer wants can have bizarre, frivolous, or even immoral origins, and an admirable case can still be made for a society that seeks to satisfy them. But the case cannot stand if it is the process of satisfying wants that creates the wants. For then the individual who urges the importance of production to satisfy these wants is precisely in the position of the onlooker who applauds the efforts of the squirrel to keep abreast of the wheel that is propelled by his own efforts.

That wants are, in fact, the fruit of production will now be denied by few serious scholars. And a considerable number of economists, though not always in full knowledge of the implications, have conceded the point. Keynes noted that needs of "the second class," i.e., those that are the result of efforts to keep abreast or ahead of one's fellow being, "may indeed be insatiable; for the higher the general level the higher still are they." And emulation has always played a considerable role in the views of other economists of want creation. One man's consumption becomes his neighbor's wish. This already means that the process by which wants are satisfied is also the process by which wants are created. The more wants that are satisfied the more new ones are born.

However, the argument has been carried farther. A leading modern theorist of consumer behavior, Professor Duesenberry, has stated explicitly that "ours is a society in which one of the principal social goals is a higher standard of living. . . . [This] has great significance for the theory of consumption . . . the desire to get superior goods takes on a life of its own. It provides a drive to higher expenditure which may even be stronger than that arising out of the needs which are supposed to be satisfied by that expenditure." [1] The implications of this view are impressive. The notion of independently established need now sinks into the background. Because the society sets great store by ability to produce a high living standard, it evaluates people by the products they possess. The urge to consume is fathered by the value system which emphasizes the ability of the society to produce. The more that is produced the more that must be owned in order

[1] James S. Duesenberry, *Income, Saving and the Theory of Consumer Behavior* (Cambridge, Mass.: Harvard University Press, 1949), p. 28.

to maintain the appropriate prestige. The latter is an important point, for, without going as far as Duesenberry in reducing goods to the role of symbols of prestige in the affluent society, it is plain that his argument fully implies that the production of goods creates the wants that the goods are presumed to satisfy.

III

The even more direct link between production and wants is provided by the institutions of modern advertising and salesmanship. These cannot be reconciled with the notion of independently determined desires, for their central function is to create desires—to bring into being wants that previously did not exist.[2] This is accomplished by the producer of the goods or at his behest. A broad empirical relationship exists between what is spent on production of consumers' goods and what is spent in synthesizing the desires for that production. A new consumer product must be introduced with a suitable advertising campaign to arouse an interest in it. The path for an expansion of output must be paved by a suitable expansion in the advertising budget. Outlays for the manufacturing of a product are not more important in the strategy of modern business enterprise than outlays for the manufacturing of demand for the product. None of this is novel. All would be regarded as elementary by the most retarded student in the nation's most primitive school of business administration. The cost of this want formation is formidable. In 1956 total advertising expenditure—though, as noted, not all of it may be assigned to the synthesis of wants—amounted to about ten billion dollars. For some years it had been increasing at a rate in excess of a billion dollars a year. Obviously, such outlays must be integrated with the theory of consumer demand. They are too big to be ignored.

But such integration means recognizing that wants are dependent on production. It accords to the producer the function both of making the goods and of making the desires for them. It recognizes that production, not only passively through emulation, but actively through advertising and related activities, creates the wants it seeks to satisfy.

The businessman and the lay reader will be puzzled over the emphasis which I give to a seemingly obvious point. The point is indeed obvious. But it is one which, to a singular degree, economists have resisted. They have sensed, as the layman does not, the damage to established ideas which

---

[2] Advertising is not a simple phenomenon. It is also important in competitive strategy and want creation is, ordinarily, a complementary result of efforts to shift the demand curve of the individual firm at the expense of others or (less importantly, I think) to change its shape by increasing the degree of product differentiation. Some of the failure of economists to identify advertising with want creation may be attributed to the undue attention that its use in purely competitive strategy has attracted. It should be noted, however, that the competitive manipulation of consumer desire is only possible, at least on any appreciable scale, when such need is not strongly felt.

lurks in these relationships. As a result, incredibly, they have closed their eyes (and ears) to the most obtrusive of all economic phenomena, namely modern want creation.

This is not to say that the evidence affirming the dependence of wants on advertising has been entirely ignored. It is one reason why advertising has so long been regarded with such uneasiness by economists. Here is something which cannot be accommodated easily to existing theory. More pervious scholars have speculated on the urgency of desires which are so obviously the fruit of such expensively contrived campaigns for popular attention. Is a new breakfast cereal or detergent so much wanted if so much must be spent to compel in the consumer the sense of want? But there has been little tendency to go on to examine the implications of this for the theory of consumer demand and even less for the importance of production and productive efficiency. These have remained sacrosanct. More often the uneasiness has been manifested in a general disapproval of advertising and advertising men, leading to the occasional suggestion that they shouldn't exist. Such suggestions have usually been ill received.

And so the notion of independently determined wants still survives. In the face of all the forces of modern salesmanship it still rules, almost undefiled, in the textbooks. And it still remains the economist's mission—and on few matters is the pedagogy so firm—to seek unquestioningly the means for filling these wants. This being so, production remains of prime urgency. We have here, perhaps, the ultimate triumph of the conventional wisdom in its resistance to the evidence of the eyes. To equal it one must imagine a humanitarian who was long ago persuaded of the grievous shortage of hospital facilities in the town. He continues to importune the passers-by for money for more beds and refuses to notice that the town doctor is deftly knocking over pedestrians with his car to keep up the occupancy.

And in unraveling the complex we should always be careful not to overlook the obvious. The fact that wants can be synthesized by advertising, catalyzed by salesmanship, and shaped by the discreet manipulations of the persuaders shows that they are not very urgent. A man who is hungry need never be told of his need for food. If he is inspired by his appetite, he is immune to the influence of Messrs. Batten, Barton, Durstine & Osborn. The latter are effective only with those who are so far removed from physical want that they do not already know what they want. In this state alone men are open to persuasion.

IV

The general conclusion of these pages is of such importance for this essay that it had perhaps best be put with some formality. As a society becomes increasingly affluent, wants are increasingly created by the process by which they are satisfied. This may operate passively. Increases in consumption, the counterpart of increases in production, act by suggestion or emulation to create wants. Or producers may proceed actively to create wants through advertising and salesmanship. Wants thus come to depend on output. In technical terms it can no longer be assumed that welfare is greater at an all-round higher level of production than at a lower one. It may be the same. The higher level of production has, merely, a higher level of want creation necessitating a higher level of want satisfaction. There will be frequent occasion to refer to the way wants depend on the process by which they are satisfied. It will be convenient to call it the Dependence Effect.

We may now contemplate briefly the conclusions to which this analysis has brought us.

Plainly the theory of consumer demand is a peculiarly treacherous friend of the present goals of economics. At first glance it seems to defend the continuing urgency of production and our preoccupation with it as a goal. The economist does not enter into the dubious moral arguments about the importance or virtue of the wants to be satisfied. He doesn't pretend to compare mental states of the same or different people at different times and to suggest that one is less urgent than another. The desire is there. That for him is sufficient. He sets about in a workmanlike way to satisfy desire, and accordingly he sets the proper store by the production that does. Like woman's his work is never done.

But this rationalization, handsomely though it seems to serve, turns destructively on those who advance it once it is conceded that wants are themselves both passively and deliberately the fruits of the process by which they are satisfied. Then the production of goods satisfies the wants that the consumption of these goods creates or that the producers of goods synthesize. Production induces more wants and the need for more production. So far, in a major *tour de force,* the implications have been ignored. But this obviously is a perilous solution. It cannot long survive discussion.

Among the many models of the good society no one has urged the squirrel wheel. Moreover, as we shall see presently, the wheel is not one that revolves with perfect smoothness. Aside from its dubious cultural charm, there are serious structural weaknesses which may one day embarrass us. For the moment, however, it is sufficient to reflect on the difficult terrain which we are traversing. We saw how deeply we were committed to production for reasons of economic security. Not the goods but the employment provided by their production was the thing by which we set ultimate store. Now we find our concern for goods further undermined. It does not arise in spontaneous consumer need. Rather, the dependence effect means that it grows out of the process of production itself. If production is to increase, the wants must be effectively contrived. In the absence of the contrivance the increase would not occur. This is not true of all goods, but that it is true of a substantial part is sufficient. It means that since the demand for this part would not exist, were it not contrived, its utility or urgency, ex contrivance, is zero. If we regard this production as marginal, we may say that the marginal utility of present aggregate output, ex advertising and salesmanship, is zero. Clearly the attitudes and values which make production the central achievement of our society have some exceptionally twisted roots.

Perhaps the thing most evident of all is how new and varied become the problems we must ponder when we break the nexus with the work of Ricardo and face the economics of affluence of the world in which we live. It is easy to see why the conventional wisdom resists so stoutly such change. It is a far, far better thing to have a firm anchor in nonsense than to put out on the troubled seas of thought.

THE NATURE OF PROPAGANDA

By Leonard W. Doob

———

AN EFFECTIVE way in Anglo-Saxon society to insult, belittle, or expose a man is to call him a propagandist. Since a propagandist is an individual who influences other individuals, apparently the influencing of others is considered dishonorable. The situation, however, is not quite so simple. For calling a man an educator reveals a respectful attitude toward him, except when he is labelled a "professor," in which case attention is also being called to his impracticality. But an educator is likewise an individual who influences other individuals.

Why, then, is "propagandist" an epithet in our society? Almost any other name sounds sweeter to most people. If a man is not called an educator, he seems to prefer to be known as a publicity agent, a public relations counsel or officer, an advertising agent or account executive, a salesman, a promoter, a barker, a preacher, a lecturer, or even a politician. What was called propaganda acquired such unpleasant connotations during the 1920's and 1930's that the word was avoided whenever possible when war began again in 1939. Both in the United States and Great Britain, consequently, the home front, allies, and neutral countries were provided not with "propaganda" but with "information." In most instances even the enemy was not weakened by "propaganda": Americans attacked him through the use of "psychological warfare" and the British via "political warfare." Sometimes Americans concerned with propaganda to the enemy called themselves "psychological warriors," the British counterpart to which naturally became "political warriors." Consider, too, the very names of the American organizations charged with propaganda functions at various times during the war: Office of Facts and Figures, Office of Government Reports, Office of the Coordinator of Information, Office of the Coordinator of Inter-American Affairs, Office of War Information, Psychological Warfare Branch (or Divisions), etc. There was only one exception: an unimportant, publicity-shunning Propaganda Branch of Military Intelligence in Washington, D. C.

More than a matter of mere semantics is involved in the efforts to dodge the word "propaganda" or "propagandist." In other countries with different cultures the word is quite respectable or at least as respectable as any of the equivalents our ingenious language and our beleaguered propagandists have devised. Its derivation, moreover, is respectable: its Latin ancestor is the word "to propagate" or "to sow." Its currency increased during the seventeenth century for an equally respectable reason: it was part of the official titles of two Catholic organizations charged with the responsibility of "propagating the faith" through foreign missions and of training priests to become missionaries. Words in general, it seems, acquire unpleasant connotations for very good reasons. The tabooed words in our vocabulary, most of which relate directly or indirectly to religion, sex, and the eliminative processes, have been more or less outlawed because the behavior they represent is in fact also taboo or strictly regulated. Similarly the prejudice against "propaganda" must mean that people are hostile toward the activity they associate with propaganda. The inquiry into why propaganda is disliked must be searching and complete. Otherwise the nature of propaganda as well as the society in which it functions cannot be understood.

EDUCATION

The inquiry can best begin by considering education, that formal part of the process of socialization in which an older or more experienced individual influences other younger or less experienced individuals. Certainly one important aim of education is to increase knowledge. The knowledge may consist of the manipulation of numbers, called arithmetic; the accepted way to write sentences, called penmanship, spelling, syntax, or grammar; the best method of repairing an automobile, called physics, engineering, or mechanics; the duties and obligations of a citizen, called civics; the correct manner of behaving in social situations, called etiquette; or the desirable beliefs concerning God, the purpose of life, and the hereafter, called religion or philosophy. A man's education is said to be good or bad. It is good if he learns a great deal *and* if he learns the "right" kinds of things. It is bad if he learns too little *or* if he learns the "wrong" kinds of things. But what is "right" and what is "wrong"?

A question like this, though profound and puzzling, cannot be relegated to jesting Pilate or the reader's intuition or prejudice. Each person must be deliberately aware of what he considers right or wrong before he can pass judgment on education or distinguish education from propaganda. The problem of values cannot be avoided.

Any child from the age of one (or less) begins to acquire his parents' language. This knowledge is essential from the viewpoint of both the child and his parents. It facilitates, for example, communication between the two. The moron's limited knowledge of language is one of his principal handicaps. The language that is learned by the child may be imperfect: it may be a class-typed dialect which forever after will make it difficult for him to rise in the social scale; it may not be so efficient or considered by some to be so beautiful as another language; or it may not belong to the linguistic family from which as an adult the child will be compelled to learn another language. At any rate, by being forced to learn the language his parents speak, the child is both psychologically and physiologically prejudiced against other versions of that language and against other languages, as any English-speaking adult knows who has vainly attempted to learn the pronunciation, for example, of the letters *l* or *r* in German, French, or Spanish. The child, in acquiring the language of his parents, has been educated; but the education has been dictatorially if unconsciously imposed without his permission and has biased him against all other ways of talking.

The grade-school teacher is giving a spelling lesson. She tells the children that the correct spelling of "through" is "t-h-r-o-u-g-h." One boy, who is neither bright nor stupid, asks her why it is not spelled phonetically: "t-h-r-u." She tells him that only her version is the correct one and that his is unacceptable except to a few radicals and crackpots who advocate simplified spelling. Thereafter he always writes "t-h-r-o-u-g-h" and throughout his life is prejudiced against "t-h-r-u." Or the same teacher writes the word "itch" on the blackboard and then explains that other words in English containing the sound of "itch" are similarly spelled; for example, she jots down this word-family:

> pitch
> ditch
> stitch
> hitch
> witch
> bitch

She then may lose her job not because she is a poor teacher—after all, *rich, niche,* and *which* all contain the sound of *itch* although the letter *t* is absent—but because American children are not supposed to be taught to spell a word like *bitch.* "But, Mr. Superintendent, I was only illustrating what happens when a *b* is added to *itch,* and I was thinking of a type of dog, not of the filial expression you have in mind."

Another school teacher—and here an illustration will be constructed on the basis of one suggested by Freeman (5)—is planning an arithmetic lesson and wants to select an exercise from one of the following:

1. Divide 60 by 80.
2. A man wishes to borrow $80, but his friend lends him only $60. What percentage of the amount he wanted does he obtain?
3. Medical and health authorities agree that a family of four requires a minimum wage of $80 per week. The John J. Jones Company in our town pays most of its workers only $60 per week. What percentage of a decent minimum wage do these workers receive?
4. If we do not use our atomic bombs against Russia within the near future, Russia will design her own atomic bomb to use against us. Ac-

cording to General John J. Jones, 60 out of every 80 people in a city struck by an atomic bomb are likely to be killed and the rest will be severely hurt. What percentage of people in our city will be killed by the atomic bomb which Russia will explode in our midst?

The identical arithmetical process is involved in all four exercises. The first is straight arithmetic. No teacher in the United States would hesitate to use the second because borrowing money is both frequent and respectable in American society. But the third raises a problem: even though the pupils only have to divide 60 by 80, there is the suggestion—which might more properly be expressed by union organizers or even communists—that the John J. Jones Company underpays most of its workers who therefore must be suffering from malnutrition and who certainly are not able to follow the good life. And the fourth illustration seems to possess an anti-Soviet undertone which has little to do with arithmetic; it might be more acceptable to some school boards than the third.

Spelling and arithmetic are ordinarily considered to be "pure" subjects which do not give rise to controversy. A child has to learn to spell and calculate, and that is that. Other subjects involving the child's or even the college student's social environment are recognized as problem-producing. They can be briefly illustrated by intercepting a few remarks which an American teacher or instructor might make in the classroom:

1. *History:* "You know that in the North where I was born and lived until I came here a few years ago that war is called the 'Civil War.' Personally I would much rather call it that than the 'War Between the States.' And I want you to. For it really was a civil war: the North wanted to prevent the South from seceding and from having slaves, and the South. . . ."

2. *Civics:* "What we really have been talking about is the way our city government is supposed to work according to the charter we have. In practice, though, the picture is quite different. Our councilmen don't vote as they wish or as the people they represent wish. They do what the political bosses tell them to do. Graft also is involved because. . . ."

3. *Geography:* "The capital of Puerto Rico is San Juan and the island has an area of 3,435 square miles. Most of the million and a half inhabitants are of Spanish or Negro origin and all of them have been helped in some way or other by the United States. In fact ever since we liberated Cuba from Spain and undertook to spread our civilization to Puerto Rico. . . ."

4. *Economics:* "We shall begin our study of economics by reading Karl Marx. Your first assignment is Chapters 1-3, inclusive, of his *Capital*, which I consider to be the most penetrating book ever written on our economic system. After you have understood Marx thoroughly, you will be in a better position to evaluate the classical economists who talk about supply and demand, the so-called law of diminishing returns. . . ."

Perhaps it is no longer necessary to belabor the point that the curriculum of formal education is permeated with value-judgments. It is tempting to do so, however, because it is not easy to stand off and detect those judgments: the individual's knowledge and attitudes make him frequently incapable of perceiving bias in his own thinking. The New Englander who shares the approach to the "Civil War" which the teacher from that area is using in a Southern classroom would think it right and proper to present the war from the Northern viewpoint; but the Southern parents of the children might call the teacher a "Northern propagandist." Few people would disagree that the formal functioning of municipal government should be explained in the school, but many might wonder whether a realistic approach to ward politics is a proper subject for immature minds which might thereby grow disillusioned. No one doubts that the capital of Puerto Rico is San Juan and that this United States possession contains so-and-so-many square miles; but readers of the *New Republic* and the *Nation* might disagree with the particular version of American colonial policy being taught. The illustration from economics is not an imaginary one: it represents a more or less accurate quotation from the introductory remarks of an instructor in a foreign country whose approach to the subject shocked the writer completely since he had previously studied economics as economics is taught in American colleges.

Ultimately the values involved in what is called education can be assayed by considering the effect of the teaching on those who are taught. Sixty divided by 80 is .75 when the operation is carried to two decimal points—this is a true statement. But the effect of learning to carry on the operation can be a function of the example's context, whether that context be a loan between friends, sub-standard wages, or atomic warfare. That there was a conflict in the United States which began in 1861 and ended in 1865 is a fact, but the interpretation of that conflict being given by the Northern teacher is one which is not considered quite accurate by historians (including those in the North) and any interpretation inevitably produces different responses in Northampton, Mass., from those which occur in Natchez, Miss. Whether or not ward politicians control councilmen is a question of fact which can be settled by investigation, but teaching the fact—if it be one—may have the disillusioning effect the advocates of idealism suggest or it may produce more politically sophisticated citizens. Karl Marx—and not Adam Smith, George Washington, or Winston Churchill— did write *Capital* which is therefore a book in economics to be found in many civilized libraries, but the economic and social views of a student who reads that book and no other treatise in economics are likely to be quite different from those held by a contemporary who has been assigned a text written by a classical or neo-classical economist.

The implications of this discussion can best be summarized by defining education as *the imparting of knowledge or skill considered to be scientific or to have survival value in a society at a particular time.* This definition, like most so-called intensional or connotative definitions, does not resolve perplexing problems but rather calls attention to their existence. In the first place, what is scientific knowledge? It is knowledge which competent men in a society agree is correct and which is therefore subject to verification. Water contains two molecules of hydrogen and one of oxygen, a fact which chemists can verify in their laboratory and which laymen, if they wish to achieve the competency of chemists, can also verify. As of this moment and among us, therefore, the teaching of this fact and its accompanying theoretical structure is education. The parents in a primitive society who tell their child that the sun is a large lake reflecting the light from the earth are teaching him an alleged fact with which the competent of their society —perhaps the priests—presumably agree, but it is a pre-scientific fact which cannot be verified. From our viewpoint, consequently, the parents are not educators but from theirs they are.

The teaching of the belief about the sun, moreover, may be absolutely essential in that particular society. The adolescent who has not learned the "fact" will be debarred from entering the religious society he must join if he is to be allowed to select a wife, to grow his own pigs, to win prestige in inter-tribal warfare, etc. The knowledge possesses survival value in the society at the particular time. No question of science or of verification is involved in calling such knowledge part of the socialization process of this group and hence education.

Scientific skill consists of a system of responses which are best adapted to the problem at hand. The novice who is told that to apply the foot brakes on an automobile it is most efficient to lean down and press the right pedal with his left hand is acquiring a rather foolish skill in terms of both the construction of the car and his own body; he is not being educated. The learning of the parental language, imperfect as it may be, is essential for the child; it is part of his education and so considered by everybody, including even this writer.

The foregoing definition of education is deliberately relativistic: whether knowledge or skill is to be called education depends on the state of science at the time and on what is broadly considered necessary for survival by the society or particular sub-groups therein. A swift glance at any anthropological treatise (*cf.* 8) is usually sufficient to convince the student of man that almost any type of behavior, including kinds which seem horrible or barbarous to people in our society, has been tolerated or encouraged somewhere or by people at some period in their development. Values in this sense are relativistic, as are the goals of socialization.

Science, too, is relativistic since what is considered or can be demonstrated to be true or false changes as men's knowledge accumulates. Until the acceptance of Galileo's conception of the universe, the well-educated man in European society had to subscribe to the Ptolemaic view that the earth is the center of the universe. Now the hypothesis is thought to be false or inadequate, and it has been discarded from all modern educational systems except those advocated by certain religious sects. At this point there arises again a troublesome difference between the natural and the social sciences. In the natural sciences facts and theories can be decisively if only eventually verified or disproved by the observation of the competent: there is a definite procedure to determine truth or falsity. In the social sciences, on the other hand, verification is much more difficult in almost all instances because observation of people is more complicated and hence the methods of ascertaining truth or falsity are less clear-cut (3). The well-educated Soviet economist, for example, is grounded in Marxism and his American counterpart in Adam Smith or one of Smith's modern successors; the difference here is a function not only of the social acceptability accorded the doctrines but also of their scientific character concerning which men of corresponding competency in both societies are unable to agree. Similarly there are historical facts, which means that there is convincing evidence at hand to show that certain events occurred in the past, but the interpretation of those events—the attempt, for example, to establish cause-and-effect sequences—gives rise to argument and leads to little or no agreement. Much of the content of social science, as a result, cannot be considered education in the present sense of the word. Frequently all that a social science has to offer as education is a scientific way of approach to the study of man, in addition to some facts and a few hypotheses which in all honesty ought always to be clearly labelled as tentative.

In short, the "right" kind of education consists of learning facts and theories which can be verified or of subscribing to points of view which are considered "good," "just," "beautiful," or "necessary" in the society. The "wrong" kind promotes unverified or unverifiable facts and theories as well as "bad," "unjust," "ugly," or "unnecessary" points of view. The educator has prestige in our society because it is presumed that he teaches what people want and need to be taught, in order to be socialized according to our standards. If he mixes radicalism with arithmetic or exposés with civics, he is branded a propagandist by the majority of people in the United States. If he mixes imperialism with geography or capitalism with economics, he is likewise angrily labelled a propagandist certainly not by the majority but by the radical-minded minority. Pick your science or the values you consider important in your society, and then you can decide what education is.

The Scope of Propaganda

Propaganda is not education as education has been here defined. Propaganda can be called *the attempt to affect the personalities and to control the behavior of individuals toward ends considered unscientific or of doubtful value in a society at a particular time.* What has been said of education applies to propaganda but in a reverse manner. The imparting knowledge which has not reached the scientific stage is propaganda, as is the teaching of a skill which is not adapted to the situation at hand. The dissemination of a viewpoint considered by a group to be "bad," "unjust," "ugly," or "unnecessary" is propaganda in terms of that group's standards.

This severe distinction between education and propaganda on the basis of science and survival value does not mean that the influence of an individual upon his contemporaries is clearly either one or the other. What almost always occurs is a combination of the two, or the influence can be variously appraised by observers with different conceptions of science and value. The learning of the parents' language by the child is education, for clearly it involves survival or the acquiring of a skill most suited to its particular environment. Not spelling "through" in simplified fashion is education, the majority of people in our society would say, but it is propaganda against simplified spelling, according to the advocates of this reform. The avoidance of the word "bitch" during the spelling lesson is an educational gesture by the teacher who knows that the use of this word in our society is maladaptive except among restricted groups of dog fanciers or among some individuals who feel impelled to make an unflattering reference to a male's maternal ancestry or a female's obnoxious characteristics. The rules and principles involved in arithmetical calculations are part of our educational process, but the illustrations employed for practicing those calculations have an educational or a propaganda effect related not to arithmetic but to values considered important or unimportant, good or bad, etc. The social sciences as usually taught are mixtures of education and propaganda: to the extent that they teach verifiable facts or a scientific approach to a problem, they are education; to the extent that they rely upon dogmatism and obscurantism, they are propaganda from a scientific viewpoint but nevertheless also education in terms of the values possessed by special groups in a society.

To discriminate between education and propaganda, therefore, is not always easy. The individual attempting the discrimination must be aware of the state of scientific knowledge on a subject and must be conscious of the value judgments he is employing in his own thinking. It is tempting to say—as a popular cliché phrases it—that propaganda is what the other fellow is doing, but all that is being thereby expressed is disagreement with or antagonism toward the objectives that other fellow is seeking to attain. Individuals in Anglo-Saxon society do not like to be called "propagandists" because they recognize the hostility toward their scale of values which is thus implied. Propaganda is supposed to be underhanded or anti-social, but in fact operates when there is no science or when people's values are in conflict.

Propaganda acquired its bad reputation in this country during the 1920's when countless writers and scholars exposed the lies which the propaganda machines of both sides disseminated throughout World War I. In addition, "propaganda" is disliked in a democratic society because people feel naively that their decisions should be made by themselves and not by someone else. The feeling is naive because decisions result from past experiences, many of which are usually culturally determined; but it is certainly in keeping with the belief of our society that man, if he only will, can shape his own destiny.

Admittedly the conception of propaganda here outlined is broad and, it may be said, includes phenomena which ordinarily are not so classified. It is felt, however, that no sharp distinction can be made between the propaganda and educational implications of most social processes and that by focusing upon the science and values which they contain a more useful insight into their nature can be obtained. Other attempts to distinguish between education and propaganda, moreover, seem to be relatively sterile or unincisive.

Toward the close of the debunking 1920's when the word "propaganda" was particularly unpopular, Martin (10) stated a point of view which continues to be widespread:

> . . . Education aims at independence of judgment. Propaganda offers ready-made opinions for the unthinking herd. Education and propaganda are directly opposed both in aim and method.
>
> The educator aims at a slow process of development; the propagandist, at quick results. The educator tries to tell people *how* to think; the propagandist, *what* to think. The educator strives to develop individual responsibility; the propagandist, mass effects. The educator fails unless he achieves an open mind; the propagandist unless he achieves a closed mind.

Martin's is the credo of a thinker in a democracy who wishes to praise education and decry propaganda. But his phrases are too general. Certainly the label "poison" on a bottle of rubbing alcohol offers a "ready-made" opinion which should not be disregarded; there can be nothing "slow" about the "process of development" through which individuals must go if they are to profit from the warning; "what" should be the nature of thoughts people have concerning the contents of the bottle is scarcely left in doubt; and it would be foolhardy for anyone to question the label on his own "individual responsibility" in order thus to demonstrate that he has "an open mind" on the subject. It is, consequently, a purely verbal matter whether the label is called a propaganda or an educational attempt to affect people's behavior regarding the contents of the bottle. In addition, it is not possible to learn "how to think" unless the thinker thinks about something. That something may have propaganda implications, just as the exercise of a purely arithmetical principle may affect the individual's attitude toward certain social practices of his society.

Efforts have also been made to characterize propaganda in terms of the characteristic method which it allegedly employs. Lumley (9), for example, considers propaganda a form of "veiled" promotion and thus identifies certain activities which he chooses to attack. This crucial adjective, however, is vague; "veiled" from whose point of view it is legitimate to ask. More recently Henderson (6) has surveyed the definitions of propaganda which have wide currency and has decided that the essence of propaganda is the propagandist's effort to limit the "freedom of choice" available to the propagandees. It is true that propagandists do seek to restrict the responses which the propagandees can make, but educators likewise desire to eliminate responses from their students' repertoire—the false or the incorrect ones. The writer (2) once attempted to establish a sharp psychological distinction between education and propaganda: he maintained that education employs "suggestion" and propaganda does not. The difficulty here, he now realizes, is that he sought to dodge the problem of value and faced only the problem of science. To say, as he did, that what is learned in propaganda depends on the method of learning (*i.e.*, on suggestion) is to assume that only questions of fact are involved; but, since the customs prevalent in a society are also learned with or without the kind of learning he chose to call suggestion, the distinction has only a limited applicability.

The conclusion may be drawn that education and propaganda are special cases of learning which are evaluated in terms of certain specified or unspecified criteria. If the criteria are disregarded in making the analysis, then a distinction between education and propaganda need not be made. Both can be subsumed under some neutral concept like learning, tuition, instruction, presentation, expression, inducement, transmission, diffusion, or communication. It would be, perhaps, more efficient to use any one of these innocuous words which do not arouse violent or abusive emotions. Such a semantic manipulation, however, has one important shortcoming: the neutralization of terminology avoids even raising the problems of truth and goodness. After the explosion of the first few atomic bombs, many modern physicists no longer confined their thoughts to the description, prediction, and production of atomic energy—their traditional role in connection with any problem in physics—but of necessity began to make proposals concerning the control of this tremendous force. Both the work of the chairman of an adult forum studying a modern social problem and the deeds of a fifth columnist before the outbreak of a war are indeed illustrations of simple or complex "communication" and both involve suggestion or learning; but the problem of deciding what proportion of education and propaganda each communicates remains, if their efforts are to be fully evaluated. The words "education" and "propaganda," then, should be retained but with some misgiving because of the social connotations they have come to possess and because they are too frequently used as epithets.

It must be fully recognized, moreover, that propaganda is being employed here in a neutral sense to describe the influence of one person upon other persons when scientific knowledge and survival values are uncertain. From this viewpoint, propaganda is absolutely inevitable and cannot be exorcised by calling it evil-sounding names. All knowledge has not reached a scientific stage, and men who are thought to be competent do not always agree as to what is a scientific fact or theory even in our society. In the realm of social, political, and economic values, there is even less agreement and more prejudice. The faith of a free society is in its varied systems of values, each seeking expression and survival. At a given moment, none but a fool or a prophet will state which ultimately is true or untrue, which good or bad. Man's struggle to conquer his environment, to control himself, and to regulate his relations with his fellows is waged with half-truths which emotionally convince some and leave others unmoved, which fluctuate from generation to generation, and which cannot be eternally experienced or expressed. Only a complete dictatorship is free from propaganda, for then there is a single "truth" to be promoted and that "truth" must be considered true and good within the society. But those who by living in another country are not crushed by this dictator or who within the country have their own internal attitudes refer in shouts or whispers to the "propaganda" on which the regime is founded and subsists.

The last two sentences are a mixture of education and propaganda. They are educational to the extent that their characterization of dictatorship is accurate and would find agreement among those competent to judge. They are propaganda, too, since their mode of expression casts aspersions upon dictatorship and thus seeks to prejudice the reader still more against this form of government. The writer believes that dictatorship is "bad," but he cannot prove this belief in the sense that a chemist can demonstrate the distribution of hydrogen and oxygen in water. Even without completely convincing proof, however, he prefers to retain the belief and to propagandize in its behalf.

THE PROPAGANDIST'S INTENTION

There is an obvious but important difference between the individual who deliberately attempts to influence other people and the individual who unwittingly has a similar effect upon them. The advertising agent wants to promote the sale of a particular product, but the housewife who spontaneously praises the product in the presence of a friend is working toward the same end. The school teacher who has recently been converted to communism or vegetarianism prepares her lessons self-consciously and seeks an opportunity to score a point in favor of her new philosophy; but the spinster, who teaches her pupils after the gospel of the Republican party and other respectable doctrines which are prevalent in an American community and to which she herself subscribes, almost automatically absorbs and transmits these views of society. The enemy agent is paid to spread demoralizing stories, but the rumor-monger helps diffuse the tales not because he wishes to do so but because he thereby relieves some of his own personal anxiety. The advertising agent, the communist or the vegetarian school teacher, and the enemy agent are aware of a propaganda objective; whereas the housewife, the Republican and respectable school teacher, and the rumor-monger are rather blissfully unaware of the propaganda objectives their respective activities nevertheless achieve. The first group can be called intentional and the second unintentional propagandists. Intentional propagandists *deliberately* attempt to affect or control the behavior of a group of individuals, unintentional propagandists *unwittingly* do so.

Ordinarily the term "propagandist" refers only to an intentional propagandist whose efforts, when they are known, clearly represent an attempt to change people and their society. The unintentional propagandist, on the other hand, frequently is seeking to maintain the status quo, and hence his efforts are considered praise-worthy and educational. In addition, he does not or cannot appreciate the consequences of what he is doing and is usually horrified to be called a propagandist. Often the intentional propagandist can function more effectively than the unintentional propagandist because he can systematically vary the techniques he is employing to achieve his chosen objectives. But this advantage does not always exist. The unintentional propagandist occupies a position in society which enables him to have greater access to the media of communication. He behaves "naturally" and hence his propagandees have no reason to suspect his motives: "he may be prejudiced but he means well. . . ."

A propagandist can almost never anticipate the complete consequences of his own propaganda and therefore it must be said that some of those consequences are achieved unintentionally. One investigator (11), for example, produced attitude changes in American high school children on a variety of issues (such as capital punishment and the agricultural policies of the Roosevelt administration) by presenting them with clearcut points of view on the subjects. The average changes were in the direction of the propaganda materials. When "no conscious attempt" was made to change attitudes on the issue of divorce, no appreciable changes occurred. These changes, therefore, were in harmony with the propagandist's intentions and they tended to persist over a period of six months. Propaganda concerning labor unions made students, on the average, less favorably disposed toward these organizations, and, in addition, "sharply divided the group into two opposing tents." This last effect apparently was unforeseen; it was not observed in connection with the other issues; it must be called unintentional. Similarly, Chen (1) in the early thirties manipulated the attitudes of various groups of American college students toward the Sino-Japanese conflict over Manchuria by having them listen to intentionally pro-Chinese or pro-Japanese "propaganda" speeches. What he considered in one instance to be "neutral material"—because it presented only the so-called "facts"—actually and to his own surprise made the students less pro-Chinese.

A group of investigators (4) who studied the effects which orientation films had on men in the United States Army during the last war discovered that sometimes changes in attitude would occur which were not desired or intended by the producers. The Soviet Union was not mentioned, for example, in a motion picture on "The Battle of Britain." After seeing the film, however, slightly fewer men thought that Russia "will keep on fighting until the end" of the war against Germany and that "if Germany is beaten before Japan, the Russians will probably help us fight the Japanese"; and slightly fewer disagreed with the statement that "after we help Russia beat the Germans the Russians are liable to turn around and start fighting us." According to the investigators, "the presentation of Britain's outstanding effort in holding off the Nazis" resulted in "a release of the men's former suspicion of Russian integrity that had been inhibited by their respect and obligation to Russia since she had currently been doing the bulk of the fighting."

Many intentional propagandists eventually admit that they are surprised by some of the results of their own propaganda. James A. Farley, for example, was Mr. Roosevelt's first campaign manager. He strove mightily to have Mr. Roosevelt elected and then re-elected a second time. Apparently, as he realized later, he himself had not appreciated in advance all the consequences of the New Deal. He did not and perhaps he could not guess that one of the effects of his successful propaganda would be to produce reforms and policies with which he would disagree, especially after his personal relations with the President had deteriorated and after he himself had acquired the ambition to become President.

There have been objections to a distinction between intentional and unintentional propaganda by those who would restrict the term "propaganda" to the intentional variety. Some critics have contended that, if unintentional propaganda be included in a discussion of propaganda, then the concept embraces too wide a field. It is true that the meaning or referent of the word is thus extended, but extension is legitimate since the phenomena included thereunder are identical with respect to psychological methods and social consequences and differ only in regard to the motivation of the propagandist. Others have maintained that the distinction is difficult to make unless the personality of the propagandist is known. This criticism is certainly correct, for the most effective propagandists of our time have not allowed themselves to be subjected to prolonged interviewing or to psychoanalysis. The inaccessibility of propagandists, however, does not mean that the problem of analyzing them and their motives should be completely neglected. Frequently on the basis of scanty information it is possible to formulate rather sagacious hypotheses concerning them. The analyst who is unacquainted with the intimacies of an advertiser's motives need not despair and block himself from concluding that the man supervises the writing of copy to increase sales. Such a conclusion is sufficient from a propaganda viewpoint, even though psychologically his real motive may be to compensate for the strict cleanliness training he received as a child.

Lasswell (7) "rejects the category of 'unintentional propaganda'" once proposed by this writer. He says that the "unintentional circulation of Communist symbols is not propaganda, but may be a result of propaganda." Yes, but such circulation may have no relation whatsoever to previous propaganda: it can be the consequence of social or economic events in which intentional propaganda has played little or no part. By making "manipulation" or "premeditation" the keystone in his conceptualization of propaganda, Lasswell restricts the term to instances in which the propagandist is conscious of his objectives. Certainly he knows that the dividing line between the conscious and the unconscious is frequently most difficult to discern.

Sometimes it appears useful for practical or administrative purposes to call one kind of propaganda "education" or "information" and another kind "propaganda," but the utility of the distinction should lead no one to believe that it is an absolute one. During the last war, for example, overall policy for England's propaganda to neutral and allied countries came from the Ministry of Information and to her enemies from the Political Warfare Executive. The "information" from the M. of I. tended to contain more facts on any standard than the "propaganda" of the P.W.E., although at times their radio programs were indistinguishable. The objectives of the two agencies, however, were different: the M. of I. sought to reinforce Britain's reputation over a period of time extending beyond the war and hence had to be more "truthful," whereas the P.W.E. was necessarily interested in short-range effects directly related to the war effort and hence was less "truthful." Since the objectives were different, different types of propagandists and of propaganda techniques were employed by each organization. In the United States, the Office of the Coordinator of Inter-American Affairs prevented itself from becoming a part of the Office of Strategic Services and then of the Office of War Information by maintaining with a false grin on a not very competent face that its propaganda to Latin America was "informational" and therefore should not be contaminated with "propaganda" or "psychological warfare." Within the Office of War Information, which was for the United States the equivalent of both the M. of I. and the P.W.E., the distinction was maintained on an organizational basis. Such semantic and political considerations, in fact, led one of the O.W.I.'s propagandists (13) to write after the war that "information is one thing—propaganda quite another," in support of which he could repeat only the trite and psychologically meaningless dichotomy between "reason" and "emotion."

Types of Propaganda

A classification of phenomena into types is usually a makeshift arrangement that is evolved for some practical reason. Women may be called vaguely or precisely "tall" or "short" in order to indicate which size coat they should buy or which size man they should love or marry. When a particular woman is so classified, obviously only her height is being considered and not the thousand-and-one other characteristics she possesses.

Innumerable schemes are available which can serve as the basis for classifying propaganda campaigns. All of them are arbitrary and hence the selection of one rather than another is a function of which aspect of propaganda is being emphasized at a given moment. Types of propaganda, then, may refer to the motive of the propagandist; the methods he employs; the recognition or non-recognition of his objectives by the propagandees; or the consequences of his propaganda.

A classification of the basis of the propagandist's motives has already been suggested: propaganda may be intentional or unintentional. This distinction refers only to the propagandist's awareness of what he is doing: is he deliberately or unwittingly attempting to influence other people? It does not take into account all the other ways in which propaganda may be characterized, nor should it be required to.

It is difficult to classify propaganda on the basis of methods because those methods are so diverse. A dichotomy may be derived from a moral judgment and then propaganda can be called "honest" or "dishonest." Or propaganda may be labelled with reference to a particular method: there is "repetitious" and "non-repetitious" propaganda. Propaganda may also be characterized in terms of the media of communication employed: "newspaper," "radio," "motion-picture," "magazine," "leaflet," and "rumor" propaganda are the principal categories. Each of these schemes has its merits and each, consequently, should be employed as the occasion demands.

An extremely useful criterion for classifying propaganda is to refer to the propagandees' recognition or non-recognition of the propagandist's objectives. Every normal adult in American society, for example, knows that the goal of an advertisement is to increase sales: the presence of the propaganda is thus appreciated and variously evaluated. The praise lavished upon the product by a housewife may be considered quite disinterested and objective, as indeed it is if she is merely an unintentional propagandist. Conceivably, however, she may be an intentional propagandist who is simply not revealing her interested motive to the propagandee: she or her husband may own stock in the company manufacturing the product or she may be paid to recommend the product as part of the company's promotion campaign. Regardless of her conscious intention, she is affecting the person with whom she is talking, and that person is not aware of the fact that he is being propagandized. Propaganda, consequently, may be *revealed, concealed,* or concealed at first and then revealed (*delayed revealed*).

Propaganda is revealed when the propagandees are aware of the fact that propaganda is affecting them. Voters during a campaign never or seldom forget that the candidates' immediate objective is to be elected. Concealed propaganda, in contrast, affects people even though they do not know that someone else—intentionally or unintentionally—is seeking to control their reactions. Fifth columnists pose as sincere patriots and try to prevent people from learning that they are being paid and directed by some outside power.

The division between revealed and concealed propaganda cannot be clearcut for two reasons. In the first place, the nature of the propaganda may be concealed at first but then later—because the propagandist makes the decision or is forced to make it or because the propagandees secure additional insight—it is revealed. The shrewd street-corner speaker does not reveal his purpose until he has attracted a crowd and aroused their interest; then he names his party or nostrum. Then, secondly, propagandees differ in their reactions to the propaganda which is affecting them: some may and others may not know what is happening to them. The same item on a radio newscast, for example, is revealed propaganda for the few who appreciate its origin and social implications, but it is concealed propaganda for the greater number who consider it an objective, important presentation of the "facts." Since minute analyses of propagandees are usually impossible and since, consequently, their own appraisal of the propagandist's objective cannot be obtained, any classification of propaganda into one of the three types must always be somewhat arbitrary. Sometimes a sample of the propagandees can be interviewed or otherwise observed, but the representativeness of the sample may remain open to question. More frequently it is possible to make reasonably probable inferences about the propagandees' reactions from the stimuli which constitute the propaganda. No investigation is required to decide that a political speech is a form of revealed propaganda for American adults, but one is necessary to determine whether members of a radio audience are able to recognize that a "news" item about a candidate has been smuggled into the press association's file.

Propaganda may also be classified in terms of its objectives. It may be called "good" or "bad" on the basis of some social, philosophical, or simply prejudiced criteria. The most obvious and distinguishing characteristic to single out is the field of human activity which the propaganda is attempting to affect. Common sense suggests types such as commercial propaganda, political propaganda, war propaganda, anti-semitic propaganda, communist propaganda, etc.

Sometimes it is useful to refer to the effort of one individual to influence others as *counter-propaganda*. This term emphasizes the negative objective of weakening customary responses which people make or of preventing responses desired by an opponent from occurring or being reinforced. In a sense, however, all propaganda involves some counter-propaganda, inasmuch as the drive strength of pre-existing competing responses must be weakened before learning can occur. The manufacturer may have a monopoly and therefore he is not forced to carry on counter-propaganda against a competitor, but he nevertheless is competing with other interests possessed by the propagandees. The term "counter-propaganda," therefore, has little psychological significance and should be employed only when it is necessary to indicate that a propagandist is seeking, intentionally or unintentionally, to counteract a competing propaganda which has been previously, is concurrently, or may eventually begin operating.

* * * *

REFERENCES

1. Chen, William Keh-Ching. The influence of oral propaganda material upon students' attitudes. *Archives of Psychology*, 1933, v. 23, no. 150. Pp. 23, 27-28.
2. Doob, Leonard W. *Propaganda*. New York: Holt, 1935. Pp. 79-88.
3. ————. *The plans of men*. New Haven: Yale University Press, 1940. Chaps. 3-6.
4. Experimental Section, Research Branch, Information and Education Division, U. S. War Department. *Experimental studies of army educational films*. 1948. Chap. 2.
5. Freeman, Ellis. *Social psychology*. New York: Holt, 1936. Pp. 263-265.
6. Henderson, Edgar H. Toward a definition of propaganda. *Journal of Social Psychology*, 1943, v. 18, pp. 71-87.
7. Lasswell, Harold D. & Blumenstock, Dorothy. *World revolutionary propaganda*. New York: Knopf, 1939. Pp. 10-11, footnote.
8. Linton, Ralph. *The study of man*. New York: Appleton-Century, 1936.
9. Lumley, Frederick E. *The propaganda menace*. New York: Appleton-Century, 1933. P. 44.
10. Martin, Everett D. Our invisible masters. *Forum*, 1929, v. 81, pp. 142-145. P. 145.
11. Remmers, H. H. Propaganda in the schools—do the effects last? *Public Opinion Quarterly*, 1938, v. 2, pp. 197-210.
12. Smith, Bruce Lannes; Lasswell, Harold D.; & Casey, Ralph D. *Propaganda, communication, and public opinion*. Princeton: Princeton University Press, 1946. P. 121, italics theirs.
13. Warburg, James P. *Unwritten treaty*. New York: Harcourt, Brace, 1946. P. 17.

PUBLIC RELATIONS AND MASS COMMUNICATION

By *Charles S. Steinberg*

THERE IS AN element of paradox in placing the function of public relations in the universe of discourse of mass communication. There is no practitioner of public relations and, indeed, few social scientists who would deny the assumption that the practice of public relations is related, directly or peripherally, to the mass media and to the process of opinion formation —and, some would add, to propaganda. Yet, no empirical method of research has identified public relations itself as mass communication, as distinguished from identifying the process as a by-product of the development of mass communication.

It is no random conjecture, however, to assume for public relations a vital role in the whole process of mass communication. Mass media and public relations are facets and results of the competitive, mercantile economy of the twentieth century. Both are as much a part of the contemporary society as the Industrial Revolution was a distinguishing feature of American society of a century ago. Both are related to the process of information, public opinion formation and consensus in a dynamic and democratic society.

Yet, public relations in itself is not a mass medium. It is not a channel between communicator and receiving audience. Its identification with the whole process of mass communication is a dual one. First, pragmatic public relations—public relations in action involving the dissemination of information in the form of communication content—is mass communication in action. At the same time, public relations also utilizes one or more of the mass media as pipelines to public opinion. In one sense, therefore, public relations itself is mass communication. In another sense, it utilizes, through identification, the various media of mass communication. It is both intrinsically and extrinsically related to the whole nexus of the communication process. There have been some doubts expressed as to the effectiveness of various mass media on public opinion. There can be little doubt that public relations can affect public opinion very significantly.

It was not fortuitous that public relations and the mass media developed together as aspects of the mass culture of twentieth century society.

Expanded from an article by Charles S. Steinberg in the *Journal of Public Relations,* June 1961.

The technological developments of the last fifty years prepared the social environment for the development of mass media capable of harnessing remarkable new technical devices, particularly such tools of communication as the radio and television. And the development of media capable of reaching, simultaneously, audiences of a scope and dimension never dreamed of in the past, offered an opportunity for the development of newer, more refined, more powerful techniques of informing and influencing public opinion. In this environment, the art and the science of public relations came to be a tremendously important factor in public information and in mass persuasion. Its spectacular growth after the last war was given impetus, direction and ethical orientation by communication research, by public relations courses in the colleges and by the formation of national associations such as the newly merged Public Relations Society of America and the American Public Relations Association, as well as by the establishment of the American College Public Relations Association. These professional organizations have given a working code and a sense of direction to public relations, which has become a mass communicator of signal influence in contemporary society.

The most compelling factor in the rapid and still proliferating growth of public relations is the presence of mass media, geared to reach audiences never before reached in the history of mankind. Other factors existed, to be sure. An increasingly competitive economy made it both necessary and prudent to develop advertising, publicity and promotional techniques capable both of confronting competition and of reaching many potential "publics" with a degree of immediacy and over a widely dispersed area. A greater demand for information on the part of the public instigated new techniques for the distribution of information, sometimes purveyed as unvarnished fact, sometimes thinly overlaid with opinion. Persuasion became an important ingredient of the communication process, particularly in the practice of public relations. Most significantly, the "public be damned" philosophy became more than untenable. It was at variance with the new creed of public relations wherein the good will of the public and the good name of the institution became as important as growth or profits—indeed, became necessary for growth and profits, and even for survival. The orientation of institutions of all kinds—business, professional and educational—was directed toward maintaining, as a steady goal, the good will of the public. Even high educational administrators are chosen as much for their adeptness in public relations as for their academic experience or their administrative abilities.

That so powerful a tool of persuasion would generate serious considerations of value judgments and of ethical principles was inevitable. Hence, the growth of professional organizations and the call for criteria of behavior similar in substance to the canons of journalism of the newspaper publishers. Over the last decade, in fact, there has been an increasing re-

gard for the ethical overtones of public relations. The development of un-
dergraduate courses, as well as of graduate research, in the philosophy and
technique of public relations has helped to identify public relations more
closely with the social sciences and with the broader problems of public
opinion and the motivation of consent. On the other hand, David Riesman
looks upon the public as one vast lonely crowd, "other-directed" by the
manipulation of public relations men and conditioned to an unhealthy
concern for status and the good opinion of the peer group, rather than toward independence of thought and action.

The significance of public relations probably lies somewhere between
two disparate polarities, one of which would accept its techniques uncritically and as an inevitable concomitant of mass communications in a
mass society, while the other would reject it as unhealthy and unsavory
propaganda. Practiced ethically, public relations serves as a valuable catalyst
between the institution and the public it serves. Its usefulness is internal
as well as external. Indeed, in recent years, the public relations counsel
has done much to improve management approaches to the whole area of
human relations and to steer management institutions toward a more responsible recognition of their obligations to the press, as well as to the
public. In the struggle for the survival of a free and competitive economy in
a democratic society, public relations has played a constructive role. It must
be noted, too, that public relations as we know it, could not be amenable
to totalitarian philosophy, for its techniques are competitive as well as persuasive. The able public relations practitioner is as much as communicator
as the professional journalist, and serves a useful function in the whole
process of news gathering and dissemination, as Walter Lippmann pointed
out a quarter of a century ago in his book on public opinion. At its best,
public relations serves as a genuine two-way street between management
and the public, interpreting each to the other through the instrumentality
of the media of mass communication.

In large measure, both public relations and mass media reflect society.
In a lesser sense, both also attempt to meet public needs and to create
consent within the necessary circle of those goals and values which the
public has come to decide are worth achieving. If public relations functions
to inform and to influence public opinion, it should be recognized
that the increasing influence of public opinion also generated a need for
public relations and for the development of mass communications. The
news and informational media would function without the public relations middleman, but they would not function as well, or as smoothly.
Mass media helped make public opinion articulate and important. They
also helped to make public relations a useful tool in the interaction between institutions and the public they serve.

The development of mass media provided one impetus to the rise of
public relations. The development of a mass society, with a growing re-

moteness between the institution and its public, contributed also to the development of public relations techniques. Other peripheral factors contributed as well. An increasingly literate public generated greater demands on the press and other media, both for information and entertainment. Critics of the "bigness" of business instigated a healthy respect for consumer opinion—a concern for social and business ethics which began with the muckraking tracts of Lincoln Steffens, Ida Tarbell and their contemporaries. The need for an effective method of communication between management and the public resulted in the development of public relations for this purpose. Finally, public relations came to be considered an integral part of the healthy functioning of modern management, primarily because reputable public relations practitioners developed concepts of human relations and criteria for acting in the public interest as basic creeds of institutional behavior. Good deeds in the public interest has become more than the communication of an abstract idea. It is practiced with increasing vigor by those institutions which take their obligations to the public interest seriously.

The author has stated elsewhere[1] the conviction that training in the social sciences is an important and necessary ingredient for the work of the successful public relations practitioner. This means, in effect, a deeply rooted interest in, and understanding of, the recent empirical research in public opinion, as well as a familiarity with the possibilities and limitations of language and general semantics. It is the presence of semantic roadblocks in the communication process, particularly in verbal communication, which make difficult a definition and delineation of the place of public relations in the realm of discourse of the social sciences. Public relations-motivated statements and news releases which are based on flimsy fact, heavily overlaid with bias and opinion, are frequently a result, not merely of venality or propagandistic ends, but rather of ignorance of these semantic roadblocks to effective discourse. To adhere to a dictionary definition of public relations is to end in tautology, for public relations is an aspect of the communications process which bears best a functional or operational definition. It is more denotative than connotative in nature, but based on the concept of a philosophy of managment which places, as a primary goal, a favorably inclined public opinion as the result of "good deeds in the public interest."

What can distinguish ethical and effective public relations from the blandishment of press agentry is the recognition that it is an integral part of contemporary mass communications, that it is linked inextricably with the twenty-four hour news-gathering function of the press and that, above all, its activities are most successful when they are predicated on empirical studies and the findings of the social sciences. To exploit public opinion by press agentry is not to inform and influence it by public relations. Pub-

[1] *Public Relations Journal*, June, 1961, pp. 13-14.

lic relations, then, functions as a two-way street in two related contexts. It interprets public opinion (the viewpoint of the "publics") to management; and it interprets management's viewpoint to its "publics" by means of the mass media. Within the framework of, and from the content of, the mass media, public relations extracts soundings of opinion and, having appraised these in terms of their meaningfulness (i.e., their semantics or logic), it reacts to public opinion by the utilization of the very same mass media.

It is clear, then, that there is more involved in the activity of public relations than the writing and distribution, willy-nilly, of press releases. Public relations, as a "mass communicator," may involve one or more— usually all—of four procedures.[2] Primarily, the techniques of the social scientists are immeasurably helpful in providing information about public opinion, a force in itself about which there are vast differences of opinion. How much "reach" do mass media have in engendering opinion change? What is their effect in the political, social, cultural, economic areas? Does the press in a generic sense give the public what it wants, or what the editors would like the public to have—or an interaction between both? Are polls to be accepted in terms of sheer factual objectivity, or is there validity in conclusions subjectively arrived at as a result of reading in the mass media and of informal questioning of discrete "publics?"

In any event, such procedures and the promulgation of these questions offer information to public relations which is only as valuable, in terms of practice, as the skill with which these data are interpreted and evaluated. The public relations practitioner who is trained in the social sciences is in a better position to evaluate than the one who is not. Certainly this information provides a direction finder from which a philosophy of management, or an operating creed, is devised. The plan to build a factory in a prevailingly residential area, for example, may result in a mixed expression of opinion—affirmative, because of the imminence of jobs and other community benefits; and dubiety or negation, because of the downgrading of zoning and property values. This information can be used skillfully by the public relations practitioner by emphasizing to management that certain standards of excellence must be observed in building the plant, and by informing the public that the plant will be built by an outstanding industrial architect, that it will provide unusual community recreational opportunities, that it may well enhance property values and the general economy of the area.

As a result of the three steps of preliminary analysis, interpretation to management and implementation, the public relations practitioner can launch into the fourth step, the direct phase of action—the distribution of information to the public by means of the media of mass communication.

[2] Steinberg, Charles S. *The Mass Communicators: Public Relations, Public Opinion and Mass Media.* New York: Harper & Bros., 1958. Chapter 16, pp. 198-202.

In other words, public opinion research offers data which are essential to the construction of policy. But policy is, at best, an abstraction, and it becomes operative and dynamic through one or more steps in the process of mass communication. Mass media—newspapers, radio, television—are instrumental in servicing the public with information now devised in the form of a press release, a verbal statement at a press conference, a letter to stockholders and other related public relations efforts. In this way, the process of public relations becomes identified with the process of mass communication.

In the twentieth century, with its revolutionary changes in production, distribution and consumption and with the increasing remoteness between institutions and the publics they serve, it is evident, then, that effective public relations can be practiced best if it is aware of the methods of the social sciences. Certainly, practical public relations would create no consensus, would have little or no influence on public opinion were it not for the availability of mass media. For the media of mass communication not only function as a catalyst in the two-way-street relationship between management and the public; mass media are intrinsic to the very practice of public relations, since they are the avenues by which public relations content goes forth from source to receiving audience. The newspaper editor and the guardians of the wire services and syndicates might perform an adequate service to their readers and listeners without the catalyst of publicity, but few editors would deny that the most able public relations men are akin to the most able journalists, and that they perform an immensely valuable function in the whole process of purveying news to the public. The function of the public relations man is to seek the kernel of news that makes his message worth printing. The function of the editor is to find the kernel, separate it from narrow, vested interests or parochialism and print it, either as straight news or as attributed opinion that makes news.

What distinguishes public relations from overt propaganda are the very differences which distinguish reporting in a democracy and in an authoritarian state. The differences are freedom, responsibility, and competition. Where there is little regard for a free and responsible press, there is need for a ministry of propaganda, but not for public relations. For the practice of contemporary public relations is implicitly competitive. It aims to inform and to persuade and, in a society where pluralistic viewpoints are heard, the very process of influencing public opinion is implicitly controversial and competitive. There is no absolute truth in any public relations content that cannot be appraised by competitor or editor—or the public itself. This element of implicit controversy and explicit competitiveness offers an effective brake on the temptation to aggrandize the importance of motivation research, subliminal advertising and the cult of catering to status and the peer-group.

The public relations function at its best is an integral part of the daily operation of mass media. It contributes to the daily news-gathering job of the press. And, because it is not content to rest on the status quo and to prod activity into the future, it offers an affirmation of positive values. This is not to say that techniques of mass persuasion cannot be harmful or disruptive. It is, rather, to indicate that, given certain levers, public relations is a valuable adjunct to the contemporary process of mass communication. These levers are, first, the training, education and ethical standards of the public relations practitioner; second, the responsibility of journalists and editors; third, the responsibility of management. Finally, in a democratic society, there is ultimately a clear-cut regard for the power, however intangible, of public opinion, a respect for facts and for the effort to maintain a free and responsible press.

The public relations function may be said to have developed its own dialectic, its own logic of practice. Practiced with venality, it relies on conventional stereotypes. Practiced responsibly, it has a healthy regard for the ethics of the news-gathering process. The dynamics of public relations involve the transmission of written, oral or pictorial symbols to the receiving audience through the instrumentality of the mass media. If it is to be practiced intelligently, it must rely on the findings of the social scientists and upon the disciplines of language and meaning. Otherwise, the publicity and advertising message will succumb to the easy tendency to confuse words and things, which is simply a confusion of the symbols of reality and reality itself. Facts become half-facts, heavily overladen with opinion. All labor leaders become Frankensteins, all business becomes "big business," all scholars become "absent-minded." Words are the substance of communication, but they are not reality—not the thing in itself, but a representation of it. Confusion about this principle results in a confusion of meanings. Cognitive meanings become confused with emotive meanings and emotive meanings become confused with directive ones. Facts are not facts if heavily colored with directive or emotive meanings. They are facts only with application to a specific situation as defined.

Responsible public relations, then, practiced as an integral aspect of mass communication and as an adjunct to the mass media, is implicitly an aspect of the social sciences, relying upon their findings and disciplines. In no other way can it seek to understand and to inform and influence public opinion, which is its ultimate purpose and objective. But public relations and mass media can accomplish more than the understanding and influencing of public opinion. Through a healthy regard for truth, they can help to make public opinion operative and intelligent. And, in this way, they can contribute to the effective role of articulate public opinion in a democratic society.

10

THE EFFECTS OF MASS MEDIA

David Riesman
THE SOCIALIZING FUNCTIONS OF PRINT

Raymond A. Bauer and Alice Bauer
AMERICA, 'MASS SOCIETY' AND MASS MEDIA

Carl I. Hovland
EFFECTS OF THE MASS MEDIA OF COMMUNICATION

10

THE EFFECTS OF MASS MEDIA

THE question of the effects of the mass media of communication has become a consuming one for students, and has engaged increasingly the attention of social scientists in recent years. Although there have been sporadic studies in the effects of mass media, the pace of research has quickened considerably. Included here are a summary of some literature on the effects of mass media (Hovland); a segment of a larger canvas in which the effect of mass media is discussed as part of the author's point of view on American social behavior (Riesman); and a particular point of view on the relationship between mass media and mass society (the Bauers).

Although the concern of David Riesman and his associates is with group behavior, with the emergence of a "tradition-directed" society, the "lonely crowd" of Riesman's study involves that very society whose days and nights are permeated by almost constant exposure to the mass media. In one sense, mass communication is a result of a "tradition-directed" society which tends to attach a unique significance to the opinion of the peer group, with a deadly conformity the inevitable result. Crucial to Riesman's analysis is the attitude and reaction toward print media in the transition from an inner-directed to an other-directed society. In the dynamic individualism of the former, print satisfied a hunger. It served a socializing function. In the other-directed society, however—a period of incipient population decline—this satisfaction has reached a point of fulfillment leading to satiety and to new hedonism, rather than toward any serious inclination for knowledge. Print had its psychological problem children in an inner-directed period, in those who could make little or no "characterological" adjustment to its newness and its unlimited horizons. This is evident, for example, in the furor over censorship and control which resulted from the emergence of print.

Riesman's point is that print media, in a stage of inner direction (that period when the individual was dependent upon personalized goals, rather than on the opinion of other-directed peer groups) functioned to help the individual adjust toward the responsibilities of adult life. One may question whether this was literally true when one recalls that Horatio Alger was a literary product of that era. Furthermore, does not some literature serve the same purpose of allowing the reader to act out adult roles by means of fantasy even in an other-directed society? Print, or any other medium for that matter, tends to reflect societies and, in turn, is reflected by group needs and aspirations.

There is a distinction, Riesman points out, between literature which promises that every boy, with effort, might become President and literature that emphasizes consumer interests and status rather than goals. Periodical print media of today, therefore, reach the child in large measure in order to sell products. The child audience becomes the child market in which professional storytellers present a world in which every youngster sees what every other sees, not as each child might one day see the world with adult eyes. This "bombardment," Riesman states, is evident in radio and comic books, as well as in other media. All literature becomes patterned to the peer group habits of a tradition-directed society. And the crucial problem is that there tends to be concentration on ends, rather than on means or moral values. The conclusion is overwhelmingly important. The route to the goal, by fair means or foul, becomes totally irrelevant in the emphasis on ends rather than means.

The discussion of "America, Mass Society and Mass Media" evaluates the relationship between mass society and its system of communication. While there is no question that the development of mass media as instruments of information and entertainment must depend to a large extent on technological developments, as well as on economic wealth and social leisure, the growth of mass communication is also a specific result of the spread of literacy among the masses and the increasing emphasis on the process of education, as the authors indicate.

While it is true that contemporary civilization has created a demand for the functions of the mass media—although it must be reiterated that the mass media tend to reflect society—the authors believe that mass communication has become, to a great extent, a substitute for "real" experience. The crux of the Bauers' paper is that mass media are not as trenchant a force as some of their advocates would believe. Critics, both "theoretical" and "empirical" tend to overstress the impact and effect of mass media on the mass society. The authors make the significant, if moot, point that the more study there is in the effects of mass media, the less emphasis there will tend to be on the omnipotence of mass media, one reason being the greater resistance to "propaganda" after World War II. Nevertheless, if it be true that the results of research efforts show a diminution of the myth of omnipotence of the mass media, many professional critics and special interest groups still behave as if mass communication was increasing, rather than decreasing, in its influence on society. While it may be true that people do not, in general, change their political stand as a result of the impact of mass media, this is not invariably or exhaustively true. It is probably not true in terms of the effect of mass media on other aspects of our culture, apart from political influence.

While mass media may have limited effectiveness under many conditions, they also have maximum effect under many other conditions, as Robert K. Merton has shown in his study of the effect of a Kate Smith radio broadcast on behalf of War Bonds—and as the now famous Orson Welles "Men From Mars" radio broadcast indicated many years ago.[1]

The authors emphasize a significant stress on informal communications, a valid point and worth stressing in an age of "atomized" culture. There is, they assert, an importance for the entire society of "micro-systems" as well as a "macro-system."

Professor Hovland, in his study of the effects of mass media, touches upon the same problem attacked by the Bauers—the "actual role" of mass media in social life and human behavior. Professor Hovland's presentation summarizes the major findings, based on empirical research, of the effects of the mass media and follows with a discussion of the major factors which influence the effect of mass communication, one of these being the nature of the communicator.

Of particular significance is Hovland's emphasis on the urgent need for further research, because the status of mass communication within the total framework of the social sciences is relatively new and experimental. Particularly neglected, as such an authority as Berelson has shown, is the whole problem of evaluating the effects of mass media. Professor Hovland's contribution is all the more valuable, in that it not only summarizes major findings of fairly recent date, but attempts to relate these to "basic principles of communication analysis."

Summarized by Hovland are discussions of the earlier work of reading by Bernard Berelson and others; the work of Lundberg and others on the effect of the newspaper (the conclusion that reading the newspaper has little effect on the political opinion or action of the reader is significant, but omits the social, economic and cultural influence of the newspaper); the finding, by Lazarsfeld, Berelson and Gaudet, that newspapers have greater effect on specialized audiences; the conclusion by Lazarsfeld that radio listening tends to be complementary to the other media.

What is equally important as, if not more important than, the content and effects of mass media is the "who" in the now classical presentation "who says what to whom and with what effect." This is the role of the communicator. Hovland's findings here bear out what social psychologists have indicated. Those who hold the same opinion as the communicator usually feel "justified" in their conclusions. Furthermore, emotionally motivated propaganda tends to have greater credibility impact for the re-

[1] Merton, Robert K. *Mass Persuasion.* New York: Harper & Bros., 1946.

cipient than logical analysis. Finally, the findings on effects appear to indicate that oral presentation is more effective than printed matter in generating opinion change—a point which some social scientists would still consider highly conjectural.

*   *   *   *

RELATED READING

Bauer, Raymond A. "The Communicator and the Audience," *Journal of Conflict Resolution*, II (1958), 67-77.

Berelson, Bernard. "The Effects of Print upon Public Opinion," in Waples, Douglas (ed.), *Print, Radio, and Film in a Democracy*. Chicago: University of Chicago Press, 1942.

Cantril, H. (assisted by Hazel Gaudet and Herta Herzog). *The Invasion from Mars*. Princeton: Princeton University Press, 1940.

Gould, Jack. "What TV Is Doing To Us," *New York Times*, June 24-30, 1951.

Hamilton Robert V. and Lawless, Richard H. "Television Within the Social Matrix," *Public Opinion Quarterly*, XX (1956), 393-403.

Hyman, Herbert H. and Sheatsly, Paul B. "Some Reasons Why Information Campaigns Fail," *Public Opinion Quarterly*, XI (1947), 412-23.

Klapper, J. T. *The Effects of Mass Media*. New York: Columbia University Bureau of Applied Social Research, 1949. (Mimeo.)

Lazarsfeld, P. F. *Communication Research and the Social Psychologist*, in W. Dennis (ed.), *Current Trends in Social Psychology*, pp. 218-273. Pittsburgh: University of Pittsburgh Press, 1948.

Lazarsfeld, Paul F. and Stanton, Frank (editors). *Communications Research, 1948-49*. New York: Harper, 1949.

Merton, R. K. (assisted by Marjorie Fiske and Alberta Curtis). *Mass Persuasion*. New York: Harper, 1946.

Schramm, Wilbur. *The Process and Effects of Mass Communication*. Urbana: University of Illinois Press, 1954.

THE SOCIALIZING FUNCTIONS OF PRINT

By David Riesman

A. I like Superman better than the others because they can't do everything Superman can do. Batman can't fly and that is very important.
Q. Would you like to be able to fly?
A. I would like to be able to fly if everybody else did, but otherwise it would be kind of conspicuous.

From an interview with a twelve-year-old girl.*

The Socializing Functions of Print in the Stage of Inner-Direction

When societies enter the phase of transitional growth of population, formal schooling increases, in part to train people for the new, more specialized tasks of industry and agriculture, in part to absorb the young who are no longer needed on farms and whose schooling can be supported by the greater productivity of the society. Of course, these young people learn to read. But old as well as young are affected by the excitement and novelty of literacy: there is a widespread hunger for the press and for books—a hunger that the technology and distributive facilities arouse but do not entirely satisfy. This excitement, this hunger, is a sign of the characterological revolution which is accompanying the industrial one.

In the United States, as in other countries of incipient population decline, this hunger has abated; indeed, it has been succeeded for many by a kind of satiety with serious print, coupled with insatiability for the amusements and agenda of popular culture. To remind ourselves of the older pattern we can look at countries such as Mexico and Russia, now undergoing industrialization, where the old are avid for print and the young admired for learning. Some of this we can still see among the largely self-educated Negroes of the deep South who live among our surviving stratum of white and black illiterates.

How this development aided the shift from tradition-direction to

---

* Katherine M. Wolfe and Marjorie Fiske, "The Children Talk About Comics," *Communications Research, 1948-1949*, ed. Paul F. Lazarsfeld and Frank Stanton (New York, Harper, 1949), pp. 26-27.

inner-direction can be vividly traced in Thomas and Znaniecki's *Polish Peasant*.[1] These writers describe the way in which the Polish rural press helped to restructure attitudes and values among the peasantry at the turn of the last century. They show that an individual peasant who learned to read at that time did not merely acquire a skill with little impact on his character; rather he made a decisive break with the primary group, with tradition-direction. The press picked him up at this turning point and supported his uncertain steps away from the primary group by criticizing the values of that group and by giving him a sense of having allies, albeit anonymous ones, in this move.

In this way the press helped link the newly individuated person to the newly forming society. The Polish press also supported very specific "character-building" measures, such as temperance and thrift, and fostered scientific farming as the American agricultural extension services have done; science was viewed as a kind of inner-directed morality as against the superstition of the remaining, tradition-directed peasantry. These attitudes, expounded in newspaper non-fiction, were reinforced in the same media by highly moralistic fiction.

Thus the reader could escape into print from the criticisms of his neighbors and could test his inner-direction against the models given in the press. And by writing for the press himself, as he occasionally might do as local correspondent, he could bring his performance up for approval before an audience which believed in the magic attached to print itself—much like the Americans who, in the last century, contributed poetry to the local press. By this public performance, no longer for a face-to-face audience, the former peasant confirmed himself on his inner-directed course.

The Whip of the Word

The tradition-directed person had not only a traditional standard of living but a traditional standard of how hard and long he should work; and print served, along with other agencies of socialization, to destroy both of these standards. The inner-directed man, open to "reason" via print, often develops a character structure which drives him to work longer hours and to live on lower budgets of leisure and laxity than would have been deemed possible before. He can be driven because he is ready to drive himself.

Words not only affect us temporarily; they change us, they socialize or unsocialize us. Doubtless the printing press alone cannot completely assure any particular form of social coercion—and of course not all children, even in the inner-directed middle class, were readers. But print can powerfully rationalize the models which tell people what they ought to be like. Reaching children directly as well as through their parents and teachers, it can take the process of socialization out of the communal chimney corner

[1] W. I. Thomas and Florian Znaniecki, *The Polish Peasant in Europe and America* (New York, Knopf, 1927), II, 1367-1396.

of the era depending on tradition-direction and penetrate into the private bedrooms and libraries of the rising middle class: the child is allowed to gird himself for the battle of life in the small circle of light cast by his reading lamp or candle.

To understand this more fully we must realize that the rise of literacy affects not only the content and style of the literary and journalistic genres but also their audience reception. The increased quantitative flow of content brings about an enormous increase in each child's power to select, as compared with the era of tradition-direction. As a result, more and more of the readers begin to see messages not meant for them. And they read them in situations no longer controlled and structured by the teller—or by their own participation. This increase in the number, variety, and "scatter" of the messages, along with the general impersonalization in print which induces these specific effects, becomes one of the powerful factors in social change. The classic instance in western history, of course, is the translation of the Vulgate into the spoken languages, a translation which allowed the people to read a book which only the priests could read before.

Some of the difficulties of discussing the shift from the era depending on tradition-direction to that of inner-direction arise from the teleological drift of the language we are likely to use. For example, we are prone to overlook the unintended audience because it is always easier to assume that a given medium was deliberately aimed at the audience it actually succeeded in reaching. Yet there is no proof that the media have ever been so accurate in aim. The very impersonality of the situation in which print is absorbed helps to increase the chances of under-reception or over-reception. Thus the aristocrats were often displeased by what they considered the over-reception to mobility themes in many they would have liked to keep "in their place."

The over-effects I have most in mind, however, are those in individuals whose characterological guilts and tensions were increased by the pressure of print. Their character structure simply could not handle the demand put upon them in a society depending on inner-direction. Their gyroscopes spun wildly and erratically. Not finding justification in print—not finding, as many modern readers do, a "union of sinners," the "One Big Union" of mankind extending back through the past—they experienced print simply as an intensified proof of their maladjustment. A colonial divine armed with print could get his readers to cast themselves into hell-fire on weekdays, even if he could only address them in person on Sundays.

Thus, while the myths and symbolism of the societies depending on tradition-direction support the tradition by integrating the rebellious tendencies of the listener into a pattern of the culture, the word-in-print may disorient as well as orient its audience. This is evident in the cry for censorship which goes up as soon as literacy becomes widespread. And not only formal censorship. In America the increasing piety of print, if we compare, for instance, today's press with that of the early republic, may be in part explained by the sheer weight of the informal pressure put by near-universal literacy on editors who take their responsibility seriously. As the editor of a metropolitan paper used to say if his staff verged on bawdry: "Don't forget, gentlemen, that this paper goes into the *homes.*" Or as the *New York Times* puts it: "All the news that's fit to print."

While it is beyond my ability to measure precisely to what degree the media of the early capitalist period might have been "dysfunctional," by reaching unintended audiences in unintended ways, it seems reasonable to suppose that print contains more noise along its channels than does oral, face-to-face transmission.

Models in Print

One main purpose of print in the period dependent on inner-direction is to teach the child something about the variety of adult roles he may enter upon and to permit him to "try on" these roles in fantasy. Life during the period of transitional population growth differs from earlier epochs in that the adult frequently engages in activities which the growing child no longer observes or understands. He needs not only the rich vicariousness of print but also a mode of internal direction other than tradition to guide him in unaccustomed places and situations. Both the printed media and other forms of popular culture meet this need by adding their own spurs to the parents' admonitions on behalf of ambition as well as by offering more specific guidance about the variety of new paths to success.

These new paths, in both northern and southern lands after the Renaissance, are conceived and described in adult terms. For in the earlier stages of population growth adult life is not long, on the average; the age difference—and perhaps the difference in maturity—between the literate child and the full-grown adult is less than in the period of incipient decline of population. Moreover, while the distribution of imagery and print becomes wider and cheaper than ever before, there are still many people excluded by poverty from the storyteller's market; some of these are also the overworked young. In such a society the adult stories and adult styles of narrative are often made to do for children. Even when the trick, later so prevalent, of using the child's own language, gets started, the storyteller works on the notion that he can more successfully instill adult ideas if he uses the language of children.

Among the earliest signposts erected on the printed path to success, aside from the indirect guides of catechism and religious teaching, were the great authorities on etiquette. A volume like Castiglione's *The Courtier,* for example, was meant for adults; but there was nothing else on the subject for the near-adult to read. At the same time people were willing to assume, as Lord Chesterfield did, that the young man was ready in his teens to operate successfully in situations requiring etiquette. In the Protestant lands and classes however, after 1600 or so, the purpose of print is concerned more and more directly with how to succeed not in love or diplomacy but in business. Then follows the commercial inspirational literature that reached a sort of climax in Victorian England with the success biographies written by Samuel Smiles—and in the United States with the Horatio Alger books, which come closer to being slanted for the teen-age market.

Franklin's *Poor Richard's Almanack*, the text selected by Max Weber as a typical self-inspirational document of the period of the Protestant ethic, was preceded by books such as *Pilgrim's Progress* or *Robinson Crusoe* which, while not explicitly concerned with proper conduct for would-be enterprisers, nevertheless purvey many similar exhortations. Thus, in *Pilgrim's Progress* we can trace the motive of social election and salvation which can so easily become secularized, while in *Robinson Crusoe* the motive of economic self-sufficiency is expressed in its classical paradigm. Both works aim to fire the ambition and élan, spiritual and adventurous, of inner-directed youth. Thus, with an expanding bourgeois market, marked changes occur in the style of myth, as contrasted with the pre-industrial era dependent on tradition-direction. In the Middle Ages, for example, the individual learns about human nature from accounts no less realistic because couched in symbolic language—whether Christian, classical, or folk. Often, as is well known, they are not in verbal form at all, like the superabundance of messages in the glass and stone of a cathedral. The child is trained to understand—or, better, he is not trained away from understanding—symbolic meanings. As against this, the rising middle class dependent on inner-direction establishes for itself a new style of realism from which any direct use of symbolism is rigorously excluded.

This documentary style is one literary index of an era increasingly dependent on inner-direction. There is leisure in such an era for fiction—but little for fantasy. Defoe may be taken as archetypical. He used a variety of techniques, such as first-person narration, elaborate descriptions of food, clothing, and shelter, diary-like accounts of money transactions, and collaborative witnesses, to provide a realistic setting for his wildly adventurous tales. In this respect he is certainly the ancestor of the comic book, which excels in exploiting realism of detail as a distraction to hide improbability of situation. Such handling of literary material is connected in subtle ways with the handling of life experiences generally for the inner-directed middle-class Protestant. For him life is lived in its detailed externals; symbolic meanings must be filtered through the strenuously concrete.

Gradually, the early naturalism of Defoe gives way, both in England and on the continent, to a more detailed handling of the complex interpersonal relations of town life that arise in the era of transitional growth of population when people are pouring into the cities. With the growth of social classes in the modern sense, the novel begins to concern itself with subtle class differences between individuals: rises, falls, and collisions of status are perhaps its prime preoccupation. The child is instructed in an ambiguous social world, into which he will later move, by learning to recognize the subtly individualizing traits that bespeak class position and class morality.[2] Thus fiction as well as almanac and manual provide vocational (and status-oriented avocational) guidance.

To us today many of the individuals in the early Victorian novels, or in American Victorian melodrama like *East Lynne* or *Intolerance*—or even in some of Balzac's novels—appear as stereotypes. To their earliest audiences, however, these studies of personality and class in a society of shifting possibilities—a society of more people, and more people moving around—were perhaps not clichés which hindered understanding but explorations of a confusing world, helping to make sense of that world for the young. One can still attend a modern rural high school production of *Aaron Slick of Punkin Crick* and see to what extent an unsophisticated inner-directed audience will respond to the characterological "realism" of the play in terms of the older stereotypes of class, ambition, and virtue.

Biography as well as fiction allows children, in a society dependent on inner-direction, to move in imagination away from home and into a rationalized world—cooperating in this way with the parental installation of internal, self-piloting processes. In the George Washington myth, for instance, little boys learn that they may grow up to be president and are given scales by which to measure and discipline themselves for the job during boyhood: If they do not tell lies, if they work hard, and so on—if, that is, they act in their boyhoods as the legendary Washington acted in his—then they may succeed to his adult role. The role, moreover, by its very nature, is a continuing one; somebody is always president; thus its heroes do not have the once-for-all quality of those in the myths and legends of the earlier era. In fantasy the little boy not only identifies with young Washington in the French and Indian wars but also with the adult role of president —either role will take him far from home, socially and geographically.

What the story of George Washington could be for a white child the story of Booker T. Washington could be for a black one. Booker T. Washington's whole career could be described as an effort to turn the Negro away from dependence on tradition-direction toward dependence on inner-direction. One of his books addressed to Negroes was called *Character Building;* and *The Negro Worker,* a journal published at Tuskegee, with its strong emphasis on thrift, diligence, and manners, is one of the laggard remnants (of course, under violent attack from northern urban Negroes) of a vast literature concerned not with improving "personality" but with improving "character."

2 Compare the brilliant discussion by Lionel Trilling in "Art and Fortune," *Partisan Review,* XV (1948), 1271.

The Oversteered Child

There is, however, a danger for the child in such pious biographical portraits of exemplary persons and roles because of the very fact that he can read in isolation, without the intervention either of adults or peers; he can be "oversteered," that is, find himself set on a course he cannot realistically follow. The inner-directed child, trying to shape his character according to the ideals presented in print, does not see these models, any more than he sees his parents, in a state of undress. There is none of the familiarity with the hero, even the gods in the guise of heroes, to be found in the orally-mediated myths of the society depending on tradition-direction. Thus, Washington or Cromwell, Garibaldi or Bismarck, Edison or Ford, take on some of the awesomeness of the Calvinist God. The result for many is a dreadful insecurity as to whether they live up to their exalted models. This insecurity not even the parents (when they do not themselves make matters worse by trying to be such models) can easily assuage.

Nevertheless, this unmitigated pressure for inner-directed activity in pursuit of goodness and fame succeeded, as we know, in producing in many cases an "adjusted" person because social conditions rewarded inhibitions and solaced insecurities. In other cases, however, the gap between the demand for inner-direction and the capacity for it became too great and the individual broke down—the revival meeting both released and renewed, at one class level, some of the emotional pressures of such a conflict.

I want to emphasize here the dangers of putting some of the task of socializing the child onto other than the face-to-face adults. Just as the whipping Kachinas of the Hopi Indians can tailor their punishing or initiatory blows to a particularly sensitive child, so the adults in the era of tradition-direction can see to it that the bite of the story is not too grim for any in the audience. The child in the inner-directed era, however, leaves home both to go to school and to go to books and other mass-media products; and here such mediation is no longer possible.

Moreover, the child in a period of rising literacy is much more likely than his parents to be able to read. Thus, while some children learn from books and plays how to act in a career which will be different from that of their parents—or indeed that it is possible to have such a career—other children, less able to conform in the characterologically prescribed ways, less self-disciplined and systematic, for instance, learn from precisely the same media how lost they are. They learn this particularly if their parents are lacking in the proper ethos and have not been able to give them the proper early training in inner-direction. Others may find that print reinforces their feelings of inadequacy vis-à-vis their parents if they are characterological black sheep unable to live up to steep demands of the home.

While the stream of print has many dangers, it is seldom without some alleviating tendencies, even in the theocratic regimes. Almost always there is an underground of a more picaresque sort in which the growing boy, if not his sister, can take some refuge. To be sure, the power of the parents in an era dependent on inner-direction may keep out such literature, just as the pastors in puritan countries might also keep it out of the community. But they can hardly destroy the refuge of print itself—and we must not forget that the great reading-hour storehouse of the era depending on inner-direction is the Bible and that the Bible is not one book but many, with an inexhaustible variety of messages.

Such a refuge may encourage and permit the child to free himself from his family and primary group; and he may learn to criticize what he leaves behind, as did the self-emancipating readers of the Polish peasant press. It opens up to him a whole range of models—the "five-foot wardrobe" from which he can try on new roles. The Renaissance is itself testimony to this potency of the written word. Individualistic strivings find support as well as oversupport in the variety of paths of life described in print and drama. To be alone with a book is to be alone in a new way.

The Mass Media in the Stage of Other-Direction

The Child Market

As we have already seen, in the era of incipient decline of population children begin their training as consumers at an increasingly young age. In America middle-class children have allowances of their own at four or five; they have, as opinion leaders in the home, some say in the family budget. The allowances are expected to be spent, whereas in the earlier era they were often used as cudgels of thrift. Moreover, the monopolistic competition characteristic of this era can afford, and is interested in, building up in the child habits of consumption he will employ as an adult. For he will live long, and so will the monopoly. Monopoly is, in fact, distinguished by this very ability to plan ahead, because it can afford specialists to do the planning as well as resources saved from profits to pay for it and its later implementation.

For all these reasons, then, it has become worth while for professional storytellers to concentrate on the child market; and as the mass media can afford specialists and market research on the particular age cultures and class cultures involved, the children are more heavily cultivated in their own terms than ever before. But while the educator in earlier eras might use the child's language to put across an adult message, today the child's language may be used to put across the advertiser's and storyteller's idea of what children are like. No longer is it thought to be the child's job to understand the adult world as the adult sees it; for one thing, the world as the adult sees it today is perhaps a more complicated one.[3] Instead, the mass

[3] Certainly the adult literature is more complicated and/or more salacious on its top

media ask the child to see the world as "the" child—that is, the *other* child —sees it. This is partly the result of the technical advances that make it possible for the movies to create the child world of Margaret O'Brien and her compeers, for the radio to have its array of Hardys, Aldriches, and other juveniles, and for advertising and cover art to make use of professional child models. The media have created a picture of what boyhood and girlhood are like (as during the war they created the picture of the GI, again using the considerably edited language of the soldier) and they force children either to accept or aggressively to resist this picture of themselves.

The child begins to be bombarded by radio and comics from the moment he can listen and just barely read. The bombardment—which of course inevitably over- and under-shoots—hits specifically at very narrow age-grades. For example, there seems to be for many children a regular gradation of comic-reading stages: from the animal stories like *Bugs Bunny* to invincible heroes like *Superman,* and from there to heroes like *Batman* who, human in make-up, are vulnerable, though of course they always win. The study from which the quotation at the head of this chapter is taken finds that the children themselves are aware of the progression, aware of those laggards who still read romper media when they should have graduated to blue jeans.

To be sure, the change from the preceding era of inner-direction in America is not abrupt; such changes never are. Formerly the mass media catered to the child market in at least three fields: school texts or homilies, magazines designed for children, and penny dreadfuls. But when these are compared with the contemporary media we are at once aware of differences. The appraisal of the market by the writers of this earlier literature was amateurish in comparison with market research today. Moreover, they aimed generally to spur work drives and stimulate mobility rather than to effect any socialization of taste. The English boys' weeklies, as Orwell describes them,[4] usually opposed liquor and tobacco—as did the clergyman authors of school and church readers. Such admonitions remind us of the "crime doesn't pay" lesson of the comics, a façade for messages of more importance. The boys' weeklies and their American counterparts were involved with training the young for the frontiers of production (including warfare), and as an incident of that training the embryo athlete might eschew smoke and drink. The comparable media today train the young for the frontiers of consumption—to tell the difference between Pepsi-Cola and Coca-Cola, as later between Old Golds and Chesterfields.

We may mark the change by citing an old nursery rhyme:

---

levels, as compared with the earlier era when both child and adult could read Mark Twain even at his most bitter, Dickens even at his most crude, H. G. Wells even at his most involved.

4 George Orwell, *Dickens, Dali & Others* (New York, Reynal & Hitchcock, 1946), p. 76.

"This little pig went to market;
This little pig stayed at home.
This little pig had roast beef;
This little pig had none.
This little pig went wee-wee-wee
All the way home."

The rhyme may be taken as a paradigm of individuation and unsocialized behavior among children of an earlier era. Today, however, all little pigs go to market; none stay home; all have roast beef, if any do; and all say "we-we."

Winner Take All?

Yet perhaps the most important change is the shift in the situation in which listening and reading occur. In contrast with the lone reader of the era of inner-direction, we have the group of kids today, lying on the floor, reading and trading comics and preferences among comics, or listening to "The Lone Ranger." When reading and listening are not communal in fact, they are apt to be so in feeling: one is almost always conscious of the brooding omnipresence of the peer-group. Thus the Superman fan quoted at the head of the chapter cannot allow herself to identify with Superman —the others would think her foolish—while they would not think her foolish for believing that flying is very important.

In a society dependent on tradition-direction children are, as we have seen, introduced to stories by adult storytellers. The latter do not feel themselves to be in critical competition with the young. Hence they can encourage, or at least patronize, children's unsophisticated reactions of alarm or excitement at the tales they are told—and, later on, encourage the youngster's own tall talk and tale embroidery. But the peer-groupers who read or listen together without the protective presence of adults are in no such cozy relation of "listen my children and you shall hear . . ." They cannot afford to let go—to fly.

One correlate is that the comic book differs from the fairy tale in several important respects. In the fairy tale the protagonist is frequently an underdog figure, a younger child, an ugly duckling, a commoner, while the villain is frequently an authority figure, a king, a giant, a stepmother. In the comics the protagonist is apt to be an invulnerable or near-invulnerable adult who is equipped, if not with supernatural powers, at least with two guns and a tall, terrific physique. Magical aid comes to the underdog— who remains a peripheral character—only through the mediation of this figure. Thus, whereas Jack of *Jack and the Beanstalk* gains magical assistance chiefly through his own daring, curiosity, and luck, a comic-book Jack would gain magical assistance chiefly through an all-powerful helper. While vaguely similar themes may be found in the stories of Robin Hood and

Sir Galahad, the comics show a quantitative increase in the role of the more or less invulnerable authority-hero.

The relative change in this pattern[5] is not the "fault" of the comics. These merely play into a style of reception that is fitted to peer-group reading. Indeed, if other-directed child comic fans read or hear stories that are not comics they will read them as if they were comics. They will tend to focus on who won and to miss the internal complexities of the tale, of a moral sort or otherwise. If one asks them, then, how they distinguish the "good guys" from the "bad guys" in the mass media, it usually boils down to the fact that the former always win; they are good guys by definition.

But of course the child wants to anticipate the result and so looks for external clues which will help him pick the winner. In the comics this is seldom a problem: the good guys *look it*, being square-jawed, clear-eyed, tall men; the bad guys also look it, being, for reasons of piety, of no recognizable ethnic group but rather of a generally messy southern European frame—oafish and unshaven or cadaverous and oversmooth. But in movies (and in some comics with slinky beauties in them) this identification is not easy: the very types that are good guys in most comics may turn out to be villains after all. A striking example I have observed is the bafflement of several young comic fans at the movie portrayal of the Countess de Winter (Lana Turner) in *The Three Musketeers*. If she looked so nice, how could she be so mean?

Thus we come to a paradox. The other-directed child is trained to be sensitive to interpersonal relations, and often he understands these with a sophistication few adults had in the era of inner-direction. Yet he can be strikingly insensitive to problems of character as presented by his favorite storytellers; he tends to race through the story for its ending, or to read the ending first, and to miss just those problems of personal development that are not telltale clues to the outcome. It looks as though the situation of group reading, of having to sit on the jury that passes out Hooper ratings, forces the pace for the other-directed child. He cannot afford to linger on "irrelevant" detail or to daydream about the heroes. To trade preferences in reading and listening he need know no more about the heroes than the stamp trader needs to know about the countries the stamps come from.

Fairy tales and the Frank Merriwell books also emphasize winning; hence it is important to see the precise differences introduced by the contemporary media as well as by the changed focus of the readers. One striking difference is that between the older ambition and newer "antagonistic

[5] Here, too, the abruptness of the change from inner-direction should not be exaggerated. Eliot Freidson, studying the ability of young children to remember stories, found them much more apt to recall a few traditional fairy tales like *Goldilocks* or *The Three Little Pigs* than either Golden Books or comics or movies. "Myth and the Child: an Aspect of Socialization" (Master's thesis, University of Chicago, 1949).

cooperation." Ambition I define as the striving for clear goals characteristic of the period of inner-direction; it may be a striving for fame or for goodness: to get the job, to win the battle, to build the bridge. Competition in the era depending on inner-direction is frequently ruthless, but at the same time people are in no doubt as to their place in the race—and that there is a race. If they feel guilt it is when they fail, not when they succeed. By contrast, "antagonistic cooperation" may be defined as an inculcated striving characteristic of the groups affected by other-direction. Here the goal is less important than the relationship to the "others." In this new-style competition people are often in doubt whether there is a race at all, and if so, what its goals are. Since they are supposed to be cooperative rather than rivalrous, they may well feel guilt about success and even a certain responsibility for others' failure.

Certainly, it is ambition that strikes us as an outstanding trait of the heroes of boys' literature in the era of inner-direction. Moreover, it is an ambition with which the child reader can identify, even if the particular goal—to fight Indians or find the treasure or North Pole or swim icy rivers or detect crime—is at the moment a remote one; that is, the reader could in fantasy emulate the moral qualities of the hero, such as his bravery and his self-control. Thus, while these heroes, like the modern heroes, almost invariably won, the reader was encouraged to be concerned not only with the final victorious outcome but with the inner struggles that preceded it and made it possible.

It is sometimes loosely said that the comic strip merely continues this older set of themes in a new medium, but the fact is that the themes change and the identifications change even more. Where, as often happens, children prefer comics in which the hero is not man but Superman or Plastic Man, possessing obviously unique powers, identification languishes; no amount of willpower, no correspondence course with Lionel Strongfort, will turn one into Superman even in the wildest flight of fantasy. And such flights of fantasy appear to be less available today. Exposed to ever more sophisticated media, the children are too hep for "unrealistic" daydreams; at the movies they soon learn the fine points and will criticize a Western because the hero fired seven shots running from his six-shooter. The media in turn encourage this realism with their color effects and sound effects, which exceed by far the realism of petty detail which Defoe and his successors strove for. The characters in much fiction of the era dependent on inner-direction were props—stereotypes of the sort indicated in the preceding section. In Jules Verne, for instance, it is the adventures, the mechanical details, not the characters, that are sharply delineated; the latter are loose-fitting uniforms into which many boys could fit themselves. The imaginative, tenebrous illustrations of an artist like Howard Pyle also left openings for identification on the part of the reader who wanted to picture himself as the hero.

Little of this looseness of fit remains for the imagination of the modern reader or listener to fill in. Though comic-strip and comic-book characterization is, if anything, less sharp, externals are pinned down conclusively: every detail of costuming and speech is given. This is the more necessary because, with so many mass-media heroes competing for attention, their portrayers must engage in marginal differentiation in search of their trade-mark. Bodies by Milton Caniff must be as instantly recognizable as bodies by Fisher.

There is paradox in the reception of this realism. On the one hand, every additional brush stroke of the comic-strip artist rules out identifications for millions; the small-breasted girl, for example, may find only disapproval for herself in the comics. On the other hand, the same realism is one source of the fear of being conspicuous in our little Supergirl cited at the chapter head. If she were Superman, she would be instantly recognizable. She would lack the privacy of narcissism permitted the reader of an earlier day who could gloat over the fact that he was M. Vidocq or Sherlock Holmes—only nobody knew it.

These generalizations need not be pushed too far. There are children —at least one has heard of them—who identify with Superman, or, more easily, with Terry or the Saint. Nor is it out of the question to identify, at the same time, on one level of consciousness with the hero and on another level with the person he rescues. And while the heroes of the comics are ageless, having discovered the secret of eternal youth, the growing child can move from one hero to another who better fits his own changing needs and aspirations. These counter-tendencies are encouraged by the gadgetry —Superman cloaks, and so on—that relates children to their radio, movie, and comic-book heroes. But it would be a mistake to assume that each wearer of Superman cloak identifies with Superman; he may only be a fan, wearing his hero's colors.

Perhaps it is also significant that the comic book compresses into a few minutes' reading time a sequence which, in the earlier era, was dragged out in many pages of print. Think of the Count of Monte Cristo's years in jail, his suffering, his incredible patience, and the industry and study of the abbé's teaching; both his gain and his vengeance are moralized by these prolongations, and he is an old man when, after many chapters, he wins. By contrast, the comic-book or radio-drama hero wins almost effortlessly; the very curtailment of the telling time itself makes this more apparent. To be sure, like his movie counterpart, this hero does frequently get beaten up, but this adds to excitement, not to morality or inner change, and helps justify an even worse beating administered to the "crooks."

Still another aspect of this change is worth looking at. If one does not identify with the winner but is at the very same time preoccupied with the process of winning itself, as the best handle by which one grasps a story, one is prepared for the role of consumer of others' winnings. One is prepared, that is, for the adult role of betting on the right horse, with no interest in the jockey or horse or knowledge of what it takes to be either. The content of the identification is impoverished to the point where virtually the only bond between reader and hero is the fact of the hero's winning. The spectator—the same holds for a quiz game, a sport contest, and, as we shall see, a political contest—wants to become involved with the winner simply in order to make the contest meaningful: this hope of victory makes the event exciting, while the game or contest or story is not appreciated for its own sake.

The victory of the hero, then, is only ostensibly a moral one. To be sure, vestiges of older moralities hang on, often as conventions enforced by censorship or the fear of it. But morality in the sense of a literary character's development, rather than morality in the sense of being on the side of law and right, is not depicted. Consequently, morality tends to become an inference from winning. Just as in a whodunit all appear guilty until they are retroactively cleared by finding the real killer, so the victory of the hero retroactively justifies his deeds and misdeeds. "Winner take all" becomes a tautology.

AMERICA, 'MASS SOCIETY' AND MASS MEDIA [1]

By Raymond A. Bauer and Alice Bauer

I. What Model of Study Can Be Used

THERE SEEMS TO BE little doubt that there is some determinate relationship between a society and its system of communications. Certain gross relationships seemed obvious. It is certainly more than an accident that the society most developed technologically should also be the society in which mass communications are also most developed. The history of the growth of the American system of communications can be written largely in technological and economic terms. The extensive development of the mass media for transmission of information and entertainment depended on a high level of technological advance and a great deal of wealth and social leisure. It is equally certain that there is also a determinate relationship in the other direction, that a society as complex and extensive as ours requires a flow of information and ideas that could not be handled by more primitive means. It has also been suggested—although this is a moot point—that our civilization generates a demand (apart from and beyond opportunity) for the vast amount of diversion and entertainment that is produced by our press, radio, movies, and television.

There is a considerable body of speculation and generalization concerning the relationship of the mass media of communication to American society. While there is a wide variety of assertions—optimistic and pessimistic, specific and general, informed and uninformed, sophisticated and naive—on this topic, there is only one position of prominence which approximates a coherent "theoretical" statement, the so-called theory of mass

[1] In the several years since this essay was written in 1956-1957 (as part of a larger study of American society being conducted by Professor Walt W. Rostow in the Center for International Studies, M.I.T.) a good deal of material has continued to appear on this topic. In our judgment the newer material (essays and empirical data) would not cause us to change the positions we took at the earlier period. There is, of course, a temptation to cite such newer data when it seems to favor one's foresight. However, rather than succumb to such a temptation we have limited ourselves in mid-1960 only to such editorial revisions as seemed needed for additional clarity. The arguments (and the sources) stand as of mid-1957.

Reprinted from the *Journal of Social Issues*, Volume XVI, No. 3, 1960, by permission of the Journal of Social Issues and the authors.

society and mass culture. We use the word "theoretical" in quotation marks because we agree with Bell [2] that the statements of the proponents do not in fact constitute a set of interrelated propositions of sufficient coherence to justify the label of a theory. Nevertheless the "theory of mass society" must, by virtue of its provocativeness, the articulateness of its supporters, and its prevalence among intellectuals, be taken as the point of departure in a discussion of the role of the mass media in America.

The essentials of the theory are rather familiar.[3] Bell summarizes them briefly:

> The conception of "mass society" can be summarized as follows: The revolutions in transport and communications have brought men into closer contact with each other and bound them in new ways; the division of labor has made them more interdependent; tremors in one part of the society affect all others. Despite this greater interdependence, however, individuals have grown more estranged from one another. The old primary group ties of family and local community have been shattered; ancient parochial faiths are questioned; few unifying values have taken their place. Most important, the critical standards of an educated elite no longer shape opinion or taste. As a result, mores and morals are in constant flux, relations between individuals are tangential or compartmentalized rather than organic. At the same time greater mobility, spatial and social, intensifies concern over status. Instead of a fixed or known status symbolized by dress or title, each person assumes a multiplicity of roles and constantly has to prove himself in a succession of new situations. Because of all this, the individual loses a coherent sense of self. His anxieties increase. There ensues a search for new faiths. The stage is thus set for the charismatic leader, the secular messiah, who, by bestowing upon each person the semblance of necessary grace and fullness of personality, supplies a substitute for the older unifying belief that the mass society has destroyed.[4]

The key event in the evolution of the mass society (not always explicitly acknowledged) was the development of printing. Once it was possible to disseminate printed material to large numbers of persons at low cost, a number of things began to happen. The intellectual and artistic level of printed material, it is argued, was watered down to suit the popular taste. With successive technological advances—movies, radio, television—the economics of mass communications demanded that a successively broader audience be reached and hence that the level of performance be

---

[2] Daniel Bell, "The Theory of Mass Society," *Commentary*, July, 1956, 75-83.
[3] A representative statement of this view may be found in C. Wright Mills, *The Power Elite*, New York, Oxford University Press, 1956, Chapter 13, "The Mass Society." Bernard Rosenberg and David Manning White, editors, *Mass Culture*, Glencoe, Ill., The Free Press, 1957, contains a good sample of representative essays by proponents of the notion of the mass society and mass culture. This volume contains also a number of well presented dissents.
[4] Bell, *op. cit.*, p. 75.

more and more accommodated to the least common denominator of taste. On the one hand, the public (the alternate term is "masses") became the patron of the arts. On the other hand, the broad mass of people also became the victims of mass communications. Being "atomized" by industrial society they developed an insatiable appetite for narcotizing diversion, a circumstance which makes them susceptible to the machinations of the few who control the media of communications. One result of this process, it is alleged, is that the groundwork is laid for totalitarianism. Another result is the progressive deterioration of the arts and of cultural taste. The general argument is bolstered by a number of subsidiary propositions. The mass media, by portraying debauchery and violence, stimulate the same sort of behavior in the masses. The mass media became a substitute for "real" experience, etc.

Many of these features of mass communications are blamed by some critics on specific groups or individuals who are regarded as being in a position to correct the abuses and improve the quality of information and entertainment (more properly, to replace entertainment by art since in these discussions the two are often placed in opposition to each other). However, the pure version of the "theory of mass society" treats the possibility of such reform as an illusion:

> There are theoretical reasons why Mass Culture is not and can never be any good . . . The mass man is a solitary atom, uniform with and undifferentiated from thousands and millions of other atoms who go to make up "the lonely crowd," as David Riesman well calls American society. . . . My own feeling is that, as in the case of the alleged responsibility of the German (or Russian) people for the horrors of Nazism (or Soviet Communism), it is unjust to blame social groups for this result. Human beings have been caught up in the inexorable workings of a mechanism that forces them . . . into its own pattern. I see Mass Culture as a reciprocating engine, and who is to say, once it has been set in motion, whether the stroke or the counterstroke is "responsible" for its continued action? [5]

A number of writers accept a large portion of the "theory of mass society" but view the role of the mass media more optimistically. Authors such as Lyman Bryson and others see the mass media as binding the industrial society together, as serving as a latter-day town meeting, folk ceremony, town crier, etc.[6] This is to say they agree with much of what the critics of mass society have to say, but are less pessimistic about the side effects of mass communications and more optimistic in general about the fate of our society. For the most part, the position of the defenders of mass communications is less well developed, does not cut so deep, nor does it pose

[5] Dwight Macdonald, "A Theory of Mass Culture" in Rosenberg and White, editors, *op. cit.* These quotations are taken from pp. 69-72. Although they do not occur in sequence in the text they form the essence of Macdonald's argument.
[6] Lyman Bryson, editor, *The Communication of Ideas; a Series of Addresses,* New York: Institute for Religious and Social Studies, distributed by Harper & Bros. 1948.

so many meaningful problems. It is not out of disrespect for the proponents of the more optimistic view that we have decided to focus our attention on the critics; it is rather that the critics constitute more of a challenge by virtue of their numbers, the plausibility of many of their dire predictions, and the elaborate machinery of scholarship they have mobilized.

The over-all approach we would like to adopt is that of a parallel comparison of the "pure" form of the theory of mass society as it applies to the role of mass communications with the findings and the theoretical models of empirical researchers of mass communications. In doing this, we will have, of course, to indulge in certain exaggerations. The distinction between the "theorists" and the "researchers" is difficult to maintain empirically, since there is at many points a considerable overlap of personnel. Furthermore, not all the "theorists of the mass society" agree at all points with the more extended version of that position. Nevertheless, the attempt seems worth the effort. Where there is an appropriate body of data, we will ask whether or not it squares with the theory of mass society. Where there are no direct data, we will compare the assumptions of the researchers with the assumptions of the "critics of mass society." It does not follow inevitably, of course, that the assumptions of the researchers are necessarily more correct than the assumptions of the commentators. However, the assumptions of the researchers are more likely to be conditioned by their direct contact with empirical data. For this reason it seems worthwhile to proceed on an assumption of our own, that the assumptions of the researcher are likely to be closer to "reality."

The reader may perhaps be alert to the oft-made assertion that the researchers were hired to prove to advertisers that the mass media could influence buying habits.[7] This could lead one to anticipate that the researchers are therefore prejudiced in favor of the mass media. Though honest men, they may in fact be so prejudiced. If they are, then our general observation that it was precisely the attempts to "prove" (or, more neutrally, assess) the effects of the mass media which led to a realization of their limitations, is all the more remarkable.

II. THE COMMUNICATION MODEL'S ASSUMPTIONS[8]

The Myth of the Omnipotent Media

Prior to World War II a substantial portion of the literate Americans seemed morbidly preoccupied with the power of the mass media. Exposés

[7] cf. David Riesman, "Listening to Popular Music," in Rosenberg and White, editors, *op. cit.*, 408-409.
[8] The same line of argument as we employ in this section will be found in Elihu Katz and Paul Lazarsfeld, *Personal Influence*, Glencoe, Illinois: The Free Press, 1955. These authors assemble a good deal of research evidence in support of the researcher's model of communication. While our presentation agrees with theirs, our own view of the researcher's model evolved independently, although largely out of the same evidence.

were written of the "lords of the press," of the domination of the mass media by "special interests," and of the low, conniving, sinister, and—of course—spectacularly successful tactics of such "propagandists" as George Creel, Ivy Lee, and Edward L. Bernays. Undergraduates were offered courses in "public opinion and propaganda" in which a good portion of the course time was devoted to training them in the analysis and detection of distortion in the press and radio. The Institute for Propaganda Analysis were formed. Adult education sessions were held. The U. S. Senate conducted an investigation of "munitions industry propaganda" upon our entrance into World War I. Readers, writers, researchers, social critics, almost everyone who viewed the mass media, whether from inside or out, shared the common tacit impression of their omnipotence. The predominant view was that there was almost a one-to-one relationship between the content of the media and their impact on the public. A recent critic of the mass media says: "The opinion-maker's belief in the media as mass persuaders almost amounts to magic . . ." [9] This belief in the magic of the media was not in the past confined to the opinion maker, but shared with him by the researcher and the critic.

Katz and Lazarsfeld point out that the mass media were regarded historically either with optimism as being potentially the functional equivalent of the "town meeting" in the new urban society, or pessimistically "as agents of evil aiming at the total destruction of democratic society"—this latter view corresponding to that of the present-day critics of the mass media. Both parties, however, shared the same implied premises:

> From one point of view, these two conceptions of the function of the mass media appear widely opposed. From another viewpoint, however, it can be shown that they are not far apart at all. That is to say, those who saw the emergence of the mass media as a new dawn for democracy and those who saw the media as instruments of evil design had very much the same picture of the *process* of mass communications in their minds. Their image, first of all, was of an atomistic mass of millions of readers, listeners and movie goers prepared to receive the Message; and secondly, they pictured every Message as a direct and powerful stimulus to action which would elicit immediate response. In short, the media of communication were looked upon as a new kind of unifying force—a simple kind of nervous system—reaching out to every eye and ear, in a society characterized by an amorphous social organization and a paucity of interpersonal relations. [10]

It is ironic, or perhaps inevitable, that this view is retained in substantial fashion by only the critics of the mass media. We say that it is perhaps inevitable that this group retains this image because without this image they could not maintain their present level of alarm over the impact of the

[9] Mills, *op. cit.*, p. 315.
[10] Katz and Lazarsfeld, *op. cit.*, p. 16.

mass media. It would still be possible to be critical, but not with the same degree of intensity, and with the same degree of assurance that the content of the media could be equated with their effect on the populace.

There were many sources, some negative and some positive, of this earlier exaggerated view of the power of the mass media. One of them was the bragging of World War I propagandists, such as George Creel. Their boasting, and the horrified reactions of the exposers of wartime propaganda reenforced each other. Secondly, a relatively few newspapers and then radio chains began to dominate the mass media. The absolute number of daily newspapers began to shrink after the first decade of the century, even though the population was growing rapidly. As far as the remaining newspapers were concerned, their independence was prejudiced by the growth of newspaper chains, and the wire services. In the thirties, radio, the new medium, appeared to be becoming even more "monopolistic" than the press. To these actual developments we must add a third factor, the attitude of Marxists toward capitalist society. Even if there had been no changes in the structure of the American mass media, or the experience of World War I propaganda, it is likely that many American intellectuals of the thirties would have been concerned with the fact that the mass media were owned by capitalists and largely financed by the advertising of other capitalists.

To the above factors must be added a fourth negative one. Most communications research prior to World War II was concerned with the structure of the media, with their content, and with the nature of their audience or readership. The study of effects was much more poorly developed. It is highly improbable that any one of these researchers in response to a direct question, would have said that there was a direct linear relationship between the content of the communications he was studying and the effect of this content on the audiences he studied. Yet, either this assumption was built into his work, or he had to question it directly by studying effects rather than taking them for granted. Needless to say, effects were studied and the more they were studied, the more vulnerable became the notion of the omnipotence of the mass media. Effect studies date back well into the early twenties. However, it was not until approximately the beginning of World War II that their full impact was felt and the researchers' model of the role of the mass media began to diverge explicitly from that which is still held by many commentators on mass communications.

We will dwell at some length on the developments in communications research which challenged the notion of the omnipotence of the mass media. For this reason we shall pause briefly to note a convergent trend arising out of the practical experience of the "operators," the opinion makers. This development is recorded by Kris and Leites in their essay on "Trends in Twentieth Century Propaganda." [11] The authors note that there was a

11 Ernst Kris and Nathan Leites, "Trends in Twentieth Century Propaganda," reprinted

great disparity between the propaganda of World War I and that of World War II. There were three areas of difference: World War II propaganda was less emotional; it was less moralistic; "propaganda during the second World War tended to put a moderate ceiling on grosser divergences from presently or subsequently ascertainable facts, divergences that were more frequent in propaganda during the first World War." [12] In other words, despite the greater development of the mass media in the latter period, they were employed with a more modest conception of their powers.

Kris and Leites place two interesting qualifications on their generalizations. The trend they note became more marked as World War II progressed. Second, it is more true of the propaganda of the Western democratic countries (which, by the way, were the areas in which communications research predominated) than of the propaganda of Germany and Russia.

They attribute this trend, at least in part, to the development of resistance to propaganda among the Western peoples during the period between the wars. There seems to be little doubt that there is a large measure of truth in this point. It is scarcely probable that both the communicators and their audience were not affected by the spate of propaganda exposés in the period preceding World War II, and that the communicators as a consequence were more alert to creating conditions of confidence. To the extent that this factor carried weight, it is possible that the "myth of omnipotence" was *more* accurate in the prewar period. It is our suspicion, however, that it was extremely inaccurate even then. But, whatever weight we give to the argument of Kris and Leites as to cause of this shift, the fact remains that World War II propagandists became progressively more conservative in their estimate of what could be accomplished by the skillful manipulation of words.

Dissolution of the Myth

In the Foreword to Katz and Lazarsfeld's *Personal Influence*, written in 1955, Elmo Roper comments:[13]

> As the result of my own research into public attitudes I have come to the tentative conclusion that ideas often penetrate the public as a whole slowly and—even more important—very often by interaction of neighbor on neighbor without any apparent influence of the mass media.

Perhaps some statement of this sort might be found among the public utterances of opinion pollers of the prewar era. However, Roper's phraseology implies what our own judgment suggests, that it is highly unlikely

in Wilbur Schramm, editor, *The Process and Effects of Mass Communication*, Urbana: University of Illinois Press, 1955, 489-500.

[12] *Ibid.*, p. 491.

[13] Elmo Roper in the Foreword to Katz and Lazarsfeld, *op. cit.*, p. xv.

that any one would even have asked himself the relevant question. In this question we would like to trace the sequence of events that led to the dissolution of the myth of the omnipotence of the mass media in the minds of the researchers.

During the thirties, concern over control of the press by representatives of limited interest groups was naturally most actively focused on the field of politics. In an era when Franklin D. Roosevelt enjoyed overwhelming popular support, the press was overwhelmingly opposed to him. Recalling as best we can the feel of the mid-thirties, we have the impression that Roosevelt's victory was regarded as a personal triumph. Politically it seemed to be a fluke. While this might have led to doubts about the role of the press, there was in fact, no strong initial tendency to question the power of the press. Rather the lesson that was learned from the 1936 election was that the press did not represent majority opinion; and therefore, one had all the more reason to fear its power.

The turning point in the communications researcher's view of the model of mass communications came during the 1940 electoral campaign. True, Roosevelt won again in the face of a hostile press. But more pertinently, Lazarsfeld *et al.* did a study of voting behavior in Erie County, Pennsylvania.[14] This study was designed to test the influence of the mass media on voting in a presidential election. The results of this portion of the investigation were essentially negative. There was little evidence of people changing their political stand as a result of the influence of the mass media. As we have indicated above, negative results from effect studies had earlier precedents. The status of the Erie county study as a turning point, therefore, must be attributable to several novel factors:

(1). Since this was a large-scale, very carefully conducted survey employing the panel technique of following the opinions and behavior of a sample of people over several months, the Erie County findings were perhaps the most convincingly negative to that time.

(2). The gathering of additional data permitted a provisional exploration of an alternative model, that of the "two-step flow of communications." This two-step model was suggested by the fact that the persons who actually changed their voting intentions, had done so as a result of personal contact rather than under the influence of the press or radio.

(3). The notion of the "two-step flow" was not permitted to die. The continuing research interests of Paul Lazarsfeld and his colleagues and the existence of the Bureau of Applied Social Research at Columbia University, resulted in an active exploration of this new model in a series of studies aimed at locating "opinion leaders" and patterns and processes of personal influence.

(4). As so often happens, "the times were ripe," and other studies produced convergent results.

[14] Reported in the now famous, Paul Lazarsfeld, Bernard Berelson, and Hazel Gaudet, *The People's Choice* (2nd ed.), New York: Columbia University Press, 1940.

This was most marked with respect to wartime informational programs. The World War I propagandist was free to ply his trade unhampered by any feedback from his audience. But, between the wars, the technique of survey research had been developed, as had social psychological methods of experimental evaluation of the impact of communications.

Some of the survey assessments of the success of public information campaigns produced dismally discouraging findings. The following example is merely illustrative:

> . . . a survey was conducted early in the war to determine why people bought war bonds. Most of them (65 per cent in April, 1943) said it was to finance the war; at this time 14 per cent said it was to help inflation. A tremendous advertising campaign was conducted in the next few years, with the prevention of inflation an important theme. In June, 1945, 68 per cent of the people thought bonds should be bought to help finance the war and 14 per cent thought they should be bought to help prevent inflation.[15]

The Research Branch, I & E Division of the War Department, conducted careful experimentation on the effects of mass communications.[16] Other experimental studies in the past had been premised upon the differential effect of various types of communications and media. But these experiments, being larger in scale than any previous research program of like nature, and coming at a time when field research was producing such marked negative findings, drove one more wedge into the image of an omnipotent mass communications system by showing that communications are highly differential in their impact. To cite as an example one of the most famous of these experiments, whether a one-sided or two-sided presentation of an argument was more effective depended on the initial attitude of the audience.[17]

Even though experimental studies demonstrated the variability of response to communications, such studies were by no means as persuasive as were additional field studies which continued to demonstrate the limited effectiveness of mass communications under many conditions. Whereas social scientists of the prewar period wrote exposés of "principles of propaganda," those of the postwar period wrote articles such as "Some Reasons Why Information Campaigns Fail." [18]

One of the most conspicuous failures of an information campaign was the attempt in 1947-1948 to bring information about the United Nations

[15] Mason Haire, *Psychology in Management*, New York, McGraw-Hill, 1956.
[16] Reported in Carl I. Hovland, Arthur A. Lumsdaine, and Fred D. Sheffield, *Experiments in Mass Communications*. Princeton, Princeton University Press, 1949.
[17] *Ibid.*, Chapter 8.
[18] Herbert H. Hyman and Paul B. Sheatsley, "Some Reasons Why Information Campaigns Fail," reprinted in Guy E. Swanson, Theodore M. Newcomb and Eugene L. Hartley, editors, *Readings in Social Psychology*, 2nd ed., New York: Henry Holt and Co., 1952, 86-95.

to the people of Cincinnati.[19] In an effort to stimulate interest in and convey information about the United Nations, two organizations literally bombarded the city of Cincinnati with an informational campaign over a period of six months. Radio stations scheduled 150 spot broadcasts a week. The newspapers played up United Nations news over the six months' period. This use of the mass media was supplemented by less formal means. Hundreds of movies were shown. "In all, 59,588 pieces of literature were distributed and 2,800 clubs were reached by speakers supplied by a speakers' bureau." "The objective was to reach in one way or another every adult among 1,155,703 residents in Cincinnati's retail trading zone." [20]

The National Opinion Research Center conducted a survey of the local opinions and attitudes toward the United Nations at the beginning and at the end of this six months' period. As far as increasing knowledge of the United Nations was concerned, the campaign was a failure: ". . . the before and after scores remained remarkably constant; for example, in September, 34 per cent said they had heard of the United Nations' veto power and 7 per cent could explain how it worked; in March these figures were almost unchanged—37 per cent and 7 per cent." [21] This was approximately the picture on all items. While a few improved over the six months' period, others became worse, and still others were unchanged.

The major explanation of the failure of the informational campaign lay in the fact that the people who were initially best informed and least in need of information were precisely those who were most likely to be exposed to the communications. The less well informed people, who in fact indicated their own need and desire for information, simply were not reached; their interest was not sufficient to cause them to attend the communications.

We have, of course, no intention of maintaining that the mass media have no effect. We do believe, however, that the accumulated evidence of communications research challenges sharply three premises that underlie, either implicitly or explicitly, the model of communications still held by the "critics of mass society" and which have been abandoned by the researchers: (1) that informal communications play a minor role, if any, in modern society; (2) that the audience of mass communication is a "mass" in the sense of being socially "atomized"; (3) that content and effect may be equated.

The Role of Informal Communication

Certainly no single individual has ever said that there were no informal communications in an industrial society. Yet, inevitably, in studying the differences between communications in a modern industrial society

---

[19] Reported in Shirley A. Star and Helen MacGill Hughes, "Report on an Educational Campaign: The Cincinnati Plan for the United Nations," *American Journal of Sociology*, January, 1950, 55, 389-400.
[20] *Ibid.*, p. 390.
[21] *Ibid.*, p. 392.

and a folk society, one tended to emphasize the relative unimportance of informal communications in a society dominated by the mass media. The obvious thing to study was the distinctive, new phenomenon of a system of mass communications. The tacit assumption of both social theorists (whether optimistic or pessimistic in their approach to the media), and of communications researchers up to World War II, was that informal communications played no crucial role in a "mass society."

Probably the main support for this assumption was, as suggested above, the amount of attention devoted to such significant social events as the development of the press, the growth of the movie industry, and the emergence of radio broadcasting. Additional support was found in the belief that primary groups had little role in a modern industrial society. As Shils points out in his review of the study of the primary group,[22] American sociologists of two or three decades ago tended to regard primary groups as an anachronism.[23] European social theorists (among them, Marx), whether pessimistically or optimistically, looked forward to the "new society" in which informal primary groups would disappear. Marxist utopianism, it will be remembered, eulogized rather than deprecated the dissolution of such primary groups as the family. While the present day "theorists of mass society" deprecate rather than eulogize, they follow in the tradition of assuming that primary groups dissolve under the impact of industrialization.

As so often in this essay, we are confronted with convergent phenomena when we analyze the transmutation of the social scientist's model of mass communications. The importance of the primary group in American society began to assert itself in various areas of inquiry sometime around the mid-thirties. In the field of practical endeavors this rediscovery of the primary group was most dramatic in industrial sociology and psychology. Since the classic studies of Mayo, Roethlesberger, and others at the Harvard Business School, the field of industrial relations and business administration has been dominated by a concern over informal human relations in industry. Simultaneously social science researchers such as Lewin and Moreno turned their efforts to studying small groups. The reasons for the increased interest of social scientists in the study of small groups and interpersonal relations are, of course, complex. But the fact remains that, in this alleged mass society of atomized individuals, the most active area of research in American sociology and psychology has been precisely that sphere of human behavior which was supposed to disappear, or at least to atrophy radically.

In the field of communications research it was the aforementioned

---

[22] Edward A. Shils, "The Study of the Primary Group" in Daniel Lerner and Harold D. Lasswell, editors, *The Policy Sciences; Recent Developments in Scope and Method*, Stanford: Stanford University Press, 1951, 44-69.
[23] It is true, as Shils notes, that members of the Chicago School of Sociology (Thrasher, for example) did studies of primary groups, but these groups were not regarded as an integral part of the evolving society.

Erie County Study which marked the turning point in the attention which researchers devoted to informal communications. Under the stimulus of the "two-step" model of communications, researchers from the Bureau of Applied Social Research began the search for "opinion leaders" who mediated between the media and the broad mass of the population. Successive studies indicated that the original two-step model was somewhat overly simple.[24] "Opinion leaders" were not a single type of person. They varied with the subject matter under consideration. They exercised their influence in varying fashion. The flow of influence was not always "downwards," but sometimes "upwards" and "sidewards." The network of communications is a socially structured one depending upon established patterns of social relations.

Since the Bureau of Applied Social Research has spearheaded this work on informal communications, one of its most recent products may be taken as an example of the new focus of interest in research. Menzel and Katz report a study of the spread of the use of a new drug in the medical community.[25] In this study, the established pattern of interrelations of the doctors in the community, both socially and professionally, is taken as the matrix within which the pattern of interpersonal influence takes place. The point of entry of information about the new drug into a New England medical community was studied, together with the time of adoption of the drug (measured by the date at which it was first prescribed), and the patterns and mechanisms of influence. The pattern of findings is too complicated to permit summarization. However, we may quote the authors' concluding remarks about the basic communications model:

> . . . we have found it necessary to propose amendments for the model of the two-step flow of communications: by considering the possibility of multi-step rather than two-step flow; by noting that sources other than printed publications may be the channels to the outside world maintained by the opinion leaders; by noting that the model may not apply to channels of low prestige and usually easy accessibility; and by differentiating various kinds of leadership, especially by emphasizing the differential roles of the innovator or pioneer on the one hand and the opinion leader or arbiter on the other.[26]

Obviously the subject matter of this study, the adoption of a drug in the medical community of a specific city, is not one which is ordinarily handled by the mass media, and it is equally clear that a group of doctors

[24] Since the following passage was written, an article by Elihu Katz has been brought to our attention in which he makes virtually every one of the points contained in the next several pages. Elihu Katz, "The Two-Step Flow of Communication: An Up-to-Date Report on an Hypothesis," *Public Opinion Quarterly*, Spring, 1957, 21, 61-78.
[25] Herbert Menzel and Elihu Katz, "Social Relations and Innovation in the Medical Profession: the Epidemology of a New Drug," *Public Opinion Quarterly*, Winter, 1955-1956, 19, 337-352.
[26] *Ibid.*, p. 352.

is not a representative segment of the population. What is relevant about this study, however, is that attempts to trace patterns of informal communications associated with topics dealt with in mass communications led to the use of a sociometric design rather than to a traditional sample survey.

The use of the sample survey, which has virtually dominated communications research in recent decades, accepted implicitly the notion of the "atomized" individual. A sample of individuals is selected out of a population which may or may not be characterized by structured interpersonal relationships. (We are arguing, of course, that such structured relationships invariably exist in the population from which the sample is drawn.) The nature of the data inclines one to accept the individuals in the sample *as individuals,* or at best to look at them as representative of certain categories in the population; i.e., the young *vs.* the old, the poor *vs.* the rich, etc. Any attempt to reconstruct the *structure* of interrelationships from which the sample was drawn may not be impossible, but is in the nature of things a *tour de force.* Any attempt to trace the actual flow of communications is even more difficult.[27] Hence, an effort to trace out the network of communications and influence, as Menzel and Katz did, demanded the identification and study of the whole of some subsystem within the over-all societal communications network.

Interest in informal communications has by no means been confined to scholars working at the Bureau of Applied Social Research. It is exemplified in the work of the Program on International Communications at M.I.T., and in the entire area of recent attitude and opinion research. A perusal of the pages of the *Public Opinion Quarterly* will quickly establish the fact that this is the burgeoning area of investigation. Just as sociologists and psychologists have turned to the study of small groups, so are communications researchers tending progressively to concentrate on microsystems rather than macro-systems such as the entire American society.

The fact that so much of communications research is currently focused on informal communications does not, of course, prove the importance of this type of communications in American society any more than the absence of such research proved the lack of importance in the prewar period. There are many reasons why scholars concentrate their efforts on certain types of problems. However, interest in this area arose out of a growing sense of the limitations of the mass media. Furthermore, the researchers have presented sufficient evidence for their position that they have been able to get financial support from advertisers, manufacturers, and, most amusing, from the publishers of such mass media as Time, Inc., and Macfadden Publications, Inc. Whether the researchers be right or wrong,

[27] Whether or not it is necessary to say so, we would like to be explicit in stating that the above comment is not intended as a serious criticism of sample surveys *per se,* nor as a forecast that they will decline in use. At the present stage of the study of *informal* communications, however, there are advantages to working with a total, though small and specialized group.

their *assumptions* about the role of informal communications in American society square poorly, if at all, with the notion of "the mass society."

In closing this discussion of research on informal communications, we would like to comment on an interstitial area in which there has been relatively little work done, but which is pertinent to the model of the "mass society." It is one of the postulates of the "theory of mass society" that among the primary groups which are dissolving under the impact of social change is the neighborhood community. Morris Janowitz, in his study of the community press in the Chicago metropolitan area[28] builds the thesis that local newspapers are serving to give cohesion to the neighborhood communities in metropolitan areas.

Certainly neither Janowitz nor the present writers would contend that a Chicago neighborhood held together by a weekly newspaper was not qualitatively different than a seventeenth century European village. However, his work contributes to the evolving realizations that the distinction between folk and urban society can be and has been largely overdrawn.

While we do not share the belief of the "theorists of mass society" that totalitarianism is the logical extension of industrial society, it is worth noting that informal relationships continue to play a crucial role in even so brutally a total society as Stalin's Russia, and furthermore that the very nature of totalitarianism serves to solidify some and create other primary groupings.[29] Certainly it was Stalin's intent to create a social order which closely approximated the bugaboo of the mass society. The divergence between the reality of the Soviet system and Orwell's 1984 is a good measure of the irreducible, minimal role which primary groups and informal processes play in any society.

This section on the study of informal communications must close on an ironic note. We have at various points talked about the convergence of different areas of investigation. Now we must note one conspicuous failure to converge. For years, rural sociologists (significantly for this point, a group low in the prestige hierarchy of sociology) have been working on the pattern of interpersonal communications and influence in connection with the introduction of innovation into farm communities.[30] The systematic problem is identical with that which concerns the student of informal communications, yet the work of the rural sociologists has had virtually no impact on the main body of communications research.

---

[28] Morris Janowitz, *The Community Press in an Urban Setting*, Glencoe, Illinois, The Free Press, 1952, *passim*.

[29] Cf. Raymond A. Bauer, Alex Inkeles, and Clyde Kluckhohn, *How the Soviet System Works*, Cambridge, Harvard University Press, 1957, *passim*.

[30] For an example of the former, cf. "Sociological Research on the Diffusion and Adoption of New Farm Practices: A Review of Previous Research and a Statement of Hypotheses and Needed Research," Lexington, Ky.: University of Kentucky, 1952 (pamphlet).

The Mass Audience as a "Mass"

We have already pointed to the fact that communications researchers have become preoccupied with the role of informal communications in modern society. The issue to be discussed here is a related but distinct one, namely, the influence of social factors on the individual in his relation to the mass media. Whereas previously we were concerned with the way in which informal communications *via* established social relationships supplemented more formal communications, we are now concerned with the way in which use of and reaction to mass communications is affected by social relationships. We take as our point of departure the contention of the theorists of "mass society" that such societies are characterized by an "atomization" of interpersonal relationships.

Communications in a folk society take place in a social context. The primitive child hears a folk tale sitting around the fire in the company of his family and peers. Modern man, on the other hand, reads the newspaper in lonely solitude on the crowded subway. His wife listens to the soap opera in isolation, etc.

Critics such as Herbert Blumer have argued that the word "mass" has two meanings in the term mass communications. Not only are these communications directed at large numbers of people, but this "mass of people" is also a mass in the sense of being socially disorganized. As a matter of fact, it is argued that modern man turns to the mass media precisely because he is alone, lonesome, hollow, atomized. The mass media are the twentieth century opiate of the masses. They are alleged to be the substitute for healthy, rewarding interpersonal relations.

There is unquestionably a good deal of truth in Merton's observation that the manner of many radio and TV personalities is deliberately designed to create a *"pseudo-gemeinschaft,"* a feeling of togetherness (begging the question of its complete desirability) more characteristic of a folk society. However, there is a certain *prima facie* naiveté to the view that the target of mass communications is "atomized." Certainly the amount of discussion generated by telecasts of the World Series, by news of the latest rape or murder, or by last night's quiz show, cannot have escaped the attention of the critics. While it may be argued that these communications follow after "atomized" exposure to communications, reference group theory tells us that it is virtually certain that these anticipated audiences influence the individual at the time of exposure, and that while he is physically alone he is psychologically in the company of others.

The notion of "mass" as applied to mass communications, as Freidson has pointed out, stands in opposition to a good deal of data. Moviegoing, once selected by Blumer as an example of isolated, individualized communications behavior, is very much a social phenomenon. The decision to attend movies is socially determined; they are attended in the company of others; and they are discussed afterwards.[31] Riley and Riley[32] have shown that children's selection and reaction to TV programs is a function of their relations to their peer groups and their families. Rossi and Bauer, and Bauer and Gleicher,[33] found that communications behavior in the Soviet Union was a function of the individual's involvement in the Soviet system. Eisenstadt has similar findings among Israeli immigrants.[34] Addiction to popular singers or movie stars generates face-to-face fan clubs among adolescents (and adults). Newspapers are read for the raw material with which to impress one's fellows.

There are dissenters of the interpretation we put on these data, however. Maccoby, for example, found that television brings the family closer together, but that the resultant social life is "parallel" rather than interactive.[35] We cannot quarrel with these investigators' interpretations of their own data. They do, however, find that radio listening and TV viewing take place in a social context.

It would be senseless to maintain for a moment that there are not fundamental qualitative differences between communications behavior in a society dominated by mass media and in a traditional folk society. We would only maintain, along with Freidson, that:

> On the basis of this material and on the experience and behavior of members of the audience, it is possible to conclude that the audience, from the point of view of its members, at least, is *not* anonymous, heterogeneous, unorganized and spatially separated. The individual member of the audience frequently does not manifest the selective activity characteristic of the mass, and when such selection has been observed to occur, it appeared to rise out of the stimulation of organized social processes rather than merely the individual's personal interests. Given this, it is possible to conclude that the concept of the mass is not accurately applicable to the audience.[36]

While Freidson's conclusion may be accepted as a conservative reflection of extant research findings, the following passage by Katz and Lazarsfeld suggests what future research may uncover:

> We have learned over the last decade that there is good reason to suspect—although there is really no empirical evidence available—that

---

[31] Eliot Freidson, "Communications Research and the Concept of the Mass," *American Sociological Review*, June, 1953, 18, 313-317.
[32] Matilda Riley and John W. Riley, Jr., "A Sociological Approach to Communications Research," *Public Opinion Quarterly*, Fall, 1951, 15, 445-460.
[33] Peter H. Rossi and Raymond A. Bauer, "Some Patterns of Soviet Communications Behavior," *Public Opinion Quarterly*, Winter, 1952-53, 16, 663-666. Raymond A. Bauer and David B. Gleicher, "Word-of-Mouth Communication in the Soviet Union," *Public Opinion Quarterly*, Fall, 1953, 17, 308-309.
[34] S. N. Eisenstadt, "Conditions of Communicative Receptivity," *Public Opinion Quarterly*, Fall, 1953, 17, 363-374.
[35] E. E. Maccoby, "Television: Its Impact on School Children," *Public Opinion Quarterly*, Fall, 1951, 15, 424-429.
[36] Freidson, *op. cit.*, p. 316.

some of the most effective radio broadcasts involve the presence of planned listening groups rather than isolated individuals. Father Cough-lin's radio success, for example, appears to have been built on group lis-tening. And we know from a recent study of communications in Soviet Russia that the channels of communication there depend heavily on in-person presentations to organized groups and that mass communications are superimposed upon this interpersonal framework. A related point— that individuals will reject a communication which seeks to separate them from their group—is a central finding of Shils and Janowitz (1948) in their study of allied propaganda to German troops during World War II.[37]

In summary, the researchers, in addition to being impressed with the role of informal communications in American society, are also impressed with the role of interpersonal relationships in affecting the way one re-sponds to mass communications. The communications model of the re-searchers diverges from that of the critics of mass society in these respects, as well as in the degree of power of the mass media, and in the inferences which may be made as to the relationship of content to effect.

The Equation of Content and Effect

The last of these premises, that content and effect may be equated, may well be denied by the critics of mass society. Yet we believe it is im-plicit in their position. The mainstays of their case are content analysis, argument, and illustrative anecdote. The arguments are invariably per-suasive and sophisticated,[38] and since there is little doubt that the mass me-dia play a varied role, there can be equally little doubt that their arguments offer an accurate description of the processes at work in *some* segment of the population. But, it is precisely this diversity of effect that makes illustrative anecdotes and content analysis devices of limited validity for assessing effect. (We have *no* criticism of many other uses of content analy-sis.) There can be little doubt that, in a population of more than 150 mil-lion persons, TV has precipitated acts of violence in some portions of the populace—just as did the advent of the lollypop and the ice cream cone. However, as much as one may deprecate vulgar quantification, the rele-vant questions are quantitative ones.

More to the point is the use of content analysis. We are told that there were X number of murders, and Y acts of violence shown on TV in a given period of time; or that heroes and heroines are depicted in such-and-such a fashion in a given sample of movies or magazine articles. Such findings serve well to alert us to the low artistic state of the media, and they may give us a good deal of insight into our culture and values. But it is precari-ous indeed to infer from this content its impact on its audience. Lest we

<hr>

[37] Katz and Lazarsfeld, *op. cit.*, p. 28.
[38] Cf. as an extreme example, Frederick Wertham's work on children and comics, *Se-duction of the Innocent*, New York: Rinehart & Company, 1954.

seem to cavil unduly we prefer to quote the distinguished sociologist Robert Merton in his introduction to Dallas Smythe's content analysis of New York television. Smythe had found that nearly 3,000 acts of violence had been portrayed on New York television programs during the course of a week. Merton comments:

> Nothing in these figures can tell us about the psychological and social effects upon television audiences of these numerous episodes of violence, nor does Mr. Smythe move beyond his evidence to guess at the effects. It cannot simply be taken for granted that violence on the scene is emotionally damaging to the spectator. When violence becomes conventionalized, for example, as in the well-grooved patterns of the Western movie, it may not cause the least distress or damage to children who know that the noble hero will irresistibly triumph over the blackhearted villains but that, for this to happen in proper style, the good men and bad men must first work their way through a sequence of ambushes, fist fights, and gun play in which injuries and even occasional death become more symbolic than real.[39]

In general our contention that content and effect of communications cannot be equated rests on the evidence presented throughout this essay as to the variability of response to communications. We pause here only to record our reservations; and also to draw forcibly the distinction between imputation of effect, and the moral and aesthetic issues on which content analysis may be extremely pertinent. That is to say, the statement of Merton, with which we concur, that violence on the TV screen cannot be assumed to be emotionally damaging to the spectator, is neutral with respect to the quality of TV programming itself. The critics of the mass media would be on far firmer ground if they were to keep these two issues separate.

[39] From Robert K. Merton's Introduction to Dallas W. Smythe, *New York Television: January 4-10, 1951-1952.* New York TV Monitoring Study No. 4, Urbana, Ill.: N.A.E.B., 1952, v.

EFFECTS OF THE MASS MEDIA OF COMMUNICATION

By Carl I. Hovland *

ONE OF THE MOST striking characteristics of the twentieth century is the fact that we live in an age of mass communication. Newspapers, radio, television, motion pictures, cheap magazines, and pocket-sized books have become the principal purveyors, in our society, of fact, fiction, entertainment, and information.

The technological revolution in production and distribution that has made mass communication possible on such a scale is of relatively recent origin. Fifty years ago three of the most potent of the mass media were practically unknown; and the other, the cheap press, had not yet reached the proportions it has presently assumed.

The rapid rise of the mass media, their ubiquity, and their potential influence have led many to wonder about the actual role they play in social life and behavior. Some writers suggest that mass communications are all-powerful, that they determine thought and action to a major degree. These persons cite the tremendous impact of propaganda during World War I, when the newspapers "got us into war." They also point out that advertising, via the mass media, has become a vital factor in our way of life.

Other analysts, however, are inclined to minimize the effects of the mass media. They point to the fact that many political candidates, enthusiastically supported by the press, are not actually elected to public office and, in general, they regard many interpretations of the power of the mass media as being quite extreme.

The existence of widely differing opinions concerning the effects of the mass media highlights the pressing need for further objective research. Indeed, the editors of the most recent book of readings in this field believe that investigation of "effects" is "the most neglected area in communication research" (Berelson and Janowitz, 1950, p. 395).

Considerable research on the effects of communication has already

* The author wishes to acknowledge the helpful criticism and suggestions of Leonard W. Doob, Fred D. Sheffield, Irving L. Janis and Edmund H. Volkart. He also wishes to thank Gerald Wiener for his generous assistance in procuring books and journals from the various libraries and Ruth Hays for her careful editing of the next-to-final draft of the manuscript.

---

been done, but much of it is of a practical rather than of an analytical or theoretical character. At the same time there is a growing body of data on basic principles of communication that are relevant to the effects of mass media. The purpose of this chapter, then, is to summarize some of the major studies and to relate the large number of empirical findings to basic principles of communication analysis. In the first section there will be a brief review of some of the principal studies of the major media during the last decades. In the second section analytical studies attempting to assess the major influences affecting the impact of communications will be discussed. Here the concern will be with the nature of the communicator, the communication, the medium, and the audience. This section will conclude with a brief review of the variety of different types of behavioral change subsumed under the rubric "effects."

Numerous definitions of mass media have been advanced. Wiebe (1952b) restricts the term to media which are readily available to *most of the public*, "including a sizable number of people in all major subgroups," and whose "cost is so small to the individual that they are available to these same people in a financial sense" (pp. 164f.). For many purposes this is a useful definition. But for purposes of analyzing and interpreting the effects of mass media it does not appear desirable to limit the coverage of studies to those which have been done on extremely large audiences. What does appear critical is that the results bear on methods which could be utilized with mass audiences. Accordingly, we shall follow Klapper (1949) in including researches done with impersonal transmission media regardless of the size of audience. Studies done with radio, movies, books, newspapers, and magazines are included by this definition, but those involving personal address, the drama, and other face-to-face communications are excluded. It must be emphasized, however, that principles may often be uncovered in the latter situations which will enable us to understand better the type of communication which is involved with mass media. Studies of psychotherapy, for example, may help illuminate general problems of communication. But because they are complicated by methodological difficulties of controlling the interaction effects between communicator and communicatee, they cannot be directly generalized to mass media problems.

The emphasis in the present review will be on the analysis of the "effects" of communication. This results in the omission of discussion of content analyses of the various media, methods of control of communication, the economic and social characteristics of major communicators, and similar topics which must be included in a complete analysis of the communication process. A second emphasis is on empirical quantitative investigations. This involves the exclusion of a large number of brilliant essays by communication experts suggesting hypotheses not backed by research results. References to some of these other phases of communication will be found in the excellent bibliography of Smith, Lasswell and Casey, *Propa-*

ganda, Communication, and Public Opinion (1946), and in the supplementary bibliography by Fearing and Rogge (1951).

SURVEY OF GENERAL STUDIES

Before proceeding to a discussion of the specific factors influencing the impact of communications, a brief review of some of the major studies of the over-all effects of the principal mass media will be presented. These studies, primarily done within the last two decades, indicate some of the general effects on behavior produced by reading, movies, and radio. The relatively few studies done on the newest medium—television—will also be briefly reported.

Effects of Books, Magazines, and Newspapers

What Reading Does to People, by Waples, Berelson, and Bradshaw (1940), summarizes the major studies concerning the effects of printed media. It is disappointing to find how few solid quantitative data are available here. But there are such formidable difficulties in the way of accurate analyses of the effects of reading books and newspapers—created by problems of evaluating exposure over the long period of time during which effects are produced and of determining the interaction between the effects of reading and other media—that one must be patient and not expect quick research answers.

Waples, Berelson, and Bradshaw have provided a very useful analysis of the types of effects which reading may produce. They distinguish five broad categories of effects: (1) *Instrumental.* These are primarily concerned with the utilization of information in print for a variety of the individual's practical and personal problems. (2) *Self-esteem or prestige.* Articles praising the group to which the reader belongs are avidly read for this reason. Sometimes the reading results in the mitigation of guilt and inferiority feelings, and at other times it invites identification with those who have achieved goals toward which the individual is striving. (3) *Reenforcement.* Support is sought for a position already taken on controversial issues. Conversions are rare and are more extreme responses to controversial reading. (4) *Enriched aesthetic experience.* (5) *Respite.* This is a transient type of response to reading which is characterized by such terms as "forgetting worries," "having a good laugh," and "killing time." The authors also present a number of interesting suggestions for research in this little-investigated area.

The five principal classes of print upon which research has been conducted involve (1) books, (2) newspapers, (3) magazines, (4) comic books, and (5) leaflets.

Books. We are all aware of the profound effects which certain books have had upon society; this may particularly be observed in the case of such books as the *Bible, Uncle Tom's Cabin,* and *Das Kapital.* The task of evaluating these effects is largely in the realm of the social historian. An excellent example of this type of analysis is found in *Books that Changed Our Minds*, edited by Malcolm Cowley (1939). A summary of the historical studies, with appropriate references, is provided by Waples, *et al.*, as follows:

> Reinforcement of their own function and position in society was a result of the reading done by the bourgeoisie in Elizabethan England. The influence of London was extended throughout Britain with the growth of a reading public in the provinces in the late eighteenth century. The radical ideas of the French Revolution were brought to the attention of the working classes through popular pamphlets, and opportunities for such readings are supposed to have stimulated an interest in reading among them. The specific titles read by the Victorians reinforced many of the political, moral, and religious attitudes of the time.
>
> The literary culture and literary production of early colonists in the United States are reflected in and explained by their reading. Propaganda in early American fiction, an outgrowth of the propaganda pamphlets of the Revolutionary War, was directed at various social reforms. The extension of the American reading public in the middle nineteenth century, documented in both general histories and specialized studies, is attributed to the democratization of education and the introduction of cheap and inviting mass publications (pp. 105f.).

Newspapers. The effects of newspapers have also been studied from a historical standpoint by a number of writers (cf., e.g., Bent's *Newspaper Crusades*, 1939). A frequent concern is the effect of newspapers on voting. One of the earliest attempts to secure an assessment of the influence of the press on political behavior was made by Lundberg (1926). He interviewed a random sample of 940 residents of Seattle concerning their views on four public questions which had been given prominent press discussion during the preceding eight months. In a different connection each individual interviewed was asked what newspaper he read most frequently. Only a very slight relationship was found between the stand taken on each issue by the newspaper and the opinion of the reader of that newspaper. The slight relationship could readily be explained by selective factors working in the reverse direction; i.e., some readers selected papers with whose editorial position they agreed rather than that the editorials influenced their position. Lundberg concluded from the data he assembled that: "A modern commercial newspaper has little direct influence on the opinions of its readers on public questions. It probably seeks to discover and reflect that opinion rather than to make it." . . . "The stand of a newspaper on public questions is a negligible factor in the reader's estimation in selecting his newspaper" (pp. 712f.).

More recently, Mott (1944) has made an extensive analysis of the position of newspapers in presidential elections from 1792 to 1940. Wide discrepancies between newspaper support and popular voting were frequently found. Mott's conclusion is that "there seems to be no correlation, positive or negative, between the support of a majority of newspapers during a campaign and success at the polls" (p. 356).

While there may be no gross correlation between the position of the newspapers and voting in these studies, it appears to the reviewer that the conclusion that newspapers have no effect on opinion is clearly unwarranted. First of all, the studies are set up on the expectation of the effects being so pronounced that they will show up in the gross figures. From what is known about the mass media we should expect the effects to be of a magnitude which would require more careful and detailed analysis to test the relationship. In the second place, the election issues which have been studied are typically major ones, concerning which the public is usually moderately well informed. It is possible that on minor issues and local candidates the effect of the newspaper is considerably greater. Finally, editorials and news stories within the same newspaper often do not agree and hence there may be cancellation of effects. Separate analyses of the influence of editorials, news reports, and syndicated columnists would be most interesting.

The impact of the newspaper on behavior is a major concern of Lazarsfeld, Berelson, and Gaudet (1944). Much of their discussion and analysis is devoted to the problem of who reads the material in the newspapers dealing with the election issues. Their most general finding is that newspaper reading is done by those most interested in the campaign, and these are people who have already made up their minds long before the election. ". . . People with most interest were most likely to make their vote decision early and stick to it throughout the campaign. What we now find is that the people who did most of the reading about and listening to the campaign were the most impervious to any ideas which might have led them to change their vote. Insofar as campaign propaganda was intended to change votes, it was most likely to reach the people least susceptible to such changes" (p. 125). No definitive data are presented of the effects on individuals exposed and not exposed to the newspaper, but interviews did show that at least two-thirds of the voters mentioned that the newspaper was a source from which they obtained much information leading to their voting decision.

While the number of researches in naturalistic settings concerning the effects of reading have been few, there are a number of studies in which the reading of material has been controlled by the experimenter and the effects determined on information and opinion. Swanson (1951) presents a preliminary report of research carried out in this manner. A sample of 209 Minneapolis residents was interviewed on four successive occasions. On the first interview demographic and biographical data were secured. During the second interview a "before" test of information and attitude was administered, together with a five-item disguised intelligence test. During the third interview the respondent was asked to read several sections from the newspaper. "After" tests of the material read on the third interview were secured on the fourth interview. On the basis of the results obtained to date Swanson advances a number of hypotheses as to factors influencing the learning and retention of items concerning government contained in the daily press. The data indicate that there is considerable consistency, over a period of time, in an individual's habits of reading, and that on the basis of verbal ratings of interest one can effectively predict patterns of information acquisition. Those of his results bearing on the assimilation of information by men as compared with women and by brighter as compared with less bright members of the audience will be discussed below in connection with individual differences.

A frequently cited early study of the effect of reading on attitude was conducted by Annis and Meier (1934). Stories were "planted" in the university daily concerning a little-known Australian prime minister. To ensure exposure, the planted articles were included with other material read by the students during class sessions. Some of the students were exposed to material favorable to the prime minister, Mr. Hughes, while others were given statements which were uncomplimentary to him. The material read had considerable potency in influencing the attitudes of the students. Ninety-eight percent of those who read the favorable editorials were biased in the favorable direction and 86 percent of those who read the unfavorable editorials were biased against Mr. Hughes.

Another study using newspapers as the stimulus material is by Britt and Menefee (1939). Reports of the Dies Committee were read in newspaper form by students. Attitudes toward various individuals cited in the reports were strongly influenced by the reading.

Magazines. While there have been numerous surveys of who reads which magazines, the effects produced on those who do read them have not been extensively studied. Investigations of the effects of magazine advertising on sales are numerous but seldom made available publicly. It is doubtful that there are many distinctive effects associated with magazines which are not also characteristic of books and newspapers. One difference noted by Lazarsfeld, Berelson, and Gaudet (1944) is that magazines may be quite effective in reaching specialized audiences. Thus small specialized magazines may have considerable influence. It was found that the *Farm Journal* was mentioned as a concrete influence upon changes in vote intention as frequently as *Collier's*, despite the considerable discrepancy in circulation; and the Townsend publication was referred to as frequently as *Life* or the *Saturday Evening Post*.

Comic books. A new influence in the American pattern of reading is that of the comic books, which have skyrocketed in circulation. Seldes (1950) states that the number of copies printed is 700 million per year.

They have been widely decried as injurious to morals and responsible for the lowering of tastes. But little research on their effects is available, and the results reported are conflicting. Wertham (1948) refers to extensive "clinical studies" carried out by himself and associates which indicate that "comic books represent systematic poisoning of the well of childhood spontaneity" (p. 29) and set the pattern for later aggressive crimes. Wolf and Fiske (1949), on the other hand, report that the child finds in animal comics "subjects for his early projective needs, and later, in invincible heroes, he finds subjects for ego-inflation" and from comic classics material to "supplement the facts and insights he gains from more formal reading of history and current events and from experiences with real people" (p. 20). Objective research in this area is greatly needed.

Leaflets. In a number of investigations the effects of leaflets have been evaluated. The study by Hartmann (1936) on the use of political leaflets to influence voting is discussed elsewhere in this chapter. Leaflets have been extensively used in psychological warfare and there is keen interest in their effectiveness for this purpose. The problem of determining their impact in this situation is a difficult one methodologically. The kinds of data which may be secured and some of their implications are discussed by Herz (1949). Evidence concerning effectiveness was based on such criteria as the number of leaflets found on prisoners, the recall of the content by the prisoners, comments on allied leaflets by the enemy, etc. Simple ideas were judged to be much more effective than more complicated ideological discussions. Additional work on leaflets with better experimental procedures is currently being done by the military services but is still in the classified category.

A number of other studies of the effects of reading have been done with specially prepared material read by the subjects, usually with attitude scales for the measurement of effect. Some of these are cited elsewhere in this chapter. They include the investigations of Bateman and Remmers (1941), Bird (1927), Cherrington and Miller (1933), Hartmann (1936), Hovland and Weiss (1951), Knower (1936), Sims (1938), and Wilke (1934).

Motion Pictures

From the standpoint of effects, the motion picture has probably been more extensively studied than any other medium. This is partly because a movie is an expensive and permanent thing (as Lazarsfeld, 1948, suggests) but also because it is believed to be a particularly potent medium, utilizing both sight and sound. Also the conditions for research on its effects are a little easier to arrange because the audience is ordinarily physically present in a public place, whereas with newspapers, books, radio, and television the audience is scattered over a wide area, and it is a major task to identify those who become exposed and those who do not.

Movies, like the other media, may have a long-lasting effect on social behavior which can only be assessed by the social historian. Thus the effects of *Birth of a Nation* can be evaluated only superficially by short-term measurement. But the difficulties of long-term evaluation are very grave, and the majority of motion pictures are designed in terms of their more immediate effects. Most of them are produced for entertainment, and are considered effective if they have good box office sales. This review is not concerned with these. Our interest is primarily in those motion pictures designed to provide knowledge or to change opinions, beliefs, and overt behavior. Pictures of this nature are many fewer in number and have received much less attention than the "popular" variety, but they are sufficiently different in objective to justify questioning the common assumption of movie producers that the techniques which have been time-tested for entertainment purposes will prove equally effective for providing information and modifying opinions.

There is an extensive literature on the utilization of films for straight instruction. This field is now so large and rapidly growing that it will be impossible to review it in the present chapter. Brief mention of the early studies must suffice. A more comprehensive treatment will be found in the recent bibliography by Hoban and van Ormer (1951).

One of the pioneer studies of the impact of motion pictures on both attitudes and overt behavior was that of Lashley and Watson (1922). They were asked by the United States Interdepartmental Social Hygiene Board to investigate the informational and educative effect upon the public of a film used in various campaigns for the control, repression, and elimination of venereal diseases. The film studied, *Fit to Win*, used a dramatic treatment to depict the consequences of venereal disease and of continence on World War I soldiers. Approximately 5000 individuals, made up of business groups, literary clubs, employee groups, soldiers, sailors, and youth groups, were shown the picture. The film was quite effective in conveying information about venereal disease. Questionnaire responses indicated a temporary increase in fear of venereal disease. But the evidence revealed no decrease in exposure to venereal disease afterwards.

During the decade from 1920 to 1930 there was intense activity in research on the utilization of the film as a medium of instruction, and during this period studies by Freeman (1924), Wood and Freeman (1929), Knowlton and Tilton (1929), and others were reported. These researches greatly increased our understanding of the scope and limitations of the movie medium.

Studies of considerable importance concerning the effects of films on opinions, attitudes, and behavior were done during the early thirties under the sponsorship of the Motion Picture Research Council, with financing from the Payne Fund. Perhaps the best known is that of Peterson and Thurstone (1933) on the effects of films (silent) on attitudes of school age children. Attitude scales were administered before and after the presentation of a variety of movies dealing with crime, war, and foreign groups. Sizable changes were produced which lasted over a considerable period of time. Table 1 presents some of the results obtained by these investigators.

TABLE 1

EFFECTS OF MOTION PICTURES ON ATTITUDES
(from Peterson and Thurstone, 1933)

Film	Attitude Scale	N	Mean Score Before	Mean Score After	Diff/P.F. diff.
"Four Sons"	Germans	130	5.66	5.28	5.37
"Sons of the Gods"	Chinese	182	6.72	5.50	17.5
"All Quiet on the Western Front"	War	214	4.33	3.65	14.98
"Birth of a Nation"	Negro	434	7.41	5.93	25.5

Another frequently cited book in the Payne Fund series is that by Blumer and Hauser (1933) devoted to an analysis of the effects of motion pictures on delinquency. They employed detailed interviews and diaries to ascertain whether the types of crimes and their frequency were influenced by motion picture attendance. They conclude:

Several important indirect influences disposing or leading persons to delinquency or crime are discernible in the experience of male offenders. Through the display of crime techniques and criminal patterns of behavior; by arousing desires for easy money and luxury, and by suggesting questionable methods for their achievement; by inducing a spirit of bravado, toughness, and adventurousness; by arousing intense sexual desires; and by invoking daydreaming of criminal roles, motion pictures may create attitudes and furnish techniques conducive, quite unwittingly, to delinquent or criminal behavior.

One may detect in the case of delinquent girls and young women influences similar to those spoken of in the case of young men. Motion pictures may play a major or minor role in female delinquency and crime by arousing sexual passion; by instilling the desire to live a gay, wild, fast life; by suggesting to some girls questionable methods of easily attaining them; by the display of modes of beautification and love's techniques; by the depiction of various forms of crime readily imitated by girls and young women; and by competing with home and school for an important place in the life of the girls. (pp. 198-199)

Another approach to the problem is represented by the investigation of Shuttleworth and May (1933). They compared the attitudes and conduct of grade school students who attended the movies two or more times a week with an equated group who attended once a month or less. They report: "No significant differences were found in the conduct tests of persistence, self-control, and honesty in out-of-school situations, nor in measures of moral knowledge and social attitudes on a wide variety of topics most of which were unrelated to the movies, nor on a great many types of attitudes which are definitely related to the movies" (p. 84). These data suggest that the picture presented by Blumer and Hauser may be somewhat exaggerated. The wide divergence in the estimate of effects derived from the two investigations is pitilessly attacked by Adler (1937). This is, of course, an area with tremendous methodological difficulties. Controlling exposure to rule out self-selection effects is difficult enough, but the evaluation of cumulative effects of a number of movies over a considerable period of time is also a formidable problem. As a consequence, evaluations of the effects of films on crime have been done characteristically with less rigorous methods, and serious loopholes exist in the interpretation of the results.

Other studies in the Payne series are those of Holaday and Stoddard (1933) on the acquisition of knowledge, and of Blumer (1933) on general conduct. There is a good summary of the series by Charters (1933).

Considerable use was made of motion pictures by the military services during World War II not only for training in skills but also for "orientation" and "indoctrination." A report of some of the experimental studies carried out to determine the effectiveness with which films modified attitudes was presented by Hovland, Lumsdaine, and Sheffield (1949). They summarize their results on the *Why We Fight* films as follows:

> The *Why We Fight* films had marked effects on the men's knowledge of factual material concerning the events leading up to the war . . . Highly effective presentation methods are possible with this type of film.
>
> The films also had some marked effects on opinions where the films specifically covered the factors involved in the particular interpretation . . . Such opinion changes were, however, less frequent and in general less marked than changes in factual knowledge.
>
> The films had only a very few effects on opinion items of a more general nature . . . which were considered the criteria for determining the effectiveness of the films in achieving their orientation objectives.
>
> The films had no effects on the items prepared for the purpose of measuring effects on the men's motivation to serve as soldiers, which was considered the ultimate objective of the orientation program. (pp. 64f.)

A number of hypotheses are discussed by the authors as to factors limiting the effectiveness of films for indoctrination purposes. Analyses are made of the effects of films on individuals of differing intellectual ability, and with varying interpretations of the real purposes behind the showing of the films. In some respects the conditions of utilization of films for civilian purposes may be different from those involved in army usage. But the situation within the army was ideal for this particular type of investigation because the pictures could be shown under conditions which were exactly those involved in nonexperimental utilization and the evaluation could therefore be carried out with a minimum of knowledge on the part of the subjects that any experimentation was involved.

There have been a number of very useful studies of individual films. An early investigation by Rosenthal (1934) indicated that a single 40-minute film on radicalism changed socio-economic attitudes closely related to its content but had little effect on other related items not specifically covered. A recent study by Cooper and Dinerman (1951) is of considerable interest because it is concerned with the possible effects of motion pictures on prejudice. Both questionnaire evaluation and individual and group interviews were employed. The authors report that the film *Don't Be a Sucker*, which shows that prejudice is a device manipulated by agitators for their own gain, was successful in directing specific messages to specific target groups. But there were a number of "boomerang effects," in which changes were produced opposite to those intended. They also found that messages stated in a generalized form are not likely to be accepted by any significant portion of an audience, and that messages which are not explicitly stated are likely to be entirely lost upon the less intelligent members of the audience. The latter point receives support from a recent experimental study by Hovland and Mandell (1952a) which showed that with complex material an explicit drawing of the conclusion is more effective than leaving it to the audience to derive.

Radio

Radio as a medium of mass communication has been studied quite extensively. The progress in this field is attributable in good measure to the establishment of an Office of Radio Research, first at Princeton and then at Columbia, financed by the Rockefeller Foundation. Nearly half of the citations in this section represent studies carried out under these auspices.

Among the very early studies of the effectiveness of radio programs in modifying attitudes was one conducted by E. S. Robinson (1932). A series of four programs during successive weeks was presented on the topic "Unemployment. What the Voter Should Know." An experimental group of 419 listened to the programs, while a control group of 45 did not listen. Tests were administered before and after the series. The first effect of the programs noted was an increase of about 16 percent in the number of solutions for unemployment suggested by the exposed group. The new suggestions were heavily concentrated in the categories discussed in the programs. An interesting incidental finding was the tendency for the listeners to accept a large number of ideas presented, even though some of the ideas were clearly inconsistent with others.

Another early investigation of the effects of radio was that of Cantril and Allport (1935). In addition to making comparisons between media (a topic to be discussed later), they performed a series of experiments on "effective conditions for broadcasting," investigating the effects of length of sentence, length of program, value of repetition, and so on. For that period (1935), this book stands as a very good pattern of research and interpretation. Later studies have, of course, modified and extended its conclusions.

A major utilizer of radio, largely for information purposes, has been the government. The effects of various radio programs directed at farmers have been studied by W. S. Robinson (1941) and by Umberger (1932). Umberger interviewed 532 farm families to determine their radio listening patterns and the extent to which they reported changes in their farming practices attributable to various sources of influence. His survey indicated that radio was responsible for 5.9 percent of the changes reported and that it ranked above circular letters, exhibits, posters, and several other types of influence. Considering the fact that radio reaches families less accessible to other Department of Agriculture informational services, the author considered it highly effective. Robinson is much less impressed with the importance of radio in changing opinions and practices. Among his rural listeners he found relatively few changes in opinion brought about by radio; in nearly every case the listeners reported turning off the radio when a point of view opposed to their own was presented. A bibliography of other studies of the influence of radio on farmer groups is presented by the author.

An interesting study of the impact of radio was reported by Cantril (1940) on the panic reactions of listeners to the Orson Welles broadcast of the War of the Worlds. Detailed interviews of 135 persons were conducted, primarily among individuals who were known to have been upset by the broadcast. The varieties of reaction of different listeners are described. The authors stress the importance of radio in these terms:

> The fact that this panic was created as a result of a radio broadcast is today no mere circumstance . . . Radio has inherently the characteristics of contemporaneousness, availability, personal appeal, and ubiquity. Hence, when we analyze this panic, we are able to deal with the most modern type of social group—the radio audience . . . [which] consists essentially of thousands of small, congregate groups united in time and experiencing a common stimulus—altogether making possible the largest grouping of people ever known. (p. x)

Studies of the utilization of radio for changing attitudes and opinions as part of a propaganda program are reported in Childs and Whitton (1942). Although little controlled experimentation is reported, there is a wealth of case material on the effects of the short wave broadcasts by both Axis and Allied sources. A particularly stimulating chapter is that of Edrita Fried on Techniques of Persuasion.

A number of detailed studies of individual radio programs have been reported. Particularly interesting is the series by Wilson (1948a), who obtained experimental measures of the effectiveness of documentary program broadcasts in influencing attitude. One of the programs was an hour-long broadcast on problems of juvenile delinquency, entitled *The Eagle's Brood.* This program stressed the underlying causes of juvenile delinquency and the present inadequate means of dealing with the problem, and presented an action plan at the community level to cope with the situation. Before the program 42 percent of the panel considered our present system of dealing with delinquency "poor" or "very poor." This figure jumped to 66 percent after the broadcast. The effectiveness of individual points made during the broadcast is reported. (The interpretation of some of these is open to question. For example, the item judged to have been most effectively influenced, "Most juvenile delinquents are just naturally bad," is given an "Effectiveness Ratio" of 67 percent, but the data reveal that this is derived from the fact that only three percent of the audience had this opinion before the broadcast and one percent had it afterwards. No account is taken of the unreliability of such small changes.)

In the Wilson report there is a good analysis of one of the programs which failed to reach its objective. *The Empty Noose* dramatized the crimes against humanity which brought the leading Nazis to the gallows at Nuremberg, and attempted to show the threat inherent in certain home-grown types of Fascism.

> Research findings showed that failure to provide a broad enough base for listener identification severely limited the impact of the broadcast. Listeners of the Jewish faith and strong liberals were terrifically moved by it; others were either antagonistic or lukewarm in their interest and approval. The latter groups tended to regard the problem of fascism as mainly of concern to minorities. (p. 25)

In the case of radio there has been very extensive study of the immediate reactions of the audience to programs. The Columbia Broadcasting System, over a period of years, has studied the reactions of small panels of listeners to a large number of its programs, using pushbutton and polygraph recording, with subsequent interviews. The methods used, described by Hollonquist and Suchman (1944), help to locate points of low interest and permit modification of the programs to improve dull spots. The recording of likes and dislikes often brings out points which are unclear to the audience (in the case of documentaries and lectures), and points which are otherwise ineffective.

Another type of approach is the detailed interviewing of individuals who do and who do not listen to particular programs. This method is best exemplified by Merton's (1946) analysis of the Kate Smith war bond radio program. Excellent case material is provided which is suggestive of important predispositions of the audience and of the manner in which appeals relate to these predispositions in bringing about action. The use of liberal quotations from the respondents adds enormously to the interest of the book.

The effects of radio listening on responses to other media have been examined by Lazarsfeld (1940) in *Radio and the Printed Page*. Considerable evidence is presented that radio listening is not necessarily in competition with book, magazine, and newspaper reading, but may be complementary. In a substantial number of instances, the stimulation for reading books and articles was derived from listening to a program over the radio. Radio and reading also interact in influencing voting behavior, according to Lazarsfeld, Berelson, and Gaudet (1944). People who listened to radio discussions of the campaign issues tended to read political news also, and those who were not exposed to one generally were not exposed to the other. When asked which medium helped them to make up their minds about voting, 68 percent of the respondents mentioned radio and 66 percent mentioned the newspaper. An interesting finding, but one which is highly specific and not likely to be generalizable, was that the individuals who changed their voting intention from Republican to Democratic were more likely to attribute the change to radio than to newspapers, while those who shifted to the Republican position were more likely to attribute the change to the newspapers. This is thought to be attributable to the fact that Roosevelt was a much more effective radio personality than Willkie, while the newspapers were solidly Republican.

A number of other studies which are discussed elsewhere in this chapter had as an incidental purpose the analysis of the effect of radio on opinions and behavior. These included investigations by Dietrich (1946), Gaskill (1933), Heron and Ziebarth (1946), and Wilke (1934).

Television

Television is, of course, the wonder child of the mass media. Its rise has been so rapid and dramatic that systematic research on it is far behind that of the other media. As short a time as five years ago Wilson (1948b) complained that "we have difficulty in locating television set owners" [in New York City!]. Today there are over three million television sets there.[1]

The possibilities of television for instruction are enormous, and there are numerous studies showing how it can be used to transmit information. A good review of the research on educational utilization of television will be found in Finn (1953). The military services are beginning to explore the potentiality of the new medium for their instructional programs, and several recent research reports have appeared under the auspices of the Navy's Special Devices Center [cf., e.g., Rock, Duva, and Murray (not dated)]. As an instructional medium under classroom conditions it is doubtful that there will be any major differences between it and motion

[1] This number has since increased substantially. (Ed.)

pictures. Under naturalistic conditions interesting differences may be expected.

While doubtless research is in progress regarding the effects of television on beliefs, opinions, and attitudes, little of this work has been reported to date. Illustrative of the type of investigations being made is one by Wiebe (1952a), concerned with public reactions to the televised broadcast of the hearings on crime and corruption in New York City. Since one of the objectives of televising these hearings was to arouse public concern and reduce apathy, Wiebe asked the sample he interviewed after the hearings what their reactions were. A high percentage indicated an aroused interest and concern, but few of these reported taking any action calculated to improve the conditions described. "The phenomenal impact of the Hearings dwindled to rather minor productivity insofar as it was mirrored in the reported behavior of our respondents and in their own opinions of the significance of what they did" (p. 185).

One question that is being asked by television researchers is: How does television compare in effectiveness with radio in producing sales? Several preliminary investigations have been reported indicating the superiority of television, and the flood of advertising dollars into this medium shows that the advertisers are convinced of television's effectiveness by their own confidential data.

Another question posed for research on television is the extent to which this new medium alters the pattern of life of the typical family. One of the early studies on the effect of television on leisure time activity was by Coffin (1948). He reported a decrease in attendance at movies and sports events. Radio listening had declined by 68 percent during evening hours, and reading had dropped off some 18 percent. Substantially similar results were reported by McDonagh (1950). The latter investigator also noted decreases in pleasure driving, visiting, and conversation.

Swanson and Jones (1951) report data that closely parallel those just mentioned. Their sample went to fewer movies and said they spent less time listening to the radio. Television appears to have interfered less with reading of newspapers and magazines. Television viewers appeared to be less well informed on current events than were nonviewers, but it is difficult to assign the appropriate cause.[2]

The decreased attendance at sports does not necessarily indicate a decreased interest in sports. A high percentage of the television owners studied reported that they had an increased common family interest in sports, according to Riley, Cantwell, and Ruttiger (1949), who also found that with children TV is not a substitute for other media, but rather an added activity. This has also been reported by Maccoby (1951). She found that children increased the total amount of time they spent on mass media.

The results of investigations in England are substantially the same as

[2] News and public affairs programs make this no longer true. (Ed.)

those reported in the United States. Silvey (1950) studied a random sample of 1000 television households which was selected and compared with a matched control group. A decrease in radio listening and visiting away from home as a result of watching television was less than that reported in the studies in this country. It is to be expected that some of these effects of television will be confined to its period of novelty, but others may continue for a long time.

Major Factors Influencing Effects

The preceding researches have been concerned primarily with the over-all effects of the various mass media. The studies which will be discussed in the present section have concentrated upon particular aspects of communications in an attempt to analyze major determinants of effect. These factors can all be subsumed under the conventional descriptive formula of *"who* says *what* in which *channel* to *whom* with what *effect"* (Smith, Lasswell, and Casey, 1946). Accordingly, our treatment will be concerned with the analysis of the communicator, the communication, the medium, the audience, and the effect.

The Communicator

Who says something is usually as important as *what* is said in the determination of the impact of a communication. Surprisingly, however, the influence of this factor on the effectiveness of the mass media has not been extensively investigated. There are a large number of studies of communicators, but the emphasis in these analyses is usually on the characteristics of the communicators and their role in society rather than on their effects.

In the general analysis of social psychological factors, variations in the effectiveness of different communicators are usually subsumed under the rubric "prestige effects." But the studies are seldom done in a communication setting. The typical investigation consists of an examination of the changes in the subject's responses to statements when different labels are attached to them. A sample of studies of this type is an early one by Arnett, Davidson, and Lewis (1931). A series of statements of attitude and belief were presented to graduate student subjects, who were asked to indicate their own positions on each item. They were then told how a group of educators had marked each statement. Later, when they again filled out the questionnaires, their ratings had changed in the direction of those attributed to the educators. This technique has subsequently been used primarily to determine the relative prestige of various groups.

A study of communicator effects designed to simulate the conditions which obtain in mass communication situations was recently reported by Hovland and Weiss (1951). College students were given communications to read which were represented as excerpts from newspaper and magazine articles. Half of the communications were attributed to sources found from an earlier questionnaire to be considered highly trustworthy, and half were attributed to those considered untrustworthy. For example, an article on the feasibility of developing an atomic submarine was attributed to Robert Oppenheimer in half of the cases and in the other half to *Pravda*. Questionnaires were administered before and after the reading, with several key opinion items inconspicuously included. Tests of information and evaluations of the fairness and justifiability of the presentations were also obtained.

Marked differences in the initial evaluation of the fairness and justifiability of the presentations were obtained when identical articles were attributed to different authors. The initial position of the reader also affected his evaluation.

> Identical communications were regarded as being "justified" in their conclusions in 71.7 percent of the cases when presented by a high credibility source to subjects who initially held the same opinion as advocated by the communicator, but were considered "justified" in only 36.7 percent of the cases when presented by a low credibility source to subjects who initially held an opinion at variance with that advocated by the communicator. (p. 650)

Sizable differences were found in the immediate effects of the two types of communicators on opinions. In 23 percent of the cases, subjects changed their opinions in the direction advocated by the communicator when the high credibility source was used, but less than 7 percent changed when the low credibility source was used. The results for the individual topics are shown in Table 2. The differences in opinion did not appear to be mediated by differences in attention or care in reading because substantially

TABLE 2

NET CHANGES OF OPINION IN DIRECTION OF COMMUNICATION WITH
"HIGH CREDIBILITY" AND "LOW CREDIBILITY" SOURCES*
(from Hovland and Weiss, 1951)

	Net percentage of cases in which subjects changed opinion in direction of communication			
Topic	*High credibility sources*		*Low credibility sources*	
Antihistamines	$(N = 31)$	22.6%	$(N = 30)$	13.3%
Atomic submarines	$(N = 25)$	36.0	$(N = 36)$	0.0
Steel shortage	$(N = 35)$	22.9	$(N = 26)$	−3.8
Future of movies	$(N = 31)$	12.9	$(N = 30)$	16.7
Average	$(N = 122)$	23.0	$(N = 122)$	6.6
Diff.		16.4%		
$P_{diff.}$		<.01		

* Net changes = positive changes *minus* negative changes.

the same amount of information was acquired whether the material was attributed to a high or a low credibility source.

Confirmation of these results was obtained in a later study of Kelman and Hovland (1953) with high school subjects. Students were invited to listen to a recording of an educational radio program. The "communicators" were three guest speakers assigned different roles. All took the same position on the topic, which was that extreme leniency should be employed in the treatment of juvenile delinquency. The three communicator versions, differing only in the introductory characterization of the guest speaker, may be labelled "positive," "negative," and "neutral." In the *positive* version the communicator was identified as a judge in a juvenile court—a highly trained, well-informed, experienced authority on criminology and delinquency; sincere, honest, and with the public interest at heart. In the *neutral* version, the speaker was identified as a member of the studio audience, chosen at random. No information about him beyond his name was given. In the negative version, the speaker was also presented as a man from the studio audience, but in the introductory interview it was revealed that he had been a delinquent as a youth and currently was involved in some shady transactions, being out on bail after an arrest on a dope-peddling charge. He showed low regard for the law and great disrespect for his parents. It was plainly evident that he was self-centered and that his leniency view was motivated by self-interest.

Audience reactions to the various speakers were obtained directly after the communication, and the results are summarized in Part A of Table 3. The "negative" source was judged as less fair and trustworthy than the "positive" source. Reaction to the "neutral" source was intermediate.

The opinion results closely parallel these reactions. In Part B of Table 3 it can be seen that the group hearing the communication from the "positive" source has opinions more in line with those advocated by the communicator than those hearing it from the "negative" source. (The higher scores indicate a more lenient position.) The generalization drawn by the authors of the above studies is that the characterization of the communicator as trustworthy or biased has relatively little effect on the learning of factual material but markedly influences the degree to which the communicator's conclusions and recommendations are accepted. They consider the extent of change in belief to be a joint effect of the learning of the content and the acceptance of the message communicated.

Surveys of audience reactions to the communicator may throw considerable light on the factors affecting degree of acceptance. In this category belongs Merton's (1946) interesting study of Kate Smith's bond-selling marathon. One of the principal themes of the book is the audience's perception of Kate Smith as a very sincere individual and the relevance of this factor in explaining her effectiveness. The respondents viewed the eighteen-hour marathon itself as validating this characteristic and the

TABLE 3

AUDIENCE EVALUATIONS AND OPINION CHANGE WITH "POSITIVE," "NEUTRAL," AND "NEGATIVE" SOURCES DELIVERING THE SAME COMMUNICATION ON JUVENILE DELINQUENCY
(from Kelman and Hovland, 1953)

A. Audience Judgments concerning Expertness and Trustworthiness

	Nature of the source		
	Positive $(N = 105^*)$	Neutral $(N = 59^*)$	Negative $(N = 100^*)$
Percent judging him to be highly qualified to speak on the topic of juvenile delinquency . . .	78%**	33%	9%
Percent judging him as giving a "completely fair" or "fair" presentation . . .	73%**	63%	29%
Percent saying they would trust his judgment "completely" or "some"	87%**	66%	25%

* The number of subjects answering each question varies slightly. These are the smallest N's for any of the three judgments.
** Positive versus negative is significant at beyond the .001 level.

B. Immediate Effects of Communicators on Opinion Scores*

Group	N	Mean**
"Positive" source	97	46.7
"Neutral" source	56	45.7
"Negative" source	91	42.8

* A high score represents the position of leniency advocated in the communication.
** $t_{\text{pos-neg}} = 4.11$ $p = .001$
$t_{\text{pos-neutr}} = 0.79$ $p = .21$
$t_{\text{neutr-neg}} = 2.36$ $p = .01$

steady listeners were more convinced of the purity of Kate Smith's motives for conducting the campaign than were those who only listened occasionally or did not listen at all. The author attributes this largely to the effects of successive broadcasting in building up a public image of Kate Smith. It is also possible, of course, that the chain of causation is in the opposite direction—that only those with the favorable image became steady listeners. The contrast between Kate Smith's sincerity and the usual pretenses, deceptions, and dissembling of daily experience is stressed. Informants appear to feel themselves the objects of manipulation:

> They see themselves as the target for ingenious methods of control, through advertising which cajoles, promises, terrorizes; through propagandas that, utilizing available techniques, guide the unwitting audience

into opinions which may or may not coincide with the best interests of themselves or their affiliates; through cumulatively subtle methods of salesmanship which may stimulate values common to both salesman and client for private and self-interested motives. (p. 142)

Further data concerning audience reaction to different types of communicators and the relation of these perceptions to the effect of the communication are furnished in a recent study by Hovland and Mandell (1952a) which had as its main purpose a comparison of the effects of conclusion-drawing by the communicator and audience. Recordings of a program on devaluation of currency were made on tape. In one version the communicator was introduced as being a prominent importer (who would have something to gain by devaluation), and in the other as an economist from a specified large American university. Pronounced differences in the subject's evaluation of the adequacy and fairness of the presentation were obtained, as indicated in Part A of Table 4. But the net percentage of the subjects who changed their opinions in the direction advocated by the communicator was not very much greater with the "nonsuspicious" than with the "suspicious" communicator. *Thirty-seven* percent of the subjects who heard the version attributed to the impartial economist were influenced, while in the case of the suspicion-arousing communicator the percent changed was *twenty-five*. With somewhat over one hundred cases in each group, this difference is not significant (Part B of Table 4).

A related type of study has been done in the field of public speaking by Haiman (1949), employing the concept of the "ethos" of the speaker. Introducing a recorded speech concerning compulsory health insurance as delivered by the Surgeon General of the United States, a communist, or a college sophomore produced significantly different amounts of opinion change.

Two types of studies have been discussed: one in which characterizations of the communicator have been experimentally varied, and the other in which differences in the audience's perceptions of the communicator were analyzed through interview. It will be seen that these two types of research give distinctive but complementary information. The type of interview study typified by Merton's (1946) investigation is particularly useful in analyzing the factors to which the audience is reacting when a particular communicator is involved. It is well suited to the exploration of a genuine real-life communication where strong emotional factors may be involved. Experimental investigation, however, is necessary to determine whether the differences in audience evaluation of a communicator really affect the capacity of the communicator to modify belief, attitude, and overt behavior. The study by Hovland and Mandell emphasizes this point: although there were pronounced differences in evaluations of the trustworthiness of the communicator, there were no significant

TABLE 4

AUDIENCE EVALUATIONS AND OPINION CHANGE WITH IDENTICAL COMMUNICATIONS PRESENTED BY "SUSPICIOUS" AND "NONSUSPICIOUS" COMMUNICATORS
(from Hovland and Mandell, 1952a)

A.   Audience Judgments concerning Adequacy and Fairness of Communication

	"Nonsuspicious" communicator ($N = 113$)		"Suspicious" communicator ($N = 122$)
Percent of subjects believing communicator did "A very good job" in giving the facts	41.1		21.1
Difference		20.0	
p		$<.001$	
Percent of subjects saying communicator gave a "fair and honest" picture	52.7		36.7
Difference		16.0	
p		$<.01$	

B.   Percent of Subjects Changing Opinion on "Devaluation" from Before to After Communication

	Direction of change*	Conclusion not drawn by communicator %	Conclusion drawn by communicator %
"Nonsuspicious" communicator	Positive	30.9	53.4
	No change	60.0	44.8
	Negative	9.1	1.8
	Net % changing	21.8 ($N = 55$)	51.6 ($N = 58$)
"Suspicious" communicator	Positive	30.5	49.2
	No change	55.9	46.0
	Negative	13.6	4.8
	Net % changing	16.9 ($N = 59$)	44.4 ($N = 63$)
Combined ("suspicious" and "nonsuspicious" communicators)	Positive	30.7	51.2
	No change	57.9	45.5
	Negative	11.4	3.3
	Net % changing	19.3 ($N = 144$)	47.9 ($N = 121$)
Mean Diff. =			28.6
$p =$			.001

* Positive is here defined as changing in direction of position advocated by communicator, negative as changing in direction opposite that advocated by communicator. Net % changing = percent changing in positive direction minus percent changing in negative direction.

differences in the extent to which opinions were changed by the two types of communicator.

The Communication

How are the effects of mass media influenced by the character and content of the communication? In answering this question one must consider both the types of appeals employed and the arrangement of the elements sequentially.

Appeals. One way in which the nature of appeals is frequently discussed is in terms of the relative effectiveness of "emotional" *versus* "rational" appeals. Thus in the experiment of Hartmann (1936) two types of appeals were compared in terms of their efficacy in inducing voters to cast their ballot for the Socialist party. One type of leaflet employed a strong emotional appeal, stressing the implications of socialism for freedom from war, want, and fear, and its positive effects for home, comfort, and country. The other ("rational appeal") version employed a quiz game in which the arguments favoring socialism were stressed. In one set of voting districts every family was given the emotional leaflet, while in a second set the rational appeals leaflet was distributed. A third set of wards was retained as a control. The emotional appeal leaflet was most effective. Fifty percent more socialist votes were cast in these wards than in the previous election, while the increase was only thirty-five percent in the "rational appeal" wards. (The control wards showed an increase over the previous election of 24 percent.) (Figure 1.)

Superiority of emotional propaganda over logical argumentation was also obtained by Menefee and Granneberg (1940). The remaining studies have failed to find clear-cut superiority of one type of appeal over the other. In studies by Knower (1935, 1936) the two methods appeared to be of approximately equal effectiveness in influencing attitudes toward prohibition. But it was found that individuals favoring prohibition were more affected by logical argument, and those opposed by persuasive argument. Dietrich (1946) reports that in the case of radio commentator programs there were no significant differences between a "conversational" and a "dynamic" delivery in shifting attitudes. Subjects tended to label the dynamic delivery as "propaganda" more frequently than the conversational delivery. No differences were found between "commentator" and "dramatic" radio transcription by Hovland, Lumsdaine, and Sheffield (1949) in changing the opinions of soldiers about the probable length of the war.

The lack of consistency in outcome suggests the need of further research on the conditions which affect the relative advantage of the two types of appeals. These two types of appeal are not, of course, truly alternative, since the effectiveness of emotional appeals may depend to a large extent on persuading individuals to consider rationally certain issues raised, and of course rational arguments depend for their effectiveness

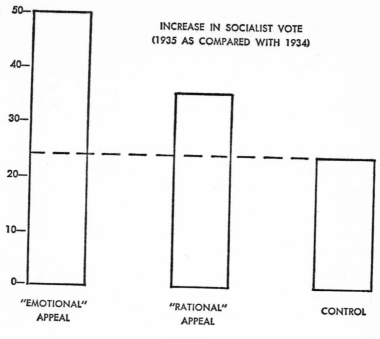

FIGURE 1.

on some appeal to the individual's motives. A study of individual differences, determining which members of an audience are most affected by the various types of appeals, would be particularly instructive. Certainly educational differences should appear, associated with emphasis during schooling on the "virtues" of the rational and the deprecation of the emotional. Personality and cultural differences are also to be expected.

Another research formulation in this area is that of "positive" as compared with "negative" appeals. The appeal in the former is oriented toward the attainment of some desirable outcome, while in the latter it is couched in terms of how to avoid some unpleasant outcome. In advertising there appears to be a general trend toward an increased use of negative appeals (Lucas and Britt, 1950), and this may be based on confidential data concerning its effectiveness. Lucas and Benson (1930) obtained sales records for extension courses, a test campaign, and a book promotion program. Sixteen of the comparisons favored the positive and twelve the negative appeals. Some of the products appeared to sell better with negative appeals and others better with positive ones, despite a lack of over-all difference in effectiveness. Again there is a need for further research to determine why one is more effective under particular conditions than the other.

In the experimental literature there is relatively little evidence concerning the use of various types of appeals in communication. A good share of our knowledge of this problem comes from commercial research done in connection with radio, newspaper, and magazine advertising. Most of this work is rather uncontrolled and is set up along empirical rather than theoretical lines. The types of results available in the advertising literature concerning appeals and methods of presentation will be found in some of the publications on the psychology of advertising. Books by Burtt (1938) and Lucas and Britt (1950) are particularly complete in this area.

Extremely interesting data on the use of appeals in mass communication come from the Merton (1946) study of the Kate Smith campaign, referred to earlier. A content analysis was made of the various types of appeals used, and then cross comparisons were made between the appeals and the comments of the individuals interviewed. For example, content analysis revealed that "sacrifice" was frequently used as a theme. From the comments the author infers that:

> . . . this triangulation of sacrifice, this three-cornered pressure—the boys' sacrifice, other listeners' sacrifice, Smith's sacrifice manifested in the marathon—developed in many listeners a strong sense of unworthiness and guilt. . . . Only by matching the sacrifices of the other three—converting the triangle into a square as it were—could tension be relieved.

This is then illustrated by the following case study:

> Then, after the purchase, there was strong evidence of catharsis. Duty had been done and guilt swept away. . . . "After I called up, I felt good, *I felt that I had done something real on the phone. I got it, and just to bring the boys home.*" (pp. 54f.)

It will be seen that this type of research, based largely on matching comments and appeals, has important methodological difficulties. The comments may or may not have any close relationship to the reasons for bond purchases. Such research is, however, very suggestive of hypotheses for more rigorous investigations where appeals of various types may be experimentally introduced and the changes in attitudes and behavior studied.

An example of an experimental attack on the problem of optimal utilization of appeals in mass communication is the study by Janis and Feshbach (1953). The effects of three different intensities of fear appeal were investigated in a communication on dental hygiene. A fifteen-minute talk was prepared in three versions which contained the same essential information about causes of dental disease and the same recommendations for proper care of teeth, but which differed in the amount of fear-arousing material. Version I used a strong fear appeal, emphasizing the painful consequences of tooth decay and showing illustrative slides on diseased gums and other results of poor dental hygiene. Version II used a moderate appeal in which the dangers were presented in milder form. Version III used a minimal fear appeal in which more neutral material appeared. Both the verbal material and the accompanying slides varied in the degree to which they contained threats concerning the consequences of not conforming to the recommended course of action concerning oral hygiene.

The freshman class of a large high school was divided into four groups —three experimental groups (one for each of the appeals) and one control. Evidence that the three appeals differed in the amount of emotional tension they aroused was obtained from questions asked of the audience concerning their worry about the condition of their own teeth. A clear progression appeared, with 74 percent of the "strong fear" group, 60 percent of the "moderate" group, and 50 percent of the "minimal" group reporting feeling "some worry" during the presentation.

The principal results of the experiment bear on the extent to which the recommendations were accepted and followed. The greatest change was obtained in the minimal fear-arousal condition (Table 5). This was in line with the authors' expectation that fear arousal, if intense, may lead to adverse effects, such as hostility toward the communicator. As a result the communication may not be accepted. Another way of checking the effects was employed by re-exposing the audience to a second communication, which discounted the recommendations of the first. Again the talk of minimal fear arousal was found to be most effective in that the audiences in the other groups were more inclined to accept the countercommunication which discounted the original talk.

Sequence of arguments. The impact of a communication is also influenced by the order in which the various points are presented.

TABLE 5

Effect of Different Degrees of Fear Appeal on Conformity to Dental Hygiene Recommendations
(From Janis and Feshbach, 1953)

Type of change	Strong Fear appeal group (N = 50)	Moderate Fear appeal group (N = 50)	Minimal Fear appeal group (N = 50)	Control Group (N = 50)
Increased conformity	28%	44%	50%	22%
Decreased conformity	20%	22%	14%	22%
No change	52%	34%	36%	56%
	100%	100%	100%	100%
Net change in conformity	+8%	+22%	+36%	0%
pdiff.	.03		.01	

One characteristic problem concerns the relative effectiveness of arguments presented toward the beginning or toward the end of the communication. This is frequently phrased as the effect of "climax" as compared with "anticlimax" order. In the former the strongest arguments are saved for the end, while in the latter the strongest arguments are used at the outset.

Several studies of the relative effectiveness of the two alternative arrangements have been made. One carried out by Sponberg (1946) used communications concerning the desirability of wartime marriages. Each communication was divided into three parts: "large" (eight minutes long and containing the line of argument rated as of greatest importance by speech judges); "medium" (five minutes of an argument of intermediate importance); and "small" (three minutes of the least important argument). These were presented to one group of 92 college students in "climax" order (with most important arguments last), and to another group of 93 students in the reverse ("anticlimax") order. Opinion questionnaires dealing with the over-all issue and with each of the three supporting arguments were administered immediately before the communication and again immediately after, followed by a third administration from ten to thirteen days after the communication. While the shifts of opinion on the main proposition were not significant, opinion change on the "large" argument was clearly greater when it was presented at the beginning of the communication (in "anticlimax" order).

Another major study was made by Cromwell (1950). He presented recorded speeches to four groups of college students, totaling 441 subjects. The topic concerned the desirability of federal medical aid. Half of each communication was a speech containing strong arguments for the position advocated; the other half was a speech of the same length but weaker in argumentative content and organization. The characterization of the speeches as "strong" or "weak" was also checked in terms of the ratings of effectiveness assigned to them by trained judges. One group of subjects listened to a "strong" affirmative speech followed by a "weak" affirmative speech. Another group listened to the same speeches in the opposite order. Two other groups heard strong and weak speeches on the negative side of the question. Attitude scores were given before the speeches and after each of the two speeches.

The mean shift in audience attitude was significantly greater for speeches in the weak-strong (climax) order than in the opposite, anticlimax order. Only 27 percent of the auditors who heard the speeches presented in anticlimax order made a shift greater than one standard error, whereas 42 percent of the listeners who heard the speeches in climax order made a shift toward the side of the proposition advocated.

Sponberg's results support an anticlimax order, while those of Cromwell indicate the superiority of a climax sequence. There seem to be two major variations in the procedures of the two experiments that may have affected the outcomes. In Sponberg's study the differences in emphasis were confined to two portions of a single speech, while in the Cromwell study the difference was in the strength of two different speeches on the same topic. The other variation was that in the Sponberg study the difference in strength of argument was determined primarily on the basis of the amount of time devoted to it in the talk, while in the Cromwell research the speeches were of equal length but were designed to differ in convincingness.

It appears unlikely that one or the other order of presentation will turn out to be universally superior. Research is therefore needed as to what factors are responsible for the differences in outcome. Hovland, Janis, and Kelley (1953), in analyzing this problem, discuss the role of attention, learning, and acceptance. In connection with *attention arousal* the hypothesis is suggested that the presentation of the major arguments at the outset (anticlimax order) will be most effective where the audience is initially little interested in the communication. Studies of *learning* in serial order are discussed, showing that learning difficulty is greatest in the middle portions and that both the beginning and the end are easier to learn than the items in the center. Various hypotheses are suggested as to how the structure of the communication may affect the *acceptance* of the communication. One hypothesis derived from learning theory is that the climax order will be more effective in regard to acceptance, when other factors are kept constant, because with the anticlimax order the failure to fulfill the expectations created by the initial portions may produce frustration and consequent extinction.

A second problem of sequence which also goes under the name "primacy-recency" is that involved when opposed sides of an issue are being presented. Does the side presented first have a better chance of influencing opinion than that presented second? This is of considerable importance in connection with debates, court trials, propaganda, and so on.

One of the first studies of this problem was by Lund (1925). Communications were presented first on one side of an issue and then on the other. The positions were suitably counterbalanced so that the relative effectiveness of the first presented could be compared with that of the second. His results indicated that the first presentation invariably changed opinions more than the second changed them back. Diametrically opposite results were obtained by Cromwell (1950), who found that the last presented results were more effective in persuasion. A recent study by Hovland and Mandell (1952b), which repeated the Lund procedure, found neither primacy nor recency consistently.

Again the research task is to separate out some of the factors contributing to the differences in results obtained by various experiments. The factors of attention, learning, and acceptance may all be involved.

The relative effect of primacy may be different when the audience is interested in the issue than when the initial communication must first arouse interest and then present the arguments. The presentation of both sides represents the standard reproductive interference design in classical verbal learning research. From the studies done in this area, we should expect that the time interval between the two presentations and between the initial presentation and the testing for opinion change would be critical elements. Acceptance may depend on the evaluation of the communicator and the degree of commitment produced by answering the questionnaire items in a particular manner. Both factors may have contributed to Lund's results. Since the experimenter was the regular instructor the class may have accepted the first communication as Lund's own position, but they may have been confused and mystified by the switch when the same instructor presented the second side. Also, questionnaires were administered after each communication, so that some commitment to the position taken after the first communication was involved [although the results of Hovland and Mandell (1952b) suggest that this is not a crucial factor]. Thus a great deal of further research is needed before the Lund phenomenon can be truly named, as Lund entitled it, "*The Law* of Primacy in Persuasion."

A final type of problem in the arrangement of arguments is involved when one is faced with the decision as to whether arguments on both sides of the question should be discussed, or whether the arguments should be confined to only one side. When one is successively exposed to first one side and then the other of a controversial subject, as in a debate, the typical result is that the individual is left at approximately his initial position. This comes out most clearly in the study by Sims (1938), where the same individuals were exposed to both sides of a communication on TVA. Each side alone produced a significant effect, but in combination cancellation of effects was obtained. Substantially similar results were obtained by Schanck and Goodman (1939) using propaganda favoring or not favoring civil service. Related studies on the effects of debates and discussion groups are summarized in Brembeck and Howell (1952).

A quite different problem is raised when the same communicator takes into account both sides of an issue but is himself in favor of one side. Klapper (1949) has labelled this problem that of "partial impartiality," in reporting the study by Hovland, Lumsdaine, and Sheffield (1949). These investigators presented communications to two experimental groups of 214 soldiers each and to a control group of 197 soldiers on the question of an early end of the war with Japan following Germany's surrender. Beliefs concerning the issue were tested before the communication and immediately after the communication. One experimental group was given a fifteen-minute talk presenting only the arguments for thinking that the war with Japan would be a long one. The material presented contained much factual information stressing Japan's advantage and resources. The second experimental group was given a communication which contained an additional four minutes of information woven into the presentation stressing United States advantages and Japanese weaknesses.

To evaluate the effectiveness of the two programs, subjects were asked to estimate the probable length of the war with Japan after VE Day. The hypothesis studied was that those opposed to an issue would rehearse their own counter-arguments during a one-sided presentation and would regard a one-sided presentation as biased. Their data, presented in Fig. 2, sup-

NET PER CENT OF INDIVIDUALS CHANGING OPINION
IN DIRECTION OF POSITION ADVOCATED
BY COMMUNICATOR

A. Among men initially <u>opposed</u>
to communicator's position

| PROGRAM I (ONE SIDE) | 36% |
| PROGRAM II (BOTH SIDES) | 48% |

B. Among men initially <u>favorable</u>
to communicator's position

| PROGRAM I (ONE SIDE) | 52% |
| PROGRAM II (BOTH SIDES) | 23% |

FIGURE 2.

port the hypothesis by showing that the "net effects" were different for the two ways of presenting the material, *depending on the initial stand of the listener.* The program giving both sides was more effective for men initially opposed, that is, for men who, contrary to the programs, expected a short war (less than two years). On the other hand, the program giving the one-sided picture was more effective for men initially favoring the stand taken, that is, for the men who agreed with the point of view of the programs that the war would take at least two years.

Another expectation was that the better educated men would be less affected by a conspicuously one-sided presentation and, conversely, would be more likely to accept the arguments of a presentation that appeared to take all factors into account in arriving at a conclusion. On the other hand, the consideration of both sides of an issue could weaken the immediate force of the argument for the less well educated insofar as they are less critical and more likely to be impressed by the strength of the one-sided argument without thinking of objections. The results, when analyzed according to educational level, showed that the program which presented both sides was more effective with better educated men and that the program which presented one side was more effective with less educated men.

When education and initial position were considered together, it was found that the communication giving both sides proved to be more effective among the better educated regardless of initial position, whereas the one-sided presentation was primarily effective with those who were already convinced among the less well educated group. From the results obtained it would be expected that the total effect of either kind of program on the group as a whole would depend both on the group's educational composition and on the initial division of opinion in the group. Thus, obtaining information about the educational level and initial position of an audience might be of considerable value in choosing the most effective type of presentation.

An extension of this type of investigation was carried out by Lumsdaine and Janis (1953). Here audiences were exposed to a communication contrary to the initial communication after having heard either both sides or only a single side. The results indicate that the two-sided presentation is particularly effective in "inoculating" the audience against the effects of subsequent countercommunication.

The Medium

In the literature of communications there are a considerable number of studies comparing one medium with another in terms of achieving some desired effect. Such comparisons present some very grave methodological problems. For one thing, the uses of two different media are often so distinctive that direct comparison is not meaningful. For example, determining whether radio or television is more effective in conveying to an audience the characteristic techniques of different sculptors would not be worthwhile, since it could be predicted in advance that television would be superior.

A second problem is the differential selection of audiences by different media. Comparisons of naturally self-selected audiences have one meaning, while comparisons between audiences which have been experimentally subjected to one or the other medium may have a different meaning. Thus comparisons involving captive audiences which have been given one or the other medium may not sustain generalization to real life situations where a high degree of self-selection obtains.

The third difficulty is to obtain a sufficiently large sample of different communications using the same medium to permit valid generalization about a population of cases involving some particular medium. The bulk of the literature involves a comparison of say one radio presentation and one directly given speech. The obtained results may be attributable to unique characteristics of the particular comparison made.

One generalization derived from comparisons of media is that the oral presentation of material appears to be more effective than the printed presentation in changing opinion. The three major studies of this problem all appeared at about the same time, in 1934-36. Wilke (1934) compared the effects of oral, radio, and printed presentations on attitudes toward war, distribution of wealth, birth control, and God. A total of 341 college students were studied. One group heard the speech delivered in person, another listened to it over a closed radio circuit, while the third read a mimeographed version labeled as the text of a speech to university classes. Subjects served in the experimental group for one topic and the control group for another. All three methods had significant effects. The speech made in person produced the greatest changes and the printed pamphlet the least. Particularly in the case of radio, some individuals were changed in a direction opposite to that intended.

Comparisons of oral versus printed presentations of persuasive arguments were also made by Knower (1935, 1936). The topic studied was prohibition, two of the versions favoring it and the other two opposing it. Attitude scales were administered before and after the communications. Oral argument was found more effective in producing changes in opinion than printed argument.

The studies by Cantril and Allport (1935) represent another attack on the problem. In these investigations not only were there comparisons of the over-all effect of communications, but also extensive observations were made concerning the reactions of the audience during the presentations. In general, simpler materials were used, designed more for transmittal of information than for persuasion. From the comparison of directly transmitted speech as compared with radio presentation the authors conclude that "the radio situation is more solidly structured than the face-to-face situation, less easily analyzed and regarded less critically by the listener" (p. 139). The latter point is not consistent with the results of Wilke mentioned above. From a comparison of listening to radio and reading carried out by Carver, Cantril and Allport draw the following conclusion: "If other conditions are kept constant, the mental functions of recognition, verbatim recall, and suggestibility seem more effectively aroused in listening; whereas critical attitudes and discriminative comprehension are favored by reading" (p. 159).

The differences found by Cantril and Allport between listening to a lecture directly and hearing it over a loudspeaker were found to be relatively slight. Studies by Ewbank (1932) and by Heron and Ziebarth (1946) have tended to support this result, although Gaskill (1933) found some superiority in broadcast lectures over direct hearing.

Contrasted with the laboratory investigations of the relative effectiveness of the printed page as compared with the radio are investigations which take account of the complex naturalistic setting of the alternative media. In *Radio and The Printed Page*, Lazarsfeld (1940) presents an extensive report of the types of interest satisfied by the two media, differences in their characteristics, and some data on their effectiveness. One of the striking findings is the interdependence of the two, in which one of the clear-cut effects of radio is the promotion of reading. In Lazarsfeld, Berelson, and Gaudet (1944) there is an extensive comparison of the extent to which individuals base their voting decision on one or the other medium. Both are judged about equally effective in having an influence, but radio is more often given as the factor which was *most decisive*. Results on this point are shown in Fig. 3.

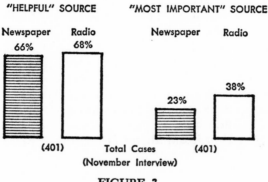

FIGURE 3.

Films have been frequently compared with other media for effectiveness. Much of the literature is in the area of teaching which we have arbitrarily excluded from the present review because of its extensiveness. Hoban and van Ormer (1951) report over twenty studies devoted entirely to the comparison of films with other methods of instruction in teaching various types of subject matter. The conclusion derived by these authors from the studies reported is that effective films are approximately equal to an instructor for the presentation of facts and the demonstration of concepts.

There are beginning to appear a few comparisons of television with other media. Those which appear in the trade publications are primarily concerned with the relative efficacy of television as compared with radio in producing sales. The results generally favor television. There has been one laboratory-type study of the comparative effectiveness of a radio and television transmission of the same program (Goldberg, 1950). The results indicate that television viewers were able to name the sponsor of the program and the products advertised more frequently than were those in the radio group. They also remembered more details concerning the content of the program. Again we must await further research to determine whether the superiority of television is primarily attributable to its present novelty. In another study television was compared with a movie version of the same program in the training of officers and enlisted men. The two were found to be equally effective and about as effective as the typical method of face-to-face instruction [Rock, Duva and Murray (not dated)].

Factors responsible for differences in effectiveness of media. Comparisons between the various media, discussed in the preceding section, have not proved fruitful in providing important scientific generalizations. This is primarily attributable to the fact that there are a sizable number of differences between the different media and some of these may operate to increase and others to decrease the effects studied. At the same time, the studies have frequently been done under somewhat artificial conditions so that they have likewise not been too useful for practical application under naturalistic conditions. It would seem profitable for future research, therefore, to employ controlled variation of particular factors in which the media differ. Simultaneously research will have to be conducted to determine the realistic conditions under which the generalizations are to be applied. Some of the general factors which are involved in media comparisons will be briefly discussed in terms of their effects in (a) attracting and holding an audience, (b) providing information, (c) changing attitudes and opinion, and (d) inducing action along particular lines.

Attracting an audience. The first respect in which media may differ is in the kind of audience they attract and the degree to which they hold the attention of the audience attracted. The effects of communications are inextricably bound to these factors. Generalizations in this area will be concerned with which media attract which types of individuals. Research on this topic is represented by the work of Beville (1939) and Herzog (1944) on audiences for radio programs, Berelson (1949) on readership of books, Schramm and White (1949) on newspaper readership, Lazarsfeld and Wyant (1937) on magazines, and Handel (1950) on movies. Much information of this type is already available, and additional data, based on surveys of who are reached by various media, are in the hands of commercial agencies.

The second facet of the problem, having to do with the degree of attention aroused by the various media, is less fully investigated. It is alleged that television is particularly compelling and that individuals give it their undivided attention to a much greater extent than radio, but this is not too well documented and merely highlights the need for numerous comparative studies. One would suspect that the difference between the immediacy of an event transmitted via television and a subsequent movie version of it would be the type of factor to be investigated, but differences in conditions of viewing would also have to be taken into account.

Conveying information. The second general area of studies would involve comparisons among the media in terms of their efficacy in transmitting knowledge and imparting skills. In this area gross comparisons of the media will probably have to be supplemented by detailed investigations of particular factors within each medium. The characteristic of media which has been most extensively investigated in this connection is the sense modality involved. A large number of studies of this problem have been made, many of which are summarized by Klapper (1949). The majority of the studies have found higher retention of simple material when it is presented orally rather than visually. Almost all show that the combination of visual and auditory presentation is more effective than either alone. But further work is needed to define the conditions under which one or the other is superior. There is suggestive evidence that the superiority of oral presentation is greater with the less intelligent subjects. There are also likely to be differences in terms of what type of material is to be learned; for some material, seeing the objects may be absolutely essential. Comparisons of sound versions with silent films on various topics may shed considerable light on these problems.

Another factor which may be involved in comparisons of media is in the extent to which presentation with motion is permitted. What are the conditions under which the *motion* involved in motion pictures as compared with the still presentation of sound slides with identical recordings is effective? Illustrative of the type of studies required is one by Hovland, Lumsdaine, and Sheffield (1949) comparing the points which are equally well learned from a sound film and a sound slide on map reading with those which are learned more effectively with one or the other medium. More extensive data on this and related topics are being compiled by the training film researchers of the Air Force (Lumsdaine, 1953).

The extent to which exposure to the material is controlled by the subject is a third factor to be explored. It has been mentioned frequently as an advantage of reading that it permits the reader to control his own pace and to go over the material if it is not completely assimilated on the first trial. This factor needs further investigation in isolation, where its effects are not confounded with all of the other differences between the media. Comparisons of fixed and variable rates of presentation within a single medium are relevant here.

Lastly, the efficiency of media for imparting information and skills may be dependent on the extent to which they involve active or passive conditions of learning. Results from laboratory experiments (cf. review by Hovland, 1951) and from communication studies using sound slides (Hovland, Lumsdaine, and Sheffield, 1949) and films (Hoban and van Ormer, 1951) indicate that the greater the participation and involvement of the subject in the learning, the greater will be the acquisition. Can some of the differences in effectiveness between the media be attributed to this factor? According to Cantril and Allport (1935) reading differs from radio presentation in this respect. Radio permits greater passivity. Movies, on the other hand, are frequently said to be particularly potent in terms of involving the subject in the communication (Blumer, 1933).

Changing opinions and attitudes. When the objective of the communication is the changing of opinion and attitude the factors previously mentioned play a role to the extent that change in attitude or opinion is dependent on learning what the communicator is saying. But an additional group of factors is introduced by the requirement that the communication become *accepted* by the recipient. The differences in various media in terms of acceptance need further exploration.

One factor influencing the extent to which a message in a mass medium is accepted is the prestige of the medium. Various writers have stressed the fact that one medium may be more prestigeful than another (e.g., Doob, 1948). But this generalization would need further specification in terms of "prestige for whom?" Research in our own country suggests that for some, radio may be more prestigeful, for others print, and so on. During its period of novelty, television may be more prestigeful for certain segments of the population. In foreign countries radio may be more prestigeful than newspapers, possibly as a result of differences in political control. The latter point suggests that the media may in certain circumstances differ also in credibility and that the medium judged by an individual to be most trustworthy may be most effective.

A second factor which might be expected to affect the comparison of media would be the extent of social interaction. Knower (1935) reports that hearing a speech when a member of an audience is less effective than hearing it individually. On the other hand, Cantril and Allport (1935) suggest that radio may be more effective than print precisely because the individual feels himself part of a larger group listening simultaneously to the program. Detailed investigation of this problem is certainly needed.

The extent to which the medium provides flexibility of appeals constitutes a third factor. Here the comparisons would center about the relative advantages of various media in catering to special interests and differences in comprehension. Print is alleged to be particularly effective in terms of this factor, providing for specialized interests and tastes to a greater degree than other media. Flexibility is stressed by Lazarsfeld, Berelson, and Gaudet (1944) as an explanation for the efficacy of personal influence: "The clever campaign worker, professional or amateur, can make use of a large number of cues to achieve his end. He can choose the occasion at which to speak to the other fellow. He can adapt his story to what he presumes to be the other's interests and his ability to understand. If he notices the other is bored, he can change the subject. If he sees that he has aroused resistance, he can retreat, giving the other the satisfaction of a victory, and come back to his point later. If in the course of the discussion he discovers some pet convictions, he can try to tie up his argument to them. He can spot the moments when the other is yielding, and so time his best punches" (pp. 153f.). A learning theory formulation concerning temporal factors in mass communication yields a similar analysis (Hovland, 1948b). During the political campaign just passed attempts were made to increase flexibility of fixed presentation media by employing a two-way communication network between the studio and the listener. Questions raised by the man-in-the-street could thus be answered immediately by the political candidate in the television studio.

Inducing action. Still another objective of some communications is to precipitate action. The factors mentioned earlier may all be involved in convincing the recipient that the suggested action is appropriate, but additional ones are involved in producing the desired response. The primary new factors here seem to be immediacy, flexibility, and surveillance. From Merton (1946) it appears that one of the reasons for Kate Smith's effectiveness was the timeliness of the action. Thus a rebroadcast where all elements were the same except for immediacy would have been expected to be less effective. It is possible that similar differences may be found in comparisons of television and film transcriptions of same programs, particularly when events of public interest are presented.

Flexibility of appeals is relevant here again. This may have been involved as an explanation of Cartwright's (1949) finding that personal solicitation was much more effective than mass media appeals. There may also have been a third factor: personal appeals have the advantage that they can constitute a pressure to carry out an action and can provide surveillance as to whether the suggested action is carried out. This is a phenomenon well known to salesmen, who try to sign up the prospect on the spot. For a discussion of some of the psychological aspects of this problem, the reader is referred to Kelman (1953).

The foregoing analysis suggests that in many instances the superiority of one medium over another is based on a large number of different factors. Thus face-to-face communication is almost universally reported to be more effective than that by radio, but to what extent this is due to oral versus visual plus oral presentation, to flexibility, "feedback," surveillance, attention value, or other factors is not at all clear. Over-all empirical generalizations about media tend to overlook the number of different factors and their interaction. It is much to be hoped that future research will help clarify the problem by attention to some of the basic theoretical variables involved.

REFERENCES

Adler, M. *Art and prudence.* New York: Longmans, Green, 1937.

Annis, A. D., & Meier, N. C. The induction of opinion through suggestion by means of "planted content." *J. soc. Psychol.*, 1934, 5, 65-81.

Arnett, C. E., Davidson, Helen H., & Lewis, H. N. Prestige as a factor in attitude changes. *Sociol. soc. Res.*, 1931, *16*, 49-55.

Barry, H., Jr. A test for negativism and compliance. *J. abnorm. soc. Psychol.*, 1931, *25*, 373-381.

Bartlett, F. C. *Remembering*. Cambridge, Eng.: Cambridge Univ. Press, 1932.

Bateman, R. M., & Remmers, H. H. A study of the shifting attitude of high school students when subjected to favorable and unfavorable propaganda. *J. soc. Psychol.*, 1941, *13*, 395-406.

Bent, S. *Newspaper crusaders*. New York: McGraw-Hill, 1939.

Berelson, B. *The library's public*. New York: Columbia Univ. Press, 1949.

Berelson, B., & Janowitz, M. *Reader in public opinion and communication*. Glencoe, Ill.: Free Press, 1950.

Bettelheim, B., & Janowitz, M. Reactions to Fascist propaganda—a pilot study. *Publ. Opin. Quart.*, 1950, *14*, 53-60.

Beville, H. M., Jr. *Social stratification of the radio audience*. Princeton: Princeton Univ. Press, 1939.

Bird, C. The influence of the press upon the accuracy of report. *J. abnorm. soc. Psychol.*, 1927, *22*, 123-129.

Blumer, H. *Movies and conduct*. New York: Macmillan, 1933.

Blumer, H., & Hauser, P. M. *Movies, delinquency, and crime*. New York: Macmillan, 1933.

Brembeck, W. L., & Howell, W. S. *Persuasion*. New York: Prentice-Hall, 1952.

Britt, S. H., & Menefee, S. C. Did the publicity of the Dies Committee in 1938 influence public opinion? *Publ. Opin. Quart.*, 1939, *3*, 449-457.

Burtt, H. E. *Psychology of advertising*. Boston: Houghton Mifflin, 1938.

Cantril, H. (assisted by Hazel Gaudet and Herta Herzog). *The invasion from Mars*. Princeton: Princeton Univ. Press, 1940.

Cantril, H., & Allport, G. W. *The psychology of radio*. New York: Harper, 1935.

Cartwright, D. Some principles of mass persuasion. *Hum. Relat.*, 1949, *2*, 253-267.

Carver, M. E. Listening versus reading. In H. Cantril & G. W. Allport, *The psychology of radio*. New York: Harper, 1935. Pp. 159-180.

Charters, W. W. *Motion pictures and youth*. New York: Macmillan, 1933.

Cherrington, B. M., & Miller, L. W. Changes in attitude as a result of a lecture and of reading similar materials. *J. soc. Psychol.*, 1933, *4*, 479-484.

Childs, H. L., & Whitton, J. B. (Eds.). *Propaganda by short wave*. Princeton: Princeton Univ. Press, 1942.

Coffin, T. E. Television's effects on leisure-time activities. *J. appl. Psychol.*, 1948, *32*, 550-558.

Cooper, Eunice, & Dinerman, Helen Analysis of the film "Don't be a Sucker": A study in communication. *Publ. Opin. Quart.*, 1951, *15*, 243-264.

Cooper, Eunice, & Jahoda, Marie The evasion of propaganda: How prejudiced people respond to anti-prejudice propaganda. *J. Psychol.*, 1947, *23*, 15-25.

Cowley, M. (Ed.), *Books that changed our minds*. New York: Doubleday, Doran, 1939.

Cromwell, H. The relative effect on audience attitude of the first versus the second argumentative speech of a series. *Speech Monogr.*, 1950, *17*, 105-122.

Dale, E., Dunn, Fannie W., Hoban, C. F., & Schneider, Etta   *Motion pictures in education.* New York: H. W. Wilson, 1937.

Dietrich, J. E. The relative effectiveness of two modes of radio delivery in influencing attitudes. *Speech Monogr.*, 1946, *13*, 58-65.

Dietze, A. G., & Jones, G. E. Factual memory of secondary school pupils for a short article which they read a single time. *J. educ. Psychol.*, 1931a, *22*, 586-598.

Dietze, A. G., & Jones, G. E. Factual memory of secondary school pupils for a short article which they read a single time. *J. educ. Psychol.*, 1931b, *22*, 667-676.

Dodd, S. C. *A controlled experiment on rural hygiene in Syria.* Beirut, Lebanon Republic: American Press, 1934.

Doob, L. W. *Public opinion and propaganda.* New York: Henry Holt, 1948.

Duncker, K. Experimental modification of children's food preferences through social suggestion. *J. abnorm. soc. Psychol.*, 1938, *33*, 489-507.

English, H. B., Welborn, E. L., & Killian, C. D. Studies in substance memorization. *J. gen. Psychol.*, 1934, *11*, 233-260.

Ewbank, H. L. Exploratory studies in radio techniques. In Josephine H. MacLatchy (Ed.), *Education on the air.* 3rd Yearbook. Institute for Education by Radio. Columbus, Ohio: Ohio State Univ., 1932. Pp. 231-245.

Fearing, F., & Rogge, Genevieve   A selected and annotated bibliography in communications research. *The Quart. of Film, Radio, and Television*, 1951, *6*, 283-315.

Finn, J. D. Television and education: A review of research. *Audio-Visual Communic. Rev.*, 1953, *1*, 106-126.

Fiske, Marjorie, & Lowenthal, L. Some problems in the administration of international communications research. *Publ. Opin. Quart.*, 1952, *16*, 149-159.

Flowerman, S. H. Mass propaganda in the war against bigotry. *J. abnorm. soc. Psychol.*, 1947, *42*, 429-439.

Freeman, F. N. (Ed.), *Visual education.* Chicago: Univ. of Chicago Press, 1924.

Fried, Edrita   Techniques of persuasion. In H. L. Childs & J. B. Whitton (Eds.), *Propaganda by short wave.* Princeton: Princeton Univ. Press, 1942. Pp. 261-301.

Gaskill, H. V. Research studies made at Iowa State College. In Josephine H. MacLatchy (Ed.), *Education on the air.* 4th Yearbook. Institute for Education by Radio. Columbus, Ohio: Ohio State Univ., 1933. Pp. 322-326.

Glock, C. Y. The comparative study of communications and opinion formation. *Publ. Opin. Quart.*, 1952, *16*, 512-523.

Goldberg, H. D. Liking and retention of a simulcast. *Publ. Opin. Quart.*, 1950, *14*, 141-142.

Gosnell, H. F. *Getting out the vote.* Chicago: Univ. of Chicago Press, 1927.

Haiman, F. S. An experimental study of the effects of Ethos in public speaking. *Speech Monogr.*, 1949, 16, 190-202.

Handel, L. A. *Hollywood looks at its audience.* Urbana, Ill.: Univ. of Ill. Press, 1950.

Hartmann, G. W. A field experiment on the comparative effectiveness of "emotional" and "rational" political leaflets in determining election results. *J. abnorm. soc. Psychol.*, 1936, 31, 99-114.

Heron, W. T., & Ziebarth, E. W. A preliminary experimental comparison of radio and classroom lectures. *Speech Monogr.*, 1946, 13, 54-57.

Herz, M. F. Some psychological lessons from leaflet propaganda in World War II. *Publ. Opin. Quart.*, 1949, 13, 471-486.

Herzog, Herta What do we really know about daytime serial listeners? In P. F. Lazarsfeld & F. N. Stanton (Eds.), *Radio research, 1942-3.* New York: Duell, Sloan & Pearce, 1944. Pp. 3-33.

Hoban, C. F., & van Ormer, E. B. Instructional film research (Rapid mass learning) 1918-1950. Technical report No. SDC 269-7-19. Washington, D. C.: Dept. of Commerce, Office of Technical Services, 1951.

Holaday, P. W., & Stoddard, G. D. *Getting ideas from the movies.* New York: Macmillan, 1933.

Hollonquist, T., & Suchman, E. A. Listening to the listener. In P. F. Lazarsfeld & F. N. Stanton (Eds.), *Radio research, 1942-3.* New York: Duell, Sloan & Pearce, 1944. Pp. 265-334.

Hovland, C. I. Psychology of the communication process. In W. Schramm (Ed.), *Communications in modern society.* Urbana: Univ. of Ill. Press, 1948a. Pp. 59-65.

Hovland, C. I. Social communication. *Proc. Amer. Philos. Soc.*, 1948b, 92, 371-375.

Hovland, C. I. Human learning and retention. In S. S. Stevens (Ed.), *Handbook of experimental psychology.* New York: Wiley & Sons, 1951. Pp. 613-689.

Hovland, C. I., Janis, I. L., & Kelley, H. H. *Communication and Persuasion.* New Haven: Yale Univ. Press, 1953.

Hovland, C. I., Lumsdaine, A. A., & Sheffield, F. D. *Experiments on mass communication.* Princeton: Princeton Univ. Press, 1949.

Hovland, C. I., & Mandell, W. An experimental comparison of conclusion-drawing by the communicator and by the audience. *J. abnorm. soc. Psychol.*, 1952a, 47, 581-588.

Hovland, C. I., & Mandell, W. Is there a "law of primacy in persuasion"? Paper read at the Eastern Psychol. Assn., Atlantic City, Spring, 1952b.

Hovland, C. I., & Weiss, W. The influence of source credibility on communication effectiveness. *Publ. Opin. Quart.*, 1951, 15, 635-650.

Inkeles, A. *Public opinion in Soviet Russia.* Cambridge, Mass.: Harvard Univ. Press, 1950.

Janis, I. L. Personality correlates of susceptibility to persuasion. *J. Pers.*, 1954, 22, 504-518.

Janis, I. L., & Feshbach, S. Effects of fear-arousing communications. *J. abnorm. soc. Psychol.*, 1953, 48, 78-92.

Janis, I. L., Lumsdaine, A. A., & Gladstone, A. I. Effects of preparatory communications on reactions to a subsequent news event. *Publ. Opin. Quart.*, 1951, 15, 487-518.

Kelley, H. H. Salience of membership and resistance to change of group-anchored attitudes. *Amer. Psychologist*, 1952, 7, 328-329. (Abstract)

Kelley, H. H., & Volkart, E. H. The resistance to change of group-anchored attitudes. *Amer. Sociol. Rev.*, 1952, 17, 453-465.

Kelman, H. C. Attitude change as a function of response restriction. *Hum. Rel.*, 1953, 6, 185-214.

Kelman, H. C., & Hovland, C. I. "Reinstatement" of the communicator in delayed measurement of opinion change. *J. abnorm. soc. Psychol.*, 1953, 48, 327-335.

Kendall, Patricia L., & Wolf, Katherine M. The analysis of deviant cases in communications research. In P. F. Lazarsfeld & F. N. Stanton (Eds.), *Communications research, 1948-49*. New York: Harper, 1949. Pp. 152-179.

Kishler, J. Prediction of differential learning from a motion picture by means of "indices of identification potential" derived from attitudes toward the main character. *Amer. Psychologist*, 1950, 5, 298-299. (Abstract)

Klapper, J. T. *The effects of mass media*. New York: Columbia Univ. Bureau of Applied Social Research, 1949. (Mimeo.)

Klineberg, O. Tensions affecting international understanding. *Soc. Sci. Res. Council Bull.*, 1950, 62.

Knower, F. H. Experimental studies of changes in attitude. I. A study of the effect of oral argument on changes of attitude. *J. soc. Psychol.*, 1935, 6, 315-347.

Knower, F. H. Experimental studies of changes in attitude. II. A study of the effect of printed argument on changes in attitude. *J. abnorm. soc. Psychol.*, 1936, 30, 522-532.

Knowlton, D. C., & Tilton, J. W. *Motion pictures in history teaching*. New Haven: Yale Univ. Press, 1929.

Kriesberg, M. Cross-pressures and attitudes. *Publ. Opin. Quart.*, 1949, 13, 5-16.

Lashley, K. S., & Watson, J. B. *A psychological study of motion pictures in relation to venereal disease campaigns*. Washington, D. C.: United States Interdepartmental Social Hygiene Board, 1922.

Lazarsfeld, P. F. *Radio and the printed page*. New York: Duell, Sloan and Pearce, 1940.

Lazarsfeld, P. F. Communication research and the social psychologist. In W. Dennis (Ed.), *Current trends in social psychology*. Pittsburgh: Univ. of Pittsburgh Press, 1948. Pp. 218-273.

Lazarsfeld, P. F., Berelson, B., & Gaudet, Hazel *The peoples' choice*. New York: Duell, Sloan and Pearce, 1944.

Lazarsfeld, P. F., & Merton, R. K. Mass communication, popular taste and organized social action. In L. Bryson (Ed.), *The communication of ideas*. New York: Harper, 1948. Pp. 95-118.

Lazarsfeld, P. F., & Wyant, Rowena   Magazines in 90 cities—Who reads what? *Publ. Opin. Quart.*, 1937, 1, 29-41.

Lewin, K. Group decision and social change. In G. E. Swanson, T. M. Newcomb, & E. L. Hartley (Eds.), *Readings in social psychology* (Rev. Ed.). New York: Holt, 1952. Pp. 459-473.

Lewin, K., & Grabbe, P. Conduct, knowledge, and acceptance of new values. *J. soc. Issues*, 1945, 1, No. 3, 53-64.

Lippmann, W. *Public opinion.* New York: Harcourt, Brace, 1922.

Lucas, D. B., & Benson, C. E. Some sales results for positive and negative advertisements. *J. appl. Psychol.*, 1930, 14, 363-370.

Lucas, D. B., & Britt, S. H. *Advertising psychology and research.* New York: McGraw-Hill, 1950.

Lumsdaine, A. A. Audio Visual Research in the United States Air Force. *Audio Visual Communication Review*, 1953, 1, 76-90.

Lumsdaine, A. A., & Janis, J. L. Resistance to "counterpropaganda" produced by a one-sided versus a two-sided "propaganda" presentation. *Publ. Opin. Quart.*, 1953, 17, 311-318.

Lund, F. H. The psychology of belief. *J. abnorm. soc. Psychol.*, 1925, 20, 174-196.

Lundberg, G. A. The newspaper and public opinion. *Soc. Forces*, 1926, 4, 709-715.

Maccoby, Eleanor E. Television: its impact on school children. *Publ. Opin. Quart.*, 1951, 15, 421-444.

McDonagh, E. C. *et al.* Television and the family. *Sociol. & Soc. Res.*, 1950, 35, 113-122.

Marrow, A. J., & French, J. R. P., Jr. Changing a stereotype in industry. *J. soc. Issues*, 1945, 1, 33-37.

Menefee, S. C., & Granneberg, Audrey G. Propaganda and opinions on foreign policy. *J. soc. Psychol.*, 1940, 11, 393-404.

Merton, R. K. (assisted by Marjorie Fiske and Alberta Curtis) *Mass persuasion.* New York: Harper, 1946.

Mott, F. L. Newspapers in presidential campaigns. *Publ. Opin. Quart.*, 1944, 8, 348-367.

National Research Council. *Manual for the study of food habits.* Report of Comm. on Food Habits, 1945, Bull. No. 111.

Newcomb, T. M. *Personality and social change.* New York: Dryden, 1943.

Perentesis, J. L. Effectiveness of a motion picture trailer as election propaganda. *Publ. Opin. Quart.*, 1948, 12, 465-469.

Peterson, Ruth C., & Thurstone, L. L. *Motion pictures and the social attitudes of children.* New York: Macmillan, 1933.

Ramseyer, L. L. Measuring "intangible" effects of motion pictures. *Educ. Screen*, 1939, 18, 237-238.

Remmers, H. H. Propaganda in the schools—do the effects last? *Publ. Opin. Quart.*, 1938, 2, 197-210.

Riley, J. W., Cantwell, F. V. & Ruttiger, Katherine F. Some observations on the social effects of television. *Publ. Opin. Quart.*, 1949, *13*, 223-234.

Riley, Matilda W., & Riley, J. W., Jr. A sociological approach to communications research. *Publ. Opin. Quart.*, 1951, *15*, 445-460.

Robinson, E. S. Are radio fans influenced? *Survey*, 1932, *68*, 546-547.

Robinson, W. S. Radio comes to the farmer. In P. F. Lazarsfeld & F. N. Stanton (Eds.), *Radio research, 1941*. New York: Duell, Sloan & Pearce, 1941. Pp. 224-294.

Rock, R. T., Jr., Duva, J. S., & Murray, J. E. Training by television: The comparative effectiveness of instruction by television, television recordings, and conventional classroom procedures. *Hum. Eng. Rept.*, 476-02-2. Special Devices Center (undated)

Rose, A. M. Studies in reduction of prejudice. Chicago: American Council on Race Relations, 1947. (Mimeo.)

Rosenthal, S. P. Change of socio-economic attitudes under radical motion picture propaganda. *Arch. Psychol.* (New York), 1934, No. 166.

Schanck, R. L., & Goodman, C. Reactions to propaganda on both sides of a controversial issue. *Publ. Opin. Quart.*, 1939, *3*, 107-112.

Schramm, W., & White, D. M. Age, education, economic status: factors in newspaper reading. *Journalism Quart.*, 1949, *26*, 149-159.

Seldes, G. *The great audience.* New York: Viking Press, 1950.

Shayon, R. L. *Television and our children.* New York: Longmans, Green, 1951.

Shuttleworth, F. K., & May, M. A. *The social conduct and attitudes of movie fans.* Bound with Ruth C. Peterson & L. L. Thurstone. *Motion pictures and the social attitudes of children.* New York: Macmillan, 1933.

Silvey, R. Television viewing in Britain. *Publ. Opin. Quart.*, 1950, *14*, 148-150.

Silvey, R. The intelligibility of broadcast talks. *Publ. Opin. Quart.*, 1951, *15*, 299-304.

Simms, V. M. Factors influencing attitude toward the TVA. *J. abnorm. soc. Psychol.*, 1938, *33*, 34-56.

Smith, B. L., Lasswell, H. D., & Casey, R. D. *Propaganda, communication, and public opinion.* Princeton: Princeton Univ. Press, 1946.

Smith, F. T. *An experiment in modifying attitudes toward the Negro.* New York: Teacher's College, Columbia Univ., 1943.

Sponberg, H. A study of the relative effectiveness of climax and anti-climax order in an argumentative speech. *Speech Monog.*, 1946, *13*, 35-44.

Stouffer, S. A. A sociologist looks at communications research. In D. Waples (Ed.), *Print, radio, and film in a democracy.* Chicago: Univ. of Chicago Press, 1942. Pp. 133-146.

Suchman, E. A. Invitation to music. In P. F. Lazarsfeld & F. N. Stanton (Eds.), *Radio research, 1941.* New York: Duell, Sloan and Pearce, 1941. Pp. 140-188.

Swanson, C. E. Predicting who learns factual information from the mass media. In H. Guetzkow (Ed.), *Groups, leadership and men.* Pittsburgh: Carnegie Press, 1951.

Swanson, C. E., & Jones, R. L. Television owning and its correlates. *J. appl. Psychol.*, 1951, *35*, 352-357.

Umberger, H. The influence of radio instruction upon farm practices. In Josephine H. MacLatchy (Ed.), *Education on the air.* 3rd Yearbook. *Inst. Educ. by Radio.* Columbus, Ohio: Ohio State Univ., 1932. Pp. 274-290.

Waples, D., Berelson, B., & Bradshaw, F. R. *What reading does to people.* Chicago: Univ. of Chicago Press, 1940.

Wegrocki, H. J. The effect of prestige suggestibility on emotional attitudes. *J. soc. Psychol.,* 1934, 5, 384-394.

Wertham, F. The comics . . . very funny! *Sat. Rev. of Lit.,* 1948, 31, No. 22, 6-7; 27-29.

Wiebe, G. D. Merchandising commodities and citizenship on television. *Publ. Opin. Quart.,* 1951, 15, 679-691.

Wiebe, G. D. Responses to the televised Kefauver hearings: Some social psychological implications. *Publ. Opin. Quart.,* 1952a, 16, 179-200.

Wiebe, G. D. Mass Communications. In E. L. Hartley & Ruth E. Hartley, *Fundamentals of social psychology.* New York: Knopf, 1952b. Pp. 159-195.

Wiese, Mildred J., & Cole, S. G. A study of children's attitudes and the influence of a commercial motion picture. *J. Psychol.,* 1946, 21, 151-171.

Wilke, W. H. An experimental comparison of the speech, the radio, and the printed page as propaganda devices. *Arch. Psychol.,* N. Y., 1934, No. 169.

Williams, R. M., Jr. The reduction of intergroup tensions. *Soc. Sci. Res. Council Bull.,* 1947, 57.

Wilson, E. C. The effectiveness of documentary broadcasts. *Publ. Opin. Quart.,* 1948a, 12, 19-29.

Wilson, E. C. The listening audience. In W. Schramm (Ed.), *Communications in modern society.* Urbana: Univ. of Ill. Press, 1948b. Pp. 117-125.

Wolf, Katherine M., & Fiske, Marjorie The children talk about comics. In P. F. Lazarsfeld & F. N. Stanton (Eds.), *Communications research, 1948-1949.* New York: Harper, 1949. Pp. 3-50.

Wood, B. DeK., & Freeman, F. N. *Motion pictures in the classroom.* New York: Houghton Mifflin, 1929.

APPENDIX

A) *Canons of Journalism:*
AMERICAN SOCIETY OF NEWSPAPER EDITORS

B) *Production Code:*
MOTION PICTURE ASSOCIATION

C) *Television Code:*
NATIONAL ASSOCIATION OF BROADCASTERS

CANONS OF JOURNALISM

"CODE OF ETHICS OR CANONS OF JOURNALISM—THE AMERICAN
SOCIETY OF NEWSPAPER EDITORS

"THE PRIMARY function of newspapers is to communicate to the human race what its members do, feel and think. Journalism, therefore, demands of its practitioners the widest range of intelligence, or knowledge, and of experience, as well as natural and trained powers of observation and reasoning. To its opportunities as a chronicle are indissolubly linked its obligations as teacher and interpreter.

"To the end of finding some means of codifying sound practice and just aspirations of American journalism, these canons are set forth:

"I. Responsibility

"The right of a newspaper to attract and hold readers is restricted by nothing but considerations of public welfare. The use a newspaper makes of the share of public attention it gains serves to determine its sense of responsibility, which it shares with every member of its staff. A journalist who uses his power for any selfish or otherwise unworthy purpose is faithless to a high trust.

"II. Freedom of the press

"Freedom of the press is to be guarded as a vital right of mankind. It is the unquestionable right to discuss whatever is not explicitly forbidden by law, including the wisdom of any restrictive statute.

"III. Independence

"Freedom from all obligations except that of fidelity to the public interest is vital.

"1. Promotion of any private interest contrary to the general welfare, for whatever reason, is not compatible with honest journalism. So-called news communications from private sources should not be published without public notice of their source or else substantiation of their claims to value as news, both in form and substance.

"2. Partisanship, in editorial comment which knowingly departs from the truth, does violence to the best spirit of American journalism; in the news columns it is subversive of a fundamental principle of the profession.

"IV. Sincerity, Truthfulness, Accuracy

"Good faith with the reader is the foundation of all journalism worthy of the name.

"1. By every consideration of good faith a newspaper is constrained to be truthful. It is not to be excused for lack of thoroughness or accuracy within its control, or failure to obtain command of these essential qualities.

"2. Headlines should be fully warranted by the contents of the articles which they surmount.

"V. *Impartiality*

"Sound practice makes clear distinction between news reports and expressions of opinion. News reports should be free from opinion or bias of any kind.

"1. This rule does not apply to so-called special articles unmistakably devoted to advocacy or characterized by a signature authorizing the writer's own conclusions and interpretation.

"VI. *Fair Play*

"A newspaper should not publish unofficial charges affecting reputation or moral character without opportunity given to the accused to be heard; right practice demands the giving of such opportunity in all cases of serious accusation outside judicial proceedings.

"1. A newspaper should not invade private rights or feelings without sure warrant of public right as distinguished from public curiosity.

"2. It is the privilege, as it is the duty, of a newspaper to make prompt and complete correction of its own serious mistakes of fact or opinion, whatever their origin.

"*Decency*

"A newspaper cannot escape conviction of insincerity if while professing high moral purpose it supplies incentives to base conduct, such as are to be found in details of crime and vice, publication of which is not demonstrable for the general good. Lacking authority to enforce its canons the journalism here presented can but express the hope that deliberate pandering to vicious instincts will encounter effective public disapproval or yield to the influence of a preponderant professional condemnation."

MOTION PICTURES: PRODUCTION CODE

FOREWORD

Motion picture producers recognize the high trust and confidence which have been placed in them by the people of the world and which have made motion pictures a universal form of entertainment.

They recognize their responsibility to the public because of this trust and because entertainment and art are important influences in the life of a nation.

Hence, though regarding motion pictures primarily as entertainment without any explicit purpose of teaching or propaganda, they know that the motion picture within its own field of entertainment may be directly responsible for spiritual or moral progress, for higher types of social life, and for much correct thinking.

On their part, they ask from the public and from public leaders a sympathetic understanding of the problems inherent in motion picture production and a spirit of cooperation that will allow the opportunity necessary to bring the motion picture to a still higher level of wholesome entertainment for all concerned.

THE PRODUCTION CODE

GENERAL PRINCIPLES

1. No picture shall be produced which will lower the moral standards of those who see it. Hence the sympathy of the audience shall never be thrown to the side of crime, wrong-doing, evil or sin.

2. Correct standards of life, subject only to the requirements of drama and entertainment, shall be presented.

3. Law—divine, natural or human—shall not be ridiculed, nor shall sympathy be created for its violation.

PARTICULAR APPLICATIONS:

I. CRIME:

1. Crime shall never be presented in such a way as to throw sympathy with the crime as against law and justice, or to inspire others with a desire for imitation.

2. Methods of crime shall not be explicitly presented or detailed in a manner calculated to glamorize crime or inspire imitation.

3. Action showing the taking of human life is to be held to the minimum. Its frequent presentation tends to lessen regard for the sacredness of life.

4. Suicide, as a solution of problems occurring in the development of screen drama, is to be discouraged unless absolutely necessary for the development of the plot, and shall never be justified, or glorified, or used specifically to defeat the ends of justice.

5. Excessive flaunting of weapons by criminals shall not be permitted.

6. There shall be no scenes of law-enforcing officers dying at the hands of criminals, unless such scenes are absolutely necessary to the plot.

7. Pictures dealing with criminal activities in which minors participate, or to which minors are related, shall not be approved if they tend to incite demoralizing imitation on the part of youth.

8. Murder:
   (a) The technique of murder must not be presented in a way that will inspire imitation.
   (b) Brutal killings are not to be presented in detail.
   (c) Revenge in modern times shall not be justified.
   (d) Mercy killing shall never be made to seem right or permissible.

9. Drug addiction or the illicit traffic in addiction-producing drugs shall not be shown if the portrayal:
   (a) Tends in any manner to encourage, stimulate or justify the use of such drugs; or
   (b) Stresses, visually or by dialogue, their temporarily attractive effects; or
   (c) Suggests that the drug habit may be quickly or easily broken; or
   (d) Shows details of drug procurement or of the taking of drugs in any manner; or
   (e) Emphasizes the profits of the drug traffic; or
   (f) Involves children who are shown knowingly to use or traffic in drugs.

10. Stories on the kidnapping or illegal abduction of children are acceptable under the Code only (1) when the subject is handled with restraint and discretion and avoids details, gruesomeness and undue horror, and (2) the child is returned unharmed.

II. BRUTALITY:

Excessive and inhumane acts of cruelty and brutality shall not be presented. This includes all detailed and protracted presentation of physical violence, torture and abuse.

III. SEX:

The sanctity of the institution of marriage and the home shall be upheld. No film shall infer that casual or promiscuous sex relationships are the accepted or common thing.

1. Adultery and illicit sex, sometimes necessary plot material, shall not be

explicitly treated, nor shall they be justified or made to seem right and permissible.

2. Scenes of passion:
    (a) These should not be introduced except where they are definitely essential to the plot.
    (b) Lustful and open-mouth kissing, lustful embraces, suggestive posture and gestures are not to be shown.
    (c) In general, passion should be treated in such manner as not to stimulate the baser emotions.

3. Seduction or rape:
    (a) These should never be more than suggested, and then only when essential to the plot. They should never be shown explicitly.
    (b) They are never acceptable subject matter for comedy.
    (c) They should never be made to seem right and permissible.

4. The subject of abortion shall be discouraged, shall never be more than suggested, and when referred to shall be condemned. It must never be treated lightly or made the subject of comedy. Abortion shall never be shown explicitly or by inference, and a story must not indicate that an abortion has been performed. The word "abortion" shall not be used.

5. The methods and techniques of prostitution and white slavery shall never be presented in detail, nor shall the subjects be presented unless shown in contrast to right standards of behavior. Brothels in any clear identification as such may not be shown.

6. Sex perversion or any inference of it is forbidden.

7. Sex hygiene and venereal diseases are not acceptable subject matter for theatrical motion pictures.

8. Children's sex organs are never to be exposed. This provision shall not apply to infants.

IV. VULGARITY:

Vulgar expressions and double meanings having the same effect are forbidden. This shall include but not be limited to such words and expressions as chippie, fairy, goose, nuts, pansy, S.O.B., son-of-a. The treatment of low, disgusting, unpleasant, though not necessarily evil, subjects should be guided always by the dictates of good taste and a proper regard for the sensibilities of the audience.

V. OBSCENITY:

1. Dances suggesting or representing sexual actions or emphasizing indecent movements are to be regarded as obscene.

2. Obscenity in words, gesture, reference, song, joke or by suggestion, even when likely to be understood by only part of the audience, is forbidden.

VI. BLASPHEMY AND PROFANITY:

1. Blasphemy is forbidden. Reference to the Deity, God, Lord, Jesus, Christ, shall not be irreverent.

2. Profanity is forbidden. The words "hell" and "damn," while sometimes dramatically valid, will if used without moderation be considered offen-

sive by many members of the audience. Their use shall be governed by the discretion and prudent advice of the Code Administration.

VII. COSTUMES:

1. Complete nudity, in fact or in silhouette, is never permitted, nor shall there be any licentious notice by characters in the film of suggested nudity.
2. Indecent or undue exposure is forbidden.
    (a) The foregoing shall not be interpreted to exclude actual scenes photographed in a foreign land of the natives of that land, showing native life, provided:
        (1) Such scenes are included in a documentary film or travelogue depicting exclusively such land, its customs and civilization, and
        (2) Such scenes are not in themselves intrinsically objectionable.

VIII. RELIGION:

1. No film or episode shall throw ridicule on any religious faith.
2. Ministers of religion, or persons posing as such, shall not be portrayed as comic characters or as villains so as to cast disrespect on religion.
3. Ceremonies of any definite religion shall be carefully and respectfully handled.

IX. SPECIAL SUBJECTS:

The following subjects must be treated with discretion and restraint and within the careful limits of good taste:
1. Bedroom scenes.
2. Hangings and electrocutions.
3. Liquor and drinking.
4. Surgical operations and childbirth.
5. Third degree methods.

X. NATIONAL FEELINGS:

1. The use of the flag shall be consistently respectful.
2. The history, institutions, prominent people and citizenry of all nations shall be represented fairly.
3. No picture shall be produced that tends to incite bigotry or hatred among peoples of differing races, religions or national origins. The use of such offensive words as Chink, Dago, Frog, Greaser, Hunkie, Kike, Nigger, Spig, Wop, Yid, should be avoided.

XI. TITLES:

The following titles shall not be used:
1. Titles which are salacious, indecent, obscene, profane or vulgar.
2. Titles which violate any other clause of this Code.

XII. CRUELTY TO ANIMALS:

In the production of motion pictures involving animals the producer shall consult with the authorized representative of the American Humane Association, and invite him to be present during the staging of such animal action. There shall be no use of any contrivance or apparatus for tripping or otherwise treating animals in an unacceptably harsh manner.

REASONS SUPPORTING THE CODE

I. Theatrical motion pictures, that is, pictures intended for the theatre as distinct from pictures intended for churches, schools, lecture halls, educational movements, social reform movements, etc., are primarily to be regarded as entertainment.

Mankind has always recognized the importance of entertainment and its value in rebuilding the bodies and souls of human beings.

But it has always recognized that entertainment can be of a character either helpful or harmful to the human race, and in consequence has clearly distinguished between:

a. Entertainment which tends to improve the race, or at least to re-create and rebuild human beings exhausted with the realities of life; and

b. Entertainment which tends to degrade human beings, or to lower their standards of life and living.

Hence the moral importance of entertainment is something which has been universally recognized. It enters intimately into the lives of men and women and affects them closely; it occupies their minds and affections during leisure hours; and ultimately touches the whole of their lives. A man may be judged by his standard of entertainment as easily as by the standard of his work.

So correct entertainment raises the whole standard of a nation.

Wrong entertainment lowers the whole living conditions and moral ideals of a race.

Note, too, the effect on ancient nations of gladiatorial combats, the obscene plays the unhealthy reactions to sports like cockfighting, bullfighting, bear baiting, etc.

Note, too, the effect on ancient nations of gladiatorial combats, the obscene plays of Roman times, etc.

II. Motion pictures are very important as art.

Though a new art, possibly a combination art, it has the same object as the other arts, the presentation of human thought, emotion and experience, in terms of an appeal to the soul through the senses.

Here, as in entertainment,

Art enters intimately into the lives of human beings.

Art can be morally good, lifting men to higher levels. This has been done through good music, great painting, authentic fiction, poetry, drama. Art can be morally evil in its effects. This is the case clearly enough with unclean art, indecent books, suggestive drama. The effect on the lives of men and women is obvious.

Note: It has often been argued that art in itself is unmoral, neither good nor bad. This is perhaps true of the thing which is music, painting, poetry, etc. But the thing is the product of some person's mind, and the intention of that mind was either good or bad morally when it produced the thing. Besides, the thing has its effect upon those who come into contact with it. In both these ways, that is, as a product of a mind and as the cause of definite effects, it has a deep moral significance and an unmistakable moral quality.

Hence: The motion pictures, which are the most popular of modern arts for the masses, have their moral quality from the intention of the minds which produce them and from their effects on the moral lives and reactions of their audiences. This gives them a most important morality.

1. They reproduce the morality of the men who use the pictures as a medium for the expression of their ideas and ideals.

2. They affect the moral standards of those who, through the screen, take in these ideas and ideals.

In the case of the motion picture, this effect may be particularly emphasized because no art has so quick and so widespread an appeal to the masses. It has become in an incredibly short period the art of the multitudes.

III. The motion picture, because of its importance as entertainment and because of the trust placed in it by the peoples of the world, has special moral obligations.

A. Most arts appeal to the mature. This art appeals at once to every class, mature, immature, developed, undeveloped, law abiding, criminal. Music has its grades for different classes; so have literature and drama. This art of the motion picture, combining as it does the two fundamental appeals of looking at a picture and listening to a story, at once reaches every class of society.

B. By reason of the mobility of a film and the ease of picture distribution, and because of the possibility of duplicating positives in large quantities, this art reaches places unpenetrated by other forms of art.

C. Because of these two facts, it is difficult to produce films intended for only certain classes of people. The exhibitors' theatres are built for the masses, for the cultivated and the rude, the mature and the immature, the self-respecting and the criminal. Films, unlike books and music, can with difficulty be confined to certain selected groups.

D. The latitude given to film material cannot, in consequence, be as wide as the latitude given to book material. In addition:

a. A book describes; a film vividly presents. One presents on a cold page; the other by apparently living people.

b. A book reaches the mind through words merely; a film reaches the eyes and ears through the reproduction of actual events.

c. The reaction of a reader to a book depends largely on the keenness of the reader's imagination; the reaction to a film depends on the vividness of presentation.

Hence many things which might be described or suggested in a book could not possibly be presented in a film.

E. This is also true when comparing the film with the newspaper.

a. Newspapers present by description, films by actual presentation.

b. Newspapers are after the fact and present things as having taken place; the film gives the events in the process of enactment and with the apparent reality of life.

F. Everything possible in a play is not possible in a film:

    a. Because of the larger audience of the film, and its consequential mixed character. Psychologically, the larger the audience, the lower the moral mass resistance to suggestion.

    b. Because through light, enlargement of character, presentation, scenic emphasis, etc., the screen story is brought closer to the audience than the play.

    c. The enthusiasm for and interest in the film actors and actresses, developed beyond anything of the sort in history, makes the audience largely sympathetic toward the characters they portray and the stories in which they figure. Hence the audience is more ready to confuse actor and actress and the characters they portray, and it is most receptive of the emotions and ideals presented by its favorite stars.

G. Small communities, remote from sophistication and from the hardening process which often takes place in the ethical and moral standards of groups in larger cities, are easily and readily reached by any sort of film.

H. The grandeur of mass settings, large action, spectacular features, etc., affects and arouses more intensely the emotional side of the audience.

In general, the mobility, popularity, accessibility, emotional appeal, vividness, straightforward presentation of fact in the film make for more intimate contact with a larger audience and for greater emotional appeal.

Hence the larger moral responsibilities of the motion pictures.

REASONS UNDERLYING THE GENERAL PRINCIPLES

I. No picture shall be produced which will lower the moral standards of those who see it. Hence the sympathy of the audience should never be thrown to the side of crime, wrong-doing, evil or sin.

    This is done:

    1. When evil is made to appear attractive or alluring, and good is made to appear unattractive.

    2. When the sympathy of the audience is thrown on the side of crime, wrong-doing, evil, sin. The same thing is true of a film that would throw sympathy against goodness, honor, innocence, purity or honesty.

Note: Sympathy with a person who sins is not the same as sympathy with the sin or crime of which he is guilty. We may feel sorry for the plight of the murderer or even understand the circumstances which led him to his crime. We may not feel sympathy with the wrong which he has done.

The presentation of evil is often essential for art or fiction or drama.

This in itself is not wrong provided:

    a. That evil is not presented alluringly. Even if later in the film the evil is condemned or punished, it must not be allowed to appear so attractive that the audience's emotions are drawn to desire or approve so strongly that later the condemnation is forgotten and only the apparent joy of the sin remembered.

b. That throughout, the audience feels sure that evil is wrong and good is right.

II. Correct standards of life shall, as far as possible, be presented.

A wide knowledge of life and of living is made possible through the film. When right standards are consistently presented, the motion picture exercises the most powerful influences. It builds character, develops right ideals, inculcates correct principles, and all this in attractive story form. If motion pictures consistently hold up for admiration high types of characters and present stories that will affect lives for the better, they can become the most powerful natural force for the improvement of mankind.

III. Law—divine, natural or human—shall not be ridiculed, nor shall sympathy be created for its violation.

By natural law is understood the law which is written in the hearts of all mankind, the great underlying principles of right and justice dictated by conscience.

By human law is understood the law written by civilized nations.

1. The presentation of crimes against the law is often necessary for the carrying out of the plot. But the presentation must not throw sympathy with the crime as against the law nor with the criminal as against those who punish him.

2. The courts of the land should not be presented as unjust. This does not mean that a single court may not be represented as unjust, much less that a single court official must not be presented this way. But the court system of the country must not suffer as a result of this presentation.

Reasons Underlying Particular Applications

I. Sin and evil enter into the story of human beings and hence in themselves are valid dramatic material.

II. In the use of this material, it must be distinguished between sins which repel by their very nature, and sins which often attract.

a. In the first class come murder, most theft, many legal crimes, lying, hypocrisy, cruelty, etc.

b. In the second class come sex sins, sins and crimes of apparent heroism, such as banditry, daring thefts, leadership in evil, organized crime, revenge, etc.

The first class needs less care in treatment, as sins and crimes of this class are naturally unattractive. The audience instinctively condemns all such and is repelled.

Hence the important objective must be to avoid the hardening of the audience, especially of those who are young and impressionable, to the thought and fact of crime. People can become accustomed even to murder, cruelty, brutality, and repellent crimes, if these are too frequently repeated.

The second class needs great care in handling, as the response of human nature to their appeal is obvious. This is treated more fully below.

III. A careful distinction can be made between films intended for general distribution, and films intended for use in theatres restricted to a limited audience. Themes and plots quite appropriate for the latter would be altogether out of place and dangerous in the former.

Note: The practice of using a general theatre and limiting its patronage during the showing of a certain film to "Adults Only" is not completely satisfactory and is only partially effective.

However, maturer minds may easily understand and accept without harm subject matter in plots which do younger people positive harm.

Hence: If there should be created a special type of theatre, catering exclusively to an adult audience, for plays of this character (plays with problem themes, difficult discussions and maturer treatment) it would seem to afford an outlet, which does not now exist, for pictures unsuitable for general distribution but permissible for exhibitions to a restricted audience.

I. CRIMES AGAINST THE LAW

The treatment of crimes against the law must not:

1. Teach methods of crime.

2. Inspire potential criminals with a desire for imitation.

3. Make criminals seem heroic and justified.

Revenge in modern times shall not be justified. In lands and ages of less developed civilization and moral principles, revenge may sometimes be presented. This would be the case especially in places where no law exists to cover the crime because of which revenge is committed.

Because of its evil consequences, the drug traffic should not be presented except under careful limitations.

II. BRUTALITY

Excessive and inhumane acts of cruelty and brutality have no proper place on the screen.

III. SEX

Out of regard for the sanctity of marriage and the home, the triangle, that is, the love of a third party for one already married, needs careful handling. The treatment should not throw sympathy against marriage as an institution.

Scenes of passion must be treated with an honest acknowledgment of human nature and its normal reactions. Many scenes cannot be presented without arousing dangerous emotions on the part of the immature, the young or the criminal classes.

Even within the limits of pure love, certain facts have been universally regarded by lawmakers as outside the limits of safe presentation.

In the case of impure love, the love which society has always regarded as wrong and which has been banned by divine law, the following are important:

1. Impure love must not be presented as attractive and beautiful.

2. It must not be the subject of comedy or farce, or treated as material for laughter.

3. It must not be presented in such a way as to arouse passion or morbid curiosity on the part of the audience.

4. It must not be made to seem right and permissible.

5. In general, it must not be detailed in method and manner.

6. Certain places are so closely and thoroughly associated with sexual life or with sexual sin that their use must be carefully limited.

IV. VULGARITY

This section is intended to prevent not only obviously vulgar expressions but also double meanings that have the same effect.

V. OBSCENITY

Dances which suggest or represent sexual actions, whether performed solo or with two or more; dances intended to excite the emotional reaction of an audience; dances with movement of the breasts, excessive body movements while the feet are stationary, violate decency and are wrong.

This section likewise applies to obscene words, gestures, references, songs, jokes and gags.

VI. BLASPHEMY AND PROFANITY

It is clear that neither blasphemy nor profanity should be permitted on the screen.

VII. COSTUMES

General principles:

1. The effect of nudity or semi-nudity upon the normal man or woman, and much more upon the young and upon immature persons, has been honestly recognized by all lawmakers and moralists.

2. Hence the fact that the nude or semi-nude body may be beautiful does not make its use in the films moral. For, in addition to its beauty, the effect of the nude or semi-nude body on the normal individual must be taken into consideration.

3. Nudity or semi-nudity used simply to put a "punch" into a picture comes under the head of immoral actions. It is immoral in its effect on the average audience.

4. Nudity can never be permitted as being necessary for the plot. Semi-nudity must not result in undue or indecent exposures.

5. Transparent or translucent materials and silhouette are frequently more suggestive than actual exposure.

VIII. RELIGION

The reason why ministers of religion may not be portrayed as comic characters or as villains so as to cast disrespect on religion is simply because the attitude taken toward them may easily become the attitude taken toward religion in general. Religion is lowered in the minds of the audience because of the lowering of the audience's respect for a minister.

IX. SPECIAL SUBJECTS

Such subjects are occasionally necessary for the plot. Their treatment must never offend good taste nor injure the sensibilities of an audience.

The use of liquor should never be excessively presented. In scenes from American life, the necessities of plot and proper characterization alone justify its use. And in this case, it should be shown with moderation.

X. NATIONAL FEELINGS

The just rights, history, and feelings of peoples and nations are entitled to most careful consideration and respectful treatment.

XI. TITLES

As the title of a picture is the brand on that particular type of goods, it must conform to the ethical practices of all such honest business.

XII. CRUELTY TO ANIMALS

The purpose of this provision is to prevent the treatment of animals in films in any unacceptably harsh manner.

THE TELEVISION CODE OF THE
NATIONAL ASSOCIATION OF BROADCASTERS

PREAMBLE

Television is seen and heard in every type of American home. These homes include children and adults of all ages, embrace all races and all varieties of religious faith, and reach those of every educational background. It is the responsibility of television to bear constantly in mind that the audience is primarily a home audience, and consequently that television's relationship to the viewers is that between guest and host.

The revenues from advertising support the free, competitive American system of telecasting, and make available to the eyes and ears of the American people the finest programs of information, education, culture and entertainment. By law the television broadcaster is responsible for the programming of his station. He, however, is obligated to bring his positive responsibility for excellence and good taste in programming to bear upon all who have a hand in the production of programs, including networks, sponsors, producers of film and of live programs, advertising agencies, and talent agencies.

The American businesses which utilize television for conveying their advertising messages to the home by pictures with sound, seen free-of-charge on the home screen, are reminded that their responsibilities are not limited to the sale of goods and the creation of a favorable attitude toward the sponsor by the presentation of entertainment. They include, as well, responsibility for utilizing television to bring the best programs, regardless of kind, into American homes.

Television and all who participate in it are jointly accountable to the American public for respect for the special needs of children, for community responsibility, for the advancement of education and culture, for the acceptability of the program materials chosen, for decency and decorum in production, and for propriety in advertising. This responsibility cannot be discharged by any given group of programs, but can be discharged only through the highest standards of respect for the American home, applied to every moment of every program presented by television.

In order that television programming may best serve the public interest, viewers should be encouraged to make their criticisms and positive suggestions known to the television broadcasters. Parents in particular should be urged to see to it that out of the richness of television fare, the best programs are brought to the attention of their children.

I. ADVANCEMENT OF EDUCATION AND CULTURE

1. Commercial television provides a valuable means of augmenting the educational and cultural influences of schools, institutions of higher learning, the

home, the church, museums, foundations, and other institutions devoted to education and culture.

2. It is the responsibility of a television broadcaster to call upon such institutions for counsel and cooperation and to work with them on the best methods of presenting educational and cultural materials by television. It is further the responsibility of stations, networks, advertising agencies and sponsors consciously to seek opportunities for introducing into telecasts factual materials which will aid in the enlightenment of the American public.

3. Education via television may be taken to mean that process by which the individual is brought toward informed adjustment to his society. Television is also responsible for the presentation of overtly instructional and cultural programs, scheduled so as to reach the viewers who are naturally drawn to such programs, and produced so as to attract the largest possible audience.

4. In furthering this realization, the television broadcaster:
   a) Should be thoroughly conversant with the educational and cultural needs and desires of the community served.
   b) Should affirmatively seek out responsible and accountable educational and cultural institutions of the community with a view toward providing opportunities for the instruction and enlightenment of the viewers.
   c) Should provide for reasonable experimentation in the development of programs specifically directed to the advancement of the community's culture and education.

II. ACCEPTABILITY OF PROGRAM MATERIAL

Program materials should enlarge the horizons of the viewer, provide him with wholesome entertainment, afford helpful stimulation, and remind him of the responsibilities which the citizen has towards his society. The intimacy and confidence placed in Television demand of the broadcaster, the network and other program sources that they be vigilant in protecting the audience from deceptive program practices. Furthermore:

   a) (i) Profanity, obscenity, smut and vulgarity are forbidden, even when likely to be understood only by part of the audience. From time to time, words which have been acceptable, acquire undesirable meanings, and telecasters should be alert to eliminate such words.

   (ii) Words (especially slang) derisive of any race, color, creed, nationality or national derivation, except wherein such usage would be for the specific purpose of effective dramatization such as combating prejudice, are forbidden, even when likely to be understood only by part of the audience. From time to time, words which have been acceptable, acquire undesirable meanings, and telecasters should be alert to eliminate such words.

   b) (i) Attacks on religion and religious faiths are not allowed.

   (ii) Reverence is to mark any mention of the name of God, His attributes and powers.

   (iii) When religious rites are included in other than religious programs the rites are accurately presented and the ministers, priests and rabbis portrayed in their callings are vested with the dignity of their office and under no circumstances are to be held up to ridicule.

c) (i) Contests may not constitute a lottery.

(ii) Any telecasting designed to "buy" the television audience by requiring it to listen and/or view in hope of reward, rather than for the quality of the program, should be avoided. (see *Contests, page 515*)

d) Respect is maintained for the sanctity of marriage and the value of the home. Divorce is not treated casually nor justified as a solution for marital problems.

e) Illicit sex relations are not treated as commendable.

f) Sex crimes and abnormalities are generally unacceptable as program material.

g) Drunkenness and narcotic addiction are never presented as desirable or prevalent.

h) The administration of illegal drugs will not be displayed.

i) The use of liquor in program content shall be de-emphasized. The consumption of liquor in American life, when not required by the plot or for proper characterization, shall not be shown.

j) The use of gambling devices or scenes necessary to the development of plot or as appropriate background is acceptable only when presented with discretion and in moderation, and in a manner which would not excite interest in, or foster, betting nor be instructional in nature. Telecasts of actual sport programs at which on-the-scene betting is permitted by law should be presented in a manner in keeping with Federal, state and local laws, and should concentrate on the subject as a public sporting event.

k) In reference to physical or mental afflictions and deformities, special precautions must be taken to avoid ridiculing sufferers from similar ailments and offending them or members of their families.

l) Exhibitions of fortune-telling, occultism, astrology, phrenology, palm-reading and numerology are acceptable only when required by a plot or the theme of a program, and then the presentation should be developed in a manner designed not to foster superstition or excite interest or belief in these subjects.

m) Televised drama shall not simulate news or special events in such a way as to mislead or alarm. (*see News, page 510*)

n) Legal, medical and other professional advice, diagnosis and treatment will be permitted only in conformity with law and recognized ethical and professional standards.

o) The presentation of cruelty, greed and selfishness as worthy motivations is to be avoided.

p) Excessive or unfair exploitation of others or of their physical or mental afflictions shall not be presented as praiseworthy.

q) Criminality shall be presented as undesirable and unsympathetic. The condoning of crime and the treatment of the commission of crime in a frivolous, cynical or callous manner is unacceptable.

r) The presentation of techniques of crime in such detail as to invite imitation shall be avoided.

s) The use of horror for its own sake will be eliminated; the use of visual or aural effects which would shock or alarm the viewer, and the detailed presentation of brutality or physical agony by sight or by sound are not permissible.

t) Law enforcement shall be upheld and, except where essential to the program plot, officers of the law portrayed with respect and dignity.

u) The presentation of murder or revenge as a motive for murder shall not be presented as justifiable.

v) Suicide as an acceptable solution for human problems is prohibited.

w) The exposition of sex crimes will be avoided.

x) The appearances or dramatization of persons featured in actual crime news will be permitted only in such light as to aid law enforcement or to report the news event.

y) The use of animals, both in the production of television programs and as a part of television program content, shall at all times, be in conformity with accepted standards of humane treatment.

z) Quiz and similar programs that are presented as contests of knowledge, information, skill or luck must, in fact, be genuine contests and the results must not be controlled by collusion with or between contestants, or any other action which will favor one contestant against any other.

aa) No program shall be presented in a manner which through artifice or simulation would mislead the audience as to any material fact. Each broadcaster must exercise reasonable judgment to determine whether a particular method of presentation would constitute a material deception, or would be accepted by the audience as normal theatrical illusion.

III. RESPONSIBILITY TOWARD CHILDREN

1. The education of children involves giving them a sense of the world at large. However, such subjects as violence and sex shall be presented without undue emphasis and only as required by plot development or character delineation. Crime should not be presented as attractive or as a solution to human problems, and the inevitable retribution should be made clear.

2. It is not enough that only those programs which are intended for viewing by children shall be suitable to the young and immature. (*Attention is called to the general items listed under Acceptability of Program Material, page 507.*) Television is responsible for insuring that programs of all sorts which occur during the times of day when children may normally be expected to have the opportunity of viewing television shall exercise care in the following regards:

a) In affording opportunities for cultural growth as well as for wholesome entertainment.

b) In developing programs to foster and promote the commonly accepted moral, social and ethical ideals characteristic of American life.

c) In reflecting respect for parents, for honorable behavior, and for the constituted authorities of the American community.

d) In eliminating reference to kidnapping of children or threats of kidnapping.

e) In avoiding material which is excessively violent or would create morbid suspense, or other undesirable reactions in children.

f) In exercising particular restraint and care in crime or mystery episodes involving children or minors.

IV. Decency and Decorum in Production

1. The costuming of all performers shall be within the bounds of propriety and shall avoid such exposure or such emphasis on anatomical detail as would embarrass or offend home viewers.

2. The movements of dancers, actors, or other performers shall be kept within the bounds of decency, and lewdness and impropriety shall not be suggested in the positions assumed by performers.

3. Camera angles shall avoid such views of performers as to emphasize anatomical details indecently.

4. Racial or nationality types shall not be shown on television in such a manner as to ridicule the race or nationality.

5. The use of locations closely associated with sexual life or with sexual sin must be governed by good taste and delicacy.

V. Community Responsibility

A television broadcaster and his staff occupy a position of responsibility in the community and should conscientiously endeavor to be acquainted fully with its needs and characteristics in order better to serve the welfare of its citizens.

VI. Treatment of News and Public Events

News

1. A television station's news schedule should be adequate and well-balanced.

2. News reporting should be factual, fair and without bias.

3. Commentary and analysis should be clearly identified as such.

4. Good taste should prevail in the selection and handling of news:

Morbid, sensational or alarming details not essential to the factual report, especially in connection with stories of crime or sex, should be avoided. News should be telecast in such a manner as to avoid panic and unnecessary alarm.

5. At all times, pictorial and verbal material for both news and comment should conform to other sections of these standards, wherever such sections are reasonably applicable.

6. Pictorial material should be chosen with care and not presented in a misleading manner.

7. A television broadcaster should exercise due care in his supervision of content, format, and presentation of newscasts originated by his station, and in his selection of newscasters, commentators, and analysts.

8. A television broadcaster should exercise particular discrimination in the acceptance, placement and presentation of adveritising in news programs so that such advertising should be clearly distinguishable from the news content.

9. A television broadcaster should not present fictional events or other non-news material as authentic news telecasts or announcements, nor should he permit dramatizations in any program which would give the false impression that the dramatized material constitutes news. Expletives (presented aurally or pictorially) such as "flash" or "bulletin" and statements such as "we interrupt this

program to bring you . . ." should be reserved specifically for news room use. However, a television broadcaster may properly exercise discretion in the use in non-news programs of words or phrases which do not necessarily imply that the material following is a news release.

10. All news interview programs should be governed by accepted standards of ethical journalism, under which the interviewer selects the questions to be asked. Where there is advance agreement materially restricting an important or news-worthy area of questioning, the interviewer will state on the program that such limitation has been agreed upon. Such disclosure should be made if the person being interviewed requires that questions be submitted in advance or if he participates in editing a recording of the interview prior to its use on the air.

Public Events

1. A television broadcaster has an affirmative responsibility at all times to be informed of public events, and to provide coverage consonant with the ends of an informed and enlightened citizenry.

2. Because of the nature of events open to the public, the treatment of such events by a television broadcaster should be effected in a manner to provide for adequate and informed coverage as well as good taste in presentation.

VII. Controversial Public Issues

1. Television provides a valuable forum for the expression of responsible views on public issues of a controversial nature. In keeping therewith the television broadcaster should seek out and develop with accountable individuals, groups and organizations, programs relating to controversial public issues of import to his fellow citizens; and to give fair representation to opposing sides of issues which materially affect the life or welfare of a substantial segment of the public.

2. The provision of time for this purpose should be guided by the following principles:

a) Requests by individuals, groups or organizations for time to discuss their views on controversial public issues, should be considered on the basis of their individual merits, and in the light of the contribution which the use requested would make to the public interest, and to a well-balanced program structure.

b) Programs devoted to the discussion of controversial public issues should be identified as such, and should not be presented in a manner which would mislead listeners or viewers to believe that the program is purely of an entertainment, news, or other character.

VIII. Political Telecasts

Political telecasts should be clearly identified as such and should not be presented by a television broadcaster in a manner which would mislead listeners or viewers to believe that the program is of any other character.

IX. Religious Programs

1. It is the responsibility of a television broadcaster to make available to the community as part of a well-balanced program schedule adequate opportunity for religious presentations.

2. The following principles should be followed in the treatment of such programs:

   a) Telecasting which reaches men of all creeds simultaneously should avoid attacks upon religion.
   b) Religious programs should be presented respectfully and accurately and without prejudice or ridicule.
   c) Religious programs should be presented by responsible individuals, groups and organizations.
   d) Religious programs should place emphasis on broad religious truths, excluding the presentation of controversial or partisan views not directly or necessarily related to religion or morality.

3. In the allocation of time for telecasts of religious programs it is recommended that the television station use its best efforts to apportion such time fairly among the representative faith groups of its community.

X. Subliminal Perception

The use of the television medium to transmit information of any kind by the use of the process called "subliminal perception," or by the use of any similar technique whereby an attempt is made to convey information to the viewer by transmitting messages below the threshold of normal awareness, is not permitted.

XI. Production Practices

The broadcaster shall be constantly alert to prevent activities that may lead to such practices as the use of scenic properties, the choice and identification of prizes, the selection of music and other creative program elements and inclusion of any identification of commercial products or services, their trade names or advertising slogans, within a program dictated by factors other than the requirements of the program itself. This expressly forbids the acceptance by producer, talent or any other personnel of cash payments or other considerations in return for including any of the above within the program.

XII. Presentation of Advertising

1. Ever mindful of the role of television as a guest in the home, a television broadcaster should exercise unceasing care to supervise the form in which advertising material is presented over his facilities. Since television is a developing medium, involving methods and techniques distinct from those of radio, it may be desirable from time to time to review and revise the presently suggested practices:

   a) Advertising messages should be presented with courtesy and good taste; disturbing or annoying material should be avoided; every effort should be made to keep the advertising message in harmony with the content and general tone of the program in which it appears.
   b) A sponsor's advertising messages should be confined within the framework of the sponsor's program structure. A television broadcaster should avoid the use of commercial announcements which are divorced from the program either by preceding the introduction of the program (as in the case of so-called "cow-catcher" announcements) or by following

the apparent sign-off of the program (as in the case of so-called "trailer" announcements). To this end, the program itself should be announced and clearly identified, both audio and video, before the sponsor's advertising material is first used, and should be signed off, both audio and video, after the sponsor's advertising material is last used.

c) Advertising copy should contain no claims intended to disparage competitors, competing products, or other industries, professions or institutions.

d) Since advertising by television is a dynamic technique, a television broadcaster should keep under surveillance new advertising devices so that the spirit and purpose of these standards are fulfilled.

e) Television broadcasters should exercise the utmost care and discrimination with regard to advertising material, including content, placement and presentation, near or adjacent to programs designed for children. No considerations of expediency should be permitted to impinge upon the vital responsibility towards children and adolescents, which is inherent in television, and which must be recognized and accepted by all advertisers employing television.

f) Television advertisers should be encouraged to devote portions of their allotted advertising messages and program time to the support of worthy causes in the public interest in keeping with the highest ideals of the free competitive system.

g) A charge for television time to churches and religious bodies is not recommended.

h) The role and capability of television to market sponsors' products are well recognized. In turn, this fact dictates that great care be exercised by the broadcaster to prevent the presentation of false, misleading or deceptive advertising. While it is entirely appropriate to present a product in a favorable light and atmosphere, and techniques may be used to depict the characteristics of the product as they appear in actuality, the presentation must not, by copy or demonstration, involve a material deception as to the characteristics, performance or appearance of the product.

XIII. ACCEPTABILITY OF ADVERTISERS AND PRODUCTS—GENERAL

1. A commercial television broadcaster makes his facilities available for the advertising of products and services and accepts commercial presentations for such advertising. However, a television broadcaster should, in recognition of his responsibility to the public, refuse the facilities of his station to an advertiser where he has good reason to doubt the integrity of the advertiser, the truth of the advertising representations, or the compliance of the advertiser with the spirit and purpose of all applicable legal requirements. Moreover, in consideration of the laws and customs of the communities served, each television broadcaster should refuse his facilities to the advertisement of products and services, or the use of advertising scripts, which the station has good reason to believe would be objectionable to a substantial and responsible segment of the community. The foregoing principles should be applied with judgment and flexibility, taking into consideration the characteristics of the medium and the form

and content of the particular presentation. In general, because television broadcasting is designed for the home and the family, including children, the following principles should govern the business classifications listed below:

a) The advertising of hard liquor should not be accepted.

b) The advertising of beer and wines is acceptable only when presented in the best of good taste and discretion, and is acceptable only subject to Federal and local laws.

c) Advertising by institutions or enterprises which in their offers of instruction imply promises of employment or make exaggerated claims for the opportunities awaiting those who enroll for courses is generally unacceptable.

d) The advertising of firearms and fireworks is acceptable only subject to Federal and local laws.

e) The advertising of fortune-telling, occultism, astrology, phrenology, palm-reading, numerology, mind-reading, character reading or subjects of a like nature is not permitted.

f) Because all products of a personal nature create special problems, such products, when accepted, should be treated with especial emphasis on ethics and the canons of good taste. Such advertising of personal products as is accepted must be presented in a restrained and obviously inoffensive manner.

The advertising of intimately personal products which are generally regarded as unsuitable conversational topics in mixed social groups is not acceptable.

g) The advertising of tip sheets, race track publications, or organizations seeking to advertise for the purpose of giving odds or promoting betting or lotteries is unacceptable.

2. Diligence should be exercised to the end that advertising copy accepted for telecasting complies with pertinent Federal, state and local laws.

3. An advertiser who markets more than one product should not be permitted to use advertising copy devoted to an acceptable product for purposes of publicizing the brand name or other identification of a product which is not acceptable.

4. "Bait-switch" advertising, whereby goods or services which the advertiser has no intention of selling are offered merely to lure the customer into purchasing higher-priced substitutes, is not acceptable.

XIV. Advertising of Medical Products

1. The advertising of medical products presents considerations of intimate and far-reaching importance to the consumer, and the following principles and procedures should apply in the advertising thereof:

a) A television broadcaster should not accept advertising material which in his opinion offensively describes or dramatizes distress or morbid situations involving ailments, by spoken word, sound or visual effects.

b) Because of the personal nature of the advertising of medical products, claims that a product will effect a cure and the indiscriminate use of such words as "safe," "without risk," "harmless," or terms of similar meaning should not be accepted in the advertising of medical products on television stations.

XV. Contests

1. In addition to complying with all pertinent Federal, state and local laws and regulations, all contests should offer the opportunity to all contestants to win on the basis of ability and skill rather than chance.

2. All contest details, including rules, eligibility requirements, opening and termination dates should be clearly and completely announced and/or shown, or easily accessible to the viewing public, and the winners' names should be released and prizes awarded as soon as possible after the close of the contest.

3. When advertising is accepted which requests contestants to submit items of product identification or other evidence of purchase of product, reasonable facsimiles thereof should be made acceptable.

4. All copy pertaining to any contest (except that which is required by law) associated with the exploitation or sale of the sponsor's product or service, and all references to prizes or gifts offered in such connection should be considered a part of and included in the total time allowances as herein provided. (*See Time Standards for Advertising Copy*.)

XVI. Premiums and Offers

1. Full details of proposed offers should be required by the television broadcaster for investigation and approved before the first announcement of the offer is made to the public.

2. A final date for the termination of an offer should be announced as far in advance as possible.

3. Before accepting for telecast offers involving a monetary consideration, a television broadcaster should satisfy himself as to the integrity of the advertiser and the advertiser's willingness to honor complaints indicating dissatisfaction with the premium by returning the monetary consideration.

4. There should be no misleading descriptions or visual representations of any premiums or gifts which would distort or enlarge their value in the minds of viewers.

5. Assurances should be obtained from the advertiser that premiums offered are not harmful to person or property.

6. Premiums should not be approved which appeal to superstition on the basis of "luck-bearing" powers or otherwise.

XVII. Time Standards for Advertising Copy

1. In accordance with good telecast advertising practices, the time standards for advertising copy are as shown in the table on the next page.

2. Reasonable and limited identification of prize and statement of the donor's name within formats wherein the presentation of contest awards or prizes is a necessary and integral part of program content shall not be included as commercial time within the meaning of paragraph 1, above; however, any oral or visual presentation concerning the product or its donor, over and beyond such identification and statement, shall be included as commercial time within the meaning of paragraph 1, above.

3. Station breaks (spot announcements scheduled between programs) shall consist of not more than two announcements plus the conventional sponsored 10

Length of Pgm. (in Minutes)	5:00	10:00	15:00	20:00	25:00	30:00	35:00	40:00	45:00	50:00	55:00	60:00
"AA" and "A" Time	1:00	2:00	2:30	2:40	2:50	3:00	3:30	4:00	4:30	5:00	5:30	6:00
All Other Time	1:15	2:10	3:00	3:30	4:00	4:15	4:45	5:15	5:45	6:10	6:35	7:00

Length of Pgm. (in Minutes)	65:00	70:00	75:00	80:00	85:00	90:00	95:00	100:00	105:00	110:00	115:00	120:00
"AA" and "A" Time	6:30	7:00	7:30	8:00	8:30	9:00	9:30	10:00	10:30	11:00	11:30	12:00
All Other Time	7:35	8:10	8:45	9:20	9:55	10:30	11:05	11:40	12:15	12:50	13:25	14:00

Above time standards are for sponsored programs. "Participation" programs, carrying announcements for different individual advertisers, may not exceed one minute of advertising per five minutes of programming. (See paragraph 4.)

---

second station ID. However, the aggregate total of the announcements shall not exceed 70 seconds within the station's highest rate period for announcements. Station break announcements shall not adversely affect a preceding or following program.

4. Announcement programs are designed to accommodate a number of announcements, which are carried within the body of the program and are available for sale to individual advertisers. Commercial announcements may not consume more than 6 minutes for any 30 minute program and no program shall have commercial content in excess of this ratio. Not more than 3 announcements shall be scheduled consecutively. Where the program exceeds 30 minutes in length, the required ID, not exceeding 10 seconds, may be in addition to these commercial time allowances.

5. Programs presenting women's services, features, shopping guides, market information, and similar material, provide a special service to the listening and viewing public in which advertising material is an informative and integral part of the program content. Because of these special characteristics the time standards set forth above may be waived to a reasonable extent.

6. Any casual reference by talent in a program to another's product or service under any trade name or language sufficiently descriptive to identify it should, except for normal guest identifications, be condemned and discouraged.

7. Stationary backdrops or properties in television presentations showing the sponsor's name or product, the name of his product, his trade-mark or slogan may be used only incidentally. They should not obtrude on program interest or entertainment. "On Camera" shots of such materials should be fleeting, not too frequent, and mindful of the need of maintaining a proper program balance.

8. The above commercial time standards do not include opening and closing "billboard" announcements which give program or announcement sponsor identification. Each opening and closing "billboard" regardless of the number of sponsors shall not exceed 20 seconds in programs longer than one half-hour or 10 seconds in programs of one half-hour or less.

XVIII. DRAMATIZED APPEALS AND ADVERTISING

1. Appeals to help fictitious characters in television programs by purchasing the advertiser's product or service or sending for a premium should not be permitted, and such fictitious characters should not be introduced into the advertising message for such purposes.

2. Dramatized advertising involving statements or purported statements by physicians, dentists, or nurses must be presented by accredited members of such professions.

XIX. Sponsor Identification

Identification of sponsorship must be made in all sponsored programs in accordance with the requirements of the Communications Act of 1934, as amended, and the Rules and Regulations of the Federal Communications Commission.

INDEX

A

Aaron Slick of Punkin Crick, 420
Abie's Irish Rose, 258
Abrams, Earl A., 290 *n.*
Abstractness, of language, 38
Academic Freedom in the United States, 84 *n.*
Acceptance, of communication, 473, 474, 481
Acheson, Dean, 111 *n.*
"Acquaintance with," as type of knowledge, 127, 128, 130, 131
Acta Diurna, 53
Acton, Lord, 99
Adams, Charles Francis, 50
Addison, Joseph, 101, 274
Adler, M., 456
Adventures of Ozzie and Harriet, The, 270, 276
Advertising, 23, 45, 67, 182, 375, 376; development of, 66; direct mail, 279; estimated total, 53 (table); expenditures for (1956), 380; in magazines, 169, 170, 172, 187, 193, 279; in newspapers, 52, 57, 62, 279, 288; radio, 63, 247, 279, 286, 287, 292; subliminal, 406; television, 63, 239, 279; and Television Code, 512–14, 515, 516, 517; wants created by, 380 and *n.,* 381
Advertising Age, 182 *n.,* 183 *n.*
Aesthetic experience, as effect of reading, 449
Affluent Society, The, 375, 378 *n.*
"Age of Anxiety," 217 *ff.*
Agence France Presse, 356, 361
Agenzia Nazionale Stampa Associata, 356, 361
Albatross Modern Continental Library, 303, 304
Alcoa Hour, The, 263
Alden, Henry Mills, 189 and *n.*
Alembert, d', Jean, 102 and *n.*
Alexander, Jerome, 31
Alger, Horatio, 412, 419
Algren, Nelson, 263
Allen, Frederick Lewis, 185 and *n.*
Allen, Steve, 276
Allport, Gordon, 79 *n.,* 457, 477, 481
AM broadcasting, 248, 249, 250, 253, 254, 287
American Association for State and Local History, 181
American Behavioral Scientist, The, 61
American Booksellers Association, 326
American Brewers Foundation, 213
American Broadcasting Company, 248, 264, 287
American College Public Relations Association, 402
American Heritage magazine, 181, 182
American Home magazine, 173
American Journal of Sociology, 94 *n.,* 127 *n.,* 438 *n.*
American Library of Useful Knowledge, 304
American Machinist magazine, 178

American Magazine, 173, 187
American Mercury, 191
American News Company, 305, 308
American Newspaper Publishers Association, 58
American Past, The, 221 *n.*
American Public Relations Association, 402
American Review, 173
American Revolution, 450
American Scholar, The, 184, 320 *n.*
American Scholar Forum, 320–45
American Society of Newspaper Editors, 493
American Sociological Review, 444 *n.*
American Telephone and Telegraph Company, 279, 280 and *n.,* 281, 285, 295
American Weekly, 190
Americanization, 115–16
Americanization of Edward Bok, The, 196 *n.*
Amerika, 363
Amos 'n' Andy show, 271
Anchor Books, 326, 338, 339
Anderson, Jim, 271, 272
Anderson, Sherwood, 261
Anesta news agency, 362
Annis, A. D., 452
"Antagonistic cooperation," defined, 426
Anthropology, social, 137
Anticlimax order, of argument in communication, 472, 473
Antioch Review, 56 *n.*
Appleton and Company, D., 305
Aptitude tests, 33
Architectural Forum, 173
Aristophanes, 274
Aristotle, 45, 137
Armstrong Circle Theater, 263
Army-McCarthy hearings, 274
Arnaz, Desi, 276
Arnett, C. E., 462
Art, in United States, 222–23, 224
Art and Criticism, 148 *n.*
Art of Television, The, 262
As I Lay Dying, 273
Asheim, Lester, 300, 301; as participant in *American Scholar* Forum, 320, 324, 326, 329, 330, 333, 335, 336, 339–43 *passim,* 345
Associated Press, 354, 355, 356, 361, 362, 363
Atlantic Monthly, 56, 169, 173, 174, 181, 189–90
Attention arousal, in communication, 473
Auden, W. H., 217
Audience: appeals employed in communication with, 468–71; attracted to different kinds of media, 479; for mass media, 153, 316, 317, 443–45, 479; reactions to communicator, 459, 464, 465 (table), 466, 467 (table), 475; sequence of arguments addressed to, 471–76
Audience of Nine Magazines, The, 291*n.*